The Dynamics of Asian Economic Development

Hitoshi Hirakawa · Ferdinand C. Maquito

The Dynamics of Asian Economic Development

Understanding Asia and Its Ways Forward

Springer

Hitoshi Hirakawa
Nagoya University
Nagoya, Japan

Ferdinand C. Maquito
College of Public Affairs and Development
University of the Philippines Los Baños
Laguna, Philippines

ISBN 978-981-97-3105-3 ISBN 978-981-97-3106-0 (eBook)
https://doi.org/10.1007/978-981-97-3106-0

This Springer imprint is published by the registered company Springer Nature Singapore Pte Ltd.
The registered company address is: 152 Beach Road, #21-01/04 Gateway East, Singapore 189721, Singapore

Dedicated to the late Columbus Maquito, who understood our collaboration more than anyone

Acknowledgements

A quarter of a century has passed since the two of us, Hirakawa and Maquito, first met. During this time, our research was supported by Ms. Junko Imanishi, the Chief Representative of the Sekiguchi Global Research Association of the Atsumi International Foundation, who connected the two of us, and continued to support the regular holding of the Sustainable Shared Growth Seminar series, not only financially but also emotionally. Some of the major ideas developed in this book were born from there.

Hirakawa's perspective on Asian studies in the context of the global economy was especially influenced by Dr. Yoshihiko Motoyama, Prof. Emeritus at Kyoto University and Director of the International Economy and Work Research Institute, Osaka, Japan and Dr. Young-Ho Kim, Professor Emeritus at Kyungpook National University and ex-Minister of Trade, Industry and Energy, South Korea. Maquito's journey in studying in Japan would not have been possible without the warm welcome of the late Dr. Akira Takahashi, Professor at the University of Tokyo. We are also grateful to Prof. Damcelle T. Cortes of the College of Public Affairs and Development, University of the Philippines Los Baños, for her co-authoring Chap. 11.

In addition, for the publication of this book, we would like to mention Mr. Yutaka Hirachi of Springer Nature Japan, who warmly watched over the submission of the manuscript. Without his encouragement, we would not have been able to complete this book. Finally, we would like to take this opportunity to express our gratitude to Hirakawa's spouse, Mayumi, and Maquito's mother, Luvisminda, who provided us with internal strength throughout our collaboration.

* Chapters 2, 4, and 5 in this volume were supported by the Japan Society for the Promotion of Science (JSPS) Grant-in-Aid for Scientific Research (C) "Research on Globalization and Transfer of Knowledge-Based Economic Activities to Emerging Countries" (Project No. 16K03656, Research Period: 2016-2022).

Contents

1 Introduction 1
References 9

Part I The Asian Economy and the Transformation of the World Economy

2 The Impact of Trade Wars and Pandemics on the Asian Economy 13
2.1 Introduction 13
2.2 The Circumstances and Structure of the U.S.-Sino Trade War 14
2.2.1 The Birth of the Trump Administration and the Trade War with China 14
2.2.2 U.S. Policy Against China and Its Determination Mechanism 16
2.3 The COVID-19 Pandemic and U.S.-Sino Conflict 22
2.3.1 COVID-19 Pandemic 22
2.3.2 COVID-19 and the Growing U.S.-Sino Distrust 27
2.3.3 The Trump Administration's Decoupling Policy and China's Response 30
2.4 Biden Administration and the U.S.-Sino Conflict 31
2.4.1 The Biden Administration's Principle of International Cooperation and China's "Wolf Warrior" 32
2.4.2 U.S.-Sino Conflict and Decoupling Under the Biden Administration 38
2.4.3 The Realignment of the Global Value Chain 40
2.5 The Geopolitics of Indo-Pacific 49
2.5.1 The Realignment of the Global Value Chain 49

2.5.2 ASEAN at the Intersection of China's BRI and U.S.-Led Indo-Pacific ... 52
2.6 Concluding Remarks ... 56
References ... 56

3 Asia's Changing Mechanism of Development and the Global Economy ... 59
3.1 Introduction ... 59
3.2 The Globalization of the Economy and the Development of Asia's Emerging Economies ... 60
3.2.1 Emerging Asian Economies and China ... 60
3.2.2 Asian Emerging Economies and Globalization ... 64
3.2.3 "Population Bonus" and the Emergence of the Middle Class ... 72
3.3 BRICs and Asian Emerging Economies ... 75
3.3.1 'BRICs' and Acceptance as a Concept ... 75
3.3.2 Foreign Direct Investment and the Development of Asian Emerging Economies ... 80
3.4 The Dynamics of Asia's Development ... 85
3.4.1 Foreign Direct Investment and Asian Newly Emerging Economies ... 85
3.4.2 The Changing Development Model of Asia: From NIEs to PoBMEs ... 93
3.5 Asian Development Dynamics and Remaining Issues ... 98
References ... 100

4 China's Belt and Road Initiative and Its Prospect ... 105
4.1 Introduction ... 105
4.2 President Xi Jinping and BRI ... 106
4.2.1 The Birth of BRI ... 106
4.2.2 The Development of China's Economy and BRI ... 108
4.2.3 The Two Aspects of BRI: Between Global Public Goods and Hegemony ... 114
4.3 The Development Concept of the "Belt and Road" Initiative ... 115
4.3.1 The "Belt and Road" Initiative as a China-Led International Cooperation Initiative ... 115
4.3.2 BRI and East Asian Development Experience ... 117
4.4 The Deployment of BRI and Countries Along the Line ... 120
4.4.1 BRI and the Response of the Countries Along the Line ... 120
4.4.2 BRI Project Progress and Rising Criticism ... 125

4.5 BRI Amidst the International Community, and Its Prospects 130
4.5.1 The Impact of U.S.-Sino Trade War, and COVID-19 on BRI: From "Mask Diplomacy" to "Vaccine Diplomacy" and COVAX 130
4.5.2 BRI Member Countries and the Debt Problem Under COVID-19 134
4.6 Concluding Remarks 143
References 144

5 Another Way of Development Through ICT: Possibility and Vulnerability 149
5.1 Introduction 149
5.2 Advancement of Digital Technology and Developing Economies 150
5.2.1 Data-Driven Digital Economy and Its Issues 150
5.2.2 Global Trade and Service Exports 153
5.3 "Leapfrogging", "Premature" Deindustrialization, and Jobless Growth 158
5.3.1 *Service-Led Development in Asia, especially India and* "Leapfrogging" 159
5.3.2 ICT and Premature Deindustrialization 165
5.3.3 Impact of Automation on Emerging Economies/ Developing Countries 170
5.4 Offshoring and Development of IT-BPO in India, the Philippines, and Vietnam 174
5.4.1 Development of IT-BPO Industry and Major Destinations 174
5.4.2 COVID-19 Pandemic and BPO Industry in India, the Philippines and Vietnam 180
5.4.3 IT-BPO Industry and Gender 186
5.5 Online Offshoring/Outsourcing to Asia 190
5.5.1 Global Firms and Online Labor Platforms 190
5.5.2 Online Workforce and Asia 193
5.6 Concluding Remarks: Possibility and Vulnerability in Developing Asia 196
References 197

6 The Case of the Philippines in the Asian Economy 203
6.1 Introduction 203
6.2 "Ground Zero" of the Shared Growth Discourse 204
6.3 Mechanisms of Shared Growth from Japan 206
6.3.1 Japan's Developmental Financing 207
6.3.2 Developmental Financing in the EAM Report 210
6.3.3 Japanese Organizational Structure: The Keiretsu and FDI 213

6.3.4 The Flying Geese Model and Japanese EX/IM (Trade) ... 215
6.3.5 Strategic Complementarities in the FDI-ODA-EXIM Trinity ... 219
6.4 The Philippines in Relation to the ODA-FDI-EXIM Trinity of Shared Growth ... 221
6.4.1 The Philippines and Japanese ODA ... 221
6.4.2 The Philippines and Japanese FDI ... 222
6.4.3 The Philippines and Japanese Export–Import ... 228
6.5 Some Challenges Facing the Philippines in Flying Together ... 229
References ... 230

Part II The Roots of Asia's Development Economies After the World War Two

7 The East Asian Export-Led Industrialization in the Global Economy ... 235
7.1 Introduction ... 235
7.2 East Asia's Industrialization and Approaches of Main Economic Schools ... 237
7.2.1 The Growth Chain of the "National Economy" Approach ... 237
7.2.2 The Corporate Approach ... 248
7.2.3 The World Economy Approach of East Asian Industrialization ... 249
7.3 East Asia's Development as a Model of Late Industrialization ... 257
7.3.1 The Development Models of the 20th Century and the World Economy ... 257
7.3.2 Late Industrialization and the World Economy ... 259
7.4 East Asia's Industrialization and the World Economy ... 264
7.4.1 Dynamic Comparative Advantage and Technology Learning ... 264
7.4.2 Global Value Chain and Development of Domestic Firms ... 270
7.4.3 The Technological Development of NIEs and Economic "Upgrading" ... 280
7.5 Concluding Remarks ... 283
References ... 284

8 The Road to and from the East Asia's Currency and Economic Crisis 289
8.1 Introduction 289
8.2 The Impact of Currency and Economic Crisis on Asian Countries 290
8.3 Understanding East Asia's Currency and Economic Crisis and Its Transition 294
8.3.1 Popular Understanding of the Crisis and Controversies 295
8.3.2 Subsequent Arguments Regarding Liberalization and Regulations on Short-Term Capital Movement 303
8.4 The East Asian Currency and Economic Crisis and Japan 306
8.4.1 The Emergency Thailand Financial Support Meeting in Tokyo in August 1997 and the Asian Monetary Fund 306
8.4.2 The New Miyazawa Initiative in 1998 308
8.5 Groping for a New Regional Financial Cooperation Order in East Asia 312
8.5.1 Necessary of a Regional Financial System 312
8.5.2 Groping for the Stability of East Asian Currencies 314
8.5.3 Grouping Toward Regional Cooperation in East Asia 317
8.6 Concluding Remarks 319
References 321

9 Advancing Regionalism and Economic Cooperation in Asia 325
9.1 Introduction 325
9.2 Regionalism in the 20th Century and Its Development 326
9.2.1 Regional Integration Concepts and Decolonization Under 20th Century Imperialism 326
9.2.2 The 1960s: The Development of Two Asian Regionalisms 332
9.2.3 The 1970s to the 1990s: Two Coexisting Regionalisms 336
9.3 The Asian Currency Crisis and the Institutionalization of Regionalism 344
9.3.1 The Outbreak of the Asian Currency Crisis and the Institutionalization of Regional Cooperation in East Asia 345
9.3.2 ASEAN Community and Economic Integration 348
9.3.3 Two "East Asian Community" Initiatives 351

9.4 East Asian FTAs/EPAs Moving from Bilateral to Mega 352
9.4.1 Progress in Bilateral Regional Economic Integration 353
9.4.2 ASEAN+3 and APEC Wide-Area FTAs/EPAs Initiatives 357
9.4.3 Economic Effects of RCEP and CPTPP 362
9.5 Characteristics and Structure of East Asian Economic Integration 365
9.5.1 Promotion Structure of RCEP and CPTPP 365
9.5.2 Asian Economic Integration and China 371
9.6 Concluding Remarks 376
References 378

10 The Historical Roots of Unshared Growth: The Case of the Philippines 385
10.1 Introduction 385
10.2 Historical Context of Philippine Economic Development 386
10.2.1 Development Features (Post War) 386
10.2.2 Pre-modern Phase: 1500s to 1940 387
10.2.3 Agricultural Phase: 1945 to 1950 389
10.2.4 Import-Substitution Industrialization (ISI) Phase: 1950s to 1970s 390
10.2.5 Export-Oriented Industrialization Phase: 1980s to 1990s 392
10.2.6 De-Industrialization Phase: 1990s to Present 392
10.2.7 No EAM Report Part II 394
10.3 Lack of Strategic Sequencing 396
10.3.1 Dichotomy of Import-Substitution and Export-Oriented Industrialization 397
10.3.2 Premature Industrialization and Deindustrialization 401
10.4 Conclusion: Unshared Growth as a Critical Factor 407
References 408

11 Decentralization in the Philippines: From Inclusive to Shared Growth 411
11.1 Introduction 411
11.2 Systematic Review of Literature Methodology 414
11.2.1 Problem Identification 415
11.2.2 Literature Search 419
11.2.3 Data Evaluation 421
11.2.4 Data Analysis and Presentation 421

11.3 A Systematic Review of Literature on Horizontal Imbalance (Equity) 423
11.3.1 Pathways 424
11.3.2 Level 2 Literature 426
11.3.3 Level 3 Literature 428
11.3.4 Level 4 Literature 429
11.3.5 Some Observations 430
11.4 A Systematic Review of Literature on Vertical Imbalance (Efficiency) 431
11.4.1 Level 1 Literature 432
11.4.2 Level 2 Literature 434
11.4.3 Level 3 Literature 435
11.4.4 Level 4 Literature 436
11.5 Synthesis 438
References 440

Part III Toward a Better-Balanced Economic Development

12 Akamatsu's Flying Geese Model of Development in East Asia and Beyond 447
12.1 Introduction 447
12.2 The International Acceptance of the Flying Geese Model 448
12.3 The Birth and Succession of Akamatsu's FGM 450
12.3.1 Akamatsu's FGM: Prototype and Its Problem Awareness 451
12.4 The Birth of FGM 454
12.4.1 The Basic Model of Akamatsu's Flying Geese Theory 459
12.4.2 Succession and Development of Akamatsu's Flying Geese Model 461
12.5 Akamatsu-Kojima Flying Geese Model: Some Discussion Points 478
12.5.1 The Flying Geese Model and Dialectical Epistemology 478
12.5.2 The Characteristics of the Flying Geese Theory as a Theory of Industrialization of the Less Developed Countries 481
12.5.3 Changes in the Structure of the International Division of Labor and the Flying Geese Theory 490
12.6 Akamatsu's Flying Geese Theory and the Development of Less Developed Countries 495
References 498

13 New Structure of the Asian Economy for Trade and Resiliency 505
13.1 Introduction 505
13.2 Current Stage of Asia's Economic Development and Its Challenges Toward Shared Growth 506
13.3 Multi-layered Understanding and Empowerment of Asian Economic Development 511
13.4 Regionalization and Decentralization 515
13.5 Global Society at a Turning Point and Challenges for the Development of Asia 519
References 521

About the Authors

Hitoshi Hirakawa received his Ph.D. in economics from Kyoto University in 1996. He is currently a Professor Emeritus at Nagoya University and a Visiting Professor at Kokushikan University, Japan. He is also a Visiting Professor at Nankai University, Tianjin, China since 2005, and was a Chief Expert Professor at the Institute for Northeast Asian Studies, Zhejiang Yuexiu University of Foreign Languages, China between 2019 and 2020. He has previously taught at Nagasaki Prefectural University, Tokyo Keizai University, and other academic institutions in Japan. His research fields are modern Asian economic development in the global economy, and economic relations between Japan and Asian emerging economies from a historical perspective. He is author and co-editor, including NIES: The World System and Development (Tokyo: Dobunkan, 1992, in Japanese); Japan and Singapore in the World Economy: Japan's Economic Advance into Singapore, 1870-1965 (in collaboration with H. Shimizu, London and New York: Routledge, 1998); Codesign for a New East Asia after the crisis (co-editor with Y-H, Kim, Tokyo, Berlin, and Heidelberg: Springer Verlag, 2004); Servitization, IT-ization, and Innovation Models: Two-Stage Industrial Cluster Theory (co-editor with Tokumaru, N., Shinkai, N. et al., Oxon: Routledge, 2013); Innovative ICT Industrial Architecture in East Asia (co-editor with N. Takahashi, Ferdinand C. Maquito et al., Tokyo: Springer, 2017); "COVID-19 Pandemic and 'Emerging & Developing Economies'" (Kokusai Keizai, edited by the Japan Society of International Economics, Vol. 73, 2022, in Japanese).

Ferdinand C. Maquito received his Ph.D. in Economics from the University of Tokyo in 1996. He is currently an Assistant Professor at the Institute of Governance and Rural Development of the University of the Philippines Los Baños and an Affiliate Faculty of the Management and Development Studies at the University of the Philippines Open University. Before this, he received his BS Degree in Mechanical Engineering from the University of the Philippines Diliman, and through scholarships from the Center for Research and Communication, the Japanese Ministry of Education, and the Atsumi International Foundation, he was able to finish his MS in Industrial He is an author and co-author of various works about the Philippines:

"Decentralization, the Internal Revenue Allotment, and Shared Growth: An Examination of Correlations", Journal of Public Affairs and Development Volume 4, No. 1, 2017. "Firipin Keizai: Tei Seichou kara Dasshutsu no Kanousei" (The Philippine Economy: The Possibility of Escaping Low Growth) in ASEAN Keizai Shin Jidai to Nihon (ASEAN Economy's New Era and Japan) Tran Van Tho, et.al. (eds) Bunshindo 2016); "Kaigai Firipin Jin Roudousha no Ryuushutsu Pataan" (Pattern of Flows of Overseas Filipino Workers) in "Higashi Ajia Keizai to Roudou Idou" (The East Asian Economy and Labor Movements) Tran Van Tho, et. al. (eds), Bunshindo 2015; "KyouyuuGata Seichou Toshiteno Higashi Ajia Tougou" (An East Asian Integration as Shared Growth), Chapter 21 (co-authored with Hitoshi Hirakawa) in "Higashi Ajia no Shin Sangyou Shuseki: Chiiki Hatten to Kyouryoku/Kyousei" (New Industrial Agglomeration of East Asia: Regional Development in Cooperation and Symbiosis), Hitoshi Hirakawa, Makoto Tawada, Ryuhei Okumura, Nobuyoshi Yamori, Jong-He Seo (eds.), Tokyo: Gakujutsu Shuppankai, November 2010. He has also worked on Japan's unique features as applied in the Philippines: "Towards a Strategy for Manufactured Exports to Japan" Philippine-Japan Economic Partnership Agreement: Strengthening the Foundation for Regional Cooperation and Economic Integration Vol. 2 Philippine Institute of Development Studies 2014; "A Comparative Economic Analysis of Japanese-Style Labor Contracts from a Shared Growth Perspective" Philippine Journal of Labor and Industrial Relations Vol. 31, Nos. 1&2, 2011 (co-authored with Hitoshi Hirakawa); and "Rediscovering Japan's Leadership in Shared Growth Management". His long stay in Japan has imbued him with a deep interest in shared growth (efficiency with equity). With the untiring support of the Atsumi International Foundation and the collaboration of various educational institutions, he has led the organization of over 40 sustainable shared growth seminars.

Chapter 1
Introduction

The subject of this book is the economic development of Asia and its challenges, which has driven the structural transformation of the global economy over the past half-century or more, and has now brought China to challenge the United States. Asia's development has been achieved in the context of its engagement with the global economy, but has the mainstream economic school adequately captured this region's dynamics? This book attempts to get closer to the reality of Asian economic development by focusing on empirical facts and clarifying the issues involved. It also attempts to unravel some of the complex and diverse issues we face in the modern world today and to find clues to their solution.

Since the development of Asian economies, particularly those of East Asia, came to widespread attention in the 1970s, this region's development has been the subject of attempts to interpret it from various approaches. But to put it simply, the economic development of East Asia has far exceeded the expectations of economics in terms of its speed and spatial expansion. The mainstream school of economics, partly because the development was deeply related to trade, intuitively and deductively applied its abstract model to the development of East Asia and relied on this model as a basis for its own analysis. Although this analysis has been strongly criticized by scholars, who focus on the realities of development, such criticisms apparently have not only been ignored but prescriptions based on the mainstream model have been imposed on developing countries.

The neoliberal ideology initiated by British Prime Minister M. Thatcher and U.S. President Ronald Reagan in the 1980s became even more influential in policy circles as the universal ideology of capitalism with the fall of the Berlin Wall in late 1989 and the subsequent dissolution of the Soviet Union. It also became more influential in the academic world, both in the domestic policies of individual countries and in international development policies. Neoliberal economics, which has solidified its position in the mainstream, has applied its theories deductively to the development success stories of East Asian economies already on a development trajectory. Moreover,

H. Hirakawa and F. C. Maquito, *The Dynamics of Asian Economic Development*,
https://doi.org/10.1007/978-981-97-3106-0_1

international financial development institutions have imposed their policy packages on other emerging economies and developing regions based on these theories.

Joseph Stiglitz, a Columbia University professor and Nobel economist who has served as a Senior Vice President of the World Bank, has been a sharp critic of neoliberal economics. He criticizes mainstream economics in relation to the development of East Asian countries as follows.

> What is clear is that these countries did not follow the market fundamental model: markets played a critical role in their success, but it was managed markets, managed for the benefit of society as a whole, not for that of a few shareholders or managers; it was a market economy in which the government played the role of an orchestra conductor. It catalyzed growth, investing heavily in technology, education, and infrastructure (Stiglitz, 2015: 311).

Harvard University Professor Dani Rodrik is another economist skeptical of neoliberal economics. He carefully traces the history of the conflict between the "revisionist" school of economics (revisionist = statist), which emphasizes the importance of national industrial policies, and the mainstream school of economics that sees the development of emerging economies as the result of neoliberal policies. It describes how the East Asian research project, funded by the World Bank in an attempt to get the Japanese government to recognize its role in the development of Japan and East Asian countries, ultimately failed to achieve its goal of criticizing neoliberal policies, forcing the report to arrive at an ambiguous conclusion. The report, "The East Asian Miracle," acknowledges the role of government in the chapter analyzing the liberalization of financial markets, but fails to recognize the role of government in other chapters on industrial policy, thus obscuring whether the success of Asian countries was due to industrial policy or free market development. Rodrik, however, referring to the example of China's development, writes as clearly as Stiglitz that it was not a case of the neoliberal economic model.

The Chinese leadership resisted the conventional advice in opening their economy because removing barriers to trade would have forced many state enterprises to close without doing much to stimulate new investments in industrial activities. The Chinese decided to experiment with alternative mechanisms that would not create too much pressure on existing industrial structures. In particular, they relied on

> Special Economc Zones. ... [where in Foreign investors] were the source of technology, and they dominated exports. ... But, if China welcomed foreign companies, it always did so with the objective of fostering domestic capabilities (Rodrik, 2011: 152–153).

Kenichi Ohno, a Japanese economist and professor at the National Graduate Institute for Policy Studies (GRIPS), Japan, who was also an economist at the International Monetary Fund (IMF), wrote from his own experience that "apparently many economists at international organizations, despite leading market transition reforms in their countries, have never seriously considered even the definition of a market economy, let alone its historical creation process" (Ohno -J, 2000: 14). He relates his own experience at a conference on Central Asian economies in Washington, DC in the late 1990s, where Stanford University Professor Anne Krueger, who was the World Bank's Chief Economist, was asked, "Why don't international organizations study the history of marketization and industrialization in the West, the predecessor countries?" to which she replied, "I don't think it is an effective use of time for the IMF or the World Bank to study history" (Ohno -J, 2000: 37).

Ohno writes the following based on his experience in providing development assistance mainly to developing countries.

The World Bank, which is supposed to lead development policy, seems to be intellectually split within its ranks, with adherents of the old neoclassical school who thoroughly reject the term "industrial policy" itself, and economists who are comfortable with promoting industrial policy with certain conditions attached. The policy direction must be carried out by people or organizations with a deep understanding of the country-specific circumstances in order to avoid the folly of imposing identical solutions in each country. There is a huge gap between the intellectual contribution that developing country governments truly need and the knowledge that modern economics can provide (Ohno -J, 2013: 36–37).

Similarly, Toru Yanagihara, who was a party to a dispute of the Overseas Economic Cooperation Fund (OECF) with the World Bank over Japanese aid in the 1990s, also criticized the structural adjustment approach promoted by the World Bank, writing that the neoclassical economics paradigm is "essentially ahistorical and non-evolutionary", and thus "misses important strategic issues in the course of economic development". The World Bank's basic policy approach is a "framework" approach based on neoclassical economics, which assumes that the autonomous adjustment mechanism of the market is all-powerful, and the government and companies that are the actors in development are treated as a black box. In contrast to this, the interest of the Japanese policy approach, which is an "ingredients approach", seeks to "foster and develop firms and industries under governmental leadership and guidance" (Yanagihara, 1997: 1, 9–10). More than 20 years have already passed since Ohno and Yanagihara's criticisms. Attempts, since then, by researchers gathered at development finance institutions, the Institute of Developing Economies, and other institutions to theorize economic cooperation in the context of Japan's development experience have since been largely abandoned. Japanese academia have, by in large, chosen to follow the trend of mainstream economics, and Japan's interest in theorizing its development experience was lost.[1] Despite it all, Japan has gone through several lost decades since neoliberal thinking started to gain prominence in the 1980s, even eliciting a mea culpa from a prominent economist involved at the highest levels in the liberalization thrust of Japan (Nakatani, 2011). Moreover, the Philippines too was caught in the grip of neoliberal policies, and embarked on an aggressive pursuit of liberalization policies since the 1980s, which has not really prevented its economy,

[1] In a 2008 essay, Y. Sawada, who received a degree from Stanford University and became an Associate Professor at the University of Tokyo, pointed out that Japan development research rarely appears in prestigious international development research journals. It is a quasi-intellectual production that summarizes reports of international organizations and existing research, and it cannot be said that it has been useful for international intellectual dissemination with long-term effects" (Sawada, 2008). Mainstream economics in Japan failed to understand the significance of the controversy with the neoclassical school of economics that emanated from Japan's development experience.

particularly its industrial sector, from falling behind its cohorts (Aldaba, 2013). It is safe to say that criticisms of mainstream economics have still not lost their validity.

The cognitive problems of mainstream economics are similarly ironically pointed out by Israeli historian Yuval N. Harari. "Many neo-liberal economists and political scientists argue that it is best to leave all the important decisions in the hands of the free market. They thereby give politicians the perfect excuse for inaction and ignorance, which are reinterpreted as profound wisdom" (Harari, 2015: 439). This laissez faire attitude of neoclassical economics, however, is not confined to the issue of efficiency, but also extends to the concept of equity.

Although not directly related to the development of East Asia, it is not useless to reiterate the point made by Carl B. Frey of Oxford University regarding the cognitive characteristics of neoclassical economics. He critically writes as follows, using as an example Kuznets' formulation of the so-called inverted U-shaped curve, an experience from the U.S. case study, which has had a great influence on economics, that income inequality increases in the early stages of industrialization but eventually shrinks as the economy grows. "Like the doomsday economists of the Industrial Revolution, twentieth-century economists were unfortunately fond of developing iron laws of economics that could be used to explain the trajectory of capitalist development for every time and place, though it is not hard to understand their appeal. Kuznets's theory, which shaped how economists thought about inequality for half a century, was intuitive and straightforward". Needless to say, Frey rejects this supposed universal Kuznets curve, citing rebuttals by researchers such as Paris School of Economics Professor Thomas Piketty (Frey, 2019: 206–211). What is certain is that the development of East Asian countries was not simply the result of neoliberal policies and the functioning of market mechanisms alone.

This book, like Stiglitz and Rodrik, sees Asian economic development beginning with East Asia as a different case from the neoliberal model of development. It also tries to view Asian economic development from a multifaceted perspective as a development within the global economy. Based on the authors' empirical understanding of the actual situation, the development of this region is not a development phenomenon as a mere aggregation of one country's economy, but a development phenomenon, on one hand, in the Asian region deeply related to the international expansion of developed country enterprises, and on the other hand, a development phenomenon achieved through the involvement of development actors in less-developed countries. Therefore, we are attempting to approach the issue using both a global economy approach and a local economy approach.

Although economic globalization has been actively discussed since the 1990s, it did not begin in the 1990s. As this book reveals, Newly Industrializing Economies (NIEs) have already begun to develop since the late 1960s, mainly by accepting the international expansion of Japanese enterprises, which were met with appropriate policy responses from East Asian countries. The juxtaposition of (a) the world economy surrounding Asia as the ruling factor, and (b) the policy-oriented development efforts of the least developed countries at the national level, began in this period.

The following examples will help us understand this. The World Bank report "The East Asian Miracle," which Rodrik also noted, excludes China from consideration because its ownership structure and the way China's economy is run and governed by corporations and citizens differ from those of other countries. However, Japan, Hong Kong, South Korea, Singapore, Taiwan, Indonesia, Malaysia, and Thailand are grouped together as High-performing Asian economies (HPAEs) because of their common characteristics, such as rapid export growth, and more broadly, shared growth (World Bank, 1993).

The authors note here that the Philippines is also excluded from the report. It is not at all the case that the Philippines has not pursued development. In the 1950s, the Philippines was the country with the highest level of development in Asia and the most promising future prospects. Despite its early adoption of development policies, the Philippines lagged behind its East Asian neighbors and was excluded from growth studies in the 1990s. How did this come about?

In this century, the "middle-income trap" theory has emerged as an economic analysis of such cases. The "middle-income trap" theory has been widely analyzed since two authors, I. Gill and H. Kharas, published the World Bank report An East Asian Renaissance in 2007. The report's main concern was whether East Asian countries, especially China, which had risen from low-income to middle-income status in the World Bank's income grouping, could continue to develop toward high-income status. The report considered this a problem to be avoided by shifting to the economic structure of advanced economies. The report examined various issues, including the shift of the economy's center of gravity from investment to innovation, the education system and the development of skilled labor, economies of scale, cohesion and inequality, and corruption (Gill & Kharas, 2007: 17–39).

The epistemological feature of this approach is that it takes economically successful countries and enumerates the challenges from its analysis. It certainly appears objective. However, it is flawed by the weak perspective of the parties involved on the developing country side. Countries and societies aiming for development should, of course, learn from the lessons of developing countries that have succeeded in development, but from the perspective of the development of developing countries, they can only formulate policies based on their own domestic conditions. The development policies of the developing countries are in an evolutionary process of linking their economies directly and indirectly to the various elements of globalization in accordance with their own realities. Simply looking at only those countries that have succeeded in development and identifying the common threads of success only captures the opposite side of the effectiveness of development policies. Although this may seem objective at first glance, from the standpoint of those involved in development, the specific aspects of developing countries are missing. There must be a movement toward inclusion of developing economies from the side of economic globalization and policy attempts to catch up from the side of the least developed countries under the pressure or inducement of globalization.

The following case may be instructive. Since the 1960s, export processing zones, free trade zones, and special economic zones (SEZs) have been established in Asia and other developing regions of the world. In most cases, the significance of the establishment of such zones differs between the party entering the zone and the party hosting the zone. While the main purpose of establishing special economic zones for foreign enterprises on the entry side was to take advantage of low-cost labor, the purpose of establishing special economic zones for developing countries on the receiving side was to gain foreign currency, secure employment, and at the same time protect domestic companies and markets while acquiring foreign product manufacturing technology, business management technology, and information on overseas markets. The significance of the same policy measure differs between the capital entry side and the capital receiving side. The development of East Asia must be viewed as a synthesis of these two vectors. Many Asian developing countries have gone through these policy steps to develop local firms, to increase their economic independence, and now to give birth to market economies. This process has naturally led to some enterprises entering the region through Foreign Direct Investment (FDI) but failing and withdrawing, with some of the later developing countries losing out in the competition to attract companies from other countries.

Some countries have adopted inconsistent policies in attracting FDI, while others have failed to achieve success in absorbing firms and technology. This is because it is a process of evolution that entails some path dependency. The study of economic development in the emerging and developing economies of East Asia will have limited policy effectiveness if the evolutionary process of development is excluded from the framework of the study of development. It should be noted that there are perspectives that are left out from merely considering the causal relationships among success stories.

A regional overview of the development of East Asian economies would be too formalistic if it were merely a collection of country-by-country analyses. Why did the development of East Asian developing economies begin in the NIEs and eventually spread to the Association of Southeast Asian Nations (ASEAN) countries and China? The combination of the international strategies of multinational corporations in developed countries and the responses of developing countries to those strategies must be examined across national borders. Otherwise, we will not be able to follow the development trajectory of East Asian countries.

The reason this book was authored by two authors was our desire to examine the changes that have occurred in the East Asian region from an economic perspective in line with the realities of the region. One of the authors, Hitoshi Hirakawa, has emphasized that, at the regional level in East Asia, economic development in the region was initially achieved through the international business activities of multinational corporations of advanced nations, mainly Japanese firms. Here, the international activities of multinational corporations from advanced economies require special attention. International capital flows are not merely quantitative capital flows. It is characterized by the transfer of various economic factors such as product technology, production technology, business management technology, commodities, and market information through direct investment. From the multinational corporation's perspective, the objective is to strengthen market competitiveness by efficiently transferring their technology and information to the emerging Asian countries that are less developed as part of their corporate activities. However, as explained in the above-mentioned example of export processing zones, the latecomer Asian countries that accept the Multinational Corporations (MNCs) have their own policy intentions. The development of Asia has occurred in the combination of the two.

Another author, Ferdinand C. Maquito examined the evolution of development, particularly from the side of developing countries, using the Philippines as a case study. One of his main interests has been to look at the Japanese development experience and connect this to the local level of development of the Philippines. As noted above, neoliberal economics has virtually no economic policies conducive to developing countries, and Maquito looks at the Philippines' attempts at development in this context, but also considers the Philippines' development potential in the context of other East Asian countries as well as in relation to developed country enterprises, especially Japan.

In this book, we have examined the reality that the economic development of Asian countries, starting with East Asia, has been achieved, in the postwar world economy since the 1960s and the progress of economic globalization, through a process of evolution on the part of the developing countries. This book also examined the reality of the new challenges that the region faces both internationally and domestically. In this context, we attempted to discover the dynamics of East Asia and Asia as a whole.

Part One "Asian economy and transformation of the world economy" consists of five chapters. Here, we discuss how the U.S.-Sino trade war, initiated by President Trump in 2017 under the banner of "Make America Great Again" and "America first," deepened into a struggle for supremacy between the U.S. and China after a pandemic of a novel coronavirus. Furthermore, we will examine the economic development of China, which became the main actor in this struggle for hegemony, within the context of the development mechanism of East Asia. Next, we trace the development of China's "One Belt, One Road" initiative as a global strategy and consider its significance and challenges. Finally, automation and the digital economy brought about by advances in ICT are creating new development paths in South Asia, especially India, and in Southeast Asia, including the Philippines. We also examined the possibilities and challenges of this development. The titles of the chapters are as follows: Chap. 2 "The Impact of Trade Wars and Pandemics on the Asian Economy"; Chap. 3 "Asia's Changing Mechanism of Development and the Global Economy"; Chap. 4 "China's Belt and Road Initiative and Its Prospect"; and Chap. 5 "Another Way of Development Through ICT: Possibility and Vulnerability".

Part two "The roots of Asia's development experience after the World War Two" consists of five chapters. In this part, first, we will examine the development of East Asian developing economies chronologically, beginning with the NIEs and tracing the paths by which their development spilled over into the East Asian region, in order to understand the characteristics of East Asian regional economic development in relation to the world economy. Next, we look at the Asian currency crisis that broke out in the late 1990s and the subsequent swell of regionalism and regional cooperation. We will also extract the characteristics of the Philippines' policies in economic development during this period, and examine how these policies are deeply rooted in history. The chapter titles are as follows: Chap. 6 "The Case of the Philippines in the Asian Economy"; Chap. 7 "The East Asian Export-Led Industrialization in the Global Economy"; Chap. 8 "The Road to and from the East Asia's Currency and Financial Crisis"; Chap. 9 "Advancing Regionalism and Cooperation in East Asia"; Chap. 10 "The Historical Root of Unshared Growth: The Case of the Philippines"; and Chap. 11 "Decentralization in the Philippines: From Inclusive to Shared Growth".

In Part three "Toward a better-balanced economic development", we will trace in detail the development process of Kaname Akamatsu and Kiyoshi Kojima's theory of the flying geese pattern, which has attracted attention as an explanatory theory of East Asian development since the late 1980s, and reexamine its significance today. The titles of the two chapters are as follows. Chap. 12 is "Akamatsu's Flying Geese Model of Development in East Asia and Beyond." Chap. 13 is "A New Structure of the Asian Economy for Trade Peace and Resiliency".

Note that this book has hosted over 40 online study sessions since 2019, and all chapters have been reviewed. It is literally a book of collaborative research. We chose to jointly author this book because we felt that there were barriers that could not be overcome by our individual research alone. The authors believe that by jointly authoring this book, the development of the less developed economies and the challenges they face have become even clearer. Therefore, there is no need to divide the authors of this book, but the chapters have been written by the two authors based on their previous research results, with one chapter written in collaboration with a faculty member of the University of the Philippines Los Baños. The writing assignments are as follows. Chaps. 1, 2, 9, 10, 12, and 13 are collaborations of H. Hirakawa and F. C. Maquito, Chaps. 3–5, and Chaps. 7 and 8 written by H. Hirakawa, and Chap. 6, and 10 written by F. C. Maquito, and Chap. 11 jointly written by F. C. Maquito and Damcelle T. Cortes of the College of Public Affairs and Development of the University of the Philippines Los Baños.

A quarter of this century has now passed. During this period, Asia has grown remarkably and, as a result, has made dramatic progress in the structural transformation of the world economy. The struggle for hegemony between the U.S. and emergent China has intensified, and decoupling in areas related to advanced technology and security has been progressing, giving rise once again to what has been called the new "Cold War". In addition, the development of ICT is accelerating changes in the international community through the digitization of the economy and the birth of Artificial Intelligence (AI). The U.S.-China trade war, the COVID-19 pandemic, the development of ICT and the deepening of the digital economy, global warming, the war in Ukraine, the Israel-Hamas war, and many others have occurred since the late 2010s. These events are challenging the current order, rules, and common sense established in the twentieth century. Global environmental problems and global warming have emerged as an issue that the world cannot avoid. It is as if the state of modern civilization is being confronted with an enormous challenge from both the past and the future.

The world is increasingly seeing a resurgence of nationalism and violence. But at the same time that the framework of economic development transcends national borders, the solution of these challenges calls for international cooperation that is fundamentally premised on the framework of national borders. We cannot solve today's challenges if we fall into narrow-minded nationalism, either at the national level or at the local level. What we need to learn is to recognize each other's local diversity and deepen mutual understanding beyond national borders, while at the same time striving to strengthen social foundations at the local level. No doubt the resolution of today's challenges will take time, with no shortcut in sight.

One thing that we can say is necessary, however, is that in a changing world, there is a need for reflection on the state of economics, with its market economy-oriented universalism. Avoiding such reflection and simply following changes in the phenomenological aspects will not only leave behind the challenges that remain to be solved today, but will also deepen the crisis.

Turning to the economies of Asia, this book attempts to clarify the mechanisms of dramatic development over the past half-century, while at the same time focusing on the economic issues that have been neglected in this development. The development problems of the developing regions of the world, including Asian countries, require diversity and harmonious development in the global economy. To this end, this book looks at the relationship between the regional and local levels within the global economy. It will be of great pleasure to the two authors if this book can be of any help to the development of the developing countries.

References

**Documents with a symbol (-J) after the author's name are Japanese documents*

Aldaba, R. (2013). Twenty years after Philippine Trade Liberalization and Industrialization: What has happened and where do we go from here, Manila: *PIDS Discussion Paper Series* no. 2013-21.

Frey Carl, B. (2019). *The technology trap*. Princeton University Press.

Gill, I., & Kharas, H. (2007). *An East Asian renaissance: Ideas for economic growth*. World Bank.

Harari Yuval, N. (2015). *Homo deus: A brief history of tomorrow*. Vintage.

Nakatani, I. -J. (2011). *Shihon shugi naze jikai shita no ka "Nihon saisei" he no teigen (Why did capitalism self-destruct: a proposal for "Japan's revival")*. Shueisha Bunko.

Ohno, K. -J. (2000). *Tojokoku no gurobarizeshon* (*Developing countries in globalization*), Tokyo: Toyo Keizai Shinposha.

Ohno, K. -J. (2013). *Sangyo seisaku no tsukurikata* (*How to create industrial policies*). Yuhikaku Publishing Co., Ltd.

Rodrik, D. (2011). *The globalization paradox: Why global markets, states, and democracy can't coexist*. Oxford University Press.

Sawada, Y. -J. (2008). Kaihatsu enjo kenkyuryoku takameyo (Boost research capacity in development assistance). *Keizai Kyoshitsu*, Nihon Keizai Shimbun, October 31 (Posting on *RIETI Column* on November 11, 2008. Research Institute of Economy, Trade, and Industry), https://www.rieti.go.jp/jp/papers/contribution/sawada/01.html.

Stiglitz Joseph, E. (2015). *The great divide*. W.W. Norton & Company (2016 Penguin Books).

World Bank. (1993). *The East Asian miracle: Economic growth and public policy*. Oxford University Press.

Yanagihara, T. (1997). Economic system approach and its applicability. In: Yanagihara, T., & Sambommats, S. (Eds.), *East Asian development experience: Economic system approach and its applicability*. Institute of Development Economies.

Part I
The Asian Economy and the Transformation of the World Economy

Chapter 2
The Impact of Trade Wars and Pandemics on the Asian Economy

Abstract The U.S.-Sino trade war, which started in 2018 and was followed by the novel corona (COVID-19) pandemic, has dramatically intensified the U.S.-Sino conflict with the "America First" policy of the 45th U.S. President Trump directed against China. The point of conflict, which started from the trade deficit, has spread beyond the escalation of tariffs by both countries, to include invasion of intellectual property rights, unfair industrial policies, cyberattacks, technology hegemony, national security risks, human rights, and the system or ideology of the state. Keeping in mind an emergent China, the new Biden administration of the U.S. born in 2021 moved towards strengthening ties with the pro-human rights democrats. On the other hand, China is aiming for the upgrading of its domestic industrial structure in a bid to become more self-reliant and maintain a hardline diplomatic stance as it moves forward with BRI in external relations. Revolving around China's BRI, the intensification of the U.S.-Sino rivalry has promoted infrastructure provision and would be able to give birth to the possibility of Asian expansion into the Afro-Eurasian economic zone in the future. At the end of this chapter, we will briefly discuss the effects and issues posed by a gigantic China on the emerging economies of Southeast Asia.

Keywords U.S.-Sino trade war · "Trump Deal" · COVID-19 · Trade deficit · Intellectual property rights · Technological hegemony · Human rights violation

2.1 Introduction

2020 to 2021 would probably be determined as the years when the world economy shifted from the past development track. The novel corona pandemic (COVID-19) spread quickly across the globe after a mass outbreak in China. Overlapping with the trade war between the two largest economies in the world, this pandemic brought about large changes in the globalization that started nearly half a century ago.

Economic globalization was already underway around the 1970s. This was accelerated from the 1990s by the dramatic development of Information and Computer

H. Hirakawa and F. C. Maquito, *The Dynamics of Asian Economic Development*,
https://doi.org/10.1007/978-981-97-3106-0_2

Technology (ICT). The COVID-19 virus used the very channels built up by this globalization to move goods and people to launch what may look like a simultaneous attack by terrorists on the hubs of this global network. During these two years, it was shown how overly optimistic the early prognosis was held by governments, international institutions, and many people. COVID-19 accelerated the structural changes in the world economy that had started before its outbreak.

Needless to say, the biggest driver of these changes is China, which rode on and surpassed the bounds of the wave of East Asian economic development. From a less developed country of Asia, communist China rode the wave of globalization in the last quarter of the twentieth century and in this century grew out of its Asian shell to land on the world stage, challenging the U.S. With the aggressive policies taken by the Trump administration against China and the ensuing COVID-19 outbreak, this challenge has taken on the character of a conflict that is giving birth to a new world economic structure.

In this chapter, we first discuss the features of the U.S.-Sino conflict by tracing back the policies of the 45th president of the U.S., Donald Trump, vis-a-vis Asia, especially with regards to China. We also look into the intensification of this conflict due to the attack of COVID-19 in the final year of the Trump administration. The after taste of President Trump even now holds the attention of the U.S. We shall consider what his China policy has brought about to China and the world.

2.2 The Circumstances and Structure of the U.S.-Sino Trade War

In this section, we shall consider the trade policy towards China called the "Deal" of the 45th President of the U.S., Trump whose trade negotiations with China are strongly idiosyncratic. By tracing the structure of circumstances of these negotiations, we shall clarify the reasons and features of the U.S.-Sino trade war.

2.2.1 *The Birth of the Trump Administration and the Trade War with China*

In January 2020, the "First Phase Agreement" of the "U.S.-Sino Trade War" was reached. The U.S.-Sino trade war was initiated by the 45th President Trump (hereafter simply President Trump) in March 2018. This is related to the idiosyncrasies of the "Trump Deal", which he prefers to use and its tendency to dramatically escalate a conflict from the outset. The "Trump Deal" is not limited to negotiations between the U.S. and China, but it is where the "Trump Deal" is particularly evident. In this chapter, we shall first look at this.

The first task of Donald Trump, who was inaugurated in January 2017 as President, was to sign the Presidential Decree of withdrawing from the Trans-Pacific Partnership 12 (TPP12). He considered the U.S. trade deficit as a defeat and was the result of "unfair" transactions. Incidentally, the U.S. trade deficit in 2017 was US$793.4 billion, of which US$375.4 billion (47.3%) was with China.

On March 8, 2018, President Trump announced the addition of a 25% and a 10% tariff on steel and aluminum imports, respectively, ignoring the rules of WTO international agreements, citing Section 232 of the 1962 Trade Expansion Act of the U.S. The tariffs were imposed on the 23rd of the same month. Section 232 allows the imposition of tariffs without Congress approval in the case where the national security of the U.S. is threatened. With the levying of the tariffs, however, President Trump not only broke the WTO rule but also did not discriminate between allied and non-allied countries. In treating the U.S. allies as a threat to U.S. national security, this measure posed a contradiction that made it an unacceptable sanction to the Northern American and European allies of the U.S. Unaligned China and Russia considered this as a disregard for internationally-agreed WTO rules and proclaimed retaliatory measures against imports from the U.S. (Nihon Keizai Shimbun, Dec. 30, 2018, hereafter, it was written as Nikkei-J, -J means in Japanese).

President Trump, in the presidential elections of 2016, adopted the slogans "America First" and "Make America Great Again". This was spectacularly concretized in the execution of Section 232. Based on this domestic law, the WTO international rule was broken, and an interpretation of the domestic law was forced upon Congress. Not only this, but the law's execution also contradicted its essence of upholding national security when it imposed sanctions even on U.S. allies.

A series of additional tariffs aimed at China was initiated. On March 22nd, a day before the promulgation of Section 232 of the Trade Expansion Act, President Trump announced additional tariffs on Chinese products on the basis of Section 301 of 1974 Trade Act. There were additional tariffs of 25% on 50 to 60 billion dollars worth of Chinese products. Under the instructions of the President in August 2017, the U.S. Trade Representative (USTR) section undertook a survey of China's coercive and unfair technology transfer policies, as well as the violations of intellectual property rights, among others. The results of the survey legitimized the execution of Section 301 (White House Presidential Memorandum, 2018).

This of course broke the WTO rules. China promptly announced a countermeasure. Since then, concessions could not be seen in the U.S.-China negotiations. For three consecutive months, as shown in Fig. 2.1, a series of additional tariffs were imposed on Chinese imports from July 2018, for the first to the third round, a total of US$250 billion worth of imports were subjected to additional tariffs. China has sought the adjudication of the WTO. In September of the next year, the fourth round of additional tariffs were imposed on US$110 worth of imports.

However, the US$150 billion imports of Chinese goods by the U.S. is merely about a third of China's exports. By the third round, China's countermeasures were reaching a sense of stalemate as it became unable to adopt proportionally equivalent countermeasures. There was an increasing awareness that discussions were becoming unfavorable for China. Nevertheless, the U.S.-Sino discussions went on to the fourth

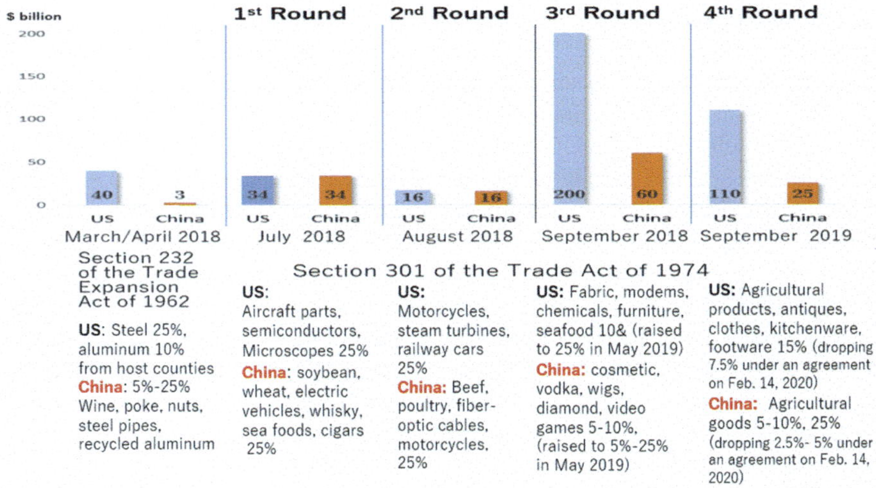

Fig. 2.1 The U.S.-Sino additional tariffs since March 2018: Tariffs, by percentage rate, imposed by the U.S. and China on each other (*Source* created by Hirakawa from JETRO Business Brief, Feb. 21, 2020, Bloomberg News, Sep. 15, 2020, etc.)

round. This conflict went on for nearly two years, and in January 2020, the "first phase agreement" was reached, leading to the partial lowering of additional tariffs in the following month. Figure 2.1 summarizes the additional U.S.-Sino tariffs.

2.2.2 *U.S. Policy Against China and Its Determination Mechanism*

U.S.-Sino trade talks are called "trade wars". The negotiation technique of the "Trump Deal", which is preferred and used by President Trump himself, has a tendency to call the talks as such. From the outset, "Trump's Art of the Deal" is different from the usually assumed negotiation style, as it starts with a "threat" element. The "Trump Deal" could be summarized into about four components or characteristics, with three distinguishable actors, and, if intensively conducted, could be finished in four rounds of negotiations, as summarized in the Table 2.1.

The four components or characteristics of the Trump Deal are: 1. a disregard of rules and a one sided demand based on self-righteousness; 2. escalation of sanctions; 3. an intuitive judgment of policies; and 4. dealers meeting. The actors are: the President himself; anti-China hardliners of the administration; and Congress.

Trump's extremist negotiation technique stands out in each phase. However, looking back at the negotiations, we notice that the role played by anti-China hardliners and congress is extremely big. Among the anti-China hardliners are Peter Navarro (all occupations below are contemporaneous), who was an adviser during the presidential elections, Robert Emmet Lighthizer (U.S. Trade Representative or

Table 2.1 Four rounds of the U.S. President Trump

Trump deal round number	Date and place	Description
1	May 2018 @ Washington DC	U.S.: to "temporarily withhold" sanctions and retaliatory tariffs China: promised large purchases of agricultural and energy products President Trump unilaterally scrapped the agreement, and announced the imposition of additional tariffs against China → 3 rounds of additional tariffs on U.S. imports from China; China imposes retaliatory tariffs
2	Dec. 2018 @G20 Summit	Ceasefire China, however, rejected the White House's announcement that promises were exchanged regarding matters beyond the trade deficit
3	Dec. 2019 @G20 Summit	Ceasefire U.S.: activation of the 4th round of additional tariffs was suspended, and agreement was reached to relax the transactions ban of U.S. firms with Huawei China: promised increased imports of agricultural products, and it is thought that it proposed a summit meeting between Trump and Kim Jong-un of North Korea
4	Oct. 10, 2019–Jan. 15, 2020 @Washington DC	Phase 1 Agreement reached (for re-presidential election) China: promised to import agriculture products and others over two years US$200 billion worth, and to protect intellectual assets, to abandon forced technological transfer, and to liberate financial services. Reduced additional tariff rates in half on agricultural imports and others of $7.5 billion worth (See also Fig. 2.1)

(*Source* Made by Hirakawa)

USTR), and Mike Pompeo (Secretary of State). They have a strong distrust of China's system and its diplomatic methods, and could be considered as a decoupling faction that seeks to sever the relations of U.S. firms with China. Like the anti-China hardliners in the administration, Congress has viewed, beyond republican-democrat party lines, China with a strong sense of distrust and a threat in various areas such as intellectual property rights violations, unfair industrial policies, technology hegemony risks, and national security risks (Hirakawa -J, 2021a, 2021b).

Trade negotiations were naturally triggered by the U.S. trade deficit, and sought to reduce the deficit. However, as the negotiations wore on the points of discussion were essentially shifting to those emphasized by the anti-Chinese hardliners in the administration and congress, such as unfair trade and industrial policies, technological hegemony and national security, human rights, and ideological systems. In

December 2018, on the day that President Trump and Chairman Xi Jinping had a meeting, the deputy chair of the board of Huawei was arrested in Canada.[1] By 2019, the chief negotiator changed from Treasury Secretary Steven Mnuchin, a moderate who focused on the reduction of America's trade deficit, to the hardliner Robert Lighthizer, who focused on trade policy and frontier technology theft. During this period, the latter's concerns were being brought to fore. Looking more concretely at the "deal", we can discern a gap between President Trump's direct intentions and the content of the negotiations. Here we could see the positions of the anti-China hardliners with those in the Congress. But, before we go into its explanation, let's start by pointing out that this was a unilateral sanction. The White House initially announced sanctions on a scale of US$50 billion. However, this was later raised by the President to US$60 billion. The amount of reduction of the trade deficit with China was initially US$100 billion and was doubled to US$200 billion by May. During the first round of negotiations, the sanctions for the second round were publicly disclosed, while the sanctions for the third round were publicly disclosed in the second round. It was a technique of threatening even larger sanctions if the proposed sanctions are not accepted.

The first "Trump Deal" was observed in May 2018. In trade talks held in Washington, Treasury Secretary Steven Mnuchin and China's Deputy Prime Minister Liu He reached an agreement to "temporarily withhold" sanctions and retaliatory tariffs. In return, China promised large purchases of agricultural and energy products. At the end of the same month, however, President Trump unilaterally scrapped the agreement, and announced the imposition of additional tariffs against China. Just before this, however, in April he instructed the Department of Commerce to lift its transaction ban on ZTE Corporation, a large Chinese communications device company. On a direct request from President Xi Jinping, President Trump decided to lift the transaction ban on the ZTE Corporation as a "personal favor" (Bloomberg -J, May 15, 2018; Nikkei -J, May 16, 2018). In July, the transaction ban was lifted upon ZTE Corporation's payment of the US$1 billion fine (News Japan, May 30, 2018; Nikkei -J, June 20, 2018; Bloomberg News, July 24, 2018). With this, ZTE Corporation, whose manufacturing operations were paralyzed by the sanctions, has weathered a difficult storm.

The President, on one hand, reneged on the official agreements of the negotiating team, while, on the other hand, shelved the state sanctions on firms that violated U.S. laws so as to prioritize "personal favors" to the Chinese leaders. Such lopsided handling of agreements by Trump also means that the anti-China hardliners within his administration held the leading position in the negotiations.

Since the establishment of the Xi Jinping Order around 2013, the U.S. was steadily becoming more and more distrustful of China. Under Xi Jinping's order, coral reefs in the South China Sea were being landfilled for the construction of military facilities, signaling the start of the BRI construction. The industrial policy based on "China

---

[1] In September 2021, the U.S. Prosecutor's Office reached a Deferred Prosecution Agreement (DPA) with CFO Meng Wanzhou, and announced the ending of criminal actions. With this Meng was released from custody and went back to China.

Manufacturing 2025" was crafted in 2015, and the "national intelligence law" was enacted in 2017. This law imposed on all organizations and citizens of China the "obligation to cooperate in the country's intelligence activities". In the following year, the constitutional limit to the president's term was abolished. These series of events were considered by liberalist factions as the resurgence of dictatorship that could be a threat to national security of the U.S. Clearly stating China as a military threat, the U.S. announced its National Security Strategy (NSS) in 2017, and its National Defense Strategy (NDS) in 2018. In this same year, the Office of Trade and Manufacturing Policy (OTMP),[2] which is under the direct supervision of the President, issued a report claiming that China is seeking to dominate the world market, and is obtaining intellectual assets through the use of unfair means. In the summer of the same year, Congress passed the "National Defense Authorization Act", and sought prohibiting the transactions with five companies including Huawei and ZTE Corporation.

These series of events became the focus of Vice-President Spence's talk at the Hudson Institute. In his talk, he launched an all-out criticism of the Chinese Communist Party, claiming that China is: interfering in the democratic affairs of the U.S.; scheming of dominating frontline technology industries with "China Manufacturing 2025"; conducting currency manipulation, coercive technology transfer, and theft of intellectual property rights; and setting up "debt traps" in the developing regions. He considered a deterioration in the U.S.-Sino relations as inevitable, and concessions in top negotiations to be unlikely.

In the U.S.-Sino leader's meeting held at the G20 Summit in Buenos Aires, Argentina in December of the same year, however, a "ceasefire" of the trade war was agreed upon. This is the second part of the "Trump Deal." President Trump was proud of the fruits of the negotiation that agreed on China lowering the additional tariffs or even abolishing the additional tariffs on automobiles. The additional tariffs of 25% on US$20 billion worth of imports, for the third round planned for January of the next year, 2019, was suspended for 90 days.

China, however, rejected the White House's announcement that promises were exchanged aiming for the agreement in such matters as efforts to correct the trade imbalances with China during the grace period, coercive technological transfer, intellectual asset protection, non-tariff barriers, and cyber attacks. Later on, the chief U.S. negotiator Mnuchin was replaced with the hardliner Lighthizer.

Actually, the focus of the negotiations shifted from the trade deficit to other matters such as the abandonment of the industrial policy "China Manufacturing 2025" and frontier technology theft. As was mentioned above, in the high-level talks of December, Huawei Vice President Meng Wanzhou was arrested. At the end of the same year, President Trump also activated the "International Emergency Economic Powers Act". This Act prohibited U.S. firms from procuring, from the overseas communication devices market, Huawei and ZTE Corporation products (Reuters, Dec. 27, 2018).

---

[2] OTMP is an organization established by Presidential Decree and has Peter Navarro as Director.

In the vice-ministerial trade talks that started from January 2019, China proposed that it will increase its "imports of energy, agricultural, and industrial products from 12 sectors" and in six years will bring down its trade surplus with the U.S. to zero (Bloomberg News, Jan. 19, 2019). At the end of the same month, China presented, among other things, the schedule of structural reforms and intellectual asset protection. In the negotiations of late February, President Trump assessed that a "big leap forward" has been made, and suspended the raising of additional tariffs of the upcoming third phase. It seems that Chinese leaders worked very hard on the negotiations. The Chinese side did not admit to subsidizing the regional governments with "China Manufacturing 2025", but accepted the abolition of central government subsidies for R&D. Having the bitter experience of conceding to an unfair agreement in the past, however, the Chinese leadership would agree on the condition that additional tariffs are immediately and evenly removed by both sides. The Trump administration, however, did not accept this request.

As it turned out, in May 2019, President Xi Jinping reduced to a hundred pages the agreement proposal document of around 150 pages, of which around 90% was already completed, and sent it to the U.S. According to Reuters, "the promise of a legislation reform, which was to resolve issues in protection of intellectual assets and corporate secrets, competition policies, access to the financial services market, and manipulation of foreign exchange, was scrapped" (Reuters -J, May 9, 2019). On the other hand, Xi Jinping, together with Liu He, at the Jiangxi memorial hall for the departure area of the long march, called for a "New Long March", while visiting the rare earth enterprises of the province. The "Long March" is considered as the "Arduous March" which led to the success of the Chinese revolution through a strategic retreat that span 12,000 km during the civil war between the Chinese Communist Party and the Nationalist Party. In short, Xi Jinping urged the Chinese leadership and citizenry to be prepared for a long struggle, while impressing upon both local and foreign audiences that China is in possession of a strategic material. Incidentally, this means that the negotiations were back where they started.

Looking at China's response, on May 5th, Trump announced the raising, on May 10th, to 25% the additional tariffs on US$200 billion worth of imports in the third round of additional tariffs, putting pressure on China. On June 10th, Xi was pressured to hold a top-level meeting at the G20 Summit to be held in Osaka in the same month, otherwise additional tariffs would be immediately imposed on the remaining US$300 billion worth of imports from China.

This third "Trump Deal", which materialized in the G20 summit, once again reached a "cease fire." The activation of the additional tariffs of the fourth phase was suspended, and agreement was reached to relax the transactions ban of Huawei with U.S. firms. China promised increased imports of agricultural products.[3] It is thought, considering the circumstances before and after the Trump-Xi meeting, that it proposed a summit meeting between Trump and Kim Jong-un. After the closing of

---

[3] In June 2020, the previous Presidential Advisor, John Bolton, in his memoirs, "The Room where it happened: A White House Memoir" revealed that the President requested President Xi to expand agricultural imports in order to gain an advantage in the presidential elections.

the G20 Summit on the 29th, President Trump announced the agreement to meet with Kim Jong-un, and on the next day (the 30th) headed for Panmunjom North–South Demilitarized Zone to meet with Kim, and agreed to the reopening of North Korean Denuclearization Talks. Ultimately, he chose to accomplish something in foreign affairs.

In the month prior to the high-level meeting, however, the U.S. Department of Commerce placed Huawei in the "entity list" due to the company's being a national security concern. This enhanced restrictions on Huawei prompted its buyers, such as Google, Intel, and Qualcomm, to seek for a reconsideration, but with the high-level meeting a month away, all parties decided to go against the relaxation of restrictions on Huawei (Bloomberg News, Jun. 24, 2019). Despite the agreement between Trump and Xi Jinping to suspend sanctions on Huawei, the Presidential Advisor Navarro announced that the sanction relaxation would be in the order of US$1 billion (Nikkei -J, July 3, 2019). Ultimately, Trump's agreement with Xi could not be fulfilled.

On July 30th, the U.S.-Sino Talks were restarted but it immediately fell into a stalemate. Barely two days later, President Trump announced the levying of a 10% tariff, effective one month later, on the remaining imports from China worth US$300 billion.[4] On the 13th of the same month, the National Defense Authorization Act of fiscal year 2019 came into force, prohibiting the purchase of goods from Huawei and five other Chinese firms. In November, the U.S. Federal Communications Commission (FCC) prohibited firms, receiving subsidies from FCC, from procuring Huawei products, while the Department of Commerce also announced its plans to regulate the procurement of Huawei products. These were aimed to close all the "loopholes" concerning the entry of Chinese products into the U.S. market, as concerns over espionage ran high.

The 4th "Trump Deal" could be seen to have transpired from October 2019 to the reaching of the "Phase 1 Agreement". On October 10th, President Trump announced that agreement has been reached with China over such matters as expansion of agricultural imports from the U.S., further protection of U.S. intellectual assets, restraint on foreign exchange rate manipulation, and the further opening up of its financial center. On December 13th, he stated that "both countries are in the last stages of an 'extremely big deal'", and reported that the world has reached the "Phase 1 Agreement" (Reuters -J, Nov. 13, 2019; Bloomberg News, Nov. 26, 2019; WSJ, Nov. 26, 2019; Bloomberg -J, Dec. 13, 2019; Nikkei -J, Dec. 13, 2019; Newsweek -J, Dec. 16, 2019). In the same month of December, however, the National Defense Authorization Act was approved by both lower and upper houses. Keeping the "Trump Deal" in mind, this Act included the prohibition of procuring from Huawei and other Chinese state-owned enterprises, for fear of information leakages, and the prohibition as well of the lifting of the trade embargo.

The "Phase 1 Agreement" was signed in Washington D.C. by the President and Vice Premier Liu on Jan 15, 2021. China promised, among others, to import over two

[4] Actually, additional tariffs were levied on US$110 billion worth of imports, affecting domestic consumers.

years US$200 billion worth, to protect intellectual assets, to abandon forced technological transfer, and to liberate financial services. The issue of industrial subsidies, however, was excluded from the agreement (Bloomberg -J, Jan. 1, 2020). The additional tariffs on the US$110 billion worth of imports for the 4th round (List 4A) were lowered to 7.5%, and were postponed for the remaining US$160 billion worth of imports (List 4B). On the same day, China lowered the tariffs from 5 to 2.5% on 4th round imports amounting to US$75 billion. The lowering of tariffs by both countries was implemented in February.

This "agreement" did not go beyond the existing levels promised by China. It could be said that this outcome was the hurried result of President Trump amidst the impending Presidential elections. It did not eliminate the distrust held by the U.S. Congress and anti-China hardliners. Moreover, the "Phase 1 Agreement" was soon displaced by the outbreak of the COVID-19 pandemic.

2.3 The COVID-19 Pandemic and U.S.-Sino Conflict

In this section, we shall take a look at the timeline of events of the COVID-19 outbreak and its features. We shall show the spiral of distrust brought about by COVID-19 within the international community, focusing on U.S.-Sino relations. We shall then discuss how this spread to economic relations arising from the U.S.-Sino conflict and the decoupling of corporate networks.

2.3.1 COVID-19 Pandemic

In December 2019, there was an outbreak of an unknown cause in Wuhan City, China. Investigation of the matter started in the city on the 29th of the same month. It was on January 4, 2020 that a laboratory in Shanghai detected the culprit to be a novel coronavirus. On January 23rd, the World Health Organization (WHO) held an emergency meeting of the committee for novel corona infection, and issued the first statement. The WHO declared a state of emergency on January 30th, named the novel coronavirus as COVID-19 on February 11th, and proclaimed a COVID-19 pandemic on March 11th. In just a few months, COVID-19 has already spread throughout the globe.

The infection first hit Europe and the U.S., and then rapidly spread to India, Brazil, and other countries. New varieties, with higher infectiousness, emerged at the destinations, repeatedly infecting people as they moved from one country or region to another. According to data collected by John Hopkins University (Fig. 2.2), the number of infected people in the world reached 100 million by January 26, 2021 (2.15 million dead). About eight months later, on August 4th, this number broke through the 220 million mark (4.25 million dead). By the following September, this number reached 230 billion people.

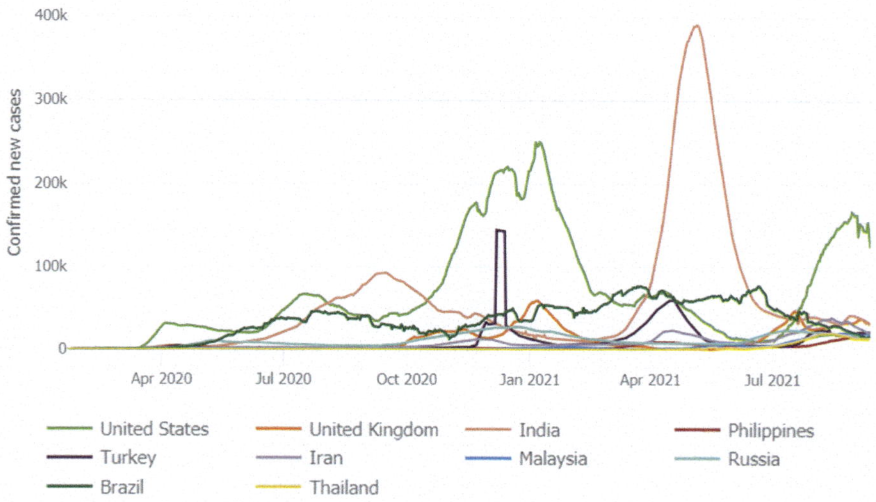

Fig. 2.2 New COVID-19 cases in highly-infected countries (7-day moving average as of September 13, 2021) (*Source* Johns Hopkins Univ. Coronavirus Resource Center. Accessed Sep. 15, 2021)

Based on a genetic analysis, the path of the COVID virus during the early months could be traced. Figure 2.3 shows such an analysis as of January 2, 2020. It suggests that COVID first took a southern path in the days soon after the outbreak in China.[5]

This path roughly coincides with that suggested by the risk ranking of cities outside China, shown in Table 2.2. The figure shows the highest risk countries based on the number of people traveling by air from 18 high-risk cities in China one week before and ten weeks after the Lunar New Year's Day in 2018. The 18 high-risk cities in China are those cities that had received a lot of COVID-infected travelers from Wuhan during the 2020 Lunar New Year migration. From Fig. 2.4 we can see that the highest risk countries are mostly South of China, and includes an Australian City. Figure 2.5 shows a positive correlation between the number of imported cases reported for various Chinese provinces and the risk of importation via travelers. Both these figures could explain the southward movement of infections shown in Fig. 2.3.

From these countries, including the Chinese cities, the virus spread quickly across the world, through the channels created by globalization. Within a week of each other Western Europe and the U.S. were hit by the virus. It is as if COVID-19 was a simultaneous terrorist attack, hitting the hubs of the global economic network. Entering 2021, various mutations of the virus emerged, resulting in dramatic increases in infections. Vaccinations were hard pressed to stem the wave of infection.

Looking at the accumulated data on infections by country, we notice something very interesting. Figure 2.5 shows that surges in infection starts from the U.S. and is followed by surges in India, Brazil, Russia, France, Turkey, the UK, and Italy. This

[5] The curvature of the lines joining the hotspots, indicated by the shaded circles, indicate direction of flow based on a counterclockwise rule. The lines shown in Fig. 2.3 correspond to the downward side of the counterclockwise movement, indicating the flow of infection is downwards.

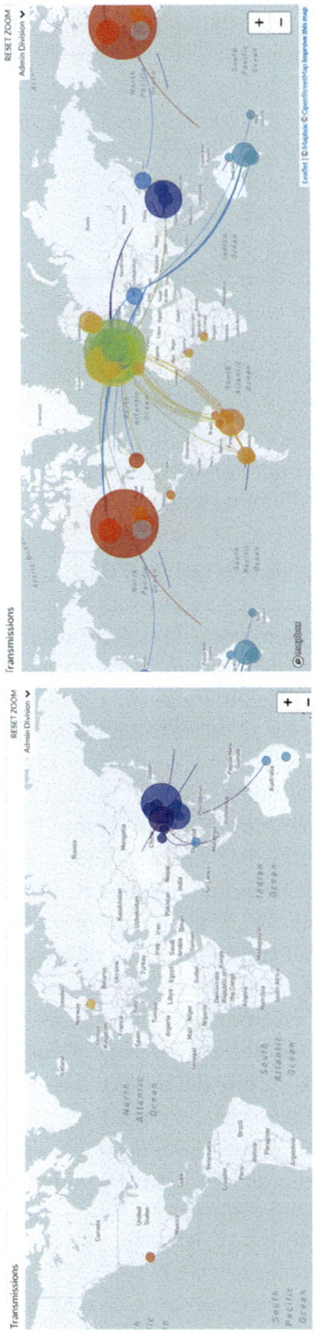

Fig. 2.3 Diffusion of COVID-19 (Left frame: as of January 2, 2020; Right frame: as of March 3, 2020) (*Source* Nextstrain https://nextstrain.org/ncov/2020-03-20?d=map&dmax=2020-01-10&dmin=2020-01-02&l=clock&p=full. Accessed Dec. 13, 2021)

Table 2.2 High risk cities outside of China

Rank	City	Country/region	Volume (in thousands)	Risk (%)
1	Bangkkok	Thailand	1062.9	7.86
2	Hong Kong	Hong Kong SAR, China	1001.7	7.41
3	Taipei	Taipei, China	857.5	6.34
4	Seoul	South Korea	757.9	5.61
5	Tokyo	Japan	714.3	5.28
6	Singapore	Singapore	568.1	4.20
7	Phuket	Thailand	492.8	3.65
8	Osaka	Japan	434.1	3.21
9	Kuala Lumpur	Malaysia	382.7	2.83
10	Macau	Macau SAR, China	260.4	1.93
11	Denpasar Bali	Indonesia	222.2	1.64
12	Sydney	Australia	207.4	1.53
13	Chiang Mai	Thailand	156.9	1.16
14	Melbourne	Australia	154.5	1.14
15	Los Angeles	United States	154.5	1.14
16	New York	United States	145.9	1.08
17	Dubai	United Arab Emirates	144.9	1.07
18	Nha Trang	Vietnam	143.0	1.06
19	London	United Kingdom	142.1	1.05
20	Ho Chi Minh City	Vietnam	142.0	1.05
	Total		13,514.9	100.00

(https://www.worldpop.org/events/china Accessed Dec. 14, 2021)
Note Risk (%)* is "defined as the percentage of airline travelers received by each city out of a total volume of travelers leaving high-risk cities (18 cities) based on the air travel data from February to April 2018, obtained from the International Air Travel Association (IATA). The Lunar New Year in 2018 started from February 16, 2018

pattern remains basically the same in 2021. In short, the major infected countries are the U.S., followed by BRICs, and then major countries in Europe.

There are exceptions. The U.S. and China have completely opposite experiences with respect to infections, as can be seen from Table 2.3. While there's extremely many total cases in the U.S., in China it is exceptionally few. China forcibly stopped the movement of people, suppressing the infection. On the contrary, the Trump administration's infection awareness and disregard of countermeasures triggered an infection explosion. This trend continues even up to the point that coronavirus was seen to be on the way out, just before omicron. More sobering is the disparity of the infection and death rates between the U.S. and China. It can also be seen from Table 2.2 that the low incidences in China are also in stark contrast with those of its fellow BRIC countries. Medical systems (especially, health care workers), population density, and income inequality are among the possible determinants of

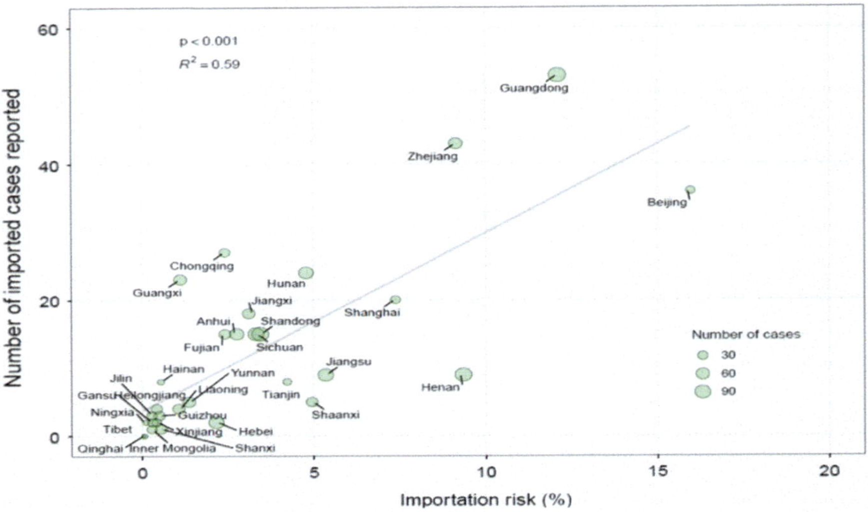

Fig. 2.4 Correlation between imported cases and the importation risk (*Source* https://www.worldpop.org/events/china Accessed Dec. 14, 2021). *Note* Risk of importation at the provincial level = % of incoming travelers to the total number of travelers leaving Wuhan within two weeks before and since the first day of the 2020 Lunar New Year

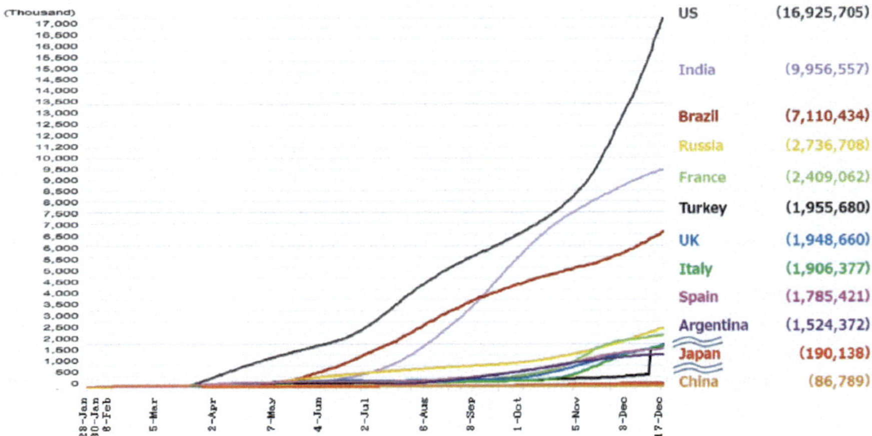

Fig. 2.5 Cumulative confirmed cases of COVID-19 by country, January 23–December 18, 2020 (*Source* Ministry of Foreign Affairs, Japan. https://www.anzen.mofa.go.jp/covid19/country_count.html Accessed Jan.6, 2021). *Note* The number of confirmed cases in China excludes carriers without symptoms. Turkey began including carriers without symptoms in its numbers starting Dec. 11

Table 2.3 Comparative death rates due to COVID-19

Country	Total cases	Total cases per million	Deaths per million
USA	49,099,590	147,122	2,395
China	98,672	69	3
Russia	9,604,233	65,772	1,876
India	34,580,832	24,717	335
Brazil	22,080,906	102,853	2,861
World	261,926,070	33,603	669.7

(*Source* Worldometer, as of Nov. 21, 2021)

COVID-related deaths.[6] Even with the new Biden administration, the obstacles left by the Trump administration could not be removed.

We would like here to focus on the countries called BRICs and emerging economies, which together with advanced industrial countries have become major infected countries. The economic development potential of these countries has gained much attention, entering this century. In short, these are countries that leveraged economic globalization for their economic development. This channel provided the route of infection. Next to Wuhan, Europe and the U.S. followed with their own lockdowns and border closings. This is but natural for hubs of economic globalization. This soon spread from the cities to the rural areas.

2.3.2 *COVID-19 and the Growing U.S.-Sino Distrust*

On January 23, 2020, the WHO issued its first statement about the outbreak, of unknown origin, at the end of 2019 in Wuhan. At which time, the U.S. ordered the evacuation of Americans and their families from Wuhan, and within one week allowed U.S. government staff and their families to leave China. On the 31st, foreigners with a history of traveling to China, as well as those coming directly from China were forbidden to enter the U.S. On February 2nd, the U.S. announced the mandatory quarantine of Americans, who have stayed in Hubei Province for two weeks prior to entering the U.S. (U.S. Visa Information Service information, Feb. 3, 2020). In response, the Chinese government criticized that through such measures, the U.S. is causing panic, and "spreading fear" (BBC News, Feb. 3, 2020). At this time, the WHO also did not consider the novel corona outbreak as extremely dangerous.

On the other hand, in China, Wuhan City was locked down on January 23rd, and rushed the construction of emergency hospitals in the span of ten days. On the Chinese Lunar Year, the 27th of January, holidays were extended up to February 2nd

[6] For example, see The Economist, July 31, 2021 "Why have some places suffered more covid-19 deaths than others? Income inequality is a big part of the answer" https://www.economist.com/finance-and-economics/2021/07/31/why-have-some-places-suffered-more-covid-19-deaths-than-others (Accessed Dec. 29, 2021).

in major cities and enterprises, and overseas travel was prohibited. The movement, however, of a large number of Chinese, including those from Wuhan to other cities within the country, already began on the 20th.

In hindsight, the Chinese government's response was a bit late, but once mobility was strongly restrained, the outbreak within China began to wane by the end of February, causing the economy to restart. On April 8th, the Wuhan lockdown was lifted.

In contrast, infection started surging in the U.S., various European countries, and Asia. At the end of January, infection spread to 22 countries, starting with the U.S., and then Russia, Italy, and the UK (New York Times, Jan. 31, 2020). In Japan, on February 3rd, the cruise tour ship Diamond Princess docked at Yokohama port and caused a COVID-19 panic. Out of the 439 people on board, 135 tested positive (Japanese Ministry of Health bulletin, Feb. 10, 2020). On March 9th, Italy implemented a nationwide lockdown, Europe's first such case. According to economic growth projections of the IMF (2020), published in April 2020, China grew by 1.2%, while the U.S. and advanced countries dropped by 5.9 and 6.1%, respectively. These figures were reduced in the June economic predictions to +1.0% for China and −8.0% for the U.S. and advanced economies.

2020, however, was the year of the U.S. presidential elections. This was the biggest reason for the "first phase agreement" in the U.S.-Sino Trade War. Signing of the agreement in Washington took place on January 15th of the same year. The lowering of part of the additional tariffs took effect on February 14th. At this point, COVID-19 made its appearance. In contrast to China, the U.S. fell into a severe economic crisis. There ensued a series of events that stirred up a growing distrust between the U.S. and China.

Firstly, there was the failure of the Chinese government's early response to the COVID-19. Ophthalmologist Li Wenliang, who was infected and died on February 6th, revealed from his hospital bed the fact that he was under pressure from the Wuhan City authorities to be silent, on the grounds that he was "disturbing the social order" (BBC News, Feb. 6, 2020, Feb. 7, 2020). Dr. Li early on became aware of the dangers of COVID-19, and conveyed this fact in a chat group with other physicians. This action was suppressed by the authorities. There were those, even within China, who praised Dr. Li, but the U.S. and the rest of the Western world viewed this matter as a particularly shocking attempt of the Chinese government to conceal the truth.

President Trump criticized China, and in July warned that the U.S. will withdraw from the WHO, which he considered as "China's puppet" when WHO Director-General Tedros Adhanom Ghebreyesus commended China's early infection countermeasures. In March, President Trump declared COVID-19 as a "Chinese virus", while U.S. Secretary of State Mike Pompeo called it the "Wuhan virus". At the G7 Foreign Ministers Meeting of the same month, the State Secretary was planning to issue a joint statement criticizing the lack of transparency of the Chinese government's response to COVID-19. The G7 Foreign Ministers Meeting postponed the crafting of the joint statement (CNN, March 25, 2020).

Early February, the quarrel between the U.S. and China was also stoked by the Wall Street Journal article on "China is the Real Sick Man of Asia", which casted doubt on the economic development of China, the source of COVID-19. The Chinese government demanded an apology, citing the racial discriminatory tone of the article's title, among others. This demand went unheeded leading to the deportation of three journalists of the journal. In response, the U.S. State Department designated five U.S.-based companies, including Xinhua, as "Foreign Country Propaganda Outlets", and in early March ordered the 40 percent reduction of U.S.-based Chinese staff of four China state-owned newspapers. In retaliation, the Chinese government revoked the press passes of the WSJ, Washington Post, and New York Times (WSJ, Feb. 3, 2020; Bloomberg News, Feb. 19, 2020, March 3, 2020, March 18, 2020).

On March 16th, Xi Jinping in a telephone call to the COVID-19 crisis-stricken Italian Prime Minister Giuseppe Conte, offered a "Heath Silkroad", where masks and medical equipment were sent to Italy, together with medical teams, initiating a "Mask Diplomacy" with various countries. On the other hand, the Chinese press let out the news that the U.S.-Europe response to the infections have been lukewarm, and, on the contrary, China contributed to the containment of the coronavirus. Press Secretary Zhào Lìjiān, who will be later called as China's "wolf warrior diplomat", in his personal twitter, asserted that America brought in the virus to Wuhan (Nikkei -J, Mar. 17, 2020, Mar. 18, 2020). Still in March, in the U.S. State of Florida, individuals and firms filed lawsuits against the Chinese government for economic damages arising from the corona crisis. Similar actions were taken in other places such as Texas, Nevada in the U.S., the UK, Italy, Germany, Nigeria, Egypt, and India. According to Japanese internet news, a Hong Kong economic daily report estimated the compensation demanded from China has reached US$100 trillion, and called for opposition to the demands that brought to mind those made by the U.S. and European major powers to the Chinese people during the Boxer Rebellion of 1900 (Nikkei -J, April 1, 2020; Yahoo Japan News -J, June 2, 2020).

In April, Australia sought for an "independent investigation" of the virus source, as well as the response of the WHO to COVID-19. This investigation was at first rejected by the Chinese government (BBC News, April 24, 2020), but at the WHO General Assembly in May, a resolution was passed for a "fair, independent, and comprehensive" investigation. Even with certain conditionalities, Xi Jinping had no choice but to accept the investigation. China, however, applied high tariffs on imports from Australia such as beef, wine, and coal, in what is perceived as a reprisal.

Australia concluded an FTA with China in 2015, deepening economic relations. With the change of the Prime Minister in August 2018, however, it quickly banned Huawei and ZTE products in the construction of the 5G network, in tune with the policies of the Trump administration (BBC News, Aug. 23, 2018). It next requested for an independent investigation of the COVID-19 infection source. It could be said that China chose to retaliate via exports that had rising dependence on China.

Around this time, China's belligerent diplomatic posture came to be called "wolf warrior diplomacy", "Wolf Warrior" was the title of a 2017 blockbuster action movie about a Chinese patriot that fought with enemies led by the U.S. It came to be used as a term by patriots to praise Chinese diplomats who opposed the severe criticisms of China. This also became the diplomatic posture of the Chinese government (WSJ -J. May 20, 2020; CNN, June 6, 2020). To the outside world, however, this term showed the tyranny of China. The same term acquired completely opposite meanings outside and inside China. Either way, it is a term to mean Xi Jinping's departure from Deng Xiaoping's diplomatic policy "to hide one's light under a bushel".

In what was considered by Western countries led by the U.S. as abandoning the international pledge of "one country two system", the Law of the People's Republic of China on Safeguarding National Security in the Hong Kong Special Administrative Region was carried out in Hong Kong on July 1st. On the other hand, U.S. State Secretary Pompeo announced sanctions against China for human rights violations on a minority group in the Xinjiang Uygur Autonomous Region.

On July 3rd, then Secretary of State Mike Pompeo asserted that the Chinese Government's 9-dash-line claim in the South China Sea is "completely illegal," on the grounds of the International Arbitration Court's ruling on the case filed by the late president of the Philippines, Corazon Aquito, and announced the economic sanctions on Chinese-related firms, citing human rights violations of the Xinjiang Uyghur minority group. The following day, President Trump signed the Hong Kong Autonomy Act, which enables the sanctioning of individuals, groups, and financial institutions that violate Hong Kong's autonomy.

In a speech made on July 23rd following the October 2018 speech of Vice President Spence, State Secretary Pompeo made a scathing criticism of China. He called for "a new alliance of democracies" to oppose China, perceiving that the "involvement" policy, starting with former President Nixon's visit to China in 1972, was a mistake (Pompeo, 2020). On the same day, the Trump administration also ordered the closing of the Chinese Consulate General in Huston on the grounds of intellectual property theft (BBC News, July 23, 2020, July 24, 2020) The U.S. Senate also passed the National Defense Authorization Act (NDAA) for fiscal year 2021. Just after passing the Act, Senator Inhofe said. "Right now, the main challenge to our security comes from authoritarian regimes that stand against our values—namely, China and Russia—and this bill stands up for our people and our democratic values (U.S. Committee on Armed Services 2020).

2.3.3 The Trump Administration's Decoupling Policy and China's Response

Citing cyber-attacks, leading technologies and national security risks, human rights violations, and ideological conflict, among others, the Trump administration's sanctions on China in 2020 consisted of disconnecting the global supply chain that linked the U.S. and China.

Until the summer of 2020, the transaction by the U.S. Government ban on Huawei and others leading the next generation 5G cellular technology spread from American firms to third country firms. Transactions were also banned with 24 construction firms involved in the construction of military bases in the South China Sea. The plan to invest the U.S. federal employees' pension fund in China was suspended. Listing to the U.S. stock market has been regulated. The plan to directly connect with China through a submarine cable communication network was also suspended. The sale of the U.S. operations of the Chinese video site TikTok, and the prohibition of the WeChat messaging and messenger app were also announced.[7]

On the other hand, since August 2020, China passed a series of commercial laws focusing on opposing the U.S. The revised "export prohibition and export technology restriction list" (Commercial Sector and Scientific Technology Sector Public Notice 2020 Number 38) was passed in August, the "Unreliable Entity List" (Commercial Law 2020 Number 4) in September, and the China Export Administration Act in December. In the Export Administration Act, "opposition" to overseas regulations was clearly written (Nikkei -J, Dec. 17, 2020). Come January 2020, "Counteracting Unjustified Extra-territorial Application of Foreign Legislation and Other Measures" came into force. This provides the legal basis, from the point of view of the Chinese government, for Chinese firms to demand compensation from American firms that broke transactions following U.S. government regulations banning transactions with Chinese firms (CISTEC Secretariat -J, 2021; Nikkei -J, Jan. 10, 2021; MOFCOM, 2021). Strengthening the control of rare earth as a strategic resource was also announced (Nikkei -J, Jan. 16, 2021).

The legislative basis is naturally crucial. But, in the case of Chinese laws, there is a strong resemblance to the legal basis of regulations against China by the Trump administration. Related to territorial issues, the Chinese Coast Guard Law took effect in February 2021. The Chinese Coast Guard can use arms against foreign vessels that do not obey commands.

Within the first four years of the Trump administration, China's diplomatic posturing visibly changed. The strong-arm policy taken against China by the Trump administration appears to have incited China to embark on a foreign policy that is clearly a mix of irritation and a sense of superiority.

2.4 Biden Administration and the U.S.-Sino Conflict

The birth of the Biden administration in the U.S. returned the policy on China towards the principle of international cooperation. Biden's policy on China focused on foreign policy to win the competition with China in leading technologies, the economy, and the military. The conflict changed from one between the U.S. and China to one between the Western advanced nations and China, leading to a stronger decoupling

[7] In response, TikTok won an appeal to Washington's Federal Regional Court to suspend the prohibition, but the court battles continue. Ultimately in June 2021, President Biden, revoked the Presidential Decree of former President Trump. However, in December 2022, when it became clear that TikTok had attempted to illegally obtain the location information data of a reporter in charge of reporting on TikTok, there was a move to regulate it again. The U.S. House of Representatives Foreign Relations Committee passed a bill banning TikTok from being used in the U.S. on March 1, 2023.

in the fields of leading industries and scientific technologies. Asia is changing into a region of competition between these two forces.

2.4.1 The Biden Administration's Principle of International Cooperation and China's "Wolf Warrior"

In January 2021, Joe Biden, who won the presidential elections in November of the previous year, became the 46th U.S. President. However, even before the presidential inauguration of Biden, Trump did not acknowledge his defeat in the presidential elections, and rejected the legitimacy of the new administration. His agitation even caused the occupation of the Capitol Building by his supporters on January 6th. The Biden administration was born amidst a crisis of democracy in a divided society.

The Biden administration's policy towards China could be viewed as partly reconciliatory, but it did not turn out that way. The basic policy of the new administration changed into deploying its policy towards China with the cooperation of U.S. allies, while continuing the hard-line posture of the Trump administration. Fulfillment of Trump's "First Phase Agreement" was sought for, but due to the COVID-19 outbreak, China's imports were less than that promised. In 2020, China's import was US$99.9 billion, which was only 58% of the promised US$173.1 billion (Brown, 2021). China's trading and economic systems would be main items in the second phase negotiations. It could be said that the Biden administration has prioritized the international relations with its allied countries.[8]

The first four years of the Trump administration greatly changed the relation between the U.S. and Asia. The TPP12, from which Trump boastfully withdrew in 2017, was inaugurated at the end of 2018 as the Comprehensive and Progressive Agreement for Trans-Pacific Partnership (CPTPP) formed by 11 countries, without the U.S. The Regional Comprehensive Economic Partnership (RCEP) Treaty, to which China has joined, took eight years to negotiate, and in November 2020 was signed by 15 countries, excluding India.[9] Its members consist of the ASEAN 10 countries, Japan, China, South Korea, Australia, and New Zealand. For the first time in history, the birth of an Asian regional economic coordination treaty is imminent. China's diplomatic offensive took on a stronger push. As soon as the signing of RCEP was done, China showed its willingness to join the CPTPP, filing its official application in September 2021.[10] With respect to COVID-19 response, China embarked

---

[8] In October 2021, the U.S. government announced the reopening of the trade negotiations. The U.S. sought for the compliance to agreements made, such as protection of intellectual property rights, and demanded reforms in the issue of excessive subsidies to state-owned enterprises, among others (JETRO Business Brief -J, Oct. 5, 2021). This would undoubtedly be an important as well as difficult negotiation related to world trade rules.

[9] RCEP took into effect in January 2022.

[10] With the official application of China for CPTPP membership, Taiwan was compelled to apply. China opposes Taiwan's participation in an international institution. With China's formal application to the CPTPP, Taiwan has been forced to also apply. Should China's application be accepted, the

quickly on a "vaccine diplomacy" by supplying the main member countries of BRI, outstripping the U.S., with which it had a deepening political and social conflict.

The Biden administration's Asia policy rebuilt its China policy by linking up with Western advanced countries under the principle of international cooperation that pivoted on the ideology of democracy and human rights. In February, the President symbolically alludes to this in his first speech where he says, "America is back." He actually had the U.S.-based Taiwan representative attend the presidential inauguration in January. This was the first time for this to happen since the normalization of ties in 1979, which led to the adoption of the "one China" policy. In his Presidential inauguration speech to both Lower and Upper Houses, he bared his basic position as he identified China as a military hegemony with human rights issues. In March, he led the Quad online summit meeting that would unite the U.S., Japan, Australia, and India. The meeting was continued face to face in September, where agreements were reached on "increasing production and access to safe and effective vaccines" as well as "infrastructure partnership" among others (U.S. White House Fact Sheet, Sep. 24, 2021). In April, he met up with Japanese Prime Minister Yoshihide Suga in Washington and agreed on the common values, as well as the peace and stability in the Taiwan Strait. Such strengthening of relationships with allied countries led to the holding of the "Democracy Summit" of December 2021.

In the first high-level diplomatic meeting between the U.S. and China in March 2021, U.S. Secretary of State Blinken, amidst an intense conflict, directly expressed his apprehensions to China over human rights and hard-line diplomacy. In the same month, the U.S. State Department issued the human rights violation report. State Department Secretary Blinken criticized China's Uighur repression as "genocide." The May G7 Foreign Ministers Meeting clearly cited the peace and stability in the Taiwan Strait. In the G7 Summit Meeting in June, a pledge was made of supplying one billion doses of vaccine to the COVID-19 pandemic-stricken world. At the same time, there were deliberations over issues such as the sharing of common values, a strong concern over China's human rights problem, Taiwan, and cyber-attacks. There was agreement to support infrastructure construction in low- and middle-income countries. In August, Vice President Harris visited Singapore and Vietnam, calling for the strengthening of ties. At the end of the same month, President Biden resolutely carried out the withdrawal of US troops from Afghanistan, allowing to focus on pushing his China policy.

The big change that came with the Biden administration was the taking of coordinated action with the EU in the diplomatic field, and the appearance of military links in the Asia Pacific region. As the former State Secretary Pompeo stated the territorial claims of China over the South China Sea have no basis, and in September 2020, the UK, France, and Germany jointly sent a letter to the UN officially renouncing the territorial claims of China in the South China Sea (Economic Times, Sep. 20, 2020). In the EU-China Leaders Meeting video conference held in the same month, there was an expression about the "need for China to refrain from unilateral actions

possibility of China joining will be most certainly lost. Membership to the CPTPP has become mired in international politics.

in the South China Sea and to promote international peace and security" (European Council International Summit, Sep. 14, 2020). Incidentally, Japan sent diplomatic letters renouncing the South China Sea territorial claims in January 2021.

In March 2021, the EU Parliament imposed sanctions on Chinese related to the human rights violation of minorities in the Xinjiang Uyghur Autonomous Region. The EU Parliament Diplomatic Committee deliberated on the "EU-Taiwan Relations and Cooperation" on September 1st of the same year. There 60 yeas, 4 nays, and 6 abstains, leading to an overwhelming agreement to strengthen ties with Taiwan. While taking this not to be a revision of EU's "One China" policy, the report expressed a deep concern for China's military pressure on Taiwan, and chose the position of "protecting Taiwan's democracy and the status of this island as an important partner of the EU".

Incidentally, the committee, four days prior to the deliberations, changed the name of the Taiwan office to "European Union Office in Taiwan" from "the European Economic and Trade Office in Taipei" (Focus Taiwan, Sep. 2, 2021; Bloomberg News, Sep. 2, 2021). In the same month of September, the "Asia–Pacific Strategy" was adopted. It mentioned the problems in the South China Sea and East China Sea, as well as the escalation of the territorial claim conflict in the Taiwan Strait. It also pointed out the threat to the principles of democracy and human rights.

In April 2021, the U.S., Japan, Australia, India, and France conducted their first joint naval exercises in Bengal Bay. In August, a German battleship was deployed to the Asia Pacific, the Philippine Sea. Joint exercises were also conducted by the U.S., Japan, Australia, France, South Korea, and New Zealand. In September, the U.S. and UK announced the construction and deployment of nuclear submarines to Australia, giving birth to a new security framework (Aukus) consisting of the U.S., UK, and Australia.[11] In consideration of its relations with China, Germany requested for its dispatched vessels to call on the port of Shanghai, but is reported to have been rejected (DW, Sep. 15, 2021). In October, the U.S., UK, Japan, the Netherlands, Canada, and New Zealand conducted joint military exercises off the coast of Okinawa (Nikkei -J, Oct. 5, 2021).

From around 2020, East European countries are also conducting adjustments in their directions with regards to their China policies. In August 2020, Czechoslovakian Senate speaker Milos Vystrcil, despite strong warnings from China, led a group of around 90 lawmakers, businessmen, and researchers to visit Taiwan, and signed agreements of high-tech manufacturing and environmental management (Nikkei Asia, Aug. 30, 2020; AP News, Aug. 31, 2020; VOA East Asia, Sep. 4, 2020). In February 2021, an online meeting of EEC 17+1 was organized for the first time by President Xi Jinpin, but the leaders of the three Balic countries of Lithuania, Latvia, and Estonia did not participate. Only the leaders of Poland, Czechoslovakia, Serbia, Montenegro, Bosnia Herzegovina participated (Turcsanyi, 2021).

[11] When Aukus was announced, Indonesia and Malaysia showed concern over the increase of military power. Moreover, strong French opposition grew with Australia's sudden annulment of the nuclear submarine construction contract it had with France.

This reflects the strong disappointment among many CEE countries over China not meeting their expectations of the BRI project. This was also due to the strong distrust of the Chinese government's policies involving the Uighur ethnic group, the Hong Kong issue, and the exclusion of Taiwan in the WHO. In May 2021, Lithuania announced its withdrawal from the EEC17, and in July established the "Taiwan Representative Office" in Taiwan. It requested that Taiwan be invited to the WHO general assembly towards an international response to the COVID-19 pandemic. Czechoslovakia also supported Taiwan's participation in the WHO. In October 2021, a group of French lawmakers paid a visit to Taiwan. A senior French senator was reported to have stated that Taiwan should be called a country (Reuters, Oct. 5, Oct. 8, 2021; France 24, Oct. 6, 2021).

Against this backdrop in Europe and the U.S., China's wolf warrior diplomacy, taken during the Trump administration, appears to have some bearing. The EU prohibited the entry to Europe and froze the assets of four government officials of the Xinjiang Uyghur Autonomous Region, and one organization, as sanctions for their human violations of the Xinjiang Uyghur ethnic group in March 2021. In response, China immediately applied retaliatory measures on five EU Parliament members of five countries, as well as four EU organizations. Treating the human rights foreign policy of Europe and the U.S. as "interference in domestic matters", China strongly criticized the "EU double standard", citing Europe's history of human rights violations, and asking it "to stop preaching about human rights". However, given these circumstances, the action taken by the EU Parliament in May was freezing the ratification deliberations for the EU-China Comprehensive Agreement on Investment, which was broadly agreed upon at the end of the previous year. The freezing of the ratification deliberations was resolved by an overwhelming majority of 599 yeas against 30 nays, with 58 abstains (European parliament News, 2021).

The Chinese foreign minister Wang Yi criticized the above-mentioned Czech Senator's visit to Taiwan, warning that a "heavy price" will be paid (VOA East Asia, Sep. 4, 2020). Vystrcil later stated that the Czech Republic would not bow down to the objections raised by Beijing (Gupta, 2020). In 2019, Prague terminated its sister city relationship with Beijing, rejecting the principle of "one China", and in January 2020 formed a sister city relationship with Taiwan. Shanghai has terminated its friendship with Prague (Reuters, January 14, 2020; Turcsanyi, 2021). When the plan to visit Taiwan by the French Senators was made in February 2021, the Chinese embassy in France sent a letter of protest to the representative of the senate group. This letter was criticized by a French researcher, whom the Chinese embassy came to refer to as a "thug" or a "wild dog dressed in a scholar's coat", among others. The French Department of Foreign Affairs called the Chinese embassy to protest the "rise of unacceptable comments by the Chinese embassy insulting and threatening lawmakers and scholars" (NHKWeb -J, Mar. 23, 2021; Asahi -J, March 23, 2021).

At a top-level meeting in March of the same year, agreeing that both the U.S. and China are superpowers, China countered that it has its own "Chinese Style Democracy", while denouncing racial discrimination in the U.S. This possibly led to the publication of the "China Democracy" White Paper, in opposition of the Biden administration's Democracy Summit in December of the same year. China more and more took a wolf warrior posture, even within the military sphere. From September of the same year, there was an increase in the invasion of the Taiwanese Air Defense Identification Zone. During the Chinese National Day on October 1st, the numbers of fighter plane invasions were 38, on the 2nd it was 39, on the 4th it rose to 56. It clearly was a show of force towards Taiwan (Nikkei -J, Oct. 5, 2021).

There was an excuse of course for the hard line military posture. From the point of view of the Chinese Communist Party, the Taiwan issue is the unsolved liberation problem of the imperial period. Based on the basic principle of "One China" normalization of U.S.-Sino ties of 1972, the Taiwan problem is a domestic problem. The normalization, however, also promised the "peaceful resolution" of the Taiwan problem. China's opposition and rejection of the interference in domestic affairs, on issues of democracy and human rights by the Western countries, is a return to the pre-normalization sentiments. 2021 was the 100th year of the Communist Party. It was a good opportunity to recall the legitimacy of the Communist Party.

The wolf warrior diplomacy, however, that China pursued amidst this recent conflict appears to have brought about the opposite reaction against China, not only from the democratic peoples of Europe and the U.S, but also from an overwhelming number of Asians.

In the Pew Research Center's, 2021 survey in 17 advanced economies regarding sentiments towards China, "unfavorable" responses reached historically high levels, continuing from last year. The overall median was 69% versus 27%, with the majority choosing "unfavorable" (Pew Research Center, 2021: 12, 21). In the 2021 survey, the COVID-19 countermeasures of China, including various European countries, were given high ratings. Despite that, why is China not liked? A common response shared across regions was that the Chinese government "did not respect freedoms". Even in Singapore, where responses of China "respects freedoms" were exceptionally high, the share of such responses was only 35%. This, however, is not the whole story. If we exclude the exceptionally high share (70%) of "confidence" responses of Singapore, the assessment of President Xi Jinping's handling of world affairs was extremely low for all countries. The median for the 17 countries surveyed for "no confidence" responses was 77%, as against 20% for "confidence" responses. Next to Singapore, the highest share of "confidence" responses was Greece with 36%, and the Netherlands and Taiwan both with 25%. With regards to the handling of President Xi Jinping of overseas affairs, the response was "practically or absolutely" not trusted. The survey report summarizes it as follows: "Majorities in all but one of the 17 publics surveyed have little or no confidence in Chinese President Xi Jinping's handling of world affairs" (Pew Research Center, 2021: 21).

In the 2021 survey of Australia's Lowy Institute of citizens of eight major countries, the countries with the high-trust response shares, excluding Australia, were the UK and Japan (87%), and the U.S and India (61%), while that of China was just 16%. With respect to the responses of Australians' trust in China, 47% responded "not at all", and 37% "not very much" (Lowy, 2021: 6). It should be noted, however, that Australia's sentiments towards China changed dramatically from 2018 to 2020. With regards to the question as to whether China was an economic power or more of a security threat, the 2018 survey showed 82% responded "economic power", but in

2021 this drastically dropped to 34%. Instead, the responses of "more of a security threat" rose sharply from 12 to 63% (Lowy, 2021: 6, 12). These big changes form part of China's retaliatory measures against Australia with the COVID-19 outbreak.

With respect to China's economy, Asia's posture changes. When asked "with which country, the U.S. or China, should economic relations be strengthened", excluding Singapore, all countries responded the U.S. Nevertheless, when asked "which of two issues, human rights or strengthening economic relations with China while sacrificing human rights" should be prioritized, an increasing number of Asian countries chose to prioritize the economy. Let's look at Fig. 2.6. South Korea and Singapore have more than half of their responses emphasizing economic ties with China, even if it means sacrificing liberties. Taiwan and Japan also show high shares. This is clearly different from the tendencies in Europe and the U.S. Here lies the history of authoritarian-driven development. In Singapore, it was Lee Kwan Yew, in South Korea it was Park Chung Hee. It could be said that such experiences may bring about different political philosophies.

Southeast Asians also have mixed feelings towards China. In a 2021 survey of ASEAN 10 countries by the ASEAN Studies Center, et al., there was an overwhelming 76.3% who chose China as the most influential economic power in the Southeast Asian region. Towards this influence, however, 72.3% responded "worry", while 27.7% responded "welcome". Next, the survey asked which country would be the most influential political and strategic power. Only 49.1% chose China, but this was still 1.5 times bigger than the 30.4% that chose the U.S. Among those who responded to this, 88.6% chose "worry" while only 11.4% chose "welcome" (ASEAN Studies Center et al., 2021: 20, 22).

Figure 2.7 shows the changes in the breakdown of the confidence level in China. "No confidence" responses, which include "little confidence" responses, rose from 51.5% in 2019 to 63.0% in 2012. For both years 37.0 percentage points is from "little confidence" responses. On the other hand, "confidence" responses fell from

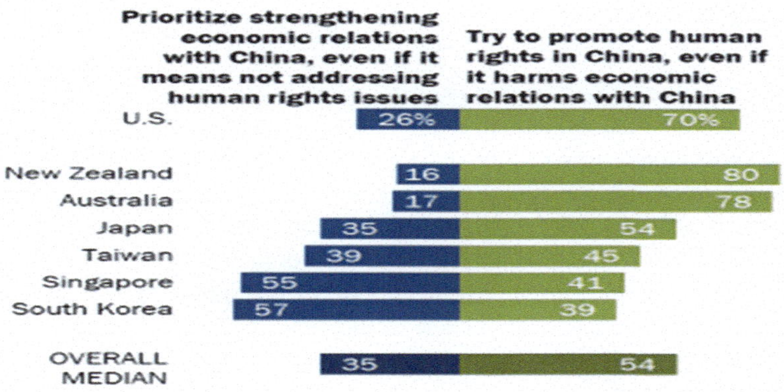

Fig. 2.6 Asian-Pacific public priorities for relationship with China (*Source* Pew Research Center, 2021: 22). *Note* Those who did not answer were not shown. *Source* Spring 2021 global attitudes survey. Q20. "Large majorities say China does not respect the personal freedoms of its people"

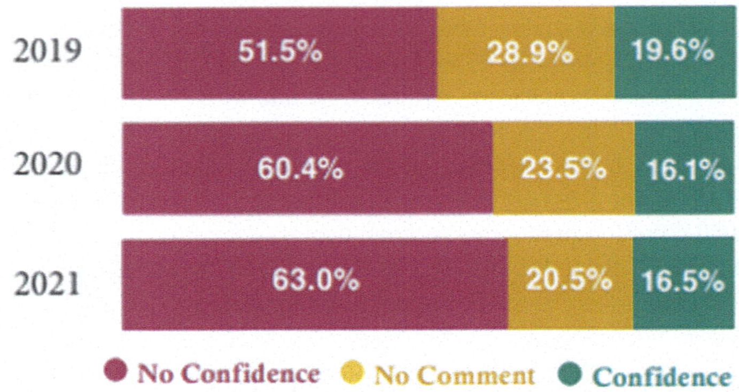

Fig. 2.7 Changes in confidence towards China, 2019–2021 (*Source* ASEAN, 2021: 42)

19.6 to 16.5%, of which 1.5 percentage points is from "very confident" responses. The distrust towards China is extremely strong (ASEAN Studies Center, 2021: 42). Citing distrust as a reason, 51.8% of the responses said that "China's economic and military power could be used to threaten my country's interest and sovereignty", while 24.0% said that "I do not consider China a reliable power". With regards to interests in the South China Sea issue, 62.4% of the responses chose "China's militarization and assertive actions", and 59.1% chose "Chinese encroachments in the exclusive economic zones and continental shelves of other littoral states". There is confusion among an overwhelming number of ASEAN peoples, when confronted with the gigantic Chinese influence (ASEAN Studies Center, 2021: 15). Depending on the actions of China, there is a growing share of ASEAN people becoming distrustful.

2.4.2 U.S.-Sino Conflict and Decoupling Under the Biden Administration

In April 2021, the U.S. Department of Commerce announced its putting seven Chinese supercomputer development firms and research institutions on the Entity List, which essentially was a trade embargo (USDOC, 2021). It was indicated that these firms and research institutes were involved with the manufacturing of super computers for the People's Liberation Army. Moreover, the use of Chinese IT devices by U.S. domestic firms was not allowed without government permission. Reports say that at most 4.5 million firms have been affected by this. In the same month, the IT firm Intel announced that, at the behest of the U.S. government, it has embarked on the domestic manufacture of semiconductors on a commission-basis, and have been commissioned by "more than 50 companies". A Presidential Decree banning investment in 59 Chinese firms has also been signed. The certification of five Chinese communication device companies, including Huawei, has been prohibited. The other four companies are ZTE, Hikvision (security cameras), Dahua Technology, Hytera (2-way radios).

In July of the same year, additions to the Entity List included 14 Chinese organizations which were involved in the human rights violations in the Xinjiang Uyghur Autonomous Region, as well as 34 organizations that were considered as supporting the Iranian and Russian military (Bloomberg News, July 9, 2021). At the same time, a recommendation to industry was issued, urging them to carefully check that sanctioned firms are not in their production supply chain (Bloomberg News, July 9, 2021; FT, Sep. 23, 2021). This is a renewal of Trump's policy implemented a year ago. The USTR warned that firms that do not withdraw from Xinjiang Uyghur are at risk of violating the law (Nikkei Evening -J, July 30, 2021). On the other hand, the Biden administration in July announced the strengthening of the Buy American Act, and the raising of the local domestic content of government-procured products from 60% and above to 75% beginning 2029.

Since early July, 50 Chinese companies were preparing for an Initial Public Offering (IPO) to the New York Commodity Exchange, but come August none was successful. Up to that time, Chinese companies were able to avoid the screening by the Public Company Accounting Oversight Board (PCAOB). This avoidance turned out to be unacceptable to the market.

Moreover, the Biden administration has been crafting a policy to counter China by allying with Japan and others with regards to the patent of the next generation communication G6. The Quad Summit in September 2021 has reached agreement on the creation of a semiconductor network by the four countries, as a major field of cooperation. Under the auspices of the U.S. government, around 30 countries or regions, including the U.S., Europe, and Japan, held an online meeting of ministers in October regarding measures against cyber-attacks. This meeting also discussed measures against "ransomware" attacks, wherein files are encrypted and ransom is demanded in exchange for unlocking the files. Considered as "involved in malicious activities", China and Russia were excluded from the meeting (Nikkei -J, Oct. 14, 2021).

On the other hand, the Chinese government tightened its control on large internet companies, beginning 2021. In June of the same year, the data security act (implemented in September) and in August the personal information protection act (implemented in November) were enacted. There would be several reasons for these laws. Besides vigilance over data leakages from firms publicly traded abroad due to U.S.-Sino conflict, there could also be the intent to prevent the concentration of power of internet firms that transcend the state. In April, a fine of about 18.2 billion Yuan was imposed on the Alibaba group for violation of antitrust laws. At the end of June, the Chinese government started to investigate DiDi, which was listed in the New York Securities Market, on possible violation of the National Security Act and the Cyber Security Act. On-site investigations of the company have been conducted. Moreover, the Chinese government's internet authority announced that it will review all the overseas listings of companies having more than one million users. Owing to this, the stocks of DiDi, which was able to obtain equity infusions of US$4 billion from the American market, dropped by US$18.0 billion in July alone (Nikkei -J,

Sep. 5, 2021). The company eventually announced at the start of December that it was delisting from the New York Securities Exchange and has been preparing to list itself in Hong Kong. It has been reported that pressure from the Chinese government was behind this (Nikkei -J, Dec. 3, 2021).

The Chinese central government in May notified the regional governments about the Auditing guidelines for government procurement of imported products (2021 issue). Covering mostly medical equipment, the document sets the local content requirements of 25 to 100% for purchases of Chinese companies of 315 items, including marine and geological and geophysical equipment (Reuters, Aug. 3, 2021; Nikkei -J, Aug. 12, 2021).[12] The local procurement of Huawei, which cut transactions with U.S. firms, was 30% for its old smart phone model. With the new smart phone model, local procurement has reached 60%.

Ultimately, U.S. and Chinese leading technology firms have mutually erected bypasses in their domestic products and transactions with allied countries, related to the national security risks and technological hegemony. What is interesting here is the trends in Japanese firm behavior. In July, it was reported that 5000 Japanese firms are planning to connect the online system being managed by seven companies, including NTT Data and Mitsubishi Corporation, to mutually monitor the product material procurement data among Japan, Taiwan, Thailand, Singapore, Australia, and New Zealand, and to draw up an import–export plan (Nikkei -J, July 10, 2021). The U.S.-Sino conflict has steadily driven the separation of two large camps. This is decoupling.

2.4.3 *The Realignment of the Global Value Chain*

For the past half century, especially even in this century, China's sustained rapid growth has come to gain for itself a high position as a market in the global economy.[13] Entering this century, U.S. firms made foreign direct investments in China, and created a global supply value chain among Asian companies, mainly in manufacturing. On the other hand, China has increased its investments in the US since the 2010s, deepening U.S.-Sino economic interdependence. In changing its demands from reduction of the trade deficit to issues regarding industrial policy, leading technology and national security risks, and hegemony, the Trump administration ultimately was moving towards severing this supply chain. It is at this point that the COVID-19 pandemic struck.

[12] The document sets local content requirements of 25 to 100% for 315 items. They include medical equipment, ground-based radar equipment, testing machinery, optical instruments; items used for animal husbandry; seismic instruments, and marine, geological and geophysical equipment, the former official said. However, this notice violates the agreement made as a member of the WTO. One congressional staff member said. "By not releasing it publicly, the PRC could deny it and say it's just guidance" (Reuters, Aug. 3, 2021).

[13] We call such newly emerging economies as Potentially Big Market Economies (PoBMEs), which will be discussed more in Chap. 3.

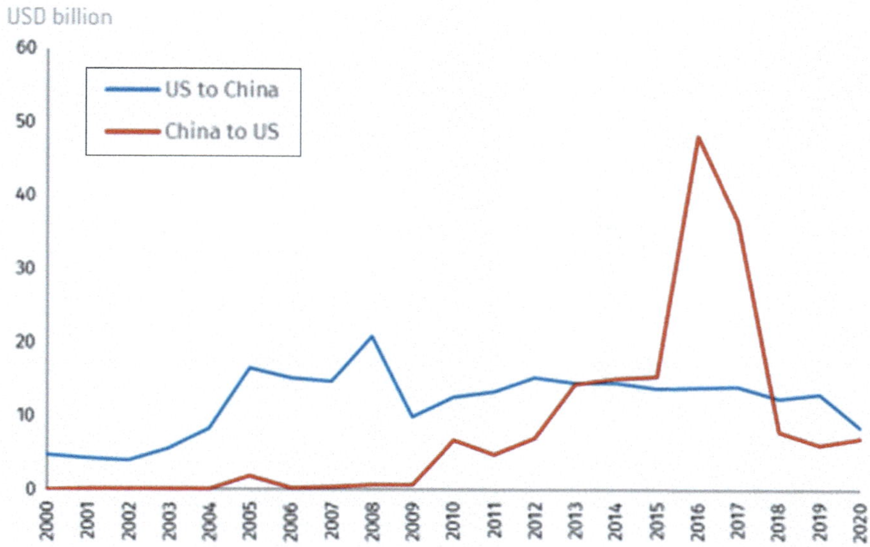

Fig. 2.8 Annual value FDI transactions between the U.S. and China, 2000–2020 (*Source* Hanemann et al., 2021: 9). *Note* Collected by the Rhodium Group

Figure 2.8 shows the changes in FDI for the U.S. and China since 2000. U.S. FDI to China has been steady, excluding the early years of the 2000s. The drop in 2009 shows the effect of the global financial crisis. The FDI in 2020 dropped a third of the previous year's US$13.1 billion to US$8.7 billion, which is the lowest recorded since 2004. It goes without saying that the U.S.-Sino trade war was behind this.

The major U.S. FDI to China in 2020 was by Walmart and Tesla. On the other hand, after showing dramatic increases in 2016–2017, FDI to the U.S. by Chinese firms dropped suddenly from 2018. In 2020, China's FDI to the U.S. was US$7.2 billion, which showed a slight increase from US$6.3 billion in 2019. These were due to the acquisitions of the Universal Music Group and the Harbin Pharmaceutical Group Co. Ltd by Tencent.

When comparing the form of FDI by both countries in Figs. 2.9 and 2.10, we can clearly see a difference. While the U.S. FDI to China are mostly greenfield investments, China's FDI are mostly acquisitions. The Rhodium Group reports as follows

> Whereas the earliest investments focused on labor-intensive manufacturing, interest in the 2000s and early 2010s shifted towards Chinese consumer-oriented sectors like food and autos. Over the past five years, American investors have increasingly targeted high-tech and advanced services sectors. Investment in sectors that are subject to high regulatory scrutiny, such as semiconductors, aviation or infrastructure, has largely disappeared (Hanemann et al., 2021: 15, 20).

These investments suddenly dropped in 2018.

In July 2019, a year after the trade war started, a Nikkei Shimbun survey of the reactions of Asian, primarily Japanese, firms found that over 50 major firms based

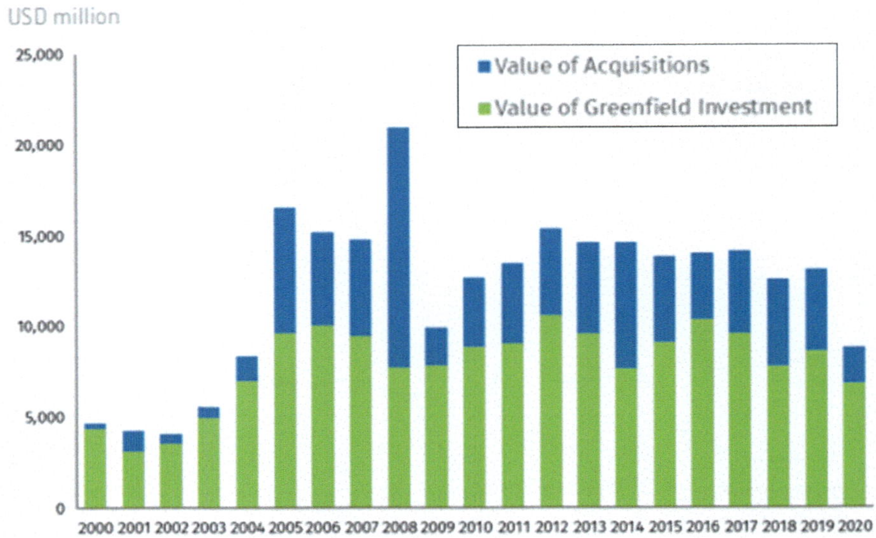

Fig. 2.9 Value of U.S. FDI transactions in China, 2000–2020 (*Source* Hanemann et al., 2021: 14)

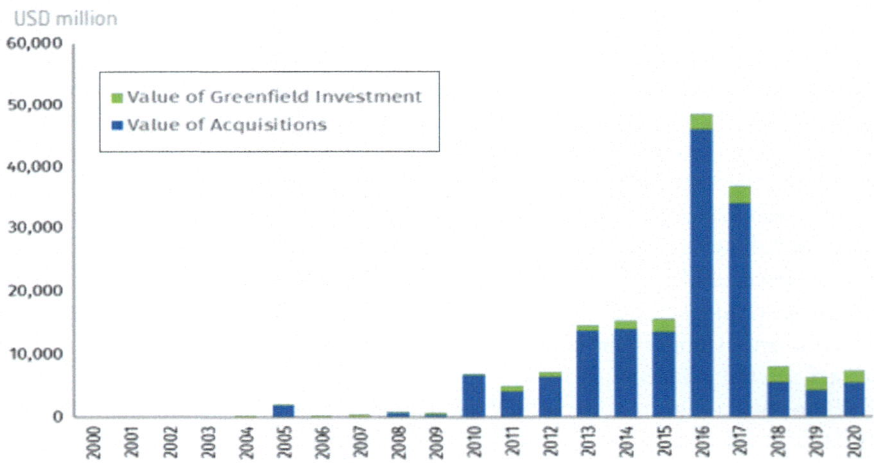

Fig. 2.10 Value of Chinese FDI Transactions in the US, 2000–2020 (*Source* Hanemann et al., 2021: 19)

in China have transferred their production operations from China back to their home country or to a third country. The transfer of operations were to such countries as Vietnam, Thailand, Japan, the U.S., India, Taiwan, and Mexico (Nikkei -J, July 18, 2019).

COVID-19 has further strengthened the decoupling policy of the U.S. Based on a COVID-19 impact survey of financial officers of manufacturing firms in Asia, the

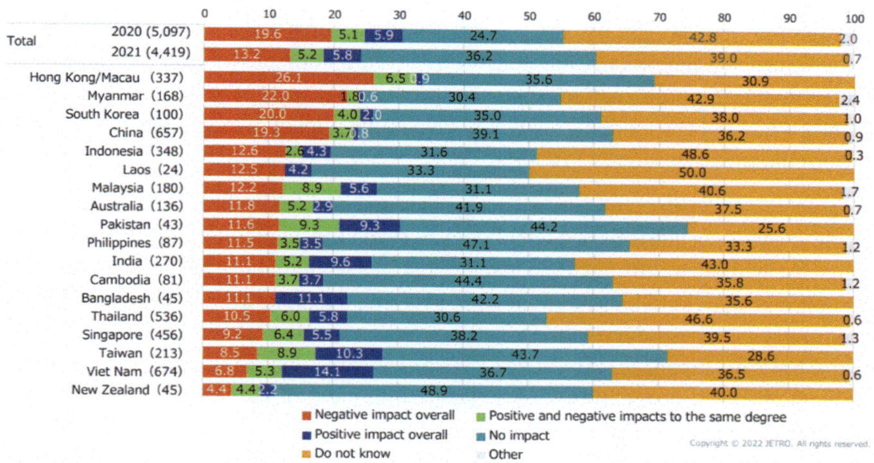

Fig. 2.11 Impact of changes in the trading environment on business performance for the Next 2–3 years (%, August–September 2020 Survey) (*Source* JETRO, 2020). *Note* Countries and regions with at least 20 valid responses

Swiss financial institution, UBS, reported in June 2020 that 76% of U.S. firms based in China, and 85% of North Asian firms including Japanese and Korean, and 60% of Chinese manufacturers moved their production out of China.

The U.S. was a target for relocating capacity for 82% of U.S. firms shifting production. Canada was 2nd at 38%, with Japan and Mexico at 29 and 23%, respectively.

For the case of Japan, Taiwan, and South Korea, transfer destinations were firstly the home country, followed by Vietnam, Thailand, and India. For the case of China-based U.S. firms, roughly 89% of health care and consumption product firms responded as transferring part of their production outside of China (UBS -J, 2020). According to an internet news in August, after the results of the UBS survey was published, a survey of entrepreneurs from China, North Asia (South Korea, Japan), and the U.S., who responded that they will transfer out from China part of their production capabilities were 60, 85, and 76%, respectively (excite News, Aug. 11, 2020).

Figure 2.11 shows the JETRO survey of the summer of 2020 about the performance prospects for the next two to three years of Japanese firms in Asia, due to changes in the environment. Based on this, more than 40% of the respondents say that prospects are not very clear, but there were many respondents who stated a concern over the deterioration of the business environment in Hong Kong and China, as well as gave good assessments of Vietnam, Bangladesh, India, and Taiwan. The main transfer destinations from China are Vietnam and Thailand. India is expected to take over China as a growth pole.

- Looking at the impact on business performance over the next 2–3 years, "Do not know" was the highest at 39.0%. Although this was 3.8 points lower than

in the previous survey (42.8%), there is still a strong sense of uncertainty about the future. On the other hand, 36.2% answered that there would be "No impact", meaning 11.5 points increase from the previous survey (24.7%).
- Only 13.2% of respondents answered "Negative impact overall", down 6.4 points from the previous survey (19.6%).

Table 2.4 shows the withdrawal by region based on a basic survey of operations of Japanese overseas subsidiaries conducted by METI in September 2020. According to this, the withdrawal from China is relatively higher than those of the other regions. The share is also high, but the number of overseas subsidiaries withdrawing has not particularly increased due to the U.S.-Sino trade war. The transfer of manufacturing from China by Japanese, American, and other firms can be seen, but it does not imply an all-out transfer from China. The realignment of the supply chain network prompted by the U.S.-Sino conflict and COVID-19 does not mean that firms are forced to choose between China, their homeland, or a third country. It is "China plus one" or "China plus". This is natural, given that a big market has already been developed in China, and, not only that, the market of the future would be in China. The realignment is one of risk diversification from a complete dependence of the production base on China. At the same time, it is a further widening of firm activity to ASEAN members and India.

Table 2.4 Changes in the withdrawal rate of Japanese firms' overseas subsidiaries by region

	Changes in the number or share of overseas subsidiaries by region									
	Number of withdrawing overseas subsidiaries					% Share of withdrawing overseas subsidiaries				
	2015	2016	2017	2018	2019	2015	2016	2017	2018	2019
All regions	724	650	725	612	603	2.8	2.5	2.8	2.3	2.3
North America	103	76	94	61	76	3.1	2.3	2.8	1.8	2.3
Asia	466	435	472	402	385	2.7	2.6	2.8	2.2	2.2
China	278	269	270	232	219	3.4	3.5	3.5	2.9	2.8
ASEAN10	121	119	141	117	123	1.8	1.6	2	1.5	1.7
Europe	93	79	80	8	76	3.1	2.7	2.7	2.7	2.6

(*Source* METI (2020) "50th Basic Survey on Overseas Business Activities. Conducted in September 1, 2020, covering 10, 345 firms in Japan, with 10,415 firms responding for a response rate of 73.8%)
Notes 1. Overseas subsidiaries that were newly established or initiated equity participation during the fiscal year of the survey were considered as newly established overseas subsidiaries
2. Withdrawal means "dissolution, withdrawal: transfer" as well as "decrease in investment ratio" (Japan side's investment ratio is between is more than 0% but less than 10%)
3. Withdrawal Ratio = number of overseas subsidiaries that withdrew in fiscal year 2018/(total number of overseas subsidiaries in fiscal year 2018 + number of overseas subsidiaries that withdrew in 2017) × 100.0
4. Covering 10, 345 firms in Japan, with 10,415 firms responding for a response rate of 73.8%

Leading technology sectors, such as semiconductors, however, touch on the issue of hegemony, so such industries would more strongly feel the effects of the U.S.-Sino conflict. The world's largest semiconductor contractor, Taiwan's TSMC (Taiwan Semiconductor Manufacturing) was forbidden to transact with Huawei during the Trump administration, and in May 2020 announced a construction plan for a semiconductor factory in the state of Arizona. In September of the same year, it completely stopped transactions with Huawei (Nikkei XTECH -J, May 18, 2020; Toyo Keizai Online -J, July 22, 2020).

The COVID-19 shock has accelerated the digitalization of advanced economies and societies, and increased the demand for leading edge technology products even in infrastructure provision. Adding to the problem is regulations due to the U.S.-Sino conflict, come the second half of 2020, a lack of supply of semiconductors emerged. Owing to this, the world's semiconductor companies announced, one after the other, plans to invest in equipment. These investment plans were encouraged by the subsidy policies of major countries which aim to have the production of leading edge products come back home, given their geopolitical assessments.

Table 2.5 compiles a summary of the investment plans of semiconductor companies that was announced in 2021. We can see that investment plans of companies such as Apple, SMTC, Intel, TSMC, and Samsung are directed towards the production in the home country as well as major markets. This is the differentiation in production and supply between the western advanced economies of the U.S. and Europe, and China.

Actually, President Biden signed into law the CHIPS and Science Act of 2022, or the so-called CHIPS+Act in August, 2022. The White House announcement said that "Spurred by the passage of the CHIPS and Science Act of 2022, this week, companies have announced nearly $50 billion in additional investments in American semiconductor manufacturing, bringing total business investment to nearly $150 billion since President Biden took office" (White House, 2022).

Under Xi, China aimed for the strengthening of science and technology power and the upgrading of the manufacturing structure and has taken great strides towards a "strong country". Huawei is already ahead of U.S. companies in G5 technology and market dominance. In the digital service field, internet companies, born in the domestic market, are rapidly increasing their shares in the global market. Gaps are steadily being closed even in science and technology power. According to the report of the National Science Board (NSB), the value-added output of high-level R&D-intensive industries as a share of world output in 2003 was 38% for the U.S. and 6% for China. These were reduced to 32% for the U.S. and 21% for China in 2018. For mid-range R&D-intensive industries, however, the value added for the same period shrank from 25% (U.S.) versus 19% (China) to 22% (U.S.) versus 26% (China). China is already overtaking the U.S. For the same period, the number of S&E papers in 2018 showed a reversal, with China catching up, from 28% (U.S.) versus 5% (China) to 17% (U.S.) versus 21% (China) (NSF, 2020).

As COVID-19 was contained in May 2020, the Politburo Standing Committee of the Communist Party of China Party raised up the "Dual Circulation" Strategy. As a remedy to the shrinking of the local and foreign economy due to the COVID-19

Table 2.5 Investment plans of major semiconductor companies (announced in 2021 and 2022)

Company name	Investment destination	Publication month	Content
Apple (USA)	Germany	March 2021	Put in one billion Euro in the next ten years to set up a Silicon design center based in Munich. It will serve as the largest European base for development of wireless semiconductor and software and is scheduled to start operations from 2022. Plan for 100% renewable energy
SMIC (China)	China	March, September 2021	Tie up with Shenzhen City government-owned enterprise, Shenzhen Major Industry Investment Group. Invest US$2.35 billion. Provide manufacturing of integrated circuits and technology services. Expected to manufacture 40,000 12 inch wafers every month, starting from 2022. Construction of a semiconductor factory in Shanghai through a joint venture of the Shanghai City government. Investment of US$8.87 billion. Product with more than 28 nm circuit line width. Start of operations is undetermined
Intel (USA)	USA	March, July 2021; September 2022	Invest US$20 billion for construction of two new factories in Arizona. Set up semiconductor foundry (Intel Foundry Service: IFS) based in the U.S. and Europe to cope with increase in demand for semiconductors. Contract manufacturing of 2 nano-semiconductors announced. Groundbreaking ceremony held for new state-of-the-art semiconductor manufacturing plant in Ohio. Initial investment of more than $20 billion, scheduled to start operations in 2025

(continued)

Table 2.5 (continued)

Company name	Investment destination	Publication month	Content
TSMC (Taiwan)	Taiwan, USA, Japan	April 2020; October 2021; December 2022	Expected to invest about US$30 billion, subject to later adjustments, in 2021 (including equipment expansion in the state of Arizona, USA). Plan to invest US$100 billion into equipment and R&D in the next three years. In collaboration with Sony, construction of a US$70 billion factory in Kumamoto, Kyushu, Japan. Operations to start by 2024. Built a new factory in Arizona. Start of operation in 2026
Samsung (South Korea)	South Korea, USA	May, November 2021	Increase investments to about US$150 billion by 2030 on system LSI and foundry, accelerating leading edge semiconductor processing technology and the construction of new manufacturing factories. Construction of a new production line in Pyeongtaek City, with plans to operate from the second half of 2022. Announced the construction of a $17 billion foundry factory in Texas, USA, scheduled to start operation in 2024
Bosch (Germany)	Germany	June, 2021	Strengthen in-house production of semiconductors. Open up a semiconductor factory by merging Dresden AI and IoT, with an investment of US$1.2 billion
FFEN (Japan)	USA	March 2022	Fuji film Electronics Materials (FFEM) announced an additional $88 million investment in its existing Arizona plant to strengthen its semiconductor manufacturing business
GlobalWafers (Taiwan)	USA	June 2022	A plan to build a 300 mm silicon wafer factory in Texas. Construction of a silicon wafer factory in the U.S. for the first time in 20 years
SkyWaterTechnology, Inc. (USA)	USA	July 2022	Announced the construction of the state's first semiconductor research and production facility at $1.8 billion in Indiana. Groundbreaking scheduled for 2023

(continued)

Table 2.5 (continued)

Company name	Investment destination	Publication month	Content
SK Hynix (South Korea)	South Korea	July 2022	Announced a $15 billion investment in semiconductor research and development, materials development, advanced packaging, and the establishment of test facilities. New facility to break ground in 2023, full operation in 2025–26
Sumitomo Chemical Co. Ltd. (Japan)	USA	September 2022	Established a new company in Texas through Dongwoo Finechem (Korea), a wholly owned subsidiary. Announced the construction of a plant for process chemicals for semiconductors. Scheduled to start operation in 2024
Micron Technology (USA)	USA	October 2022	Plans to build a semiconductor manufacturing plant worth up to $100 billion in New York State. Construction is scheduled to begin in 2024, with operations scheduled to begin in the late 2020s. Planning to manufacture advanced DRAM memory
IBM (USA)	USA	October 2022	Announced plans to expand its semiconductor R&D ecosystem by investing $20 billion in New York State
JX Nippon Mining & Materials (Japan)	USA	October 2022	JX Nippon Mining & Metals USA held a groundbreaking ceremony, initiating the construction of a new state-of-the-art electronic materials manufacturing plant in Arizona. The new plant will be operational in early 2024,creating more than 100 jobs by 2025
Edwards Vacuum (UK)	USA	November 2022	Invested $319 million in New York State to build a semiconductor dry pump factory. Plan announced to create about 600 jobs over the next seven years

(*Source* Made from Kashiwase -J, 2021; Isobe -J, 2022, Reuters -J Sep. 3, 2021, Nikkei -J Sep. 4, 2021, Nikkei -J Oct. 8, 2021, JX USA Oct. 5, 2022) shock, the policy is to also promote the international economic cycle, while expanding domestic demand.

In October of the same year, Communist Party 19th Central Committee 5th General Meeting voted that by 2035 there would have been a significant increase in economic, technological, and national powers, in the rural and urban incomes, as well as in the upgrading of innovation and industry. It was also decided "To take a significant step" also in the modernization of national defense and the military (People's Daily -J, Oct. 30, 2020).

On March 13, 2021, marking the 100th anniversary of the Chinese Communist Party, the 13th National People's Congress (NPC) decided that the real economic growth rate for fiscal year 2021 would be more than 6%, and adopted the compendium of long-term goals of the 14th 5-year development plan (2021–2025) and up to 2035. It extols an innovation-driven development strategy, green development, and the people's welfare (JETRO Business News -J, Sept. 3, 2021). This would strengthen the relation between the infrastructure construction of BRI member countries and investment, while expanding the domestic cycle. Ultimately, the formation of the BRI economic network would be China's basic international strategy.

Even under the Biden administration, the decoupling policy initiated by President Trump, centered on leading edge technology industries, has not eased up. This has intensified from a bilateral conflict between China and the U.S. to a multilateral conflict between China and the advanced economies such as the U.S., the EU, and Japan.

2.5 The Geopolitics of Indo-Pacific

The U.S.-Sino rivalry that started with Trump's U.S.-Sino trade war has been intensified by COVID-19. China has responded with wolf warrior diplomacy. The conflict between the U.S. and China is promoting a restructuring of international production networks built in East Asia, centered in China. ASEAN region increases its importance economically as well as politically as an intersection of U.S. and China rivalry.

2.5.1 The Realignment of the Global Value Chain

Entering this century, the economies of large countries of China and India have been growing, instantly attracting attention as new growth regions. As such, the focus of the growth of East Asia has shifted from the Asian NIEs of the fourth quarter of the twentieth century to heavily populated countries. In particular, China's rise and BRI overseas policy, as will be discussed in Chap. 4, have decidedly attracted attention to this region. This has shifted the political and economic frontier from "Asia Pacific"

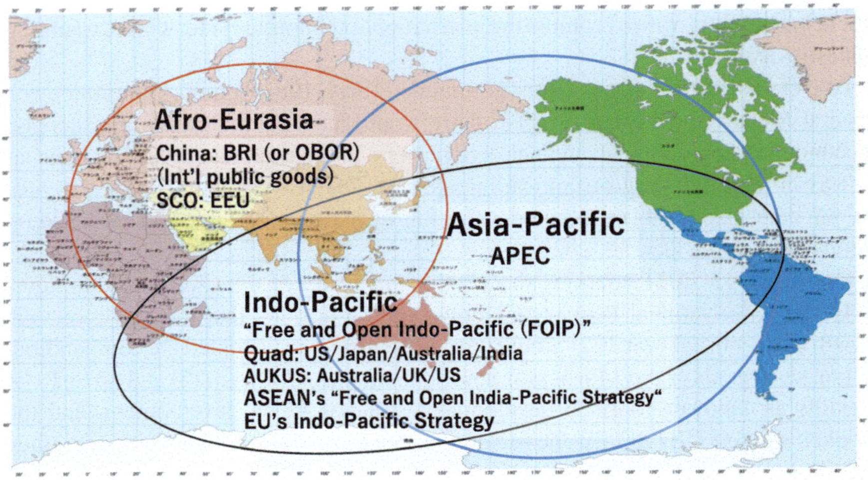

Fig. 2.12 From Asia-Pacific to BRI and Indo-Pacific (*Source* made by Hirakawa). *Notes* ASEAN: Association of Southeast Asian Nations; SCO: Shanghai Cooperation Organization, EEU: Eurasian Economic Union

to "Indo-Pacific" (Fig. 2.12). We shall look into below the birth of the Indo-Pacific concept and the issues thereof.

The "Indo-Pacific" concept is not a new one. For example, in 2013, the State Secretary during the Obama administration, John Kerry announced the "Indo-Pacific Economic Corridor" in the U.S.-India strategic dialogue[14] (Sundararaman, 2017; Wallar, 2015).

The generalization of "Indo-Pacific" here could be traced, for one, to the "Free and Open Indo-Pacific" (FOIP) advocated by then Japan Prime Minister Shinzo Abe in the 4th Africa Development Conference (Tokyo International Conference on African Development: TICAD IV) held at Nairobi, Africa in August 2016. Cognizant of China's aggressive maritime push in the East China Sea and the South China Sea beginning this century, this initiative is later on decided as Japan's main foreign policy, as is shown in diplomatic bluebooks and ODA White Papers from the following year (MOFA Japan, 2017a: 26, 2017b: 2–3).

At the Abe-Trump U.S.-Japan Summit Meeting in November 2017, it was agreed that FOIP will be a common foreign policy. At the APEC-CEO Summit held in Vietnam in the same month, President Trump used this term in his speech. At the end of May of the next year, the "U.S. Pacific Command" based in Hawaii changed its name to the "Indo-Pacific Command" (Hirakawa -J, 2018a). At the ASEAN Summit

[14] Together with Hillary Clinton's proposal in 2011 to link Central and South Asia in a "New Silk Road", Kerry's concept may have given some hint on China's BRI, but in the case of the U.S., this remained as a concept. In 2011 then U.S. Secretary of State Hillary Clinton proposed the State Department's "New Silk Road" concept to Afghanistan and Tajikistan, to link, by roads, railroads, and electric power infrastructure, Afghanistan, Pakistan, India and the various Central Asian countries of the former Soviet Union (AKDN, 2011; Kucera, 2011).

in June 2019, the "ASEAN Outlook on the Indo-Pacific" was adopted, and proclaimed the basic policy of making the Asia–Pacific a region of "cooperation not conflict" (ASEAN Secretariat, 2019). The EU Parliament adopted the "EU strategy for cooperation in the Indo-Pacific" in September 2021, which determines EU's basic posture in relation to the Indo-Pacific from both political and economic aspects, bearing in mind a stronger China (European Commission, 2021). The four leaders of "Quad" led by President Biden have announced their common vision of a "Free and Open Indo-Pacific". In September of the same year, the Quad summit at the White House, in a joint statement, confirmed the "free, open, rules-based order, rooted in international law" of the Indo-Pacific (Reuters, Sep. 25, 2021). Cooperation was promised in areas such as the provision of more than 1.2 billion doses of vaccine, including those to COVAX, as COVID-19 countermeasures of "democratic partner countries having a common vision", digital connectivity, climate change, and the building of a semiconductor supply chain (Quad Leaders' Summit, Fact Sheet, Sep. 24, 2021). In the same month of September, Australia, the UK, and the U.S. inaugurated a national security cooperation framework, Aukus, the objective of which is to counter the growing military power of China in the Indo-Pacific. In May 2022, President Biden also launched the Indo-Pacific Economic Framework (IPEF) as a system of re-entry into the East Asian economy that President Trump lost when he withdrew from the TPP in 2017, and 13 countries, including Japan, Australia, and India, participated in it.

Now, India historically has taken a non-allied neutralism as its foreign policy. This tradition is not rejected even by Quad. In June 2020, a confrontation occurred between the military forces of India and China at the India-China border, where for the first time in 45 years, there was one death. Since then, India's sentiments towards China have soured. India has been overly concerned about China's encirclement of India known as China's so-called "pearl necklace" policy, and has also been troubled by the flood of Chinese products, including high-tech products, into the Indian market. This national stress has led to India boycotting and prohibiting the use of Chinese-made smartphone applications. India's joining Quad is a balancing foreign policy and has an important significance as part of its national security policy.

The Biden administration's principle of international cooperation, however, has not gone totally well. The issue of the construction of nuclear submarines in Aukus has sown the seeds of distrust with France.

On the other hand, China has not limited itself to the BRI strategy, as it builds new networking relationships in Eurasia. One such initiative is the Shanghai Cooperation Organization (SCO), which emerged after the fall of the Soviet Union in 1994, as China played a central role in forming the Shanghai 5 consisting of Kazakhstan, Kyrgyzstan, Russia, and Tajikistan, with Uzbekistan joining in 2001. The Eurasian Economic Union (EEU), which was inaugurated in 2015 by Russia together with Belarus, Kazakhstan, Armenia, and others, has strengthened its links with the SCO. In 2015, the 15th SCO Summit and the 7th BRICS Summit were jointly held in Ufa, Russia. At that time, agreement was reached over China's constructive role through BRI. Furthermore, membership of Pakistan and India was approved at the Ufa SCO Summit. At the 21st SCO Summit held in Dusan, Tajikistan in September 2021, the membership of Iran, which participated as an observer since 2005, was formally approved, and is now being processed. The U.S. has imposed economic sanctions on Iran over the nuclear development issue. Iran's entry into the SCO has strengthened its political position over the nuclear development issue. Through their conflict with the U.S., China and Russia have expanded and strengthened their home camps. This is a big plus for BRI.

We should say that the two large countries of the U.S. and China have become the axis of a conflict structure of the "New Cold War". As such, the Indo-Pacific region has become more and more important as a strategic region in global geopolitics. From a purely economic perspective, this will give rise to competitive relations over infrastructure construction, which opens up the possibility of economic development.

2.5.2 ASEAN at the Intersection of China's BRI and U.S.-Led Indo-Pacific

What would be the effect on Asia's emerging economies of the global structural change in political economy and conflict? Here, let us take a brief look at ASEAN, as it is caught in the middle of this conflict between the U.S. and China. As will be discussed more in the next chapter, Southeast Asia has played a large role in the development of the regional economy since the second half of the 1980s. China has also come to regard the Southeast Asian regions as a strategic and high priority region. In November 2002, ACFTA[15] was formed. RCEP also reached an agreement in December 2020, after eight years of negotiations, and was inaugurated in January 2022. ASEAN is a member in both treaties. The Southeast Asian region is also an important region along the BRI circuit.

ASEAN's relationship with China, however, is complicated. With its economic development being acknowledged from both within and without in the 2010s, China's policy towards the ASEAN region has clearly become increasingly belligerent. Based on the so-called "Nine-Dash Line", China has built military facilities on land reclamations on what used to be coral reefs, deepening its conflict especially with the Philippines and Vietnam. Such maritime incursions of China have brought about a rift among ASEAN members. In the ASEAN Foreign Ministers meeting in 2012, agreement on the South China issue was not reached, neither was a joint statement issued. While the Philippines and Vietnam sought for the inclusion of the South China Sea issue in a joint statement, the Chair Country, Cambodia, rejected the proposal. This is a historical first for ASEAN. Given this, the Philippines in January 2013 brought an arbitration case against China to the International Permanent Court of Arbitration, based on the United Nations Convention on the Law of the Sea, to seek a solution to the territorial dispute. China has rejected the arbitration. In July 2016, the Court of Arbitration ruled in favor of most of the Philippines' assertions.

---

[15] Formally called the Framework Agreement on Comprehensive Economic Cooperation between the Association of Southeast Asian Nations and the People's Republic of China.

On the other hand, ASEAN has high expectations of China with regards to funding the region's further development. Even before the launching of China's BRI in 2013, ASEAN was already working towards economic integration. In 2010, ASEAN formulated the Master Plan on ASEAN Connectivity (MPAC 2010) towards the building of the "ASEAN Community" in 2015, initiating 19 projects on physical, institutional, and people connectivity[16] (ASEAN Secretariat, 2019). Furthermore, the 2009 Asia Development Bank report announced the "Infrastructure for a Seamless Asia", estimating an infrastructure demand of about US$8 trillion in Asia over the period 2010 to 2020. Financing this infrastructure demand is a big issue for ASEAN, but China's BRI responded to such expectations of ASEAN. Established in October 2014, the Asia Infrastructure Investment Bank (AIIB)[17] was quickly accepted by ASEAN countries even at its planning stage. ASEAN members were also establishing members.

For China, the ASEAN region is an important region along the BRI circuit. Once BRI has started, Chinese firms, funded by China, would actively deploy across the region. In Malaysia, Thailand, Indonesia, and others, plans for and construction of high-speed railroad systems are already underway. There have been reports of rampant problems related to such matters as construction delays, debt repayments, environment, and corruption. Overcoming the COVID-19 crisis, however, is the high-speed railroad system connecting Kunming and Vientiane, Laos in early December 2021.

In actuality, ASEAN and China's economic relations have rapidly progressed during these past ten years. The U.S.-Sino trade war and COVID-19 have in fact worked positively for ASEAN's trade. The U.S.-Sino trade war has forced China-based firms, including Chinese ones, to transfer part of their production outside China, as part of their "China plus one" policies. Vietnam and China have become the major destinations of these firms. In this way, the ASEAN trade structure is starting to change.

Looking at the changes in the past ten years, let us compare ASEAN's trade structure in 2010 and 2020. During this period, intra-regional and Japan trade shares in ASEAN's total trade (exports and imports) dropped from 24.5 to 21.4%, and 11.0 to 7.8%, respectively. In contrast, China and U.S. trade shares rose from 12.0 to 19.4%, and 9.2 to 11.2%, respectively. This reflects the ASEAN region as a business center for trade with the U.S. ASEAN's export value to China doubled during this period, increasing the share from 10.8 to 16.1% of total export value. Similarly, exports to the US also doubled in value, expanding its share from 9.6 to 14.4%. Moreover, the value of imports from China in 2020 exceeded ASEAN intra-regional imports, making China currently the largest source of imports (Kitami, 2021). Awareness of

[16] At the 2003 ASEAN Summit it was agreed to build the ASEAN Community by 2020. This was advanced to 2015 at the 2007 Summit, due to the rapid advance of the region's development at that time.

[17] AIIB was established in December 2015 and started operations from January 2016. There were 57 member countries at the beginning, but by 2020, the number has grown to 103 (AIIB HP, Accessed Dec. 10, 2021). America and Japan were the only major advanced countries that were not participating.

the risk of concentrating manufacturing bases in China due to the U.S.-Sino trade war and COVID-19 has spurred the transfer of production to ASEAN, trade with China, and exports to the U.S. We expect that this structure will continue to hold for some time.

As was mentioned above in the survey results of Sect. 2.4.1, ASEAN's trade structure has confronted the ASEAN region with a dilemma. The high level of economic dependence on China increases the political risks. The contradiction among the regional countries is also spreading. The deepening dependence of Cambodia and Laos on China may prevent the unity of cooperation within ASEAN. The case of Myanmar's dictatorship following the military takeover in February 2021 poses a big problem to ASEAN cooperation. These have become existential issues for ASEAN.

ASEAN Way as a decision-making method for the ASEAN has developed a unique management method, which extols principles such as non-interventionism and consensus, different from those common in American and European organizations. As such, there is sometimes a feeling of disappointment. Besides, decision-making takes time. The organization, however, acquires flexibility. The organization has been sustained for more than half a century since its establishment in 1967, while holding up ambitious goals and achieving results. These achievements are by any means only those of ASEAN. An institutional base and international public good were provided to link Japan, China, and South Korea. We started this chapter with a discussion of how Trump applied his art of the deal in international trade negotiations with China. Xi Jinping has shown that he is equally willing to play hardball. What seemed at first as a zero-sum game (ZSG) has now degenerated into a game of chicken (GOC). The worst-case scenario in a ZSG is that one side loses, while in a GOC both sides lose, making it a more dangerous game to play, not only for the two countries but also for the rest of the world.

With regards to the phase one agreement, however, we cannot help but feel that the gains of this deal, at this point, have been in favor of China. Additional tariffs were not that effective in reducing the U.S. deficit vis-a-vis China, and served only to increase the prices paid by American consumers without improving the performance of the industries being protected by the tariffs.[18] In short, China has outmaneuvered yet once again the U.S.

This is not the first time China has done this. We could go all the way to China's opening up in the 1980s and see how it has outmaneuvered the capitalist countries, in general, and the U.S., in particular. In fact, a famous saying from Sun Tzu's Art of War, which was written around 500 BC in China, captures very well what China has done through these four decades: Appear weak when you are strong, and strong when you are weak. The first part of the saying is essentially a strategy of luring the enemy in, while the second part is a strategy of repelling the enemy. The "weakness" here, as it would be perceived by more democratic states, would be China's communist political system. China's "strength" lies in its economy. Capitalist countries were strongly

[18] See "How China won Trump's Trade War and got Americans to foot the bill" (Bloomberg News, Jan. 12, 2021) https://www.bloomberg.com/news/articles/2021-01-11/how-china-won-trump-s-good-and-easy-to-win-trade-war (Accessed Dec. 29, 2021).

attracted to China because of its large supply of cheap skilled labor, and vast markets, even going to the extent of offering access to more advanced production technology in exchange for access to the Chinese labor pool and markets. The opportunity to convert a communist country into democracy has also been cited as a reason for embracing China, albeit this would not really be given top priority until perhaps much later. Ultimately, the Chinese economy grew by leaps and bounds thanks to capitalism. China, however, retains its "weakness" of being a communist country, while strengthening its economy. This to us is one of the greatest outmaneuvering of capitalist countries by a communist country in the era where capitalism has been declared the de-facto victor.

This outmaneuvering, however, does not stop here. China now has a dominating presence in the South China Sea, where it had practically none during the Cold War and all the way to the early 1990s, when the U.S. still had major military bases in the Northern Philippines. Even after observing the Chinese incursions in the South China Sea, the Obama administration presented no solid resistance that would deter China's further expansion.

As discussed briefly above, the South China Sea actually offers a way out of the GOC following, not the Art of the Deal, but the Art of War. ASEAN, which also has claims in the South China Sea, may be easier to play hardball with than the more formidable U.S., but doing so would most likely end up in China spreading too thinly in several fronts and would have wasted a golden opportunity to regain trust where it is easier to do so. The better way of playing the game would be that of Sun Tzu where war[19] is avoided if it is at all possible.[20] It is a true warrior that deeply understands the value of peace. As Sun Tzu recommends, alliances with contiguous states should be formed at the "intersecting highways".

ASEAN is in the very midst of changes in the Asian structure, and is confronted with many challenges for which solutions would not be easy. Reflecting on its more than half a century of accumulated experience, ASEAN would be able to maintain a certain individuality, which does not lean to either side, while being in a region over which the U.S. and China camps compete. In doing so, ASEAN is in a position to play an important role in defusing the escalation of the GOC between the two superpowers. How the various parties negotiate with each other has been and will be a key factor.

---

[19] Here, the term "war" is taken to involve a series of exchanges of blows between two parties, not necessarily military in nature.

[20] "Supreme excellence consists in breaking the enemy's resistance without fighting" (Sun Tzu (translated by Lionel Giles) 1910: 41), Art of War: The Oldest Military Treatise in the World. London: British Museum, 41).

2.6 Concluding Remarks

As the 45th President of the U.S., Donald Trump's "America First" has thrown relations with China into a series of rude threats and retaliations, lending substance to the use of the term "trade war" instead of "trade friction". Moreover, the point of conflict has widened, without any rule to go by, from the trade deficit to a wider set of issues, including hi-tech theft, national security risks, systems, ideologies, and human rights. Although the "Phase 1 Agreement" was reached in early 2020, it has not built a trusting relationship between the two countries.

The COVID-19 pandemic has only served to further deepen this distrust, as China was initially able to successfully contain the contagion where the U.S. failed to do so. The Trump administration has blatantly deployed a policy of decoupling with China, which responded plainly with its "wolf warrior diplomacy." Bringing this to bear on countries and people who were critical of China. While soliciting support within China, the wolf warrior diplomacy has brought about historically high anti-Chinese sentiments and distrust among the peoples of Western advanced countries and the emerging countries around China. President Biden's foreign policy of returning to the principle of international coordination has changed the structure of conflict with China from China-versus-the U.S. to China-versus-the U.S. and its allies. As such, BRI and the Indo-Pacific have become the axis of conflict of what has deepened into a "new cold war".

The COVID-19 pandemic and political confrontation between the United States and China poses risks to the East Asian region, and has a great impact on ASEAN countries as an intersection of two forces. However, it also restructures the new production supply chain and brings the possibility of further development when that decisive conflict could be controlled.

References

**Documents with a symbol (-J) after the author's name are Japanese documents*

AKDN. (2011). *Press release: US Secretary of State Hillary Clinton discusses New Silk Road Initiative*. Aga Khan Development Network. https://www.akdn.org/press-release/us-secretary-state-hillary-clinton-discusses-new-silk-road-initiative-lauds-akdn-

ASEAN Secretariat. (2019). *ASEAN outlook on the Indo-Pacific*. https://asean.org/asean2020/wp-content/uploads/2021/01/ASEAN-Outlook-on-the-Indo-Pacific_FINAL_22062019.pdf

ASEAN Studies Center and Institute of Southeast Asian Studies. (2021). *The State of Southeast Asia: 2021 survey report*. ISEAN.

Brown, C. P. (2021). *US-China phase one tracker: China's purchases of US goods*. PIIE Research, September 27, https://www.piie.com/research/piie-charts/us-china-phase-one-tracker-chinas-purchases-us-goods

CISTEC Secretariat -J. (2021). Regarding the enforcement of the promulgation of the Chinese Commerce Department's 'Counteracting Unjustified Extra-territorial Application of Foreign

Legislation and Other Measures'. Center for Information on Security Trade Control, January 12.

European Commission. (2021). The EU strategy for cooperation in the Indo-Pacific, September 16.

European Parliament News. (2021). The EU strategy for cooperation in the Indo-Pacific, September 16.

Gupta, P. (2020). The "17+1" initiative: Is China losing its charm in Central and Eastern Europe? *ORF Young Voice*, September 18.

Hanemann, T., Rosen, D. H., Witzke, M., Bnennion, S., & Smith, E. (2021). Two-way street: 2021 update: US-China investment trends. A Report by the US-China Investment Project, May.

Hirakawa, H. -J. (2018a). Indo taiheiyo wa atarashii Keizai furontia (The 'Indo-Pacific' is the new economic frontier). *World Economic Review* IMPACT, no. 1130, August 13.

Hirakawa, H. -J. (2018b). Sekai Keizai furontia sosyutsu no kanousei (The Possibility of creating a world economic frontier). *Gendai no Riron* (Modern Theory), Summer.

Hirakawa, H. -J. (2021a). Tranpu Seiken no beikoku daiichi to kokusaikankei (The Trump Administration's 'America First' and international relations). *Kikan Gendai no Riron* (Quarterly Modern Theory), no. 25, February, http://gendainoriron.jp/vol.25/feature/hirakawa.php

Hirakawa, H. -J. (2021b). Tranpu daitoryo to COVID-19 ha sekai keizai wo do kaeru ka (How will President Trump and COVID-19 change the global economy: Focus on US-Sino relations). *Kokusai Keizai* (Annual Report of the Japan Society of International Economics), no. 72.

Isobe, S. -J. (2022). Beikoku de moriagaru handotai sangyo no Shinko to yusyutsu kanri (Promotion and export control of the booming U.S. semiconductor industry). JETRO Chiiki Bunseki Repooto, December 28.

IMF. (2020). *World economic outlook*. International Monetary Fund, April.

JETRO. (2020). *Survey on business conditions of Japanese companies operating overseas (Asia and Oceania)*, December 23.

Kashiwase, A. -J. (2021). Sekai keizai wo tenbo suru kii waado Handotai: Juyo kyuzo, kakkoku de kyokyuu noryoku kyoka wo isogu (Semiconductors, a Keyword for the prospects of the global economy: Rapid increase in demand, countries speeding up the strengthening of supply capabilities). JETRO Chiiki/Bunseki repohto (Regional and Analytical Report), September 24.

Kitami, S. -J. (2021). Boeki matorikkusu de miru ASEAN shijo no seicho to boeki aite no hensen (Growth of ASEAN market and changes in trade partners as seen from trade matrix). JETRO Chiiki/Bunseki Repohto (Regional and Analytical Report), June 23.

Kucera, J. (2011). *Clinton's dubious plan to save Afghanistan with a 'New Silk Road'*. The Atlantic, November 3, https://www.theatlantic.com/international/archive/2011/11/clintons-dubious-plan-to-save-afghanistan-with-a-new-silk-road/247760/

Lowy Institute. (2021). Poll 2021: Understanding Australian attitudes to the world, June 23.

MOFA Japan. (2017a). *Diplomatic bluebook 2017*. Ministry of Foreign Affairs of Japan.

MOFA Japan. (2017b). *White paper on development cooperation 2017*. Japan's International Cooperation.

MOFCOM PRC. (2021). *MOFCOM Order no.1 of 2021 on rules on counteracting unjustified extra-territorial application of foreign legislation and other measures*. Ministry of Commerce, January 9.

NSF. (2020). *The State of U.S. science and engineering 2020*. National Science Foundation, USA.

Pew Research Center. (2021). *Large majorities say China does not respect the personal freedoms of its people: Unfavorable views of China also near historic highs in most of the 17 advanced economies surveyed*. June 30, PG_2021.06.30_Global-Views-China_FINAL.pdf

Pompeo, M. R. (2020). *Communist China and the free world's future*. U.S. Department of State, July 23, https://www.state.gov/communist-china-and-the-free-worlds-future/

Sun Tzu (L. Giles, Trans.). (1910). *Art of war: The oldest military treatise in the world*. British Museum.

Sundararaman, S. (2017). *Indo-Pacific economic corridor: A version in progress*. ORF Commentaries, February 10, https://www.orfonline.org/research/indo-pacific-economic-corridor-a-vision-in-progress/#_ftnref3

Turcsanyi, R. Q. (2021). *Unrewarding show: Online summit of China-CEE 17+1 Platform.* Italian Institute for International Political Studies (ISPI), February 26.

UBS. (2020). *Supply chains are shifting: How much and where?* UBS Evidence Lab inside, June 15, https://www.ubs.com/global/en/investment-bank/in-focus/covid-19/2020/supply-chains-are-shifting.html

USDOC. (2021). Commerce adds seven Chinese supercomputing entities to the entity list for their support to China's military modernization, and other destabilizing efforts, April 8.

Wallar, J. (2015). *Indo-Pacific economic corridor for U.S., Indian, & ASEAN statesmanship.* CSIS Asia Program, September 2, http://www.cogitasia.com/indo-pacific-economic-corridor-opportunity-for-u-s-indian-asean-statesmanship/

White House. (2022). Fact Sheet: CHIPS and Science Act will lower costs, create jobs, strengthen supply chains, and counter China, August 9.

White House Presidential Memorandum. (2018). *Presidential memorandum on the action by the United States related to the Section 301 investigation.* March 22, https://trumpwhitehouse.archives.gov/presidential-actions/presidential-memorandum-actions-united-states-related-section-301-investigation/

Chapter 3
Asia's Changing Mechanism of Development and the Global Economy

Abstract In this chapter, we confirm that the development of the Asian economy from the 1990s to the early part of this century was achieved amidst a deep relationship with the change in the world political economy. At the same time, we will trace the development of the Asian economy for the past half century, and consider this development, not as the product of universal development policies, but as the result of the interplay of simultaneously changing global and regional economies which are deeply related to the foreign direct investment (FDI) of advanced economies. Extracting the main points of the mechanism of this development is the main objective of this chapter. At the end of this chapter, we determine how, through such a mechanism, Asia's development is promoting a structural shift of the global political economy, and the new issues arising thereof.

Keywords BRICs · Emerging economies · FDI · Middle class · PoBMEs · Population dividend (bonus)

3.1 Introduction

In the 1990s, globalization garnered a lot of attention. During the second half of the twentieth century, the trade-led global economy was transformed into a global economy wherein multinational companies are actively engaged in foreign direct investment. The international division of labor also went through big changes. These changes were supported by the end of the ideological conflict between capitalism and socialism in the twentieth century, with the collapse of the Soviet Union, and the progress in Information and Communication Technology (ICT). The collapse of the Soviet Union, in one fell swoop, opened up the possibility of the integration of the Eastern economy with the Western economy, and the possibility of removing the space–time constraints facing economies, through the development of ICT. Towards the twenty-first century, it was becoming generally known that a global economy, which has at its core the advanced capitalist economies, was born.

H. Hirakawa and F. C. Maquito, *The Dynamics of Asian Economic Development*,
https://doi.org/10.1007/978-981-97-3106-0_3

From the 1990s up to the early twenty-first century, however, was a period wherein the developing economies, which historically occupied a subordinate position, began to show a presence that could not be ignored. Owing to the continued spectacular growth of the East Asia-centered Asian economy, it was a period that also changed the structure of the world economy. That change was also reflected in the birth of various coined words, and new international fora. Developing economies have been dubbed with terms such as "emerging markets" or "emerging economies." The G20 framework was born in this period. Coined words such as "population bonus", "BRICs", and "middle income trap" are also deeply related to the Asian developing economies and newly emerging economies.

In our consideration of the development of Asian economies in this chapter, we will first take the development of Asian economies, not as a collection of the development of individual countries, but as the development of a regional economy amidst the global economy. In so doing, we will determine the features of the Asian economic development mechanism, as well as its concomitant issues. Next, we will focus on the driving force of the development of the emerging economies, its changes and background. In the third section, we clarify the dynamic changes in the development mechanism and attempt to arrive at its prospects. In the fourth section, we attempt an inquiry of the issues that arise from mutual interaction of development of East Asia and economies of individual countries. We will synthesize at the end.

3.2 The Globalization of the Economy and the Development of Asia's Emerging Economies

The development of the Asian economies, which centered on East Asia since the 1990s, have brought about dramatic structural changes in both the global and Asian economies. We shall clarify such dramatic development and then discuss the structural changes within the region that accompany such changes.

3.2.1 Emerging Asian Economies and China

The rapid growth of the Asian economies has already been attracting interest since the 1970s, however, it could be said that this development has only been tied to the development of the Asian region beginning the 1990s. Up to then the Asian economies were studied as individual country economies, following the predominant economic methodology, and as such, most studies were country-specific appreciations of development. The interest in the Asian economy during the 1960 and 1970s was generally based on the high growth of the Japanese economy, and not so much on the Asian developing economies. The OECD focused on the manufacturing export of a group of less developed countries to advanced economies, and in 1979 labeled these less

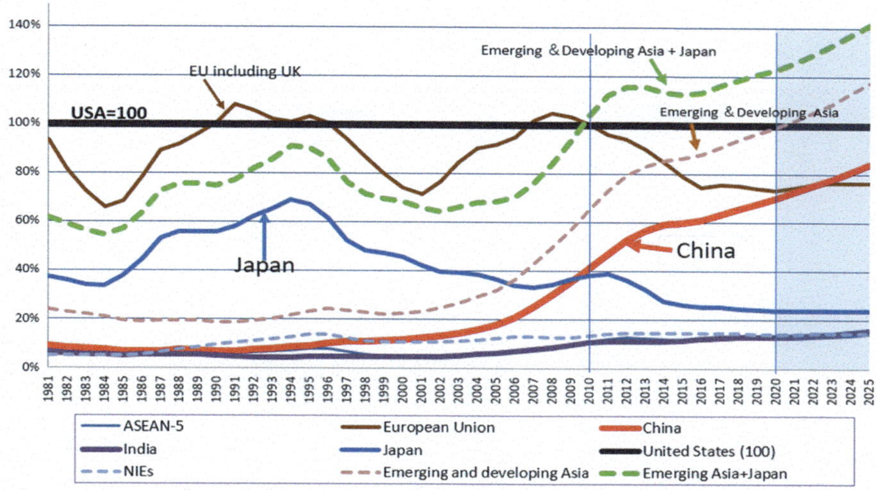

Fig. 3.1 Economic size of major countries/regions relative to the U.S. 1981–2025 3-Year moving average (*Source* IMF World Economic Outlook Database, April 2021). *Note* Values from 2020 are estimated. NIEs consist of Hong Kong, Korea, Singapore, and Taiwan. ASEAN-5 consists of Indonesia, Malaysia, Philippines, Thailand, and Vietnam. East Asia consists of NIEs, ASEAN-5, China, and Japan. 'Emerging and developing Asia' follows the IMF definition

developed countries as the Newly Industrializing Countries (NICs) (OECD, 1979). The research interest at that time was not on Asian but Latin American and European NICs.[1] Interest on Asian NICs heightened from the latter part of the 1980s, particularly in the 1990s, when they were the only group of countries sustaining high growth. The came to be called Newly Industrializing Economies (NIEs) instead of NICs.[2] Until then, Asia was presumed to be an impoverished and stagnant region.

Figure 3.1 shows the structural changes of the global and Asian regional economies. From this figure, we can see the relative relationship of the global and Asian economies since the 1980s. We can see first of all that the EU zone is the largest economy next to the U.S., and that the total scale of the economy of the Asian region only accounted for 60–70% of the U.S. The Japanese economy occupied an overwhelming share of the Asian economy. During the 1980s up to the first half of the 1990s, Asia was rapidly catching up with America, led by the development of Japan. It was at this time that the Japan–U.S. trade friction heated up.

[1] The late Professor Emeritus K. Kojima of Hitotsubashi University, Tokyo gave the author a note at the time of the Asian Development Seminar sponsored by Science Council of Japan (March 27, 1993), that said the main interest of the researchers participating in the OECD's NICs research project was "not on the Asian NICs but rather European NICs, Latin American NICs".

[2] According to the late Japanese diplomat H. Kitamura, who attended the 1988 Toronto Summit, the Canadian leader Sherpa suggested that the NICs be called NIEs. The reason was to avoid calling Taiwan and Hong Kong a country because of their political relationship with China (Kitamura, 1988).

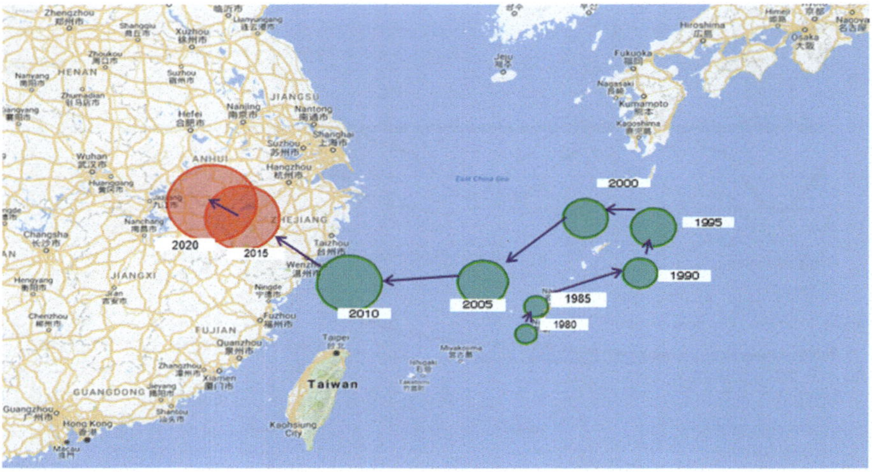

Fig. 3.2 Center of gravity shift of East Asia + Australia, New Zealand, and India economy 1980–2020 (*Source* Revised version from Hirakawa et al., -J, 2009; Hirakawa, 2010. Data from IMF, World economic outlook database October 2016). *Note* We calculated and illustrated the circle of the Asian regional economy using the GDP of East Asia + three countries (Australia, New Zealand, and Inndia) using the total GDP to indicate the size of the circle, and using the GDP-weighted location of each country's capital to indicate the center of each circle. East Asia includes the four NIES countries/regions (South Korea, Taiwan, Hong Kong, and Singapore), and the nine ASEAN countries (Indonesia, Malaysia, the Philippines, Thailand, Brunei, Cambodia, Laos, Myanmar, and Vietnam). The map was drawn based on the scale in current dollar terms. Illustrated on Google map. The illustrations were first made in 2009 with the help of then graduate school students of Nagoya University, Dr. M. Abe and Mr. A. Mizutani

From the second half of the 1990s, however, there was a structural shift. At this time, the Japanese economy showed a remarkable shrinking relative to the American economy, Japan had ceased to become a challenger to America. In the former's stead emerged China. From the 1990s, China has been steadily catching up with Japan, and in 2010 surpassed the size of the Japanese economy. China's presence in East Asia has also grown overwhelmingly. Figure 3.2 shows the shifting of the economic center or equilibrium point of the region based on the GDP of East Asia + Australia, New Zealand and India.[3] The center of gravity, which had been drawn toward Japan until the mid-1990s, has since then been drawn toward China, and by the turn of the century, it has been located on the Chinese mainland.

Incidentally, 2010 was the year when the size of East Asian economies, including Japan, surpassed that of America. Adding India to the mix, puts the overtaking of the American economy one year earlier. Ten years later in 2020, as the global economy

[3] There was a paper by Quah (2011), which dealt with shifts in the center of gravity of the global economy with a similar idea of this figure. The author's figure, although quite simple, was first created in 2009 with the cooperation of then students of the Graduate School of Economics at Nagoya University, and the figure was first used in a paper published in Octpber 2009 (Hirakawa et al., -J, 2009). I would like to thank two graduate students at that time, Dr. Masaru Abe and Mr. Akito Mizutani.

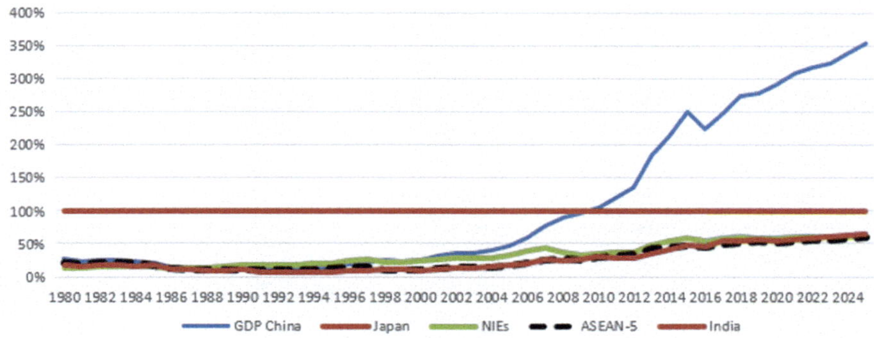

Fig. 3.3 Economic scale of China, NIEs, ASEAN-5, India relative to Japan 1980–2025 (*Source* IMF World Economic Outlook Database, April 2021). *Note* Values after 2020 are estimates. Definition of regional groups is the same as that of Fig. 3.1

sinks into the Corona crisis, China was able to suppress the COVID-19 infection, and maintain its growth, growing to 70% of the American economy. Now, the East Asian economy is not only represented by China but, even without Japan, is becoming the biggest regional economy in the world on par with the American economy. Having quickly suppressed COVID-19 as soon as it started in 2020, China, at the end of 2020, became more realistically able to talk about projections of overtaking America.[4]

Figure 3.3 was created to show the structural changes in the major countries/ economies of the Asian region for the same period as the previous figure. With Japan as a reference point, we can glean two features from the figure. One is China's fast catching up with and overtaking Japan. At the start of 1990, China's economy was just about one-ninth that of Japan. It was a quarter in 2000, a half in 2005, surpassed Japan in 2010, and is now about three times bigger. This great reversal happened in less than a quarter of a century. One more glaring point is the steady catching up of NIEs, ASEAN, and India with Japan, albeit at a slower pace than that of China. Any of the four classes of economies above have reached a scale of 60–70% that of Japan. In Asia, it is not only China, but also NIEs, ASEAN, and India that are growing. For sure, Asia's emerging economies are also growing and developing as a region.

[4] In 2022, there was an explosion of corona infections in China, and the Chinese government continued the so-called "Zero Corona" policy throughout 2022, until December 2022. However, the infection continued for several months after the full lifting of Covid restrictions in January 2023, and the economy stagnated. As a result, previous predictions that China would overtake the United States in the 2020s to 2030s have been delayed even further. According to Bloomberg's forecast in September of the same year, the overtaking is now set to occur in the mid-2040s or later (Bloomberg News, Sep. 5, 2023).

3.2.2 Asian Emerging Economies and Globalization

When we comprehend the remarkable development of the Asian emerging economies since the 1990s, it becomes necessary to focus on three causes brought about by the international economy and community at that time. One is the G5 Finance Ministers and Central Bank Governors meeting held in 1985 at the New York Plaza Hotel. Another one is the collapse of the Eastern Communist bloc, starting with the fall of the Berlin Wall and the dismantling of the Soviet Union. Lastly is the start of the accelerated development of Information Communications Technology (ICT) at that time.

The G5 Finance Ministers and Central Bank Governors meeting reached the Plaza Accord for the correction of disequilibrium in the balance of payments and the strong dollar. As a result, the Japanese yen rapidly appreciated against the U.S. dollar, which in turn brought about a chain of new economic development in East Asia. Right before the Plaza Accord, at the end of August 1985, the exchange rate was one US$ to 237 Japanese yen. At the end of September, the yen appreciated to 217, and at the end of April 1987 crossed 140, for a 70% appreciation or *endaka*, which led to throwing Japan into a disconcerting *endaka* recession. Japanese companies, however, rode on a wave of foreign direct investment to the NIEs, ASEAN, and China, triggered by the internationally stronger yen.

Along with the overlapping currents of declining interest rates in international financial markets and the drop in oil prices, the NIEs were able to achieve economic growth. This in turn was called the NIEs currency appreciation, which led to direct investments of NIEs companies into ASEAN countries and China. In this way, an organic union was created within the Asia region, through intra-regional investment and trade with Asian companies as core (Hirakawa -J, 1992: 257).

The development of Asian NIEs will be discussed in more detail in Chap. 7. Suffice it to say at this point that it was a "growth triangle" structure, wherein Japanese companies investing into the NIEs imported capital and intermediate goods from Japan, processed this, and exported the resulting goods to the U.S. The Plaza Accord triggered the upgrading of the triangle structure, with the participation of NIEs companies. Incidentally, ASEAN countries and China responded with an export-led development policy that was open to foreign direct investment.

Many ASEAN countries up to this period pursued an import-substitution type of development policy. changing to an export-led type of policy. In 1978, China threw away its self-reliance approach, embarked on an opening up reform, and, after Deng Xiaoping's "Southern Tour Lectures" in 1992, established a "communist market economy" approach. China built special economic zones along the coastal area, attracted foreign companies, and connected domestic firms to the world market. The special economic zones played important roles not only for the growth of NIEs and China but also for other Asian countries (ADB, 2015).

According to the Asian Development Bank (ADB), the growth rate of global FDI in 1983–89 reached 29%, which was three times that of global exports and four times that of GDP. The global FDI during this period was mostly directed to advanced economies. To this was added Asia's emerging economies that provided promising investment opportunities for multinational companies. Moreover, investments to Asia, by Japanese companies followed by companies that succeeded in Asia's emerging economies, played a big role. ADB writes as follows.

> Worldwide foreign direct investment made by Japan increased at a rate of 62% per annum between 1985 and 1989, and expansion of foreign direct investment by the NIEs was equally rapid. Developing Asia, primarily the NIEs, the ASEAN-4 and China, was also in the forefront as a host region. Its share (excluding Hong Kong and Taipei, China) of foreign direct investment in all developing countries increased from 30% in the early 1980s to 65% in 1990 (ADB, 1992: 63).

The share of investments by host countries in 1990 was 19% for South Korea and Singapore, 12% for China, 24% for the ASEAN-4 (Indonesia, Malaysia, the Philippines, and Thailand), and 10% for other Asian developing economies (ADB, 1992: 66).

The resulting East Asian investment and growth chain was especially viewed as a manifestation of the "Flying Geese Type of Development", which was brought to the limelight, of course by Japan, and by international institutions.[5] This is the theory formulated by Akamatsu Kaname in the 1930s drawn from his empirical research on the industrial development of Japan and developing countries. An industry, or an economy for that matter, will, in succession, go through import, production, and then export. This is accompanied by industrial upgrading and the transfer of failing firms to countries at a lower stage of industrialization, leading to an international division of labor. In East Asia's development, much attention has been given to the internationalization mechanism of the Flying Geese Theory. In the 1994 White Paper, a trade specialization coefficient ((export − import))/(export + import)) on different goods of different East Asian countries was used to explain the regional development as follows.

> Looking at this (trade specialization coefficient), we can see that it rises, declines and becomes negative. On a country (or regional) level, this pattern first appears in Japan, and then the NIEs, and then ASEAN, and then China. From an industry level, the order is from non-durable consumption goods to durable consumption goods to capital goods. As such, we can clearly observe a flying geese type of development, where the lead country (Japan) is being pursued by the other countries, and where there is continuous shifting of the industrial weight to higher value-added sectors. In particular, the developing countries of ASEAN and China are greatly shortening their catching up process (MITI -J, 1994: 304).

The phrase "greatly shortening their catching up" in the above quotation has in mind the achievement of this development through the foreign direct investments mainly of Japanese companies.

---

[5] Using the Flying Geese model of development, a series of reports came out explaining Asia's development, such as Japan's former Economic Planning Agency, the Cabinet Office's 1994 "White Paper" and "Global Economy White Paper", the 1995 World Investment Report and 1996 Trade and Development Report of the United Nations Conference on Trade and Development (UNCTAD). We shall discuss in detail the development of the Flying Geese model and theoretical issues in Chap. 12.

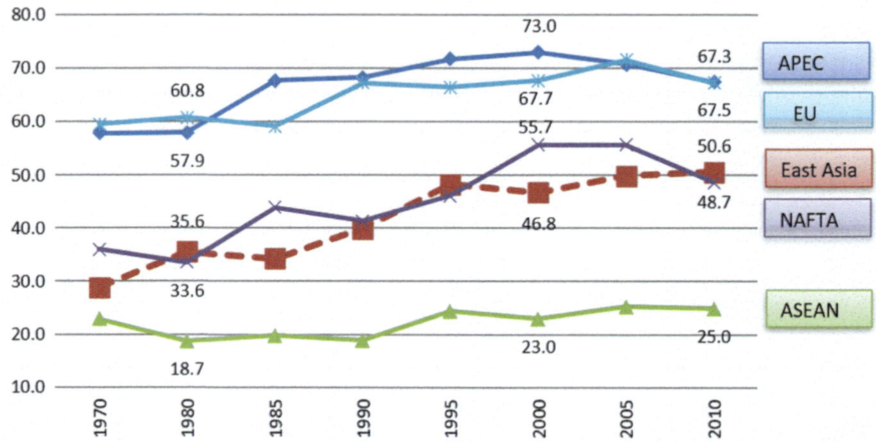

Fig. 3.4 The intra-regional trade (exports) of major economic zones 1970–2010 (*Source* World Bank, 2005, 2011, 2012). *Note* The East Asia intra-regional export ratio was derived from the 2010 JETRO World Trade Matrix

In this manner, the development of Asian emerging economies upgraded the above-mentioned Japan-NIEs-U.S. growth triangle structure, and pushed East Asian regional countries and economies towards integration. Figure 3.4 shows the changes in the share of intra-regional trade (exports) of the world's major economic zones. The intra-regional share of Japan, NIEs, ASEAN and China combined increased from 35.6% in 1985 to 48.3% in 1995, or 13 percentage points over ten years. The intra-regional share in 2020 for "Asia", including India, reached 60%(UNCTAD, 2020: 20).

Next is the collapse of the former Socialist zone. Francis Fukuyama viewed this as the "End of History" (Fukuyama, 1992). The world came to view this as the victory of liberalism and capitalism over socialism. The constituent countries of the former Soviet Union gained independence and came to be called "transition economies". In economics, neoliberalism and market fundamentalism came to hold sway.

The development of the Asian NIEs came to be viewed as good examples of the victory of liberalism and capitalism. In 1987, South Korea and Taiwan achieved a shift in their political systems from authoritarianism to democracy. The major global economies, without exception, came to pursue liberalist policies with regards to trade and investment. International financial and developmental institutions strongly sought for the liberalization of trade and investment in developing regions.

Figure 3.5 collates the number of countries and cases from 1991 to 2020 with respect to FDI-related laws as collected by UNCTAD. Since the 1990s, the number of countries and cases that set up FDI-related laws went through repetitive ups and downs. Cross-referencing this with Fig. 3.6, which distinguishes FDI-related laws by characteristic, we could divide the period into two phases, with phase 1 extending up to 2000, followed by phase 2. There was a strong acceptance of global FDI in phase 1 due to FDI-related laws, while a shift to more regulations began in phase

2. In terms of the number of countries and cases, there are two valleys. The 2000–2001 valley is the collapse of the American IT bubble. The valley in 2008 could be associated with the global financial crisis. Regulation started during the period of the economic stagnation due to the IT bubble, but since the 2008 global financial crisis, the relationship between FDI and regulation became more antagonistic.

What measures were taken to attract FDI? UNCTAD sorts the 248 laws by characteristic as follows. 36% were for more liberal entry and operational conditions,

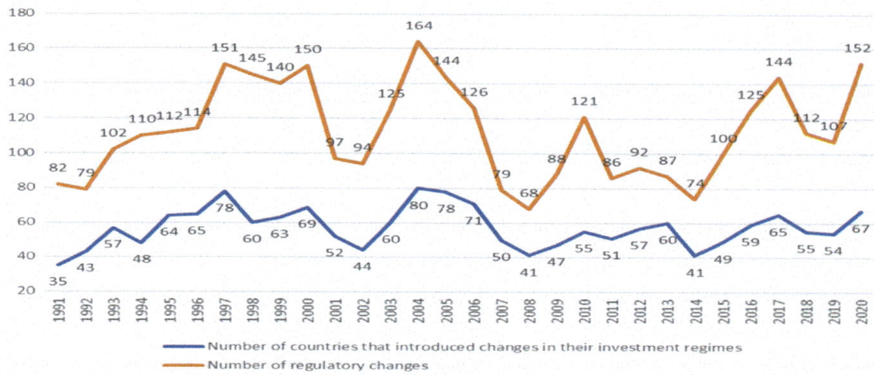

Fig. 3.5 Number of countries and changes that introduced FDI-related changes, 1991–2020 (*Source* UNCTAD, 2003: 21, 2015: 102, 2021: 109). *Note* Since the data varied by report in terms of number of countries and cases, we basically used the data from the latest version of the report. Reports were used from which a ten-year data could be obtained

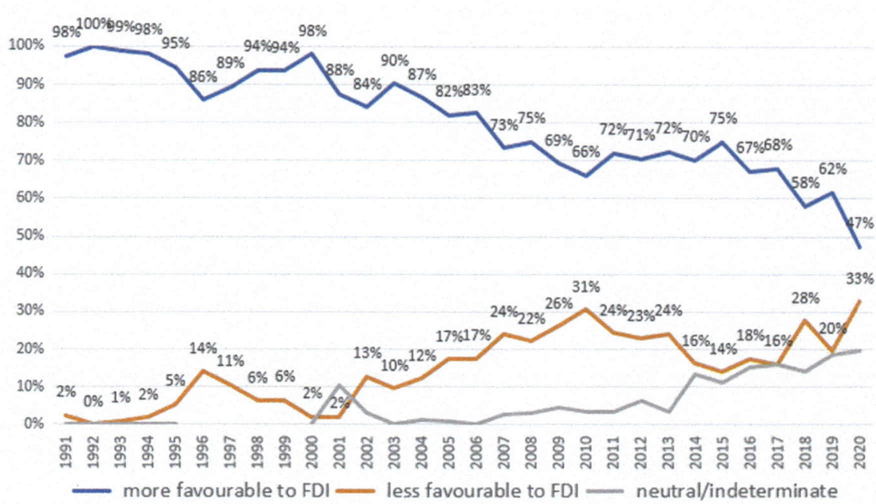

Fig. 3.6 Changes in national investment policies, 1991–2020 (*Source* UNCTAD, 2003: 21, 2011: 94, 2021: 109). *Note* The same with Fig. 3.4

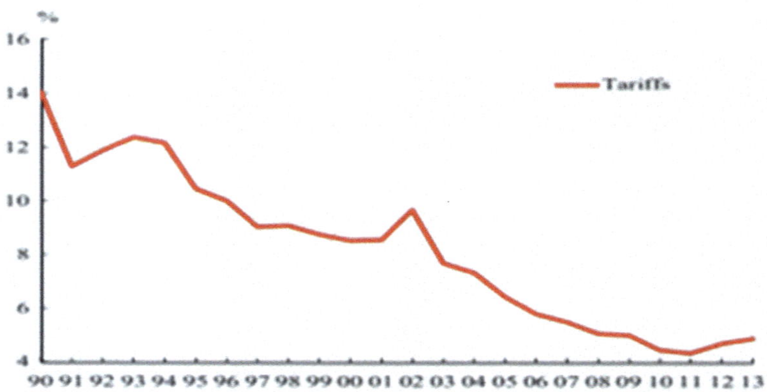

Fig. 3.7 Global tariffs 1990–2013 (*Source* Nakajima et al., 2016: 24). Note Vertical axis is the average global tariff rate, horizontal axis is the year

31% were for more promotion, including incentive, 20% were for more guarantees, and not more than 5% were for more control or restrictions (UNCTAD, 2003: 21).

From the 1990s up to about the 2010s, liberalization was actually promoted in both trade and investment fronts. Although there was the Asian financial crisis in 1997, this did not stop the liberalization trend. After the 2008 global financial crisis, various regulatory measures on trade, particularly in advanced economies, came to be clearly accepted (ADB, 2013: 20). At the start of this century, however, liberalization became a major global trend. Figure 3.7 shows the global average tariff rate from 1990 to 2013. Tariff rates greatly dropped from 14% in 1990 to 4% in the 2010s.

Asia, especially East Asia, aggressively rode on this liberalization trend. Policies were adopted to attract FDI. One third of the world's FDI-related laws enacted in 2010 aimed to regulate. In the case of advanced countries, the ratio reached one half. The developing countries were open to the enactment of related laws, with Asia being the most aggressive. In the same year, "Asia stands out, with a total of 46 out of 56 measures being more favourable to FDI" (UNCTAD, 2011: 94).

Treaty member countries of FDI-related laws generally agree on bilateral investment treaties (BITs) and double taxation treaties (DTTs). A BIT aims to protect one's companies from risks such as discrimination and expropriation in the host country. A DTT aims to avoid the double taxation of the incomes of the investing firm and its deployed employees. In 2002, 76 countries agreed to 82 BITs, while 64 countries agreed to 58 DTTs. From 1990 to 2002, the total number of treaties consisted of 2,181 BITs and 2,256 DTTs. The most active developing countries in entering treaties was China with 107 BITs and India with 81 DDTs (UNCTAD, 2003: 21). UNCTAD writes that "Many countries in the Pacific have not yet signed a BIT, and Angola, Cambodia and Nicaragua have not signed a DTT", clarifying the geographical distribution of these FDI-related arrangements. Amidst the declining trend of global FDI after the 1997 Asian financial crisis, up to the start of this century, advanced countries as well as Asian emerging economies aggressively adopted liberalization measures (UNCTAD, 2003: 21–22).

The end of the Cold War colored the awareness of the global economy with a liberal capitalism. The Asian emerging economies were not only birthed by but also sustained this large wave. For the record, this structural change created a current of regulation in advanced economies entering this century.

The last cause is the intensification and structural change in the international division of labor due to the developments in ICT. The development of ICT in the 1990s has brought about the diffusion of ICT devices into industry and promoted the creation of networks. This facilitated the entry of companies abroad, and at the same time changed the structure of division of labor.

R. Baldwin added a new interpretation, from a historical perspective to the economic globalization that was speeding up in the 1990s. According to him, the development of transportation technology at the start of the nineteenth century lowered the cost of trade, giving rise to the first globalization. This created the divergence between today's advanced and developing countries. He calls this the first unbundling. This globalization proceeded into the second globalization of the 1990s. The development of ICT that greatly lowered the cost of moving ideas. and the opening up of the possibility of transferring a part of the production process to developing countries, brought about the industrialization of the emerging countries. This wave is called the second unbundling (Baldwin, 2016).

In the first unbundling, factories in advanced countries manage the production process and the jobs that support it. The produced final goods become internationally traded goods. The development of ICT, however, made possible the fragmentation and dismantling of the production process and its supporting jobs, adding intermediate goods, consisting of parts and processed goods, to internationally traded goods. The intensifying competition among multinational companies forced further cost reductions. As such, intermediate goods became major trading goods. This promoted the globalization of manufacturing (Baldwin, 2016: 165–168). More precisely, this was the major trend of economic globalization even after the global financial crisis up to the regime change due to the U.S.-Sino trade war and the novel corona pandemic.

Since the 1990s, intermediate goods trade actually came to account for an overwhelming share of the trade of Asia, especially East Asia. Figure 3.8 shows the share of intermediate goods (parts and components) in trade of major East Asian countries and regions in 1990 and 2003. From the figure we can see that intermediate goods trade during this period was growing very fast. Moreover, we can also see that the share of trade was expanding in absolute terms. In particular, changes were large in the Philippines and Malaysia. In 2003, the former's exports and imports grew by 55.6 and 4.8.8% respectively, while the latter's grew by 39.5 and 47.9%, respectively. Taiwan, Japan, and South Korea followed, the share of which was about 20–30%.

Figure 3.9 compared this change in the goods composition of EU and NAFTA (USMCA). From this figure, we can confirm the salient features of the export goods structure of the East Asian economy. During the 1990s, East Asia, unlike the two other economic zones, rapidly increased its share of parts exports, with its intermediate goods share being well over 60% of the trade value. On the other hand, its share in

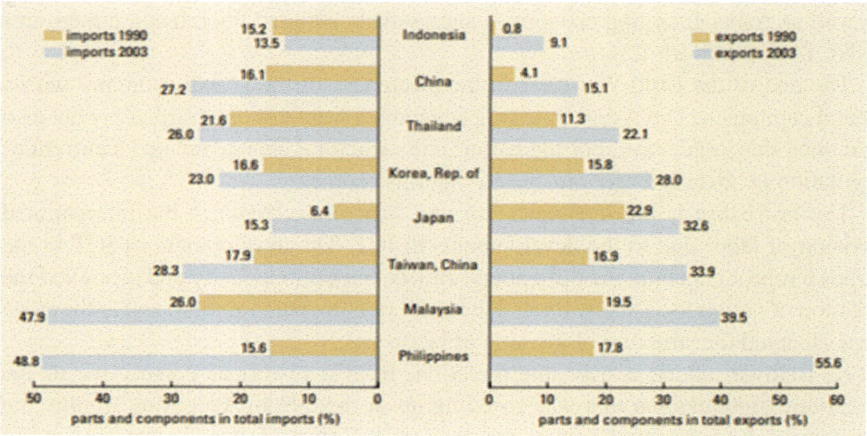

Fig. 3.8 Share of parts and components in total exports and imports in East Asia 1990, 2003 (*Source* Gill & Kharas, 2007: 21)

consumption goods was greatly reduced. The share of consumption goods, however, changed very little in the EU and NAFTA export structure. From the 1990s to the start of this century, the East Asian economy quickly developed an organic relationship.

Let us point out one more fact. Figure 3.10 shows Japan's exports by goods and region. We can see that exports to Asia from the 1990s to the 2000s greatly grew, with processed goods, parts, and capital goods rapidly increasing. Exports to America and the EU showed a slight tendency to increase. Comparing this, however, with East Asia, the growth is clearly different. We can ascertain Japan's position in the intra-regional trade of East Asia.

Such changes brought about the upgrading of the triangle structure, which was the growth pattern of NIEs. The NIEs development pattern, which gained popular

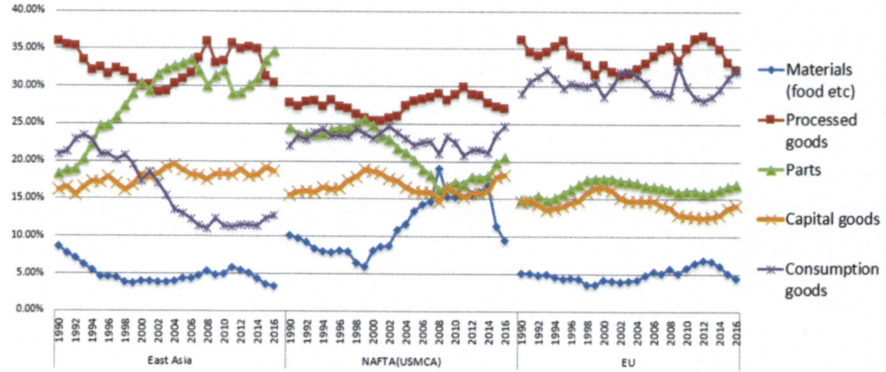

Fig. 3.9 The composition of the intra-regional trade by goods of the 3 big economic zones 1990–2016 (*Source* Japan IETI-TID Database). *Note* Definitions of goods are based on METI Japan

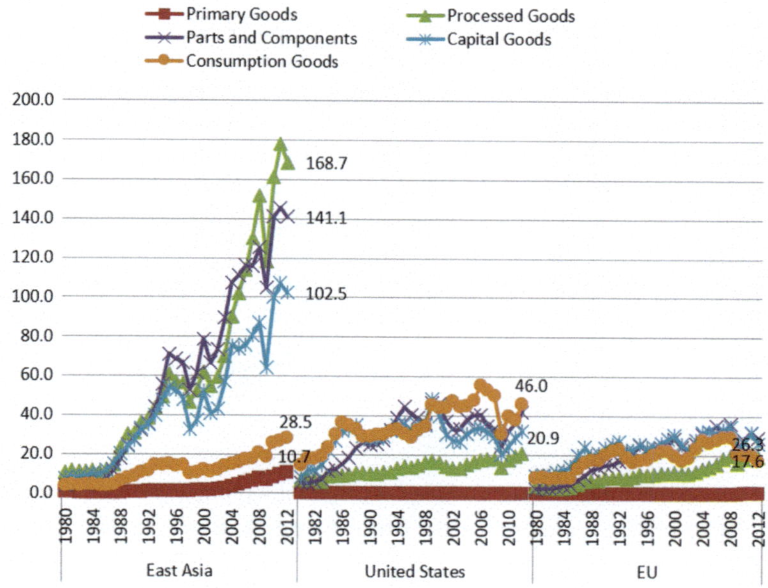

Fig. 3.10 Changes in the export of Japan's partners by region and by good 1980–2012 (*Source* METI -J, 2014: 414). *Note* Figure is revised

attention in the 1970 and 1980s, was as follows. Capital and raw materials were imported from Japan, these were assembled or processed at the low NIEs wages, and then the resulting finished goods were exported to America. This pattern spread spatially and was also upgraded content-wise.

According to Japan's 2005 METI White Paper, NIEs together with Japan have been promoted to producing intermediate goods of high value-added, the NIEs position is now occupied by China and ASEAN, which produce final goods using the intermediate goods procured from Japan and NIEs. The final goods are then exported to the U.S. and EU forming a triangle structure(METI -J, 2005: 166–67). This brought about a larger value-added for Asia. According to the 2008 White Paper, the gross value-added of manufacturing of: East Asia (ASEAN + 6[6]) reached US$2.55 trillion; and EU27 reached US$2.5 trillion, surpassing NAFTA's US$1.83 trillion (METI -J, 2008: 143).

According to the U.S. National Science Board, the global total value-added of the high-technology manufacturing industries of the OECD, consisting of communications and semiconductors, pharmaceuticals, scientific instruments (medicine, precision/optics, aerospace, and computers and office machinery increased from US$720 billion in 1995 to US$1.2 trillion in 2000. The distribution of value-added, however, greatly changed. The share production value-added by region in 2007 was 25.0% for the EU, and 30% for America, which were not significantly different from the

[6] ASEAN + 6 consists of ASEAN member nations, China, South Korea, India, Australia, New Zealand and Japan.

shares in the 1990s. It was different, however, in Asia. China, including Hong Kong saw its global share rise from 2.6 to 13.7%, and the Asian 9 countries from 8.9 to 10.3%. In contrast, only Japan saw its share drop by 16 percentage points from 26.8 to 10.6%. This means that China and the Asia 9 countries[7] took away some of Japan's value-added share (NSB, 2010: 6–18, & Appendix Table 6-5).

The progress of the intra-regional trade of Asia, centered on East Asia, had one feature that distinguished it from other economic zones. North America and Europe pushed integration through the formal institutions of NAFTA and EU, respectively. Asia, however, started negotiations for free trade institutions only at the beginning of the twenty-first century. In short, Asia's integration was a de facto integration (Hirakawa, 2018). The formation of an international division of labor, which transcended the national borders of multinational firms, and production network gave birth to the integration of East Asia.

3.2.3 "Population Bonus" and the Emergence of the Middle Class

In the second half of the 1990s, there appeared research on "population bonus", whereby the growth rate of the employed population surpassed the growth rate of the unemployed population. This was considered as enabling the development of the Asian emerging economies. This research quickly gained attention. Andrew Mason, in 1997, published a paper that considered the declining birthrate as contributing to East Asian miraculous growth in Japan, South Korea, Taiwan, and others. A month after his publication, David E. Bloom and Jeffery G. Williamson published a working paper at the National Bureau of Economic Research. They claimed that population cannot be considered as a decisive cause but one third of Asia's miracle can be explained by population (Bloom & Williamson, 1997). The following year, the United Nation Population Fund also came out with the interpretation that Asia's high economic growth can be explained by the employed population growth rate surpassing that of the unemployed population, Mason writes as follows.

> Have slower rates of population growth accelerated economic development in East Asia? The answer is yes. Experience over the past 30 years demonstrates that a rapid decline in fertility, in conjunction with effective economic policies and other favorable conditions, can have a strong positive impact on economic growth. Rapid growth of the working population has been likened to a "demographic bonus" because an increase in the proportion of the population earning incomes can produce an increase in the overall income per capita. In East Asia, demographic conditions will favor high rates of economic growth for several decades. Population will be heavily concentrated at the working ages, high rates of investment in education will ensure an educated, productive labor force, and high rates of saving will support additional capital deepening (Mason, 1997: 1, 3, 4).

[7] Asia-9 consists of India, Indonesia, Malaysia, the Philippines, Singapore, Korea, Taiwan, Thailand, and Vietnam.

The United Nations Population Fund explains population bonus as follows.

> Lower birth rates in today's developing countries offer the possibility of demographic bonus in the next 15–20 years, as a "bulge" of young people comes into the workforce while fewer children are born. If jobs can be found for them, the "workforce bulge" can be the basis for more investment, greater labour productivity and rapid economic development. This will generate revenues for social investments like health, education, and social security, to meet the needs of both old and young and secure the basis for future development (UNFPA, 1998: 4).

Indeed, if there is an environment where the population composition is such that the ratio of the employed population to the unemployed population is high, and the energetic young age group enter the labor market, more of income would be allocated to hygiene and education, and savings to investment, increasing productivity. In the second half of the 1990s, the "population bonus" theory has greatly changed the popular thinking, which up to then negatively looked at population. As such, the so-called "Malthus Trap" has been dislodged. East Asian economic development is premised on employment. We think that this change in thinking has spread beyond the issue of population theory research. In particular, the effect had been great on investors and managers looking for new investment destinations amidst globalization.

Putting that aside, the population bonus composition, where young workers participate in the economy, eventually gives rise to the stage where the unemployed labor population is relatively larger than the employed population (population onus). The stage of the aging society draws near. Could the emerging economies transition into advanced economies, before reaching this stage? This is an issue that draws our interest.

This interest, however, is at the same time, directed towards the reality confronting Asia's emerging economies, which extolled population bonus at the turn of the century. The conditions that continue to support growth are the supply of labor and newly emerging markets, since these portends the future economic development.

The middle class was starting to gain attention in the 1990s, and, in fact, income for a certain class in Asia has been rapidly rising. The 2010 ADB report based on household income survey data, focusing on the middle income class ($2-$20 income/expenditure per person per day) confirms the dramatic increase of the middle class in the Asian emerging economies (Fig. 3.11). During this period, this region's middle class population rose from 2.692 billion to 3.384 billion, with per capita incomes rising 3.5 times from US$721 to US$2564 (PPP). The overwhelming share was occupied by big population countries China and India (ADB, 2010: 6).

Looking back, the World Bank Report "East Asia Miracle" was published in 1993 and highlighted the remarkable development of East Asian economies. It discovered not only rapid growth sustained over several decades, but also the reduction of income disparities, which went against the accepted economic common sense that at the early stages of industrialization income disparities would widen. The world bank called this phenomenon "shared growth". Such acknowledgement of East Asian development appeared to have been temporarily lost due to the 1997–98 Asian financial crisis. Completely opposite to Latin America's experience in the 1980s of falling into stagnation. East Asia later staged an astonishing comeback, and returned to a

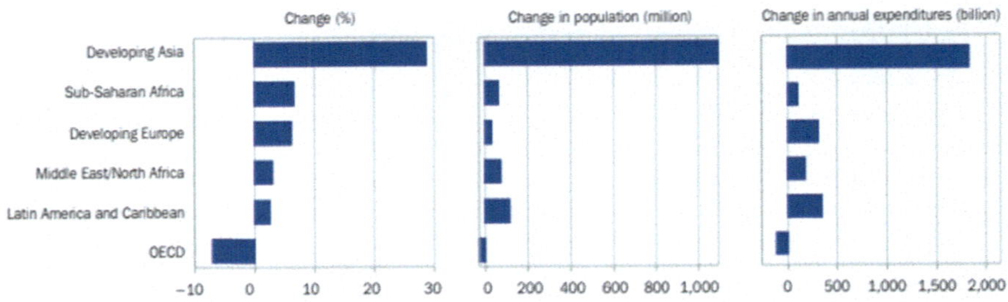

Fig. 3.11 Change in size of middle class by region (1990–2008, based on household survey means) (*Source* ADB, 2010: 7). Original: Chun (2010: 11). *Note* **Developing Asia** = Armenia, Azerbaijan, Bangladesh, Cambodia, China, India, Indonesia, Kazakhstan, Kyrgyz Republic, Lao RDR, Malaysia, Mongolia, Nepal, Pakistan, Philippines, Sri Lanka, Tajikistan, Thailand, Turkmenistan, Vietnam. **Developing Europe** = Albania, Belarus, Bosnia and Herzegovina, Bulgaria, Latvia, Lithuania, Macedonia, Moldova, Poland, Romania, Russian Federation, Turkey, and Ukraine. **Latin America and Caribbean** = Argentina, Brazil, Chile, Colombia, Costa Rica, Dominican Republic, Ecuador, El Salvador, Guatemala, Honduras, Jamaica, Mexico, Nicaragua, Peru, Uruguay, and Venezuela. **Middle East/North Africa** = Algeria, Djibouti, Egypt, Iran, Jordan, Morocco, Tunisia, and Yemen. OECD = Austria, Belgium, Denmark, Finland, France, Germany, Greece, Ireland, Italy, Luxemburg, the Netherlands, Norway, Portugal, Slovak Republic, Spain, Sweden, the UK. and the U.S. **Sub-Saharan Africa** = Botswana, Burkina Faso, Burundi, Cameroon, Central African Republic, Ethiopia, Gambia, Ghana, guinea, Guinea-Bissau, Kenya, Lesotho, Madagascar, Malawi, Mali, Mauritania, Mozambique, Niger, Rwanda, Senegal, Sierra Leone, South Africa, Swaziland, Tanzania, and Uganda. Yearly expenditure values are converted to US$ using PPP exchange rates

growth trajectory.[8] The effect of the Asian currency crisis on China was negligible, allowing it to continue growing.

Around 2004–2005, however, there appeared in China the phenomenon of labor scarcity in the coastal areas of Shanghai, the Pearl River Delta, and others. This gave rise to rising wages that started to spread beyond the coastal areas up to the inner continent. This led to the pessimistic view that China's export-led development depending on low wages is reaching its limits. In short, it is a "middle income trap". In the regions, however, the birth of the "middle income class" is gaining attention. East Asia, especially China, continues to gain interest as a country having a high growth potential. This is because a mammoth population is an indicator of potential, in terms of labor supply as well as in terms of markets.

[8] In response to the rapid recovery of emerging economies in Asia after the global financial crisis of 2008, the Economist magazine looked back at the case of the Asian currency crisis of 1997–98 and reported that the recovery of emerging Asian economies was an "astonishing rebound" (The Economist, August 13, 2009).

3.3 BRICs and Asian Emerging Economies

In this section, we will first consider the understanding of the coined word BRICs that emerged early in the twenty-first century. We will then arrive at a mechanism of Asia's development through an East Asian regional approach that goes beyond the general approach of economics. As the core concept for this, we present the Potentially Bigger Market Economies (PoBMEs), which we have coined to replace BRICs and Next-11.

3.3.1 'BRICs' and Acceptance as a Concept

In the first year of the twenty-first century, the investor report of the American investment company Goldman Sachs (GS) carried the paper of the head of its Global Economic Research Department, Jim O'Neill entitled "Building better global economic BRICs". BRICs is a word coined from the acronyms of the four countries of Brazil, Russia, India, and China.

The paper makes the following claims. In 2001 and 2002, the real GDP of BRICs grew faster than that of the G7. Moreover, in 2000, BRICs' economic size in current dollars was 8.9% of the world, but its purchasing power parity (PPP) reached 23%. For the next ten years BRICs saw its economic importance rising. Considering its future influence on global fiscal policy and financial policy, BRICs should be added to the international discussion (O'Neill, 2001). In 2003, two subordinates of J. O'Neill published a paper on the simulation results regarding BRICs growth up to 2050, which caused interest on BRICs to snowball. The simulations showed that the total BRICs economy will surpass the G6 in 2050 and will be more than half of the G6 economy by 2025. Within the current six advanced economies, only the U.S. and Japan will remain (Wilson & Prushothaman, 2003). In GS papers of 2005 and 2007, the Growth Environment Score (GES) was developed, and was used to select the next eleven countries (N-11) as the newly emerging countries following BRICs (O'Neill et al., 2005; Wilson & Stupnytska, 2007).

The GES ranks countries as follows. A country's performance on each measure of 13 sub-variables of five basic areas (macroeconomic stability, macroeconomic conditions, technological capabilities, human capital, and political conditions) on a 0–10 scale and create overall score (O'Neill et al., 2005: 14). Figure 3.12 shows the resulting selection of BRICs and N-11 by projected growth.

In H. McGregor's article, O'Neill, however, says the following with regards to the definition of BRICs.

> My definition of a BRIC economy is a country that is materially influencing the world economy- that is either at 3% of world GDP or is likely to become so. The Next 11 includes countries by population size (McGregor, 2011: 28).

In actuality, J. O'Neill confessed that 9.11 of 2001 brought about in him a sense of the "end of American-led globalization", which led to the conceptualization of

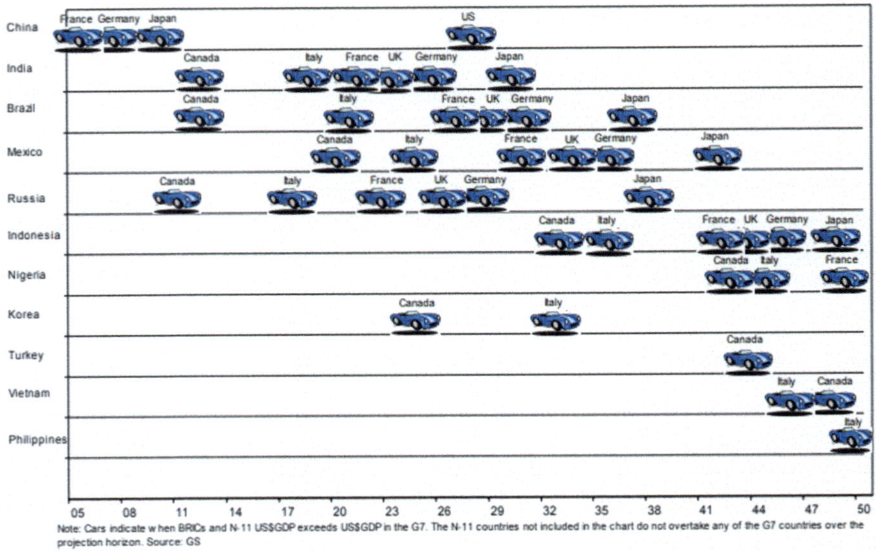

Fig. 3.12 Overtaking the G7: When BRIC's and N-11's GDP would exceed G7 (*Source* Wilson & Stupnyska 2007: 3). *Note* Cars indicate when BRICs and N-11 US$GDP exceeded US$GDP in the G7. The Next-11 countries not included in the chart do not overtake any of the G7 countries over the projection Horizon

BRICs. In short, O'Neill discovered BRICs as a fund manager. Through his eyes as a financial investor, BRICs were emerging economies that had promising potential. He states as follows. "I am perplexed" about BRICs including South Africa, since it only has a population of 45 (or 50) million" (Nikkei -J, July 7, 2011; McGregor, 2011: 27). With respect to adding Nigeria to the Next-11, he says "because Nigeria is one of them, with a population constituting 20% of the African continent" (McGregor, 2011: 28).

What we would like to point out here is that O'Neill's interest is not on the population composition ratio as in the Population Bonus theory, but rather on the absolute population size. In reality, a big obstacle to continuing rapid growth in newly emerging economies is the ability to supply labor, with population size able to explain a large part as "potential". This size is one viewed from the external sector rather than from the internal sector. For a given growth, the bigger the population size, the bigger the economy. This is because the size of the market, in this case, is determined by the size of the population. It could be said that O'Neill very early on became aware of this potential.

In the field of economics, there has been a series of research around the world on BRICs 4 or BRICS 5, which includes South Africa. Most of such research, however, looks for the potential of development from the internal sector of BRICs. As such, these researches inquire into the differences in such things as industrial and export structure rather than on the commonalities. Following O'Neill's coining, the BRICs discussion becomes simply one of lining up the economies of four or five countries.

For example, Japan's 2005 METI White Paper explained "The newly emerging economies called BRICs have been sustaining their economic growth in recent years. The share of BRICs' GDP to the world economy is not that big at 9%, but these countries are blessed with area, population, mineral resources, and others, giving rise to high expectations with regards to the group's growth potential" (METI - J, 2005). The report of the Vienna Institute for International Economic Studies, which inquires into EU policies, also cite the commonalities such as big land size, large population, and fast economic growth, as well as indicate the difference in the development models of the four countries. Brazil is a 'domestically oriented service economy', Russia is 'heavily dependent on energy and raw material resources', India is 'essentially service-led, supported by exports, and China is 'manufacturing exports and investment-driven' model (Ghosh et al., 2009: 1).

We did a comparison of BRICs and NIEs mainly using trade indicators (Hirakawa & Than, 2011: 48–49). This is shown in Table 3.1. The periods of comparison are the periods of high growth for each. One thing that we can readily observe is the big variation in population size. Compared to the units in millions of NIEs, BRIC figures are in the hundreds of millions. While the trade ratio and manufactured goods export of NIEs sharply rose, BRICs' dependence on trade was small, with the exception of China. Variance among countries is large. India stands out sharply with a high trade in services. As is well known, India is a country that rapidly increased its soft service amidst the advances in globalization and ICT. Incidentally, the breakdown of India's services trade in 2008 shows that computer and information communication-related businesses accounted for 72% (World Bank, 2010). In short, BRICs do not have any commonalities in the trade aspect. It is not shown here, but the common point would be in the large influx of FDI and population size, and land area.

In the 2010s, a negative view of the coined word BRICs emerged. 2015 Nobel Laureate in Economics, Angus Deaton, in a publication (2013), states as follows, conceding these concepts as not capable of elucidation in economics.

> The two largest countries (China and India) in the world have been among the most successful, at least over the past quarter of a century. Is this because they are large, or is it simply that the two countries that did so well happened to be the largest?/The "BRIC" countries (Brazil, Russia, India, and China) certainly reap some advantages from their size. A diplomatic corps, a competent bureaucracy, a few well-trained leaders, and the faculty of a world-class university cannot all be filled with only a handful of good people, and larger countries have larger pools from which to choose./Whether these advantages to scale are enough to elevate growth rates, or whether larger countries tend to grow faster for other reasons, are open questions (Deaton, 2013: 169).

In 2014, Japan's researcher of Asia, Suehiro Akira, asserted that "BRICs, Next 11, and the like cannot be called as concepts that could endure a scientific inquiry" (Suehiro -J, 2014: 5).

Nevertheless, BRICs became a word that symbolizes the age of globalization at the start of the twenty-first century. The National Intelligence Council (NIC), tasked with handling America's national security, in a 2004 report, brought up 'BRICs' in its prospects of the global economy in 2020. This report wrote as follows, taking China and India as the "new major global players" of the twenty-first century.

Table 3.1 Comparison of NIEs and BRICs: Population, trade ratio, manufactures export and service export ratio

	Population (Million)	Trade ratio[a]			Manufactures export ratio[b]			Service export ratio[c]	
	1970	1970 (%)	1976 (%)	2006 (%)	1970 (%)	1976 (%)	2006 (%)	1995 (%)	2006 (%)
Korea, Republic of	31.9	38	68	71	77	82	89	14	14
Taiwan	14.7	63	90	180	79	85	91	12	12
Hong Kong SAR	3.9	182	183	225	93	97	91	15	18
Singapore	2.1	225	252	386	31	43	80	17	20
	2000	1995 (%)	2000 (%)	2006 (%)	1995 (%)	2000 (%)	2006 (%)	1995(%)	2006 (%)
Brazil	170.4	16	23	26	54	59	51	10	16
Russian Federation	145.6	44	71	55	26	22	17	15	16
India	1015.9	23	28	48	74	79	70	14	48
China	1262.5	44	50	74	84	88	92	12	10

(*Source* World Bank 2008, & Council for Economic Planning and Development, Republic of China, 2008).
Note [a]NIEs: Merchandise trade/GDP, BRICs: Merchandise and service trade/GDP. [b]Manufacturers exports/Marchandise exports, [c]Service exports/(Marchandise + service exports).

> Given its enormous population—and assuming a reasonable degree of real currency appreciation—the dollar value of China's gross national product (GNP) may be the second largest in the world by 2020. For similar reasons, the value of India's output could match that of a large European country. The economies of other developing countries, such as Brazil and Indonesia, could surpass all but the largest European economies by 2020. The likely emergence of China and India, as well as others, as new major global players—similar to the advent of a united Germany in the nineteenth century and a powerful United States in the early twentieth century—will transform the geopolitical landscape, with impacts potentially as dramatic as those in the previous two centuries. In the same way that commentators refer to the 1900s as the "American Century," the twenty-first century may be seen as the time when Asia, led by China and India, comes into its own (NIC, 2004: 30–31, 47).

A 2008 report by the same council, predicting 2025, sheds light on global uncertainty, while at the same time accepting the coined word BRICs as a term referring to four countries. With the benefit of hindsight, the prediction is off target, but the report has an optimistic view of the four countries, as "state capitalism".

> Growth projections for Brazil, Russia, India, and China (the BRICs) indicate they will collectively match the original G-7's share of global GDP by 2040–2050. China is poised to have more impact on the world over the next 20 years than any other country. If current trends persist, by 2025 China will have the world's second largest economy and will be a leading military power. It also could be the largest importer of natural resources and the biggest

> polluter. The rising BRIC powers are unlikely to challenge the international system as did Germany and Japan in the nineteenth and twentieth centuries, but because of their growing geopolitical and economic clout, they will have a high degree of freedom to customize their political and economic policies rather than fully adopting Western norms. They also are likely to want to preserve their policy freedom to maneuver, allowing others to carry the primary burden for dealing with such issues as terrorism, climate change, proliferation, and energy security. China, India, and Russia are not following the Western liberal model for self-development but instead are using a different model, "state capitalism." State capitalism is a loose term used to describe a system of economic management that gives a prominent role to the state. However, the impact of Russia, and particularly China, following this path is potentially much greater owing to their size and approach to "democratization." We remain optimistic about the long-term prospects for greater democratization (NIC, 2008: v, x, vii),

Asian development and the BRICs have become the target of global interest, prompting many discussions regarding the sustainability of development entering this century. IMF and ADB, prior to the global financial crisis, promoted discussions on the so-called "decoupling" and "uncoupling", seeking to understand the thinning connectivity between the advanced economies and Asian newly emerging economies. The problem being studied is whether or not the Asian economies have become independent of the advanced economies (IMF, 2007, 2008; ADB, 2007, 2008).

On the other hand, the World Bank proposed the "middle income trap". Here the interest has shifted to whether or not the rapidly growing Asian emerging economies could make the transition to advanced economies. Growth theory teaches that East Asia needs three transitions. First is that development is accompanied by the disappearance of diversity of the economy in both production and employment. Second is the decline of the importance of investment, and the rise of importance of innovation. Third is the imperative for education to nurture highly skilled laborers that could adapt to the new technologies. Latin America and the Middle East, however, have not achieved these transitions over many decades. Whether or not Asia could achieve these transitions is the question (Gill & Kharas, 2007: 17–18). The "middle income trap" is related to the appearance of a tendency for wages to rise in the above-mentioned emerging economies, and has been garnering quite an interest not only in China but also in ASEAN countries.

In the 2010s, interest grew quickly over BRIC countries, especially China and India. One after another, reports were made predicting the development of Asia. In 2011, ADB published "Asia 2050", a prediction of 2050. According to this report, assuming that countries do not fall into the "middle income trap", compared to 2010 in 2050, per capita income (PPP) would have grown six times, and the share of world GDP would have risen from 27.4 to 50.6%. "Asia would regain the dominant global economic position it held some 250 years ago, before the industrial revolution. Some have called this possibility the 'Asian Century'" (ADB, 2011: 1). As the engines of the Asian century, the report cites Asia-7 economies (China, India, Indonesia, Japan, Korea, Thailand, and Malaysia), and predicted the GDP share of these economies over the 2010–2015 period to be as much as 87% of total GDP in Asia, amounting to 55% of the global GDP growth. "They will thus be the engines of not only Asia's economy but also the global economy" (ADB, 2011: 31). The report was very careful not to use the term BRICs, and to conduct its study by dividing Asia into three economic groups.[9] As far as contribution to Asia's growth is concerned, however, China and India are by far the largest. This conclusion brings us closer to the theory of BRICs and N-11.

In the following year, the Organisation for Economic Co-operation and Development (OECD) published "Looking to 2060", which predicted that "The next 50 years will see major changes in the relative size of world economies. Fast growth in China and India will make their combined GDP measured at 2005 Purchasing Power Parities (PPPs), soon surpass that of the G7 economies and exceed that of the entire current OECD membership by 2060" (OECD, 2012: 8). With regards to the country's composition in the global economy for the 50 years up to 2060, China would increase its share from 17 to 28%, India from 7 to 18%. In contrast, America would decrease its share from 23 to 16%, the Euro region from 17 to 9%, and Japan from 7 to 3% (OECD, 2012: 23).

As such, the future prospect, which is based on the economic performance of East Asia since the 1990s, will highlight the large population countries of the emerging economies. This is because if the production/income of the emerging economies converges with that of advanced economies, countries having a large population, naturally, will have a stronger presence. Such a prospect is naturally reflected in the current global awareness.

3.3.2 *Foreign Direct Investment and the Development of Asian Emerging Economies*

How was Asia's development actually possible? In the previous section, we traced East Asia's development and confirmed that the interest is headed toward large population countries. We looked at the background for this interest in BRICs. With its birth as a coined word, BRICs was rapidly accepted by the world. At the same time, economics could not come up with a persuasive response with regards to a term that is supposed to symbolize the times, or with regards to the development of big population countries. It is here that we once again consider the awareness and limits of BRICs.

As attention is focused on BRICs, a research, which was commissioned by the Japanese government's Cabinet Office to study BRICs, is profoundly interesting. The report of this research states that the reason BRICs is getting a lot of attention is its "high growth performance and large potential". The report confirmed that BRICs performance from 1997 to 2006 was an average growth rate of 6.0% as against the 4.2% of NIEs. With regards to potential, the report cites the simulation prediction

[9] Asian countries are separated into three groups based on their past performance: 'High income developed economies' (7: Brunei Darussalam, Hong Kong, Japan, Korea, Macau, Singapore, and Taiwan), 'fast growing, converging economies' (11: Armenia, Azerbaijan, Cambodia, China, Georgia, India, Indonesia, Kazakhstan, Malaysia, Thailand, and Vietnam), and 'slow or modest growth, aspiring economies' (31: Pakistan, Philippines, Sri Lanka, and others).

for 2050 of O'Neill's 2005 BRICs paper Naikakufu (Cabinet Office -J, 2006). In this manner, the analysis of the four countries was conducted. This explanation, however, still leaves a gap in our understanding of what is potential.

Here, let us widen the analytical framework to the Asian region and add a temporal axis. In doing so, a completely different structure surfaces.

Figure 3.13 charts the relationship between the growth rate of major Asian countries and population size, dividing the period 1960–2014 into three periods. As such, certain tendencies surface in the relationship between the economic growth rate and population size. The high growth rate of emerging economies firstly begins from small-population countries such as Singapore, Hong Kong, Taiwan and South Korea, and tends to shift towards China and India as time passes. Japan, which basically has a different development stage and structure, deviates from this tendency, but bigger-population countries show the upward tendency upon entering this century.

A study by Onishi and Kanae is of particular interest as it focuses on the correlation between growth rate and population size. They divide the period 1960–2010 of the Asian economies (PPP-base) into five sub-periods, and analyze the correlation between economic growth rate and population. The result is shown in Fig. 3.14 and Table 3.2. They explain the results in their paper as follows.

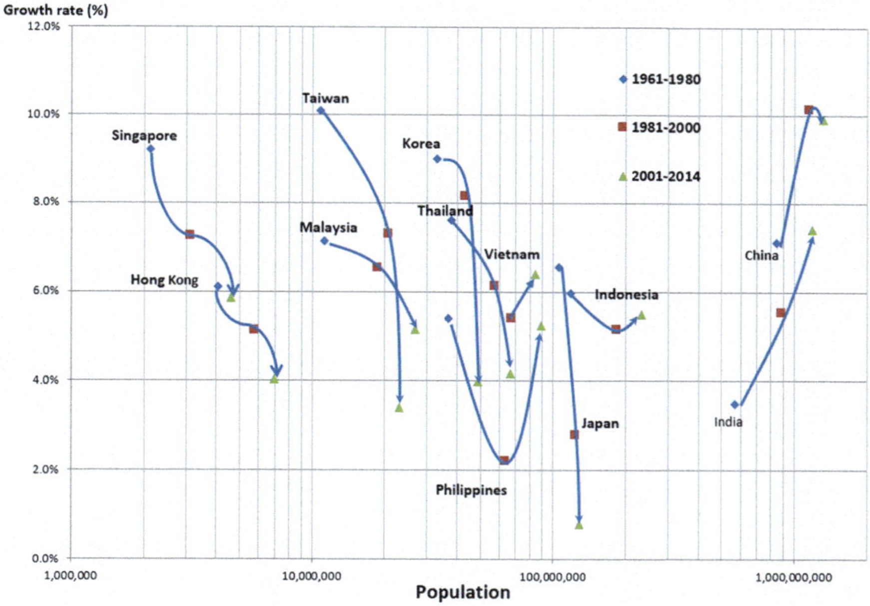

Fig. 3.13 Changes in Ave. GDP growth rate (1961–1980, 1981–2000, 2001–2014, 2005 constant $) and population size (1971, 1991, 2007) (*Source* Hirakawa -J, 2018: 86. Original data from WB 2016 World development indicators, Taiwan statistical data book, 2012). *Note* Data is from 1965 for Hong Kong and from 1984 for Vietnam

We can identify the "Age of Small-Population Economies" only in the 1960s at the 5% significance level, and the "Age of Large-Population Countries" in the 2000s at close to the 10% significance level. However, if we remove Myanmar from the figure for the 2000s, the correlation becomes significant at the 1% level. "By removing it, the correlation coefficient and its p value in the 2000s become 0.7719 and 0.001, respectively. This means that Asia has changed to the "Age of Large-Population Countries" in the new century (Onishi & Kanae, 2016: 385).[10]

Even then, why is it that in the early 1960s there is a correlation between growth and population in economies with a small population size, and why is it that at the start of this century there is a strong correlation between population size and economic growth rate in economies with a big population size? After the development of NIEs, Asia now has brought about an interest in big-population countries. NIEs upgraded the growth triangle, which spread spatially from points of small-scale economies to East Asia, enabling the structural entry of China. In this way, a large middle-income class emerged in Asia, giving birth to markets, and raising the interest on the "potential" of big-population countries. It is the discovery of "population bonus" on an absolute scale and the middle class. Excluding the factors of employment, the supply of labor population determines economic scale. Goldman Sachs' O'Neill was quick in discovering this, leading to the coining of the term BRICs. This would be the foresight on firm behavior by fund manager O'Neill. This foresight could also be considered as valid when looking at sustainability of future growth based on the relationship between population size and growth rate. Let us take a look at Fig. 3.14.

Figure 3.15 plots the per capita income and population of East Asian countries (and India), entering this century. The Box inside Fig. 3.15 shows the average growth rate of per capita GDP for Asian countries from 2001 to 2010. From this we can confirm that, entering this century, countries/regions with a high per capita GDP have small populations and low growth rates, while countries with a low per capita GDP tend to have large populations and high growth rates. This shows that countries with a large room for development and high growth rates are those with large populations. In terms of regions, the Asian region shows a lot of room for development. This confirms that the next center of the activities of the global economy is shifting towards Asia or big-population countries. Within this globalizing economy, firms will head towards such economies or regions. It is highly likely that these firms' capital and technologies will also head in that direction.

Let us touch here on whether or not the term BRICs is an appropriate word to show the features of the modern global economy. BRICs is simply the acronym

[10] The Onishi/Kanae paper quantitatively predicted economic growth for 2030, and then moved towards an analysis of historical regularities. With regards to the importance of population size, they indicated that export-led development seeks for overseas markets so population size is not important (Onishi/Kanae -J, 2014: 148). We have no disagreement with this point. NIEs were successful in launching their industrialization by attracting foreign companies that introduced capital and technology. It was after clearing this stage that interest in big-population countries blossomed. As we will see in this chapter, this process is making Asia a region of economic development.

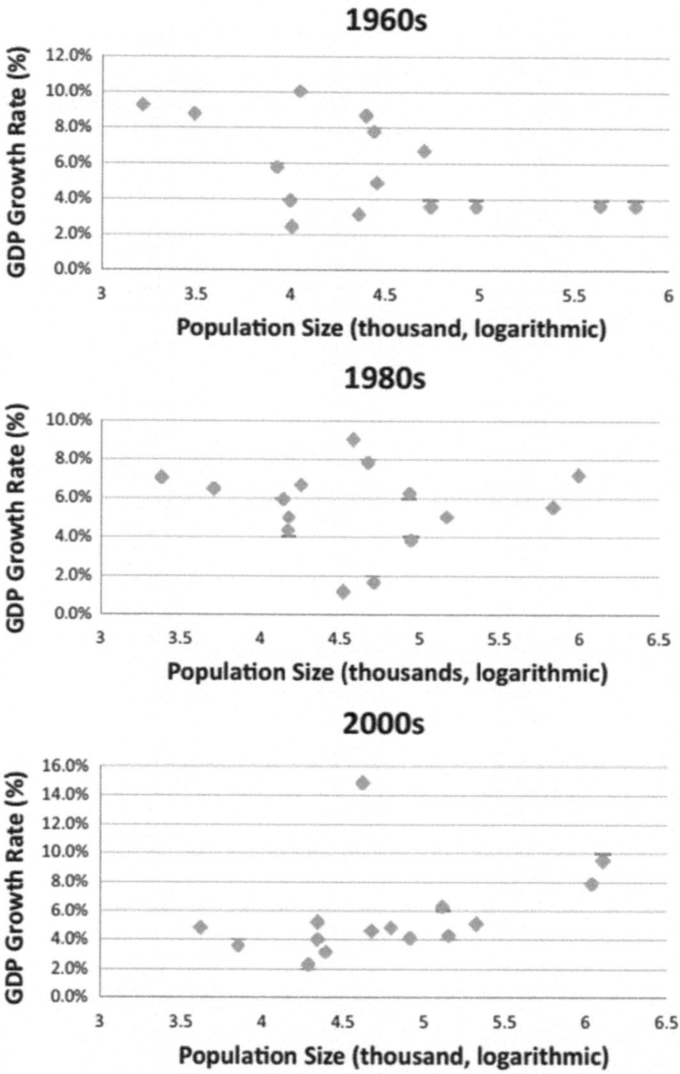

Fig. 3.14 Changes in the correlation coefficient between population size and economic growth rate for East Asian countries 1960, 1980, 2000s (*Source* Onishi & Kanae, 2016: 384). *Note* This paper was first published in Japanese in 2014, and in English two years later. In that paper, there were five correlation figures, but we only show three periods here. Sample countries were ASEAN5 (Brunei Darussalam, Indonesia, Malaysia, Philippines, and Thailand), PRC. NIEs4 (Korea, Hong Kong, China, and Singapore, Taiwan, China), and South Asia5 (Bangladesh, India, Nepal, Pakistan, and Sri Lanka)

Table 3.2 Changes in the correlation coefficient between population size and economic growth rate for East Asian countries

	1960s	1970s	1980s	1990s	2000s
Correlation coefficient	−0.5297	−0.4470	−0.0346	−0.0819	0.3950 **0.7719: excluding Myanmar**
p-statistic	(0.042)	(0.095)	(0.902)	(0.772)	(0.145) **(0.001: excluding Myanmar)**

Source Onishi & Kanae (2016: 384).

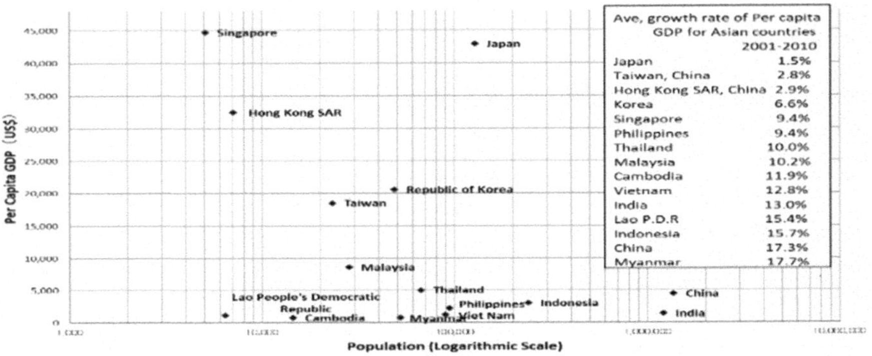

Fig. 3.15 Growth rate of per capita GDP (2001–2010) and population (2010) of Asian countries (*Source* Hirakawa -J, 2014: 29). *Note* Per capita GDP from IMF data, 2013 April; Population from UN Population Information Network data

of four emerging economies having large populations.[11] It is the same with N-11. While a country is identified, these terms do not essentially include a definition. We do not know the background for the development of these economies/countries. We would like to call this potential, which could be seen in Asia's development, Potentially Bigger Market Economies (PoBMEs), as a coined word to capture the concept of this development.[12] PoBMEs are emerging economies that tie their economic development to attracting multinational companies, which have become aware of the potential of these economies.

What is referred to here as "potential", however, does not consider severe environmental problems such as resource consumption, global warming, and climate change. It is a term that refers to economies/regions that are expected to have high

[11] Influenced by the BRICs idea, similar coined terms were created. In Japan there is VISTA (Vietnam, Indonesia, South Africa, Turkey, and Argentina), but words coined by collecting specific countries have a similar defect.

[12] One of the authors first used this in Hirakawa (2010). Since then it has been repeatedly discussed in Hirakawa and Than (2011), Hirakawa -J (2014), Hirakawa (2017, 2018), and others.

economic growth. In the next section, we discuss PoBMEs as a phenomenon of the global economy that starts from the 1990s.

3.4 The Dynamics of Asia's Development

In this section, we shall inquire into Asia's development, focusing on the capital and technology transfer mainly from the advanced economies. We will discuss the transition of this development from one that is export-oriented to one that is local market-oriented. In our analysis, we will confirm the importance of the potential growth of future markets, by concretely looking at the business activities mainly of multinational companies, as a vehicle of capital from advanced economies.

3.4.1 Foreign Direct Investment and Asian Newly Emerging Economies

As East Asia went through a rapid regional integration, Peter Drucker published a paper in the 1997 issue of "Foreign Affairs", wherein he writes as follows.

> International trade theory takes for granted that investment follows trade. Most people think of "international trade in goods" when they hear the words "international trade." But increasingly today, trade follows investment. International movements of capital rather than international movements of goods have become the engine of the world economy (Drucker, 1997: 166).

About ten years prior to this, South Korea's economist Kim Young-Ho indicated the existence of "capital/technology-intensive investment" from advanced countries was behind the industrialization of East Asia. He referred to this as the "reverse Lewis model". W.H. Lewis is a Nobel Laureate in economics, and was from Saint Lucia of the British West Indies, for his work on the "Dual Sector" theory in the 1950s, where he took the developing economy as consisting of a capitalist and subsistence sector. In this theory, he considered the "unlimited supplies of labour" from the subsistence sector to the capitalist sector as the cause of underdevelopment. Kim searched in the inflow of capital and technology for the major factors of development of East Asia, starting with South Korea, and claimed this as "economic development with unlimited supplies of capital/technologies" (Kim -J, 1988: 60). His claim means that we cannot ignore the role that the inflow of FDI from abroad, Japanese firms, in particular, played in the development of East Asia, starting with South Korea. Japanese economist Kojima Kiyoshi is also looking into the role of FDI, and thinks that, FDI as a medium, enabled the upgrading of industry from labor-intensive goods to capital-intensive and knowledge-intensive goods He writes that "the economic development of the East Asian region heavily depends on the foreign direct investment from developed countries", and that "FDI is not only capital (financing) but a packaged transfer of

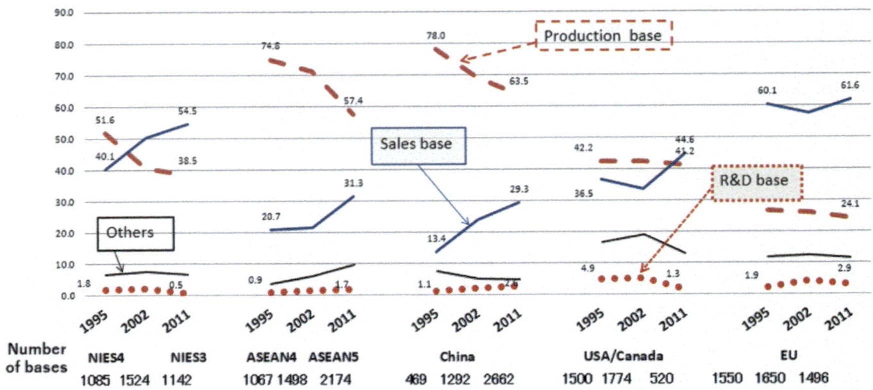

Fig. 3.16 Changes in the bases of Japanese companies by region and business content 1995, 2002, 2011 (*Source* JBIC survey reports on overseas business operations by Japanese manufacturing companies). *Note* The NIEs 4 consist of South Korea, Taiwan, Hong Kong, and Singapore (2011 does not include Singapore). ASEAN 4 consists of Indonesia, Malaysia, the Philippines, and Thailand (2011 includes Singapore)

managerial resources such as technology, management know-how, and key staff" (Kojima -J, 2006: 172).

Actually, as was indicated by the above-mentioned researchers, FDI from advanced economies have played an important role in the development process of Asian emerging economies. In this section, let us validate that from the point of view of micro firms' Asian investments.

Figure 3.16 was created from the survey data of Japanese manufacturing companies overseas, conducted by the Japan Bank for International Cooperation (JBIC) since the 1990s. We can see the changes in business activity of overseas bases of Japanese companies. The total number of bases, based on the questionnaire responses, are indicated in the lower portion of the figure.

According to this, the activity composition of Europe (EU) and America (USA and Canada) is different from that of Asia. In the 1990s, the Japanese manufacturing companies, which entered China and ASEAN, were overwhelmingly into manufacturing activities. Entering this century, however, it appears that there was a shift from production to marketing. R&D bases also show a tendency to increase, albeit slightly. In contrast, in the advanced economic region of the EU, marketing is the main activity. America and Canada are 50–50 into manufacturing and marketing, but there is a tendency for marketing to increase. For Japanese companies, East Asia is a production location, but it is also starting to be a marketing location. This is a change during the 1990s up to the turn of the century.

Next, let us look at the promising investment destination countries for the next three years from the point of view of Japanese manufacturing companies, from the 1990s up to now. Figure 3.17 shows this. The countries chosen as promising investment destinations from the 1990s to the early 2010s was, by far, China. By the 2010s, even as the Japan-Sino conflict was becoming prominent, and even as the large effects

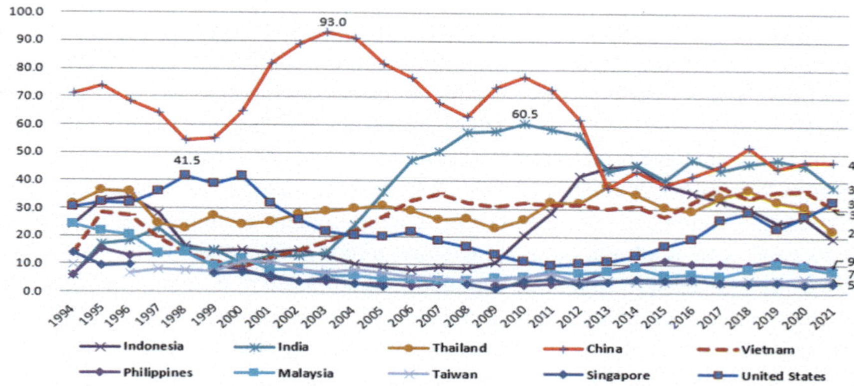

Fig. 3.17 Ranks of promising countries for overseas business operations for Japanese manufacturing companies over medium terms (over the next 3 years or so) 1994–2021 (*Source* JBIC survey reports on overseas business operations by Japanese manufacturing companies, various year issues)

on the international division of labor from the intensification of U.S.-Sino hegemonic struggle was becoming evident, most Japanese companies were still choosing China as a promising investment destination. In the second half of the 1990s, America followed China as a promising country. Entering this century, however, America has been dropping in ranking, but in the second half of the 2010s, there was a renewed appreciation of the U.S. as an investment destination. This would be due to the higher risk of emerging economies brought about by the structural shift and instability of the international society in the international political economic sphere, which reversely strengthened the confidence in advanced economies.

Even then, since the 1990s, especially entering this century, ASEAN countries, such as Thailand, Vietnam, and Indonesia and various South Asian countries emerged as promising investment destinations. In the second half of the 2000s, India quickly became an object of interest. Emerging economies such as Thailand, Vietnam, and Indonesia came to be considered as promising. These countries have large populations, and, therefore as discussed above, have a high growth possibility. In terms of population, America could also be placed in this category. The Japanese companies are keeping a close eye on these countries. Let us try to confirm from the same survey what are the reasons for the high expectations of these countries.

Figure 3.18 shows the reasons (or causes) by which Japanese companies choose promising investment destinations in the near future. From Fig. 3.18 a and b, we can see the reason for Japanese companies to choose the leading PoBMEs, China and India. The typical change tendency can be seen in the case of China. At the start of this century, the main reasons were "future growth potential of the local market", followed by "inexpensive source of labor". The share of "future growth potential" not only slightly surpasses "inexpensive labor" but more or less is sustained. The share of "inexpensive source of labor" has a downward trend. In its stead, the share of "current size of local market" is rising. This shows that, entering this century, there is a thinning of interest in low wages as an investment factor. Moreover, interest has been gradually turning to the existing market size. In short, companies looking at China have been turning their gaze from production to market. It could be deemed that in India, which is lagging behind China, this process has started.

Figure 3.18c, d, e shows the three major promising factors for Thailand, Vietnam, and America, who have been following China and India. For Thailand and Vietnam, interest in "inexpensive source of labor" is high, but, entering this century, expectations on the "future growth potential of the local market" have been on a gradual upward trend. This is similar but lagging to the trends in China and India.

Let us look at the selection of investment destinations of U.S. and other Western companies. Table 3.3 shows the top 11 countries based on Kearney's FDI confidence index for 1998–2021. From this world direct investment confidence ranking of multinational companies, China started to compete with America for the top slot entering this century, actually overtook America for nine years, from 2003 to 2012, for the

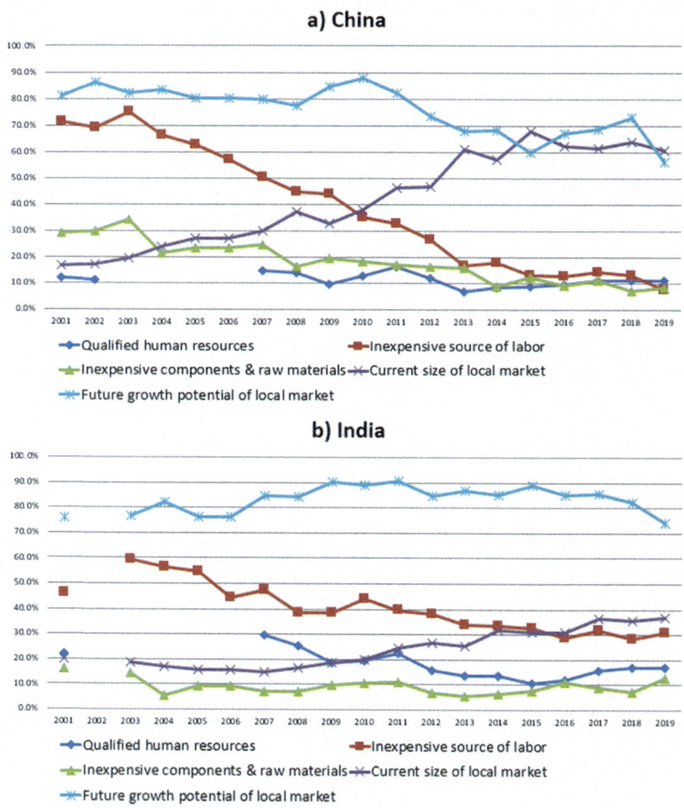

Fig. 3.18 Major countries and major Causes of the selection of promising investment countries by Japanese manufacturing companies 2001–2019 (*Source* JBIC survey reports on overseas business operations by Japanese manufacturing companies, various year issues). *Note* **a** and **b** show the reasons for the choice of the top two promising firms, **c–e** show the changes of reasons for promising countries by country

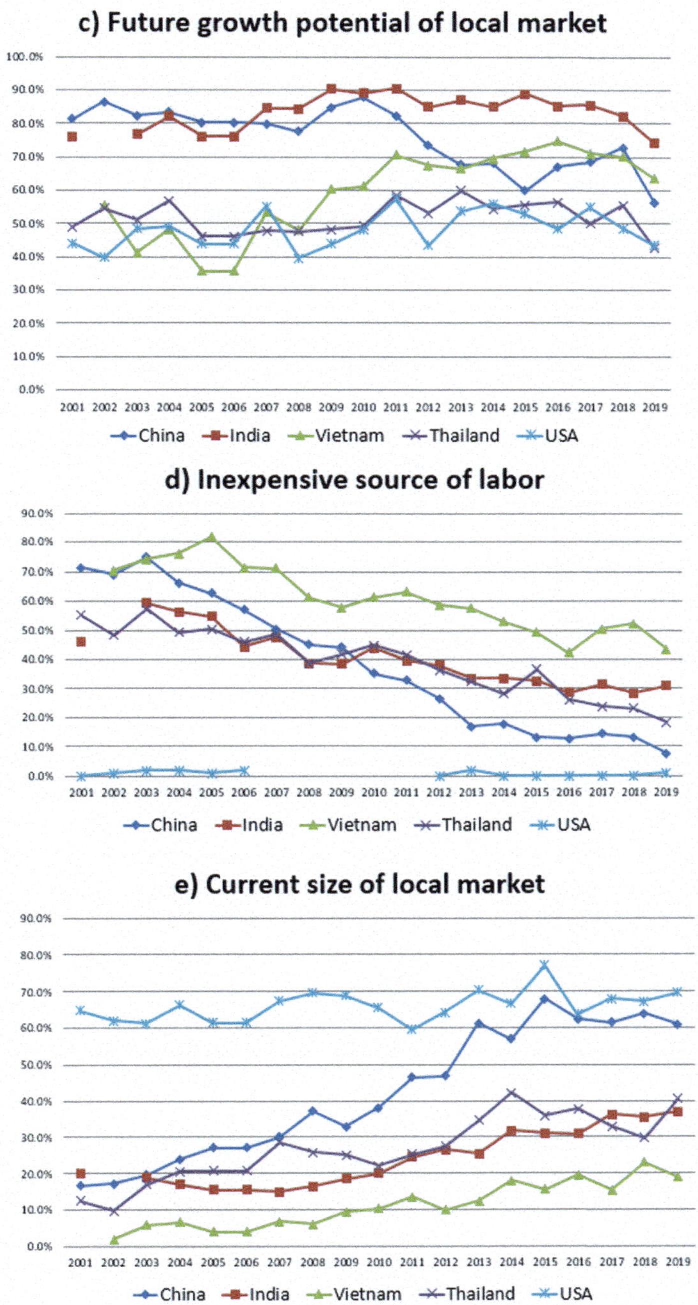

Fig. 3.18 (continued)

top slot, and was in second place for the four years from 2013 to 2016. The BRIC countries India, Brazil and Russia were also included in the top 11 during this period.

From the second half of the 2010s, China has had its rankings start to drop. In 2021, advanced economies monopolized the top rankings, with China at 12th position. The investment risk accompanying the structural change of the global economy contributed to the drop in rankings of China. There is also the risk of restructuring the global supply chain brought about by the changes in the U.S.-Sino conflict arising from the trade negotiations and the COVID-19 (Kearney, 2021: 11). In the second half of the 2010s, the increasing instability in the international society raised the risks of investing in PoBMEs. Since 2014, Russia has been embroiled in conflict with the U.S. and European countries over the Ukrainian crisis and the Crimean Peninsula. Brazil saw its GDP dropping in 2015–2016 due to the fall in natural resource prices and the chaos in domestic politics, due in part to the deepening political conflict also over the COVID-19 response. Interest in the newly emerging countries, starting with the big-population countries of BRICs, was particularly prominent from the 1990s to the 2010s.

The 2004 Kearney's FDI confidence index contains the results of a questionnaire survey whether the length of attraction, to investments in the major emerging economies of China, India, Poland, Brazil, and Mexico, was short-term (one to three years) or medium-term (ten years). According to this, investors' short-term and medium-term responses were 80 and 85%, respectively for China, 68 and 82%, respectively for India, 48 and 55%, respectively, for Poland, 41 and 55%, respectively for Brazil, 35 and 46%, respectively, for Mexico. Expectations on China and India were particularly high, but a common point was that the above-mentioned four emerging economies, without exception, were higher for the medium-term (ten years) than the short-term (one to three years) (Kearney, 2004: 15).

What is more interesting is the survey responses with regards to the attraction of China and India, shown in Fig. 3.19. The responses to reasons for choosing China are: market size with 94%, and market growth potential with 78%. While in the case of India, 78% chose a highly educated workforce, 73% management talent and rule of law, and 70% transparency. The investors to China and India have significantly different perspectives. There are different expectations for the two economies, however, expectations are the same for such things as market size, market growth potential, and skilled workers. Suffice it to say that investors are really engrossed in searching for the potential in big-population countries.

2005 was the year China and India occupied the first and second ranks of Kearney's FDI confidence index, pushing America down to third place. The survey results of responses about R&D spending plans clearly showed an awareness of the large populations of emerging economies at that time. This is shown in Fig. 3.20 where 48% responded with increasing R&D, especially to Asia Pacific, which had 50% of the responses, overwhelming those for North America and Europe.

The 2005 UNCTAD World Investment Report analyzes in detail the focusing of R&D expenditures of multinational firms towards the newly emerging developing economies.

Table 3.3 Kearney's FDI confidence index top 11 countries 1998–2021 (not every year)

Rank	June 1998	December 1998	June 1999	January 2000	2003	2005	2007	2010	2013	2015	2017	2020	2021
1	US	US	US	US	China	China	China	China	US	US	US	US	US
2	Brazil	Brazil	China	UK	US	India	India	US	China	China	Germany	Canada	Canada
3	China	China	UK	China	Mexico	US	US	India	Brazil	UK	China	Germany	Germany
4	UK	UK	Brazil	Brazil	Poland	UK	UK	Brazil	Canada	Canada	UK	Japan	UK
5	India	Germany	Mexico	Poland	Germany	Poland	Hong Kong	Germany	India	Germany	Canada	France	Japan
6	Mexico	Poland	India	Germany	India	Russia	Brazil	Poland	Australia	Brazil	Japan	UK	France
7	Poland	India	Australia	Mexico	UK	Brazil	Singapore	Australia	Germany	Japan	France	Australia	Australia
8	Argentina	Mexico	Poland	Italy	Russia	Australia	UAE	Mexico	UK	France	India	China	Italy
9	Australia	Spain	Germany	Spain	Brazil	Germany	Russia	Canada	Mexico	Mexico	Australia	Italy	Spain
10	Germany	France	France	Australia	Spain	Hong Kong	Germany	UK	Singapore	Australia	Singapore	Switzerland	Switzerland
11	Spain	Italy	Italy	India	France	Hungary	Australia	UAE	Russia	India	Spain	Spain	Netherlands

(*Source* Kearney-Global Business Policy Council various year issues).
Note China's confidence Index was first place in 2003–2012 and was kept at second place from 2013 to 2016. It dropped soon after, and in 2021 dropped out of the top 10, at 12th place.

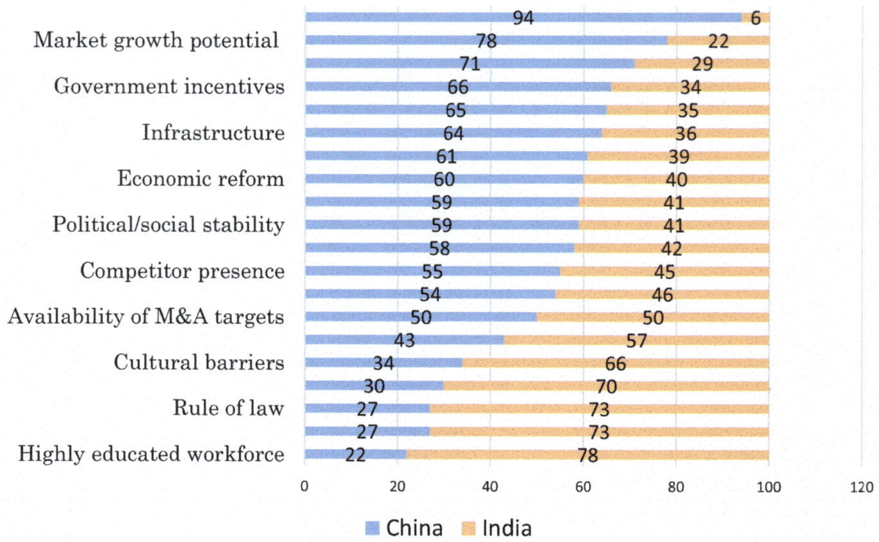

Fig. 3.19 Which is more attractive for the following FDI attributes—China or India? (*Source* Kearney's FDI confidence index, October 2004: 4)

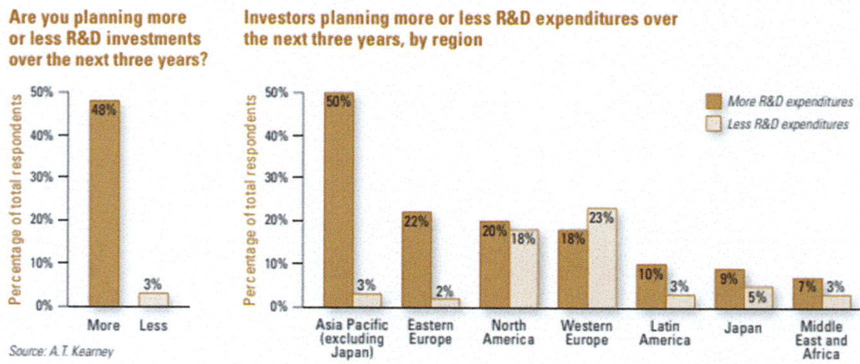

Fig. 3.20 Shift of global R&D expenditures from advanced economies to developing (emerging) economies 2005 (*Source* Kearney, 2005: 4)

Developed countries remain the main host locations of foreign R&D activities by TNC, but there is a clear trend towards location more R&D activities to developing economies, South–East Europe and CIS. This is confirmed by available national statistics as well as by corporate surveys and case studies. The kind of R&D being undertaken by TNCs in developing countries is also changing. While it has traditionally involved mainly product or process adaptation to meet local market demands, recent developments suggest that some developing, South–East European and CIS markets are emerging as key nodes in the global R&D systems of TNCs (UNCTAD, 2005: 126–127).

According to this report, the overseas R&D expenditures of U.S. multinational companies rose from U.S.$11,877 million in 1994 to U.S.$21,151 million in 2002, of which the share towards advanced economies dropped from 92.4 to 84.4%, while that towards developing economies increased from 7.6 to 13.5%. The share of developing Asia increased threefold from 3.4 to 10.0%, and that of China from 0.1 to 3.1%. In 2002, India accounted for 0.4%. "Expenditures on R&D by affiliates of United States TNCs in developing economies are concentrated mostly in five countries: China, Singapore, Brazil, Mexico and the Republic of Korea in that order. They accounted for 70% of the total R&D expenditure of United States TNCs in developing countries in 2002" (UNCTAD, 2005: 129–130).

In short, multinational companies of the world have been showing an increased interest during this period on the newly emerging developing economies and their future potentials. Global capital and technology are flowing toward the PoBMEs, especially Asian PoBMEs. Focus on Singapore is due to its historical accumulation of central functions of the Asian newly emerging economic zone.

Finally, in order to validate the above findings, let us look at the changes in the composition of the recipient region for the world's FDI for the past half century, as shown in Fig. 3.21. Looking at this figure, we first notice that the advanced economies, particularly the EU and America, were the predominant recipients of FDI up to 2010. Looking at the case of developing countries, however, we can see the share of developing countries rising again entering this century after dropping in the 1990s at the height of the Asian financial crisis. During the second half of the 2010s, shares underwent a lot of variation but the average level is significantly higher than before.

Asian newly emerging economies, particularly China, is a major destination. Entering this century, India is also starting to show its viability as a recipient of investments. Since the 1990s, there is clearly a flow of capital into developing countries, Asian newly emerging economies, especially big-population countries. With the capital, technology is moving towards Asia.

3.4.2 The Changing Development Model of Asia: From NIEs to PoBMEs

Earlier we noted that global FDI is flowing in the direction of Asian emerging economies, against the backdrop of expectations on the potential development of Asia. The investment destination has been BRICs, as discovered by O'Neill, and PoBMEs, as we are proposing. When we consider this development of the Asian emerging economies along a temporal dimension, as we do in Sect. 3.3.1, we could glean the details of its changes. This is sorted out in Table 3.3.

Table 3.4 is a matrix that considers the FDI investment goals of production and marketing, with respect to advanced economies and Asian emerging economies.

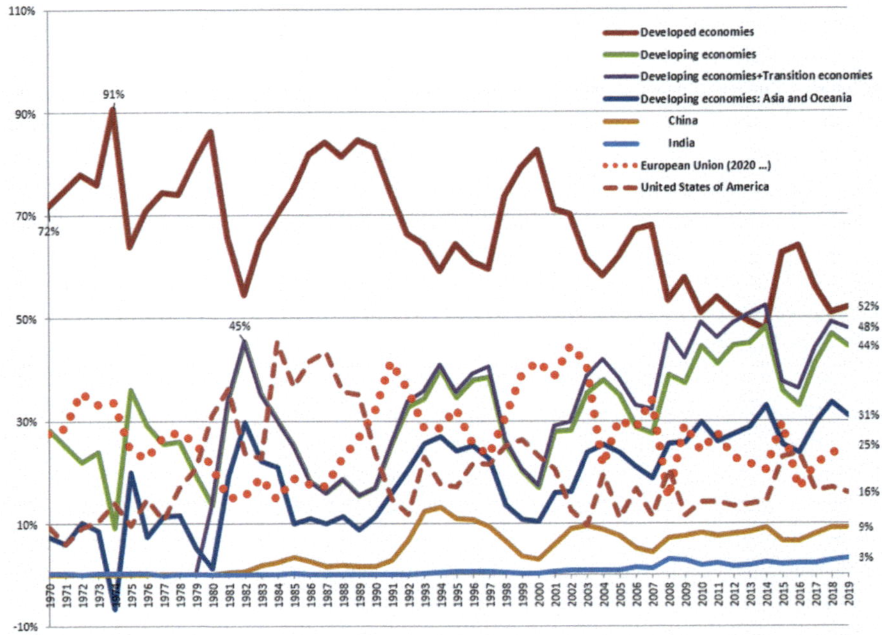

Fig. 3.21 The Composition of regions receiving global FDI 1970–2019 (*Source* UNCTAD database. Accessed August 2021)

From this, the first quadrant (upper right) depicts an FDI type which conducts production and consumption in the advanced economies. Investment is a mutual investment between advanced economies. Firm activity is completed within the advanced economy zone. The second (upper left) and third (lower left) quadrants become the development model of Asian emerging economies. The second quadrant depicts an FDI type which produces in newly industrializing economies/developing regions, and exports the products to the advanced economy markets. The third quadrant depicts an FDI type that enters a potentially bigger market economy/developing region and produces products (including intermediate goods), and sells these to domestic market or exports these to advanced and emerging economies. The difference in type of FDI between the second and third quadrants is whether the market is mainly an advanced economy or an emerging economy/developing region.

As we have confirmed, however, in this chapter, Asia developed by starting from the second quadrant and then transitioning to the third quadrant. The second quadrant FDI brought about the export-oriented development of NIEs that started from the 1960s. The third quadrant FDI could be clearly seen as supporting the development of China entering this century. FDI is recognizing, in particular, the development of potential markets. India, Thailand, Vietnam, Indonesia, and others have been following China's lead. Such newly emerging economies can be called PoBMEs. China and India are such types of economies.

Table 3.4 Matrix of 3 historical classification of FDI and the development of emerging economies

Location of primary markets	Developed economies (countries)	FDI to product for export (export-oriented FDI) NIEs-investment type of development	Mutual FDI among developed economies (developed market-oriented FDI) Developed economies-investment type of mutual development
	Emerging economies (countries)	FDI to product for domestic market (potential market-oriented FDI) PoBMEs-investment type of development	Catching Up
		Emerging economies (countries)	Developed economies (countries)
		Location of primary production	

(*Source* Revised version from Hirakawa 2016: 134, 2017: 53).
Notes 1st quadrant: Developed economies' mutual investment type of development./Transfer of capital and technology through FDI among developed economies.
2nd quadrant: NIES-investment type of development./Transfer of capital and technology to emerging economies through FDI in search of low wage labors and for export to developed economies' markets.
3rd quadrant: PoBMEs type of development./Transfer of capital and technology to big population countries with potentially bigger market through FDI. "NIEs" stand for Newly Industrializing Economies. "PoBMEs" stand for Potentially Bigger Market Economies.

This, however, does not mean that all newly emerging economies went from the second to the third quadrant types of FDI. It means that the major form of FDI shifted to the third quadrant type. Here, the potential market is the local market, but considering the reality of ASEAN, it should be taken as a broader regional local market, rather than strictly the local market within national borders.

We shall discuss more in Chap. 9, bearing China in mind, ASEAN, since the start of the 1990s, aimed for a regional integration along the lines of this development mechanism. Such a policy thrust created newly emerging economies, in addition to China and India, with enhanced potential growth capabilities. ASEAN concluded the ASEAN Free Trade Area (AFTA) in 1992, adopted the "ASEAN Vision 2020" in 1998, when the Asian financial crisis occurred, and launched the building of an ASEAN community. The inauguration of the ASEAN community was moved forward five years at the 2007 ASEAN Summit Meeting, and conducted in 2015. The ASEAN community consists of the three pillars of "Political-Security Community", "Economic Community", and "Socio-Cultural Community", with economic integration at a central position. In November 2020, the ten countries of ASEAN signed the RCEP of Japan, China, South Korea, Australia, and New Zealand. RCEP was inaugurated in January 2022. With a population of 650 million, the ASEAN region, together with the 1.4 billion of China and 1.3 billion of India, is aiming for an economy that is formed by the Asian economies.

Asia's development policies were naturally matched to the above-mentioned FDI activities. This will be discussed in more detail in Chap. 7, let us take a look at the main points in this section. The development policies adopted by developing

Fig. 3.22 Three stages of development policies in Asian emerging economies (*Source* Revised from Hirakawa/Than, 2011: 56; Hirakawa, 2013: 283, 2018: 77). Note NIEs stand for newly industrializing economies, PoBMEs stand for potentially bigger market economies

economies after the Second World War appear to be divisible into three stages. This is shown in Fig. 3.22.

Most Asian countries gained independence from colonization. The resulting newly independent states of developing countries first took the policy of import-substitution industrialization for their country's development. This first stage of industrialization policy was protectionist and depended on the local market. Based on the economic history of capitalism, it could be said that this was a justifiable policy of latecomer industrialization. This was due to an inability to nurture industries that could compete abroad. It was the export-oriented industrialization policy of the second stage that sought to overcome these limitations.

The export-oriented industrialization policy adopted by the NIEs, entering the 1960s, depended on the advanced country companies for capital, technology and markets, and hurdled the development limitations of a small-scale economy. Companies, which were attracted by the policies of NIEs, employed cheap labor to produce goods, which are then exported to the markets of advanced economies. In this way, the NIEs were able to solve their problem. This gave birth to the coining of the word NICs (becoming NIEs in the 1980s), the development of which is as shown in Table 3.1 and Figs. 3.13, and discussed in Chap. 7.

Later on, to cope with the strengthening of the yen due to the Plaza Accord of 1985, ASEAN countries and China shifted their policies towards export-led industrialization and liberal reforms, drawing in a wave of FDI from Japan and the NIEs. In this way, the triangle of growth of the NIEs expanded to Asia's triangle of growth, giving birth to intra-regional markets and opening up the path to a PoBMEs-type of development.

Figure 3.23 is a graphical stylization of Asia's development. The triangle of growth of the NIEs, through Asia's FDI, achieved an upgrading in the 1990s, and connected with the development of big-population countries that quickly appeared in the 2000s.

Let us touch briefly here on our understanding with regards to the awareness in economics of this development. We would like to point out that we do not consider

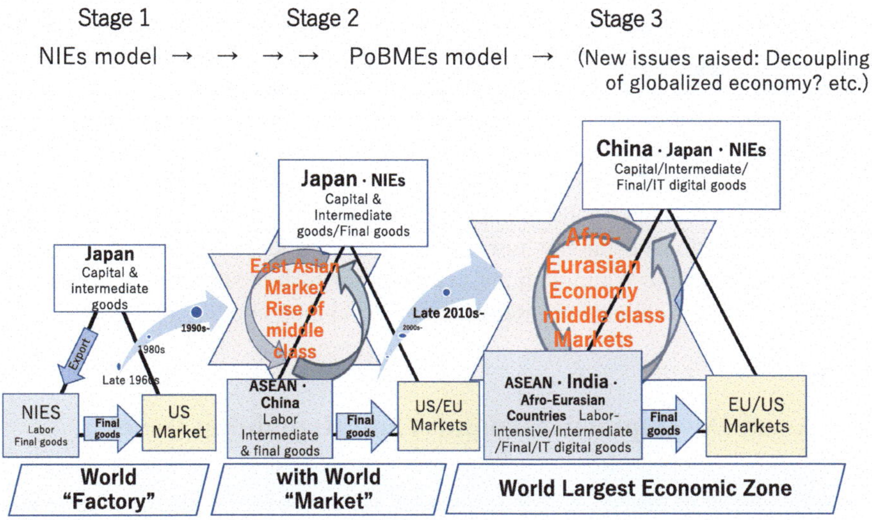

Fig. 3.23 Three development stages of Asian emerging economies (*Source* A revised version from Hirakawa, 2021: 102). *Note* "NIEs" stands for newly industrializing economies. "PoBMEs" stands for potentially bigger market economies

the export-type of development, due to the introduction of FDI from advanced economies, as a development based solely on neoliberalist policies. The introduction of capital and technology through the multinational companies from advanced countries were important to the development of PoBMEs, but at the same time these must be assimilated into the domestic economy. One indicator for this is the development of the local firms. Let us first confirm here the role of national government policies in the newly emerging economies. For that, we cite the statements of two economists, Dani Rodrik and J. Stiglitz. Dani Rodrik writes as follows.

> The Japanese government pushed the bank (WB) to prepare a study of the "Asian miracle," agreeing also to pay for the bulk of it. The miracle in question referred not only to Japan's experience but also to that of seven other East and Southeast Asian economies that had grown very rapidly since the early 1960s—South Korea, Taiwan, Hong Kong, Singapore, Malaysia, Thailand, and Indonesia. All of these countries had benefited enormously from exports and hence from globalization. But none, with the exception of the British colony of Hong Kong, came even close to being free market economies. The state had played an important guiding and coordinating role of them (Rodrik, 2011: 144–145).

Stiglitz says the following.

> What is clear that these (East Asian) countries did not follow the market fundamentalist model; markets played a critical role in their success, but it was managed markets, managed for the benefits of society as a whole, not for that of a few shareholders or managers; it was a market economy in which the government played the role of an orchestra conductor. It catalyzed growth, investing heavily in technology, education, and infrastructure (Stiglitz, 2016: 311)

The government's role in the development of Asia was extremely important. As mentioned above, however, simply citing the role of government would be insufficient, since the development of the Asian emerging economies was not achieved separately from the global economic structure. As we have seen in this chapter, the dynamics of Asia's development could not be captured simply by an analysis of the dualism between market and state. The development of the Asian newly emerging economies was achieved through the adoption of various policies that developed the national economy, in consonant with the global economic structure. This heavily depended on multinational companies, which brought about the transfer of technology to the national economy and the development of the local firms.

3.5 Asian Development Dynamics and Remaining Issues

The development of the Asian economy started with the export-led type of development of the NIEs, and even provided new markets, entering this century. In this chapter, we considered these dynamics of development as a region, and traced its movement through time covering over half a century. Entering the twenty-first century, the Asian emerging economies are certainly at a new destination. They are at the stage of a PoBMEs type of development, and presumably at long last in a position for the birth of an Asian economic zone.

This, however, means that the Asian economy has been brought to a new phase, both internally and externally. One is the changes on the global economic balance induced by the development of PoBMEs, which is appearing to be a U.S.-Sino rivalry for hegemonic supremacy. We are clearly now in a period of transition. We have discussed this partly in Chap. 2. Another is the new foreign policy of China that was initiated at the point of arrival of a PoBMEs type of development. This had great significance to Asia as well as to the international political economy. We will deal more about the situation and significance of this in Chap. 4.

Looking inside the region, there are issues that have been left unresolved. In this chapter, we have considered the deployment of FDI, but of course FDI is not a sufficient condition for development. FDI should be organically linked to the development of each economy. This will be dealt more in Chap. 7. There is also the issue related to the "middle income trap." Entry into the global economy does not promise development to all East Asian countries. An IMF paper, which sorts the high-growth debate of East Asia, states that amidst the high growth of East Asian countries, "The worst performer was the Philippines, which grew at about 2% a year (in per capita terms), about equal to the average of non-Asian countries" (Sarel, 1995: 2), confirming the issue of Philippine growth at an early stage. Economists with an interest in the rapid growth of the emerging economies, however, practically ignore the case of this country as a subject of study. The World Bank's "East Asian Miracle" is an early study that shed light on the rapid growth of East Asia, particularly, what it calls as the High Performing Asian Economies which comprise of eight countries/ economies including Japan. The Philippines was not included, for one, because of its low GDP per capita growth rate (World Bank, 1993: xvi). The same case could be seen in Japanese research (Kuchiki -J, 2007).

At this point, it would be important to cite the 2007 World Bank report "Asian Renaissance", which raises the issue of the "middle income trap". The "middle income trap" was probably brought about by a similar concern in the 1980s over the "sandwich problem". This problem refers to the environment of stagnation wherein the export-led industrialization based on low wages of the NIEs is caught in the international markets between the low value-added products of latecomer countries and the high value-added products of the advanced economies. The World Bank raised this as a problem of economic structure upgrading, or the structural transformation from an export-led economy to an advanced economy.

Looking at the middle-income trap, the 2013 IMF Regional Economic Outlook, based on the growth performance in the last 20 years and the performance after the 2008 global financial crisis, divided Asian countries into one group, which would avoid the trap, and another group, which faces the risk of falling into the trap. The dividing factor is the contribution of total factor productivity to economic growth. The report writes as follows.

> The four Asian Tigers (Hong Kong SAR, Korea, Singapore, and Taiwan Province of China) continued to grow rapidly after attaining middle-income status and thereby reached income levels comparable to those of advanced countries./With their income per capita currently standing at 10–40% of average G-7 levels, China, India, Indonesia, Malaysia, the Philippines, Thailand, and Vietnam all face the challenge of sustaining their convergence process. The main proximate driver of a sustained slowdown in growth has often been a persistent decline in the growth of total factor productivity, a crude measure of technological progress (IMF, 2013: 48).

Figure 3.24 is related to the above statement. Of note is the figure's inclusion of the trend in the per capita GDP of the Philippines. China and Malaysia appear to be on a strong trajectory of convergence to the G-7 PPP GDP per capita average, but the growth of other countries are stagnating. This trend is particularly strong in the Philippines, and is even showing a downward tendency. Recall, however, Fig. 3.7 at the early part of this chapter. At the point where her GDP per capita was stagnating, the Philippines, more than any other country, was deeply embedded in the global supply chain. It is not at all strange that the Philippines would stand in front. This, however, has not been the case. Various studies have investigated the middle income trap using macro indicators such as investment to GDP ratio, TFP trend, FDI/GDP ratio, share of higher education, and R&D expenditure ratio. From which, general policies are recommended to country policy makers. Why has the Philippines fallen into the typically observed middle income trap? There would be many causes, but there would be a problem in the economics approach. This will be mainly discussed from the Philippine perspective in Chap. 6.

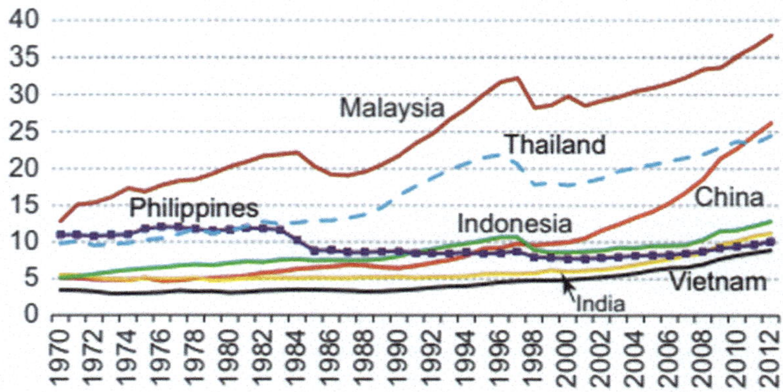

Fig. 3.24 GDP per capita convergence in seven emerging Asian economies (PPP GDP per capita as percentage G7 average PPP GDP per capita) (*Source* IMF, 2013: 48)

References

**Documents with a symbol (-J) after the author's name are Japanese documents*

ADB. (1992). *Asian development outlook 1992*. Asian Development Bank, Oxford University Press.

ADB. (2007). *Asian development outlook 2007 update*. ADB.

ADB. (2008). *Asian development outlook 2008*. ADB.

ADB. (2010, August). *Key indicators for Asia and the Pacific 2010: the 41st edition.*

ADB. (2011). *Asia 2050: Realizing the Asian century*. ADB.

ADB. (2013). Beyond factory Asia: Fueling growth in a changing world. ADB.

ADB. (2015). *Asian economic integration Report 2015*. ADB.

Baldwin, R. (2016). *The great convergence: Information technology and the new globalization*. Belknap Press of Harvard University Press.

Bloom David, E., & Williamson, J. G. (1997). *Demographic transitions and economic miracles in emerging Asia*. NBER Working Paper No. 6268, November.

Bloomberg News. (2023). *China slowdown means it may never overtake US economy*: Forecast slows. Bloomberg, September 5.

Chun, N. (2010). *Middle class size in the past, present, and future: A description of trends in Asia. ADB Economics Working Paper Series* No. 217, September.

Deaton, A. (2013). *The great escape: Health, wealth, and the origins of inequality*. Princeton: Princeton University Press.

Drucker, P., F. (1997). The global economy and the nation-state, *Foreign Affairs*, *76*(5), September/October.

Fukuyama, F. (1992). *The end of history and the last man*. International Creative Management

Ghosh, J., Havilik, P., Poplawski-Ribeiro, M., & Urban, W. (2009). *Models of BRICs' economic development and challenges for EU competitiveness*. The Vienna Institute for International Economic Studies, Research Reports No. 359, December.

Gill, I., & Kharas, H. (2007). *An east Asian renaissance: Ideas for economic growth*. The World Bank

Hirakawa, H., -J. (1992). *NIES: Sekai shisutemu to kaihatsu (NIEs: The world system and development)*. Dobunkan.

Hirakawa, H. (2010). East Asia's structural change from NIEs to potentially bigger market economies (PBM) and regional cooperation: Implications for a small economy. A paper presented at the 2nd ANDA international seminar on skills development for the emerging new dynamism in Asian developing countries under globalization, organized by Graduate School of International Development, Nagoya University, Japan, and Royal University of Phnom Penh, Cambodia, January 8–10, Phnom Penh Hotel, Cambodia. https://www2.gsid.nagoya-u.ac.jp/blog/anda/files/2010/06/2_hitoshi-hirakawa.pdf

Hirakawa, H. (2013). East Asia's integration and structural shift. In: N. Yagi, S. Yokokawa, S. Hagiwara, & G. A. Dymski (Eds.), *Crises of global economies and the future of capitalism.* Routledge.

Hirakawa, H., -J. (2014). Sekai Keizai no kozo tankan to Shinko keizai (The Structural transition of the global economy and emerging economies). *Kikan Keizai-Riron (Political Economy Quarterly) Japan Society of Political Economy, 51* (1), April.

Hirakawa, H., -J. (2016). Kozotenkan no Sekaizeizai to shinkokeizai soshite shuhenkeizai (Structural transformation of the world economy and emerging economies, and peripheral economies. In: H. Borjigin (Ed.), *Nichi-Mongoru kankei no rekishi: Genjo to tenbo (A history, present situation, and prospects of Japan-Mongolia relations).* Fukyo-sha.

Hirakawa, H. (2017). East Asia's economic development and Japanese firms' ICT-based services offshoring. In: H. Hirakawa & N. Takahashi, et al. (Eds.), *Innovative ICT industrial architecture in East Asia.* Springer Japan.

Hirakawa, H., -J. (2018). Higashi ajia keizaitogo no aratana tenbo Higashi ajia keizai togo no aratana tenbo (A new prospect of economic integration in East Asia). *Ajia Kenkyu (Asian Studies), Japan Association for Asian Studies, 64*(4), October.

Hirakawa, H. (2018). Transformation of the world economy and institutionalization of East Asian region. In: R. Boyer, H. Uemura, T. Yamada, & L. Song (Eds.), *Evolving diversity and interdependence of capitalism.* Springer Japan.

Hirakawa, H., -J. (2021b). Beicyu boueki senso oyobi Covid-19 kiki ga ajia keizai ni ataeru eikyo (The impact of US-Sino trade war and COVID-19 crisis on Asian economy), *21 seiki ajiagaku kenkyu* (Kokushikan University), March 9.

Hirakawa, H., & Than, A. (2011). Globalization and the emerging economies: East Asia's structural shift from the NIEs to potentially bigger market economies (PoBMEs). *Evolutionary and Institutional Economics Review, 8*(1).

Hirakawa, H., Kobayashi, N., & Morimoto, A., -J. (eds.). (2009). *Higashi ajia chiiki kyoryoku no kyodo sekkei (Co-designing East Asian regional cooperation).* Nishida Shoten.

IMF. (2007). *World economic outlook.* International Monetary Fund, April.

IMF. (2008). How much decoupling? How much converging? *Finance and Development, 45*(2), June.

IMF. (2013). *Regional economic outlook Asia and Pacific, April.*

MITI, -J. (1994). *Tsusho hakusho (White paper on international trade).* Tsusho Sangyo Sho (Ministry of International Trade and Industry, Japan).

Nikkei, -J. (2011). Recording: Keynote speech by J. O'Neill at Mutual Fund Special Seminar "Looking at the 2011 growth market". The Nihon Keizai Shimbun, July 7.

JBIC. (Multiple Years). Survey reports on overseas business operations by Japanese manufacturing companies.

Kearney (AT Kearney). (2004, 2005, 2021). *FDI confidence index.* Global Business Policy Council, Kearney Inc.

Kim, Y.-H., -J. (1988). *Higashi ajia kogyoka to sekai shihonsyugi (East Asian industrialization and the world economy.* Toyo Keizai Shinposha.

Kitamura, H., -J. (1988). Toronto samitto no tokucho to nihon (Characteristics of the Toronto summit and Japan). *Sekai keizai hyoron (World Economic Review),* September.

Kojima, K., -J. (2006). *Ganko gata keizai hatten ron Dai 3 kan (The Flying-geese theory of economic development III).* Bunshindo.

Kuchiki, A., -J. (2007). *Ajia sangyo kurasuta ron (Industrial clusters in Asia).* Shoseki Kobo Hayama.
Mason, A. (1997). *Population and the Asian economic miracle.* Asia-Pacific Population & Policy, No. 43, October.
McGregor, H. (2011) Jim O'Neill: Game changer. *Brunswick Review,* (4), Summer.
METI, -J. (2005). *Tsusho hakusho (White paper on international trade).* Keizai Sangyosho (Ministry of Economy, Trade, and Industry, Japan).
METI, -J. (2008). Tsusho hakusho (White paper on international trade). Keizai Sangyosho.
METI, -J. (2014). *Tsusho hakusho (White paper on international trade).* Keizai Sangyosho.
Naikakufu, -J. (2006). *BRICs keizai no seicho to sekaikeizai heno gani ni kansuru chosa kenkyu houkokusho* (The Survey Research Report on the Implications to BRICs Economic Growth and the Global Economy) Cabinet Office, Japanese Government, March.
Nakajima, J., Takatomi, K., Mori, T., & Ohyama, S. (2016). Slow trade: structural and cyclical factors in global trade slowdown. *BOJ Reports & Research Papers*, Bank of Japan, December.
National Science Board, NSFUS. (2010). Science and engineering indicators 2010.
NIC. (2004). *Mapping the global future: Report of the National Intelligence Council's 2020 project.* National Intelligence Council. USA, December.
NIC. (2008). *Global trends 2025: A transformed world.* National Intelligence Council, USA, November.
O'Neill, J. (2001). Building better global economic BRICs. *Goldman Sachs Global Economics Paper,* no. 66, November 30.
O'Neill, J., Dominic, W., Roopa, P., & Anne, S. (2005). How solid are the BRICs? *Global Economics Paper,* no. 134, December 1.
OECD. (1979). *The impact of the newly industrializing countries on production and trade in manufactures.* Report by the Secretary-General. Organisation for Economic Co-operation and Development. OECD.
OECD. (2012). *Looking to 2060: Long-term global growth prospects. OECD Economic Policy Papers,* no. 3, November.
Onishi, H., & Kanae, R. (2016). The age of large-population countries and marxian optimal growth theory. *World Review of Political Economy, 7*(3), Fall.
Onishi, H., & Kanae, R. -J. (2014, October). "Jinko taikoku no jidai" to marukusuha saiteki seicho ron ("The age of large-population countries" and Marxian optimal growth theory). *Mita Gakkai Zasshi, 107*(3).
Quah, D. (2011, January). The global economy's shifting center of gravity. *Global Policy, 2*(1).
Republic of China. (2008). *Taiwan statistical data book.* Council for Economic Planning and Development, Republic of China (Taiwan).
Rodrik, D. (2011). *The globalization paradox: Why global markets, states, and democracy can't coexist.* Oxford University Press.
Sarel, M. (1995). Growth in East Asia: What we can and what we cannot infer. *IMF Economic Issues Working Paper*, no. 1995/098, September.
Stiglitz, J. E. (2016). *The great divide.* Penguin Books.
Suehiro, A., -J. (2014). *Shinko ajia keizairon: Kyacchi appu wo koete (Emerging Asian economy: Beyond catching up).* Iwanami Shoten.
UNCTAD. (2003). *World investment report 2003.* United Nations Conference on Trade and Development.
UNCTAD. (2005). *World investment report 2005.* UNCTAD.
UNCTAD. (2011). *World investment report 2011.* UNCTAD.
UNCTAD. (2015). *World investment report 2015*, UNCTAD.
UNCTAD. (2020). *UNCTAD handbook of statistics 2020.* UNCTAD.
UNCTAD. (2021). *World investment report 2021.* UNCTAD.
UNFPA. (1998). *State of world population 1998: The new generations.* United Nations Population Fund.

Wilson, D., & Purushothaman, R. (2003). Dreaming with BRICs: The path to 2050. *Goldman Sachs Global Economics Paper*, No. 99, October 1.

Wilson, D., & Stupnytska, A. (2007). The N-11: More than an acronym. *Goldman Sachs Global Economics Paper*, no. 153, March 28.

World Bank. (1993). *The East Asian miracle: Economic growth and public policy*. Oxford University Press.

World Bank. (2005). *World development indicators 2005*. IRDB.

World Bank. (2008). *World development indicators 2008*. World Bank.

World Bank. (2010). *World development indicators 2010*, World Bank.

World Bank. (2011). *World development indicators 2011*. World Bank.

World Bank. (2012). *World development indicators 2012*. IRDB.

Chapter 4
China's Belt and Road Initiative and Its Prospect

Abstract Xi Jinping was inaugurated as President at the 12th National People's Congress held in March 2013. In September and October of the very same year, he advocated the "Silk Road Economic Belt" and the "21st Century Maritime Silk Road". These two initiatives were adopted as national strategies in the 3rd meeting of the 18th Central Committee of the Communist Party in November of the same year. In the next year, President Xi announced the establishment of the New Development Bank (BRICS Bank) in July, and the Asia Infrastructure Investment Bank (AIIB) in August, and clarified the "One Belt One Road Initiative" (BRI) to the leaders attending the APEC-CEO Summit in November. BRI was pushed at a massive scale since then, but in 2018 criticisms, such as the "debt trap" began emerging. The birth of the Trump Administration stirred up the U.S.-Sino Trade War, and the world was besieged with the COVID-19 pandemic that broke out of Wuhan, China in 2020. Amidst the turbulent global economy, what are we to make of BRI? What prospects could be drawn? In this chapter, we shall trace the development of BRI, its realities and issues, and in the process, consider what the future holds.

Keywords Afro-Eurasia · Debt trap · One Belt One Road Initiative (BRI) · Global public goods · Xi Jinping

4.1 Introduction

At its inception in 2013, the "one-belt-one-road" initiative[1] was met with mixed assessments. While it was pointed out as a new development in the emerging economies, its form was vague, and at one time was even considered as nothing more than the chants of China's hegemonic policy. Such conflicting assessments continue to this day.

[1] For the One Belt One Road Initiative (OBOR), the Chinese government uses the English term "the Belt and Road Initiative" (BRI). In this chapter, BRI is used in principle instead of one belt and one road.

H. Hirakawa and F. C. Maquito, *The Dynamics of Asian Economic Development*,
https://doi.org/10.1007/978-981-97-3106-0_4

China has actually provided massive financing to countries along the BRI route, promoting gigantic infrastructure projects. However, since 2018, various issues regarding these projects have emerged, aggravated by the "U.S.-Sino Trade War" initiated by the former U.S. President Trump, as well as the COVID-19 pandemic. As the global COVID-19 outbreak deepened, the Politburo Standing Committee of the Chinese Communist Party of May 2020, President Xi Jinping raised the concept of the "dual circulation" that stressed the domestic economy.

With a population of 1.4 billion, China holds a great potential for local demand. The dual circulation strategy seeks to develop the domestic economy and link it with the international cycle to put the economy into a new development trajectory. This development path puts weight on domestic demand, and appears to dilute the significance of BRI as a foreign policy. For the Xi Jinping administration, however, BRI holds a special significance. As the world is thrown into a "new cold war" with the deepening of the hegemony rivalry with the U.S., such significance is becoming even bigger.

In the second section of this chapter, we clarify the background that led to the birth of the BRI in China, and examine the features of this initiative. In the third section, we consider the concepts underlying this initiative and its significance. In the fourth section, we deal with the various issues accompanying this initiative and its development. In the fifth section, we take stock of the prospects of BRI after looking at developments after the global outbreak of COVID-19 and the U.S.-Sino conflict. We conclude with a synthesis.

4.2 President Xi Jinping and BRI

In this section, we organize our thinking on the background of the birth of China's BRI, focusing on the birth of a new leader and China's economic development. In doing so, we clarify the features of BRI.

4.2.1 The Birth of BRI

BRI is China's global strategy set out by President Xi Jinping in line with his long-cherished wish to build a world-class state. In the same month of his appointment as Chairman in the first assembly of the 18th Central Meeting of the Communist Party in November 2020, Xi Jinping visited the National Museum with Prime Minister Li Keqiang and six Politburo standing committee permanent members. During his tour of the on-going exhibit on the "path to recovery," he publicly made the following important comment.

> Looking at the past, those who fall behind are beaten up, so it is in developing precisely that one becomes strong. ... I think that the achievement of the great revival of the Chinese people

is their greatest dream since modernization (Beijing Weekly, Japanese version November 30, 2012).

With his inauguration as President in the 12th National People's Congress, he says the following: "The realization of the Chinese people's dream of their great revival is the realization of the prosperity of the state, the revival of the race, and the happiness of the people" (People's Daily Online, Japanese version, March 17, 2013).

Six months after his inauguration as President, he visited Kazakhstan in Central Asia, and gave a lecture at the Nazarbayev University, wherein he advocated the "Silk Road Economic Belt. In the month following, he advocated the construction of the "21st Century Maritime Silk Road". By November, in the 3rd meeting of the 18th term of the Communist Party, these two Silk Road initiatives were adopted as a national strategy.

A year later in November of 2014, the APEC/CEO Summit held in Beijing became the venue for President Xi Jinping to announce BRI to the international community. In front of the political and economic leaders, he announced the establishment of a Silk Road fund with a gross value of about 40 billion.[2] [3] In line with this APEC summit, China expressed the establishment of the New Development Bank (a.k.a. BRICS Bank) in July and the Asian Infrastructure Investment Bank (AIIB) in August of the same year. The economic weekly of Japan's megabank, MUFG Bank reported that China's biggest accomplishment in the APEC Beijing summit was the crafting of a roadmap for an Asia–Pacific free trade zone and BRI.[4]

In March of the following year 2015, BRI was referred to by the Chinese National Development and Reform Commission, Ministry of Foreign Affairs, and Ministry of Commerce as the "Initiative and Actions for the Promotion of the Joint Construction of the Silk Road Belt and 21st Century Marine Silk Road". Half a year later, in the 5th Plenary Session of the 18th Central Committee of the Chinese Communist Party held in October, this was included in the 13th Five-Year Plan (2016–2020). In the National People's Congress of March 2016, the "Outline" of the above-mentioned five-year plan explicitly mentions the BRI as the basic policy of international opening. This places BRI as a key concept in the international opening of the 13th five-year plan.

From the above sequence of events, we can see that BRI was born together with the formation of the Xi Jinping establishment, and is deeply related with the "Chinese People's Dream of Revival". In the National People's Congress of March 2018, Xi Jinping revised the Constitutional article on the President's term (originally limited to two terms and ten years), laying down the foundation for a long-term reign. This

---

[2] The Nikkei Shinbun News reported President Xi Jinping's speech at the opening ceremony of the APEC/CEO Summit as follows. Together with the establishment of the silk road fund with a gross value of $40 billion to assist infrastructure and mineral resource development projects, the President announced a plan to promote investments abroad amounting to 1.25 trillion over the next decade, He said that "[we] would like to contribute to the development of the region", which was met by a resounding applause (Nikkei -J, Nov. 9, 2014).

[3] In this chapter, values are in U.S. dollars, unless otherwise specified.

[4] Tokyo Mitsubishi UFJ Bank's title of an article is "The Biggest Accomplishment of Beijing: Kicking Off the Asia-Pacific Free Trade Zone and the BRI Strategy" (MUFG Bank (China) -J, Economic Weekly, no. 229, Dec. 19, 2014).

was a big blow to the liberalism of the West, which saw it as the birth of a dictatorship in China.

However, a sober assessment would find such developments unsurprising. Viewing China's modern history as humiliating, Xi Jinping is, almost predictably, leading China, the second largest economy in the world, to become a political superpower on the eve of the nation's 100th founding anniversary. It is necessary to keep in mind his ambition, but the problem here is that China has an enormous influence on the international community, and has adopted BRI as its foreign policy. There is a need for a deeper and careful analysis of what BRI will bring about for the international community.

4.2.2 *The Development of China's Economy and BRI*

BRI was born from a concoction of various foreign and domestic causes. The following causes, among others, definitely come into play: (a) the leadership's ambitions; (b) the emergence of the Chinese economy, having deep foreign reserves, and its shift towards a capital-exporting country; (c) national security with regards to natural resources; (d) excess domestic production and new normal measures; (e) domestic disparity in income/wealth distribution and minority policy; and (f) TPP12 policies (Hirakawa -J, 2017). We already have discussed cause "a", let us now examine causes "b" to "f".

b. China's economy surpassed Japan in 2010.[5] Since August of that year, the foreign media has come to report that China's GDP exceeded that of Japan in the second half of that year (New York Times Aug. 15, 2010; Bloomberg News Aug. 16, 2010). In 2011, there were more media reports of China as the second largest in the world. BBC News reported as follows:

> China overtakes Japan as the world's second-biggest economy. Japan's economy was worth \$5.474 trillion (£3.414 trillion) at the end of 2010, figures from Tokyo have shown. China's economy was closer to \$5.8 trillion in the same period. At its current rate of growth, analysts see China replacing the U.S. as the world's top economy in about a decade (BBC News, Feb. 14, 2011).

In actuality, China's growth performance was remarkable even at the turn of the century. In 2009, it became the number one country in the world in terms of exports. In 2006, its foreign reserves exceeded one trillion, surpassing Japan's 895.3 billion and emerging as number one in the world. Figure 4.1a, b shows the foreign reserves and FDI abroad. In 2014, China's foreign reserves ballooned to 3.9 trillion. It dropped to 3.9 trillion in 2014, but even then it was still nearly thrice the 1.233 trillion of the

[5] China's GDP in U.S. dollars surpassed that of Japan in 2010. According to later revisions of the IMF data, China's GDP in 2009 was U.S.\$ 5.714 trillion, a little over Japan's U.S.\$ 5.35 trillion. In 2010, China's GDP was 6.52 trillion and Japan's was 5.4987 trillion. There should not be a problem in citing, as it is often done so, 2010 as the year that China overtook Japan.

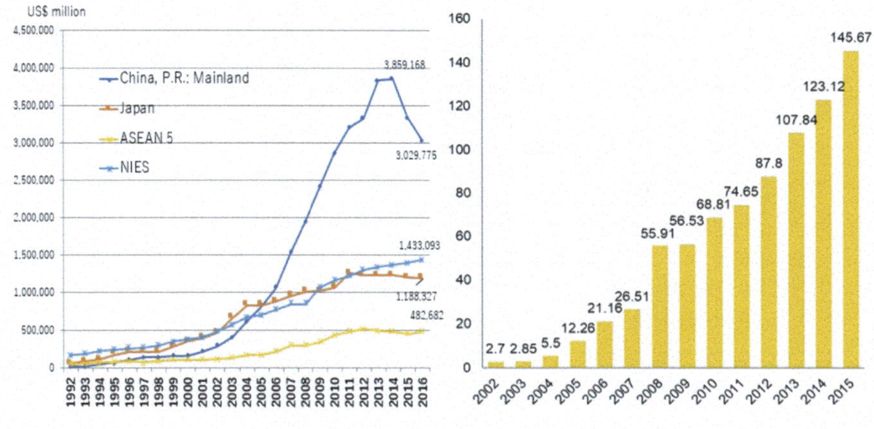

Fig. 4.1 Chinese foreign reserves and FDI. **a** Foreign reserves (million) in China, Japan, NIEs, and ASEAN 1992–2015 (right), b China's outward FDI (billion) 2002-2015 (Left) (*Source* Derived from World Bank Database). *Note* **a** Foreign reserves are a total of IMF reserves, SDRs, and gold. **b** China's outward FDI (billion) 2002–2015 (*Source* National Statistics Foreign Exchange Administration, 2014; Asahi Shimbun Newspaper -J, Sep. 22, 2016)

second placer, Japan. In 2015, its FDI surpassed that of Japan, becoming the second largest foreign investor in the world.

c. The high growth of the Chinese economy is accompanied by the rapid increase in consumption of natural resources. China's energy consumption was 2.32 billion tons, surpassing America's 100 million tons, and reached 2.97 billion tons in 2014. This accounts for 23.0% of the world share, surpassing America's share of 17.8% (Fujimori -J, 2016: 120). As shown in Fig. 4.2, China's share in world energy consumption rapidly increased at the turn of this century. By 2014, it was 57.4% for iron ore, 50.6% for coal, 56.5% for copper, and 12.4% for oil. China has no recourse but to depend heavily on natural resource imports. For a growing China, mineral resources become a matter of national security.

Figure 4.3 shows the dependence of exports to China since 2000, focusing on the developing countries. While a rise in dependence on exports to China could be seen in some high-income economies such as Hong Kong and South Korea, what is of particular interest is the remarkable rise in export dependence of developing countries such as the small countries contiguous to China, Central Asia, Africa, and Micronesia. Mongolia's share of exports to China surged during this period from less than 50% to less than 90%. North Korea and Myanmar are following suit. America has imposed economic sanctions on North Korea, which has been strikingly isolated from the international community in part due to its nuclear arms development, and Myanmar, where military rule prevails. In Central Asia, a remarkable rise in Turkmenistan could be observed. Turkmenistan completed the natural gas pipeline to China by the end of 2009, causing a surge in its exports (Yusa -J, 2013: 30–31). Uzbekistan's exports of natural gas to China have also gone into full swing (Kato, 2015: 2). The same

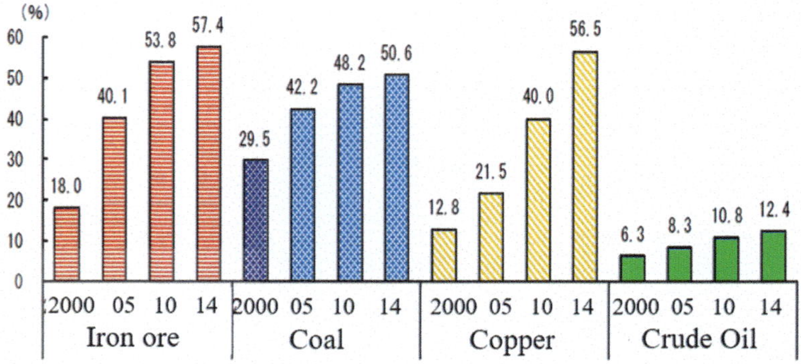

Fig. 4.2 China's share in world resource consumption 2000, 2005, 2010, 2014 (*Source* Cabinet Office, Japan -J, 2015a, : Fig. 1-1-17, 2015b)

goes for various African countries. From 1998 to 2008, the Economic Community of Central African States, such as Angola and Congo, increased their trade share with China from 4 to 25% (Schiere & Rugamba, 2011: 11). In 2006, 80% of the exports to China from various Sub-Saharan countries was oil. China's oil imports from various Sub-Saharan countries reached 30% of total oil imports. From African countries, China imports 80% of its cobalt, and 40% of its magnesium. Angola, Congo, Kenya, Sudan, and South Africa are among the major mineral exporting countries (Foster et al., 2006: 6). Behind the dramatic rise of mineral resource-rich Sierra Leone in export dependence on China is the entry of Chinese state-owned enterprises in 2011[6] (Epoch Times Japan, May 22, 2021).

In line with BRI, China undertook a series of acquisitions of companies or operating rights such as the ports of Zeebrugge (Belgium), Djibouti, Hambantota (Sri Lanka), Khalifa (UAE), Gwadar (Pakistan), and Pizzeria (Greece) (Nikkei -J Feb. 25, 2018), laying the foundations for a strong nautical nation. This is easily understood given the role of natural resources in the context of national security. In the same vein, it would not be folly to say that the aggressive incursion of China in the South China Sea,[7] and the construction of the China-Pakistan Economic Circuit (CPEC) is deeply related to national security.

d. BRI functions even as a countermeasure for excess domestic production. Recall that in September of 2008, the American investment bank, Lehman Brothers, went bankrupt in the wake of the subprime crisis in the U.S., triggering a world financial crisis. Until 2010, China was then maintaining an annual growth rate of 10% in real terms for 30 years since its opening up reforms. This has nose dived. For its 12th Development Plan (2011–2015), the real growth rate is 7.9%.

---

[6] With the outbreak of Ebola in this country and the collapse of steel prices, the value of exports to China dropped dramatically, leading to the suspension, the following year, of the airport construction funded by China (CNN Oct. 12, 2018 https://www.cnn.co.jp/business/35126924.html).

[7] Also referred to as the West Philippine Sea in the Philippines.

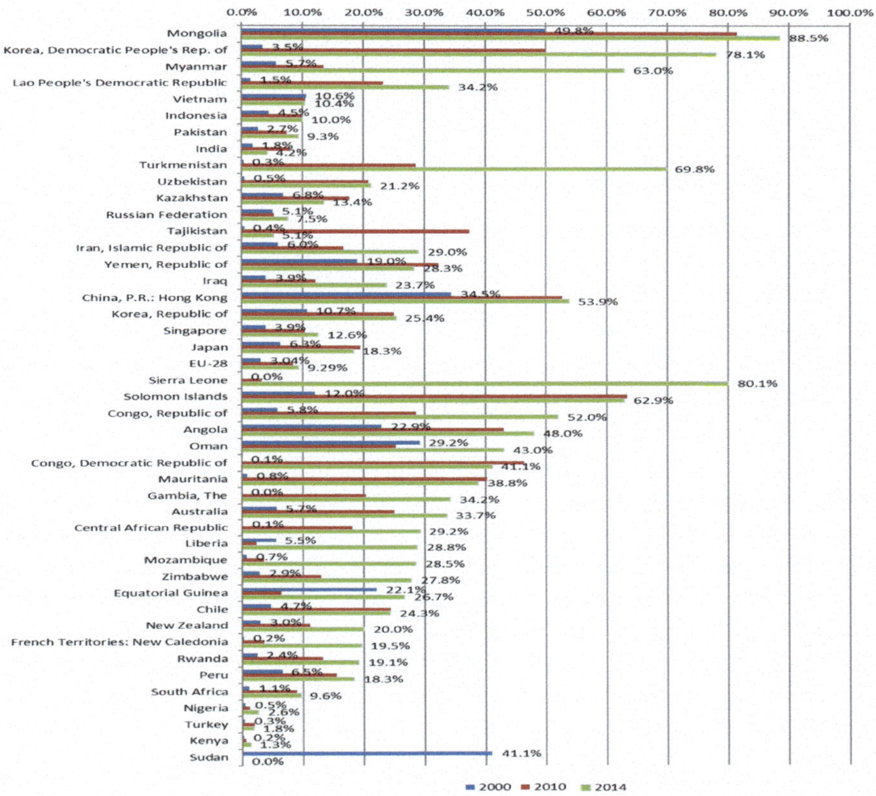

Fig. 4.3 Changes in dependence on exports to China, mainly of developing countries 2000, 2010, 2014 (*Source* Made by author. Original data: IMF Direction of Trade Statistics. And EU28 from the UN Comtrade Database). *Note* Since data for Sudan for 2000 could not be acquired, its bar was placed at the lowest position

At the onset of the financial crisis in November of the same year, China undertook a massive domestic expansionary policy, which amounted to an investment of four trillion yuan (13% of GDP) into various urban and rural infrastructure sectors such as railroads, roads, airports, and sanitation, as well as into energy conservation and environmental protection, to sustain its economic growth. This measure dramatically raised the standing of China in the international community, which saw China's efforts as preventing a global recession. This four trillion-yuan expansionary policy, however, gave birth to an excessive investment boom that eventually led to the problem of overproduction in manufacturing, especially in the infrastructure sectors. The capital investment utilization rate of China's manufacturing sector dropped from 79.4% in 2007 to 70.8% in 2013 and 71.0% in 2014. Infrastructure-related sectors suffered more severe drops in capital investment utilization rates. From 2007 to 2014, the utilization rate dropped from 81.2 to 66.1% for steel and iron processing, from

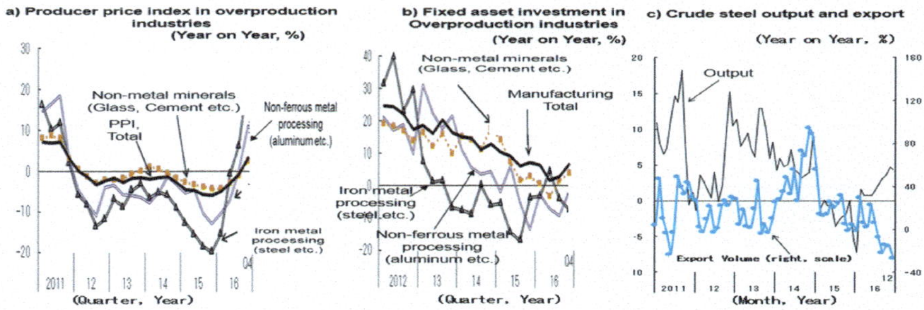

Fig. 4.4 Excess production and export after the 4 trillion-yuan counter to the Lehman Shock 2015a, 2015b (*Source* Cabinet Office, Japan -J, 2015a, 2015b: 28–29). *Note* The figure has been redrawn by adding new data from the fourth quarter of 2015 to 2016

9.7 to 66.8% for non-metal minerals such as aluminum, glass, and cement, and from 78.9 to 73.1% for transportation (Cabinet Office -J, 2015a, 2015b: 28).

Figure 4.4a–c show from 2011 to 2015, respectively, the producer price index in overproduction industries, fixed assets in overproduction industries, and crude steel output and export. For the whole manufacturing sector, a downward trend in producer price, investment, and production could be clearly seen. On the other hand, crude steel exports are prominently stable. Such export pressure, due to a domestic clamor for markets, has sparked trouble with surrounding countries that are subjected to dumping and other unfair trade practices.

e. Policies to address the domestic disparity in income/wealth distribution are also policies to address the minority issue. The policy of reform and opening up started from the opening up of the coastal area, leaving behind the development of the inner and Western regions, where most minority groups are. It could be said that the remedy of the resulting regional disparities has an element of also dealing with the independence issue of minorities. Heilongjiang Province, Inner Mongolia Autonomous Region, Xinjiang Uyghur Autonomous Region, Tibet Autonomous Region, and Yunnan Province are actually among those connected to the economic circuit of BRI.
f. There is the aspect of a TPP12 countermeasure. In November 2009, as America was recovering from the global financial crisis of 2008, then American President Obama initiated negotiations aiming to tie up the TPP, which was based on the P4 Agreement (Trans-Pacific Strategic Economic Partnership Agreement) of Singapore, New Zealand, Cile, and Brunei. The negotiations were joined that year by Australia and Peru, with Vietnam as an observer. In October of the following year 2010, Vietnam and Malaysia became formal members. Canada and Mexico joined in November 2012, while Japan joined in July 2012, forming a total of 12 negotiating countries of the TPP12. Negotiations reached a general agreement in the ministerial meeting held in Atlanta, America in October 2015. The formal signing of the TPP agreement was held in Auckland, New Zealand in February 2016. In January 2017, however, America withdrew from the TPP12. For the

newly inaugurated President Xi Jinping, a policy to counter the TPP12 was a very important political issue.[8]

America's Obama administration pushed the TPP12 with the goal of helping America's economic growth. But this was not the only goal. America's share then in the total GDP of TPP members excluding Japan, was 73%. Even including Japan, this share remained extremely high at 58%. This means that the effect on America's trade expansion due to the formation of TPP is limited (Hirakawa, 2013: 224). The real reason behind America's TPP push is the establishment of trade rules in the Asia Pacific given the disconcerting rise of China. Having reached a general agreement, President Obama stated in an emergency press conference at the White House.

> We can't let countries like China write the rules of the global economy. We should write those rules, opening new markets to American products while setting high standards for protecting workers and preserving our environment (Obama, 2015).

In the wake of this agreement, in a commentary article of one of the editors of the Nikkei Newspaper, Yasuhiko Ota, wrote as follows:

> The focus of the negotiations, heated up by conflicts and battles, is not simply limited to the essence of trade agreements. While market liberalization is needed to increase the trade of goods, the real heart of the Trans-Pacific Partnership (TPP) is the setting of unprecedentedly ambitious international rules. Behind this is the emergence of China, which has become a superpower deploying military forces into the South China Sea and state-owned "Gulliver" firms making their presence felt. China's arbitrary decisions and muscle-flexing faintly draw an unstable future landscape. Japan's defeat in the Indonesian bullet train deal would be symbolic of this (Nikkei -J, Oct. 6, 2015).

Both the Japan-U.S. statement accompanying the TPP agreement and the commentary confirm that the TPP was a setting of trade rules aware of China. Negotiations for the Asia Pacific FTA started in 2013 with the Regional Comprehensive Economic Partnership (RCEP) and the Free Trade Agreement of the Asia Pacific (FTAAP), both of which did not reach an agreement. As such, an early conclusion of the TPP would likely be the "de facto global standard", with the TPP12 applying pressure on China.

According to Yang Dongliang, there were, at that time, four patterns of response by China to the TPP. The biggest response was an America-directed conspiracy theoretical interpretation. The other forms of response were membership pessimism, cooperation counterattack, and reform deepening. Membership pessimism refers to a sense of inadequacy regarding China's economic level for membership, and being isolated. On the contrary, China already had a huge economy, and could develop through cooperation with various countries, such as BRICs, which were not members of TPP. This is the essence of cooperation counterattack. Lastly, reform deepening

[8] Simultaneous to his inauguration in January 2017, President Trump withdrew the U.S. from TPP12. Negotiations continued, without America, over the TPP11 framework (Comprehensive and Progressive Agreement for Trans-Pacific Partnership, or CPTPP), which reached a general agreement in November 2017, was signed in March 2018, and came into force in December of the same year.

was the position of treating TPP as a form of foreign pressure, and using this as a leverage to promote domestic reforms (Yang, 2016).

We could venture "the internationalization of the yuan" as one more factor behind this initiative, although its importance at the outset was considered to be small.

As it would be true for any country, any grandiose initiative would be a matter of national interest. It could be said that BRI emerged from the interplay of the abovementioned domestic and international factors.

4.2.3 The Two Aspects of BRI: Between Global Public Goods and Hegemony

While enormous, BRI is a vague concept, which a research of the European Parliamentary Research Service (EPRS) puts as one that links Europe and China, but remains a "moving concept" (Grieger, 2016). A China researcher in Japan is concerned with a move to explore a business opportunity, and warn against being manipulated by what seems to be akin to a horoscope (Takahara -J, 2018, 2021). Another China researcher writes that the folklore of 65 countries tentatively along the BRI route does not have a sound basis or consistency, and suffers from an all-encompassing policy package (Ito, 2018: 18–19). Indeed, in May 2017, the "twenty-first century nautical silkroad" was extended to include Latin America. Moreover, the "North Pole Policy White Paper" published in January 2018, incorporates into the initiative the North Polar sea route, calling it the "Ice Silk Road".

Our interest, however, would be on the indication that BRI provides a "global public goods". In his inaugural speech, President Xi Jinping mentioned that China will be providing a "public goods" to the Asia Pacific. In a press conference in March 2016, Foreign Minister Wang Yi highlighted that more than 70 countries and institutions have expressed their cooperation with the BRI, and that more than 30 countries have already concluded agreements, while referring to the belt and road as a global public goods. In the Presidential address in the "Belt and Road" International Cooperation Summit Forum of May 2017, the "One-Belt-One-Road" was again referred to as a global public goods, while emphasizing free trade (East Asia Forum May 15, 2017). In an international symposium in December 2018, Foreign Minister Wang Yi mentioned that BRI has now become the most popular global public goods, while referring to the Presidential inaugural speech that claimed the forming of cooperative ties with more than 50 countries and institutions, and more than 140 treaties (Wang, 2018). BRI as global public goods caught the interest of Masahiro Kawai, former head of the ADB Research Institute, who was very hopeful about this possibility (Kawai -J, 2016; Kawai, 2017).

Several concerns of the Chinese government could also be seen. The Chinese terminology of "Belt and Road Initiative" is "One Belt One Road" (OBOR). The direct translation of the Chinese terminology is feared to lead to misunderstandings.

OBOR tends to emphasize "one," and may convey a message of competition. Moreover, in order to avoid the criticism of being a China-centered institution-building strategy, the word "initiative" was chosen to be added (Una, 2016).

BRI is an international development cooperation initiative, which as seen in the previous section, strongly reflects China's domestic problems. While it forms part of domestic policy, it is also foreign policy. As would be true of any country, its foreign policy would more or less be a matter of national interest. Foreign policy meant to deal with domestic issues would ordinarily not be the object of criticism. The problem is that today China and its projects are gigantic in scale. As such, these projects have both hegemonic and public goods aspects.

4.3 The Development Concept of the "Belt and Road" Initiative

In this section, we consider the "one belt one road" or the "Belt and Road" development concept of China. While aiming to push transportation, energy, communication infrastructures and connectivity, the concept is heavily tinged with the development experience of East Asia. The development of the East Asian economy in the second half the twentieth century follows a series starting with Japan's Asia policy, followed by the NIEs, ASEAN, ASEAN latecomers, and then China. This experience is reflected in China's BRI.

4.3.1 The "Belt and Road" Initiative as a China-Led International Cooperation Initiative

In 2015, the "Vision and Actions on Jointly Building Silk Road Economic Belt and 21st-Century Maritime Silk Road" of the Foreign and Commercial Departments of the China National Development and Reform Commission, in line with the principle of joint construction, upholds the silk road spirit (peace and cooperation, openness and comprehensiveness, mutual learning and benefit) and the five principles based on the United Nations Charter (Mutual respect for each other's territorial integrity and sovereignty, Mutual non-aggression, Mutual non-interference in each other's internal affairs, Equality and mutual benefit, Peaceful coexistence). This framework runs through the continents of Asia, Europe, and Africa, and links the East Asian economic region with the European economic region, and is considered to promote the huge potential for economic development of many countries. "One belt" connects: China-Central Asia-Russia-Europe (Baltic Sea); China-Central Asia-West Asia-Persian Bay-Mediterranean Sea; and the China-Southeast Asia-South Asia-Indian Ocean. "One road" actually consists of two routes: one is formed by the Chinese coastal area-South China Sea-Indian Ocean-Europe; and the other is formed by the Chinese

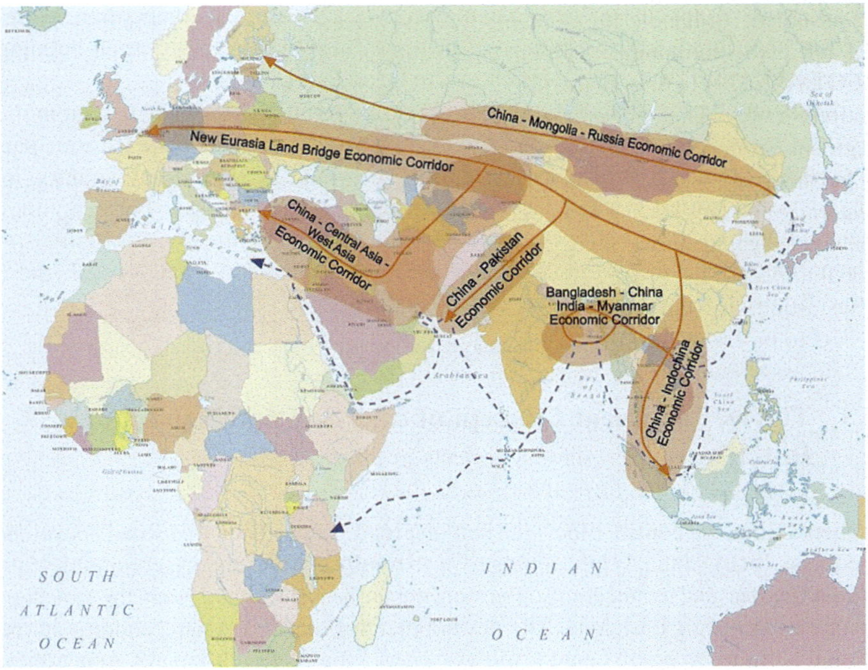

Fig. 4.5 The BRI map (*Source* Winter, 2016)

coastal area-South China Sea-South Pacific Ocean. On land, there is the construction Eurasian land bridge and the development of the economic circuits consisting of: China-Mongolia-Russia; China-Central Asia-West Asia; China-Indochina; sea-connected China-Pakistan; and Bangladesh-China-India-Myanmar (NDRC et al. 2015, Winter 2016, Fig. 4.5).

The economic circuits here also refer to environmental issues, as well as raise the connectivity through such cooperation platforms such as the establishment of economic trade and manufacturing zones, and the construction of transportation and energy infrastructure (oil and gas pipelines), and fiber cable communications networks.

With regards to developmental financing, the Asia Infrastructure and Investment Bank (AIIB) and the BRICS Bank (New Development Bank), and even the Silk Road fund, which was established by China on its own in December 2014, are assumed[9] to handle this matter. Cooperation mechanisms are not only bilateral but also multilateral, and includes the Shanghai Cooperation Organization (SCO), ASEAN+1, Asia Pacific Economic Cooperation (APEC), China-Gulf Cooperation Strategic Dialogue, Greater Mekong Subregion (GMS), and the Central Asia Regional Economic Cooperation (CAREC) (NDRC et al., 2015).

Furthermore, the dominant part of the construction projects actually are conducted bilaterally and lack transparency on such things as funding conditions. As such, one could not say that there is no discrepancy between stated principles and realities. The global impact of the projects proposed by China was extremely large. A Bloomberg News article in August 2016 reported that an IMF economist estimated the scale of BRI to be 1.4 trillion dollars, which would be 12 times the Marshall Plan of the U.S. to assist the recovery of Europe after the Second World War, and about 9% of China's GDP (Curra, 2016). An article of the Guardian in 2017 stated that China was planning to provide 150 billion dollars annually to the BRI project (Phillips, 2017). Nomura Holdings, in a 2018 report, estimated an annual investment of 150 billion dollars over ten years, or a gross total of 1.5 trillion dollars for the infrastructure projects China is already conducting in 80 countries along the BRI circuit (Nomura Holdings, 2018).

In a speech in Astana, Kazakhstan, the Deputy Chief Economist of CCIEE, Xu Hongcai states that amidst the global spread of protectionism and populism after the global financial crisis, "BRI is the new engine that will promote the sustainable development of the global economy", and a global public goods (Xu, 2017).

Incidentally, China formally denies the calling of BRI as a Marshall Plan. Beyond this issue of terms, the possibility cannot be denied that BRI is an international project that rivals or surpasses the Marshall Plan. After the initiative was hammered out, there was a dramatic expansion in the foreign projects of China.

4.3.2 BRI and East Asian Development Experience

BRI is an international development cooperation led by China, but it aims, among others, for connectivity through the construction of transportation, economic and trade manufacturing parks, and energy infrastructures.

This is remarkable not only in terms of creating an international shipping route with the construction, jointly with countries along the BRI circuit, of infrastructure for steel, expressways, ports, communications and the like. It is remarkable also in terms of promoting the overseas deployment of Chinese firms, as well as the

[9] In the Vision and Action Initiative announced by China National Development and Reform Commission-Department of Foreign Affairs-Department of Commerce in March 2015, the AIIB was also at its conception phase. AIIB was established in December 2015, became operational in July 2017, and as of July 2021 has 103 member countries. The establishment of the New Development Bank was agreed upon by the BRICS5 countries in July 2014 and was inaugurated in July 2015. The Silk Road Fund was established in December 2014 through a 40 billion dollar funding from the State Administration of Foreign Exchange and the Chinese Export-Import Bank.

internationalization of China's industries, through economic industrial parks that become key platforms in core cities along the circuit. In May 2015, Prime Minister Li Keqiang announced the "Guiding Opinions of the State Council on Promoting International Cooperation in Industrial Capacity and Equipment Manufacturing" (State Council, PRC -Chinese, 2015), which specifies the "favorable conditions for (Chinese) firms to Go Global". "International cooperation in industrial capacity" is an initiative of Chinese firms entering into other countries, especially those along the BRI circuit, and jointly developing markets. The industries that are of special interest for overseas deployment are steel, non-steel metals, construction materials, railroads, electricity, chemical, fiber, automotive, communications, construction equipment, aviation, shipping, and offshore construction (State Council, PRC -Chinese, 2015).

In December of the same year, "Some Opinions for the Speeding Up of the FTA Strategy Implementation" was also issued. According to the late Japanese China researcher, N. Ehara, this could be called it the "bible of China's FTA strategy", and indicates the level of China's conviction in its formation of free trade economic zones (Ehara -J, 2016). In short, developed countries such as Europe could also receive "international cooperation", and create BRI economic zones.

Incidentally, BRI's development approach deeply reflects the East Asian development experience. The overseas economic activities of China "is often considered as similar to the trade-investment-assistance trinity or the trade-investment-assistance-international cooperation quaternity" (Suehiro -J, 2018: 107).[10] Such policies perfectly match BRI. At the same time, this form fits Japan's post-war ODA.[11] From the end of the 1970s up to the 1980s, Japan emerged as an ODA global power, which had a comprehensive economic cooperation policy based on the trinity of foreign aid, direct investment and imports (METI -J, 1989: 2). Both Japanese and Chinese researchers admit to the similarity of the policy of both countries (Ohno -J, 2012; Wang -J, 2012). The report of the project on the foreign aid to China by Japan Institute of International Affairs reads as follows.

> There is a growing awareness that the development plan that China is putting into practice, wherein there is a connection among trade, investment, and aid, as well as an emphasis on self-reliance, is based on Japan, which initiated its assistance of Asian developing countries, while receiving aid from Europe and the U.S., as well as international institutions, after the war. Moreover, there have also been indications that this also overlaps with the (development) aid philosophy to South Korea, which has the dual experience of being an aid recipient as well as provider (Ohno -J, 2012: 10).

Japan's economic cooperation consists not so much of grants but of yen loans. Moreover, it is directed towards infrastructure construction. In the 1980s, this type of foreign aid was strongly criticized as tied loan and "commercialism" by European and American countries. In the 1990s, Japan disposed of its tied loan, but at the

---

[10] Suehiro himself finds that "the mutual relationships are not really clear when looking at the four activities across regions", so "we should be cautious when looking at China's overseas activities only from the perspective of a quaternity" (Suehiro -J, 2018: 107).

[11] The Chinese researcher, Ping Wang acknowledges the similarities between the foreign aid of China and Japan (Wang, 2012: 88–89).

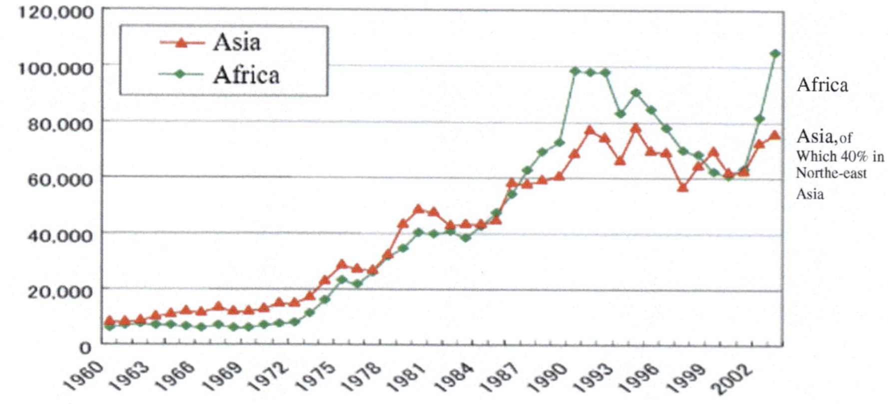

Fig. 4.6 Changes in ODA to Asia-Africa 1960–2002 (*Source* Ministry of Economy, Trade, and Industry 2005). *Note* The definition of Asia and Africa is based on the classification of OECD Development Assistance Committee

same time stressed the "self-help efforts" of the recipient countries. As shown in Fig. 4.6, the ODA amounts received by Asia and Africa are not so different. However, Asia developed in an entirely different way from Africa. In Asia the debtor country shoulders the obligation to repay. As such, the funds are used effectively, bringing about growth in Asia. This philosophy of self help efforts will be discussed in more detail in Chap. 5.

BRI is also being financed through loans for infrastructure construction. The scale of financing is very much different from China, but the form is very similar to it.

The development experiences of NIEs and China are being capitalized in BRI. In its early stage of industrialization, NIES set up export processing zones, and promoted an export-led industrialization policy. After the opening up reforms, China has set up special economic zones along the coastal area, which eventually spread throughout the country. The establishment of export processing zones is considered to be a factor in the successful economic development of East Asia (ADB, 2015; UNCTAD, 2015, 2019). Industrial Parks are reminiscent of that experience.[12]

That is to say, BRI is very close to the development framework of East Asia. It could be said to be an overseas economic cooperation policy that was actively promoted. This may be called an initiative that marks a new stage in the development of East Asia.

---

[12] Note that today's criticized large exodus of Chinese laborers (overseas labor cooperation) is reminiscent of the history of overseas Chinese. Even if the objective of labor exports after the opening up reforms was foreign exchange procurement, today's Chinese exodus has many problems. In actuality, beginning this century, China has been building the legal groundwork for the administration of overseas workers (Ohashi -J, 2012). As of April 2020, the overseas labor cooperation has deployed 787,000 laborers (China Internet Information Center -J, Oct. 5, 2020).

4.4 The Deployment of BRI and Countries Along the Line

With the launching of BRI, China became more active in its overseas deployment. As expectations on the initiative were raised, many problems eventually surfaced. In this section, we summarize the overseas investments of China up to the end of the 2010's, and then consider the various issues that appeared until 2020.

4.4.1 BRI and the Response of the Countries Along the Line

The initiative for the Silk Road Economic Belt started from Xi Jinping's speech at Nazarbayev University of Kazakhstan in Central Asia. Since their independence from the USSR, Central Asian countries have become the object of rivalry between Russia and China. In 1996, China inaugurated the "Shanghai Five", together with Kazakhstan, Kyrgyzstan, Russia, and Tajikistan, and the Shanghai Cooperation Organization (SCO) in 2001 with the joining of Uzbekistan. In response to this, Russian President Putin inaugurated the tariff alliance with Belarus and Kazakhstan in 2010, and proposed the Eurasia Economic Union (EEU) in 2011. The EEU talks were concluded in May 2014. The EEU was inaugurated in January of the following year, with the joining of Armenia, and then Kyrgyz, forming a five-country alliance. Amidst this rivalry, China launched the cooperation initiative of "one belt", backed by its economic might (Kaczmarski, 2015).

BRI and Central Asia. The focus here has been on the rivalry between China and Russia. A closer look, however, suggests quite the opposite". Russia and China have avoided direct confrontation, and could be seen to reconcile their initiatives (Kaczmarski, 2015). As China gains economic strength, Russia has tilted towards strengthening connections with China. Behind this is the international isolation of Russia due to the Ukrainian crisis in the beginning of 2014 (Gabuev, 2016). Central Asian countries have countermeasures for local terrorist organizations and anti-government forces and will choose a balancing diplomacy between Russia and China.

According to the Xinhua News Agency, at the 7th BRICs Summit Meeting and the 15th SCO Summit Meetings held jointly in May 2015 in Ufa, Russia, there was agreement on China's constructive role, as well as on the further promotion of strategic mutual trust with China and related countries (Xinhua News Agency, 2015). China pushes the silk road economic belt, Russia the route straddling the Euro-Asian route, and Mongolia the "prairie road" project, forming the China-Russia-Mongolia economic circuit.

South Asia and BRI. In the SCO Summit Meeting of 2015, India and Pakistan were promoted to formal members, Belarus to observer from dialogue country, Azerbaijan, Armenia, Cambodia, and Nepal to new dialogue countries (Puts, 2015). SCO was showing an expansionary tendency towards South Asia. India and Pakistan's joining the alliance had a great significance.

In April 2014, China signed up on the China-Pakistan Economic Circuit (CPEC), which includes the development of the Gwadar new port of Pakistan and the Arabian Sea, the express way, railroad, and energy from Gwadar to the Xinjiang Uyghur Autonomous Region, forming the flagship projects of the development push. Pakistan gave China a 43-year lease of the Gwadar port, while China provided 1.65 billion dollar funding for the construction of a hydroelectric plant, as the first financed project of CPEC. This is considered to have doubled the electricity generation of Pakistan.

CPEC, however, aroused the national security concerns of neighboring India. Ultimately, India joins the BRICS bank, but continues to take an ambiguous position without swallowing the BRI proposal. In June 2020, a confrontation occurred, after 45 years, with Chinese and Indian armies near the border, killing at least 20 Indian soldiers. Since then, the relationship has been deteriorating. Actually, India is a major promoter of the economic integration project, from South Asia to Central Asia, bypassing Pakistan. There is a plan for a trade shipping circuit to connect the expressway between Afghanistan and Zaranj-Delaram (National Road 606) with the Chabahar (Iran)-Afghanistan border through an expressway. The former was completed in 2009 by India, while the latter in 2016 by Iran. India provided financing for the construction of the Chabahar port. This infrastructure development plan is expected not only to have economic effects on the countries involved, but also political effects as measures against Afghanistan's Taliban and anti-government organizations. The same is true for the International North–South Transit Corridor (INSTC) established in 2000 and consisting of shipping-railroad-road multi-modal links. INSTC was initiated by India, Iran, and Russia, thereafter joined by Turkey and other Central Asian countries. It is an initiative to set up transportation and shipping linking St. Petersburg and Northern Europe passing through the Indian Ocean-Persian Gulf-Iran, the Caspian Sea and then to Russia (Jha, 2017). In 2018, India acceded to the Ashgabat Agreement inaugurated in April 2016 by several countries, including Kazakhstan, Uzbekistan, Turkmenistan, and Iran, with Pakistan acceding in October of the same year.

A BRI project wherein India and China are directly involved is the Bangladesh-China-India-Myanmar Economic Corridor (BCIM-EC). This initiative is an infrastructure and trading facility construction plan costing a total of 22 billion dollars, and will connect India's Calcutta with China's Kunming by air, land, and water. Conceptualized in the 1990s, the BCIM-IC has become a BRI connector project, with 4 countries signing up in December 2013. While India's development of the Calcutta port and the liberation of the economic potential of the northeastern provinces are significant in themselves, China gains one more route that bypasses the Malacca Strait.

BRI and Middle Eastern Europe. In the 17th EU-China Summit Meeting in 2015, the EU was not able to prepare a common policy towards the entry of China into Europe. Since adopting the European Neighborhood Policy (ENP) in 2003, the EU has been urging countries contiguous to EU allied countries to adopt political and fiscal reforms that would spread democracy. As the surrounding environment changed, however, the EU has "shifted from the promotion of democracy to the strengthening of stability through economic development", in an acceptance of the linking up with China. This is because China will aggressively adopt an expansionary policy of trade and investment towards EU's neighboring countries.

Since 2012, China has been regularly holding summit meetings of the Central/ Eastern Europe (CEE) consisting of 16 countries[13] (CEE 16+1 Framework) to promote cooperation in trade, investment, and finance. In the 4th China-CEE summit meeting held in November 2015, an agreement was reached on the priority areas for 2015 to 2020, with the promise of infrastructure construction and financial cooperation of Chinese state-owned enterprises. This was an alignment of the development strategies of various CEE countries and BRI (Jakóbowski et al., 2015). These developments caused the EU to be gravely concerned about what may be China's move to form, within the EU, a China-friendly faction and to create division, given that 11 of the CEE16 countries are EU member countries. In the light of this, the 17th EU-China summit meeting of 2015, which celebrated the 40th anniversary of EU-China diplomatic relations, confirmed the importance of an EU-China comprehensive strategic partnership, and mutually acknowledged each other's flagship projects, namely the European investment plan and BRI, and expressed the building of a cooperative relationship (Verlare & Putten, 2015).

Looking back to March 2015, prior to the EU-China summit meeting, the UK's joining the Asia Infrastructure Investment Bank (AIIB) triggered an avalanche with Germany, France, and Italy also joining. On the other hand, China, in July 2015, revealed its investment of several billions in euros to the new infrastructure investment fund of 300 billion euros that the EU was pushing. In the summit meeting of July 2016, it decided to invest two billion euros. Ultimately, the EU had no other choice but to connect with China's BRI so as to obtain the stability of the EU and the neighboring countries, as well as the investment opportunities presented.

At least the relationship between the EU and China in the 2010s was one where China continued its diplomatic offensive through the strengthening of relations with ECC countries. The relationship with the UK was particularly strong. Starting from around 2012, the UK was seeking to establish an offshore market for the yuan in London's City, and in July 2014 was able to establish a settlement exchange for yuan. This was followed by its decision to join the establishment of the AIIB in March 2015. This became the breakthrough for Europe's advanced countries to join the AIIB. This choice led to the realization of Xi Jinping's official visit to the UK in October of the same year. During Xi's UK visit an investment package worth 40 billion pounds, including a 30% equity investment of a state-owned enterprise in the UK's new nuclear power facility, was agreed upon.[14]

[13] The participating countries of CEE16 are: Albania, Bosnia & Herzegovina, Bulgaria, Croatia, the Czech Republic, Estonia, Hungary, Macedonia, Montenegro, Latvia, Lithuania, Poland, Romania, Serbia, Skivajua and Slovenia. Greece joined in 2019 to form the CEE17+1. The 9th Summit Meeting was scheduled for April 2020 but was canceled due to COVID-19.

[14] A press release states that the UK government is considering excluding Chinese firms from all of their country's electricity projects (Newsweek -J, July 27, 2021).

From 2015, the Anglo-Sino Trading Association and Tsinghua University issued the "Sino-Anglo BRI Case Study Research Report", which covers the joint projects with third countries in infrastructure, energy development, and logistics. It is an experiment in productivity cooperation.

Chinese companies use English companies as platforms for pushing projects in third-country markets. English companies, hence, provide the specialist knowledge and services to Chinese firms, which are lacking in international experience. In the 2016 report, examples of this include the consulting services provided to Chinese companies engaged in Bangladesh power plant and river tunnel construction (China-Britain Business Council, 2016).

BRI and Africa. Trading between Africa and China began to grow in the 1990s, and rapidly expanded at the turn of the century. The value of trade between sub-Saharan Africa and China rose by more than a hundred times during the 20-year period from 1990 to 2010. In particular, the export dependence of Africa on China dramatically increased. China rapidly increased its resource imports from various African countries, and attempted strategic investments in various enterprises. In 2006, China formulated a plan to set up 50 overseas economic and trade cooperation zones. By 2010, there were 19 such zones certified by the Chinese Ministry of Commerce, five of which were in Sub-Saharan Africa: Ethiopia, Mauritius, Nigeria (2 zones), and Zambia.。In North Africa, zones were established in Algeria and Egypt (Brautigam et al., 2010). Such a policy is inscribed in BRI.

As part of the economic cooperation framework with Africa in 2000, China has institutionalized the ministerial meetings of the Forum on China-Africa Cooperation (FOCAC), which is held every three years. A summit meeting was also held in the 3rd ministerial meeting of November 2006 in Beijing, and the 6th ministerial meeting in December 2015, during which the Beijing declaration and the Johannesburg declaration, respectively, were announced. In 2018, the 7th FOCAC became the Beijing summit meeting, where the Beijing Declaration and Beijing Action Plan (2019–2021) were announced. This was participated by 53 countries comprising the African region. As BRI is China's national strategy, it is but natural that the FOCAC summit meeting accepts this initiative. In the Johannesburg declaration, we find the African countries welcoming this initiative, and a confirmation of both sides engaging in joint development.

This is an expression of "strengthening cooperation in infrastructure projects including, but not limited to, railways, highways, regional aviation, power, water supply, information and communication, airport and ports, as well as human resource development cooperation and capacity building", through the establishment of Special Economic Zones (SEZs) (Johannesburg Summit, 2015). The Johannesburg action plan clearly states that, in order to construct the infrastructure needed for Africa's independence and sustainable development, "investment expansion is a priority through various means such as Public–Private-Partnership (PPP) between Chinese firms and financial institutions, and Build-Operate-Transfer (BOT), in support of African countries and flagship projects (Johannesburg Action Plan: 2016–2018, Section 3.3 Infrastructure Development). Moreover, President Xi promised that by the end of 2014, the total investment by more than 3,100 firms would amount to 101.0 billion dollars, and the total assistance package would amount to 60 billion dollars, including grants and non-interest loans in the three-year span up to 2018 of five billion dollars, priority financing and trade credits of 35 billion dollars, and an additional capital to the China-Africa development fund of five billion dollars.

BRI and Southeast Asia. ASEAN members such as Vietnam, the Philippines, and Malaysia are embroiled in conflict with China regarding the territorial rights to the South China Sea, but generally were receptive to BRI. The establishment of the AIIB was welcomed even from the conceptualization stage. Based on a 2009 report by the Asian Development Bank (ADB), Asia's demand for infrastructure from 2010 to 2020 was estimated to be about eight trillion dollars (730 billion dollars per year) (ADB, 2009). In addition, this addressed the dissatisfaction of developing countries over the terms of financing of international financial institutions such as the World Bank. All of the member countries joined the establishment of the AIIB, and the BRI International Cooperation Summit Forum held in May 2017. The late Surin, former Secretary General of ASEAN, in his last Japanese media interview at the end of 2017, clearly responded that BRI matches the situation of ASEAN countries in need of infrastructure financing, and is "favorably received by ASEAN." Singapore's Kishore Mahbubani, Dean of the Lee Kuan Yew School of Public Policy, stated that "most of the Asian countries would surely be quite interested in doing it together' under the condition that China avoids blatantly pursuing its national interest (Nikkei -J Dec. 5, 2017).

As was announced in the "one road' initiative by President Xi in the Indonesian Congress, for China, Southeast Asia is in a strategically important position. The winning of the bidding for Indonesia's Jakarta-Bandung high-speed railroad construction by a Chinese firm is also deeply related to the one road initiative. The reason for winning the bidding is said to be the fact that no debt guarantee was sought from the Indonesian government for China's massive infrastructure construction financing. A fact that was not anticipated by the Japanese companies bidding for the project. Considering that Japanese companies have been cooperating with construction plans, the decision to award to a Chinese firm left a very bitter aftertaste.

In 2016, Malaysia's Najib administration signed into a BRI project worth 34 billion dollars for China's financing of the construction of railways and pipelines (Diamond Online -J, Jan. 10, 2019). The construction of the Eastern Coastal Railway was one such project, with an initial construction cost reaching 81 billion ringgit ($19.7 billion) (Bloomberg News, Jan. 8, 2019). In May 2018, then Prime Minister Najib's ruling coalition as beaten by the opposition coalition led by former Prime Minister Mahathir, leading to a review by the new administration.[15]

[15] Upon taking power, Prime Minister Mahathir reviewed former Prime Minister Najib's massively debt-based plan, and exposed the rampant corruption problem of Najib himself. At this time, one end of the relation of the Najib bribery incident with the Chinese funding for the railroad and pipeline construction projects was revealed (WSJ, Jan. 8, 2019).

Accompanying the ASEAN region's economic development is an enormous demand for infrastructure. This region is considered as an important destination for overseas deployment in the wake of China's BRI.

4.4.2 BRI Project Progress and Rising Criticism

Entering this century, China leveraged BRI to further develop its growing economy. China's promise of investment and construction to BRI-affiliated countries, between 2014 and 2018 rose to 588.9 billion dollars, 81% of which went to the following four sectors: construction with 38%, shipping with 27%, real estate with 10%, and mining with 6% (He, 2019: 5).

Based on the estimate of the World Trade Organization, China's construction exports for 12 years since 2005 grew 7% annually. The export value for 2017 grew to U.S.$ 188 billion, which was about a third or 37.3% of the world's total construction export value (WTO, 2019: 27). As shown in Fig. 4.7, China's export overwhelming growth in 2017 was 12 times that in 2005, twice that of advanced countries, and nearly four times that of other developing countries. Exports were going to Africa and other developing regions, and the investments were pouring into the construction of bridges, ports, roads, and railways. Moreover, we get the following indication from the WTO regarding the significance of the exports to the construction sector.

> The construction sector is increasingly making use of advanced technology in its operations, such as drones for the aerial surveillance of building projects, replacing land surveillance, and construction through automated modular 3D printing, to cut costs and compensate for skilled labour shortages. In addition, with prefabricated construction taking place indoors in factories and just assembly work onsite, the definition of construction as a service is becoming blurred (WTO, 2019: 28).

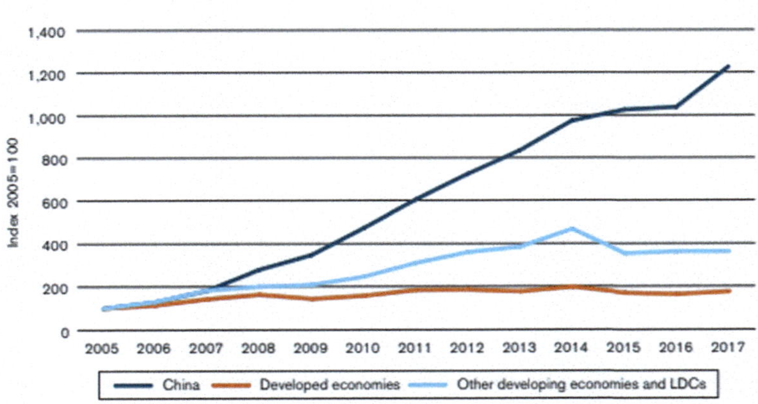

Fig. 4.7 China's construction exports: Construction exports by China, developed economies, other developing economies and LDCs (*Source* WTO, 2019: 28)

As the railroad technology of China catches up with that of the advanced countries, construction projects will surely contribute greatly to the development of China's ICT.

The investments of China towards BRI countries takes two forms: foreign direct investment (FDI) or construction contracts.

Looking at the top 10 countries for China's construction contracts and FDI in Table 4.1, there are some slight differences between the construction contract and FDI countries, but it could be seen that the main destinations are Southeast Asia, South Asia, the Middle East, and Africa. He writes "China's total value of investment and construction contracts increased greatly between 2014 and 2018, compared to the eight years (2005–2013) before the BRI was established. Nine of the 10 countries are all located within the six economic cooperation corridors (He, 2019: 6). Behind such deployment is BRI's big push.

Incidentally, firms going overseas are mainly Chinese state-owned enterprises. Their financing institutions include state-owned development banks, state-owned commercial banks, and state development funds. By the end of 2018, the total amount of funding were as follows: 45% ($341.0 billion) from two Chinese state-owned development banks (National Development Bank and Export–Import Bank), 36% ($277.2 billion) from state-owned commercial banks, 2% ($11.0 billion) from the silk road fund, among others. There are both bilateral and multilateral funds, but even the multilateral funds were actually Chinese funds (He, 2019: 13).

Needless to say, BRI projects are concentrated in the African region and LLDCs. In looking at the investment initiatives to Africa of the major five advanced and emerging countries (America, China, the UK, Russia, and France), the UNCTAD reveals that China's investment to Africa surpasses those of the other countries. As a FOCAC initiative since 2018, China has promised a financial package amounting to $60 billion, which includes $10 billion in private investment. The major projects of which are the construction of the coastal railroad in Nigeria worth $12 billion, the Addis

Table 4.1 China's construction contracts and outward direct investment: Top 10 BRI countries 2014–2018 (U.S.$ billion)

	Country	Contract value	Country	ODI value
1	Pakistan	31.41	Singapore	24.27
2	Nigeria	24.21	Malaysia	14.09
3	Bangladesh	17.54	Russia	10.44
4	Indonesia	16.77	Indonesia	9.35
5	Malaysia	15.80	Israel	7.88
6	Egypt	14.95	Pakistan	7.63
7	UAE	14.03	Laos	6.68
8	Russia	11.13	UAE	6.55
9	Laos	11.06	Nigeria	6.54
10	Iran	10.63	Bangladesh	5.30

(*Source* He, 2019: 8. *Data source* AEI and Heritage Foundation 2019).

Ababa-Djibouti railway in Ethiopia worth $1.5 billion, and the Tanzanian mega port worth $11 billion. Moreover, in the nine large-scale new investment projects reported to have gone to LLDCs in 2019, four projects were by Chinese firms. All were investments into manufacturing. The largest one was the chemical and basic chemical industries of Bolivia, amounting to $1.49 billion. There was also one investment each to Bolivia and Kazakhstan's chemical and basic chemical industry. Another project was the investment into Rwanda's fiber and clothing industry amounting to $374 million (UNCTAD, 2021: 33, 77).

Due to the Corona pandemic, there was a significant drop in the investments of Chinese firms to the developing regions, especially the LLDCs, starting with African countries, in 2020 (UNCTAD, 2021). However, up to 2019, large scale investments to LLDCs and the construction of large scale infrastructure in Southeast Asia and other developing regions along the BRI route were actively conducted. Ultimately, BRI is an extension of the "Going out" strategy at the start of this century (He, 2019: 12). There was massive deployment to infrastructure construction and resource development, and further on to labor-intensive industries. Moreover, this would be a policy that holds the possibility to play an important role in coping with the digital age brought about by the development of ICT.

However, such deployment offensive by Chinese firms due to BRI induced various criticisms around 2018. We have already touched on the non-transparent railroad construction in Malaysia. There were others that came to light, such as the administrative rights and lease of an overseas port facility. The list is a long one and includes the 43-year lease of Pakistan's Gwadar port, the 99-year takeover of Australia's Darwin port, the takeover of Greece's Piraeus port in 2016, the 35-year takeover of Harifa port terminal of the United Arab Emirates (UAE), and the operation of the Djibouti naval base from 2017. Problems also arose in dam constructions. In 2017, there was a series of cancellation of the construction of hydroelectric dams in Pakistan, Nepal, Myanmar, amounting to a total of 20 billion dollars. Reasons would vary, but there were many problems such as the lack of project transparency, excessive collateral requirements, little respect for the laws, environmental destruction, and projects prioritizing the national interest (VOA Nov. 5, 2017, Dec. 5, 2017; Irrawaddy, Jan. 29, 2019).

What really sparked greater interest was the excessive debt problem of countries along the BRI route. In March 2018, the American think tank, Center for Global Development (CGD) published a report on the evaluation of the BRI-financed projects using the end of 2016 as a base point. According to this report, out of the 68 countries that implemented BRI projects, 23 countries faced repayment risks, 8 of which particularly could face severe repayment risks in the future. These 8 countries have exceptionally high shares of debt to GDP: three middle-income countries, namely, Mongolia, Montenegro, and Pakistan; and five low-income countries, namely, Maldives, Djibouti, Laos, Kyrgyzstan, and Tajikistan (Fig. 4.8) (Hurley et al., 2018).

Also in March, Nikkei Asia and The Banker published the results of a joint survey of BRI projects, which found that a lot of the BRI projects were not able to really generate employment and appeared to have problematic debt dependence.

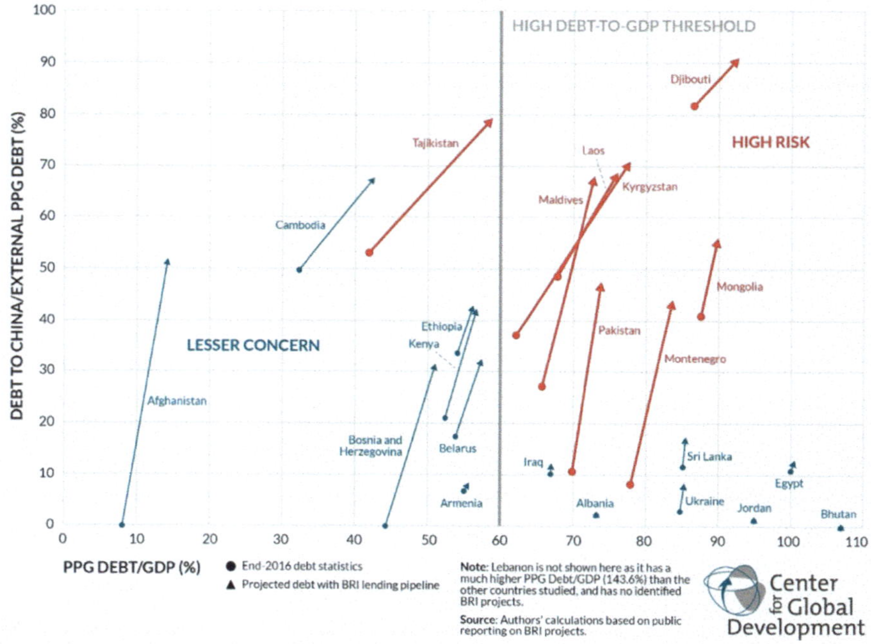

Fig. 4.8 Immediate marginal impact of BRI lending pipeline (*Source* Hurley et al., 2018: 12)

In Indonesia, the 6 billion dollar high-speed railway construction is running behind schedule, sharply raising the costs. Pakistan, Sri Lanka, Maldives, and Laos are facing high repayment risks on their loans from China. Sri Lanka and Maldives are already concerned about losing ownership rights, citing that China's concern is more about geopolitics than economics (Nikkei Asian Review, March 28, 2018). In the following April, the ambassadors to China of the 27 countries of the EU28 issued a joint critical statement against the Chinese government. This was with regards to China's ignoring free trade rules, and lacking in transparency.

This sparked the rapid global spread of a "debt trap" awareness, wherein China is viewed to be consciously scheming debt problems to beset small countries, which are particularly located in geopolitical points in the globe, so as to tie these down economically and politically. Political shifts in debtor countries have also occurred. Alongside with the above-mentioned Malaysian case, Myanmar announced in July 2018 that the big-ticket port development project in the Kyaukpyu Special Economic Zone, promised by the previous administration, has been reduced in scale (Nikkei -J, July 5, 2018). In the presidential elections of September of the same year in Maldives, the pro-China faction lost. In the same year in Sri Lanka, a pro-India administration was born.

China naturally responded to the criticism of a "debt trap". At the same time, however, it also showed a compromise with the Western global rules. In his speech at the Boao Forum for Asia in 2018, Xi Jinping denied that BRI was a "Chinese plot"

(Reuters, April 11, 2018). In the 2nd BRI International Cooperation Summit Forum in 2019, he clearly stated that infrastructure construction would "respect international rules". Foreign Minister Wang Yi, in his speech in March 2018 in Paris, stated "BRI respects international rules, and operates following market rules".

To say that excessive financing is intentionally being done by China would be too much an assertion (Albert, 2020). Instead, there is a high possibility that these problems were brought about by the lack of international experience of China's financial institutions and state-owned enterprises. Moreover, there are also a lot of cases of a lack of debt management skill on the part of the debtor countries. Incidentally, similar problems occurred during the rapid overseas investments of Japanese firms in the 1970s. Arbitrary criticisms should be avoided (Hirakawa et al. -J, 2019). RUSI (Royal United Service Institute) Senior Associate Fellow, A. Cainey says this of Chinese projects.

> Despite extensive experience building infrastructure within China, many Chinese companies are much less familiar operating outside of China. Western, Japanese, and Korean companies can bring their own experience to the table and help the success of these projects (Cainey, 2018).

In an interview posted in the South China Monitoring Post (SCMP) in November of the same year, Wang Wen, an investor of Sinosure (China Export and Credit Insurance Corporation) disclosed that Sinosure incurred a loss of $1 billion from its major railroad project in Africa (Ng, 2018). The reporter writes as follows:

> Planning behind many China-led projects abroad has been 'downright inadequate' and costly. Lessons should be drawn from the poorly executed US$4 billion Addis Ababa-Djibouti freight railway that was inaugurated early this year but has already had to restructure its debt because of underuse caused by power shortages, Wang told a belt and road infrastructure financing forum in Hong Kong earlier this month. Other China-backed projects plagued by poor preparation have included sugar refineries that have lacked a supply of sugar beet, and underused railways in Latin America (Ng, 2018).

At the end of 2018, a senior official of the Chinese government stated this in an American financial information magazine.

> Chinese authorities have noted the examples of misconduct and reassessing and tweaking their global infrastructure plans, said a senior Chinese official who asked not to be named discussing strategy. They are well aware that poorly executed projects can hurt China's reputation and are alert to the potential for resentment to spread, the official said (Marlow & Li, 2018).

Investors as well as the Chinese government understand the problem with overseas investments. The problem, however, is the reality that excessive loans have been provided and are now facing repayment difficulties. Separate from the subjective intention, responsibility must be taken for the results. Otherwise, the counterargument against a "debt trap" becomes unconvincing.

The criticism of China from the international community essentially ebbs and wanes with the intensity of the U.S.-Sino conflict. The birth of the Trump administration in 2017 saw the U.S. adopting a hardline towards its trade deficit with China, with pressure even building up on China due to the novel corona outbreak.

This will be focused on China's BRI projects and the debt problems of the newly emerging and low/middle income countries.

4.5 BRI Amidst the International Community, and Its Prospects

The U.S.-Sino trade war started with U.S. President Trump's announcement of a unilateral imposition of tariffs on a trading partner, constituting a violation of international laws but based on American domestic commercial laws. After about two years of intense conflict, both countries reached the "first phase agreement". This agreement, however, was superseded by the COVID-19 pandemic, which intensified the U.S.-Sino conflict, to the extent that China was forced to restructure the disruption of the global supply chain created amidst China's becoming the factory of the world. This is the so-called decoupling. This conflict structure sheds further light on the significance and issues surrounding BRI.

4.5.1 The Impact of U.S.-Sino Trade War, and COVID-19 on BRI: From "Mask Diplomacy" to "Vaccine Diplomacy" and COVAX

In January 2020, the U.S.-Sino Trade War finally reached a compromise with the "phase one agreement". This moment of truce, however, was broken up COVID-19 which struck the U.S., China, and the world. Taking advantage of the pandemic, the Trump administration embarked on separating U.S. companies from Chinese companies in the leading technology sector, and strengthened the regulation of Chinese-affiliated companies in the U.S. markets. On the other hand, China transformed its foreign policy posture into what would be called as "wolf warrior diplomacy".

Right after its outbreak, however, COVID-19 indeed forced great sacrifices on the newly emerging economies, mid/low income developing countries participating in BRI. The direct effects have been the curtailing of the movement of people and goods owing to the pandemic, and eventually the hibernation of projects. According to one media report, one fifth of the projects were "seriously affected", and those "adversely affected" went as high as 40% due to the stoppage in the provision of people, materials, and equipment. There were work stoppages or suspensions in countries such as Pakistan, Bangladesh, Cambodia, Kenya, Laos, Malaysia, Saudi Arabia, and Sri Lanka (Economic Times (India Times), June 28, 2020. Projects were delayed in the China-Pakistan Economic Corridor (CPEC) construction works, the construction of special economic zones in Cambodia's Sihanoukville, and the construction of coal-fired power plants in Bangladesh (Shepard, 2020; Wheeler,

2020). China, however, quickly succeeded in suppressing the infections, and moved quickly to normalize the economy.

This sheds light on the two sides of the importance of China's BRI. One is the awareness that BRI has become an even more important diplomatic policy due to the intensification of the U.S.-Sino conflict. Another one is the emergence of the massive financing repayment problem to BRI projects of middle-low income countries. In this section, we shall confirm the former.

In mid-March, President Xi Jinping in a telephone conversation assured then-Italian Prime Minister Conte of a "health silk road", and sent 300 doctors, coronavirus test kits, and artificial respirators. By the beginning of April, emergency relief goods, which included 1.8 million masks, 21,000 test kits, 36,000 personal protection equipment, artificial respirators, and thermometers, have been sent to Afghanistan, Bangladesh, Cambodia, Laos, Maldives, Mongolia, Myanmar, Nepal, Pakistan, and Sri Lanka (Wheeler, 2020). In March, 127 countries were supplied with medical goods. Amidst the global shortage of masks, however, a lot of defective goods were mixed up with the exported masks, giving rise to complaints from various countries. Owing to this, export firms were subjected to a permit system from April 1st. Due to the strengthening of China's tariff administration, the number of faulty goods confiscated between the 1st and the 13th are as follows: 31.65 million masks, 500,000 personal protection equipment, 1.18 million virus test kits, and 677 artificial respirators (Nikkei -J, Apr. 18, 2020).

Despite such problems, China, which was able to quickly suppress COVID-19, continued to supply medical goods to the rest of the world. In an announcement of the Chinese government, the quantity of exports from April to December 2020 were as follows: 224.0 billion masks, 1.8 billion test kits, 271,000 artificial respirators (State Council, PRC, 2021). Although exports were destined overwhelmingly to advanced countries such as America, Germany, and Japan, BRI countries were also recipients of these exports or donations. In doing so, China continued to be the world's supplier of medical goods.

The above supply or donation of medical goods, or "mask diplomacy" shifted, however, in 2021 with the development of vaccines, to "vaccine diplomacy". At the start, there were production shortages, so that around April to May of 2021, a big gap could be observed between high-income and mid-low income countries. In the WHO General Assembly of April, Director-General Tedros in an appeal for international solidarity, called for donations to COVAX, noting that of the 832 million vaccines 82% went to high-middle income countries, and only 0.2% to low income countries. This, he noted, meant that one in four in high income countries have been vaccinated as against one in 500 in low income countries (UN Press Release ECOSOC/7039 April 16, 2021). In a survey of the vaccine inventories of 33 major countries in September, Nikkei Shimbun found that inventories were skewed towards the vaccine producing countries of America and Europe, with a surplus of more than 150 million doses (Nikkei -J, July 18, 2021). As the vaccine exports were regulated in March due to the infection surge in India, many Asian and African countries began facing vaccine shortfalls that delayed vaccination. This created an opening, allowing the very virulent delta strain to trigger another infection explosion. Starting with Taiwan and Vietnam, which were considered to be successful in suppressing the infection, and including Indonesia, Thailand, Malaysia, and other Southeast Asian countries, as well as Latin American and African countries experienced a rapid rise in infection cases since June 2021.

Then the public's attention was drawn towards China's supply of vaccines. China had its first vaccine certified at the end of 2020, and between January and February was exporting to 43 countries (Nikkei -j, Mar. 20, 2021). By the end of May, China has sold or donated 70 billion doses of vaccines to 90 countries. The drop points for the vaccines, spreading from Chile to Egypt, from Mexico to the Philippines up to the whole world, were marked by China's flag raising and pictures of grateful officials (Kampfner, 2021).

Incidentally, together with China, Russia also started engaging in vaccine diplomacy. While initiating exports control in March due to an infection surge, India has been donating and selling 6.6 billion to 96 countries (Afifah et al., 2021: 28).

Biden became the American president in January 2021. To counter the vaccine diplomacy of China, the Biden administration in April announced that it was considering the provision of vaccines to other countries, and in May proposed that pharmaceutical companies give up their patents. This was supported by France and the EU congress, but naturally this was rejected by pharmaceutical companies in Japan and Germany, and therefore did not get approved. In June, the Biden administration announced that it will provide 25 million doses of vaccine to Asia and Latin America, as its first round of donations, and will donate 500 million doses more to poor countries, heading towards the G7 Summit. In the same month, at the G7 Summit held in the UK, the G7 agreed to provide at least one billion doses of vaccine. The vaccines will be provided either bilaterally or through COVAX. Furthermore, it was clearly written in the communique that this provision of vaccines is a cooperation to counter China's impact on world trade (BBC, June 13, 2021).

China has promised to provide ten million doses of vaccine through the COVAX, an initiative of the WHO. However, in the WHO General Assembly of May 2021, it did not pledge any vaccine to be provided through COVAX, even as it provided 1.6 million doses of vaccine, on a bilateral basis, as of mid-July 2021 (Afifah et al., 2021: 27). China's cooperation with COVAX was in the 1st Vaccine Cooperation Forum hosted by China in August, where a pledge was made of providing 100 million doses of vaccine by October of the same year (Wang, 2021).

Come September 2021, there arose the problem of the effectiveness of Chinese-made vaccines. There was an increasing case of relapse among the vaccinated even in Chile, which had a high vaccination rate. 90% of the vaccines used in Chile were Chinese-made Sinovac, while the remaining 10% were U.S.-made Pfizer. According to a column written by a Japanese national economic research institute that shared the research results of a researcher at Chile University, Pfizer and Moderna were more than 90% effective and AstraZeneca was 80% effective, while the Chinese-made vaccine was only 54% effective (Fuji -J, 2021). Owing to this, countries started to shift from Chinese-made to U.S.-made vaccines.

As shown in Table 4.2, the U.S. was first on the list of G7 countries supporting COVAX. In retrospect, at the outbreak of COVID-19, former President Trump even called the WHO "China's puppet" when WHO Director-General Tedros praised China's response to infection (Kampfner, 2021). China, however, was not aggressive in supporting the WHO, which was the only international institution dealing with COVID-19. The U.S. under President Biden came back to the WHO, and became more supportive through COVAX. The "vaccine diplomacy" of the U.S. and China has enhanced the significance of COVAX.

Ultimately, the conflict between the U.S. and China was aggravated by the trade war of the Trump administration and the ensuing COVID-19 pandemic, forcing the U.S. to resort to decoupling and China to wolf warrior diplomacy. This state of affairs was continued by the Biden administration that was inaugurated in 2021. This administration emphasized foreign policies on human rights and internationalism, as well as strengthening coordination with various Western countries. China strongly opposed this. At the first U.S.-Sino high-level talks since the establishment of the Biden administration, held in Alaska in March 2022, America raised the issue of human rights in Xinjiang Uyghur Autonomous Region and Hong Kong. Without giving up one step, China replied that the U.S. had no right to criticize China. In the same month, the EU also announced sanctions on the basis of China's human rights violations. These consisted of EU-related travel bans and the freezing of assets within the region on the authority in charge over Xinjiang Uyghur Autonomous Region plus one person, and the administrative authority over "detention facilities". In retaliation,

Table 4.2 Top 12 contributions to COVAX AMC (as of June 23, 2021)

	Country/organization	Amount $ million	% Total
1	US	3,500	36.2
2	Germany	1,097	11.6
3	Japan	1,000	10.4
4	UK	733	7.6
5	European Commission	489	5.1
6	Italy	470	4.9
7	Canada	384	4.0
8	Sweden	296	3.1
9	France	244	2.5
10	Gates Foundation	206	2.1
11	Saudi Arabia	153	1.6
12	Norway	141	1.5
Subtotal		8,713	90.2
Grand total		9,661	100.0

(*Source* Afifah et al., 2021: 14. *Original source* Gavi, 2021, Key outcomes: COVAX AMC 2021, May 10).

China banned the entry to China of ten persons, including five members of the EU Parliament, and persons from two EU organizations as well as two think-tanks.[16]

4.5.2 BRI Member Countries and the Debt Problem Under COVID-19

Through various channels, the COVID-19 pandemic is harming developing countries more severely than that experienced by advanced economies. The IMF's economic predictions for 2020 has revised its earlier predictions downwards due to the expansion of the COVID-19 pandemic, as developing economies suffer from low growth and severe debt problems.

A UNDP research using the World Bank's International Debt Statistics (IDS) has revealed the severe situation that the COVID-19 crisis has brought up in poor economies. "In 2019, long-term public and publicly guaranteed (LT PPG) external debt stock across all 120 developing (low- and middle-income) economies stood at $3.1 trillion". The Total Debt Service (TDS) in 2020 climbed to $374 billion. The poorest 73 countries account for $50 billion (13.4%) of the TDS, and depend on public credit for 70% of its debt. The dependence on public credit for other developing economies is 25%.

In 2020, the Total Debt Service (TDS) climbed to $ 374 billion, of which $50 billion (13.4%) is owned by the poorest 73 countries, with a 70% dependence on public credit. The public credit dependence of other developing countries is 25% (Jensen, 2021: 8).

Figure 4.9 confirms the rapid increase in the value of overseas lending by China, as cited by the UNCTAD research. The share of Chinese overseas lending in world GDP over the 20-year period ending in 2018 has risen from practically 0 to 2%, or $1.6 trillion. In terms of type, export credits and direct lending occupy a dominant share. Most of these loans go to low- and middle-income countries. "In total, estimates suggest that the Chinese state now accounts for a quarter of total bank lending to emerging markets" (Horn et al., 2019: 5).

The external public and publicly-guaranteed (PPG) debt stock of the Low-Income Countries (LICs) and Low- and Middle-Income Countries (LMICs) practically doubled, increasing by $1.03 trillion over the period 2010 to 2019. China's public lending to this group increased by about five times from $26.1 billion to $126 billion, causing China's lending to rise from 5 to 12% of this group's borrowings. China's average share in the top 20 countries' public overseas debt stock in 2019 went over 30%. Figure 4.10 shows the debt dependency by borrowing country. Only three of

[16] As reprisal for China's banning the entry of EU parliamentary members, the EU Parliament passed the resolution to cease the deliberation of the EU-Sino Investment Treaty broadly agreed upon at the end of 2020. The voting results showed 599 in favor, 30 against, and 58 abstained. Since the coming into force of the investment treaty requires the ratification of the EU Parliament, the early effectuation of this treaty has been put on hold (International Federation for Human Right, 2021; Nikkei -J, May 21, 2021).

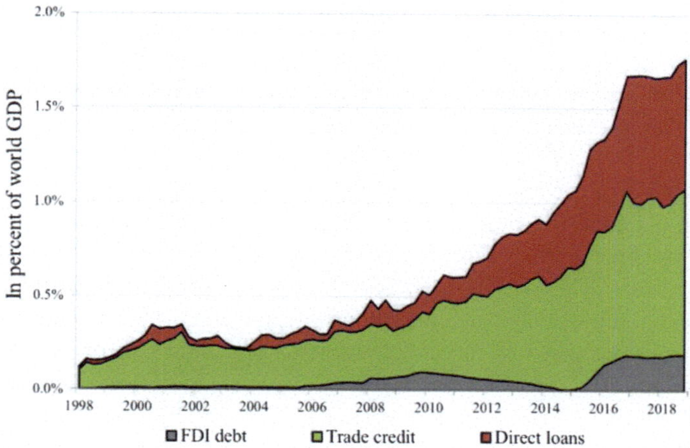

Fig. 4.9 China's overseas lending boom (*Source* Horn et al., 2019: 6). *Note* The figure represents a subset of outstanding Chinese overseas debt claims as reported in China's BoP Statistics. Trade credit includes short- and long-term trade credits and advances. Portfolio debt is excluded

these countries (shown by the blue bars) are not amongst the 72 identified vulnerable countries (Jensen, 2021: 23).

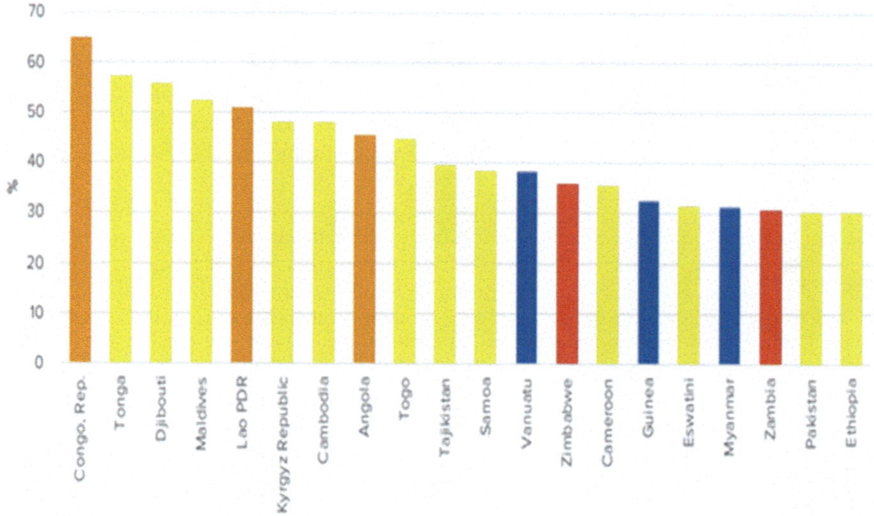

Fig. 4.10 Top 20 China's share of external PPG debt stock, 2019 (% of total) (*Source* Jensen, 2021: 23). *Note* Color-coding refers to rating categorized by Jensen, Red-coding, orange-coding, and yellow-coding means Default current or imminent, Extremely speculative/substantial risk, and highly speculative respectively. Blue means that the country is not amongst the 72 identified vulnerable countries

Figure 4.11 shows China's lending from a geographical perspective. This figure was created by a researcher from China's Central University of Finance and Economics in relation to the 52 countries that have signed a BRI MoU. From this figure, we can get an image by country, and confirm the strategic nature of the lendings.

One assertion of the above-mentioned UNCTAD research is the declining share of concessional loans in China's lending. Moreover, the fiscal position of the debtor countries was generally becoming unhealthy. Figure 4.12 shows the share of government revenues to GDP from 1990 to 2020 by country groups: advanced countries; emerging economies/middle-income countries; and low-income economies. At a glance, we can see that low-income countries are at high risk of defaulting. The situation of the LICs and MICs were already showing signs of weakening from the 2010s, and with COVID-19, further worsened (Jensen, 2021: 24). Repayment on government loans would undoubtedly become more difficult.

Then, COVID-19 deals a heavy blow to this region. Around April 2020, there was a series of debt repayment problems. In April of the same year, the survey company Rhodium Group based in New York reported, with regard to the effect of the pandemic

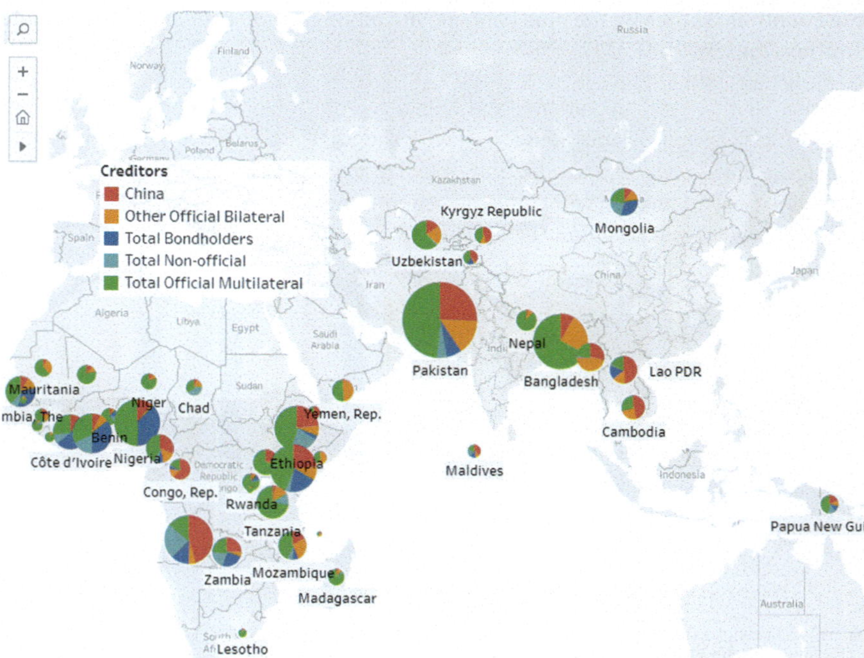

Fig. 4.11 Comparison between creditors in 52 selected BRI countries 2019 (*Source* Yue & Wang, 2020: 13). *Note* World Bank International Debt Statistics and author's depiction. Total absolute value of outstanding debt denoted in size. Explanation: From 2014 to 2019, countries like Pakistan, Angola, Bangladesh, and Kyrgyz Republic have seen an increasing share of Chinese lending, as can be seen by the increase of the red part of the pie-charts for the different countries

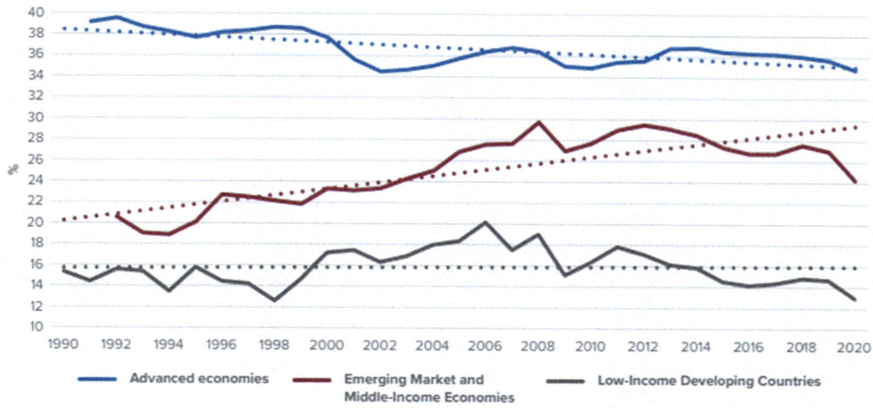

Fig. 4.12 Government revenue in % of GDP by income group (*Source* Jensen, 2021: 24. *Data source* IMF Fiscal Monitor Oct. 2020)

on BRI projects, that new lendings will shrink, but lending itself will be sustained due to the importance of overseas demand, as Chinese domestic markets shrink, and due to the political, diplomatic, and economic objectives of the Chinese government. China, however, expects an increase in renegotiations with debtor countries in 2020 to 2021, because loan repayments are supposed to start during this period, even prior to COVID-19. Loans for energy and transportation infrastructure projects under BRI are said to have a grace period of five to six years (Kratz et al., 2020). COVID-19 struck these countries as loan repayments were starting. The Rhodium Group writes as follows:

> In light of the need for debt renegotiation, it is unlikely that Beijing will return to 2016-2017 levels of new BRI commitments. That ship had sailed before the COVID crisis, and likely won't return in the near future. Instead, we would expect Beijing to focus its resources on dealing with debt renegotiation as best as it can (Kratz et al., 2020).

In actuality, China dramatically increased its investments from 2018 to 2019 towards emerging economies, LMICs and LICs along the BRI circuit. At that time, these economies were high-risk borrowers and foreign aid recipients. China brought in large-scale construction projects, from which repayment has started. Even without the COVID crisis, repayment risks were already high. While BRI has brought about an important possibility, the COVID crisis has brought about big issues. How is China trying to overcome this crisis?

China's Overseas Loans and G20 As the COVID crisis started, the G20 financial ministers and central bank governors meeting in April 2020 in coordination with the Paris Club decided to implement the first Debt Service Suspension Initiative (DSSI). The debt repayments of 73 countries, which were identified by the World Bank and the UN, were postponed from May to the end of December of the same year. Since the COVID-19 pandemic, however, did not end, the grace period was again extended for another six months in October of the same year. In April 2021, another postponement up to the end of December of 2021 was decided on. China participated, for the first time, in this international coordination of assistance, and partly shared information on lending. Amidst the growing necessity for research on China's lending, a situation shrouded in secrecy has been partly unveiled.

Based on China's disclosure of its financing to 68 developing countries to the World Bank, the Nikkei Shimbun revealed that at the end of 2018, the financing balance was at $101.7 billion, a scale nearing the $103.7 billion of the World Bank. Lendings for the past four years increased by 90% for China, 40% for the World Bank, and 10% for the IMF. The interest rate computed from the average debt balance in 2020 was 3.5% for China, and 0.6% for the World Bank and IMF (Nikkei -J, August 6, 2020).

The Kiel Research Institute attempted a systematic research to obtain the whole picture of China's lending, which has been beyond the grasp of current academic research. This research is summarized as follows:

> We document the size, destination, and characteristics of China's overseas lending systematically and estimate the drivers of Chinese cross-border flows using established empirical models. A main insight from the data is that about half of China's lending to developing countries is not picked up by the "gold standard" databases of international finance. The "hidden debts" owed to China are consequential for debt sustainability in recipient countries and pose serious challenges for macroeconomic surveillance work and the market pricing of sovereign risk (Horn et al., 2019: 2).

Let us take a look at some of the important points from this research about China's lending.

1. China has lent to over 100 countries to finance large-scale investments in infrastructure, energy, and mining.
2. The average stock of debt of the 50 most indebted recipients of Chinese direct lending accounts for 1% of GDP in 2005 and more than 15% in 2017.
3. 50% of China's commercial lending is not reported. This "hidden" loan has risen to about $200 billion by 2016.
4. Lending interest rates are relatively high, and maturity periods are short. Loans are in many aspects similar to commercial bank loans.
5. A secret clause stipulates that repayment defaults are partly insured through repayments from commercial export revenues, particularly that from oil. This system is different from the lending format of public institutions such as the World Bank、 but has similarities to China's historical experience.
6. China's credit is rarely a loan taken out by the debtor country. It is mostly provided to debtor country's state-owned enterprises through Chinese state -owned enterprises. There is a tendency for the recipient to be Chinese state-owned enterprises, hence, such debt transactions are not recorded either in the debtor country's or China's national accounting books.
7. China started reporting to the BIS in 2015, but it has not consented to publishing the bilateral financing data (by country). China adopts a "circular lending strategy" where the state-owned bank remits not to the account administered by the debtor government, but directly to the Chinese contracted firm undertaking

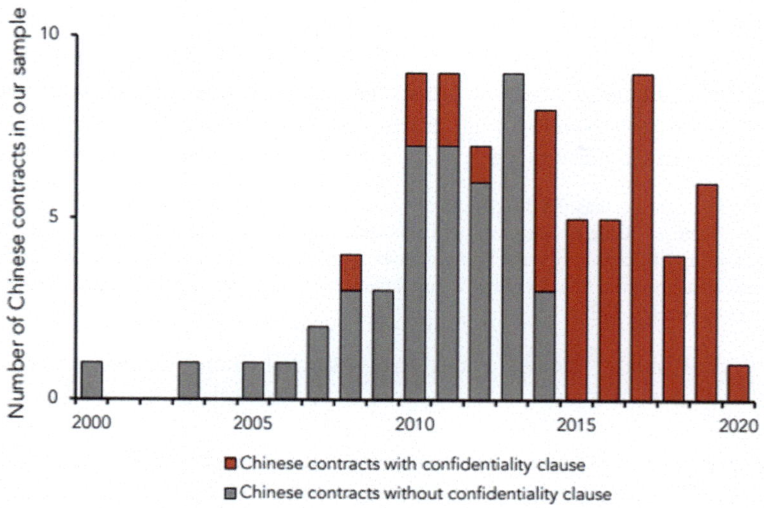

Fig. 4.13 Use of confidentiality clauses contracts over time (*Source* Gelpern et al., 2021: 23)

the construction project overseas. This type of overseas lending does not cross national borders and is not reported as overseas lending (Horn et al., 2019: 7–10).

Let us look at the research findings of the AidDATA at William and Mary's Global Research Institute about the content of China's lending contracts. We are limited to only a hundred contracts, but it still provides us with invaluable information. As can be seen in Fig. 4.13, The number of Chinese loan contracts with confidentiality clauses rapidly increased since 2014, the year that BRI was initiated.

This conditionality clause ordinarily contains a confidentiality clause, and generally entails the lender to assume some obligations. However, in the case of China's lending, the borrower is the one who assumes the obligations. In many cases, the borrowing country has the obligation not to disclose the financing terms, to allow the loan to be tied to finance, trade, and construction, and to prioritize certain debtors in any repayment to be made. Moreover, borrowing countries were increasingly subjected to the "No Paris Club" clause, where it cannot coordinate its loan repayments with lenders of the Paris Club. In conclusion, while it is not limited to China, there is a "the need for substantially greater transparency in sovereign lending, including but not confined to government-to-government loans" (Gelpern et al., 2021: 45).

The picture that emerges from the above discussion is that China's lending is deeply linked to policy and commercial-based, puts China in a superior position vis-a-vis the borrowing country, and lacks transparency. This definitely recognizes the high risks involved in BRI lending. It could be said, however, that with the COVID crisis, the level of risk has exceeded that anticipated by China when the contracts were signed.

G20's DSSI and China Normally, the external debt problems of developing countries could be dealt with by the Paris Club. Now, however, the Paris Club lenders only account for 3% of the debts of low-income countries, while China accounts for half. Given this reality, the venue for agreement for DSSI was decided to be the G20. A newspaper reports the following:

> The biggest concern was the direction that China was taking. …should a debt crisis in low-income countries occur, China's loss, as a major lending country, from defaults is going to be large, forcing China to accept the implementation of DSSI. A Japanese Ministry of Finance executive staff viewed "the reaching of agreement together with China as an achievement" (Nikkei -j, April 6, 2020).

As such, China's "hidden" loans have attracted interest. Some research has attempted to study this issue, and has partly pulled aside the veil shrouding China's loans. The G20 adopted a DSSI at the end of 2020.

The G20 applied DSSI to repayments due until the end of 2020. The optimism towards the COVID crisis, however, turned out to be ill-placed, prompting the G20 in October 2020 to apply a half-year extension of the grace period. Around that time, the debt situation was beginning to be much clearer, and the difference in awareness with China was becoming one focal point. One growing suspicion was that surplus funds generated by the DSSI might have been allocated to service the Chinese loans instead of being used to cope with COVID-19.

China has consented to the public debt repayment suspension. There is dissatisfaction, however, due to China asserting that the 100% government-funded China National Development Bank is a private enterprise. According to an article of the Nikkei Shimbun, based on an interview of the World Bank President during the G20 Summit in November 2020, China accounts for 63% of the balance of bilateral financing to the poorest 73 countries, and charges an interest rate of over 7% in contrast to the World Bank's interest rate of only 1% (LIBOR of around 0.3%, plus service charge). Moreover, the article indicated that "this G20 agreement will also be applied to Chinese state-owned banks, export–import banks, and the Industrial and Commercial Bank.

It was also revealed that the China Development Bank has ceased collecting interest payments from defaulting Zambia (Nikkei -J, Nov. 24, 2020). A translation of a Financial Times article carried by the Nikkei Shimbun also reported the World Bank's assessment of China's participation in the G20 DSSI as "slow moving", "extremely irritating", and China's contracts "in many cases, have high interest rates and lacking in transparency" (Nikkei -J, Oct. 27, 2021). It can be seen that intense negotiations between the World Bank and China are unfolding behind the scenes.

Incidentally, the above-mentioned first African default courtesy of Zambia involved a scheduled repayment of $42.5 million in October 2020, and was covered by the Guardian and Aljazeera.

> Zambia's finance minister, Bwalya Ng'andu, was quick to blame the banks and asset and fund managers who wanted to see more transparency over an estimated $3bn debt to China, but who refused to sign the necessary confidentiality agreements, he said. Ng'andu said on state television, "The position of the Chinese banks is: 'You're not going to give anybody

> any information without the confidentiality agreements in place'". Zambian government is now debating a budget that would see less money spent on healthcare and more on servicing debt repayment (Williams, 2020).
>
> Referring to a deal agreed with the China Development Bank last month (October), he said the bank had given a six-month grace period on interest payments and a three-year grace period on the principal payments for one loan. Ng'andu did not reveal the size of that loan (Aljazeera, 2020).

Incidentally, the deferral agreement of the China Development Bank is thought to be for obtaining the agreement of the lenders group to suspend interest payments. Nevertheless, an issue emerged for the international community under the COVID crisis so as to ensure the recovery of emerging and low/mid-income economies from corona. This was the importance of supporting mid-income countries and others, which have not adopted rescue measures, to participate in the DSSI of private banks and funds. There was a renewed concern over this at the re-extension of the DSSI deadline in the third G20 meeting of 2021.

In its report on the G20 Financial Ministers and Central Bank Governors General Assembly to be held in April 2021, Reuters estimates the repayment grace due to DSSI granted to about 43 poorest countries to be at about $5.7 billion. The issue of loan transparency was raised, considering the inclusion of ancillary provisions in Chinese loan contracts. With regards to considering the use of IMF's SDR, which China is also proposing, to assist the poorest countries, Reuters report has it from G7 involved parties that the act of prioritizing dollars used to procure SDR for the repayment of Chinese loans, should it even spread, is against the common framework of international agreements. Japan's media takes issue with removing state development banks, which are 100% funded by the Chinese government, from the repayment suspension framework applied to private banks. "Advanced countries think that behind this position are opaque transactions with developing countries, and demand information disclosure (Nikkei -J, Apr. 3, 2020; Reuters -J, Apr. 5, 2020). There is a lot known only to those involved amidst this lack of transparency. News reports on DSSI, however, reveal that China, as usual, does not consider state development bank funding as public funding. China would most likely be dealing with this problem on a case-by-case basis, much to the chagrin of the World Bank President.

China has to avoid a chain of default of the poorest countries. For this, coordination with the international community is indispensable. At the same time, however, abandoning the collection of capital from the massive lending is not an option. It appears to be a dilemma.

Eventually, this dilemma would require China to downscale its BRI projects or improve efficiencies. COVID-19 has challenged and revealed the great potential of the new international cooperation strategy aimed by BRI.

3 Pillars of BRI: Health Silkroad-Digital Silkroad-Environmental BRI

As we end this chapter, we would like to touch very briefly on the direction of the BRI being pursued by China. For as long as the Xi Jinping administration rules, BRI will not be abandoned. This is also clear from Xi Jinping's speech at the 100th anniversary of the Communist Party in July 2020. As such, BRI is considered to be based on three pillars.

One pillar is the "Health Silkroad", which could be seen in China's mask and vaccine foreign policy. In the keynote speech at the 3rd Belt and Road International Forum held in October 2023, President Xi extolled his country's contributions to the world, citing that China provided more than 10 billion masks and 2.3 billion doses of COVID-19 vaccines to countries, and cooperated with more than 20 countries participating BRI in vaccine production (China Radio International Online Oct.18, 2023). However, China's vaccine exports, which had drastically increased until the third quarter of 2021, sharply decreased in 2022 due to the evaluation that the protection against the Omicron strain compared to Pfizer's was low. By April of the same year, the protection evaluation had become almost zero (Nikkei -J, May 7, 2022). Further developments of the Health Silk Road cannot be expected for the time being.

Another pillar is the manner of continuing the infrastructure sector, which is now in the very middle of a big issue. As was revealed by the COVID-19 crisis, a correction is called for large construction projects towards efficient entry through digital technologies. We could call this the "Digital Silkroad". Actually, ICT infrastructure will become an indispensable information infrastructure for the world. The U.S. and China go head-to-head over 5G technology. Huawei has laid out the 820-km fiber optic of Pakistan's CPEC, at a cost of $44 million. That would be equivalent to the cost of laying out four kilometers worth of railroad. As Blanchette and Hill were quick to point out, China would be providing BRI-participating countries with projects in the digital sector (Blanchette & Hillman, 2020). This bodes of changes in the contents of infrastructure construction.

The third pillar is coping with the global trend. China in 2018, under the direction of the China Council for International Cooperation on Environment and Development (CCICED), started to put into practice the "The 2030 Agenda for Green BRI and Sustainable Development", moving towards the realization of the UN's sustainable development goals (CCICED, 2020). As could be seen from the loan repayment problems of poor countries, the adverse effect of COVID-19 has been quite severe, prompting most likely adjustments from large scale to small- and medium-scale development projects. China canceled the thermal power plant in Bangladesh due to strong local resistance. It is sure that things will go along the so-called "Environmental Silkroad" or Green BRI.

Based on the Paris Agreement at COP21 in 2015, an international framework for combating global warming, the world's attention has focused on keeping the rise in global temperatures below 1.5 °C above pre-industrial revolution levels. The International Energy Association (IEA) has proposed to reduce greenhouse gas emissions to virtually zero by 2050 and the key of achieving this goal is to reduce energy consumption through wind power, solar photovoltaic (PV) in electricity generation, and electric vehicles (EV). At COP28 climate conference in Dubai, the UAE agreed "accelerating efforts towards the phase-down of unabated coal power, phasing out inefficient fossil fuel subsidies, and other measures that drive the transition away from fossil fuels in energy systems, in a just, orderly and equitable manner" (UN

Climate Press Release, 2023). Actually, China's activities in this field are remarkable. China looks to grasp a global leadership on carbon zero emission. According to the IEA report, China's world shares of solar panel manufacturing capacity and exports of solar photovoltaic (PV) materials and devices are both overwhelming in excess of 80% (IEA, 2023). China is now one of the world's largest emitters of greenhouse gasses, and the IEA has written the following about the country that is making dramatic progress in reducing CO_2 emissions:

> Clear and ambitious targets, strong policy support, mature local supply chains and low-cost financing were all key factors in this rapid expansion of renewables. This strong foundation has enabled China to reduce unit costs very rapidly, and it is now set to achieve its current Nationally Determined Contribution's target for installed wind and solar PV capacity by 2025, five years ahead of schedule (IEA, 2023: 111).

Until very recently, China was the largest exporter of fossil fuel energy projects, but there is now no doubt that its projects in this area will be globally rolled out mainly to BRI participating countries. And, the UN and also IEA expect China to take responsibility for the attainment of the targets. China, of course, will put its national prestige on the line when promoting these projects as part of the "Environmental Silk Road" or "green BRI".

4.6 Concluding Remarks

In this chapter, we took a look at BRI, its birth, development, potentials and issues. There is great potential, but the rise of China, and its accompanying shifts in the international economy, gave birth to serious conflicts within the international community. The conflict in the trade sector with the appearance of the Trump administration in America has increased the risk of economic decoupling. China itself cannot deny the increasing savagery of foreign policies. Nevertheless, the effects of BRI not only on China but also on the BRI-participating countries as well as the Western advanced economies has been nothing but spectacular.

The effects of BRI on low-income countries cannot be ignored. For example, this could be seen in the criticism of China by the UN commission on human rights with regards to the former's implementation of the Hong Kong National Security Law in July 2020, as a violation of the "one-country-two-systems" policy. While 27 countries criticized China, there were 53 that supported her. This support was given by the developing countries participating in BRI, most of which had non-democratic states. This, however, is not the point.

On reflection, under the flag of liberalism, Western advanced countries, starting with America, have not only ignored the increasing gap within their countries, but also that within the international community. It is the same with economics. This gave way to BRI and its massive projects, under the assumption that loan repayment obligations preclude the possibility of default. The chance to develop was made available with its concomitant risks. The limits of this model were soon made clear by the COVID-19 crisis. China as well as the BRI-participating countries went through the gauntlet. It became clear, however, that the basic solution was a more efficient BRI.

The issue for China is the need for raising efficiency in lending and investing. This goes for both China and the borrowing country. China has been on the path of bilateralism while seeking for its own framework. Based on this trajectory, the best approach to improve the efficiency of BRI projects would be to overcome the issue of its transparency vis-a-vis the international community.

The conflict with Western advanced economies contributes towards the raising of the efficiency of BRI projects. BRI needs to gain the trust of the international community. Some more time would be needed for participating countries to become affluent socio-economies. Given that BRI is recognized as a genuine global public goods, China now stands at the gates of a new challenge. So it is with the international community.

References

**Documents with a symbol (-J) after the author's name are Japanese documents.*

Afifah, R.-S., Clift, C., et al. (2021). *Solidarity in response to the COVID-19 pandemic*. Research Paper, July, Chatham House.

Albert, E. (2020). What to make of China's debt relief announcement. *The Diplomat*, June 11.

Asian Development Bank. (2009). *Infrastructure for a seamless Asia*. Asain Development Bank (ADB).

Asian Development Bank. (2015). *Asian Economic Integration Report 2015: How can special economic zones catalyze economic development?* ADB.

Blanchette, J., & Hillman, J. E. (2020). *China's digital silk road after the coronavirus*. CSIS Commentary, April 13. https://www.csis.org/analysis/chinas-digital-silk-road-after-coronavirus

Brautigam, D., Farole, T., & Tang, X. (2010). *China's investment in African special economic zones: Prospects, challenges, and opportunities*. World Bank Economic Premise, no. 5, March.

Cabinet Office, Japan -J. (2015a). *Sekai keizai no chouryuII* (*World economic trends, Second half of 2015*). Naikaku-Fu, Government of Japan.

Cabinet Office, Japan -J. (2015b). *Sekai keizai no choryu II* (*World economic trends II*). Cabinet Office.

Cainey, A. (2018). *Belt and Road is not a (completely) closed shop*. Chatham House, March 22. https://www.chathamhouse.org/2018/03/belt-and-road-not-completely-closed-shop

CCICED. (2020). *Green BRI and 2030 Agenda for sustainable development (Policy Studies Release)*. China Council for International Cooperation on Environment and Development, September.

China-Britain Business Council. (2016). *China-Britain belt and road case studies report 2016*.

Curra, E. (2016). China's Marshall Plan. *Bloomberg News*, August 7.

Ehara, N. -J (2016). Fuoban kankei to Ittaiichiro sennryakuno yukue (Fuoban Kankei–Partnership—and the Whereabouts of the BRI strategy). Beijing Now, no. 34, Aug. 3.

Foster, V., Butterfield, W., Chen, C., & Pushak, N. (2006). *Building bridges: china's growing role as infrastructure finance for Sub-Saharan Africa* (Executive Summary). Trends and Policy Options, no. 5.

Fuji, K. -J (2021). *Chugoku sei koronawakuchin sessyuritu ga takai Chiri, kansen ga saikakudai ... Takoku demo kansenshaga gensho sezu* (*Infections are Rising in a Chile Highly Vaccinated with Chinese-made Vaccines ... Infection Rates not also Declining in Other Countries*). RIETI Column, Research Institute of Economy, Trade and Industry, Japan, April 10. https://www.rieti.go.jp/jp/papers/contribution/fuji-kazuhiko/251.html

Fujimori, H. -J (2016). Chugoku no bokkou to enerugi wo meguru shomondai (The rise of China and Issues Related to Energy. In: I. Hirakawa, et al. (Eds.), *Shin-ajia keizai ron* (*New Asia Economy*). Bunshindo.

Gavuevn, A. (2016). *Future approaches to China.* European Union Institute for Security Studies, April 7. https://carnegie.ru/2016/04/07/future-approachies-to-china-pub-63389.

Gelpern, A., Horn, S., Morris, S., Parks, B., & Trebesch, C. (2021). *How China lends: A rare look into 100 debt contracts with foreign governments.* A Research Lab at William & Mary University, March.

Grieger, G. (2016). One Belt, One Road: China's regional integration initiative. *European Parliamentary Research Service Briefing* (PE586.608), July.

He, A. (2019). The Belt and Road Initiative: Motivations, financing, expansion and challenges of Xi's ever-expanding strategy. *CIGI Papers* no. 225, Centre for International Governance Innovation, Canada, September.

Hirakawa, H. -J (2013). Gurobarizeishon to shinkou keizaino taitou (Globalization and the rise of newly emerging economies). In: Lim Hua Sing (Ed.), *Asia community: Its structure and issues.* Sousou Sha.

Hirakawa, H. -J (2017). Chugoku no "Ittaiichiro" kouso to afuro yurashia keizaiken no kanousei (China's "BRI" and the possibilities of an Afro-Eurasian Economic Zone). *Silkroad and Tea Road, Showa Women's University Institute of International Culture Bulletin*, vol. 23, March.

Hirakawa, H. -J (2018). Sekai keizai furontia sousyutu no kanousei (The possibility of the creation of a world economic frontier). *Gendai no Riron*, Summer Issue.

Hirakawa, H., Ishikawa, K., et al. -J (Eds.) (2019). *Ittaiichiro no seiji-keizaigaku* (*The political economy of BRI*). Bunshindo.

Horn, S., Reinhart, C., & Trebesch, C. (2019). China's overseas lending. *Kiel Working Paper* no. 2132, June.

Hurley, J., Morris, S., & Portelance, G. (2018). Examining the debt implications of the Belt and Road Initiative from a policy perspective. *CGD Policy Paper* 121, March.

IEA. (2023). *Net zero roadmap: A global pathway to keep the 1.5°C goal in reach, 2023 Update.* International Energy Association.

International Federation for Human Right: IFHR. (2021). *China: European parliament freezes controversial EU-China investment deal.* https://www.fidh.org/en/international-advocacy/european-union/china-european-parliament-freezes-controversial-eu-china-investment

Ito, A. -J (2018). Chugoku no 'ittai ichiro' koso (China's BRI Initiative). In Suehiro, A., Tajima, T. & Marukawa, T. (Eds.), *Chugoku/Shin kokoku nekusasu: Aratana sekai keizai junkan* (*China-emerging country nexus: A new global economic cycle*). University of Tokyo Press.

Jakóbowski, J., Hyndle-Hussein, & Kaczmarski, M. (2015). The China/Central and Eastern Europe summit: a new vision of cooperation, old instruments. Analysis, Centre for Eastern Studies, 2015-12-02 Warszawa, Poland.

Jensen, L. (2021). *Sovereign debt vulnerabilities in developing economies. UNDP Development Futures Series Working Papers*, March.

Jha, M. (2017). India's Eurasia policy gets a boost with long-awaited trade corridor. *The Diplomat*, December 9. https://thediplomat.com/2017/12/indias-eurasia-policy-gets-a-boost-with-long-awaited-trade-corridor/

Johannesburg Summit. (2015). *Declaration of the Johannesburg Summit of the Forum on China-Africa Cooperation.* South African Government, December 5. https://www.gov.za

Kaczmarski, M. (2015). China and Russia: Two approaches to integration. *The Diplomat*, March 30. https://thediplomat.com/2015/03/china-and-russia-two-approaches-to-integration/

Kampfner. (2021). *Vaccine competition may now be the world's best bet.* Chatham House.

Kato, M. (2015). Overview now Uzbekistan: 'Uzbek Model'—The situation of Uzbekistan Gradualism. JOI Kaigai Tohyushi, November.

Kawai, M. -J (2016). What is China's BRI? Japan Science and Technology Agency about China's BRI and Transportation Infrastructure Plan, March.

Kawai, M. (2017). *Belt and Road Initiative: Japan's perspective.* Professional Luncheon, Foreign Correspondents' Club of Japan, Tokyo, September 29. https://www.fccj.or.jp/event/professional-luncheon-masahiro-kawai-director-and-director-general-erina-and-yuqing-xing

Kratz, A., Rosen, D. H., & Mingey, M. (2020). *Booster or break? COVID and the Belt and Road Initiative.* Rhodium Group, April 15. https://rhg.com/research/booster-or-brake-covid-and-the-belt-and-road-initiative/

Marlow, I., & Li, Dandan (2018). *How Asia fell out of love with China's belt and road initiative.* Bloomberg, December 10.

Ministry of Economy, Trade, and Industry, Japan. (2005). Promoting 'The Japan ODA model based on the successful experiences of our economic cooperation. Industrial Structure Deliberation Council, Trade and Economic Cooperation Sub-Committee, Economic Cooperation Sub-Committee, July.

Ministry of Economy, Trade, and Industry, Japan. (1989). *Keizai kyoryoku no genjo to mondaiten (Current Status and Problems of Economic Cooperation).* Former Ministry of International Trade and Industry.

National Development and Reform Commission (NDRC), Ministry of Foreign Affairs, & Ministry of Commerce of the People's Republic of China. (2015). *Vision and action on jointly building Silk Roan Economic Belt and 21 st-Century Maritime Silk Road*, March 28.

National Statistics Foreign Exchange Administration. (2014). *China's outward foreign direct investment.* Ministry of Commerce, PRC.

Nomura Holdings. (2018). Belt and road: Globalization China style. *Nomura Economics*, April 16.

Obama, B. (2015). *Statement by the President on the Trans-Pacific Partnership.* Office of the Press Secretary, the White House, October 5.

Ohashi, H. -J (2012). Chugoku no hi-enjogata taigai keizai kyoryoku: Taigai keizai gassaku wo chushin ni (China's non-assistance type of foreign economic cooperation: Focus on 'Foreign Economic Collaboration'). Japan Institute of International Affairs, China's Foreign Aid.

Ohno, I. -J (2012). *Chugoku no taigai enjo to kokusai enjo syakai: Dento teki donaa to Afurica no shiten kara" (China's foreign aid and the international aid community: From the point of view of traditional donors and Africa).* Japan Institute of International Affairs, March.

Phillips, T. (2017). The $900bn question: What is the belt and road initiative? Guardian, May 12.

Puts, C. (2015). India and Pakistan to join SCO, is Iran next? *The Diplomat*, May 26.

Schiere, R., & Rugamba, A. (2011). *Chinese infrastructure investments and African integration.* African Development Bank Group *Working Paper Series,* no. 127, May.

Shepard, W. (2020). China's 'health silk road' gets a boost from Covid-19. *Forbes*, March 27. https://www.forbes.com/sites/wadeshepard/2020/03/27/chinas-health-silk-road-gets-a-boost-from-covid-19/?sh=28085ffd6043

State Council, PRC-Chinese. (2015). Guiding opinions of the State Council on promoting international cooperation in capacity and equipment manufacturing (Guo Fa, 2015 no. 30). Government Information Disclosure Column www.gov.cn

State Council, PRC. (2021). *China exports over 224 billion masks to assist global COVID-19 fight.* http://english.www.gov.cn/statecouncil/ministries/202101/14/content_WS60002f1cc6d0f72576943d4f.html

Suehiro, A. -J. (2018). Tonan ajia ni nanshin suru chugoku (China advancing southward into Southeast Asia). In: Sehiro, A., Tajima, T., & Marukawa, T. (Eds.) *Chugoku/shinkokoku nekusasu (China/emerging counties nexus)*, University of Tokyo Press.

Takahara A. -J (2021). *Izure iro aseru ittai ichiro* (*The fading away of BRI*), Wedge, April 2. https://blogos.com/article/527393/?p=1

Takahara, A. -J (2018). Ittaiichiro koso ha 'Seiza' no youna mono (BRI: Forbidding excessive expectations from a 'Horoscope'). Shukan Toyo Keizai, January 28 Issue.

UN Climate Press Release. (2023). *COP28 agreement signals "Beginning of the end" of the fossil fuels era*. December 13 https://unfccc.int/news/cop28-agreement-signals-beginning-of-the-end-of-the-fossil-fuel-era

Una, A. Berzina-Cerenkova. (2016). *BRI instead of OBOR—China edits the English name of its most ambitious international project*. Latvian Institute of International Affairs, July 28.

UNCTAD. (2015). *Enhancing the contribution of export processing zones to the sustainable development goals*. United Nations on Trade and Development.

UNCTAD. (2019). *World investment report 2019*. Geneva.

UNCTAD. (2020). *World investment report 2020*. Geneva.

UNCTAD. (2021). *World investment report 2021*. Geneva.

Verlare, J., & van der Putten, F. P. (2015). *One Belt, One Road': An opportunity for the EU's security strategy*. Clingendael Policy Brief, December. https://www.clingendael.org/sites/default/files/2016-02/One_belt_one_road_vdPutten_Verlare_Clingendael_policy_brief_2015.pdf

Wang, P. -J (2012). Chugokujin kenkyusha ni yoru nihon no ODA no kenkyu (Japan's ODA research by a Chinese researcher). Japan Institute of International Affairs, March.

Wang, Y. (2018). The Joint undertaking of the Belt and Road Initiative (BRI) enters a new phase. In *Opening address of Symposium on the International Situation and China's Foreign Relations in 2018*. Embassy of PRC in the USA, December, 11. http://www.china-embassy.org/eng/zgyw/t1621547.htm

Wang, Y. (2021). *Wang Yi hosts the First Meeting of the International Forum on COVID-19 Vaccine Cooperation*. Ministry of Foreign Affairs, PRC, Aug. 5.

Wheeler, A. (2020). Can the health silk road intervention save China's belt road initiative (BRI) from COVID-19 geopolitical fallout? *Silk Road Briefing*, April 7. https://www.silkroadbriefing.com/news/9

Williams, O. (2020). Zambia's default fuels fears of African 'debt tsunami' as Covid impact bites. The Guardian, November 25.

Winter, T. (2016). One Belt, One Road, One Heritage: Cultural diplomacy and the Silk Road. *The Diplomat*, March 29 (https://thediplomat.com/2016/03/one-belt-one-road-one-heritage-cultural-diplomacy-and-the-silk-road/)

WTO. (2019). *World trade report: Future of services trade*. World Trade Organization.

Xinhua News Agency. (2015). Spotlight: Just-conclude BRICS, SCO summits in Ufa highlight China's constructive role. July 12.

Xu, H. (2017). *The BRI is a global public goods*. China Center for International Economic Exchanges, Central University of Finance and Economics (CCIEE), March.

Yang, D. (2016). Chugoku kara mita TPP to sono taioh saku (TPP, as viewed by China, and its countermeasures). *Asia Japan Journal* (Asia-Japan Center, Kokushikan University, Tokyo), no. 11, March.

Yue, M., & Wang, C. M. (2020). *Brief: Public debt in the Belt and Road Initiative (BRI): How Covid-19 has accelerated an ongoing problem of China's lending*. International Institute of Green Finance, Central University of Finance and Economics, March.

Yusa, H. -J, (2013). Senryaku teki na izon kankei: Turkmenistan to Chugoku (Dependencies without strategy: Turkmenistan and China). Kaigai-Touyuhshi (Foreign Investment and Finance), November Issue, Kaigai Toyushi Joho Zaidan: The Japan Institute for Overseas Investment (JOI).

Chapter 5
Another Way of Development Through ICT: Possibility and Vulnerability

Abstract Since the 1990s, the importance of Information and Communications Technology (ICT)-enabled services/digitally deliverable services has steadily increased along with economic globalization. Until now, the driving force of the world economy has been world trade, mainly in goods. The digital economy has now arrived, with finance, telecommunications, software development, Business Process Outsourcing (BPO), and other service transactions becoming increasingly important, and Artificial Intelligence (AI) and big data becoming the greatest source of competitiveness. On the one hand, this economy has opened the way for some emerging and developing economies to develop through ICT and computer-based digital-based services trade, bringing great expectations to some emerging and developing economies. On the other hand, it has created increasingly difficult catch-up barriers for many developing countries. This chapter identifies the ICT-based services trade that has been the focus of much attention at the turn of the century, and refers to some of the key issues related to the development of emerging and developing economies that have been the subject of much discussion. At the same time, it examines the possibilities and challenges for the development of emerging and developing economies opened up by the development of ICTs.

Keywords Advantages of backwardness · Catching-up · Data-driven digital economy · ICT enabled services/digitally deliverable services · Information Technology (IT)-BPO · Leapfrogging · Offshoring · Premature deindustrialization

5.1 Introduction

Since the 1990s, accelerated progress in information and communications technology (ICT) has created major structural changes in the global economy, and its impact has brought a new development phenomenon to the emerging and developing economies of Asia. The world economy and society have become an era in which digitalization has hollowed out the existing legal systems of national units, and advanced economies require new international and national orders, institutions, and legal systems.

H. Hirakawa and F. C. Maquito, *The Dynamics of Asian Economic Development*,
https://doi.org/10.1007/978-981-97-3106-0_5

Incidentally, ICT innovation has given birth to a development model different from the traditional one in some emerging and developing economies. In Chap. 3 of this book, we discussed the mechanism of economic development in East Asia beginning with the Newly Industrializing Economies (NIEs), and in this century, a development model clearly different from that development model has emerged in Asia, especially in South Asian India. One World Bank report writes: "The two fastest growing regions in the world have very different growth patterns. While East Asia is a story of growth led by manufacturing, South Asia has thrived on service-led growth" (World Bank, 2009: 9). Thus, India, along with China and other countries, has become a member of the potentially bigger market economies (PoBMEs), raising expectations for its development even further.

The purpose of this chapter is to examine the reality of ICT-based services-led growth in emerging and developing economies and to address the prospects and challenges for their development. The structure of the chapter begins by reviewing the development of ICT and the changes in the digital economy and society, followed by an examination of the various debates related to the new growth and its prospects in the emerging economies of South Asia, particularly India. This will be followed by a discussion of the development potential of emerging Asian economies and developing economies and the challenges they face, focusing on the development of the IT-BPO industry in India, the Philippines, and other countries that have attracted attention in this type of development.

5.2 Advancement of Digital Technology and Developing Economies

In this section, we will see how the development of ICT is transforming the global economy and, at the same time, the digital economy, shifting the center of gravity of economic activity from goods to services, and more significantly to data and its use. The digital economy, driven by developed economies, is rapidly transforming business and society worldwide, with great potential and risks at the same time. Emerging and developing economies are emerging from this global structural change with new possibilities, but also with significant challenges.

5.2.1 Data-Driven Digital Economy and Its Issues

The development of ICT has ushered in an era of dramatic change in business and social life today, with everything connected to the Internet of things (IoT) and AI permeating society. Economic activity is shifting from goods to services, and the importance of digital data is growing dramatically. The global economy, driven by increased trade in goods and financial transactions that began at the end of the twentieth century, has begun to lose momentum this century, and has been replaced by "the new era of global flows," in which the global flow of "data" is dramatically increasing. There are four main areas of change (i) the emergence of multinational corporations on a truly global scale, (ii) the emergence of small businesses worldwide such as eBay, Amazon, Facebook, and Alibaba, which use digital platforms to reach huge consumers, (iii) the emergence of tech-based startups, and (vi) a dramatic increase in cross-border labor, learning, and communication by individuals.(Manyika, Lund et al., 2016).

The United Nations Conference on Trade and Development (UNCTAD) has also focused on these changes in the global economy this century, calling this economy the "data-driven digital economy" and examining its development and challenges from the perspective of developing countries (UNCTAD, 2019; 2021a: xv). According to the report, in the digital economy, the development of AI and the collection and accumulation of big data are concentrated in huge platform companies and research institutions in specific countries, creating a global imbalance, especially with emerging and developing countries, and also posing significant risks to the international community.

Figure 5.1 shows geographical distribution of 100 global digital platforms. The figure shows that giant ICT companies such as Apple, Microsoft, Alphabet (Google), Amazon, Facebook, Tencent, Alibaba, and Samsung dominate the global market and drive the economy. In terms of both total value and platform number, the United States and Asia are the two largest regions, with the United States and China in particular holding dominant positions in the digital economy. The report summarizes as follows.

> In terms of capacity to engage in and benefit from the data-driven digital economy, two countries stand out: the United States and China. Together, they account for half the world's hyperscale data centres, the highest rates of 5G adoption in the world, 94 percent of all funding of AI start-ups in the past five years, 70 percent of the world's top AI researchers, and almost 90 per cent of the market capitalization (UNCTAD, 2021a: xv)

But who or which country will govern the digital space in a data-driven digital economy, who will own big data, and how will it be used? The UNCTAD report devotes a chapter to the issue of governance in the data-driven digital economy, identifying three different national and regional approaches.

The three are the United States, the European Union, and China, as shown in Fig. 5.2, with the United States leaving the development to private digital companies, while China aims for strong state control and seeks to achieve global leadership through its "One Belt, One Road" foreign policy. The EU, on the other hand, is more concerned with the privacy of the individual and seeks to base its digital data regulations and rules on that value system.[1]

---

[1] In April 2023, the Cyberspace Administration of China (CAC) of the Chinese government announced proposed regulations for Alibaba and Baidu, which develop generative AI products like ChatGPT. The " content needs to reflect the core values of socialism and should not subvert state power" (CNBC April 11, 2023; NHK April 11, 2023). In May 2023, President Biden, Vice President Harris, and other senior U.S. government officials met with the heads of four major

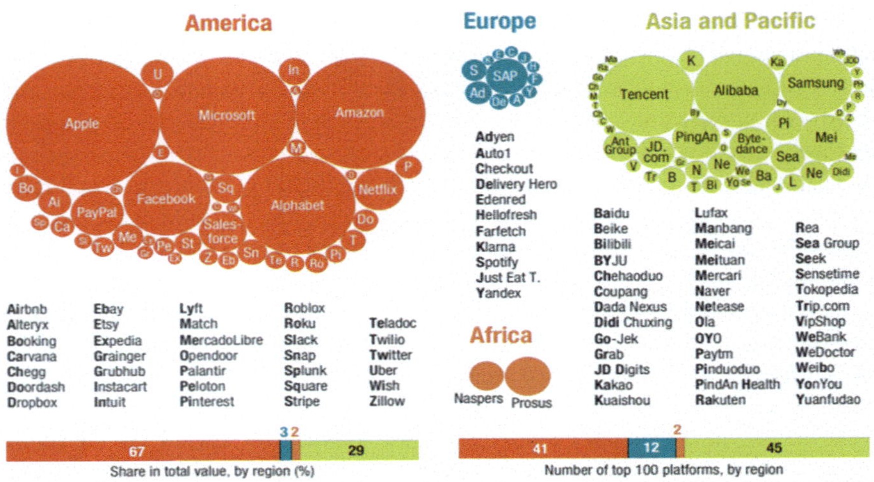

Fig. 5.1 Geographical distribution of the top 100 global digital platforms, by market capitalization 2021 (*Source* UNCTAD, 2021a: 22). *Note* Original data from Holger Schmidt, available at www.netzoekonom.de/#tab-id-1 (data as of May 2021). As a reference, the market capitalization of Apple is \$2.22 trillion, while for Mercado Libre it is \$88.7 billion, \$80.2 billion for Baidu, and \$59.7 billion for Spotify

Fig. 5.2 Approaches of the United States, European Union, and China to governing data and data flows (*Source* UNCTAD, 2021a: 98)

Within the digital economy's online infrastructure, there are two platforms with different characters. One is the transaction platform, and another is the innovation platform. "Transaction platforms are two/multi-sided markets with an online infrastructure that supports exchanges between a number of different parties. They have become a core business model for major digital corporations". "Innovation platforms create environments for code and content producers to develop applications and software in the form of, for example, operating systems (e.g. Android or Linux) or technology standards (e.g. MPEG video)" (UNCTAD, 2019: xv).

AI companies at the White House and expressed their pro-business position that the companies responsible for AI safety and privacy issues, including "ChatGPT," would be responsible for their development. On the other hand, the government will support AI innovation. (Reuters Business News, May 4, 2023).

Of course, at this stage, no consensus has been reached on international governance and international rulemaking. The data-driven digital economy is a combination of the U.S., where the evolution of AI and the accumulation of big data are advancing while being guided by the private interests of giant monopolistic platform companies, and China, which is attempting to bring it under the control of the state. While on the other hand, risks are emerging at various levels and in various domains, ranging from cyber attacks and the spread of fake news to risks related to national security, such as the struggle for supremacy in advanced technology between the U.S. and China. In addition, a large gap has emerged between the advanced economies promoting the digital economy and the overwhelming number of emerging and developing economies in terms of infrastructure sector development. There is a need for the formulation of fair rules for the international community.

5.2.2 Global Trade and Service Exports

Looking at global trade, the weight of trade in services has steadily increased over the past few decades. The expansion of services in trade and the increase in ICT-related transactions are explained by UNCTAD as follows.

> More services are increasingly tradable and possible to deliver remotely. This has given rise to an expansion of the outsourcing and offshoring of a range of business services. / Digitally delivered or ICT-enabled services are defined as services delivered remotely over ICT networks. They include insurance and pension services, financial services charges for the use of intellectual property, telecommunications, computer and information services, other business services, and audiovisual and related services" (UNCTAD, 2019: 6).

In order to understand the above quotation, let's first define the ICT-related services trade according to the UN definition (UNCTAD, 2021b: 31).

Figure 5.3 shows that 'ICT services' refers to 1.1 telecommunications and 1.2 computer services, while 'ICT-enabled services' is a broader category that includes ICT services, such as call centers and/or business process outsourcing (BPO). In recent notation, 'digitally-delivered services' and 'digitally-deliverable services' are used instead of ICT-enabled services, but it is not clear whether ICT-enabled services correspond to digitally-delivered services, and potentially ICT-enabled services correspond to digitally-deliverable services. The relationship is explained by Korka with the Division on Technology and Logistics, UNCTAD, as follows: "Potential ICT-enabled services/Digitally-deliverable = services with outputs that can be delivered remotely over ICT networks, excluding transport services (involve manipulation or transport of people, physical objects, material, or electricity), and on-site or in-person services (require on-site or personal delivery)" (Korka, 2017: 10).

In fact, as the development of ICT has given rise to a variety of services, and as many existing services are changing their labor content, trade in services is also changing its content and at the same time increasing rapidly, changing the structure of trade.

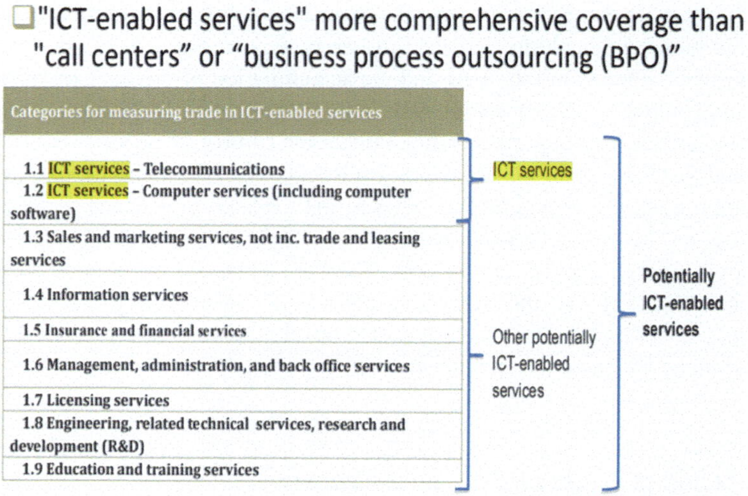

Fig. 5.3 Grouping for trade in ICT-enabled Services (*Source* Korka (2017). *Note* ICT services are an aggregation of computer and telecommunications services

Figure 5.4 uses world services export data compiled by UNCTAD at the turn of the century to identify export growth rates for three categories: digitally deliverable services; IC services; and total services exports. The following table shows the export growth rates for the three categories of digitally deliverable services, IC services and total services exports. The data shows that services exports are growing, but digitally deliverable services are outpacing this growth, and ICT services are growing even faster than digitally deliverable services. During this period (2005–2021), the growth rates were 2.3x, 3.2x, and 5.1x, respectively, and the average annual growth rates were 5.2%, 7.5%, and 10.7%, respectively.

However, focusing on 2020, the growth in total services exports is negative, while digitally deliverable services growth is moderate, and ICT services exports jump in the opposite direction. In 2020, the COVID-19 pandemic led to strong measures in major countries around the world, including city lockouts, border blockades, and travel restrictions. This led to a significant drop in traditional service exports, such as transportation and tourism, and a drop in all service exports. However, digitally deliverable services, which allow network businesses and remote work, did not decline as much during the pandemic. This was because ICT services grew significantly.

Incidentally, the UNCTAD report confirms that digitally deliverable services rose in all regions of the world in 2005–2018, but particularly in Asia, and that the nature of exports of these services tended to differ between developed and developing countries, as seen through a comparison of the share of digitally deliverable services in total services exports. The report writes:

> Developed economies accounted for more than three quarters (76%) of exports of such services. Their share was particularly high (80-90%) with respect to charges for the use of

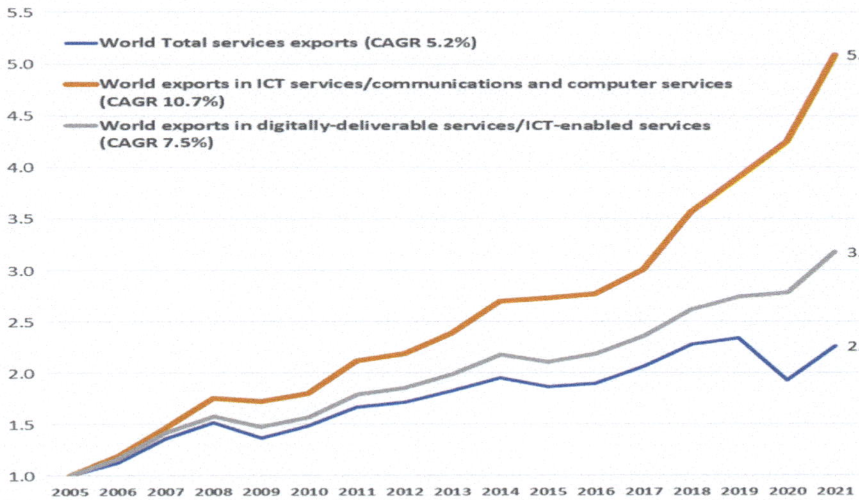

Fig. 5.4 Global exports of digitally deliverable services, ICT services, and total services, 2005–2021 (Index numbers, 2005 = 1.0) (*Source* UNCTADSTAT)

> intellectual property, financial services and audiovisual and related services. In developing countries, telecommunications, computer and information services constituted the largest share of digitally deliverable services (at 30%). In LDCs, those services accounted for 16% of all their services exports, and they more than tripled from 2005 to 2018, albeit from a very low level (UNCTAD, 2019: 66).

However, in some emerging economies in Asia, the share of digitally deliverable services in services exports rivals or exceeds that of developed economies. From pilot surveys conducted by UNCTAD in Costa Rica, India, and Thailand in 2017 for measuring digitally delivered services,[2] the differences in ICT services in emerging economies are estimated. In Costa Rica, 41% of total exports of services are digitally deliverable services, and "almost all (95%) of the digitally deliverable services were found to have been digitally delivered. Most of these exports were by large foreign-owned enterprises that were providing management, administrative, and back-office services to the United States. Meanwhile, micro and small enterprises accounted for 7.5% of the total exports of digitally delivered services" (UNCTAD, 2019: 66). However, the structure of India is entirely different from that of Costa Rica.

> In India, 70% of the total services exports were digitally deliverable in 2016. In their cases, 81% were digitally delivered, while the remainder were exported via the dispatch of ICT experts from India to the destination market. Thus, 57% of India's total exports of services were digitally delivered. Computer services were the biggest contributor, representing almost two-thirds of the total amount. For services-exporting SMEs, delivery over ICT networks constituted the predominant mode of supply (more than 99%), while for larger enterprises, many complemented remote ICT delivery with other modes of supply, notably sending experts to provide the services on site (2019: 66).

[2] Thailand's pilot survey was conducted exclusively by the Telecommunication Sector, so it is not possible to compare Costa Rica with India (UNCTAD, 2019: 66).

In retrospect, India had already begun to attract global attention in the 1990s with its rapid growth in ICT services. In the late 1990s (1996–2000), India's revealed comparative advantage (RCA) for goods and services was minus 15%, while for services it was plus 74%. 19%, travel 31%, and communication 2% in 1997–98, and 34% for software, 14% for travel, 10% for transportation, and 5% for communication in 2001–2."There has been a compositional shift in the structure of India's services exports away from traditional services such as transport and travel towards emerging services such as software and other services" (Basu, 2007: 486–487).

In this century, India's production and exports of ICT services will further accelerate. Specifically "software services and business process outsourcing (BPO) has been particularly striking". India's software services exports rose from $754 million in FY1995 to $17.2 billion in FY2004, and BPO exports also rose from only $665 million in FY1999 to $6 billion in FY2004 (Basu, 2007: 486–487). According to UNCTAD's Information Economy Report 2012, the total domestic sales and export values of India rose from $17.3 billion in 2005 to $59.3 billion in 2011, and the share of exports constantly kept 75%. In terms of export destinations, North America and European Union were respectively 62.1% and 25.7% in 2005, and 56.0% and 31.1% in 2011. Almost 90% were headed towards the advanced economies of the U.S. and Europe (UNCTAD, 2012: 40).

Looking at ICT services exports as a percentage of India's total services exports from a different perspective, the World Bank report shows that the share is around 50%, as shown in Fig. 5.5. This level is outstandingly high compared to the Philippines, and other countries such as Canada and China, which are considered to be competitors in ICT services exports with India.

Let us compare the growth of exports of goods and services in South Asia and East Asia and see their contrasting development structures as shown in Fig. 5.7. The figure shows the change in the index from 1996 to 2006, with exports of services

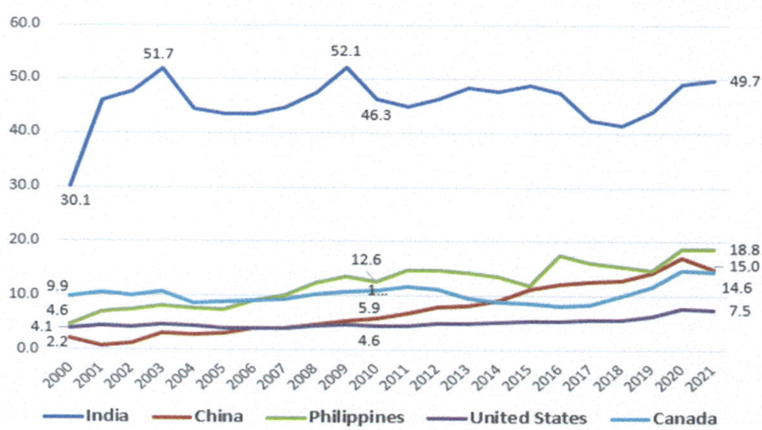

Fig. 5.5 ICT services exports as % of services exports: India, China, Philippines, United States, and Canada 2000–2021 (*Source* World Development Indicators database May 2023)

exceeding exports of goods in South Asia, while exports of goods exceed exports of services in East Asia. Moreover, the growth rate of services exports in South Asia is much higher than the growth rate of goods exports in East Asia.

In terms of absolute export value, India's exports are by far the largest in South Asia. The software exports of the four South Asian countries (Bangladesh, India, Pakistan, and Sri Lanka) in FY2007 were $29,300 million for India, and only $10 million for Pakistan, the next largest exporter. In terms of the population of engineers, Pakistan has 40,000, Sri Lanka 9,000, and Bangladesh 1,200 compared to India's 835,000. The difference between India and the other South Asian countries is of a different order of magnitude.

Separating modern services and traditional services, we see in Fig. 5.7 the changes in the RCA of services exports in South and East Asia. In South Asia, the competitiveness of modern services increased dramatically in two stages at the end of the 1990s and the beginning of the 2000s. In contrast, East Asia saw a significant decline in the competitiveness of services exports during this period. In other words, services imports generally expanded in East Asia, and the competitiveness of traditional services category exports declined in South Asia as well. Only South Asian services exports became more competitive (Fig. 5.8).

Figure 5.9 shows the growth in productivity by sector for the South Asian countries over the period 2000–2006. With the exception of Bangladesh, South Asian countries have the highest sectoral productivity in services, led by India. Although the chart is not shown, the employment growth index for the four South Asian countries for 1990–2006 shows that the service sector was the largest in India and Pakistan (World Bank, 2009: 72). As we have already confirmed, India is the dominant services export country, and it is confirmed that a development model in which modern services drive economic growth has emerged in South Asia, with India as a typical example.

Here is another figure (Fig. 5.6) on digitally deliverable services exports. This figure shows the evolution of ICT services exports and digitally deliverable services exports in value for India, the Philippines, and China over the period 2005–2021. At the beginning of this century, India was far ahead of China and the Philippines in both digitally deliverable services and ICT services exports in value. China's digitally deliverable services exports were about the same size as India's ICT services exports. However, in 2021, China ($1.95 trillion) exceeded India ($1.85 trillion) in digitally deliverable services. However, in exports of ICT services, China's exports were smaller than those of the Philippines. In other words, China's exports of digitally deliverable services are growing in the context of various services exports other than ICT services.

In the previous section, we confirmed that the digital economy is being driven by the U.S. and China. The fact that China's digitally deliverable services exports have overtaken India's can be seen as a reflection of the development of China's comprehensive ICT industry. On the other hand, India's high share of exports of ICT services, including software and BPO, keeps it ahead of other countries in this area. The Philippines, like India, is also increasing its exports, but its growth and export scale are far below India's. India is thus a representative nation of the digital age, which is rapidly developing around ICT services exports.

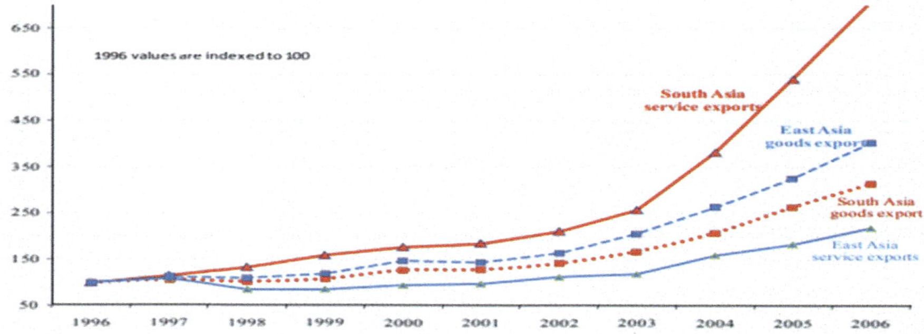

Fig. 5.6 South Asia's service export is growing faster than East Asia's goods export (*Source* World Bank, 2009: 48. Original data from IMF Balance of Payment). *Note* Exports are in current US$ terms. East Asia includes developing countries such as Cambodia, China, Indonesia, Malaysia, Philippines, Thailand and Vietnam. South Asia includes Bangladesh, India, Maldives, Nepal, Pakistan, and Sri Lanka

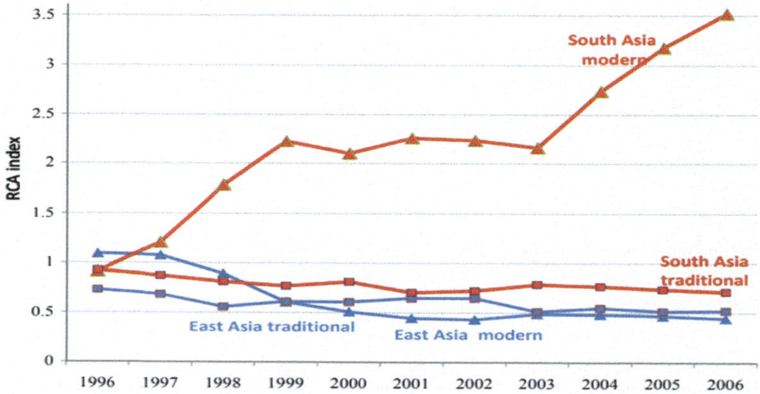

Fig. 5.7 Comparative advantage in modern services exports in South Asia and East Asia (*Source* World Bank, 2009: 28). *Note* The Revealed Comparative Advantage (RCA) index is calculated using the following concept: RCA = *(Mcj/EcT)/(Mwj/WwT)* where M = modern or traditional service exports, c = country index, j = specific sector index, w = world, T = total exports of goods and services. Modern services are communication, insurance, financial, computer, information, and other business services. The traditional services such as travel, transport, royalties, license fees, construction, and other business services

5.3 "Leapfrogging", "Premature" Deindustrialization, and Jobless Growth

In the 1990s, Asian development began to spread geographically from East Asia (Northeast and Southeast Asia) to South Asia. Moreover, it took a new form of development, different from the NIEs-type development through exports of industrial products in the latter half of the twentieth century. This has led to greater interest

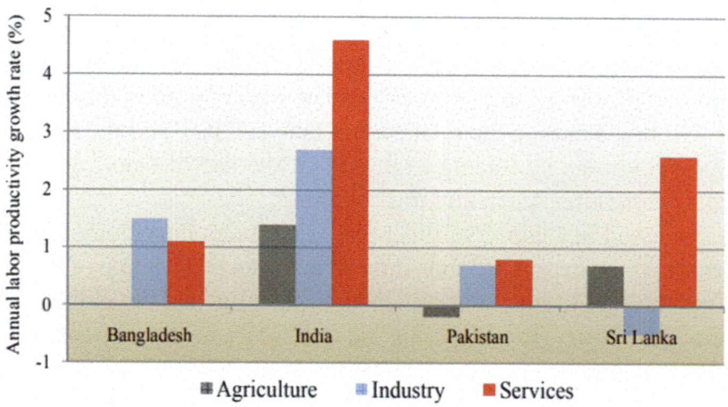

Fig. 5.8 Labor productivity growth by sector (*Source* World Bank, 2009: 17)

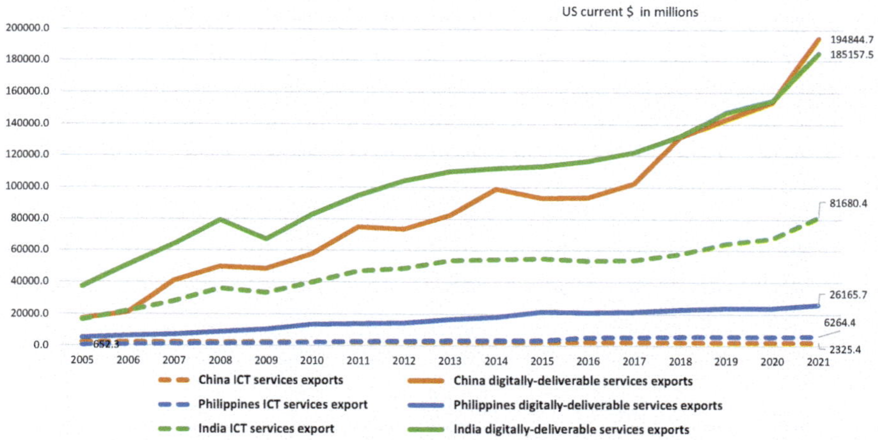

Fig. 5.9 ICT services exports and digitally deliverable services exports of India, Philippines, and China 2005–2021 (*Source* UNCTADSTAT)

in the relationship between technological innovation in advanced economies and the economic development of less developed countries. This section examines the characteristics of the development of emerging economies, focusing on the transfer of technology that supports economic development.

5.3.1 Service-Led Development in Asia, especially India and *"Leapfrogging"*

The relationship between technology and the industrialization and economic development of less developed countries has long been of interest. "Leapfrogging" is one of the terms used to describe the phenomenon of catch-up industrialization of less developed countries to advanced economies. It has also been widely used in the diffusion of ICT products to address global warming and other issues. In this section, we will first examine the relationship between ICT and the development of less developed countries by tracing examples of the use of leapfrogging, with the development of emerging Asian countries in mind.

First, as discussed in Chap. 3 of this book, East Asian development began in the late 1960s through the export of labor-intensive products. L. Soete of the University of Sussex was the first to note that this industrialization and development emerged in the electronics industry. In a book published in 1985, he drew attention to the role that technology played in the industrialization of Europe and the U.S. in the nineteenth century and Japan in the twentieth century, and further described the 'spurts' of industrialization of the electronics industry in East Asia in the late twentieth century as The paper then examines the development of East Asia from the perspective of technology transfer in relation to the development of microelectronics. The conclusion of the study was as follows, which rejects the technological panacea that the word "leapfrogging" implies: "there is little doubt that these conditions (such as competition pressures on market, rapid growth in both labor and capital productivity, 'deskilling' effects of the new electronics paradigm) are only fulfilled in a relatively small number of industrializing countries, not to mention developing countries" (Soete, 1985: 416–417).

In 1999, J. P. Singh of the American University used the term "leapfrogging development", relating the rapid development of Asian NIEs to the development of "telecommunications". He organized the usage of "leapfrogging" into three categories.

> The telecommunications literature used the word "leapfrogging" in three ways. First, it is meant to imply that telecommunications can help developing countries skip over the stages of development and become members of a post-industrial society. Second, leapfrogging is used in the "engine of growth" sense to mean that telecommunications can help developing countries accelerate their pace of development. Finally, leapfrogging is used in a technical sense to signify skipping over the technological or product cycle. Often the word "leapfrogging" is used interchangeably in both technological and economic ways (Singh, 1999: 5).

J. P. Singh devotes three chapters in his eight-chapter book to tracing the historical development of India's communications sector, detailing the privatization and liberalization policies of the Indian communications sector since 1991. The book also details the privatization and liberalization policies of the Indian communications sector since 1991. The internationalization of Indian telecommunications companies was collaborating with a number of foreign service providers and manufacturers, like Motorola, BellSouth, Bell Canada, France, and others. He titled his concluding chapter "The myth and reality of leapfrogging" and took a negative stance on the idea that technology itself can enable a latecomer to effectively catch up. (Singh, 1999).

In this century, the conceptualization of leapfrogging has deepened due to the relationship between the digital economy and the least developed countries as a result of the development of ICT. W.E. Steinmueller compared the development of firms and industries, such as steel, chemicals, and machinery, in the first industrialized countries with the development of ICT firms and industries in the second industrialized countries, extracted the characteristics of the development of industries in the second industrialized countries, and used the term "leapfrogging" to refer to the unique process of catching up (Steinmueller, 2001). He noted that according to W. W. Rostow's modernization theory, "development follows a linear, predictive path, with well-defined stages," but that the development of ICTs firms and industries do not follow such a development path. In short, "leapfrogging means bypassing stages in capability building or investment through which countries were previously required to pass during the process of economic development". Moreover, as for bypassing stages in capability, "capabilities are often constructed incrementally on the basis of experience, and the nature and extent of experience influence the evolution of capabilities in firms and industries. It is important, however, to distinguish between progress at the technological frontier, involving the discovery and invention of entirely new knowledge and capabilities, and progress in adopting and imitating technologies already in use" (Steinmueller, 2001: 194). In short、 two types of leapfrogging were identified for bypassing: acquisition of advanced technology and adoption and imitation of existing technology.

Steinmueller of the University of Sussex also cautions against optimism regarding leapfrogging in less developed countries, citing various obstacles to its realization, including the nature of the processing technology involved in producing the product, patents, and other technology transfer constraints. "By learning the 'language' of ICTs, people can discover new approaches to the social and physical world. As with any fundamental new technology, the gain from such new tools can never be fully anticipated. They remain to be demonstrated by those with vision and courage" (Steinmueller, 2001: 209).

The concept of leapfrogging was also elaborated mainly from the experience of Korea's industrial development (Lee & Lim, 2001; Lee & Ki, 2017; Lee, 2021). Keun Lee at Seoul National University focused on the research on the technological development of industrialization of the least developed countries as a process of catching up with the first developed countries, and attempted to enrich its content through the concept of leapfrogging. "Simply, leapfrogging can be defined as latecomers trying something different ahead of the forerunners, thereby leaping over them " (Lee, 2021: 123), he defined. Then, in a paper co-authored with C. Lim at Korea Christian University in 2001, he defined 'stage-skipping catch-up' and 'path-creating catch-up', and subsequently elaborated on the catch-up process (Fig. 5.10). Lee has recently proposed a "general theory of economic catch-up" consisting of three detour paths, shown in the rightmost column of Fig. 5.10. He writes: "(Lee) proposed a comprehensive theory of economic catch-up, consisting of "late entry ⇒ three detours ⇒ leapfrogging", and positioned leapfrogging as the final stage of catching-up after the detour stage of building technological capabilities" (Lee, 2021: 124).

Lee & Lim (2001)		Lee & Ki (2017)				Lee (2019, 2021)
Compared with the path of the incumbents		Two types of path creation (Path following and path creating)				A comprehensive theory of economic catch-up through three detours: Late entry ⇒ three detours ⇒ leapfrogging
1) Path-Following Catch-up:	cf) Firms adopt old technology, but cannot compete with the incumbent in the same market	**First choice (path-following catch-up)**: moving along the old technical tragectories of incumbents				**First detour**: to promote minor innovation via petit patents rather than the high level of innovation
2) Stage-Skipping Catch-up:	Following the same path as that of incumbents but skip older-generation technology	**Second choice (Stage-skipping catch-up)**: following the same path as that of incombents but skip older-generation technology				**Second detour**: to increase the share of domestic value-added in exports rather than keep relying on GVCs
3) Path-Creating Catch-up:	Exploring its own path of technological development by utilizing a new generation of technology	**Third choice (Path-creating catch-up)**: exploring its own path of technological development by utilizing a new generation technology	a) Follow-on innovation (incremental/reinvention)-based b) Radical innovation-based	a) By in-house or endogenous b) By exogenous or supplier-driven innovation	a) Inter-sectoral innovation b) Intra-sectoral innovation	**Third detour**: to specialize in short-cycle technology rather than long-cycle technologies

Fig. 5.10 Lee's development of definition of the technological catch-up and leapfrogging (*Source* Lee & Lim, 2001; Lee & Ki, 2017; Lee: 123:127). *Note* The author's summary is mainly from Lee (2021)

Lee (2021) concludes his paper with a section on "prospect of leapfrogging-based development" and identifies three groups of leapfrogging counterparts in less developed countries.[3] Group A includes China, Korea, and Brazil, and is a "public–private partnership" type of leapfrogging in which national policy plays an important role. Group B includes Malaysia, Thailand, Brazil,[4] and Mexico, which are MNC-led leapfrogging driven by FDI-based manufacturing, and Group C includes Indonesia, India, the Philippines, African countries, and Argentina, which have a weak manufacturing base. Group C is an innovation model based on 'the fourth industrial revolution (4IR)-related services startups (Lee, 2021: 152–153). This grouping gives the impression that the core drivers of industrialization are chronologically ordered from the state to MNCs to ICT/automation.

Soete and Singh, above, also used the term leapfrogging to refer to the "great spurt of industrialization" or "accelerate their pace of development" that Gerschenkron found to be characteristic of the least industrialized countries.[5] But in the research phase of Steinmueller and Lee in this century, various catch-up paths are recognized, including gradual skipping in late industrialization, but now we see that leapfrogging is being used in relation to technology, i.e., ICTs.

Incidentally, global issues such as global warming, renewable energy technologies (ERTs), etc. have further increased developed countries' interest in leapfrogging. The UNCTAD report (2011) points out that "In much of the industrial world, issues relating to climate change have begun to revolve around the notion of the 'green economy '….The 'green economy' and 'clean energies' agenda are very apparent to most developed countries but are viewed with skepticism and concern by developing countries". This is why the acquisition of technological learning and innovation by LDCs and poor countries with inferior economic and technological capacity has come to be called leapfrogging (UNCTAD, 2011: 9–10).

> The nature of recent technological advances, notably in ICT and energy, means that catch-up no longer necessarily requires following the historical paths of frontrunners, but may rather be achieved by technological 'leapfrogging' … The recent increase in attention to technological leapfrogging has been motivated in large part by the experience of the ICT sector. Rapid technological advances and associated cost reductions in ICT in recent decades have enabled some developing countries, notably in Africa, to skip the development of

---

[3] However, Lee points out that leapfrogging is not something that is automatically achieved, and depends on "each country's responses and readiness, including industrial policy, digital literacy, and skill and educational level compared to wage rates, and domestic market size and position in GVC" (Lee, 2021: 152).

[4] Brazil is included in both Groups A and B.

[5] In 1971, Japanese researcher Kiyoshi Kojima named the Flying Geese Theory the 'catching-up product cycle' (CPC) theory in reference to R. Vernon's product cycle hypothesis, and linked it to the industrial upgrading of Japan. The theory is based on the industrialization of Asia in conjunction with the industrial upgrading of Japan. See Chap. 12 for more details. Toshio Watanabe, in his paper uses the term of compressed growth ('compressed growth') to refer to 'A. Gerschenkron's 'advantages of backwardness' and/or 'the great spurt in industrialization ' (Gerschenkron, 1962: 51, 79, 204; Watanabe -J 1986: 210). Japanese studies have been exclusively concerned with the transfer of industry from Japan, overlooking consideration of the process of industrial development in the host country.

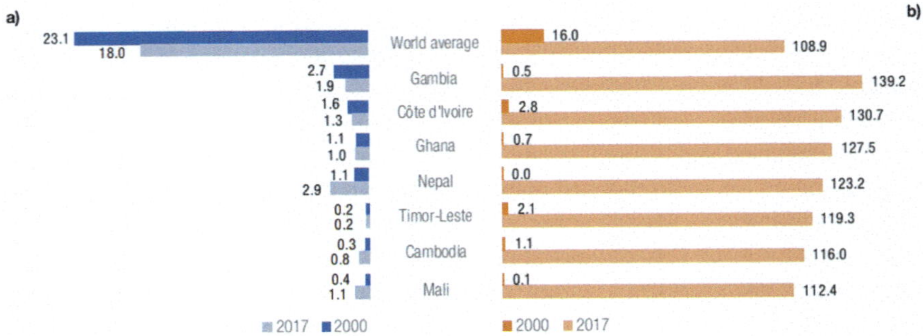

Fig. 5.11 Countries that leapfrogged to mobile technology: A comparison of (**a**) fixed-telephone and (**b**) mobile subscriptions per 100 habitants, 2000 and 2017 (*Source* UNCTAD, 2018b)

analogue landline infrastructure by moving directly to digital mobile telecommunications (UNCTAD, 2018a:84; UNCTAD, 2018b).

Mobile phones and Fin-Tech services in Africa have been widely discussed as a typical example of stage-skipping catch-up. Mobile phones have been spreading beyond the fixed-line telephony stage, which requires large initial investments, and are now being used by a large number of people in Africa (Fig. 5.11). Fin-Tech services through mobile banking systems are rapidly spreading, especially in Africa. It is the same in the case of off-grid solar power. The Financial Times Op-Ed, cites that "digital services don't replace the place of good governance". In Sub-Saharan Africa only 37% have access to electricity, but "73 m households, mostly in Africa, had access to off-grid solar power by 2017. This rapid spread, which has enabled remote parts of Africa to jump from having no electricity straight to green power, is the quintessence of the leapfrogging argument" (Financial Times, Aug.13, 2018).

UNCTAD writes that while it has been limited to employment effects and the urban sector, leapfrogging has been successful in India and the Philippines, as follows:ICTs "open up opportunities to bypass the manufacturing stages of development to leapfrog into the services economy—and some developing countries have moved in this direction, participating in global value chains through global outsourcing in ICT services" (UNCTAD, 2018a: 85; Yayboke et al., 2020).

In the energy sector, there has been a lot of discussion on the topic of "leapfrogging" in the field of renewable energy through ICT. Brazil is the world's second largest producer of liquid biofuels for transport in renewable energy technologies after the United States. China is the world's major producer of solar photovoltaic (PV) and solar thermal heating technologies (UNCTAD, 2018a: 86). Other potential applications in agriculture, providing employment opportunities for women, education, and many other areas are expected and being tested.

To be sure, ICTs do not automatically bring technological leapfrogging to less developed countries as the word suggests.[6] However, ICTs are opening pathways

[6] L. Burlamaqui at State University of Rio de Janeiro and R. Kattel at Tallinn University of Technology, Estonia argues that the perception of 'leapfrogging' is false, based primarily on Latin American development experience, that neither convergence nor catch-up has occurred, and that

for 'stage-skipping' catch-ups that bypass traditional developmental stages, and for 'path-creating' catch-ups based on new products and services that did not exist in the past.

For example, let's review Sri Lanka's expectations for its IT service sector. Sri Lanka is the country that leased the right to manage and operate the Hambantota port for 99 years to a joint venture with China in 2017, to repay its debt. Regardless of whether the criticisms are valid or not, it has attracted global attention as an example of China's "debt trap": Sri Lanka defaulted on its debt due to a sharp drop in tourism revenues caused by the COVID-19 pandemic, and a meeting of creditor nations, led by Japan, has been launched in April 2023. It is this reality that is bringing interest in the IT/ICT industry or sector to Sri Lanka.

The country's revenue and workforce of the ICT industry more than doubled between 2015 and 2020. In 2021, the industry's revenue is around $20 billion and the workforce is about 130,000. If these trends continue, Sri Lanka's ICT sector is expected to reach $600 million in revenue and 240,000 in workforce by 2030, and investment in ICT education is expected to be a key driver of this growth. According to the Sri Lanka Export Development Board (SLEDB), there are over 300 ICT companies, "a highly skilled talent pool combined with the cost-effective operational ability makes Sri Lanka's ICT industry one of the most profitable industries to date". They export software products and services to North America, the EU, Australia, East Asia, the Middle East, Africa, and Nordic regions (Karunaratne, 2022; SLEDB. Accessed June 28, 2023). The ICT sector has a number of advantages. Investment in education for this sector is highly efficient, specifically "one that can be scaled without the need for significant capital expenditure". "A significant portion of revenue generated by exporters in the manufacturing sector flows out of the country to pay for raw material imports. The IT sector also pays far better wages at all levels compared to most other key export industries".

Thus, international organizations, global corporations in developed countries, and governments, corporations, and individuals in less developed countries are now pursuing leapfrogging for policy and business interests at various levels.

5.3.2 ICT and Premature Deindustrialization

Since the 1990s, interest in China and India as drivers of global economic growth has increased, and in 2001 Jim O'Neill with Goldman Sachs coined the term BRICs from the initials Brazil, Russia, India, and China. A 2004 paper by Dani Rodrick at the Institute for Advanced Study and Arvind Subramaniam, the former Chief Economic

the development of least developed countries should be informed by Schumpeterian innovation theory (Burlamaqui, 2011; Burlamaqui and Kattel, 2016). In light of the Latin American experience, the authors seem to have expressed a strong discomfort with the term Leapfrogging, which gives the impression of being viewed as an automatic catch-up.

Advisor to the Government of India, also spoke highly of India's prospects from a different perspective in this historical context.

They estimate that India's post-1980s growth rate is double the previous growth rate—a per capita economic growth rate of 1.7% in 1950–1980 to 3.8% in 1980–2000—and that the growth rate in 2003/04 will be as high as 8%. The growth rate for the next 20 years (2005–25) was estimated at a lower bound rate of 6.7% per year, or a per capita growth rate of 5.3%, given the supply of labor force and the spread of education (Rodrick & Subramaniam, 2004: 6).

After considering the growth of total factor productivity (TFP) due to institutional reforms, building good economic and political institutions such as a stable democratic policy, reasonable rule of law and protection of property rights, building R&D facilities by foreign IT companies, and stock of human capital as positive factors of growth, and the lack of spillover effects of ICT, the quality of institutions, and agricultural issues as negative factors, they reached an optimistic conclusion as an overall judgment. The title of their paper, "Why India can grow at 7 percent a year or more," speaks volumes (Rodrick & Subramaniam, 2004: 7–14).

The following year, however, S. Dasgupta and A. Singh examined India's development prospects, mainly in relation to development economics theory. In their co-authored paper, they raised the following points: (a) According to existing development economics, manufacturing is the 'engine of growth' as taught by the Kaldorian theory of structural change. However, there are cases in which the service sector is the engine of growth in developing countries; (b) 'de-industrialization' at low levels of per capita income in a number of developing countries is occurring; (c) Jobless growth in the formal sector even in fast growing countries such as India is occurring; (d) There has been a large expansion of the informal sector in a number of both fast- and slow-growing developing countries. The result of their growth analysis is as follows.

> Finally, in relation to manufacturing versus services, our data indicates that both are closely related to the growth of GDP. In the structural analysis of economic growth, it is customary to argue that high a R-square for services does not indicate a directly causal relationship, but rather it is derived from the close relationship between manufacturing and GDP growth. The implication is that the growth of services depends largely on the growth of manufacturing.... Information technology, in particular, can be regarded more as causing the expansion of manufacturing rather than the other way around (Dasgupta, & Singh 2005: 28).

In other words, both the manufacturing and service sectors are closely related to the growth rate of GDP. (a) However, since the service sector does not statistically find a direct relationship with economic growth, the service sector must be dependent on the growth of the manufacturing sector, indicating the validity of the Kaldorian theory of the engine of growth. (b) Regarding 'de- industrialization', the share of Indian industry continued to increase throughout the 1980s and 1990s. In this respect, deindustrialization has not occurred. However, when compared to the level of employment in industry in developed countries, it is low in absolute terms. That is true for almost all of the developing countries' share of manufacturing employment.

This fact had already been found as a rule of thumb by José Gabriel Palma in his study of mainly Latin American countries. Table 5.1 above shows that no developing country exceeds the peak of manufacturing employment in the Industrial countries.

Dasgupta and Singh noted this finding of Palma when they wrote, "Palma suggests that during the 1990s, de-industrialization began at an increasingly lower level of per capita income" (Dasgupta, & Singh, 2005: 4, 9; Palma, 2005). They revisited the role of manufacturing and services in the following year's paper using a Kaldorian framework and, as did Palma, used the term "premature industrialization" to refer to the phenomenon of India, and developing countries, peaking at lower levels of manufacturing employment share and per capita income levels than the developed countries. However, they interpreted India as a special case with the development of ICT, and concluded that the service sector could make a positive contribution along with the manufacturing sector. They write:

> They (=services) fulfill the requirements of dynamic sectors in the Kaldor sense and could therefore be regarded as an additional engine of growth. In the specific case of India with the kind of primacy the country has achieved in ICT, the new engine might help India leapfrog in technological development to catch up with advanced countries (Dasgupta, & Singh, 2006: 15).

Moreover, they distinguished between two types of deindustrialization of developing countries: "There are two ideal types of deindustrialization that are occurring in the developing world. First there is the Indian kind, where manufacturing employment, including both informal and formal sector" has not declined. "The second ideal type, which more likely suggests pathological deindustrialization, has occurred in several Latin American and African countries in the 1980s and 1990s" (Dasgupta, & Singh, 2006:16).

Dasgupta and Singh view the second type of countries as effectively premature deindustrialization. They interpret this as a result of the Washington Consensus policies of international financial institutions (IFIs) debt crisis in the 1980s and 1990s,

Table 5.1 Employment in manufacturing by region (% of total)

Region	1960	1970	1980	1990	1998
Sub-Saharan Africa	4.4	4.8	6.2	5.5	5.5
Latin America and the Caribbean	15.4	16.3	16.5	**16.8**	14.2
Southern Cone and Brazil	17.4	17.2	16.2	**16.6**	11.8
West Asia and North Africa	7.9	10.7	12.9	15.1	**15.3**
Southeast Asia	8.7	9.2	10.7	13.0	**13.9**
East Asia (except China and Japan)	10.0	10.4	15.8	**16.6**	14.9
NIE-1s	10.5	12.9	18.5	**21.0**	16.1
China	10.9	11.5	10.3	**13.5**	12.3
Developing Countries	10.2	10.8	11.5	**13.6**	12.5
Industrial Countries	26.3	**26.8**	24.1	20.1	17.3

(*Source* Palma (2005: 75). Original data from ILO statistics). Note East Asia (except China and Japan): Hong Kong (China), Indonesia, Malaysia, Philippines, South Korea, Singapore, Thailand, and Taiwan (China). "NIE-1s": Hong Kong (China), South Korea, Singapore, and Taiwan (China).

which led to a considerable structural change. In their conclusion, they argued for the need for new industrial policies that contradict the interpretation of mainstream economics. "Institutional renewal of industrial policies in East Asia is far along the way with the focus being on government support of science and technology to knowledge-based industries and services". "East Asia still provides an extremely useful role model for these countries" (Dasgupta, & Singh, 2006: 16–17).

The premature deindustrialization theory that Dasgupta and Singh were interested in was noticed by D. Rodrik at Harvard Kennedy School in the 2010s (Rodrik, 2013). He argues that historically, developed countries following the UK followed a path of industrial structural transformation and a shift from an agrarian to an urban society, whereas "the developing world's pattern of industrialization has been different. Not only has the process been slow, but deindustrialization has begun to set in much sooner." He notes that, with the exception of South Korea's export-led industrialization, Brazil, India, and China have all experienced high growth over the past decade, while their peak manufacturing employment shares are lower than those of developed countries, both in terms of employment shares and per capita income levels. Thus, we point out the possible reasons for this as follows."It is not clear why developing countries are deindustrializing so early in their growth trajectories. One obvious culprit may be globalization and economic openness" (Rodrik, 2013).

D. Rodrik published a paper titled 'Premature deindustrialization' in 2015, in which he conducted a statistical analysis of the manufacturing employment share, at current and constant prices, since the 1960s, of 42 countries in Latin America, Asia and Sub-Saharan Africa, including developed countries, classifying the countries of the world into three regions (i) a high-income region that is already industrialized, (ii) one with a strong comparative advantage (or head start) in manufacturing, and (iii) the other without (a comparative advantage in manufacturing)". In short, (i) is a case of mature industrialization and is not subject to consideration. (ii) low-income regions with an increase in output and (possibly) employment, and (iii) other low income regions with a decline in both output and employment. "These consequences broadly capture the trends we have seen in the advanced economies, Asian manufacturers exports, and other developing economies, respectively" (Rodrik, 2015: 22). Economies without manufacturing industries in Latin America and in Africa need to discover new growth models. "One possibility is services-led growth. Many services, such as IT and finance, are high productivity and tradable, and could play the escalator role that manufacturing has traditionally played". However, the "bulk of other services" suffers from two shortcomings. Economies in the third region are technologically not very dynamic. Or they are non-tradable, which means that their ability to expand rapidly is constrained by income (and hence productivity) in the rest of the economy" (Rodrik, 2015: 24).

But D. Rodrik, in his 2018 book, "Straight talk on trade: Ideas for a sane world economy", reiterates his strong pessimism about India's development. He explains as follows.

> India demonstrates the limitations of relying on services rather than industry in the early stages of development. The country has developed remarkable strengths in IT services, such as software and call centers. However, the bulk of the Indian labor force lacks the skills

> and education to be absorbed into such sectors. In East Asia, unskilled workers were put to work in urban factories, making several times what they earned in the countryside. In India, they remain on the land or move to construction and petty services (where their productivity is not much higher). Structural change is limited by the growth of domestic demand for nontraditional products (Rodrik, 2018: 81).

While developed countries were able to employ 30% or more of their labor force workforce in manufacturing, the most recent laggards seldom enjoyed such benefits. In Brazil, manufacturing accounted for only 16% of employment, and in Mexico, it reached a plateau at 20%. In India, it reached 13% and then declined (in relative terms) (Rodrik, 2018: 90) and the two causes of premature deindustrialization are technology and trade (or globalization) (90–91). As early as 2004, Rodrik appreciated India's democracy and saw limitations in China's political system. However, he now evaluates China in the opposite way. Although China is a non-democracy, "its experimental approach to institutional design mimics in essence the deliberative and decision-making practices of democratic societies, taking care to ensure that reforms are well implemented in specific areas and that there is no major redistribution of wealth. Rodrik's perception changed to pessimism, as obstacles to the development of a service sector-led India are strongly perceived.

M. Atolia et al. examine structural transformation and industrialization in a globalized world in a 2018 IMF Working Paper, citing Vietnam, along with India, as successful examples. The paper argues that sub-Saharan African countries that are not competitive in manufacturing are losing out to competition in the global market and are forced to prematurely deindustrialize. Countries, such as India and Vietnam are discussed "as an incredible success story of recent times, considerably improving their public fundamentals to grow and industrialize at a rapid pace for the past 30 years. On the contrary, many SSA countries, for example, Nigeria, have suffered greatly due to poor infrastructure that has deterred investment in and upgrading of manufacturing facilities that would have enabled them to compete in international markets" (Atolia et al., 2018: 34).

For the record, a brief look at Vietnam's IT-related industries in the White Book 2020 shows that the IT, electronics, and telecommunications industry grew from 21,658 to 42,136 firms between 2015 and 2019. The breakdown is as follows: the hardware electronics industry will grow from 2,980 to 5,365, software companies from 6,143 to 12,423, digital content enterprises from 2,339 to 3,982, and IT services enterprises from 10,196 to 20,136. Revenue increased from $60,715 million to $112,566 million in total during this period, of which $100,338 million (89%) was in the hardware electronics industry in 2019 (MIC, 2020). However, the growth of the software industry is not insignificant. According to a blog (Jan. 9, 2023) by Rikkeisoft, a Vietnamese software development company, the average monthly income in Vietnam is $284, compared to India's $396 and Philippine's $1,620. The country's IT outsourcing industry is growing strongly, with an estimated growth rate of 13.47% through 2027. The number of IT engineers was 480,000, the average salary of software engineers is $655 in India, $664/month in Vietnam, $679 in the Philippines, $2954 in China, and $3658 in Singapore. Around 57,000 tech freshers were produced by more than 400 universities & education centers.[7] Vietnam, along with India, is presented as the country that can provide engineers at the lowest cost. However, unlike India, the development of the ICT industry appears to be following the development of the manufacturing industry in Vietnam. While there are significant differences in the scale and qualitative level of the industries, Vietnam's development appears to be similar to that of China.

After all, Rodrik, who saw India's future in the early twenty-first century in terms of leapfrogging, later became increasingly aware of the pessimistic premature deindustrialization scenario for India's development through the services sector. This is partly because he was influenced by China's unexpected development, but also because he noted that the knowledge-intensive service characteristics of the ICT sector were unlikely to lead directly to development at the country level, i.e., at the national economic level, and that India's social characteristics made technological spillovers difficult. Thus, Rodrik, like Dasgupta and Singh, is skeptical of neoliberal policies and recognizes the importance of policies by emerging country governments. In fact, through his own research, he seems to have become keenly aware of the fact that many emerging and developing economies are falling into the trap of premature deindustrialization due to their inability to fully develop manufacturing industries in a global marketplace where liberalism prevails. This led to his strong pessimistic perception of India.

5.3.3 Impact of Automation on Emerging Economies/ Developing Countries

Oxford University's Carl B. Frey and Michael A. Osborne's 2013 paper "The Future of Employment" has had a global impact by empirically estimating the serious impact of automation on U.S. employment. Building on previous research on computers and jobless growth, they use the 2010 U.S. Bureau of Labor Statistics data of 702 specific occupations to estimate the employment risk from the introduction of computerization. They estimated the employment risk from the introduction of computerization using the U.S. Bureau of Labor Statistics data of 702 detailed occupations in 2010, and found that 47% of U.S. jobs are at risk of being lost over the next 10–20 years, with significant negative impacts on wages and employment (Frey & Osborne, 2013). Incidentally, their estimates were also disputed. For example, an OECD study by Melanie Arntz et al. (Arntz et al., 2016) estimated an automation labor replacement rate of 9% for 21 OECD countries. Frey and Osborne's estimate was an overestimate because an occupation-based approach was used, and a task-based approach would have resulted in a replacement rate of less than one-fifth.

Incidentally, how will computerization affect employment in emerging and developing economies? While it is an extremely serious threat to the governments and industries of the countries concerned, there are two generalizations that confirm the

[7] (https://rikkeisoft.com/blog/outsourcing-in-vietnam/ Accessed August 1, 2023).

outlook: one of pessimism and one of optimism. Erich Brynjolfsson and Andrew McAfee take the former approach in their book "The Second Machine Age, 2014", which provides a historical overview of the significance of the information age and the growing inequality in the US in relation to technology. They identify the characteristics of the second machine age as computing, extraordinarily large amounts of digitized information, and recombinant innovation, and they identify these developments in the U.S. economy as well as their implications for the emerging and their impact on emerging and developing economies.

> In the long run, the biggest effect of automation is likely to be on workers not in America and other developed nations, but rather in developing nations that currently rely on low-cost labor for their competitive advantage. If you take most of the costs of labor out of the equation by installing robots and other types of automation, then the competitive advantage of low wages largely disappears. ... This can bring manufacturing back to America... A similar argument applies outside of manufacturing. For instance, interactive voice-response systems are automating jobs in call centers. ... This can disproportionately affect low-cost workers in places like India and the Philippines (Brynjolfsson, & McAfee, 2014: 184).

Martin Ford also noted in "The Rise of the Robots" in 2015 the potential for the digitization of the economy to take away routine labor and even highly educated and skilled professional jobs. He then extended his outlook to offshoring, predicting its medium- and long-term impact on emerging and developing economies. He writes it as follows:

> While the trend toward increased automation of white-collar jobs is clear, the most dramatic onslaught – especially for truly skilled professionals – still lies in the future. The same cannot necessarily be said for the practice of offshoring, where knowledge educated and skilled professionals such as lawyers, radiologists, and especially computer programmers and information technology workers have already felt a significant impact. In India, for example, There are armies of call center workers and IT professionals, as well as tax preparers versed in the American and British tax systems, and solicitors specifically trained not in their own country's legal system but in U.S. and UK law, standing ready to perform low-cost legal research for firms engaged in domestic litigation. ... Offshoring is very often a precursor of automation, and the jobs it creates in low-wage nations may prove to be short-lived as technology advances. As technology advances, we can expect that more and more of the routine tasks now performed by offshore workers will eventually be handled entirely by machines. ... huge numbers of offshore call center jobs are poised to be vaporized" (Ford, 2015: 117-118, 121).

In contrast, R. Baldwin, as mentioned in Chap. 3, takes an optimistic view of industrialization in emerging and developing economies and that offshoring will continue. His 2016 book "The Great Convergence" explains that today's globalization is in the second unbundling phase where trade costs and ICT costs are falling, and production unbundling is occurring, "making it easier to transfer more stages overseas"...these trends suggest that the unbundling of G7 factories and the offshoring of an ever wider range of production stages is likely to continue". In the future, "Firms with advanced know-how may increasingly leverage their knowledge with low-cost labor in, say, Africa or South America. Chinese firms may spearhead this new offshoring in an effort to offset the competitiveness losses that stem from rising Chinese wages"

(Baldwin, 2016: 290, 299). He saw the development of ICT instead as advancing the potential for future offshoring.

Incidentally, in its 2017 report, UNCTAD notes that digital technology creates new jobs and occupations in various sectors. New demand is generated by data analysis, software and applications (apps) development, networking, and artificial intelligence (AI), as well as designing and production of new intelligent machines, robots, and 3D printers. As in the case of the growth of American e-commerce, we could summarize as follows." As the digital economy grows, enterprises across sectors are likely to hire more people with skills related to cyber security. Estimates suggest that there are one million unfilled cybersecurity jobs worldwide, and that by 2019 the number will have risen to 1.5 million". Of course, some jobs will decline. An example of this was the BPO sector in the Philippines as 89% of jobs are at risk of being lost (UNCTAD, 2017: 63). Two years later, the UNCTAD's Digital Economy Report, noting that most studies "focus on the risk of job losses without considering the fact that new jobs will emerge in connection with digital disruptions", focused on job creation as follows:

> From the perspective of "creative destruction", the introduction of new technologies leads to some job destruction as some activities disappear, but also to job creation as new activities emerge. However, in the long-term, job creation linked to increases in productivity from digitalization may more than compensate for the job losses during the transition period. Thus, digitalization will result in both winners and losers in the job market. ... The net outcome is likely to be highly contextual, depending on different factors, such as the level of development, production and labour market structures, skills, and technological capacities (UNCTAD, 2019: 96).

The Asian Development Bank (ADB) took a similar perspective for its 2018 report, providing a detailed empirical analysis of Asian economies. While most previous studies have focused on the impact of technology on industry and service employment, the labor demand of new technology must also be taken into account. Doing so "over the past 25 years, the Asian region has created 300 million jobs annually in industry and services" (ADB, 2018: 49). The idea was that technological development has not only taken jobs away, but on the contrary, it has led to job creation, which has increased productivity and wages. However、the ADB report notes that "Indeed, that reshoring did not happen in 2005–2015 does not mean it will not happen in the near future" (ADB, 2018: 83).

The ADB report further examines the issue of job loss. Asian countries and economies are today in the 20% range of total employment in Taiwan and Vietnam, where external demand from developed countries is large, but many other Asian countries and economies, the contribution of domestic demand is significant, with employment in the 80–90% range of total employment related to domestic demand (ADB, 2018: 83). Robots have also been introduced in a) electrical and electronics industries, and automobile manufacturers, and b) producers of textiles, apparel, goods, and of food and beverages. Moreover, the shares of a) and b) in total employment by industry are 13.4% and 31.4%, respectively. This leads to the expectation that the impact of the wave of automation on employment will proceed slowly (ADB, 2018: XVI). Ultimately, the impact of future technological developments on employment

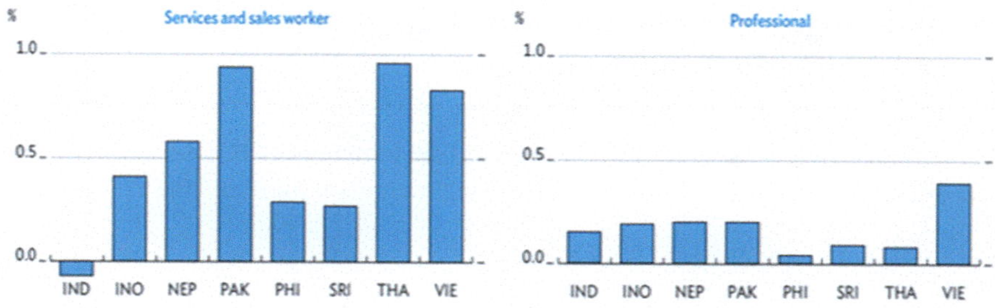

Fig. 5.12 Annual change in employment share by occupation, selected Asian economies (*Source* ADB, 2018: 85). *Note* IND = India, INO = Indonesia, NEP = Nepal, PRK = Pakistan, PHI = Philippines, SRI = Sri Lanka, THA- Thailand, VIE = Vietnam. Annual changes are: India 2000–2012, Indonesia 2000–2014, Nepal 1998–2008, Pakistan 2002–2013, Philippines 2001–2013, Sri Lanka 2004–2014, Thailand 2000–2010, and Vietnam 2000–2013

would be gradual in Asia, and appropriate job creation policies would be able to solve the employment problem, outpacing the loss of jobs (ADB, 2018).

Figure 5.12 shows the employment growth rates of services and sales workers and professionals in major Asian countries this century. The ADB's discussion above shows that, with the exception of Indonesia, all countries have seen similar growth in employment not only of services and sales workers but also of professionals, who require higher skills. The ADB's discussion above provides a relatively optimistic view of the evolution of ICT and the digital economy in the emerging and developing economies of Asia.

Frey of Oxford University, who pioneered this issue by proposing the replacement of jobs by automation, commented on the impact on employment of the recent threatening development of generative AI technology, stating that labor-intensive tasks such as pre-processing of data in its development will not decrease. He opined that this type of labor would rather increase and "benefit" (Nikkei -J, July 20. 2023). It is a perception that allows for optimism in the offshore industry in emerging economies. In the Asian region, the risk of unemployment may be smaller than at the outset.

But there are many emerging and developing economies that have been unable to participate in the global market, except for traditional exports of resources and labor-intensive goods. Technological advances, such as those seen in AI, may increase the risk of 'nearshoring' and/or 'reshoring' of the BPO industry in the future. Empirically, the potential for employment in emerging/developing economies to converge with developed economies appears to be limited to a few regions, and the gaps appear to be rather large.

Economic development is achieved through a combination of factors, including the state of the international political and economic order, the geopolitical position of the country, the strategies of multinational corporations, the industrial and financial policies of late emerging and developing economies, and the ingenuity of individuals, which may lead to cyclical booms of optimism and pessimism. It will remain as an open question and can only be concluded ex post facto.

5.4 Offshoring and Development of IT-BPO in India, the Philippines, and Vietnam

This section provides an overview of the global development of ICT services such as software development and call centers, focusing mainly on India and the Philippines.

5.4.1 Development of IT-BPO Industry and Major Destinations

American IT companies began offshoring software production in the 1970s. Initially, offshoring was done in India, Ireland, and Israel. In the 1980s, Bangladesh, Pakistan, Sri Lanka, and the Philippines began exporting software to developed countries. The engineers' main task was application development (programming).

In the 1990s, ITC-enabled services exports spread to Brazil, Bulgaria, China, Czech Republic, Hungary, Mexico, Poland, Romania, Russia, and Vietnam, and exports to developed countries via the Internet began in earnest (Dossani, 2009: Part Two 9–10). The call center business also began in India in the 1980s when American Express and General Electric, AT&T set up their first back office operations facilities in the country, followed by British Airways, United Airlines, and others until the 2000s (White, 2015; British Airways Announcement 2023; AT&T business. Accessed Dec. 2023 etc.).

In the late 1990s, multinational companies seized the opportunity to make India the world's number one ICT offshore destination by choosing to offshore their programming work to solve the Y2K bug[8] problem in 2000 (Dossani, 2009: Part Two 9–10). In the 2000s, India was the largest competitor for voice and non-voice ICT services in the world. The IT industry's direct-employment jobs increased from only 72,000 jobs in 1991 to about 4 million jobs in 2018, an additional 12 million jobs in 2018 (ADB, 2021: 110).

Table 5.2 shows the change in India's software exports, number of software companies, average revenue, and export ratio from 1980 to 2007. Exports accounted for more than 70% of revenue in 2000. Voice-based services will also dominate the global BPO market. UNCTAD wrote about offshoring destinations in early this century as below: four countries "quickly emerged as key players: Canada and Ireland among developed countries and India and the Philippines among developing countries"(UNCTAD, 2014: 8). In 2004, the global BPO market share by country was 45% in Canada, 32% in India, 9% in the Philippines, 7% in Ireland, and 7% in others. That structure will change in 2013 to 38% in India, 19% in the Philippines, 15% in Canada, 4% in China, 2% in Ireland, and 22% in others (UNCTAD, 2014: 8). As

[8] The Y2K bug refers to the fact that computer programs were written in 2 digits instead of 4 digits to reduce costs. Indian ICT companies such as Infosys and TCS became offshore destinations for Western multinationals to solve the bug problem, and India became a global exporter of ICT services.

India and the Philippines increase their dominant presence in the BPO market, their reach will expand globally (UNCTAD, 2014: 8; Hirakawa, 2017: 15–16).

India's ICT services exports grew at an annual rate of 18.2% during the period between 2005 and 2012, and increased dramatically in value from $35.08 billion in 2005 to $95.89 billion in 2012, accounting for 6.1% of GDP in 2010. The ratio to GDP was 6.1% in 2010. Incidentally, the ratio of voice-based services to non-voice voice-based services in the Indian BPO sector during this period was 60:40. However, as we will see later, the Philippines grew rapidly in the voice services BPO sector in the 2000s, becoming a threat to India's BPO industry (Hirakawa, 2017: 19–20). Figure 5.13 shows the composition of IT-BPO offshore exports in 2012. It can be seen that the composition differs greatly between India and the Philippines.

This competitive relationship, along with the threat of jobs disappearing due to automation, has been the main pressure on the Indian ICT industry to make a qualitative shift in the BPO and ICT industry with a sense of urgency. Ramit Sethi, Senior VP of global ICT company Wipro, said in 2009 "there's a sea change in revenue models in the industry.“ The National Association Of Software And Service Companies (NASSCOM), an ICT industry association, has announced that the name of BPO will be changed in 2012 to 'Business Process Management ' (BPM) in 2012. The following jobs were strengthened in order to make more competitive the BPO industry, which was greatly reliant on the call center business: "doing

Table 5.2 Growth of Indian software exports

Year	Total export ($m)	No. of firms	Average revenue per firm ($)	Average revenue per employee ($)	Exports/total revenue (%)
1980	4.0	21	1,90,476	16,000	50.0
1984	25.3	35	7,22,857	18,741	50.0
1990	105.4	700	1,50,571	16,215	n/a
2000	5287.0	816	75,98,039	32,635	71.8
2004	12,200.0	3,170	70,03,154	35,362	73.9
2007	29,300.0	n/a	n/a	33,900	74.0

(*Source* Dossani, 2009: 9-10).

Table 5.3 World Market share for BPO by destination in 2004, 2007, 2010, 2013 (%)

	2004	2007	2010	2013
India	32	35	36	38
Canada	45	27	19	15
Philippines	9	15	17	19
Ireland	7	5	3	2
China	2	2	3	4
Others	5	16	22	22

(*Source* UNCTAD 2014: 8).

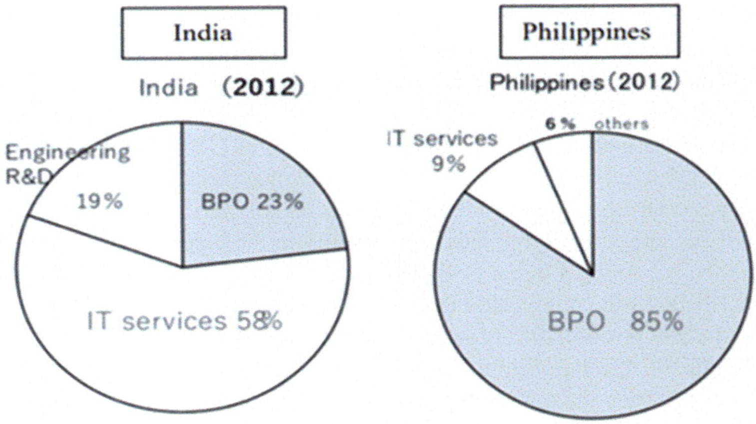

Fig. 5.13 Breakdown of offshore exports in India and the Philippines in 2012 (*Source* Hori, 2020:123).

other more complex back office work, including designing marketing campaigns, analyzing investment portfolios, advising credit card companies on collection strategies, securities market research, supply chain inventory optimization, (and) budgetary planning"(Tejaswi, 2012). BPMの It was also at this time that the shift to the term 'Knowledge process outsourcing' (KPM) was made.

NASSCOM launched the 10,000 Startup Incubate program in August 2013. This program supports incubators (warehouses) for the establishment of tech startups run by NASSCOM, supported by state governments and ICT Global Tech companies. The objective is to set up a nationwide ecosystem for startups and nurture them in a policy-oriented manner. At the same time, NASSCOM set up the 10,000 Startups Virtual Incubation program. Both programs provide market access: investor connects, access to state and government programs, Startup Kit etc. The startup kit is a key offering from 10,000 startups that includes unmatched free credits from Google Cloud, Amazon Web Services, Digital Ocean, Microsoft Azure, IBM Cloud, and 25 + others (NASSCOM HP. Accessed July 10, 2023). Google established the online training 'Startup School India' to help the program (https://startupsonair.withgoogle.com/) in July 2022. The objective was to nurture and fuel the entrepreneurial spirit in India since 2013.

The achievements of the 10,000 Startups programs from its start to 2022 is shown in Fig. 5.14. Warehouses 9,[9] 8600 + startups, 550 + funded startups, 50,000 participants, and 27,500 applications reached (NASSCOM HP. Accessed July 10, 2023). Recognized startups per sector is as follows: around 12% cater to IT services, 9% to healthcare and life sciences, 7% to education, 5% to professional and commercial services, and 5% to agriculture. The Ministry of Commerce & Industry stressed in August 2022 that "the Department for Promotion of Industry and Internal Trade (DPIIT) has recognized more than 75,000 startups—a milestone which coincides

[9] As of August 2018, NASSCOM had established 10 warehouses nationwide.

Fig. 5.14 Legacy of NASSCOM's 10,000 startup (*Source* NASSCOM HP, Accessed July 10, 2023)

with the 75th year of independence". 746, 000 jobs were created, and startups "has been a 110% yearly increase over the last 6 years, the fact that about 49% of our startups are from Tier II & Tier III (cities) is a validation of the tremendous potential of our county's youth" (Ministry of Commerce and Industry, Press Release Aug.3, 2022).

According to the DPIIT 2022–2023, the number of registered startups increased from 452 in 2016 to 84,012 in 2022, more than 900,000 direct jobs were created by them. A 64% increase in the average number of new jobs in 2022 relative to the last three years was India's recorded increase (Krishnamurthy 2023). In 2018, about 50,000 startups were born, of which 8,900–9,300 are "technology-led startups. 1,300 new tech startups were born in 2019 alone implying there are 2–3 tech startups born every day" (#startupindia, India Startup Ecosystem 2023).

Figure 5.15 shows India's productivity growth by sector (1981–2015) taken from one International Monetary Fund (IMF) study. While productivity growth has been steadily increasing this century, including in manufacturing, the growth in high-skill services has been the highest. This confirms that India continues to lead the economy through service sector growth in the face of global competition.

The Philippines: Catching up with India in Voice-Based Services (BPO)

Like India, which was a British colony, the Philippines has a history of being colonized, albeit, under the Americans. This background put the Philippines in an excellent position to catch up with India's BPO sector as a country blessed with

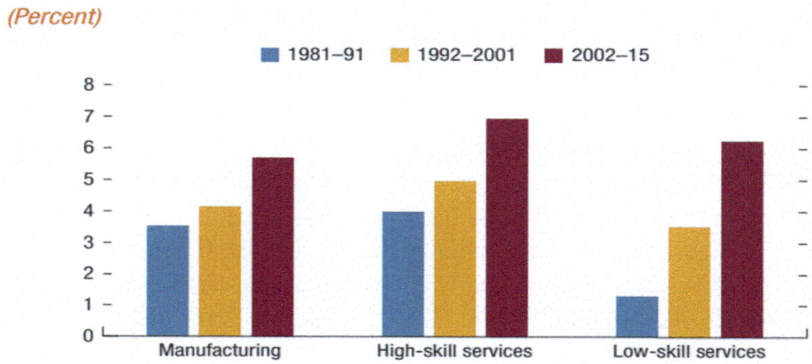

Fig. 5.15 Productivity growth across sectors in India (*Source* Salgado, & Anand eds. 2023: 198)

an English-speaking population. In fact, IT-BPO services, which specializes in the BPO sector, has arguably become the country's leading industry since the 2010s (Fig. 5.13). Tholons have ranked Manila or Philippines as the only non Indian city or country in Asia in the top five outsourcing destinations before 2010, and second-best global outsourcing destination since 2014. The USA International Trade Administration of the Department of Commerce's Official website introduces the Philippines' information and communications technology as 'a best prospect industry sector for this country'. The Philippines IT-BPO Industry and Investment Center in Berlin also introduces the Philippines as a "a top-tier destination for IT-BPM services as one of the leaders in the global IT-BPM industry" (Trade and Industry Center in Berlin, 2021),

However, as previously mentioned, the Philippine IT-BPO industry has been repeatedly pointed out to be at serious risk of job loss due to technological innovation and automation. ILO's report (2016) predicts as follows about the Philippines: because "the transition towards KPO and specialized non-voice BPO services suggest English proficiency and a service-oriented personality will not be enough", "an alarming 89 per cent of call centre workers could be replaced with computerized processes as the tasks these jobs require are repetitive in nature" (ILO, 2016: 67). Incidentally, KPO here is a prefix for Knowledge process outsourcing, which in essence refers to a highly productive, highly skilled BPO.

IBPAP launched IBPAC Research in 2017 to begin working on upgrading the BPO industry (IBPAP, 2017). Three years later in 2019, a professor of the Asian Institute of Management in Manila estimated that unless BPO workers learn new skills or upgrade their skills, "around 800,000 could lose their job in the next five years" due to the spread of Artificial intelligence (AI) (Cebu Daily News, June 13, 2019; GMA News online June 25, 2019). As will be discussed later, the outbreak of the COVID-19 pandemic in 2020 also caused great turmoil in the country. However, BPOs in the Philippines, like those in India, have been growing rapidly, defying such pessimism each time by improving the competitiveness of the BPM industry.

In retrospect, the Philippines BPO industry was born in 1992 when Frank Holz set up the Accenture Global Resource Center in the City of Mandaluyong, Metro Manila (Asiatel outsourcing blog: Featured Post). The Philippine Congress passed the Special Economic Zone Act to provide tax incentives to foreign investors in 1995. Call centers set up by Sykes, Jim Franke and Derek Holly, and others followed (Gallimore, 2023). The number of call centers was from only 4 with 2,400 employees in 2000 to 108 with 112,000 employees in 2005 (ILO, 2016: 59).

In 2004, an industry association, the Business Process Association of the Philippines (BPAP), was formed, and since then various initiatives have been taken to develop the BPO industry. In 2014, its 10th anniversary year, BPAP changed its name to the IT & Business Process Association of the Philippines (IBPAP). In 2006, BPAP developed the 2006–2010 Philippine IT-BPO roadmap and established co-developed IT-BPM courses in collaboration with the Technical Education and Skills Development Authority (TESDA), which was established in 1994. Subsequently, the 2006–2010 Philippine IT-BPO Roadmap, 2010–2015 Philippine IT-BPM Roadmap, 2012–2016 Philippine IT-BPM Roadmap, and 2016–2022 Philippine IT-BPM Roadmap were successively established and development goals were set. Currently, the Philippine IT-BPM Industrial Roadmap 2028 is being implemented (IBPAP: https://www.ibpap.org/roadmap2028).

In 2010, the Philippine BPO sector had 525,000 call center employees and indirect 1,300,000 jobs, $8.9 billion in revenue (Roadmap 2016). That year the country's IT-BPM sector overtook India's standing in voice-based services and became 'the number one provider for such services in the global economy (ILO, 2016; Gallimore, 2023).

Voce-based services were the largest contributor to the local BPO industry, accounting for 64% (493,000) of general direct employment and 67% ($7.4 billion) of total revenues in 2011. The remaining was several non-voices and complex BPO services such as healthcare information management, knowledge process outsourcing, engineering, animation, and software development, which were in a higher growth pace vis-à-vis voice-based businesses (https://www.dti.gov.ph/, accessed July 12, 2023). The number of BPO employees rose from 94,000 in 2005 to an estimated 1.3 million in 2019. BPO revenue was estimated to increase from $1.3 billion in 2004 to $26.1 billion in 2019. "This revenue accounts for about 7% of GDP and is nearly equivalent to the Philippines's annual foreign remittances inflow" (ADB, 2021: 110). IBPAP generated 1.43 million full-time employees in 2021 from 1.32 million in 2020, revenue also increased $29.5 billion from $26.7 billion between 2021 and 2020, and contributed 7.5% of GDP in 2021 (IBPAP HP-Key industry milestones. Accessed July 8, 2023).

Incidentally, Fig. 5.16 compares the composition of the Philippine IT-BPM industry by skill level in 2016 and 2022 by ADB. According to this comparison, the share of low-skill tasks will decrease by as much as 20% in 2022, while the share of high-skill and middle-skill tasks will increase significantly. Compared to India's IT-BPM industry, Philippine competitiveness is still low. However, the IT-BPO industry is also developing remarkably as a leading industry in the Philippines.

Fig. 5.16 Philippines' skills composition of the workforce as IT-BPO adjust to automation (*Source* ADB, 2018: 93). *Note* made by ADB using estimates from the IBPAP

5.4.2 *COVID-19 Pandemic and BPO Industry in India, the Philippines and Vietnam*

The first outbreak of novel coronavirus infection (COVID-19) in Wuhan, China, spread worldwide in February and March of 2020, resulting in a global outbreak. According to the information collected from 1/22/20 to 3/10/23 until Johns Hopkins University stopped collecting COVID-19 related data on March 10, 2023, the total number of infections worldwide reached 676.6 million cases and 4 million deaths. million cases, 4 million deaths. The total number of cases in India is about 44.7 million cases, and 530 thousand deaths. In the Philippines, there were a total of about 4,08 million cases, 66,2 thousand deaths (COVID-19 Map - Johns Hopkins Coronavirus Resource Center -jhu.edu).

As discussed in Chap. 2, the first outbreak of COVID-19 in China spread first to neighboring Asia, but soon spread dramatically to Europe, the United States, and the rest of the world. Figure 5.17 shows a time series of the seven-day average number of infections and deaths in India and the Philippines. The infection explosion was accompanied by the emergence of mutant strains, and a bird's-eye view shows three waves in India and four waves in the Philippines, indicating that the toll caused by COVID-19 was significant. Incidentally, India became the world's largest infectious explosion country in August–September 2020 and April-June 2021, surpassing the United States.

The impact of the COVID-19 pandemic on world trade, by the way, was to accelerate exports of digitally deliverable services, as discussed in Fig. 5.4 earlier in this chapter. Figure 5.18 shows export growth by goods, transportation and travel, and digitally deliverable services for developed and developing economies in the year of the COVID-19 outbreak. It can be seen that in contrast to the sharp decline in transportation and travel and the decrease in goods exports in the COVID-19 pandemic, there was a slight decline in exports of digitally deliverable services in developed economies and an increase in developing economies. In the course of the COVID-19 pandemic, the increase in digitally deliverable services exports from developing countries will become even clearer in the years to come.

COVID-19 and IT-BPO Industry in India

India's first COVID-19 lockdown was that of a 21-day period starting on March 24, 2020, followed by four lockdowns by the end of May (Government of India, 2020). According to journalist K. Flinders, when COVID-19 pandemic began, "the IT outsourcing market in India was not expected to be resilient to its impact". The Hindu Business Line in India estimated in April 2020 that due to the USA and the European Union, India's growth rate of IT-BPO services sector changed from over 6–8% before the COVID-19 outbreak to 3–5% (Hindu Business Line April 10, 2020). Indeed, aside from India's larger IT suppliers, BPO/BPM suppliers and smaller IT suppliers have been hit hard by the COVID-19 pandemic, which has brought up a host of issues.

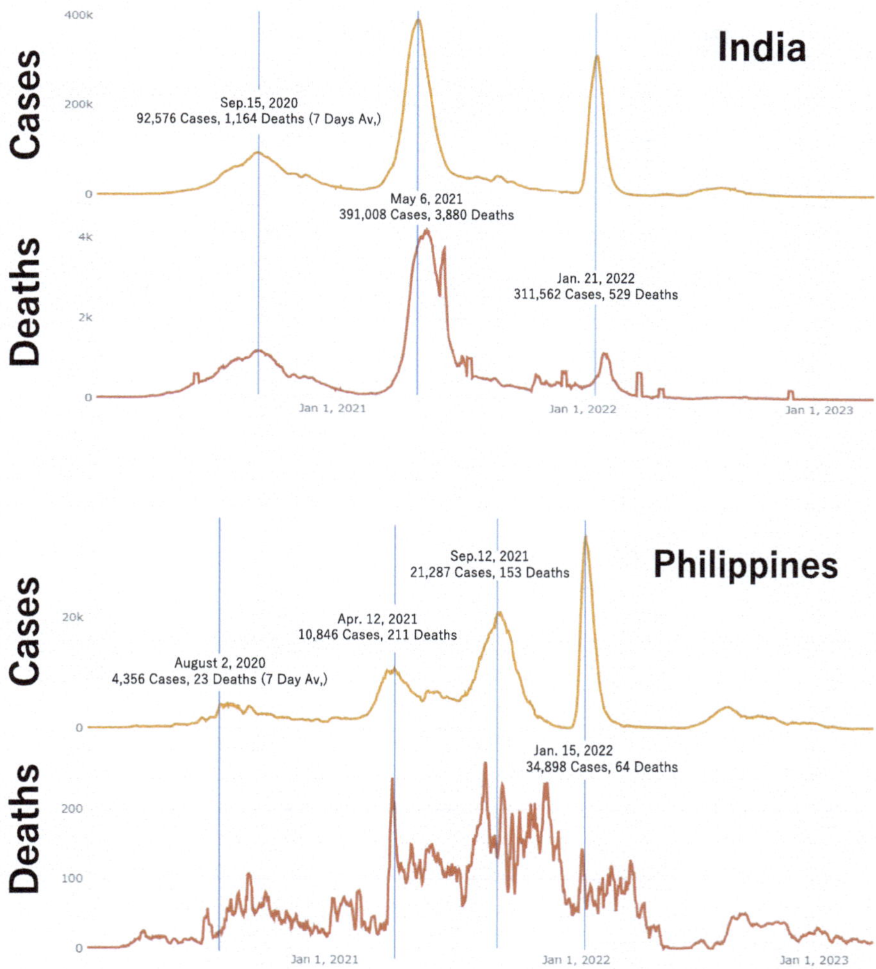

Fig. 5.17 COVID-19 disease timeline of India and the Philippines (*Source* Johns Hopkins University Coronavirus Resource Center). *Note* The vertical lines in the figure, the number of infected and the number of deaths, are the values at the peak of each infection wave (7-day average)

First, there were issues related to remote work. Chief reporter at Computer Weekly, K. Flinders wrote that once the explosive outbreak of COVID-19 started in India, NASSCOM President Debjani Ghosh "strongly reinforced the need for all companies to increase work from home for the next few weeks. … only a handful of staff will be allowed to come to the office to support the mission-critical functions and operate data centers" (Flinders, 2020). It was considered that while "the larger IT suppliers that deliver from India are well equipped to continue services amid the lockdown, BPO suppliers and smaller IT players face major hurdles". BPO suppliers and smaller IT players faced "data security issues—strict rules about protecting the data of corporate customers". "[their] offshore operations are dealing with personal

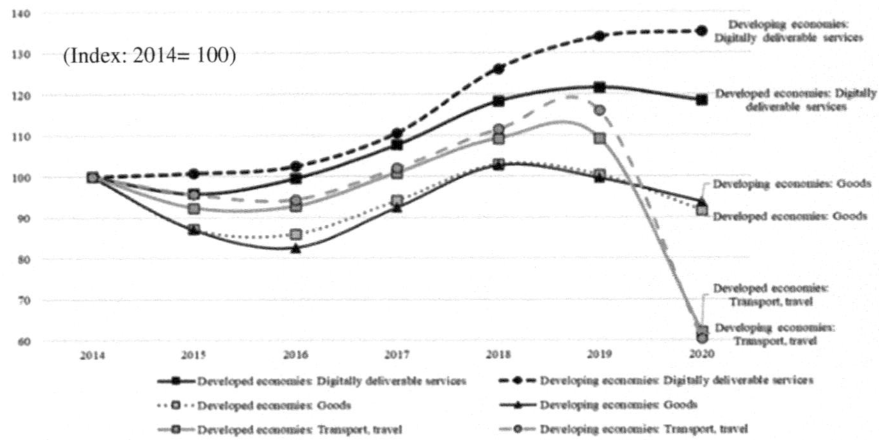

Fig. 5.18 Evolution of exports by digital- and non-digital related goods: 2014–2020 (*Source* UNCTAD, 2022: 5). *Note* Index: 2014 = 100. The classification of digitally deliverable services follows that in UNCTAD (2015)

data and consent has to be given to process personal data from home". "Working from home from an unsecured connection could be a real problem" (Flinders, 2020). Business World in India (May 29, 2020) wrote: "It seems work-from-home for BPO companies is not as easy as it was perceived. These companies are caught between mobility curbs and client protocol that disallows work-from-home" (Gupta, 2020).

There was also a weak IT infrastructure issue, which was difficult for BPO companies and employees to work-from-home. And even if work-from-home was possible, there was still the problem of connectivity capacity. The unexpectedly rapid increase in the number of users made it necessary to increase the communication capacity for remote work. Of course, there is also the issue of employees' health and employment. The government has called for BPO companies to pay the salaries of their employees. (Flinders, 2020; Gupta, 2020).

There were expectations that offshore companies would shift their policies to invest in automation due to the supply chain vulnerabilities revealed in the wake of the pandemic (Flinder, 2020). However, as previously mentioned, government and industry-wide measures to upgrade the IT-BPO sector in India had already begun before the COVID-19 pandemic. As a result, such policies were successful.

In fact, the race to develop startups is global, and India has joined the race, as shown in Fig. 5.19. Even under the COVID-19 infection explosion, the number of startups in India grew steadily from 14,532 in 2000 to 20,089 in 2021 to 23,772 in 2022. The number of new unicorns increased similarly to the number of new unicorns in 2020. In terms of the number of new unicorns, the number of new unicorns increased from 12 in 2020 to 44 in 2021 and 21 in 2022, and the total number of unicorns reached 90 as of February 2010 (Statista Data). Despite the reported significant drop in funding due to the COVID-19 pandemic (Reuters, May 11, 2020), India continued to generate startups and unicorns. The introduction of automation has helped offshore firms to

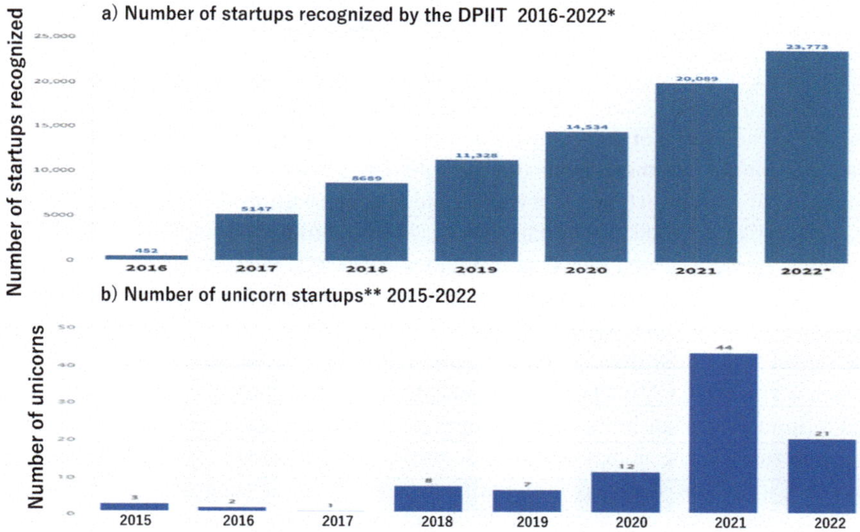

Fig. 5.19 Number of startups recognized and unicorn startups in India 2015 (2016)–2022 (*Source* **a** Pavithra, 2022; **b** Statista, 2023). *Note* **a** * startups as an entity less than ten years old with an annual turnover under one billion Indian rupees and headquartered in India. The number of startups recognized by the Indian government. The number until November 30. 2020. **b** ** privately owned companies with a valuation of one billion U.S. dollars or more. The DPIIT stands for Department for Promotion of Industry and Internal Trade in India

grow. Fears that the introduction of automation would cause offshore firms to be reluctant and nearshoring did not turn out to be a trend.

COVID-19 and IT-BPO Industry in the Philippines

The lockdown (curfew measures) to combat COVID-19 infection was first implemented in Metro Manila until April 14 in March 15, 2020 and spread throughout the Philippines by the end of April of the same year. Cebu, where the BPO industry occupied the largest share of 24% in employment in 2018, was imposed General Community Quarantine on March 17 (Carungay, 2020: 10, 16), but the Philippine government adopted a special reprieve for the BPO industry, a key industry for earning foreign currency. The Oxford Business Group (April 22, 2020) reported the following on this series of developments and their consequences.

> When quarantine measures were first imposed across Luzon from March 17, BPO companies were allowed to continue operations if they could utilize a skeletal workforce, maintain social distancing, and provide staff with temporary accommodation or a reliable shuttle service to homes within the immediate vicinity. Alternatively, BPO firms and other export-oriented companies were given a deadline to implement satisfactory work-from-home arrangements for employees. While many employees welcome the flexibility and safety of working from home, BPO firms were largely unprepared for a total work-from-home model, and had to overcome challenges related to internet access, equipment transfers, and clearance requirements from clients. In the latest Speedtest Global Index, released in March, the Philippines

was ranked 104th out of 139 surveyed countries for average fixed broadband speeds (Oxford Business Group, 2020).

Roughly 6 months later, "not all BPO employees were given the chance to work from home, and some of those who had to go on-site reported unsafe working conditions and unfair treatment from their employees". Especially smaller sized BPO companies and a certain type of services could not cope with work-from-home. And in small cities like Bacolod, public harassment, and discrimination against BPO workers as well as home-returned overseas Filipino workers (OFW) took place (Macaraeg, 2020). They were the greatest contributors to the acquisition of foreign currency before the pandemic. However, "workers in BPOs and migrants are being recast as disease vectors, rather than national heroes" (Konnektors, 2022).

A new wave of COVID-19 hit Southeast Asia in April and September of 2021, but the Philippines was late in vaccinating. In September of the same year, the Washington Post reported on the actual working conditions of BPO workers as follows. "In Quezon City … the local government found over 2,600 coronavirus cases and six deaths across 57 call centers this year. Call centers were the top venues among clusters traced to workplaces, according to the city's disease surveillance unit. … BIEN (the BPO Industry Employees' Network) estimates that outbreaks in offices and work-related facilities such as shared dorms accounted for almost 1,000 virus cases across cities including Baguio, Cavite and Davao in the first half of this year". Employees of call centers were working in "badly ventilated offices that became virus hotbeds", fearing infection and financial precarity (Washington Post Sep. 9, 2021).

At the outbreak of the pandemic, the Philippine BPO industry, which is the largest supplier to the U.S. market, was severely affected. However, "e-commerce orders and financial services enquiries temporarily boosted activity for operators with contact centers in the Philippines". IBPAP has already developed the Philippine IT-BPM Roadmap in 2016, about 75% of BPO workforce was planned to shift mid- to high-skilled positions by 2022. Healthcare services, as well as gaming, and animation services were nurtured as growth industries. Revenue growth rate through to 2022 was forecasted health segment between 7.3% and 10.8%, gaming and animation between 7.3% and 12.3%, and contact center between 3.3% and 7.4%.

However, because of the pandemic, demand for healthcare services and home entertainment options increased higher than each segment growth rate expected in the pre-pandemic period (Oxford Business Group, 2020). Trade and Industry Center in Berlin (TICB), which is part of the Philippine Foreign Trade Service Corps and Coordinating Office of the Department of Trade and Industry (DTI) , the Philippines, wrote:

> The top trends emerging in Industry 4.0 include big data and analytics (BDA), internet-of-things (IoT), automation and artificial intelligence (AI), and cloud computing, and all of which rely heavily on the IT-BPM industry. The Philippines is the leading offshore-nearshore location for healthcare services delivery and the segment is expected to grow steadily driven by the global increase in demand, especially in light of COVID-19. Thus the Philippine government has gone the extra mile to enable these sectors to continue thriving as the country paves the way to leapfrogging into Industry 4.0 (TICB, 2021).

The DTI also explained the IT-BPM industry as follows. In March 2022, former President Doterte signed the amendment to the Public Service Act, which allowed up to 100% foreign ownership of public services, including telecommunications. More than 400 U.S. and European software firms operate in the Philippines. "The Philippines' robust business processing outsourcing (BPO) industry is a strong market customer for enterprise applications. In 2020, the Philippines' ICT associations noted that the Philippine BPO industry generated $26 billion in revenue, and this figure is projected to reach $29 billion in 2022. Domestic consumers include sizable private sector entities such as financial institutions, healthcare facilities, and conglomerates with various business units seeking digitalization solutions in HR, accounting, business intelligence, and data warehousing". "The pandemic increased the demand for connectivity as more and more Filipinos were working and studying remotely and accessing online content and platforms" (DTI home page IT/BPM, Accessed July 25, 2023). Philippine economist, B. N. Villegas wrote in his article that "the COVID-19 pandemic was in a way a game changer for the better", and in early 2022, "the IT-BPM sector bringing close to $30 billion and remittances from OFWs going beyond $36 billion. The IT-BPO industry can grow by 8% annually in the next six years, growing in total revenue from $ 29.5 billion in 2021 to almost $60 billion by 2028 (Villegas, 2022). An article, titled 'The Philippine BPO Industry amidst the pandemic', reported that the BPO industry has transformed from traditional servicers to "a widely-used services for small and medium businesses in the country. … More than 80% of BPO firms now have subsidiaries or joint ventures with other businesses that operate at more than one level of the value chain" (Konnektors, Feb. 28, 2022).

However, the Tholons Global Innovation index 2020 released in August 2020 ranked the Philippines 6th, down from 5th the previous year, and the innovation city index ranked Manila 4th, down from 2nd, and Cebu 15th, down from 12th. In 2021, the index further lowered the country's ranking to 18th in the innovation index and Manila to 8th in the city index. (Tholons global innovation index 2020; 2021). Bloomberg's September 2021 ranking of 53 countries against COVID-19 in terms of resilience and response placed the Philippines at the bottom of the 2020 rankings. The low ranking was primarily due to low vaccination coverage (Business World Sep. 29, 2021). It implies that the working environment surrounding Philippine BPO employees is poor. But COVID-19, while causing great sacrifice and insecurity to IT-BPO employees or workers, has ultimately increased employment in the IT-BPM industry, which relies on low wages relative to the internationally developed economy, and has brought in new, more skilled offshore labor.

COVID-19 and IT-BPO Sector in Vietnam

Vietnam's real COVID-19 infection explosion will not occur until 2021. The country effectively contained the infection throughout 2020, but the global lockdown depressed the economy significantly: the 2019 real GDP growth rate of 7.4% fell down to 2.9% in 2020, and 2.6% in 2021. However, in the midst of this severe economic stagnation, the digital transformation has accelerated.

Incidentally, Vietnam has already started its national startups program in 2016 with a target of supporting around 1,000 startups and related projects by 2020. As of Aug. 31, 2020, around 2,500 startups and projects had received support under the program. This program exempted startups from the entire cost of land leases in industrial parks, including Hoa Lac Hi-Tech Park in Hanoi, for 50 years (Nikkei Asia, Sep. 24, 2020). And just before the COVID-19 pandemic broke out in December 20,192,019, "Make in Vietnam" by the Ministry of Information and Communications (MIC) started, aiming to promote the development of the domestic ICT industry.

Nguyen Manh Hung, Minister of Information and Communications addressed in December 2020 at the first national forum on the development of Vietnamese digital technology enterprises. "After one year, over 13,000 digital technology businesses were established, up 28 per cent on-year, resulting in a record number of such enterprises, with more than 58,000. ... The target of having 100,000 digital businesses by 2030 is now more feasible and we are likely to obtain it by 2025". He ensures that Vietnam has a cybersecurity environment, and emphasizes that Vietnam "became the fifth country in the world to pilot 5G technology, and produce 5G infrastructure devices and 5G-enabled smartphones" (Vietnam Investment Review-Special edition, Dec.31. 2020).

At the end of 2020, Indian global tech company HCL will start business operations in Hanoi, reportedly hiring 3,000 people in three years. (Business Standard, Dec.10, 2020; Vietnam Express international, Dec.13, 2020). Come 2021 、 as an article entitled "Tech firms' rapid growth amid pandemic pushes up demand for office space" reports, in Ho Chi Minh City (HCMC), the demand for grade B office spaces has been increasing (VN Express, April 7, 2021). This is due to "technology, game development, and e-commerce companies are scouring HCMC for office space as their requirements expand in step with surging growth, ... in an area close to Tan Son Nhat International Airport, offices with 300–500 square meters of space are leased by web development companies and property technology companies, most of them start-ups seeking shared office space" (Vietnam Express International, April 7, 2021; Feb. 26, 2021).

As described above, in India, the Philippines, and Vietnam, all of which had already begun to develop their IT-BPO industries in the 2010s, the pandemic had a serious direct and indirect impact on their economies and societies on the one hand. On the other hand, it was an opportunity to further the digital transformation.

5.4.3 IT-BPO Industry and Gender

In general, the global labor market is male-dominated, and this is even more so in developing countries. However, the IT-BPO industry is gaining attention as an industry where women's contributions are becoming increasingly important as it develops. The number of women in the Indian Tech sector workforce has increased from 20% in FY2004 to 30% in FY2012 and 35% in FY2020, while the number of employed women has increased from 166,000 to 1,527,000 over this period. The CAGR during this period was 6%, double the employment growth rate of all industries.

In recent years, the role of women has further increased in the IT-BPO industry. Share of women in the total technology industry base is 35%, and the share of total net new hiring is 44% in FY2020 (NASSCOM, 2020). In urban areas, women comprise around 50% of the BPOs. "Women who work night shifts in the BPO sector make up over 40 percent of the total workforce", but "in rural BPOs, this percentage is even higher. …Some rural BPOs employ more women than men, with over 60% and even up to 100% of their workplace being female" (Sourcefit outsourcing blog March 27, 2023).

Figure 5.20 shows the results of the survey conducted by the Ministry of Labour & Employment, India based on "Stratified Simple Random Sampling". The 10 highest sectors with the highest percentage of women are health, education, financial services, and IT-BPO, in that order. The share of women in the BPO industry alone is even higher than that in the IT-BPO industry.

Table 5.4 above shows data from Monster.com India, an online employment company in India, looking at the 10 largest industries recruiting women and the 10 largest industries in which women want to work. According to this data, BPO is 30%, IT/computer 24%, and banking etc. 24% in the order of recruitment, but when looking at this by the type of job desired by women, IT/computer 22%, banking/

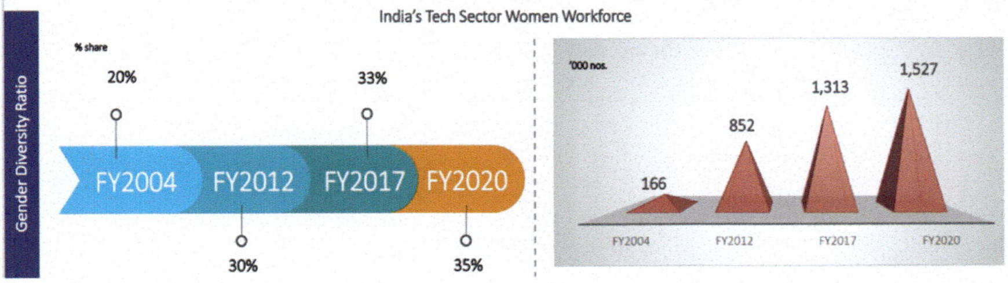

Fig. 5.20 Share and number of women workers in the Indian IT sector (*Source* NASSCOM, 2020)

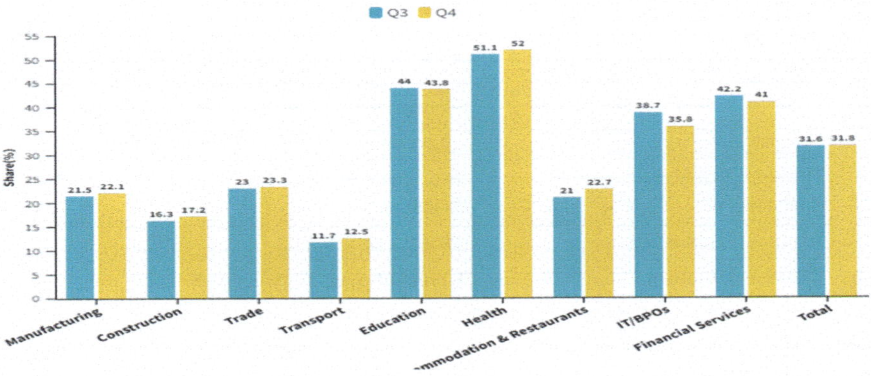

Fig. 5.21 Sector-wise share of female employees 2021–2022 (Q3, Q4, in %) (*Source* Kancharla, Oct.17, 2022. Data from the Ministry of Labour & Employment, India)

accounting 16%, education 9%, and BPO 5% in that order. However, the ranking of BPO is significantly different from that of IT/computer at 22%, banking/accounting at 16%, education at 9%, and BPO at 5%. There is a gap within the BPO industry. Although the BPO industry is the industry in which companies most desire women, it is not an industry in which women want to work.

On the other hand, in India, based on FY2017 data, there are 185 million females who cannot even write a simple sentence in any language. But, India tops the world in producing female graduates in STEM". The gross enrolment ratio of females at higher educational institutes 27.3% is more than 26.9% of male students. "The wide gap between the number of females graduating every year and those entering the workspace is an issue of paramount importance" (Samant, 2023). There is a structure in which highly educated women are moving toward sectors such as IT/computer and banking/accounting. At the same time, there will be competition among leading companies in the IT sector to take advantage of their abilities.

Table 5.4 Top 10 industries with the highest percentage share of job for women and women job seekers in India

	a Jobs for women		**b** Women job seekers	
	Industry	Shere of Jobs for women (%)	Industry	Share of women jobseekers (%)
1	BPO	30	IT/Computers—Software	22
2	IT/ Computers—Software	24	Banking/Accounting/ Financial Services	16
3	Banking/Accounting/ Financial Services	13	Education	9
4	Recruitment/Staffing/ RPO	5	BPO	5
5	IT/Computers - Hardware and Networking	5	Healthcare/Diagnostics	4
6	Education	4	IT/Computers–Hardware and Networking	3
7	Animation	4	Telecom	3
8	Hospital/Healthcare/ Diagnostics	3	Bio Technology and Life Sciences	3
9	Internet/E-commerce	3	Pharmaceutical	2
10	Travel and Tourism	3	Computing/Advisory Services	2

(*Source* Express Computer, May 8, 2022. Data of Monster.com). *Note* RPO stands for Recovery Point Objective. BPO's name in the original table is "ITes-BPO" (Information technology-enabled Services), but in this table, "BPO" is used to distinguish it from IT/Computer, The term "ITes-BPO" has come to be used to reflect this change.

Let us take a look at the case of the Philippines. According to IBPAP data, the BPO industry in 2021 generated 1.44 million direct jobs, of which about 55% are female (roughly 800,000 employees), and 3.61 million indirect jobs. 30% of total industry workforce is outside of Metro Manila (IBPAP HP, Accessed July 8, 2023; Source fit outsourcing blog March 27, 2023).

Table 5.5 shows IBPAP's analysis of the percentage of women in the IT-BPO industry at the skill level (entry, supervisory and managerial, and executive). First, in the two sub sectors excluding the BPO sector First, the percentage of women in the two sub sectors except for the BPO sector has not reached 30%. However, In terms of educational qualification, 83% of the female workforce are those with tertiary qualifications (IBPAP, 2018: 55). As in India, women's workplaces are limited.

However, despite the gender pay gap as well as extremely strong social prejudices and restrictions, the IT-BPO industry has steadily expanded employment opportunities for women. It has also developed as an employer of well-educated women. Moreover, "Women in outsourcing have comparatively high wages and benefits, enabling them to achieve greater autonomy and independence, which is empowering. Women who are well educated and working in call centers have the opportunity to gain knowledge and experience from both their local environment and the West, equipping them to be competitive in the global workforce" (Soucefit.com March 27, 2023).

The COVID-19 pandemic has reportedly reduced the labor participation rate of women. However, in the global economy, leading global IT-BPO firms are moving to attract talented female workers to enhance their competitiveness.

Table 5.5 Gender ratio by job level in IT/technology, animation, and game development in the Philippines

	Total company/ STEM roles	Entry	Supervisory and management	Executive
ITO/technology (n = 11)				
Male	56	58	52	52
Female	44	42	48	48
Animation (n = 2)				
Male	74	71	75	75
Female	26	29	25	25
Game development (n = 3)				
Male	74	76	74	74
Female	26	24	26	26

(*Source* IBPAP team's company interviews: IBPAP, 2018: 55).
Note STEM stands for science, technology, engineering, and mathematics. ITO stands for Information technology outsourcing.

5.5 Online Offshoring/Outsourcing to Asia

When the COVID-19 Pandemic broke out early in 2020, governments initially adopted a series of lockdown measures, and from 2022 onward, they embarked on a policy of coexistence between infectious diseases and the economy. At the same time, digitalization has penetrated more widely and deeply into the economy and society. Digitalization is changing the way companies do business, changing the work environment, and creating new labor markets. In this section, we will examine online outsourcing and labor market changes in the digital economy, focusing on emerging and developing Asian economies after the pandemic.

5.5.1 Global Firms and Online Labor Platforms

The COVID-19 pandemic has brought about a shift to hybrid work for ICT companies as well as for companies with a global presence. The results of the Hybrid Work Global Survey[10] that Riverbed/Aternity conducted to nearly 1500 business leaders in September 2021, in response to COVID-19, are interesting as a straightforward reflection of the characteristics of corporate responses. The results of the COVID-19 survey of nearly 1500 business leaders of Western global companies, which are also the main players in offshoring to emerging and developing economies. It is noteworthy as an indication of the potential of how the respondents will promote global digitization.

According to the survey, 94% of respondents agreed a hybrid work environment helps recruit talent and remain competitive in future. 89% of organizations plan to invest in technology to support a hybrid workforce in the next 12–18 months, which was up from 61% of last year's survey, and 42% plan to make significant investments. As for key investment areas, 86% agree that companies must increase investment into modernizing their network infrastructure (riverbed/Aternity 2021).

In order to secure talented workers and effectively utilize their abilities, major companies in developed economies are clearly investing in hybrid workplaces and building organizations. The COVID-19 pandemic has further accelerated this trend of organizational restructuring, which is incorporating ICT human resources from emerging economies and developing countries in a variety of forms within companies.

[10] Of the roughly 1,500 companies, 750 companies are business decision makers (BDMs) and 750 IT decision makers (ITDMs), with revenue above U.S.$500 million annually in the USA, United Kingdom, France, Germany, Australia, Switzerland, United Arab Emirates, and the Netherlands. Industry sectors include finance/insurance, public sector/government, healthcare/pharma, manufacturing, oil and gas, and professional services.

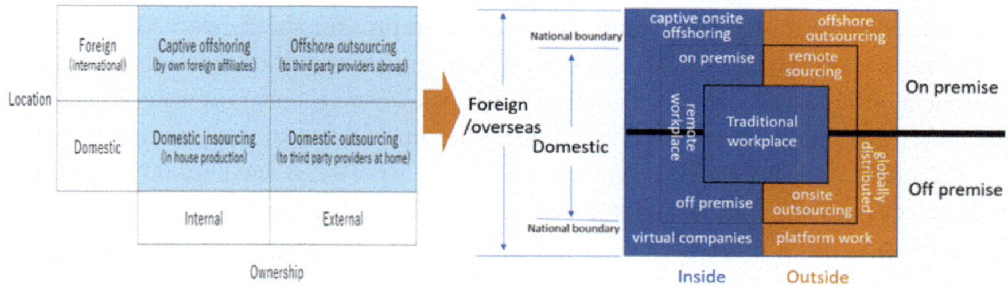

Fig. 5.22 The shift of company activity from a spatial model of offshoring and outsourcing to a virtual-added spatial model (*Source* made by Hirakawa and Maquito. Ref. Hirakawa 2017, Thomas, & Ray 2019, Norlander, & Erickson 2021, Riverbed/Aternity 2021, and Oxford online labour platform). *Note* This figure would be applicable to sourcing of goods, services, and R&D

Tessa A. Thomas and K. Ray (2019) write that multinational corporations have incorporated emerging and developing economies in three waves since the late twentieth century. They identify three waves of 'outsourcing' (as shown in Fig. 5.22 immediately below, "outsourcing" is "offshoring").[11] The "first wave of outsourcing" was the wave of overseas offshoring by manufacturing companies in the 1960s and 1970s. During this period, manufacturing firms in developed countries pursued two types of offshoring. One type was captive offshoring, in which companies expanded into developing regions to take advantage of low-wage labor and established their own subsidiaries to directly hire workers to manufacture goods (captive offshoring). The other is offshore outsourcing, in which products and parts are procured from third-party companies overseas.[12] The "second wave of outsourcing" began during the late 1990s and early 2000s when American and European firms mainly "set up operations abroad to outsource services handled by their back office, such as call centers in India". And the "third wave of outsourcing" is the ongoing online outsourcing (Thomas, & Ray 2019: 227). In the author's words, offshoring activities started with the cross-border production of goods in manufacturing, spread to the offshoring of service labor in ICT, and now we are in the midst of a huge wave of offshoring by service labor in the digital space.

Incidentally, Thomas and Ray begin the introduction to their paper with the following case study of their own journal publication process. An audio file recorded in Texas is sent to IBM Watson artificial intelligence (AI) engine, edited by it, converted to a text file by a worker in South Africa, returned again to be reviewed by a research assistant in Washington D.C., furthermore, to be marked up by author in Texas, and edited once more by another worker in the Philippines. "All of these steps

---

[11] As discussed in Chap. 7 of this book, the author attempts to provide a historical summary of late industrialization in Asia from the perspective of F. Fröber, J. Heinrichs and O. Kreye's New International Division of Labor and Y. H. Kim's Industrialization of the Least Developed Countries.

[12] In Hirakawa (2017), the author, like Thomas and Ray, divided outsourcing into domestic and foreign, and also sourcing from subsidiaries and sourcing from third party providers (non-subsidiaries), distinguishing between captive offshoring and offshore outsourcing (Hirakawa, 2017: 3).

occurred entirely through the internet, and they represent the modern-day equivalent of the assembly line". They explained the significance of online outsourcing in modern economics, using Nobel Laureate Ronald Coase's theories of transaction cost that determine the location of work and the structure of the firm. According to Coase, "transaction costs were the only barriers to efficiency between two bargaining parties. As transaction costs fall, negotiated outcomes move closer to an efficient solution. The growth of digital technology and its concomitant performance measurement, search and payment functions all help reduce transaction costs to facilitate greater trade" (Thomas, & Ray 2019: 229). "Filipinos must wait years before being allowed to live in the U.S. but can now register online to work in the U.S. through online labor markets in seconds". Moreover, women who cannot leave their homes can also participate in online markets. They assert that free trade benefits both the producer and consumer surplus globally (234).

So how are global companies attempting to reorganize themselves in the digital economy? Fig. 5.22 is a conceptual diagram showing the transition from the traditional ownership relationship between space and companies to the relationship between companies and labor, including digital space. Traditionally, companies have chosen to either produce goods within the company or procure goods from other companies. One form of development was the development of the corporate organization, which could either be a branch office or factory in Japan or a subsidiary abroad. The other was procurement from other companies, which could be done in two ways: from within the country or from outside the country. This is shown in Figure (a) on the left, and in Figure (b) on the right, the upper left square (quadrant 2) and the lower left square (quadrant 3) are in blue.

However, in the digital economy, where online work is progressing, both systems and data have shifted from on-premise to cloud computing, and new employment structures and ways of working have emerged. Companies can do their own online work spatially in-house or externally, as in remote work, and they can accept engineers dispatched by other companies into their company through online or outsource to other companies. Each of these is a procurement method or form of labor in the upper right (quadrant 1) and lower right (quadrant 4) of the orange inner cells, respectively. For example, remote work can be done at home, in an office near the nearest train station or tourist attraction, in a car, or overseas. Outsourcing may be done in-house online or outsourced to other companies. Recruitment may be done directly through an online platform or through various other forms of sourcing.

Individual and personal business contracts will also be possible on the online labor market. It will no longer matter what the worker's nationality is, or whether he or she lives in Japan or abroad; he or she can be at home. It will be a globally distributed platform for work. It is no longer unusual for the relationship between a company and a worker to be completely online. In the figure, the upper right (quadrant 1) and lower right (quadrant 4), indicated by the orange outer cells, show this relationship. The nature of offshoring will also change dramatically.

5.5.2 *Online Workforce and Asia*

The Oxford Internet Institute (OII), which was set up in Oxford University in 2001, iLabour team (2015–2021) and the ILO established the Online Labour Observatory as a digital data hub for researchers, policy makers, journalists, and the public interested in the development of online labor markets. Online Labour Observatory developed the Online Labour Index 2020 as a new, expanded version of the digital data collection and visualization system that we originally developed in the iLabour project. In the following, we will rely primarily on those results to explore trends in the online labor market.

In fact, the online labor workforce is increasing, mainly in the advanced Western economies of the U.S. and U.K., but also involving emerging economies. The number of freelancers based on the data gathered from 162 of the 351 globally relevant online freelance platforms and public data, are as follows. There are "163 million registered user accounts, of whom roughly 14 million have ever worked, and 3.3 million have worked significantly (definition applies to workers that have completed at least 10 projects or earned at least $1,000)". Adjusting for multi-homing, finally, these numbers are 9.3 million who have ever worked and 2.2 million who have worked significantly. Furthermore, "online freelancing plays an important role for economic development in rural areas and is of increasing relevance as a form of remote work in times of the global pandemic" (Kässi et al., 2021).

Oxford Internet Institute (OII), in 2081, wrote as follows. "Workers from emerging economies in particular are benefitting from these networks. … The findings … reveal that platforms such as Upwork, Freelancer and Fiverr offer companies in rich Western countries a simple and cheap mechanism to hire knowledge workers in lower income countries, without the burden of setting up offices abroad or contracting with an outsourcing company". Professor Vili Lehdonvirta at the OII says, "knowledge workers who previously worked at outsourcing companies in countries like the Philippines, for example, can now work directly for Western clients through these online platforms" (Oxford University 2018. Accessed Jul. 3, 2023). From a separate category from the 1.3–1.4 million employees working in the Philippine IT-BPM industry, an estimated 1.5 million freelancers or gig workers are on these platforms. In 2019, the number increased 35% from the previous year (Konnektors, 2022; Talmage-Rostron, 2023).

Figure 5.23 is the figure created based on the data collected by Oxford Internet Institute. Global structure of outsourcing of tasks on freelance platforms is shown in terms of county, size of outsourcing, difference of foreign employer or local employer, and median hourly earnings in US$.

The figure shows that USA, Canada, United Kingdom, Germany, Ukraine, Russia, the Philippines, Pakistan, and Bangladesh are the major suppliers of freelancers, but the supplier countries are spread all over the world. The structure is not so different in the BPO industry. In contrast, in emerging economies, employers are overwhelmingly foreign employers. The wage gap between developed economies

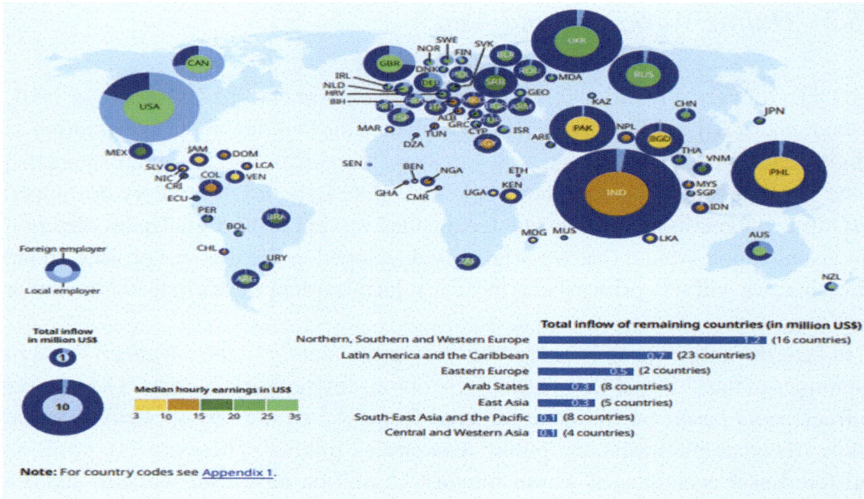

Fig. 5.23 Outsourcing of tasks on a freelance platform across countries, inflow of work and earnings, 2019 (*Source* ILO, 2021: 45). *Note* Data collected by Fabian Braesemann, Oxford Internet Institute, iLabour Project. Country codes are on the base of ISO Alpha 3

and emerging/developing economies is also extremely large. For example, median hourly earnings in the U.S. are $25-$35, while in India they are $10-$15.

As for digital labor platforms, there are two types of web-based platforms (micro-task, freelance and competitive programming) and location-based platforms in the taxi and delivery sector globally. In the world, at least 777 active platforms operated in January 2021, of which 383 were delivery sector platforms, 283 online web-based platforms, 106 taxi sectors, respectively (ILO, 2021: 47).

Since our interest is in online web-based platforms, the demand on 5 major online web-based platforms by occupation category is shown in Fig. 5.24. Incidentally, while demand in 2020 will increase in the software development occupational category, it will decrease in the three occupational categories that follow. The reason for this may be the temporary impact of COVID-19. In any case, software development and technology are by far the most in demand, followed by creative and multimedia, writing and translation, clerical and data entry, and so forth.

Figure 5.25 shows the labor supply of online web-based platforms by country and occupational category. In the occupational category, the main categories are software development, sales and marketing support, creative and multimedia, although there are some characteristics depending on the country. In the occupational category, software development, sales and marketing support, creative and multimedia are the main categories, although the characteristics vary from country to country (Fig. 5.26).

The COVID-19 pandemic incorporated remote work as one of the main forms of employment. At the same time, it has given birth to forms of employment that go beyond traditional forms, even allowing individuals to work remotely directly on web-based labor platforms. The digital economy has certainly lowered the spatial,

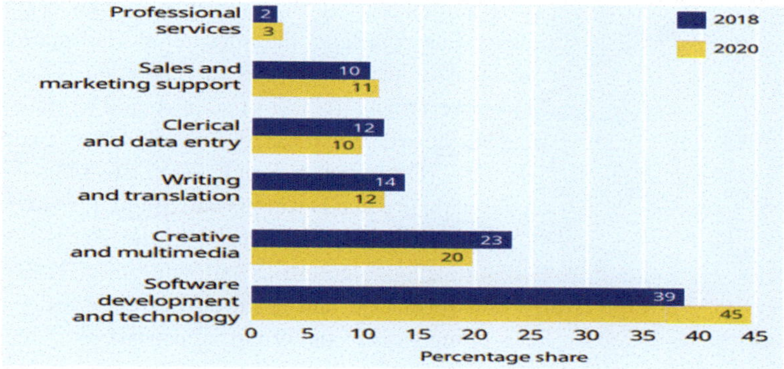

Fig. 5.24 Global demand for labor across occupational categories on 5 major online web-based platforms, 2028 and 2020 (*Source* ILO, 2021: 52)

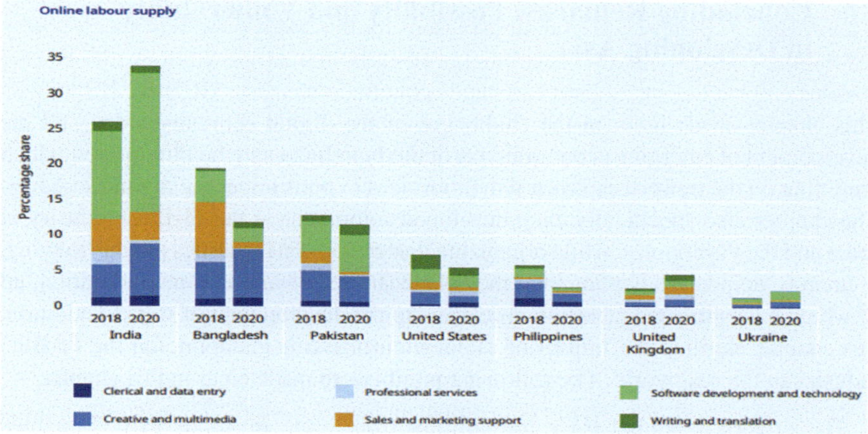

Fig. 5.25 Distribution of global labor supply on major online web-based platforms by country and occupational category, 2018 and 2020 (*Source* ILO, 2021: 53)

language, and cultural barriers that have existed in the past. It is highly likely that cross-border labor will expand in the context of global wage disparities and labor quality.

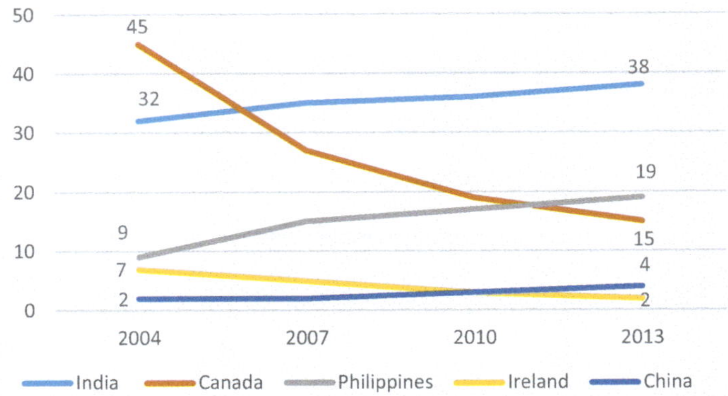

Fig. 5.26 Market share for BPO by destination 2004, 2007, 2010, 2013 (%) (*Source* Table 5.3)

5.6 Concluding Remarks: Possibility and Vulnerability in Developing Asia

This chapter sheds light on the challenges of the digital economy today and the development of emerging economies, particularly in India and the Philippines, which are riding on the trend of rapid growth in services exports under the digital economy. The chapter also specifically examines the development of the IT-BPO industry in India and the Philippines, while organizing discussions on the issues of leapfrogging, premature deindustrialization, and the disappearance of jobs due to automation, all of which have attracted attention in relation to the development of ICT. In addition, this chapter clarified the impact of the new coronavirus Pandemic on the IT-BPO industry in the real world. The following points were made clear in this chapter.

- The drivers of global trade are shifting from trade in goods to ICT-enabled services trade and data transfers. With the growing importance of trade in services, emerging Asian economies and developing countries, especially India and the Philippines, are realizing the development of IT-BPO industries.
- The term "leapfrogging" is used today to refer to the phenomenon of emerging economic development enabled primarily by the development of ICT. There are great expectations for skipping the traditional industrial development stage or opening up new development paths, but only a limited number of countries have achieved this.
- The study of premature deindustrialization has been deepened in relation to the discussion of "engines of growth," which is of interest to development economics theory. Whether the service industry can be an "engine of growth" in the development of emerging and developing economies is experientially and empirically not promising, with the exception of some Asian countries such as India and the Philippines. Moreover, even for India and the Philippines, many issues have been

pointed out as to whether they can be linked to development at the country level or at the national economy level.

- It has been suggested that automation will extinguish the BOP industry, but so far, Asia has achieved more job creation than job extinguishment. The COVID-19 pandemic has also spurred the growth of IT-BPOs. Carl B. Frey of Oxford University has also very recently pointed to the growth of employment in unskilled labor (Nikkei -J, July 20, 2023). Whether or not jobs will still be created in the future, however, depends on future trends. It can be said that policy and practical efforts to create jobs in the global economy will continue to be required.
- In the area of IT-BPO and gender issues, there is a gap between the work that women want to do and the work that the BPO industry wants women to do. The development of the ICT sector is important to bring diversity to Indian and Philippine societies.
- The digital economy is forcing global companies to reorganize the digital space organizationally, a trend reinforced by the COVID-19 pandemic. In addition to freelancers of unskilled labor through location-based platforms, online web-based platforms will create more freelancers or gig workers.

The digital economy is creating a global structure of production and employment based primarily on productivity under international wage differentials. But this ICT service exports-based industrial development does not automatically lead to the achievement of development at the national and national economy level. As Rodrik pessimistically observed of India's service-driven development, it is difficult to envision economic development at the level of a country or national economy solely on the basis of the development of ICT-related industries. The linkage and coordination with other industries in the country needs to be recognized as an important issue at the same time.

Various factors are involved in the future development of emerging economies, including what kind of international economic order the international community will create, what kind of development policies will be pursued by policy makers in emerging and developing economies at the single country and national economy level, and what kind of strategies will be used by global corporations. While services-led development is generally regarded as an outcome of liberal policies in mainstream economics, it is also important for emerging economies to position ICT at the core of their export strategies. It can be said that emerging economies need to incorporate policy perspectives that go beyond worker skill-up and the ICT-based services industry to improve the productivity of domestic industries in general.

References

A Symbol (-J) after the author's name are Japanese documents

ADB. (2018). *Asian development outlook 2018*. Asian Development Bank.

ADB. (2021). *Global value chain development report 2021*: Beyond production. Asian Development Bank.

Arntz, M., Gregory, T., & Zierahn, U. (2016). The risk of automation for jobs in OECD countries: A comparative analysis. *OECD Social, employment and migration Working Papers* No. 189. Paris: OECD Publishing.

Atolia, M., Loungani, P., Marquis, M., & Papageorgiou, C. (2018). Rethinking development policy: Deindustrialization, servicification and structural transformation. *IMF Working Paper* WP/18/223, September

Baldwin, R. (2016). *The great convergence: Information technology and the new globalization*. Cambridge: Belknap Press of Harvard University Press

Basu, K. (2007). *The Oxford companion to economics in India, Revised edition*. New Delhi: Oxford: University Press.

British Airway. (2023). *British Airways announces further investment in India, ahead of milestone anniversary*. Cision PR newswire.

Brynjolfsson, E., & McAfee, A. (2014). *The second machine age: Work, progress, and prosperity in a time of brilliant technologies*. New York and London: W.W. Norton & Company.

Burlamaqui, L., & Kattel, R. (2016). Development as leapfrogging, not convergence, not catch-up: Towards Schumpeterian theories of finance and development. *Review of Political Economy, 28*(2), April. https://doi.org/10.1080/09538259.2016.1142718

Burlamaqui, L. (2011). Development theory: Convergence, catch-up or leapfrogging? A Schumpeterian approach, Concept note for the Workshop *Novo Desenvolvimentismo e uma Macroeconomia Estruturalista do Desenvolvimento*, Centro Celso Furtado, August 15–16, Sao Paulo, Brazil.

Carungay. (2020). *The impact of the COVID-19 pandemic on implementing Cebu City's creative agenda for achieving the sustainable development goals in the Philippines*. Carungay, Municipality in the Province of Pangasinan, Philippines, November.

Chang, J.-H., Rynhart, G., & Huynh, P. (2016). ASEAN in transformation: How technology is changing jobs and enterprises. *Bureau for employers' Activities. working paper no.10*. International Labour Organization: ILO, July.

Dasgupta, S., & Singh, A. (2005). Will services be the new engine of economic growth in India? *Center for Business Research, University of Cambridge Working Paper* no. 310.

Dasgupta, S., & Singh, A. (2006). *Manufacturing, services and premature deindustrialization in developing countries: A Kaldorian analysis*. United Nations University Research Paper no..2006/49, May.

Dossani, R. (2009). Software production: Globalization and its implications for South Asia. In: World Bank (Ed.) *The service revolution in South Asia*, World Bank (Poverty Reduction and Economic Management Unit).

Erickson, C., & Norlander, P. (2021). How the past of outsourcing and offshoring is the future of post-pandemic remote work: A typology, a model, and a review. In *Faculty publications and other works, Summer 8–16–2021*. Loyola University Chicago.

Flinders, K. (2020). Coronavirus: BPO and IT services delivered from India face big challenges. Computer Weekly, April 6.

Ford, M. (2015). *The rise of the robots: Technology and the threat of mass unemployment*. Great Britain: One world Publications.

Fredriksson, T. (2016a). New methodology for measuring trade in ICT services and ICT-enabled services. In *United Nations Statistical Commission, 47th session, UNCTAD PowerPoint Presentation (un.org)*.

Frey, C. B., & Osborne, M. A. (2013). The future of employment: How susceptible are jobs to computerisation? https://www.oxfordmartin.ox.ac.uk/downloads/academic/The_Future_of_Employment.pdf

Gallimore, D. (2023). Outsourcing to the Philippines, the top destination. January 20 Outsourcing to the Philippines, the top destination|Outsource Accelerator.

Gerschenkron, A. (1962). *Economic backwardness in historical perspective: A book of essays.* Cambridge, Massachusetts: The Belknap Press of Harvard University Press.

Government of India. (2020). Press Information Bureau: Government of India issues Orders prescribing lockdown for containment of COVID19 Epidemic in the country. New Delhi, March 24, 2020.

Gupta, R. (2020). Struggle of the BPO industry during the pandemic. Businessworld, May 29.

Hirakawa, H. (2017). Global ICT-based services offshoring and Asia. In Hirakawa, H., Takahashi, N., Maquito, F.C. & Tokumaru, N., (Eds.) *Innovative ICT industrial architecture in East Asia, Tokyo:* Japan: Springer.

Hori, F. (2023). The growth of the IT-BPO industry and women's work choices in the Philippines. In: Hayashi, T., Hoshino, H., Hori, Y. (Eds.), *Base of the pyramid and business process outsourcing strategies.* Springer: Nature Singapore.

IBPAP. (2017). Digital transformation and the IT-BPM industry. Information Technology & Business Process Association Philippines (BPAP) Research No.1, December.

IBPAP. (2018). Skills and career mapping for women employment and career progression in the Philippine IT-BPM sector, IBPAP.

ILO. (2016). *ASEAN in transformation: How technology is changing jobs and enterprises.* ILO.

ILO. (2021). *World employment and social outlook: The role of digital labour platforms in transforming the world of work.* ILO.

Javaid, A. (2020). What was the Y2K bug and how it helped India's IT sector? May 15 https://www.jagranjosh.com/general-knowledge/y2k-bug-1589540224-1

Kancharla, B. (2022). Data: Share of female workers fell in IT/BPO and financial services while total employment increased by 3.5 lakh as per 4th QES. Faclty.in, October 17.

Karunaratne, M. (2022). From tuk-tuks to tech: Can we leapfrog our forex troubles? The Morning https://www.themorning.lk/articles/189142

Kässi, O., Lehdonvirta, V., & Stephany, F. (2021). How many online workers are there in the world? A data-driven assessment. Open Research Europe [version 4; peer review: 4 approved], October 15 https://doi.org/10.12688/openreseurope.13639.3

Konnektors. (2022). The Philippine's BPO industry amidst the pandemic. February 28.

Korka, D. (2017). Measuring ICT-enabled services exports project background and motivation. Presentation PPT materials for UNCTAD Expert Meeting on results from pilot surveys on exports of ICT-enabled services, 28–29 November, Geneva.

Krishnamurthy, R. (2023). Economic survey 2022–23: Indian startup ecosystem faces several challenges, causing companies to 'flip'. January 31. https://www.downtoearth.org.in

Lee, K., & Ki, J. H. (2017). Rise of latecomers and catch-up cycles in the world steel industry. *Research Policy, 46*(2).

Lee, K., & Lim, C. (2001). Technological regimes, catching-up and leapfrogging: The findings from the Korean industries. *Research Policy, 30*(3).

Lee, K. (2021). Economics of technological leapfrogging. In J. D. Lee, K. Lee, D. Meissner, S. Radosevic, & N. S. Vinortas (Eds.), *The Challenges of technology and economic catch-up in emerging economies.* UK: Oxford University Press.

Macaraeg, A. (2020). BOI companies vulnerable to COVID-19 outbreak, Rappler. https://www.rappler.com/newsbreak/in-depth/bpo-companies-vulnerable-covid-19-outbreaks/

Manyika, J., Lund, S., Bughin, J., Woetzel, J., Stanemov, K., & Dhingra, D. (2016). *Digital globalization: The new era of global flows.* McKinsey Global Institute, McKinsey & Company.

Ministry of Information and Communications, & Vietnam: MIC. (2020). *White book of Viet Nam information and communication technology 2020.* Phu Printing and Service Trading Co., Ltd.

NASSCOM. (2020). India's Tech Industry: Women for the techade. NASSCOM, March.

Nikkei, -J. (2023). Interview with C.B. Frey: Tei sukiru rodosya koso onkei, seisei AI to keizaisyakai (Law-skilled workers especially benefit, Generative AI and economic society), July 20.

Nomura Research Institute (NRI). -J. (2015). Nihon no roudou jinkou no 49% ga jinko chino ya robotto nadode daitai kanouni (the 49% of Japan's labor population can be replaced by artificial intelligence and robots etc.). *News release,* December 2.

Norlander, P., & Erickson, C. L. (2022). How the past of outsourcing and offshoring is the future of post-pandemic remote work: A typology, a model, and a review. In *Loyola eCommons*. Loyola University Chicago, Summer 8–16–2021.

Oxford University. (2021). Online labour platforms offer growing alternative to traditional offshoring. November 8. https://www.ox.ac.uk/news/2018-11-08-online-labour-platforms-offer-growing-alternative-traditional-offshoring. Accessed: July 3, 2023.

Oxford Business Group. (2020). What does the Covid-19 outbreak mean for the Philippines' BPO industry. April 22.

Palma, J. G. (2005). Four sources of "De-industrialization" and a new concept of the "Dutch disease". In A. J. Ocampo (Ed.), *Beyond reforms: Structural dynamics and macroeconomic vulnerability*. Washington D.C.: United Nations Economic Commission for Latin America and the Caribbean (ECLAC).

Palma, J. G. (2014). De-industrialization, 'Premature' De-industrialization and the Dutch-Disease. Revista NECAT - Ano 3, nº5 Jan-Jun de 2014.

Pavithra, K. M. (2022). Data: Close to 30% of Startups Recognized by The Government are into IT services, healthcare and Life Sciences, and Education. factly.in, December 13.

Reuters. (2020). Technology News: Indian start-ups get creative as coronavirus crisis fuels funding crunch, May 11.

Riverbed/Aternity. (2021). Hybrid work global survey 2021. https://www.riverbed.com/ja/press-releases/riverbed-aternity-hybrid-work-global-survey-2021/

Rodrik, D. (2018). *Straight talk on trade: Ideas for a sane world economy*. Princeton University Press.

Rodrik, D., & Subramanian, A. (2004). Why India can grow at 7 percent a year or more: Projections and reflections. *IMF working paper WP/04/118, July.*

Rodrik. D. (2013). The perils of premature deindustrialization. Project Syndicate, October 11 (Reprint, *Social Europe Journal*, October 14).

Rodrik, D. (2015). Premature deindustrialization. Revised November 2015. https://drodrik.scholar.harvard.edu/files/dani-rodrik/files/premature_deindustrialization_revised2.pdf

Salgado, R., & Anand, R. (Eds). (2023). *South Asia's path to resilient growth*. Washington D.C.: IMF.

Samant, T. (2023) Women: Education, employment, empowerment. In *Overseas Research Foundation (ORF) expert speech*, January 3.

Singh, J. P. (1999). *Leapfrogging development? The political economy of telecommunications restructuring*. State University of New York Press.

Singh, A. (2005). Will services be the new engine of economic growth in India? *CBR Working Paper no.310*. Centre for Business Research, University of Cambridge.

Soete, L. (1985). International diffusion of technology, industrial development and technological leapfrogging. *World Development, 13*(3).

Statista. (2023). Number of start-ups becoming unicorns in India from 2015 to 2022 (Published by M Rathore, Mar 14). https://www.statista.com/statistics/1238534/number-of-new-unicorns-2020/

Steinmueller, W. E. (2001). ICTs and the possibilities for leapfrogging by developing countries. *International Labour Review, 140*(2).

Talmage-Rostron, M. (2023). *Future of BPO industry in the Philippines 2023*. Nexford University, May 19. https://www.nexford.org/insights/the-future-of-bpos-in-the-philippines-and-growth-opportunities

Tejaswi, M. J. (2012). NASSCOM 'renames' BPO industry as BPM. The Times of India, September 6.

Tholons. (2020). Global innovation index 2020: Innovation at scale. Tholons.

Tholons. (2021). Global innovation index 2021: What is the future of innovation-driven growth? Tholons.

Thomas, Tessa A., & Ray, K. (2019). Online outsourcing and the future of work. *Journal of Global Responsibility, 20*(3), 2041–2568. https://doi.org/10.1108/JGR-10-2018-0039

Trade and Industry Center in Berlin: TICB. (2021) IT-BPM industry - Industry performance and outlook. Industry Briefer, October 12, 2021. https://outsourcing-journal.org/wp-content/uploads/2021/10/Briefer-IT-BPM-Industry.pdf

UNCTAD. (2012). *Information economy report 2012: The software industry and developing countries.* United Nations.

UNCTAD. (2019). *Digital economy report 2019: Value creation and capture: Implications for developing countries.* United Nations.

UNCTAD. (2011). Technology and innovation report 2011: Powering development with renewable energy technologies. New York and Geneva: United Nations.

UNCTAD. (2014). Building supply and export capacity: The case of offshored services (Services: New frontier for sustainable development). New York and Geneva: United Nations.

UNCTAD. (2017). Information economy report 2017. New York and Geneva: United Nations.

UNCTAD. (2018a). Technology and innovation report 2018: Harnessing frontier technologies for sustainable development. New York and Geneva: United Nations.

UNCTAD. (2018b). Leapfrogging: Look before you leap, Policy Brief, No.71, December.

UNCTAD. (2021a). *Digital economy report 2021*: Cross-border data flows and development: For whom the data flows. United Nations.

UNCTAD. (2021b). *Manual for the production of statistics on the digital economy, 2020 revised version*, New York: United Nations Publications.

UNCTAD. (2022). The evolving landscape of digital trade in services, Note by the UNCTAD secretariat. Trade and Development Board,TD/B/C.I/MEM.4/26.

Villegas, B.M. (2022). Human side of Economics: IT-BPM industry drives economic growth (Part 1), *Business World*, October 18. https://www.bworldonline.com/opinion/2022/10/18/481442/it-bpm-industry-drives-economic-growth/

Watanabe, T. -J (1986). *Kaihatsu keizai gaku (Development economics).* Tokyo: Nihon Hyoronsha.

World Bank. (2009). *The service revolution in South Asia.* World Bank, June.

White, K. (2015). How big is the U.S. call center industry compared to India and The Philippines? (siteselectiongroup.com).

Yayboke, E., Crumpler, W., & Carter, W. A. (2020). *The need for a leapfrog strategy.* Center for Strategic & International Studies (CSIS), April 10. https://www.csis.org/analysis/need-leapfrog-strategyd

Chapter 6
The Case of the Philippines in the Asian Economy

Abstract This chapter focuses on the context of "shared growth" to highlight the case of the Philippines in an East Asian context. The term was coined in the controversial East Asian Miracle Report of the World Bank to describe the peculiarities of the development of eight Highly Performing East Asian Economies, in which the Philippines was not included. The case of the Philippines in this context was elaborated through three international engagements of Japan, the premier model and advocate of shared growth. These engagements are also known as the trinity of ODA-FDI-EX/IM. Although the Philippines appeared to do relatively well in leveraging ODA and FDI, to the extent that it was able, the inability to ride on the flying geese dynamics which underlie Japan's trade (EX/IM) remains a challenge.

Keywords Shared growth · East Asian miracle · ODA · FDI · Trade · Flying Geese Model (FGM)

6.1 Introduction

This chapter employs shared growth as a framework for analyzing the dynamics of Philippine economic development. Shared growth here is defined as a balance between the two socio-economic goals of efficiency and equity. It should be noted that this concern over shared growth was preceded by decades of the relatively more recent explosion of interest in the distribution of income and wealth.[1] The first section discusses what is essentially ground zero of this framework in the late twentieth century, with Japan right in the epicenter. This framework links the case of the Philippines to various institutional mechanisms of shared growth that emanate from Japan. The second section augments the original discourse of shared growth by unpacking the institutional elements that form Japan's international participation in foreign direct investment, foreign aid, and trade, in the context of a broader conceptualization of shared growth. In the final section, we evaluate how the Philippines was or was not able to ride on these shared growth mechanisms. This evaluation forms

[1] Most notable of which are Piketty (2013) and Stiglitz (2012).

H. Hirakawa and F. C. Maquito, *The Dynamics of Asian Economic Development*,
https://doi.org/10.1007/978-981-97-3106-0_6

the basis for later discussions related to the case of the Philippines from a shared growth perspective.

6.2 "Ground Zero" of the Shared Growth Discourse

In 1993, the World Bank published the East Asian Miracle (EAM) Report, which focused on a peculiar pattern of development by eight highly performing East Asian economies. The report dubbed this development as "shared growth", characterized by rapid income per capita growth from 1960 to 1990 with highly equal income distributions of the following eight Highly Performing (East) Asian Economies: Japan, South Korea, Taiwan, HK, Singapore, Indonesia, Malaysia, and Thailand. Conspicuously absent from this list is the Philippines, which was not able to achieve shared growth for the period covered, especially during the turbulent decade of the 1980s which was marred by political instability.

The Philippines was actually a flashpoint in the growing international conflict that emerged with the ending of the 1st Cold War.[2] This conflict was no longer between capitalism and communism/socialism but among different forms of capitalism, and ultimately led to the EAM report. In the development assistance sector, this conflict was brewing between the World Bank and the Japanese Official Development Assistance (ODA) community, mainly represented by the Overseas Economic Cooperation Fund (OECF)[3] and the Ministry of Finance. In the 1980s the directions of the World Bank and the Japanese ODA community started diverging as the World Bank abandoned government intervention-friendly (Keynesian) principles and embraced market-friendly (virtually, neoliberal) principles. Based on a reading of the 1990 Annual Meeting Report of the World Bank, the first salvo apparently was launched by the Japanese side, which was the vanguard of an objection to the report of the Bank's Task Force on Financial Sector Operations (Okuda, 2004: 163). This task force "championed a policy of far-reaching financial deregulation for developing countries, urging removal of all interest rate controls and all directed credit programmes" (Wade, 1996: 6). The World Bank retaliated a month after the 1990 Annual Meeting Report was issued: "Citing the case of the Philippines, a senior vice-president of the Bank wrote to the President of OECF—in charge of the ASEAN-Japan Development Fund—asking him to reconsider the policy of subsidized targeted loans" (Wade, 1996: 8).[4]

More formally, the loans in question here are called Two-Step Loans (TSLs). As shown in Fig. 6.1 the donor country, in the first of two steps, provides concessional

---

[2] We consider ourselves in the midst of the 2nd Cold War.

[3] The OECF merged with the Japan Export-Import Bank in 1999 to form the Japan Bank for International Cooperation, which was assimilated in 2008, as in charge of the international sector of the Japan Finance Corporation.

[4] Interestingly, Okuda uses the more direct terminology of "we would like you to stop" instead of "reconsider" (Okuda, 2004: 163).

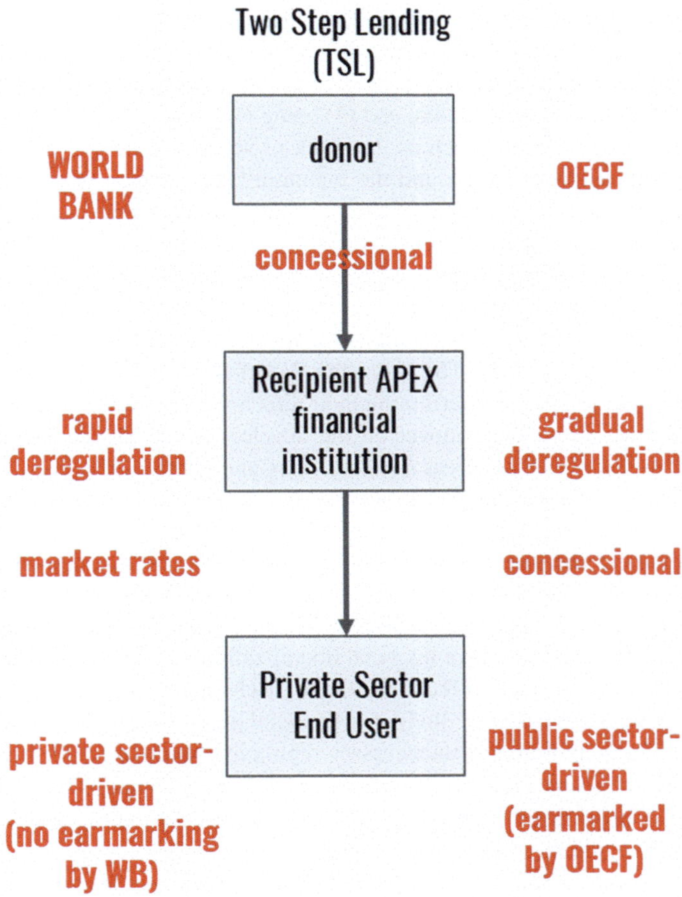

Fig. 6.1 Comparison of OECF and World Bank Two-Step Loans/Lending (adapted from Okuda, 1992, 1993)

loans to a development financing institution within the recipient country, the apex institution, which in turn lends these funds to the private sector (the second of two steps). Both the World Bank and Japan, through the OECF, have been providing TSL since the 1960s. With its conversion to neoliberalism, however, the Bank sought to do away with TSL following the directive issued by Task Force on Financial Sector Operations. Moreover, there are significant differences in the TSL of the two financial institutions.[5] In the case of the World Bank's TSL, the apex institution relends based on private sector (end-user) demand, while in the case of the OECF TSL, relending is limited to project categories that have been decided by the recipient government as priority or strategic sectors. Moreover, the Bank's TSL relending is at market interest rates while that of OECF TSL continues to be below market interest rates.

[5] Based on (Okuda, 1993: 75).

The bone of contention is that OECF TSL introduces a distortion in the financial market by: (1) introducing loans with subsidized interest rates, instead of market rates; (2) purposively channeling funds to target sectors, instead of letting the market determine the end user of the funds); and (3) being long term, instead of leaving this to other sources of financing such as the stock or securities market (Okuda, 1992: 98). While both the World Bank and the Japanese ODA community recognize the importance and underdevelopment of the financial markets of developing markets, both parties appear to have different approaches to the problem. The World Bank adopts a more drastic approach directed on improving the functioning of the financial sector through outright deregulation. The Japanese ODA side, on the other hand, prefers a gradualism that is in line with the recipient's stage of development.

Hence, the criticism of the TSL from the World Bank stems basically from its concern that Japan's TSL is undermining their reforms of the financial sector: OECF TSL "could have an adverse impact on the development of the financial sector" and hence "would create unnecessary distortions and set back the financial sector reforms' which had been supported by the IMF's Extended Fund Facility and the Bank's Financial Sector Adjustment Loan." (Wade, 1996: 8).

To the Japanese ODA side, however, this would not be a valid argument given its belief that reform of the financial sector should be in step with the development of the whole economy. "Financial liberalization policy in LDCs is quite different from that in developed countries where financial liberalization simply means deregulation of existing financial markets" (Okuda, 1993: 76), [which are premised on an already completed industrial structure].[6] "In LDCs, financial liberalization should pursue two targets, that is, the abolition of unnecessary regulations and the imposition of new regulations which are necessary for developing new financial markets" (Okuda, 1993: 76–77), which have been designed appropriately for the next industrial structure, all under the policy guidance of the government.

This disagreement came to a head with the Bank agreeing to take a closer inspection of the HPAE's post-war development on two conditions: 1. Japan shoulders the price tag of U.S.$1.2 million; and 2. Japan dropped "their opposition to the draft Operational Directive on Financial Sector Operations, which urged full scale financial deregulation." (Wade, 1996: 18). Japan agreed to both terms, resulting in the East Asian Miracle Report of 1993.

6.3 Mechanisms of Shared Growth from Japan

While being a milestone in economic development thinking, the EAM report, however, pays scant attention to certain institutional elements that we believe may have also contributed to achieving shared growth. We bring to fore these elements from the country that, as was discussed above, is at the epicenter of this shared

[6] The phrases within the brackets are based on my translation of (Okuda, 1992: 96). As could be seen, some salient points in the original Japanese version appeared to have been lost in translation.

growth discourse, Japan. While being Japan-centric, our framework focuses on the mechanisms that have an international bearing for it focuses on Japan's international engagements, namely, foreign direct investment, foreign aid, and trade.

In order to deepen our understanding of shared growth, we explore its origins within the Japanese economy. In particular, we focus on the following three institutional mechanisms of Japan by which shared growth could have been achieved: the Japanese corporate organizational structure. a.k.a. Keiretsu, Japan's development financing, and the Flying Geese Model.

The period of focus for most of our ensuing discussion would be post-war to early 2000s. To be sure, Japan's institutions have been evolving. A substantial part of this evolution during the post Cold War (1)[7] era was mainly due to its yielding to foreign pressure from other developed economies. In his mea culpa, as one of the economists deeply involved in the neoliberal reform of Japan in the late twentieth century, Nakatani Iwao deeply regrets his taking part in what he refers to as the opening of Pandora's box (Nakatani, 2008). There is a lot to regret. The lost decade, starting with the 1990s, has evolved into the lost two, three, and even four decades. Without a doubt, Japan has been dealt a paralyzing blow by the neoliberal tsunami that swept across the globe since the 1980s. For purposes of understanding Japan's different mechanisms as a reference for a developing country, the post-war period, when Japan exhibited the competitiveness of its economic institutions, would, in our assessment, be of more value to our study.

6.3.1 *Japan's Developmental Financing*

In this section, we look at two cases of Japan's developmental financing. One is international and refers to Japan's ODA, while the other is local and refers to the developmental financing studied in the EAM report practiced by the HPAEs. We shall distill the shared growth principle from these two cases.

Japan's ODA

As mentioned above, the EAM report was born out of a conflict of views between the World Bank and the Japanese ODA community. It is just fitting then that we start our shared-growth study with Japan's development financing. To further consolidate its position amidst this conflict, Japan also formulated its ODA Charter in 1992 to clarify its development assistance philosophy. One of the pillars of this Charter is the Self-Help Effort (SHE) philosophy stating that Japan is to assist the self-help efforts of recipient countries.[8]

---

[7] We consider the world to be currently in the midst of a 2nd Cold War. Post Cold War 1 covers the 1990s up to the worsening of US-Sino and NATO-Russia relationships.

[8] The SHE philosophy remains in the ODA charter even after its revision in 2003 and 2014.

There are various elaborations of the SHE philosophy, but this one I think is a good summary of its economic features (Kohama -J, 1992: 76):

1. request basis
2. no conditionality
3. local cost share
4. untied
5. loan over grants

The first four features heavily emphasize the sovereignty of the recipient country, which in turn fosters ownership of the supported project by the recipient country. Request basis implies that projects for funding are proposed primarily by the recipient country. No conditionality promotes non-interventionism in the recipient country's policy making. Local cost share requires that projects are not funded solely by ODA but involves the recipient country's sharing in the total cost. Untied aid means that ODA funds, as much as possible, do not require the purchase of donor country goods and services as inputs to the project being funded by said donor.

The fifth feature of Japanese ODA's philosophy reveals a relatively strong preference for Japan's ODA to be in the form of loans rather than grants. As we will discuss more below, this feature could be linked to the shared growth aspect of Japan's ODA. For context, we compare this feature with that of the OECD-DAC donor countries.

As could be seen in Table 6.1, the share of grants in Japan's ODA has been significantly lower than that of the DAC donors, as a whole. In fact, there appears to be a decreasing trend over the period 2012 to 2021, which goes against the overall increasing trend among DAC donor countries. The preference of Japan for loans in its ODA remains strong.

As defined earlier, Japan's SHE philosophy could be associated with shared growth, as the former's outcome. In this section, we apply the shared growth lens on Japan's ODA loans to reveal a mechanism for achieving shared growth in an international sense.

Table 6.2 shows a comparison of the stylized features of the development assistance of Japan and other donors. We focus on the distinguishing feature of Japan's ODA: the preference for loans over grants,

In terms of equity, Japan and other donors have the same intention of allocating relatively more ODA to the more backward countries. Where the two could be different is in the recovery rate of ODA. Naturally, a grant has a zero rate of recovery,

Table 6.1 Comparative grant share

Donor	Year	Total ODA	Of which: total ODA grants	Grant share (%)
DAC total	2012	181,819.94	125,576.97	69.07
DAC total	2021	154,028.07	125,285.12	81.34
Japan	2012	13,151.68	5,320.90	40.46
Japan	2021	15,403.50	5,766.65	37.44

(*Source* OECD Statistics).

Table 6.2 The efficiency and equity of the ODA of Japan and other donors

Shared growth aspects	Other donors	Japan
Equity (shared)	Allocate more ODA to more backward countries	
	Higher reliance on grants, low fund recovery	Higher fund recovery from more developed recipient countries
Efficiency (growth)	In a relatively functioning market system, grants are efficient and could adequately achieve any required income distribution	In an already, imperfectly functioning market system, inefficiency losses below-market interest rates of yen loans become irrelevant

(Adapted from Maquito 2019).

while yen loans, because of its repayment and interest obligations, have a higher rate of recovery. Recovery could be considered under the equity (shared) aspect of shared growth. In the case of Japan ODA, there is a sharing among the recipients in the sense that repayments and interest payments of one recipient could be recycled and shared with other recipients. Because of the greater reliance on grants, however, the other donors are limited in their ability to recover their ODA.

For example, in the case of Japan's ODA budget for fiscal years 1996 and 1997, funding from repayments amounted to JPY 278.8 billion and JPY 338.8 billion, respectively. These accounted for significant shares of 18.3% and 20.2% of Japan's ODA operating budget, for FY 1996 and FY 1997, respectively. (Beaudry & Chris, 1999, Appendix 4A).

The claim that less developed recipient countries tend to face less stringency is confirmed, for example, in an interview with a Japan International Cooperation Agency (JICA) staff based in the Philippines, who stated that the terms of loans become even softer (lower interest rates, longer terms of payment), the more backward the recipient country, contrary to commercial lending practices (Valenc, 2018).

Moreover, using panel data estimation,[9] we found a significantly positive relationship between the loan share of Japanese ODA and the level of development as measured by real GDP per capita for Cambodia, Indonesia, Lao People's Democratic Republic, Malaysia, the Philippines, Thailand, and Vietnam over the period 1993–2017. This confirms the hypothesis above that more developed recipient countries have higher shares of yen loans in their ODA.

With respect to efficiency, other donors, working on the assumption of functional markets, could use grants as a form of redistribution of income, and still arrive at an efficient market equilibrium.[10] Japan, however, starts with the assumption that the market system is already flawed so that any price distortion that it introduces, such as below-market interest rates, would have irrelevant consequences, and may even

[9] The Hausmann test indicates the fixed effect model as the appropriate panel-data model.

[10] The so-called 2nd Fundamental Theorem of Welfare Economics.

have good results if these are directed to strategic industries, as in the discussion of Japan's directed credit (TSL) above, and selective intervention below.

6.3.2 Developmental Financing in the EAM Report

The EAM report proposes the Functional[11] Approach to Growth framework, shown in Fig. 6.2, to explain the performance of the HPAEs. As can be seen, this framework is concerned with two kinds of outcomes. One is rapid sustained growth, which we ascribe to the economic goal of efficiency, the ability to use resources to produce more output. Another is equal distribution of income, which we ascribe to the economic goal of equity. Shared growth, therefore, could be clearly seen in the outcomes of this framework.

Shared growth could also be seen in the contest-based mechanism that is used as an alternate competitive discipline to the market mechanism in cases where the latter has failed. It is to be noted that the policy of selective intervention mainly acts through the discipline of contests. Selective intervention consists of the hallmarks of Japanese ODA: concessional interest rates, in the form of directed credit and

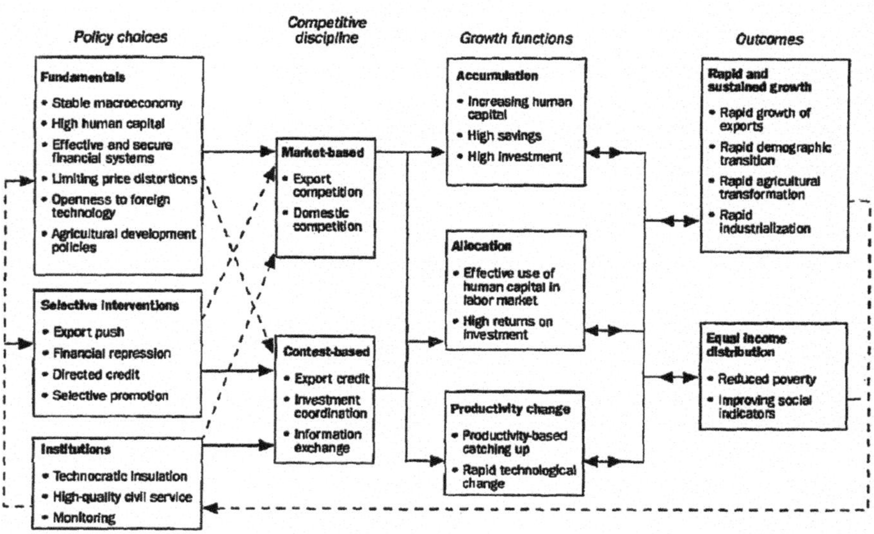

Fig. 6.2 Functional approach to growth (Adapted from: World Bank, 1993: 88)

[11] This term was a concession made to higher ups in the Bank in exchange for approval of the EAM report. The project leaders "recognized that 'strategy' and 'strategic' implied—at least to the East Asia [division] vice-presidency—a stronger argument about the efficacy of industrial policy than they wished to make, and were distracting attention from the substance of the argument about market failures. All references to strategy were therefore deleted, being replaced, where necessary, with the innocuous 'functional', as in 'a functional approach to growth" (Wade 1996: 28).

financial repression, directed towards sectors that have been selected for promotion, especially those that sell local products abroad.

Shared growth is the basic principle that imbues the political leadership the legitimacy it needs to effectively operate contest-based competition. By convincing society that it will share in whatever growth that is generated, the state is effectively endowed with the legitimacy to determine the rules, rewards, and refereeing of contests. Shared growth principles are found in the following institutional mechanisms that come in various forms in various countries: (World Bank, 1993: 157–185).

1. wealth-sharing programs designed to include non-elites in economic growth, such as universal education, land reform, support for SMEs, public housing, and health services.
2. a cadre of economic technocrats insulated from narrow political pressures
3. institutions and mechanisms to share information and win the support of the business elites, such as deliberation councils (consultation between government and industry).

The contest-based mechanism of the EAM report has not been without its share of criticism. In fact, despite admitting to the existence of selective intervention in the HPAEs, the EAM report itself ultimately gives a poor rating of the effectiveness of selective intervention in the past as well as to other developing economies.

> Our judgment is that **in a few economies**, mainly in Northeast Asia, **in some instances**, government interventions resulted in higher and more equal growth than otherwise would have occurred. However, the prerequisites for success were so rigorous that policymakers seeking to follow similar paths in **other developing countries** have often met with **failure**. (World Bank, 1993: 6) – emphases are authors'

One noteworthy criticism, which raises the critique a few more notches is that of Beason & Weinstein (1996), hereafter BM, which conducted a statistical analysis showing a negative correlation between the industry sectoral growth rates and the growth of various industrial policy instruments, namely, Japan Development Bank loans, subsidies, tax relief, and tariffs. This implies that industrial policy appears to be more generous to the slowly growing sectors of Japanese industry, contrary to the revisionist view. Instead of the Japanese government "picking the winners", it appears as if it was "picking up the losers".

To be sure there has been criticism about the methodology of Beason & Weinstein (1996).[12] Despite this, however, there appears to have been no study yet to assess the effectiveness of industrial policy instruments that overcomes the statistical problem of BM.

There is a silver lining to this cloud. The BM study prompts a closer look at the EAM report's contest mechanism, and in fact teases out a different and unexpected perspective. It actually leads one to thinking that there is room for including unconventional elements in the contest-based mechanism of the Functional Approach to Growth framework of the Bank. The contest here might not be the typical one wherein

---

[12] For example, see (Rodrik, 2021). The methodological basis of this criticism could be found in (Rodrik, 2012), which criticizes such studies as suffering from the problem of omitted variables.

the winner takes it all. In Japan, for example, there has been the practice of "recession cartels", formed by firms that essentially have lost out to the competition. "The cartels allow firms to share losses. They may also be eligible for subsidized loans to upgrade technology or restructure operations. In this way, bankruptcy or massive layoffs by one enterprise may be avoided Ito (1992)." (World Bank, 1993: 234). The bureaucracy in this case monitors the performance of such cartels to ensure that there is no abuse of the assistance that has been provided. In this way, the contest-based mechanism promotes competition, albeit tempered.

The only study we have found thus far to even suggest a shared growth interpretation of the BW study is that of Morck & Yeung (2001: 14):

> Beason & Weinstein (1996) show that Japanese government money tended to flow to the least economically viable segments of the economy, not to those with the greatest potential. This is probably because governments are properly concerned with redistributive welfare. However, this concern undermines their ability to fund creative destruction, which necessarily entails being responsible for 'destruction'.

While recognizing the role of the government to be concerned about "sharing", Morck & Yeung (2001) are skeptical that such sharing leads to growth.

This begs the question as to how the contest-based mechanism, as reimagined above, leads to shared growth?

With regards to efficiency, neoliberalism reminds us that functional markets are based on competition that breeds efficiency, as unproductive enterprises are weeded out, leaving only the more productive ones. There is an inefficiency in this process, however, when the assets involved, such as labor and capital, have the element of specificity, or being most productive only in a specific enterprise. This implies that moving such assets across different enterprises entails a social cost or inefficiency. In which case, rescuing a troubled enterprise to live and fight another day would just very well be an efficient approach, provided of course that such enterprises do not take advantage of this implicit insurance.[13]

From an equity perspective, the act of helping out in times of need by itself entails a transfer of resources from those who can afford it to those in need. This leads to a society wherein disparity in distribution of wealth would be lesser than in a situation where losers, deprived of wealth, abound. For neoliberalism, of course, this would not be a problem where markets function and there is no asset specificity.

[13] For a more elaborate discussion of asset-specificity in the context of recession cartels, see Chang (2003).

6.3.3 *Japanese Organizational Structure: The Keiretsu and FDI*

Japan's corporate structure has stylistically been referred to as the keiretsu[14] system. "The most distinctive form of network organization in Japan – and the most critical to understanding its economy—is the clusters of industrial, commercial, and financial corporations known as keiretsu." (Lincoln & Gerlach, 2004). There are basically two kinds. One is the vertical keiretsu that focuses on one market segment, and is organized around a big enterprise (e.g., assembler). Another is the horizontal keiretsu (*kigyou shudan)*, which straddles different market segments, and is organized around the council of presidents (*shachou kai)* of the main enterprises of each vertical keiretsu.

We could observe elements of shared growth in the vertical keiretsu, which is characterized by cozy, but long-term relationships, which enable various stakeholders to share in the growth of the main enterprise of the keiretsu. These long-term relationships are basically between the firm and its various stakeholders, such as laborers, stockholders, and bank.

Long-term relationships between firm and laborers empower laborers, enabling them to acquire a greater share in the value generated by the firm. This becomes a source of competitiveness, hence, growth for firms that rely on laborer skills that take a long time to develop. One manifestation of such a long-term relationship could be gleaned from the wage profiles of firms.

This relationship could be cast in sharper relief when we compare the U.S. and Japan. CEO-to-Average Worker Pay Ratios (2011–2012) in the U.S. is 354:1, while in Japan it is 67:1 (Lacmanović 2013: 171). CEO compensation is very high relative to typical worker compensation (by a ratio of 278-to-1 or 221-to-1). In contrast, the CEO-to-typical-worker compensation ratio (options realized) was 20-to-1 in 1965 and 58-to-1 in 1989. CEOs are even making a lot more—about five times as much—as other earners in the top 0.1%. From 1978 to 2018, CEO compensation grew by 1,007.5% (940.3% under the options-realized measure), far outstripping S&P stock market growth (706.7%) and the wage growth of very high earners (339.2%). In contrast, wages for the typical worker grew by just 11.9% (Mishel & Wolfe, 2019).

The long term relationship with stockholders is referred to as "stable shareholders" or *antei kabunushi* in Japanese (Sheard, 1994: 312). Stylized facts of corporate shareholding of a Japanese firm.

1. A typical Japanese firm has about 70 percent of its shares held by other corporations
2. The shares are held by a large number of firms in relatively small fractional parcels
3. The firm has some kind of transactional relationship with these corporate shareholders (banking, insurance, lending, supply of inputs, purchase of inputs)

---

[14] This word is now found in English dictionaries. Merriam-Webster defines "keiretsu" as "a powerful alliance of Japanese businesses often linked by cross-shareholding".

4. The firm holds shares in many of these firms: the shareholdings are reciprocal
5. Firms hold each other's shares as 'stable shareholders' (*antei kabunushi*)

Such stable shareholders have effectively given up the two sacred rights of shareholders: voice and exit. By relinquishing their voice, stable shareholders implicitly entrust the fate of the company to the incumbent management. By relinquishing their right to exit, the stable shareholders have given their promise to hold on and not sell off their shares. This effectively curtails the power of outside shareholders who might be unsympathetic to the long-term perspective of the firm's management. From the point of view of the shareholders, it is essentially a buy-and-hold investment strategy. The stock market, therefore, has been neutralized as a mechanism for corporate governance. This is not to say that Japanese managers are no longer in need of discipline. In the keiretsu structure, corporate governance is provided for by the main bank.

> The long term relationship with a firm's bank arises from its being identified to have a main bank, which conducts delegated monitoring, whereby the bank intervenes in case the client firm is in dire straits.
>
> ... it should be noted that this delegation or commitment to a passive, non-interventionist role ... is a state-contingent one. It obtains as long as the firm is performing well, but in times of corporate failure intervention by the main bank can be expected (Aoki, 1990; Sheard, 1989a; Sheard, 1994: 319).

A shared growth element arises from this helping out of keiretsu member firms when they are in distress. Figure 6.3 shows this very clearly.

> ..the evidence does suggest that commercial banks tend to be more procyclical when operating in more-arm's length financial systems, where a greater share of intermediation occurs through financial markets rather than through traditional relationship-based (and bank-dominated) activities (IMF, 2008: 148).

Here we have a structural feature of the keiretsu where a much stronger member helps out an ailing member, "giving an umbrella on a rainy day" instead of giving one on a clear day.

This character of the keiretsu is not limited to the vertical form. Using longitudinal data of 200 Japanese manufacturing firms and banks over the period 1965–1995, Lincoln and Gerlach (2004) established an intervention of stronger firms to help out weaker firms. The cost of such intervention is a lower growth of the stronger firms, in exchange for the continued survival and later growth of the assisted firms.

This DNA is naturally transmitted by Japanese firms to other countries through FDI. Developing countries could provide a fertile ground as these would be less subjected to the deregulation pressures that Japan underwent during the bubble era when its form of capitalism was battered by the tsunami of neoliberal globalization that swept the global economy in the 1980s. Moreover, the strengthening of the yen also was a driving force for Japanese firms to invest in various countries in Southeast Asia, leveraging the international transmission force of the Flying Geese Model.

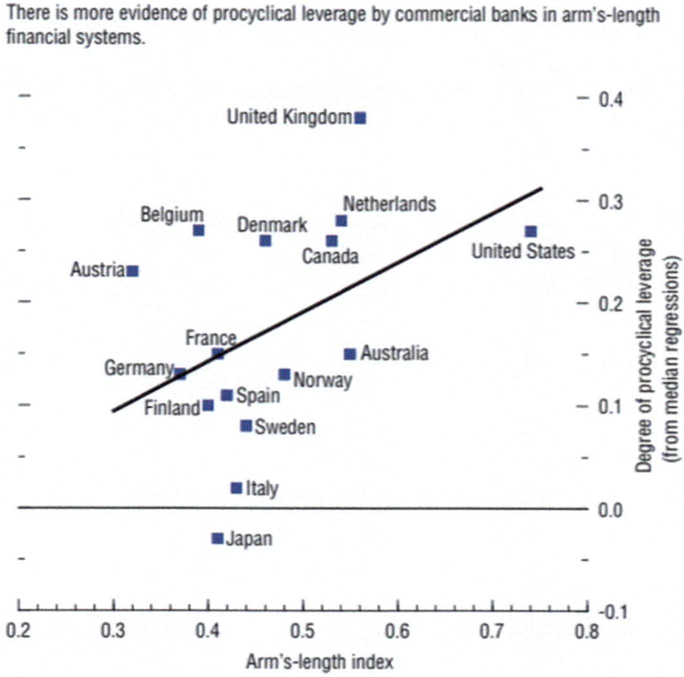

Fig. 6.3 Procyclical leverage and arm's-length financial systems (*Source* IMF, 2008)

6.3.4 *The Flying Geese Model and Japanese EX/IM (Trade)*

Another institutional mechanism that the EAM report appears to ignore is the Flying Geese Model, despite it already experiencing a renaissance in the 1980s as an explanation to the development of the East Asian region (Okita, GRIPS). In this section, we first review the Flying Geese Model, while presenting a different perspective based on nature's flying geese formation, and then discuss its associations with shared growth.

Akamatsu used the metaphor of the flying geese to describe the dynamics he observed, as the inverted U-shaped curves he was studying reminded him of the flying geese formation. The metaphor, in our view, could be extended beyond the visual association he made. It has been recently verified what has traditionally been known that the flying geese formation enables the flock to fly farther. This is due to the proper positioning of each bird within the formation, and a flapping of wings appropriately synchronized to the bird flying just ahead. This enables each bird to take advantage of lifting currents of air generated by the flock as a whole, thereby optimizing energy resources, which ultimately leads to a longer and safer migration. More specifically, there are at least two things that the geese have to accomplish: 1. Be at the proper position relative to other geese, leading to a V-formation—see

Fig. 6.4; 2. Flapping their wings up and down at the right time in sync with the lifting air waves generated by the preceding goose—see Fig. 6.5 (Wald, 2014; Yong, 2014).

From the top view of the flying geese formation, it could be seen that the geese position themselves in the zone where they could take advantage of the lift that is generated by the preceding goose.

From a side view of the flying geese formation, it could be seen that a cyclical lifting air wave is generated along the V-formation. Geese further take advantage of this by flapping their wings downward when the cyclical lift is weak, thus generating their own lift, and flapping their wing upward when the cyclical lift is strong, in effect gliding.

Although absent in Akamatsu's original naming of his model, the above elaboration should support the validity of the flying geese metaphor. Since then other

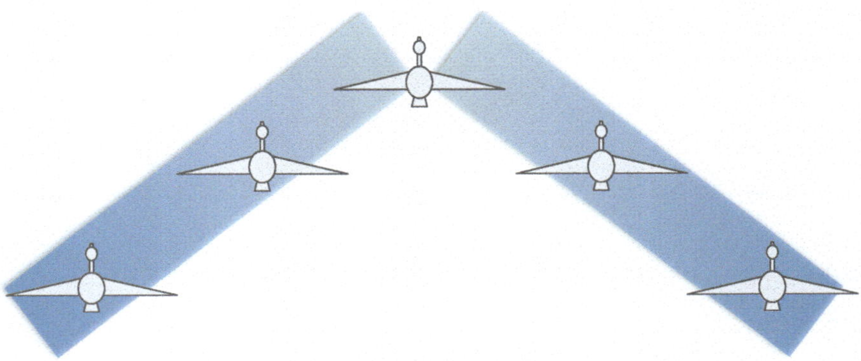

Fig. 6.4 Schematic top view of flying geese formation (*Source* by Maquito). *Note* Shaded area indicates lifting air waves

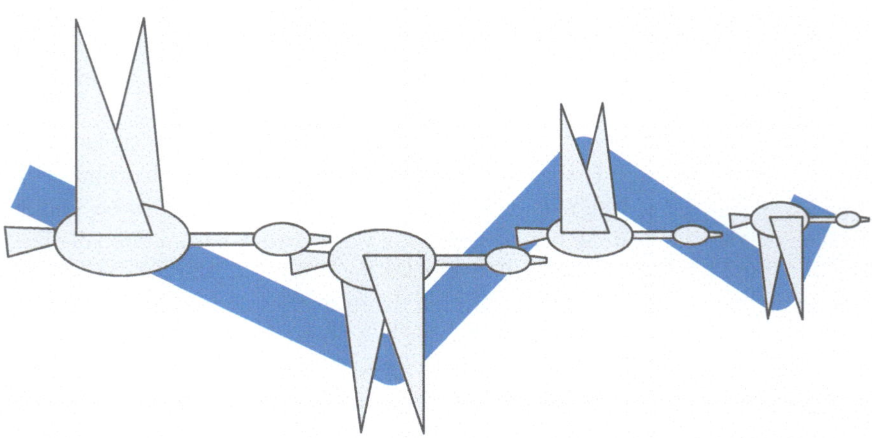

Fig. 6.5 Schematic side view of flying geese formation (*Source* by Maquito). *Note* Shaded area indicates the cycle of lifting air waves. Troughs indicate weak lift while peaks indicate strong lift

metaphors have emerged to describe the flying geese model. One is that of Kumagai (2008), who uses net export ratio as the vertical axis instead of the original value of goods, and one curve instead of the original three curves of production, import, and export. He dubs this diagram as a "flying fish diagram" as the curve for each good looks like the path of a flying fish breaking from and then reentering the surface of the water. While the curves do look that way, they do not capture the aerodynamics (or in this case the fluid mechanics) whereby geese flying in formation achieve some advantage, for the simple reason that flying fishes do not utilize such dynamics. Another metaphor is that of Lin (2012) who replaces "flying geese" to "leading dragon" to emphasize the emergence of China in the division of labor in East Asia. The flying geese metaphor still is a better one in our opinion for a couple of reasons. While the leading dragon captures the incontrovertible fact of the emergence of China as a factory of the world, the use of "dragon; is not factual since it is in the first place a mythical creature. Moreover, the flying geese metaphor already captures the possibility of the lead goose changing during the long flight.

The dynamic of the flying geese formation described earlier can be seen in the flying geese model.

Figure 6.6 shows three forces (shown numbered) in the Flying Geese Model. The horizontal force, number 1, corresponds to industrial upgrading within a country or country group through time. The diagonal force, number two, corresponds to the international transmission of industries to the other countries or country groups through time. The vertical force, number three, is essentially the resultant vector corresponding to a good division of labor across countries or country groups at any point in time. Relating this to our flying geese metaphor, each country (goose) is positioned in an industry behind the preceding country (in a V-formation), and becomes competitive in that industry (flaps its wings upwards) when it loses competitiveness (flapping wings downwards) in the preceding country. This is aided by the movement of enterprises from the preceding country to the succeeding country, akin to the lifting airwave generated by the preceding goose and passed on the succeeding goose.

As in nature's flying geese formation, this Flying Geese Model conserves the resources of countries, as economically buoyant forces help them in moving forward with their development, and as cooperation among neighboring countries prevent the wasteful expenditure of resources in excessive competition. Here lies one association of the flying geese model with shared growth. Through such a coordinated formation, all countries involved are able to go further in their development at a lesser cost.

One strategic element of the Flying Geese Model is the phase corresponding to the two important features of the flying geese formation shown in Figs. 6.4 and 6.5 above. To elaborate on this strategic element, we first have to elaborate more on the Flying Geese Model shown in Fig. 6.7.

In its complete form, the Flying Geese Model consists of the following phases, for a particular good:

1. Importation
2. Import-substitution

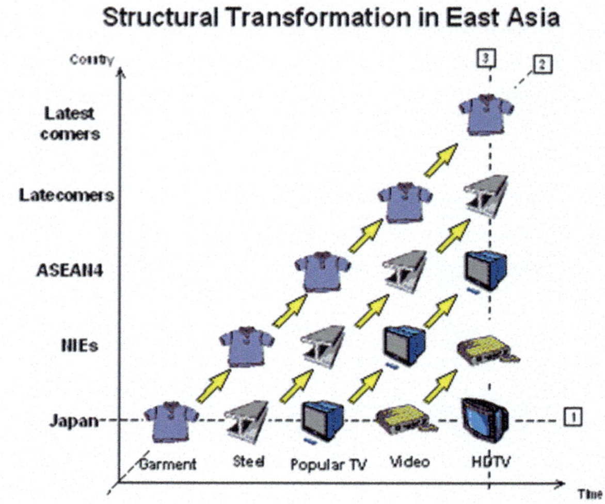

Fig. 6.6 Flying geese model forces in East Asia (*Source* https://www.grips.ac.jp/forum/module/prsp/FGeese.htm)

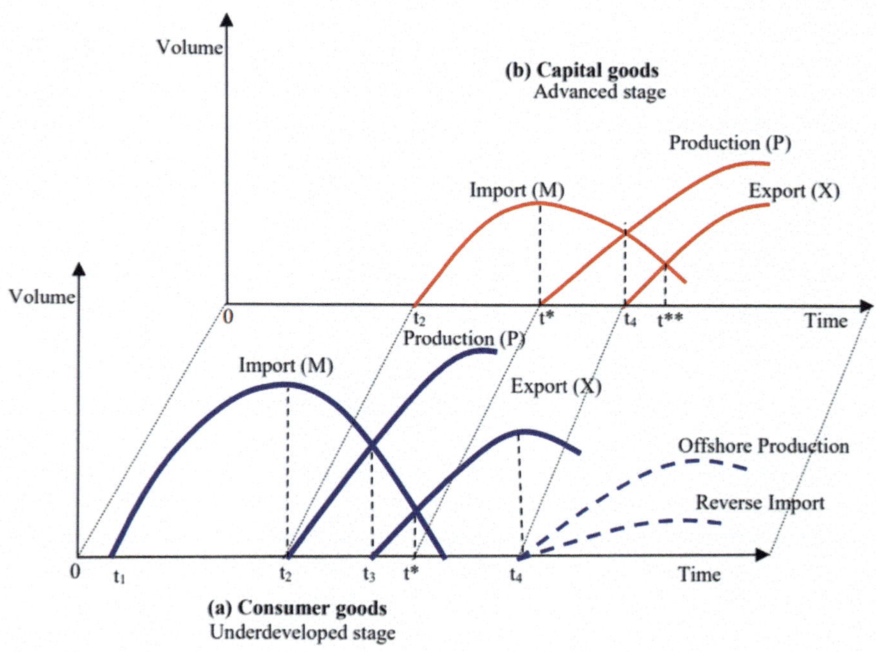

Fig. 6.7 A 3-D Depiction of Kojima's Flying Geese Model illustration (*Source* Widodo et al., 2018: 5; adapted from Kojima, 2000)

3. Exportation
4. Reverse-importation

These phases are intimately related to the competitiveness of a particular industry in the international market. Clearly the first phase of importation corresponds to the prenatal stage of an industry. In which case, the home country depends on imports of the goods produced by this particular industry. The second phase corresponds to the nascent stage of the local industry, which has embarked on producing the goods that were being imported in the first phase but not produced domestically. The third phase is when this particular industry has gained enough capabilities to compete in the international market, through exports. The final phase corresponds to the entry of latecomer countries in this particular industry in the international market, at which time, the domestic industry has lost its competitive advantage. This is not, of course, where the Flying Geese Model ends. The product cycle consisting of the four phases is assumed to continue as the domestic economy undergoes industrial upgrading (force number 1 in Fig. 6.6).

The strategic element corresponding to the positioning (Fig. 6.5) and synchronized flapping (Fig. 6.4) of nature's flying geese formation could be considered as corresponding largely to phase 2, import-substitution, where the domestic industry is positioned and striving to be competitive in an industry that a leading country is about to lose its competitive advantage. As in nature's flying geese formation, this positioning and enhancing of competitiveness is indispensable for the domestic economy to move forward at the least cost. As the position of the flying geese in the formation are fixed for a period of time while it benefits from the aerodynamics of the formation, so are the import-substitution and exportation phases referring to a particular industry. In other words, in the Flying Geese Model, the import-substitution phase could be considered as an indispensable preparation for the exportation phase of a particular industry.

6.3.5 Strategic Complementarities in the FDI-ODA-EXIM Trinity

Figure 6.8 shows the strategic complementarities among the international engagements of Japan, namely, ODA, FDI, and EXIM (export–import or trade), forming what is often referred to as a trinity.[15] As elaborated above, Japan's ODA is marked by its self-help effort philosophy, its FDI by its keiretsu type of corporate organization, and EXIM by its Flying Geese Model. The strategic complementarities among these three international engagements of Japan are as follows.

[15] To our knowledge, the term "trinity" in this context was first used by the Japanese government in MITI -J (1979) in the wake of the 5th UNCTAD and Tokyo Summit which generated high expectations for Japan to take leadership in the area of economic cooperation.

Fig. 6.8 ODA-FDI-EXIM trinity (*Source* created by Maquito)

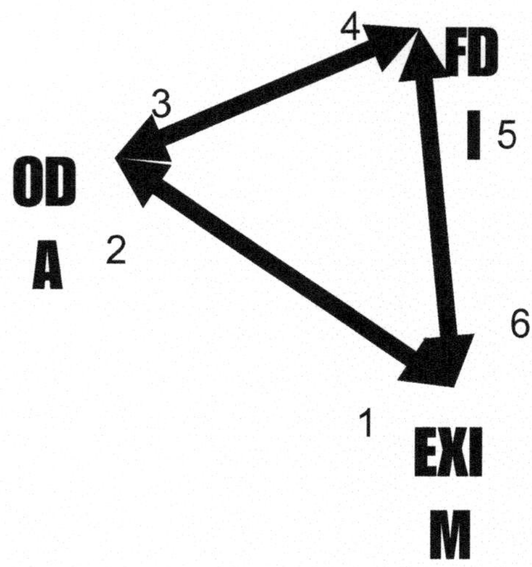

1. ODA to EXIM. The trigger for the East Asian Miracle Report of the World Bank, the two-step lending of Japan was characterized by sectoral targeting of Japan's concessional lending. This would be in support of a strategic implementation of the Flying Geese Model, which recognizes that countries had to develop particular industries given its position in the international division of labor in the East Asian region.
2. EXIM to ODA. As the targeted sector in the Flying Geese position of a recipient country gains international competitiveness, the recipient is able to earn enough to repay its concessional loans to Japan, helping in sustaining Japan's ODA program.
3. FDI to ODA. As discussed above, the corporate organizational structure of Japan, on which its FDI is mainly based, consists of a financial sector that essentially conducts financing that is countercyclical and not marked by arm's-length relationships between the financial sector and enterprises. This matches well with the unorthodox approach of Japan's ODA whereby the less advanced recipient country is given softer terms for its yen loans compared to more advanced recipient countries.
4. ODA to FDI. Higher ODA is generally allocated to countries that have higher Japanese FDI. Such ODA effectively facilitates the entry and operation of Japanese FDI within the host-recipient country.[16]
5. EXIM to FDI. As an integral part of the Flying Geese model, the international transmission of industries triggers the flight of Japanese FDI to lagging nations.
6. FDI to EXIM. Phase 2, import-substitution of the Flying Geese Model is facilitated by Japanese FDI that brings with it the technology of the industry being transmitted abroad from Japan. Ultimately, such FDI enables the host country's

[16] For example, see Blaise (2009), which finds support that Japan's ODA has been effective in promoting Japanese investment in the ASEAN 4 (Indonesia, Malaysia, Philippines, Thailand).

industry to move on to Phase 3, and compete through exports. This is referred to by Kojima as pro-trade FDI.

Another element that contributes to the strategic complementarity of Japan's ODA-FDI-EXIM is their tendency to contribute to shared growth, as discussed above. To be sure, Japan's ODA and EXIM allude to an international interpretation of shared growth, where growth is shared among a group of recipient or host countries. Japan's FDI, on the other hand, alludes to a more domestic interpretation of shared growth. This actually contributes to a complementarity and harmony between the international and domestic spheres.

6.4 The Philippines in Relation to the ODA-FDI-EXIM Trinity of Shared Growth

In this section, we situate the Philippines within the three overseas engagements of Japan, namely, ODA, FDI, and EXIM, in the context of the frameworks on which these engagements are based, namely, self-help effort philosophy, keiretsu corporate organization, and the Flying Geese Model.

6.4.1 The Philippines and Japanese ODA

With respect to ODA, Japan continues to be the Philippines' major donor country. Table 6.3 shows the sum of the grants and gross loans per DAC member country for several years to the Philippines. For the period 2013 to 2014, Japan had the highest average share among the DAC member countries at 51%, followed by the U.S. at 17%, and Australia and France at 7% each.

Recall that one core element of Japan's ODA philosophy is supporting the self-help efforts of recipient countries. A controversial feature of this philosophy is the heavier preference for yen loans, the supporting argument for which is that the obligation to repay incentivizes the recipient country to make good use of the ODA.

There is some evidence that this has indeed worked. From Table 6.3, we could see a remarkable difference in the repayments of Japan' yen loans vis-a-vis DAC donor countries, as a whole. During the period 2010–2011, the DAC's ratio of bilateral loans received (in short, repayments) to ODA gross total was about 15%, while that for Japan was significantly higher, at around 108%. This degree of difference was more or less maintained from 2018 up to 2021. This is attributable, in part, to the larger share of concessional loans in Japan's ODA, but at the same time, this is a clear indication of the recipient countries ability to repay based on their diligent self-help efforts.

Moreover, the interim report on the study of METI -J (2005) on the possibility of proposing a Japanese ODA model observed the relatively good performance of Japanese ODA recipient countries.

> In Asia and Africa, even though the amount of ODA received from Japan and other developed countries was almost the same, there was a large disparity in terms of autonomous economic development. It has focused on improving the trade and investment environment by developing economic development infrastructure, such as the development of hard infrastructure, soft infrastructure, and industrial human resource development, which will promote the vitality of the private sector. As a result, this has become one of the major factors that have led to the remarkable development of the economy and society (METI -J, 2005: 1). It is important to promote the dissemination of the Japan ODA model (METI -J, 2005: 21).

6.4.2 The Philippines and Japanese FDI

With respect to Japanese FDI, we have found indications that this has been a conduit for transmitting the praxis of Japanese corporations. In a study of special economic zones for manufacturing firms in the Philippines (Maquito & Carbonel, 2010), it was found that, based on an understanding of Japanese corporate practices at domestic and international levels, shared growth is refined to connote the following: 1. labor shares in the growth of its employing firm; 2. subcontractor firms share in the growth of the contractor firm; and 3. producer shares in the growth of its market. Data relating to manufacturing economic zones in the Philippines and trade among several countries in the automotive industry, which in the Philippines is dominated by Japanese corporations, are used to clarify certain aspects of each of the four refinements of shared growth. Using a production function framework and Philippine economic zone data, we show that indicators conceptually representing the three refinements mentioned above have positive effects on production efficiency.

Moreover, (Maquito & Hirakawa, 2011) presented two cases in the Philippines. The first case focuses on manufacturing economic zones in the Philippines, which used data provided by the Philippine Economic Zone Authority. This analysis basically shows that stable employment practices in the economic zones, along with other J-Firm features appear to promote productivity, as measured by a production function analysis. An extension of this empirical application in the second case is undertaken for a Japanese-affiliated automotive firm operating in the Philippines corroborates the economic zone findings. This implies that manufacturing economic zones and the automotive industry could provide channels by which the shared-growth DNA could be transmitted to the Philippines.

There are indications, however, that Japanese FDIs have not been leveraged by the Philippines to the same extent as other Southeast Asian countries. As could be seen in the Fig. 6.9, the Philippines has been generally at the bottom of Japanese FDI relative to its ASEAN neighbors, Indonesia, Malaysia, Thailand, and even ASEAN latecomer Vietnam.

This shows that FDI to the Philippines has been lagging behind that of its ASEAN cohorts (Indonesia, Malaysia, Thailand). This is nothing new. For the period "1973 to

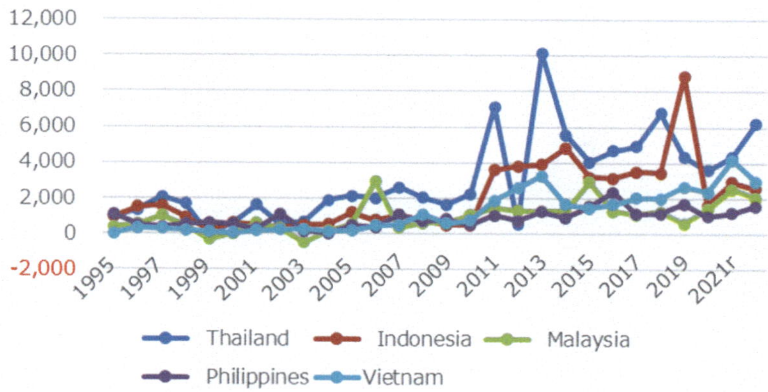

Fig. 6.9 Japanese FDI to various ASEAN countries[17] (*Source* JETRO Japanese Trade and Investment Statistics). *Note* FDI values are in million U.S. dollars

1990, FDI flows were concentrated in Malaysia, followed by Thailand and Indonesia, while the Philippines came last" (Mercado-Aldaba, 1994: 41). Using statistical analysis, it was observed that political instability was a significant negative factor affecting the FDI of the U.S., Japan, and EC Countries (Mercado-Aldaba, 1994: 64). The Philippines was embroiled in a very unstable political climate during the 1980s, with the ouster of the Marcos (Sr.) administration.

In a study we conducted for the automotive industry of the Philippines (Hirakawa, U, and Maquito 2008), we found that Japanese FDI to the Philippines tends to be behind those of Thailand. In an effort to discern the cause, we compared the country ratings of JETRO for Thailand and the Philippines across multiple factors that prospective Japanese investors considered important. "A statistical test on the difference of the means for the 62 observations (factors) for Thailand and the Philippines indicates that the null hypothesis wherein the means of the assessments of the two countries are different could not be rejected. That is to say that on the average the two countries do not significantly differ in their evaluations by investors" (Hirakawa et al., 2008: 50).

The problem, therefore, appears to be more on the side of the Philippines. This is substantiated by Table 6.5, which indicates that the Philippines is not particularly receptive to FDI compared to its East Asian neighbors. Although the Philippines was less restrictive towards FDI than the PRC, Malaysia, and Vietnam in 1997, the Philippines became the most restrictive among the listed countries since 2016. Even the later members of ASEAN, Cambodia, LDPR, Myanmar, and Vietnam appeared to be less restrictive than the Philippines.

---

[17] https//www.jetro.go.jp/en/reports/statistics.html.

Table 6.3 ODA loans and grants

	2013	2014	2015	2016	2017	2018	2019	2020	2021	2022
Australia	130.52	128.33	108.61	63.24	59.35	59.2	58.6	54.54	65.23	77.88
Austria	3.39	2.3	0.45	1.37	4.12	0.65	0.87	0.67	0.74	0.97
Belgium	6.89	8.78	6.39	6.19	4.38	5.23	5.06	4.67	5.49	3.35
Canada	68.58	61.32	18.78	17.05	12.42	12.47	10.44	12.34	11.37	15.83
Czechia	0.36	0.47	0.06	0.08	0.13	0.24	0.33	0.2	0.07	0.08
Denmark	5.39	0.39	0.39	0.06	–	0.35	0.64	0.77	0.54	2.63
Estonia	0.47	0.12	0.05	–	–	–	–	–	–	–
Finland	5.62	2.99	0.91	0.57	0.73	0.66	0.68	0.67	0.68	0.36
France	5.66	146.43	5	71.68	5.73	130.64	6.16	306.98	342.57	5.29
Germany	56.83	50.96	46.05	47.15	47.82	43.14	43.17	40.06	33.91	36.48
Greece	0.04	–	–	–	–	–	–	–	–	–
Hungary	0.03	0.13	0.04	0.07	0.04	0.17	0.45	0.38	0.6	0.94
Iceland	0.52	–	0.05	–	–	0.14	0.03	0.12	–	–
Ireland	4.3	4.7	0.56	0.34	0.21	0.04	0.12	0.39	0.52	0.73
Italy	10.05	8.94	4.34	3.93	4.96	4.99	11.88	9.63	9.28	9.21
Japan	239.42	470.79	603.53	300.66	362.48	569.75	994.22	1109.94	1175.06	1762.33
Korea	48.02	68.16	49.74	68.11	41.93	64.42	80.92	166.01	182.92	138.37
Lithuania	0.08	–	0	–	–	0.01	0	0	0	0
Luxembourg	2.57	1.51	1.84	1.98	2.03	0.73	1.19	1.79	0.5	1.28
Netherlands	8.05	0.06	–	0.53	0.66	0.68	0.67	0.39	0.65	0.7
New Zealand	10.32	6.99	7.48	3.49	2.46	6.98	3.44	5.6	2.19	3.5
Norway	18.21	10.87	2.04	2.06	3.39	1.14	1.94	4.46	1.95	1.72

(continued)

Table 6.3 (continued)

	2013	2014	2015	2016	2017	2018	2019	2020	2021	2022
Poland	0.02	0.03	0.03	–	0	0.08	0.08	0.14	2.99	0.14
Portugal	0.03	–	–	–	–	–	–	–	0	0
Slovak Republic	0.03	–	–	–	0.01	–	–	–	–	–
Slovenia	0.08	–	–	–	–	–	–	–	–	–
Spain	11.17	8.56	6.39	6.26	7.78	6.07	5.54	5.78	10.61	6.38
Sweden	21.14	9.4	5.94	6.62	7.82	7.4	6.75	6.61	8.05	3.96
Switzerland	10.14	4.59	1.69	2.04	1.71	1.5	1.17	1.62	1.68	1.51
United Kingdom	56.37	90.46	14.36	8.82	11.4	15.16	20.17	26.56	18.86	10.7
United States	215.9	327.67	312.23	301.68	174.16	131.66	154.54	160.27	172.44	145.66

(*Source* OECD Statistics).
Notes in millions U.S.$ at constant 2021 prices.

Table 6.4 Economic cooperation of Japan and total DAC countries, 2010–2021

Disbursements	Japan					Total DAC countries				
	2010–2011	2018	2019	2020	2021	2010–2011	2018	2019	2020	2021
ODA, total gross	19,555.93	17,250.01	18,922.60	20,304.03	21,951.29	145,764.47	164,803.89	161,239.60	176,879.48	199,452.94
Bilateral grants, total	7,882.10	5,278.45	5,278.10	5,469.71	5,680.33	90,187.28	99,806.40	97,935.00	101,088.60	116,823.77
Bilateral loans, total gross	7,869.46	8,006.18	9,401.75	11,417.36	12,126.28	16,303.42	19,754.07	19,887.89	27,804.96	26,862.92
Bilateral loans, amounts received	–8,483.96	–7,185.74	–7,202.41	–6,643.84	–6,186.02	–13,753.53	–14,384.77	–14,340.72	–14,100.65	–14,371.72
Other official flows, total gross	9,603.58	5,579.74	5,099.70	8,572.63	5,031.55	17,434.87	18,912.17	14,321.00	15,279.00	16,567.79
Officially supported export credits	20,842.85	10,987.32	9,374.46	6,777.56	6,841.01	62,479.91	29,208.34	23,411.79	20,065.22	40,553.32
Loans received/total gross	–107.64%	–136.13%	–136.46%	–121.47%	–108.90%	–15.25%	–14.41%	–14.64%	–13.95%	–12.30%

(*Source* OECD statistics).

Table 6.5 Restrictiveness index of various Asian countries

Country	Japan	Korea	Brunei Darussalam	Cambodia	PRC	Indonesia	LPDR	Malaysia	Myanmar	Philippines	Singapore	Thailand	Viet Nam
1997	0.079	0.532	.	.	0.625	0.479	.	0.521	.	0.501	.	0.366	0.671
2003	0.064	0.148			0.577	0.365		0.455		0.419		0.295	0.435
2006	0.057	0.143			0.468	0.365		0.445		0.417		0.295	0.371
2010	0.052	0.143			0.436	0.319		0.290		0.417		0.296	0.300
2011	0.052	0.143			0.436	0.319		0.290		0.412		0.296	0.300
2012	0.052	0.143			0.432	0.324				0.417		0.296	0.292
2013	0.052	0.135			0.432	0.368		0.255	0.442	0.417		0.291	0.281
2014	0.052	0.135			0.432	0.390		0.254	0.384	0.406	.	0.291	0.281
2015	0.052	0.135			0.395	0.390		0.253	0.390	0.406		0.291	0.132
2016	0.052	0.135		0.054	0.345	0.355	0.221	0.253	0.386	0.390		0.291	0.132
2017	0.052	0.135		0.054	0.328	0.355	0.190	0.252	0.200	0.390		0.268	0.132
2018	0.052	0.135	0.146	0.054	0.262	0.347	0.190	0.252	0.117	0.374	0.048	0.268	0.130
2019	0.052	0.135	0.146	0.054	0.244	0.347	0.190	0.252	0.110	0.374	0.059	0.268	0.130
2020	0.052	0.135	0.146	0.054	0.214	0.347	0.192	0.257	0.112	0.374	0.059	0.268	0.130

(*Source* OECD Statistics).

Notes The FDI Regulatory Restrictiveness Index (FDI Index) measures statutory restrictions on foreign direct investment across 22 economic sectors. It gauges the restrictiveness of a country's FDI rules by looking at the four main types of restrictions on FDI: (1) Foreign equity limitations; (2) Discriminatory screening or approval mechanisms; (3) Restrictions on the employment of foreigners as key personnel and (4) Other operational restrictions, e.g. restrictions on branching and on capital repatriation or on land ownership by foreign-owned enterprises. Restrictions are evaluated on a 0 (open) to 1 (closed) scale. The overall restrictiveness index is the average of sectoral scores (OECD Statistics).

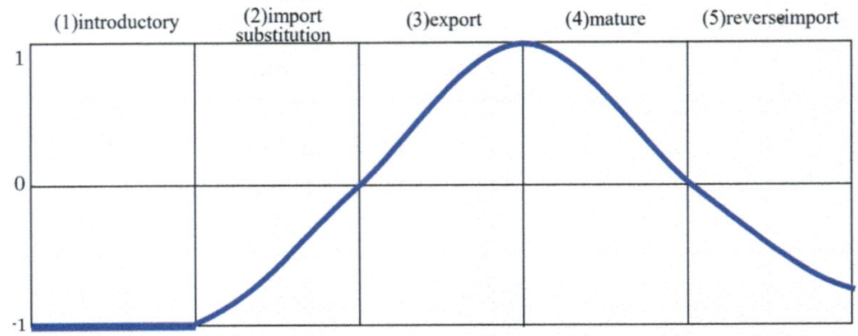

Fig. 6.10 The ICC curve according to the "Catching up" product cycle (*Source* Hiratsuka, 2005: 6)

6.4.3 The Philippines and Japanese Export–Import

Using the International Competitiveness Coefficient (ICC)[18] as a measure of the location a country with respect to a product within the four trade phases of the FGFlying Geese Model suggests the relative backwardness of the Philippines vis-a-vis its ASEAN cohorts in several product categories (Hiratsuka, 2005)

$$ICC_i = \frac{X_i - M_i}{X_i + M_i}$$

where

X_i = export value of product i.

M_i = import value of product i.

ICC varies between –1 and + 1 so that it could be used to classify countries and their products with regards to the four stages of the Flying Geese product cycle as shown in Fig. 6.10.

Based on the U.N. Standard International Trade Classification, third revised edition (SITC-R3), the products were classified into 43 product groups, and came up with the following ICC estimates for the period from 1990 to 2000.

Overall, the Philippines comes out with generally the lowest ICC over the period studied (see Fig. 6.11). It can be seen that the Philippines tends to lag (have lower absolute value of ICCs) behind its ASEAN cohorts (Indonesia, Malaysia, and Thailand) in most of the 43 product categories, with the exception of the following 9 product categories: bicycles, personal computers & peripherals, precision apparatus, natural fiber textile (IS),[19] automobile parts, machine tool parts (IS), molding (IS), aircraft parts, and vessels. This is in stark contrast to another archipelago, Indonesia, which led in 20 product categories, including in the overalls.

[18] RCA is deemed to coarse for this study's purpose.

[19] (IS) refers to import-substitution, wherein the ICC is negative, hence, "leading" means the absolute value of the ICC is lower than the cohort countries.

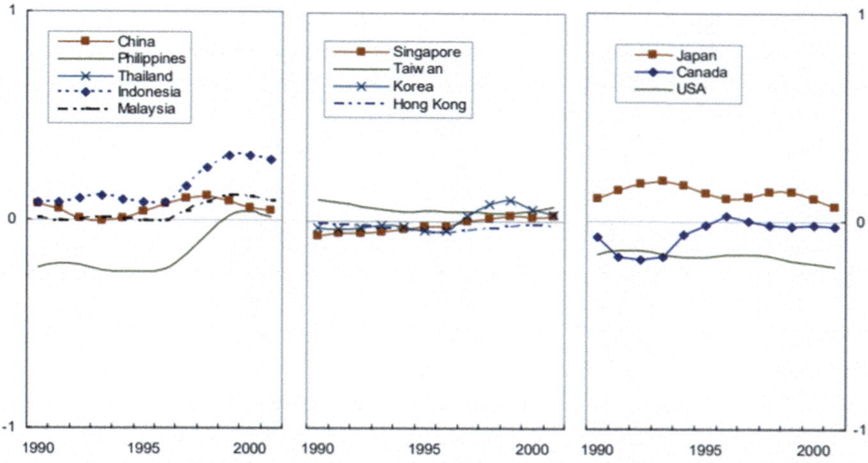

Fig. 6.11 International competitiveness coefficient for various countries (*Source* Hiratsuka, 2005: 32)

Another lackluster performance of the Philippines, with respect to the Flying Geese dynamics, is in the agricultural product and processed agricultural product categories, where the Philippines has the lowest competitiveness among its ASEAN cohorts. Moreover, in the processed agricultural product category, it is only the Philippines that has a negative ICC. Given the critical nature of agriculture in a country's economic development, this performance should be a cause for concern.

6.5 Some Challenges Facing the Philippines in Flying Together

Situating the Philippines with respect to the Japanese ODA-FDI-EXIM Trinity, we found that the Philippines appears to be responsive to the self-help effort philosophy of Japanese ODA. There is some resistance, however, in the case of Japanese FDI given that the Philippines is generally less open to FDI compared to her ASEAN counterparts. Where Japanese FDI has been able to gain entry to the country, however, there are indications that this has been effective in transmitting shared growth DNA. It is in the case of EXIM that the Philippines has been most obviously lacking in leveraging the dynamics of the ODA-FDI-EXIM trinity.

Japanese FDI and EXIM are both discussed in the Flying Geese Model. To recall, the Flying Geese Model includes the international transmission of an industry (subject industry) that has become less competitive in the home country to could be more competitive in the destination or host country. FDI plays an important role in such international transmission. (Kojima, 1973) and (Kojima, 1975) refer to this as trade-oriented or Pro-trade FDI, which is proposed to be closer to the type of FDI undertaken by Japanese companies, as this FDI eventually results in export of the goods of the subject industry. This is the case of FDI becoming a complement to trade. This is contrasted with the American type of FDI, which is depicted in the product cycle theory of (Vernon, 1966), wherein the FDI is considered to be anti-trade since it focuses on producing for the domestic market the commodity being exported by the home country (U.S.). This is the case of FDI becoming a substitute for trade.

As our discussion in the previous section indicates, the Philippines is relatively more restrictive to FDI compared to her ASEAN neighbors, which constitutes a barrier in its strategic sequencing that prevents the Philippines from leveraging the Flying Geese dynamics. The strategic sequencing here would be the shift from import-substitution to export-orientation phase. In the context of the Flying Geese model, these two phases should not be treated as separate but in fact involve the same industry. Cases of "perpetual infant industries" in the Philippines have been observed, as was also validated by the discussion in the preceding section. Moreover, the lack of strategic sequencing could also be observed in the sectoral transformation or lack thereof in the Philippines, where its agricultural sector remains to be the least productive and poorest sector of the economy, despite thrusts made in the manufacturing, and, more recently, in the services sector. Such lack of strategic sequencing could have its roots in the extractive institutions that characterize Philippine society, which is marked by a very poor distribution of income or wealth. We will discuss these issues more in Chapter nine.

References

A symbol (-J) after the author's name are Japanese documents

Aoki, M. (1990). Towards an economic model of the Japanese firm. *Journal of Economic Literature, 28*, 1–27.

Beason, R., & Weinstein, D. E. (1996). Growth, economies of scale, and targeting in Japan (1955–1990). The Review of Economics and Statistics 78, no. 2 (May): 286–295. https://doi.org/10.2307/2109930

Beaudry, M., & Chris C. M. (1999). Japan's System of Official Development Assistance (No. 1). International Development Research Centre.

Blaise, S. (2009). Japanese aid as a prerequisite for FDI: the case of Southeast Asian countries. *Asia Pacific Economic Papers* 385.

Chang, H. -J. (2003). Kicking away the ladder: Infant industry promotion in historical perspective. *Oxford Development Studies, 31*(1), 21–32. https://doi.org/10.1080/1360081032000047168

Chang, H. -J. (2011). Industrial policy: Can we go beyond an unproductive confrontation? In *Annual World Bank conference on development economics 2010, global lessons from East Asia and the global financial crisis* (pp. 83–109) N.p.: World Bank.

Ernest, C. J. (1982). *Alexander Hamilton.* New York: Scribner's.

Garcia, C. P. (1969). Third state of the nation address, January 25, 1960 | GOVPH". Official Gazette. https://www.officialgazette.gov.ph/1960/01/25/carlos-p-garcia-third-state-of-the-nation-address-january-25-1960/

Hirakawa, H., Peter Lee, U., & Maquito, Ferdinand, C. (2008). *A roadmap for shared growth through the Philippine automotive industry.*

Hiratsuka, D. (2005). The "Catching up" process of manufacturing in East Asia. *IDE Discussion Paper* 22, no. 2005.02 (February). https://citeseerx.ist.psu.edu/viewdoc/download?doi=10.1.1.886.6783&rep=rep1&type=pdf

IMF. (2008). *Financial stress, downturns, and recoveries.* N.p.: International Monetary Fund. https://www.imf.org/en/Publications/WEO/Issues/2016/12/31/Financial-Stress-Downturns-and-Recoveries

Ito, T. (1992). The Japanese Economy. Cambridge, Massachusetts: MIT Press.

Jaurigue, R. A. (2012). Steel industry development: RP's elusive dream. NSC Digest. http://www.nscdigest.com/2012/10/01/steel-industry-development-rps-elusive-dream/?preview=true

Kohama, H. -J (1992). *ODA no keizaigaku (The economics of ODA).* Tokyo: Nihon Hyouronsha.

Kojima, K. (1973). A macroeconomic approach to foreign direct investment. *Hitotsubashi Journal of Economics, 14*, 1–20.

Kojima, K. (1975). International trade and foreign direct investment: substitutes or complements. *Hitotsubashi Journal of Economics, 16*, 1–12.

Kojima, K. (2000). The 'Flying Geese' model of Asian economic development: Origin, theoretical extensions, and regional policy implications. *Journal of Asian Economics, 11*, 375–401.

Kumagai, S. (2008). A journey through the secret history of the flying geese model. *IDE discussion paper,* 158 (June).

Lacmanović, S. (2013). The relevance and effects of the executive-to-worker pay ratio' disclosure. *Economic Research-Ekonomska Istraživanja, 26*(sup1), 165–184. https://doi.org/10.1080/1331677X.2013.11517646

Lin, J. Y. (2012). From flying geese to leading dragons: New opportunities and strategies for structural transformation in developing countries. *Global Policy, 3*(4), 397–409. https://doi.org/10.1111/j.1758-5899.2012.00172.x

Lincoln, J. R., & Gerlach, M. L. (2004). *Japan's network economy.* Cambridge University Press.

Maquito, F. C., & Carbonel, H. (2010). "Rediscovering Japan's leadership in "shared growth" management." *Rikkyo business review,* 3, no. <Special Issue>*The 2nd Rikkyo university international business studies symposium "globalization, challenges for managers, and calls for leadership"* (July) (pp. 20–38). https://doi.org/10.14992/00000452

Maquito, F. C., & Hirakawa, H. (2011). A comparative economic analysis of Japanese-style labor contracts from a shared-growth perspective. *Philippine Journal of Labor and Industrial Relations, 31*(1&2), 52–77.

Maquito, F. C. (2019, November 2). 日本の共有型成長とそのODA :再考察[Japan's Shared Growth and its ODA: A Review]. In 4th International Conference. East Asian Consortium of Japanese Studies.

Mercado-Aldaba, R. A. (1994). Foreign direct investment in the Philippines: A reassessment. *PIDS research paper*, no. 94–10. https://pidswebs.pids.gov.ph/CDN/PUBLICATIONS/pidsrp9410.pdf

METI. -J (2005), *Wagakuni Keizai Kyouryoku no Seiko Keiken wa Fumaeta " japan oda model " no Suishin Chuukan Torimatome (Interim Report on the Promotion of the "Japan ODA model" based on the successful experience of japan's economic cooperation).* N.p.: Economic Cooperation Subcommittee, Trade and Economic Cooperation Subcommittee, Industrial Structure Council.

Mishel, L., & Wolfe, J. (2019). CEO compensation has grown 840% since 1978. Economic Policy Institute, August 14. https://www.epi.org/publication/ceo-compensation-2018/

MITI. -J. (1979). *Keizai Kyouryoku no Genjou to Mondaiten (The current situation and problems of economic cooperation).* Japanese Ministry of International Trade and Industry.

Morck, R., & Yeung, B. (2001). Japanese economic success and the curious characteristics of Japanese stock prices. *Center for Economic Institutions Working Paper Series* 2001–19:1–29.

Nakatani, I. -J. (2008). *Shihon Shugi Ha Naze Jikai Suru No Ka (Why capitalism self destructs).* Hardcover ed. Shueisha Bunko.

Okuda, H. -J. (1992). "Nihon gata Tsu Suteppu Ro-n: Segin Apuro-chi to Nihon Apuro-chi (Japan type two step loan: The World Bank and Japan's approaches)". *Nihon Amerika Yuroppa Kaihatsu Kyouryoku Seisaku (Japan, US, Europe Development Cooperation Policy*, 85–105. http://hdl.handle.net/2344/00013383

Okuda, H. (1993). Japanese two step loans: the Japanese approach to development finance. *Hitotsubashi Journal of Economics, 34*, 67–85.

Okuda, H. -J (2004). Washinton Konsensasu ni taisuru Nihon Seifu no Taiou (The Japanese Government's response to the Washington consensus). *Ritsumeikan Kenkyuu, 17*(2), 153–174. http://www.ritsumei.ac.jp/ir/isaru/assets/file/journal/17-2_okuda.pdf

Piketty, T. (2013). *Capital in the 21st century*. English ed. N.p.: Harvard University Press.

Sheard, P. (1989). The main bank system and corporate monitoring and control in Japan. *Journal of Economic Behavior and Organization, 11*, 399–422.

Sheard, P. (1994a). Interlocking shareholdings and corporate governance in Japan. In *The Japanese firm: Sources of competitive strength* (pp. 310–349). N.p.: Clarendon Press Oxford.

Sheard, P. (1994b). Interlocking shareholdings and corporate governance in Japan. In *The Japanese firm: Sources of competitive strength* (pp. 310–349). Oxford: Clarendon Press.

Stiglitz, J. (2012). *The price of inequality*. N.p.: W. W. Norton & Company.

Valencia, C. (2018). Special report: should we be worried about Chinese loans for infrastructure buildup? (Part 2)." Philstar Global, May 17, 2018. https://www.philstar.com/business/2018/05/17/1815829/special-report-should-we-be-worried-about-chinese-loans-infrastructure-buildup-part-2

Vernon, R. (1966). International investment and international trade in the product cycle. *Quarterly Journal of Economics, 80*(2), 190–207.

Wade, R. (1996). Japan, the World Bank, and the art of paradigm maintenance: The East Asian miracle in political perspective. *New Left Review, 1*(217), 3–36.

Widodo, T., Setyastuti, R., & Adiningsih, S. (2018). "Flying Geese" paradigm: review, analytical tool, and application. *Munich Personal RePEc Archive, 87171.*

World Bank. (1993). *The East Asian miracle: Economic growth and public policy*. Oxford, New York: Oxford University Press.

Yong, E. D. (2014). Birds that fly in a V formation use an amazing trick. National Geographic. https://www.nationalgeographic.com/science/article/birds-that-fly-in-a-v-formation-use-an-amazing-trick

Part II
The Roots of Asia's Development Economies After the World War Two

Chapter 7
The East Asian Export-Led Industrialization in the Global Economy

Abstract Today, one of the main areas of interest for the global economy is Asia, especially China. The impetus for China's development can be traced back to the development of Asian Newly Industrializing Economies (NIEs) such as South Korea, Taiwan, Hong Kong, and Singapore in the 1960s. The development of Asia, which began with the development of the NIEs, has spread to the Association of Southeast Asian Nations (ASEAN) countries and China since the late 1980s, and has spread further to South Asia since the turn of the century. How do we explain the economic development in Asia that began with the NIEs? Since the 1970s, different approaches have challenged this question and competed for explanatory power. In this chapter, we will begin by organizing various theoretical approaches related to the economic development of the Asian NIEs and their expansion to East Asia, and confirm the characteristics of their development and their world-historical character in relation to the global economy. In addition, we will discuss the new changes that will occur in this century and their characteristics.

Keywords NIEs · Innovation · Export-led industrialization · New international division of labor · Neoclassical economics · Non-neoclassical economics

7.1 Introduction

Chapter 3 of this book discusses the mechanisms of Asian economic development over the past half century. This chapter examines the basic characteristics of its development back to its early years, and discusses the industrialization and development of East Asian countries.

Looking back, the 1960s and 1970s were a time of dramatic change in the world economy. In the 1960s, Europe and Japan achieved high growth under the global spread of the U.S. dollar as the reserve currency. The developed countries enjoyed the 'golden 1960s'. However, in the 1970s, developed countries entered an era of stagnation. In 1971, the exchange of gold and dollars was suspended, and the International Monetary Fund/General Agreement on Tariffs and Trade (IMF/GATT) regime

H. Hirakawa and F. C. Maquito, *The Dynamics of Asian Economic Development*,
https://doi.org/10.1007/978-981-97-3106-0_7

"collapsed". In 1973, the first oil crisis broke out, and in 1974, the United Nations General Assembly adopted the Declaration on the New International Economic Order (NIEO). The development of East Asia began in the shadows. It is safe to say that people became aware of this development because of the 1979 report of the Organization for Economic Cooperation and Development (OECD), The impact of the newly industrializing countries (NICs).The report's preface begins with the statement, "The emergence of dynamic new exporters of manufactures in the developing world has given rise to a disquiet in advanced countries". In the report, a total of 10 countries and economies[1] in the three regions of Southern Europe, Latin America, and East Asia were selected as countries that would rapidly increase exports of manufactured goods to developed countries.

Thus, in the 1980s, the export of manufactured goods from developing regions became a major concern of the world economy, and the focus was on NICs. Initial interest in NICs was focused on South European and Latin American NICs. In the 1980s, it began to move toward Asian NICs. This is because only that region has maintained steady economic development through exports. The name "NIEs" was also proposed by the Sherpas of the Canadian government of the host country at the 1988 Toronto Summit, and the name "NIEs" became commonplace. Moreover, its coverage has spread to ASEAN countries, China, and even the less developed ASEAN countries such as Vietnam, Laos, Cambodia, and Myanmar[2] However, there was no existing theory that convincingly explained this industrialization and development. Various discussions were held to solve the mystery.

In the following, we will first approach the actual situation by organizing the main theoretical approaches to industrialization and development. Next, we will take a bird's-eye view of the global development strategies attempted in the second half of the twentieth century and extract the historical peculiarities of East Asian development. Finally, the basic structure of industrialization and development of East Asian economies is examined, focusing on the introduction and accumulation of technology.

[1] The 10 countries/economies consist of four countries in Southern Europe (Greece, Portugal, Spain and Yugoslavia), two in Latin America (Brazil and Mexico), and four in South-East Asia (Hong Kong, Korea, Singapore and Taiwan). In addition, there is also a notation that the three countries excluding Yugoslavia are OECD NICs.

[2] In this document, "NICs" (Newly Industrializing Countries) and "NIEs" (Newly Industrializing Economies) are used interchangeably. In addition, NIEs will basically be used only to refer to the four countries and economies of East Asia: South Korea, Taiwan, Hong Kong, and Singapore.

Incidentally, the industrialization of East Asia, starting with the NIEs, has also brought about a change in the concept of the region. Until then, "East Asia" had been used almost synonymously with "Far East" or "Northeast Asia". It came to include the "Southeast Asia" region. The World Bank (WB) published "The East Asian Miracle" in 1993. The term "East Asia" used in this book also uses this expanded regional concept, except in special cases.

7.2 East Asia's Industrialization and Approaches of Main Economic Schools

East Asia's industrialization and development, which have drawn significant international attention since the end of the 1970s, started from the Asian NIEs, namely, Korea, Taiwan, Hong Kong, and Singapore, which are rather small and poor in terms of population, land area, national resources, and so forth. At the time, thus, this development could be seen as an exception. However, industrialization and economic growth had to be understood in the context of East Asia as a whole, since they began to spread rapidly to ASEAN countries, and China, etc., after the second half of the 1980s. The field of research had widened from the Asian NIEs as a "point" to the whole of East Asia as an 'area', and consequently there was a need to change the theoretical framework for research into East Asia's industrialization.

There were three major contemporary approaches among the main economic schools that studied East Asia's industrialization and economic growth. The first is the growth chain of the 'national economy' approach, the second is the corporate approach, and the last is the world economy approach. Among other schools which are worthy of note, we could cite the Chinese economic zone approach, and the Confucianism approach. The Chinese economic zone approach, focusing on ethnic Chinese and overseas Chinese in East Asia, seems to confuse development factors that might become important in the future with the main factors of the established industrialization in Taiwan, Hong Kong and Singapore. There were also researchers who gave particular attention to the cultural factors, particularly Confucianism, Asian values, and "Asian ways" as development factors, and who stressed differences from Anglo-American culture. However, it is difficult to simplify the region, with its enormous diversities in terms of culture, region, historical background, and so forth, into Asian culture, value, or way of thinking. Such thinking appears to grasp Asian industrialization and its influence by reversing a causal sequence.

In this section, we would like to first divide the industrialization and economic development of East Asia into the three main approaches above, and clarify their claims and arguments.

7.2.1 The Growth Chain of the "National Economy" Approach

7.2.1.1 The Neo-Classical School's Growth Theory and the Statist/Institutional Approaches

Neoclassical economists claimed that East Asia's industrialization and economic growth were the results of market mechanisms that developed industries with relative advantage under a situation of "free trade" that was part of the states' export-oriented policies. According to these economists, East Asia's experience is a success story to be contrasted to the opposing positions of import-substitution industrialization, which was used by the newly emerging independent states after World War II, and to the centrally-planned economic industrialization adopted by the socialist countries. In the latter cases, states caused economic stagnation by intervening in the markets.

L.E. Westphal, an economist of the Development Economics Department at the World Bank confirms that Korea's development was based on political factors such as U.S. aid, foreign investment, and intervention in the labor market in the 1950~ 60s, as well as Japan imperialist rule as an initial condition. But in the end, his conclusion is as follows:

> While a variety of factors have contributed to Korea's successful development, the key fact nonetheless remains that economic policies have made a large contribution to fostering what appears to be a reasonably efficient and equitable process of industrialization. In short, given Korea's poor national resource endowment and assuming that its comparative advantage lies in labour-intensive activities, Korea provides an almost classic example of an economy following its comparative advantage and reaping the gain predicted by conventional economic theory (Westphal, 1978: 375).

"South Korea provides an example of a country which has achieved spectacular results through export-led growth and which did not alter its strategy during the period 1974–78" (World Bank, 1981: 67).

B. Balassa, a professor at John Hopkins University and a consultant at the World Bank. also saw the development of South Korea, Singapore and Taiwan as successful examples of private sector free trade policies. He divided the development strategy of developing countries during the period of the 1960s to the 1973 oil crisis into three groups and concluded that the successful countries were the first group to adopt export incentives. Countries of the first group are Korea, Singapore, and Taiwan, which "adopted an outward-oriented industrial development strategy following the completion of the first stage of import substitution". The second group is Argentina, Brazil, Colombia, and Mexico which "moved to the second stage of import substitution but subsequently reformed their systems of incentives", and countries of the third group are India, Chili, and Uruguay, which "continued to apply an inward-oriented development strategy".

The share of exports in manufactured output rose from 1% in 1960 to 41% in 1973 in Korea, from 11 to 43% in Singapore, and from 9 to 50% in Taiwan. In contrast, the shares of Latin American countries rose only from 1% in 1966 to 4% in 1973 in both Argentina and Brazil. India, Chile, and Uruguay "did poorly in primary as well as in manufactured output and showed a decline in the share of exports in manufactured exports between 1960 and 1973. India lost ground in textiles, its traditional export, and was slow to develop new manufactured exports" (Balassa, 1981: 14–15).

Thus, his conclusion is as follows:

> The evidence is quite conclusive: countries applying outward-oriented development strategies had a superior performance in terms of exports, economic growth, and employment whereas countries with continued inward-orientation encountered increasing economic difficulties. ... It has been suggested, however, that import substitution was a necessary precondition for the development of manufactured exports in present-day developing countries. In

> attempting to provide an answer to this question, distinction needs to be made between first-stage and second-stage import substitution. First-stage import substitution was of relatively short duration in the present-day industrial countries and in the three Far Eastern developing countries that subsequently adopted an outward-oriented strategy; it was longer in most other developing countries that also generally had higher levels of protection (Balassa, 1981: 16-17).

Here, the first stage of import substitution is the "easy" stage of import substitution, "entailing the replacement of the imports of nondurable consumer goods, such as clothing, shoes, and household goods, and of their inputs, such as textile fabrics, leather, and wood, by domestic production, since these commodities suit the conditions existing in developing countries that are at the beginning of the industrialization process", and the second stage of import substitution is a higher stage, involving "the replacement of the imports of intermediate goods and producer and consumer durables by domestic production (Balassa, 1981: 6–7).

At the end of the 1970s, however, the Korean government shifted towards an inward-oriented development strategy, adopting a strategy of nurturing "capital-intensive industries producing intermediate products, such as ferrous and non-ferrous metals, petrochemicals and chemicals, and heavy machineries, such as electrical power generators and heavy construction and engineering equipment". This "lowered the productivity of capital in Korean manufacturing", exports and economic growth deteriorated, and the company returned to an export-oriented strategy again in the Fifth Five-Year Plan (1982–86). It has been shown that the adoption of an outward-oriented development strategy permitted Korea to reach rapid rates of growth of exports and GDP. It has further been established that Korea, along with other outward-oriented economies, has been better able to overcome the effects of external shocks than countries pursuing an inward-oriented development strategy" (Balassa, 1985: 167, 173). In short, Balassa does not think import-substitution is effective. He simply pointed out the first and easy stage of import substitution as an exception based on actual Korean experience.

Entering the 1980s, "whether the East Asian NICs are sui generis, unique cases unreplicable elsewhere because of their unusual conditions, circumstances, and characteristics, or whether the East Asian represent models that not only can but should be emulated by other industrializing nations" became the most immediate issue (Bradford & Branson, 1987: 10). Regarding such issues, in January 1984, an international conference on the "Global implications of the trade patterns of East and Southeast Asia" organized by NBER's William H. Branson of Princeton University and Colin I. Bradford, Jr of Yale University was held.

Through this conference, Branson and Bradford, Jr reached the conclusion that "in a broad sense a factor-proportions model of comparative advantage is useful in understanding the patterns of trade of Pacific Asia". They divided the countries of Pacific Asia into three tiers, each of which developed with the export of industrial products as an 'engine of growth' in line with comparative advantage. Here, the first tier is Japan、the second tier is the "Gang of Four" (NIEs) consisting of Korea, Taiwan, Hong Kong, and Singapore, and the third tier is "ASEAN four" as the Next-tier NICs consisting of Malaysia, Thailand, the Philippines, and Indonesia

(Bradford & Branson 1987: 10). Moreover, they summarized that "public policy and government promotion of export-oriented growth strategies played a major role in the unusual success of the NICs", namely "rapid structural change in manufacturing and in exports seems to have been induced by a strategic sectoral design" (Bradford & Branson, 1987: 10, 23).

Neoclassical economics have interpreted the export-oriented development of East Asia in a wide range of ways, from those of M. Freedman claiming that it is the result of complete free trade, to those that claim that it developed by government policies that resulted in the creation of a free trade state.

In any case, these claims were met with a lot of criticism from the outset. H. Hideki Imaoka of the Institute of Developing Economies (IDE—currently IDE-JETRO) in Japan, together with his colleagues, conducted a study of industrial development in Taiwan and South Korea, and stated that "it is difficult to think as if the free trade system was realized under the export-oriented industrialization policies of both countries" and described the policy as "dual-track growth" (Imaoka, Ohno & Yokoyama, eds. -J, 1985: 5). The authors conclude that the industrialization of Asian NIEs was achieved not through a policy shift from ISI to EOI, but through an effective combination of them.

G. Gereffi also has developed a similar argument by criticizing B. Balassa. It is argued that Asian NICs (NIEs) shifted from import substitution to export-oriented industrialization in the 1960s, but in the 1970s Secondary ISI and Secondary EOI coexisted, and is not an abandonment of import substitution. According to Gereffi, Latin America, NIEs Brazil, Mexico, and Argentina, which have relatively large domestic markets, undertook a policy shift sometime in the mid 1950s from the then primary ISI that "the shift from imports to the local manufacture of basic consumer goods" to secondary ISI "using domestic production to substitute for imports of a variety of capital- and technology-intensive manufactures: consumer durables (e.g. automobiles), intermediate goods (e.g., petrochemicals and steel), and capital goods (e.g., heavy machinery)". On the other hand, a policy of accepting American and European Foreign Direct Investment (FDI) in order to deepen the industrialization process. These FDI, however, "concentrated on export-oriented projects in mining, oil, and agriculture" (Gereffi, 1989: 515).

In contrast, the growth of Asian NIEs in the 1960s "was founded on light, labor-intensive industries like textiles, garments, and electronic equipment. In subsequent phases, however, South Korea, Taiwan, and Singapore achieved success in much heavier industries like steel, petrochemicals, shipbuilding, vehicle manufacture, and computers that were less well suited to their original factor endowments" As a result, the traditional "static comparative advantage" in trade was continued in Latin America, while the "dynamic comparative advantage" was achieved in the Asian NIEs. This policy difference became clear in the 1980s.

Gereffi presented the basic data of the economies of the Asian and Latin American NIEs, highlighting their asymmetry. Looking at the changes in GDP per capita between 1981 and 1986, the Asian NIEs all grew, while the Latin American NIEs all stagnated. The Asian NIEs have achieved their development through an effective combination of import substitution and export-oriented strategies (Gereffi, 1989: 512, 515).

Figure 7.1 shows Gereffi's summary of the policy differences between NIEs in Latin America and East Asia. In fact, South Korea's heavy industrialization policy is a good example of such a secondary ISI. The Pohang Iron and Steel Company (POSCO) was planned three times by the Park Chung-Hee administration in South Korea, in 1961, 1962, and 1967. The second time was with a group of German steelmakers, and the third time with an international consortium including the World Bank. Still, the World Bank and the U.S. Export–Import Bank refused to approve the loan, and the plan did not materialize. The plan was considered to be outside the theory of comparative advantage, i.e., "considered this idea overly-ambitious" (Breen, 2011). In 1968, however, the plan finally came to fruition through Japan's postwar reparations and technical assistance (Amsden, 1989: 295; Hirakawa-J, 1992: 56; Breen, 2011).

Thus, in the 1990s, through a debate with non-neoclassical economists, neoclassical economists of the World Bank began to recognize the role of the state in the development of East Asia as compensation for market failures.

In the World Development Report 1991, the World Bank explained the growth in the East Asian countries, such as Korea and Taiwan, using the notion of the "market-friendly" approach. In The East Asian Miracle by the Bank in 1993, it accepted the conclusion that public policy had laid the institutional basis for a "miracle" for growth in these countries, including Japan and the Asian NIEs, as well as Thailand, Malaysia and Indonesia (and effectively China). After all, the state was "providing a stable

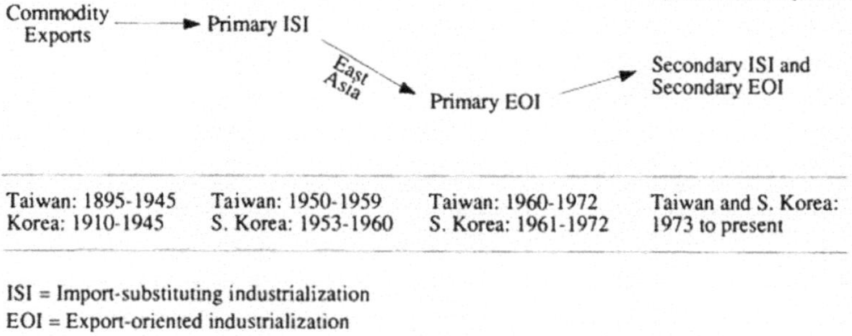

Fig. 7.1 Paths of industrialization in Latin America and East Asia: Commonalities, divergence, and convergence. (*Source* Gereffi, 1989: 517). *Note* ISI = Import-substituting industrialization, EOI = Export-oriented industrialization

macroeconomic environment and a reliable legal framework to promote domestic and international competition". Therefore, in other words, a "miracle" has occurred because East Asian countries have corrected the "failure of market functioning" through policy[3] (World Bank, 1993: 9). In addition, World Development Report 1997, which focused on "the state in a changing world", came to the clear view that countries with underdeveloped markets needed industrial policies to develop.

In contrast, the statist and/or institutional approach, which includes C. Johnson and Alice H. Amsden, asserted that states ought to assume a role which is greater than simply 'making up for market failures.

C. Johnson was an international political scientist who argued that the economic development of Japan was realized by the industrial policies of the Ministry of International Trade and Industry (now the Ministry of Economy, Trade and Industry), but he extended the analytical framework of "development-oriented countries" to East Asian countries such as South Korea and Taiwan. According to him, in South Korea and Taiwan, the "coincidence of soft authoritarianism in politics and capitalism in economics" was at the core of good economic performance (Johnson, 1985: 137).

Alice H. Amsden states in her development of "less or more skill- and capital-intensive industries" like shipbuilding and steel industries, Korea's leading sector as labor-intensive and less value-added industries "did not serve as a springboard for further industrialization in any organizational sense". Korea's heavy industrialization is a nonlinear diversification that lacks continuity in terms of technological proficiency and capital intensity, and cannot be explained by the theory of comparative advantage in neoclassical economics. Amsden, however, explained that the development of Korea's industries was due to the "dynamic comparative advantage". In this way, she explained the heavy industrialization of South Korea using the symbolic expression of "getting relative prices wrong" and clarified the role of the government, including industrial policy, in its development through concrete empirical research (Amsden, 1989: 243–268).

In the end, the axis of dispute between the neoclassical, revisionist, and/or statist schools has generally been whether states should do more than just make up for "market failures" or not. It was based on the premise of a self-sustaining "national economy", which is the basic framework of macroeconomics, and contested whether the market or the state was responsible for the essence of development.

Amsden considers Japan, South Korea, Taiwan, Malaysia, Indonesia, and Thailand to be rapidly developing industrial countries in the development of East Asia, but excludes Hong Kong and Singapore from the scope of consideration. She writes: "Singapore and Hong Kong, although prospering, are distinct because they never transformed themselves from an agrarian base, the usual meaning of 'industrialization'"(Amsden, 1991: 282). When compared with the new international division of labor theory, which will be described later, "industrialization in Singapore and Hong Kong" can be confirmed that it is a recognition of a favorable contrast.

---

[3] This report was the result of a study conducted in response to the emergence of differences in perception of development methods with economists at Japan aid agencies. The research project is funded by the Japanese government.

7.2.1.2 The "Structural Transformation Chain" and the Flying Geese Theory

Two theories that explain the spread of development from NIEs to ASEAN and China in the analytical framework of the "national economy" attracted particular attention in Japan. One is the theory of 'structural transformation chains' and the other is the flying geese theory. Both are discussed in Chap. 12, but I will summarize them in this chapter as well.

First of all, the former is an argument developed by Toshio Watanabe, who was a professor at the University of Tsukuba at that time. Watanabe was one of the first to pay attention to the industrialization of the NIEs in East Asia, including Korea, and led the study of East Asian economics in Japan by not only empirically analyzing the changes in accordance with economic theory, but also raising issues by adding intriguing interpretations to these changes. According to him, the rapid economic development of the NIEs is a reproduction in East Asia of the latecomer benefits pointed out by Gershenkron. He called this "compressed growth". He explained that this development was due to the "social competence" of the NIEs, such as high-quality workers, entrepreneurial managerial skills, and bureaucratic administrative skills (Watanabe -J, 1985: 15).

However, when development spread from the NIEs to ASEAN countries, China, and the ASEAN countries that were the less developed, and began to present development on an East Asian scale, he called it a "chain of structural transformations" and explained the development of East Asian countries as follows:

> The Western Pacific is a region in which the less developed countries react quickly to the trade and investment opportunities created by these structural changes in the first-mover countries, transform their own structures, and 'chase' the developed countries with higher growth rates (Watanabe -J, 1991: 192–193).

Here, the "rapid reaction" of each country refers to a policy shift from import substitution to export-driven. It was also the "ability to convert" that achieved a regional chain of development. It is a contextual reinterpretation of the previous "social competence". In fact, in line with the development of East Asia, he created a series of novel catch phrases such as "Asianization of Asia" and "China's Hong Kong-ization or Hong Kong's China-ization", highlighting the changes from time to time. In terms of regional concepts, he also coined a new term for "Western Pacific" instead of East Asia.

However, a major feature of his argument is that he adheres to the basic analytical framework of neoclassical economics in which each East Asian country has its own independent national economy, while at the same time using the logic that regional development has been achieved by each country adopting liberalization policies in stages and continuously. Furthermore, it has incorporated the social explanatory factors of each country into the background of its success.

Another major explanatory theory is the flying geese theory, which Kaname Akamatsu derived from the industrialization and development of Japan in the 1930s.

The flying geese theory will be discussed in detail in Chap. 12, so we will only touch on it briefly here.

The flying geese theory traces the trajectory of the industrialization of Japan, then a latecomer country, starting with imports from developed countries, followed by import substitution production, and then exports. In Japan, the theory traces the transition from consumer goods to capital goods, and from crude products to refined products. Internationally, it is a theory where comparatively inferior industries will be transferred to subsequent countries as domestic industrial structures become more sophisticated. Akamatsu called the sequence of import, import-substitution, production, and export the basic form. He called the domestic upgrading and, international expansion, the two 'secondary forms' of the flying geese pattern.

The late Kiyoshi Kojima, a protégé of Akamatsu's protégé and professor emeritus at Hitotsubashi University, focused on the role of FDI by Japanese companies and linked it to the development of East Asia since the 1960s (Kojima, 1973). Thus, in the 1990s, the flying geese theory was accepted worldwide as a theory of industrialization and development that spread to the NIEs, ASEAN, China, and other countries, with Japan at the forefront[4] (Blomqvist 1997). Moreover, it is not only a theory of East Asian development, but also a theory of Japan's Asian policy.

Here, let's check the influence of the flying geese theory in a white paper by Japan's Economic Planning Agency (now the Cabinet Office). The White Paper on the World Economy at the time explained this using the trade specialization coefficients ((export–import)/(export + import)) of Japan and East Asian countries and economies. The trade specialization coefficient has a value between + 1 and − 1, and if the coefficient is positive, it is an excess of exports, and if it is negative, it is an excess of imports. Since the basic form of the flying geese theory is that each industry or country traces the development history of imports, import substitution production, and exports, we can discern the level of development of each country and the relationship between countries through the temporal change of the coefficients.

Figure 7.2 shows one of these illustrations. The sophistication of the industrial structure of East Asian countries is indicated by the value of the export specialization coefficient of (a) capital-intensive machinery and transport equipment and (b) labor-intensive miscellaneous products. From this figure, Japan has a high level of export specialization in capital-intensive industries, but it began to show a downward trend in the latter half of the 1980s, and import specialization is predominant in labor-intensive industries. In contrast, South Korea and Hong Kong will follow Japan in capital-intensive industries and begin to reduce the export specialization coefficient in labor-intensive industries. On the other hand, Thailand, Malaysia and Indonesia are labor-intensive industries with rapidly increasing trade specialization coefficients. The Economic Planning Agency explained this by saying, "In the East Asian growth economy, the so-called [flying geese] type of economic development is progressing. "(Economic Planning Board, Japan, 1994: 122).

[4] During the Greater East Asia War in Japan in the 1940s, the wide-area economic zone described by the flying geese theory sometimes played a role in the economic theory of the Greater East Asia Co-Prosperity Sphere. This point will be dealt with in Chap. 12.

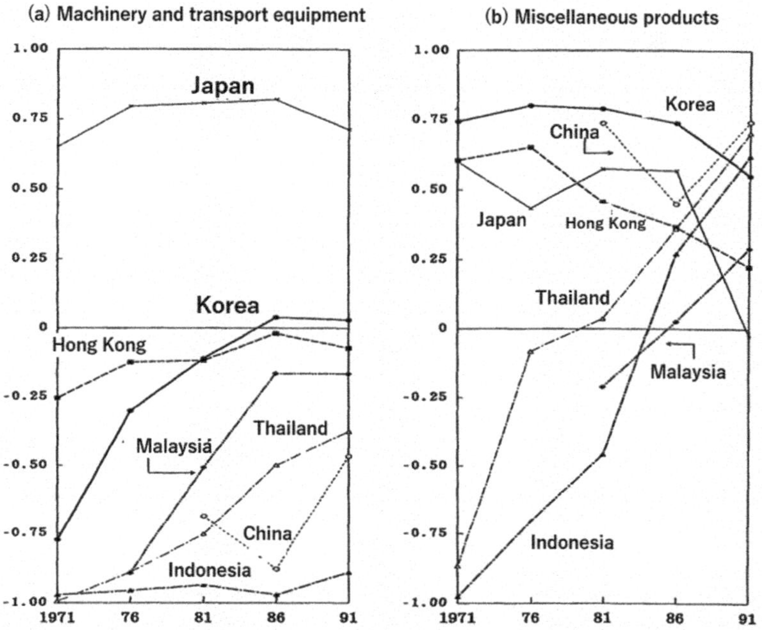

Fig. 7.2 Trade specialization coefficients of East Asian countries in 1971–1991 (*Source* Economic planning board, Japan -J, 1994: 121, Fig. 2-2-3). *Note* trade specialization coefficients = (Export − Import)/(Export + Import)

However, there were many questions about this explanation. There were a wide range of cases in major industries where the import process, which was considered to be the basic form of the flying geese pattern, was very short or non-existent (Yokota -J, 1992: 81–82; Bernard & Ravenhill, 1995; Hirakawa -J, 1997: 8–9; Kasahara, 2004: 14–15). Japan's industrialization policy was 'import substitution', while the industrialization policy of NIEs and some ASEAN countries was 'export-driven' (Hirakawa -J, 1992). Furthermore, there was criticism that the role of Japanese companies was exaggerated. The role of overseas Chinese companies was also pointed out.[5] At the turn of this century, Kojima himself pointed out the closed nature of Japan and NIEs as import markets, and this contradiction was also pointed out by Watanabe (Watanabe -J, 2004: 57).

Although little attention was paid to it, Akamatsu had one more important point. Before World War II, Akamatsu was aware of the important problem of "heterogeneity and homogenization of the world economy" from the perspective of capitalist history. In the world economy, trade tends to invigorate when the first-mover countries distinguish themselves from other countries in terms of capital accumulation (heterogeneity phase), but competition tends to intensify when the less developed

[5] M. Hobday wrote: "Although the various flying geese models attempt to see East Asia as an integrated region, one immediate difficulty is that there is no mention of the overseas Chinese in the region's development" (Hobday, 1995: 21).

countries catch up with industrialization (homogenization phase). He was one of the first to incorporate Kondratieff's research on long-term economic waves in his 1939 paper. The heterogeneity phase corresponds to the ascending period of long-term variability, and the homogenization phase corresponds to the downward phase (Akamatsu -J, 1944; Akamatsu -J, 1965: 38–59).

Apart from that, what we would like to focus on in this section is that the growth of East Asian countries has been achieved in the international networks of production and sales built by multinational corporations (MNCs) in developed countries. The form of development through the emergence of global intra-industrial trade and intra-enterprise trade cannot be grasped by the structural transformation chain theory, which is based on the "national economy" as the basic cognitive framework, or by the general flying geese theory. There was a need to consider such new phenomena from a broader perspective (Hirakawa -J, 1992; Hirakawa, 1999).

7.2.1.3 Industrialization in East Asia from the Perspective of Economic History

Political economy considerations based on the history of the East Asian (Northeast Asia) region were discussed in 1985 by B. Cummings (Cumings, 1984). Here, we will touch on the debate of economic historians in Japan. Satoru Nakamura, Professor Emeritus at Kyoto University, focused on the legacy of Japan's colonial period in particular, saying that the discussions on industrialization and economic development in East Asia in the 1970s~1990s that "focus on the policy level and do not capture the overall structure of development, have a weak historical perspective, and do not incorporate the historical conditions (domestic and international) of capitalist industrialization" (Nakamura -J, 1991: 22).

According to Nakamura's empirical research, the domination of Japan imperialism in Korea, former Manchuria, and Taiwan was caused by (a) the destruction and dismantling of the old society (pre-modern social and economic structure) through the establishment of modern land ownership relations, (b) a thorough modification of the economic structure subordinate to Japan, the colonial home country, as seen in the rice-producing proliferation program in Korea, and (c) encouraging the rapid development of a capitalist economy centered on Japan capital, as seen in the industrialization that began in the 1930s. It can be summed up as follows:

> Korea's internal development before colonization combined with the colonial rule of Japan imperialism led to Korea's rapid primary accumulation. The colonial rule of Japan imperialism in the interwar period was a new type of imperialist rule that strongly promoted the dismantling of old society = pre-modern society and fostered colonial capitalism (Nakamura -J, 1991: 165)

In this way, Nakamura argued that middle-advanced capitalism (industrialization) was achieved under the post-independence Cold War structure with the involvement of U.S. aid, reforms, and the international expansion of multinational corporations. Certainly, institutional reforms such as the agrarian reform of Japan by the United

States after World War II, and the agrarian reform carried out under the Chinese Communist Party must have been important prerequisites for industrialization.

On East Asian industrialization and NIEs, Nakamura's protégé, Professor Kazuo Hori of Kyoto University, confirmed that the trade value of China, Manchuria, Korea, and Taiwan, the trade structure, the number of factory workers, and the production of cotton products grew continuously from the 1930s to the 1960s. In other words, there is a continuity in the development of these regions from the era of Japanese imperialism to the liberation of Japan after the defeat of the war, and through the post-war international Cold War structure. This suggests that the general understanding that the economic growth of NIEs began abruptly in the 1960s ignores or downplays historical conditions (Hori -J, 1994a; 1994b).

For these reasons, Hori summarizes that "the current simple proposition of the total collapse of colonial industry is not tenable. Neither could we link the simplistic and hasty claim that industrialization during the colonial period led to the NICs of today's Taiwan and Korea,", pointing out that the historical background cannot be ignored (Hori -J, 1994a: 221).

Here we can also point out a number of issues. The biggest challenge is that there is a huge spatial discrepancy between the industrial areas of pre-war East Asia and the post-war industrial zones. As is well known, the industrial area in Korea was North Korea, not South Korea. Korea was generally a rural area. However, post-war industrialization was achieved in South Korea, and North Korea has fallen into stagnation. The same can be said for China. The industrial base was inherited from the former Manchuria region and inland China. However, the center of China's post-reform and opening-up development is the coastal areas. Today, Shenzhen, which forms the world's advanced industrial cluster, was nothing more than a freezing village before reform and opening up (Hirakawa -J, 1997: 13).

In countries that were former colonies or occupied territories of Japan, there was a very strong opposition to Japan after post-war independence. This strengthened the tendency to reject Japan's colonial heritage altogether. However, from an objective point of view, the institutional and economic foundations created during the period of Japan imperialism were a prerequisite for postwar economic development. Such a review of objective conditions was beginning to be pointed out in both Japan and the former colonial regions, mixed with great emotional friction.

The main takeaway from the historical approach is that industrialization and capitalism did not suddenly begin from scratch, but functioned as historical social and economic conditions at the starting point of postwar industrialization. If we ignore these assumptions, we will not be able to conduct an accurate analysis. However, this is not a definitive condition. We cannot ignore the historical premise, but it does not explain the industrialization of East Asia that began in the 1960s. It can be said that the historical approach teaches the importance of looking at post-war developments in the context of history.

7.2.2 *The Corporate Approach*

In the enterprise theory approach, in 1966, R. Vernon's Product Life Cycle (PLC) hypothesis can be taken up first. As mentioned above, Kiyoshi Kojima named the flying geese theory as catching-up product cycle (CPC) theory, in association with the PLC. In response to the fact that the flying geese theory remained in the economic academic community of Japan at that time and was not well known overseas, he tried to introduce it to the world using Vernon's theory. Actually Japan's role in the industrialization of East Asian countries will grow even more thereafter.

In the early 1990s, Japan was in an overwhelming economic position in Asia, and the same was true in corporate activities. In 1992, Japanese companies accounted for 90% of the top 500 companies in East Asia, and the top 34 companies were all Japanese companies. Among the top 100 non-Japan companies, South Korea's Samsung ranked 35th, and of the top 100, 90 were Japanese, six were Korean, and one each was from Taiwan, Malaysia and Indonesia. During this period, the Asian region had already grown into the largest profit region for Japanese companies, and East Asia, including China, had emerged as a major investment destination for Japanese companies (Abegglen 1994: 19).

Amidst such an environment, one of the most influential approaches to explain East Asian industrialization and development has been the 'Japanese company-ism' theory initiated by the Institute of Social Science (ISS) at the University of Tokyo in the 1980s-1990s when Japanese companies were enjoying the top place in the international economy.

Then a professor of the ISS, Hiroji Baba, the creator of the idea of 'company-ism' ('Kaisha-shugi') stated that:

> The word was originally coined to express the dualistic nature of current Japanese society, compared with the West: one is more capitalist oriented and the other more akin to socialism. This character stems from a method of capital formation which is similar to the organization of Japanese companies. And the word is also a typical expression of the mentality of Japanese employees of belonging to their company. It links the social structure, capital's distinctive features and social consciousness in our daily life, which is supported by the latter (Baba -J, 1997: 320).

According to Baba, the idea of 'company-ism' was formed in the first half of the 1960s, on Japanese rapid economic growth. It accompanied the growth during the late 1960s and provided traction power when the growth lost its speed. The center of the idea lies in Japanese industrial relations, which consist of the "trinity of life-long employment, seniority order system, and enterprise union" (Baba -J, 1991: 63, 1997: 322). This idea, as a set, spread across East Asia through the foreign investments of Japanese companies.

The multinational company research group in the ISS put forth the analysis that the direct investment of Japanese companies into the region which includes East Asia "works as a propeller with its dynamic contribution to form an economic community of great importance" (Itagaki -J. 1997: 2). The research group examined the transfer of the Japanese production system to East Asian countries and concluded that, in Taiwan and South Korea, the system in Japanese-owned main plants which assembled and made parts for electric and car manufacturing was appropriated and diffused better than in other countries such as the United States (Itagaki -J:289). Akira Suehiro, Professor at the ISS also suggested, "it is the production system of the Japanese companies itself that produces export competitiveness in the current Southeast Asian region" (Suehiro -J, 1995:188).

The mechanism that propagated Japanese management and production systems throughout East Asia is in some way supported by the flying geese model (Baba -J, 1995: 36; Suehiro -J, 1995: 183), and in another by the transfer approach through Japanese MNCs (Baba, 1997: 326). Nevertheless, compared to traditional methods of analyzing East Asia, these are new approaches that see East Asia's industrialization and economic growth through the activities of companies beyond its own borders. It would be correct to say that these understandings are underpinned by the fact that globalization is the main agency of globalization in international corporate activities, and that Japanese companies played a particularly major role in East Asia's industrialization.

However, it is not possible to understand the region's industrialization and economic growth solely through the transfer of companies' production activities and system. As we saw in the previous section and also Chap. 2, East Asian growth has been export-led, and the structure of the international division of labor, which generates more and more division of manufacturing processes, does not fit into the traditionally presupposed pattern of growth of an autonomous 'national economy'. Still, the role of states is important in the industrialization of the developing countries in East Asia, as was seen in the attention given to states' industrial policies through the debate between the neoclassical and the statist/ non neoclassical approaches. The theories of East Asian industrialization should be capable of answering the question of how to integrate companies and states.

7.2.3 The World Economy Approach of East Asian Industrialization

The world economy approach can be further divided into two approaches. One is the dependency approach, followed by the new international division of labor (NIDL) theory, and the other the world system approach. This world economy approach was significant as a paradigm change because it proposed a framework for the recognition that international economic systems and relations create underdevelopment and poverty, as opposed to the so-called theory of unilateral development, which is considered to be the theory of modernization. Unfortunately, however, its significance has lost its influence before it is understood amid the great changes of the times. In the following, I will review these arguments in contrast to the realities of East Asia's economic development in the second half of the twentieth century.

7.2.3.1 Dependency Theory and the New International Division of Labor

The dependency approach was represented by Andre G. Frank, Samir Amin,[6] and others in the 1970s and early 1980s. According to them, the world consists of a center ('metropolitan') and a 'periphery', and the poverty of the Third World (developing countries) is the result of its incorporation into 'metropolitan' capitalism. Therefore, it is extremely difficult to develop under this structure. The extreme recommendation was a "de-link" from the world economy.

The approach was almost directly adapted to the industrialization in East Asia. These theorists understand the industrialization and economic growth of Asian NIEs merely as a process of these countries becoming subcontractors for international capital so that the exploitation of cheap labor can continue, with no solution to the problem of poverty in the area.

However, the spread of industrialization into the NIEs, the ASEAN countries, and China brought rapid increases in exports, certain improvements in technology, and increases in income. Industrialization also encouraged the development of local capital. As far as these elements were concerned, adapting the dependency approach to East Asia would be seen as an "anachronism", as T. Watanabe pointed out (Watanabe -J, 1985).

It is not sufficient, nevertheless, to simply accuse the dependency view of having misjudged the situation. The question is why this school did so. Two arguments could be brought to light to explain this.

Firstly, it may be that the growth in East Asia after World War II was a new experience for the world that was simply not explainable by existing historical analysis, such as Frank's. His recognition of the dependency approach was established in *Capitalism and Underdevelopment in Latin America* published in 1967. This book was a comprehensive but empirical grasp of the relationship between trade and development in Chile and Brazil since the sixteenth century. The trouble was that it was received as a pan-historic generalization of the dependency approach.

Secondly, different sights might have emerged depending on how one interpreted the fact that some local capital was developed in a position of subcontracting to international capital. From this point of view, it is necessary to look into the theory of the 'new international division of labor' (NIDL), which offers a new perspective albeit one sympathetic to the viewpoint of the dependency school. NIDL, as presented

---

[6] A. G. Frank's early work, "The Development of Underdevelopment" in 1966 and "Capitalism and Underdevelopment in Latin America" in 1967, had a profound impact on postwar industrialization in developing countries. In addition, Egyptian-born economist, S. Amin's "Accumulation on a World Scale" in 1974 and "Unequal Development" in 1976, which are based on Amin's research on underdevelopment in Africa, also led to a major shift in perceptions of underdevelopment in the global underdeveloped region. Amin argued that the world is made up of centers and periphery, and that centers have been siphoning off wealth through unequal exchange with the periphery. All of them proposed a perspective that grasps underdevelopment and poverty from a global perspective, critically grasping the unilateralist development perception of the modernization theory that dominates in developed countries, and proposing a new perspective.

by F. Fröbel, H. Heinriches and O. Kreye at the Max-Planck Institute in Germany focuses on German industrial companies' advancement to 'free production zones' (export processing zones) in developing countries, and is an empirical and theoretical study of the transfer of production from developed industrial countries to developing areas.

Table 7.1 is given for confirmation. The table summarizes the number of developing countries with free production zones/export processing zones (EPZs) and world production factories and the number of employees in 1975 collected by the Table source. This shows that in the mid-1970s, companies in developed countries began production mainly of Asian NIEs for export from developing countries.

Table 7.1 Numbers of countries and employment in free production zones and world market factories by region, 1975

(a) Free production zones (FPZs)

	Zones in operation		FPZs under construction			
	No. of country	No. of zones	No. of country		No. of zones	
			Total	Without FPZs in operation before 1975	Total	In countries without FPZs in operation before 1975
Asia	11 (44%)	48[a] (61%)	11 (52%)	4 (36%)	20 (39%)	5 (33%)
Africa	5 (20%)	7 (9%)	3 (14%)	1 (9%)	8 (21%)	1 (7%)
Latin America	9 (36%)	24[b](30%)	7 (33%)	6 (55%)	11 (28%)	9 (60%)
Total	25 (100%)	79[b] (100%)	21 (100%)	11 (100%)	39 (100%)	15 (100%)

Notes **a**: Including 14 industrial districs in Hong Kong and 14 industrial estates in Singapore. **b**: Including 11 industrial parks in the northern boarder zone of Mexico.

(b) No. of employment in FPZs and world market factories in last available year

	Total	Of which major countries and their number
Asia	420000 (58%)	112,250 (South Korea), 105,000 (Singapore), 62,143 (Taiwan), 59,607 (Hong Kong), 40,465 (Malaysia), 16,700 (Thailand)
Africa	40000 (6%)	24,000 (Tunisia), 9952 (Mauritius), 2,800 (Ivory Coast)
Latin America	265000 (36%)	96,726 (Puerto Rico), 84,308 (Mexico), 27,650 (Brazil), 25,000 (Haiti), 6,500 (Dominican Rep.), 6,145 (El Salvador),
Total	725000 (100%)	

(*Source* Fröbel, Heinrich, & Kreye 1980: 306, and 310).

Note Employment number includes number of world market factories outside of FPZs. Nos.of Hong Kong, South Korea, Taiwan, and Malaysia in 1975, and Singapore in 1974. Nos. of Moritius in 1975, Tunisia, Ivory Coast in 1974. Nos. of Puerto Rico and Haiti, Dominican Rep., and El Salvador in 1975, Mexico in 1974, Brazil in 1973.

In fact, EPZs also played a major role in the early stages of industrialization of the NIEs, although their functions change depending on the stage of development. Taiwan established its first EPZ in Kaohsiung in 1966, and in that year, FDI in Taiwan was $11 million, of which 37.6%, or $29.3 million was invested in Kaohsiung EPZ. Since then, direct investment in Taiwan has increased dramatically, and in 1971 export processing zones were added in Nanzi and Taichung. Of the $2.252 billion in total FDI in 1979, 12.5% was invested in EPZs. In 1984, FDI doubled to $4.457 billion, of which 9.4% went to processing zones. In South Korea, the Masan Free Trade Zone (EPZ) was established in 1970, and 11.5% of the total FDI received in 1984 of $1.119 billion went to EPZs (MOFA, Japan -J, 1986: 112).

Why on earth did this production for export spread so widely in developing regions?

Fröbel et al. defined a set of three conditions for the formation of a NIDL:

(a) The development of a world-wide reservoir of potential labour-power. This reservoir is practically inexhaustible in that capital can call on several hundred million potential workers, mainly in Asia, Africa, and Latin America, and even, in one particular sense, in the 'socialist' countries.
(b) The development and refinement of technology and job organisation makes it possible to decompose complex production processes into elementary units such that even unskilled labour can be easily trained in quite a short period of time to carry out these rudimentary operations. The fragmentation of jobs, the execution of the respective fragmented operations of even very sophisticated overall processes now often requires a training period of no more than a few weeks even for unskilled labour.
(c) The development of a technology which renders industrial location and the management of production itself largely independent of geographical distance. This technology includes modern transport technology; containerization and air-freight; efficient telecommunication systems, data-processing technology, and other organisational methods (Fröbel et al., 1980: 33–36; in original German edition 1977: 51–53).

To these conditions is added competition in the international market after World War II as the intensification and global expansion of enterprises, which was enabled by technological innovation, drove the East Asian labor force to be utilized by the capital of developed industrial countries (Fröbel, 1982: 539–540; Hirakawa -J, 1992: Chap. 3).

NIDL, which was born under these circumstances, encouraged foreign direct investment by international capital/MNCs. In addition, their utilization of local capital through 'new forms of international investment', called by C. Oman, had taken place. Enterprises of advanced countries during this time formed relationships with the local enterprises of developing countries through various forms, such as international joint ventures, licensing agreements, management contracts, and international subcontracting. This relationship was broadened globally by the United States, on the one hand, with the establishment of U.S. tariff regulations 806.30 and 807.00, which imposed tariffs only on the value-added portion of imports from abroad, and Free Trade Zones (FTZs) by developing countries on the other hand (Helleiner 1983: 29–30). Oman was one of the first to recognize the consignment relationship between developed companies and local firms, and called it "new forms of international investment" (Oman, 1984: 17). Local companies were expanding their development possibilities in this relationship. As will be discussed in the next section, M. Hobday reveals that the subcontracting relationship between Asian NIEs and MNCs has become one of the trajectories of the technology accumulation and development of NIEs companies.

However, in NIEs such as South Korea and Taiwan, the development of labor-intensive industries was not limited to mere development, but heavy industrialization progressed in a visible way, and there was remarkable development in high-tech industries such as electronics. J. Henderson empirically discusses the global development of the semiconductor industry. Henderson appreciated the theory of the new international division of labor, but distanced himself from the pessimism of Fröbel et al.'s conclusions. According to the NIDL, production for the world market lacks organic linkages with the local economies of FDI destinations, technology transfer is almost unexpected, and the potential for peripheral development is extremely small. However, the results of the global systems approach, which we will see in the next section, will be used to confirm the development of the electronics industry in Hong Kong and Singapore and its "rise" in the global system. In Hong Kong and Singapore, the more advanced manufacturing processes of the semiconductor industry were mainly staffed by American companies, and a "regional division of labor" was being developed (Henderson, 1989: 17–24, Chap. 4).

D. Ernst writes as follows. Japan electronics companies viewed Asian countries only as a source of low-cost workers, but "U.S. and European, as well as Korean and Taiwanese, companies are expanding R&D functions in their overseas affiliates in Asia. In Asia, the share of Japanese companies that intend to expand R&D hovers between 9 percent, for NIEs, to 13.5 percent, for China, compared to 19 percent for the European Union and almost 23 percent for North America" (Ernst, 2006: 170).

It is important to point out that a new regional division of labor has emerged mainly in Hong Kong and Singapore. Both Hong Kong and Singapore are small countries and regions in terms of population, area, and market size, and are transit trade zones or city-states. The "National Economy" approach treated Hong Kong and Singapore as exceptions, but it does not allow the electronics industry to analyze the international division of labor across national borders. If we preempt the conclusion, we must look at the characteristics of industrialization at the end of the twentieth century. Fröbel et al. were among the first to realize that for the first time in capitalist history, industries began to move to the periphery due to the fragmentation of jobs in the production process, which was made possible by the development of transport and communication technology. Their outlook was gloomy, but they also noted the global establishment of export processing zones. In the 1980s, as East Asian NIEs developed in heavy industries such as steel and shipbuilding, as well as the electronics industry, the NIDL was regarded as one of the dependency theories and rapidly lost its influence.

However, this structure clearly continues into this century, especially in advanced industries. In the 1990s, East Asian countries, especially China, became production bases dependent on cheap labor, and by this century they had become the world's factories. It is characterized by a "new international division of labor" that is the opposite of ostensibly high growth and development. This has become clear through the analysis of the distribution structure of added value due to the evolution of the global value chain (GVC) theory and the advancement of data analysis methods, which will be described later, but here we will look at two examples.

Table 7.2 and Fig. 7.3 deconstructed the international division of labor between Japan's digital camera (A) at the beginning of this century and Apple's iPhone4 in late 2010 from the perspective of the value chain. According to an interview survey conducted by the Ministry of Economy, Trade and Industry of Japan, the value-added composition of Japan's digital camera products (A) shows that China's share of assembly products is only 8%, while Japan's parent company accounts for 49% of the parts and 37% of activities such as product development and sales. However, the factory gate price in China for products assembled in China is 63% of the total because it includes the procurement price of parts from the parent company in Japan, third countries, and other companies in China.

In Apple's production of the iPhone4, its structure is even more shocking. A value chain study of Apple's iPhone4, which has a retail price of $600 in the OECD countries, showed that the value-added portion of the iPhone in China was only 1.5%, or $6.54, as shown in Fig. 7.3. However, if we look at this from the perspective of the U.S.-China trade balance, China's factory gate price is $194.04, which is $187.5

Table 7.2 Japanese firm's parts cost composition and division of labor in the production process for digital camera A

a) Digital Camera A's Composition of parts and components production cost

Composition of parts and components production cost Share (%)	Image manipulation equipment/exterior (ex. TFT, metal exterior, etc.)		Optical system unit (e.g. filter, image sensor, lens)			Substrate (e.g. custom IC, electric parts)		Other parts		Business activities other than parts production
	Japan	China	Japan	China	Thailand	Japan	Switzerland	Japan	China	other countries
	13	1	13	6	2	17	4	6	1	37
Total 100%	**Subtotal 63%: Japan 49%, China 8%**, Switzerland 4%, Thailand 2%									**37%**

b) Digital Camera A's International divesion of labor in the production process

		Marketing/ product planning	Product development	Parts and components production	Assembly	Sale
In house division of labor	Japan (Home country)	Parent firms (Planning and development)	Parent firms (product development & Design)	Domestic related firms Procurement		Sales headquarter (Revese imports)
	outside Japan (China)			Procurement Local subsidiaries Procurement	Local subsidiaries	Local subsidearies and local distribution
	Third countries	Local subsidiaries in Europe and America				World market including Europe and America
Outsourcing				Japanese parts manufactures in China Chinese local parts manufactures Taiwanese parts manufactures in China Contract manufacturing firms in Asia other than China		

(*Source* METI -J, 2004: 165).
Note created based on interviews done by METI.

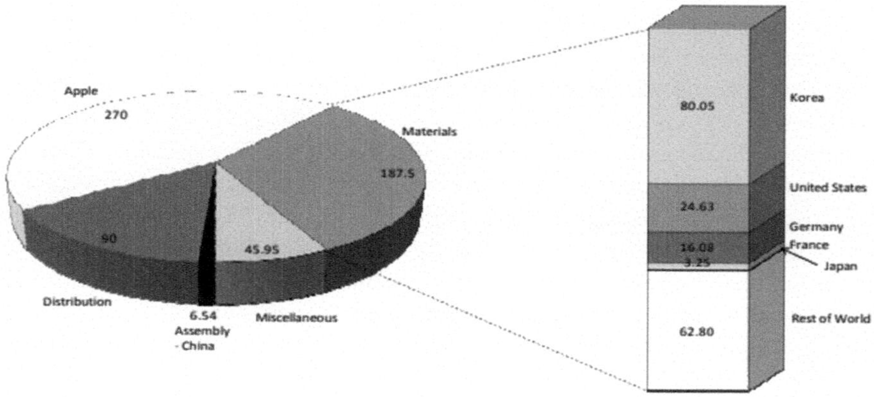

Fig. 7.3 Value creation and capturing (in U.S.$) for Apple's iPhone4 (Retail price = U.S.$600). (*Source* De Backer, 2011: 24). *Note* (1) the assignment of value to countries is based on headquarters. (2) Apple uses Toshiba as an alternative supplier to LG; the value creation/capturing for Japan changes accordingly. (3) Apple margin includes royalties and licensing fees

for parts procurement plus $6.54 for Chinese assembly. However, since this procurement included $24.63 in procurement (imports) from the United States, China's trade surplus is $169.41 (De Backer, 2011: 40). It was only through a value-added analysis from the perspective of GVCs that this structure was clarified.

However, this is not to say that this structure lacks morals. Since the 1990s, the international status of East Asian countries has certainly risen through this structure, and social changes have occurred and vitality has been generated. At the same time, its development has clearly visualized a structure that goes beyond a unilateral analytical framework. Therein lies the foresight of the NIDL's cognitive framework.

7.2.3.2 World System Approach

It was I. Wallerstein who tried to constructively grasp the capitalist market economy and underdevelopment/poverty from a global perspective in order to compensate for the deficiencies of the dependency theory. In his 1979 book, The Capitalist World-Economy, he defines the world system a "social system to be the existence within it of a division of labor, such that the various sectors or areas within are dependent upon economic exchange with others for the smooth and continuous provisioning of the needs of the area". While theorists of the dependency school grasp the world as having a dual structure of core and periphery, he considers the world's structure as consisting of three layers/parts: the core, the semi-periphery, and the periphery; and sees the semi-periphery as the most potent sphere towards some higher status (Wallerstein, 1979: 5).

So, what kind of capabilities do "semi-periphery" countries have? He defined the condition as "A wide range of countries in terms of economic strength and political background" and listed nearly 30 countries. In addition, he identified the following three strategies for rising margins: (a) seizing the chance, (b) promotion by invitation, and (c) self-reliance (Wallerstein, 1979: 76).

(a) is a strategy in which peripheral countries take advantage of the weakening of the political position of the core countries and the weakening of domestic forces linked to the center during the contraction of the world economy to raise their position in the world system through "import substitution policies" and other means. (b) is a strategy to achieve an upward trend by attracting multinational corporations during the period of global economic expansion, which he calls "semiperipheral development by invitation" through multinational corporations. (c) is an isolated development such as Tanzania. Of these, the strategy with the highest upside potential was (a) (Wallerstein, 1979: 76–80).

However, Wallerstein did not mention any of the areas or countries of the East Asian NIEs group as semi-peripheral. Surprisingly, he did cite North Korea and the other ex-socialist countries as semi-peripheral[7] (Wallerstein, 1979: 100, 103). Even in the upward trend, the industrialization of the Asian NIEs was a strategy of (b), not (a). Wallerstein could not have predicted the development of Asian NIEs at the end of the 1970s (Hirakawa -J, 1997: 16).

What does this mean? The industrialization and development of East Asia, beginning with the NIEs, was achieved in a more integrated capitalist world/global economy, beyond the expectations of Wallerstein's world system. The role of governments in developing countries cannot be ignored, but more than that, as analyzed by the NIDL theory, multinational corporations in developed countries have transferred labor-intensive industries and fragmented production processes to East Asia, and have built various networks with local companies to bring industrialization to Asian NIEs and other East Asian countries. East Asian countries took advantage of this opportunity to acquire the skills for their own development. This meant that East Asia was developing as part of the global economy.

Historically, the qualitative change in the international division of labor due to the progress of science and technology has enabled the development of East Asian countries by incorporating workers from the "periphery" countries of East Asia into their production processes. At first, the industrialization of East Asian countries, which was borne by low wages, was expected to end in integration into the world system. However, East Asian countries have achieved development beyond that. It was the reorganization of the world system and the "rise" of the countries of East Asia.

This section discusses the characteristics of industrialization and development in East Asia through a survey of the main theories of the 1980s and 1990s. There was a criticism by the nationalist approach of the neoclassical theory of market omnipotence in mainstream economics, that led to a convergence wherein a certain role of

[7] In this book, Wallerstein lists "semi-periphery" countries such as Brazil, Mexico, and Argentina in Latin America, most of Eastern Europe, Algeria, Egypt, Saudi Arabia, Israel, Nigeria in Africa, and Zambia but in Asia, Turkey, Iran, India, Indonesia, China, Korea, and Vietnam are mentioned. However, here he refers to the term "Korea" several times, but, in these cases, "Korea" signifies socialist "North Korea", not South Korea.

industrial policy was accepted. However, the two approaches, which clashed on the axis of the "market or state" debate, shared a common perception that the East Asian region was a development phenomenon through a chain of self-sustaining "national economies". Both the flying geese and the "chain of structural transformation" theories, which originated in Japan, are similar in this respect.

In the corporate theory approach, attention was paid to the transfer of Japan's management production system, and the relationship between East Asia and the international business activities of multinational corporations was shown.

The historical approach and the global economic approach have been characterized by a new level of industrialization in which the industrialization and development of the NIEs and the expansion of East Asia are defined by historical conditions but transcend them. The industrialization of East Asia is inextricably linked to the world market and the world economy, and it has developed under the international division of labor and the network of production established by the developed country MNCs. The policy of a state had, for the first time, significance within the international structure.

7.3 East Asia's Development as a Model of Late Industrialization

East Asia's industrialization and development are fundamentally outward-looking, through exports to external markets, but at the same time they are directly and/or indirectly dependent mainly on the production of Japanese- and U.S.-based multinational companies (MNCs), including NIEs-based companies. If we look at this industrialization from a historical perspective, we can identify the major characteristics of the present late industrialization.

7.3.1 The Development Models of the 20th Century and the World Economy

To begin with, let us look at the characteristics of the East Asian development experience, starting from the industrialization and development models of the twentieth century. These models can be fundamentally divided into four, if we consider China's case as a form of state capitalism.

The first was the socialist planned economy model which came out of the Russian Revolution in 1917. There was the centrally-planned economy model of the former Soviet Union, and Yugoslavia's socialist de-centralized economy model of workers' self-management that was attempted under Josip Broz Tito's government. The second model of economic development is China's socialist market economy model, which was a transition from the self-help type of socialism. The third is the import-substitution model of development, which almost all newly independent countries after World War II, adopted for their industrialization. Among them, there was India, who adopted a mixed type of development model where public and private sectors existed. And the last is the Asian NIEs' model of market economy, which has adopted the export-oriented or export-led industrialization strategies since the 1960s.

As Table 7.3 shows, among the four strategies, NIEs and Chinese type of industrialization strategies can be regarded as successful, while other two must be branded as failures.

The next question is: what strategy separates success from failure? Each model can be examined in terms of markets and the state since the debate between the two has been the bone of contention. The socialist model of the Soviet Union allowed the state to intervene in the economy, excluding the market entirely, and Yugoslavia was a decentralized economy model, which is a type of workers' self-management, but both socialist state models split and disappeared early in the 1990s. Only China's state intervention model had been growing and developing due to the changing of the self-help socialist economic model to the "socialist-market economy" model. The import-substitution industrialization model is also considered a model of state intervention in the economy which was a domestic market-based development strategy. India had adopted a mixed market-state model. But both models had an inward-looking, domestic orientation development strategy, and had fallen into stagnation.

Table 7.3 Main development/industrialization strategies in the twentieth century

Frramework of market/economy	Economic System/Model	Industrialization/Development Strategy			Policical System
Overseas-market-orientation	Laissez-faire	O Export-oriented (export-led) industrialization	O Hong Kong		O (British) colony
	Capitalist market economy/		O Singapore		O Authoritalian
	Outward-looking		O South Korea, Taiwan		O Authoritalian ⇒ Democracy
Domestic-market orientation	Market economy, mixed type economy/ Inward-looking	● Import-substitution industrialization	O Malaysia,Thailand, Philippines, Indonesia, O India	Stag-nant	O Democracy /Authoritalian ⇔ Democracy
			● Latin American countries		
Overseas-market orientation	Socialist-market economy (State Capitalism)/ Outward-looking	● Socialist-export-oriented industrialization	O China, Vietnam		O Socialism /Authoritalian
Domestic-orientation	Socialist centrally planned economy/ Non-market orientation	● Non-market Planned economy	● Soviet Union	Stag-nant; Dissolu-tion	● Socialism
	Socialist de-centralized economy/ Inward-looking	● De-centralized self-management	● Yugoslavia		● Socialism Self-management

(*Source* made by Hirakawa).
Note 1. Successful in economic growth and development. Unsuccessful, stagnant in economic growth and development 2. The Soviet Union was dissolved in 1991, Yugoslavia split into 6 countries in 1991–1992 and disappeared. The names of the countries listed here are representative examples of each model that the author considers.

NIEs' and China's strategies of outward-looking appear to be successful, which relies on the overseas market. It is not possible to identify success or failure based on the dichotomy of the state and market. The intervention of the state cannot be neglected, but is not an absolute condition. Hong Kong's economic system is a laissez faire model on the one hand, and China's economic model is called the state capitalism model on the other. In the end, it was not the state or market, but the domestic market or overseas market that separates success from failure. Furthermore, as for the Political system, democracy or authoritarianism is not a decisive condition for success, even though Hong Kong's peculiarities must be taken into account.

7.3.2 Late Industrialization and the World Economy

Let us review the experiences of industrialization of East Asia from the viewpoint of history. What is important here is that A. Gerschenkron pointed to structural differences with different industrial stages. That is, on the basis of European industrial history in the nineteenth century, the industrialization of countries can be divided into those of advanced areas, areas of moderate backwardness, and areas of extreme backwardness, with different driving forces for each stage.

As Table 7.4, cited from his book, shows, the "factory" was the driving force behind industrialization in developed regions, "banks and factory" in the moderate backward areas, and "state, banks, and factory" in the areas of extreme backwardness. This means that for the latecomers or underdeveloped countries, the greater the degree of backwardness, the larger the scale of industrialization gets, in fact, the disadvantage for backward countries becomes larger, as a broader set of capital supplying institutions becomes indispensable.

Nevertheless, the advantage of latecomers is widely accepted, for once these countries have succeeded in embarking on industrialization, the large-scale apparatus enables them to spurt towards industrialization, achieving "compressed development". The advantage of the latecomers should be assessed in terms of their disadvantage.

The achievements of Alice H. Amsden and a Korean economist and an economic historian, Kim Young-Ho deserve to be noted as analyses of East Asia's industrialization from the above-mentioned point of view.

Table 7.4 Gerschenkron's different manufacturing relationships existing with regard to sources of capital supply by stage

Stages	Advanced area	Area of moderate backwardness	Area of extreme backwardness
I	Factory	Banks	State
II		Factory	Banks
III			Factory

(*Source* Gerschenkron 1962: 355).

Amsden noted that industrialization allowed the acquisition of technology, a process in which the state played a key role. Technology was acquired through "invention" in the eighteenth century, "innovation" in the nineteenth century and "learning" of borrowed technology in the twentieth century, while the states adopted policies of protectionism and subsidy, respectively, during each stage (Amsden, 1989: Chap. 2). As for typical countries, "Japan (although in many aspects it is unique among late industrializing), South Korea, Taiwan, Brazil, possibly Mexico, and Turkey", and moreover, "this list might be expanded, but one cannot add to it the city-states of Singapore and Hong Kong, because neither began from the agrarian or raw material base that is typically taken to be the starting point of industrial transformation" was written (Amsden, 1989: 4).

Kim introduced the idea of the 'generation' approach to grasping late industrialization, which is more appropriate than the traditional analysis used to illustrate different stages (Kim -J, 1988: 17–23). Table 7.5 provides an overview of this.

As shown in Table 7.5, the first generation of industrialization is regarded as the United Kingdom at the end of the eighteenth century and the beginning of the nineteenth century, the second generation is France, Germany, and the United States in the mid-nineteenth century, the third generation is Italy, Russia, and Japan at the end of the nineteenth century and the beginning of the twentieth century, and the

Table 7.5 Industrialization generation and its standards

		(The)First Generation	Second Generation	Third Generation	Fourth Generation
Period		Late 18c - early 19c	Mid 19c	Late 19c - early 20c	Second half of 20c
Region and countries		European advanced region: England	European middle-advanced region: France, Germany, and America	European less-advanced and non-European advanced region: Italy, Russia, and Japan	Non-European less-advanced region: Taiwan, Korea, China, and others
Driving force of industrialization		Private firms (Mainly small and medium-sized firms)	Banks Private large firms	State Private large firms	State Foreign Capital (firms) Private firms**
Conditions of World system		Core type	Semi-core type	Semi-periphery type	Periphery type
Forms of international division of labor between core and periphery*	Core (Semi-core) (Semi-periphery)	Consumer manufactured goods	Consumer goods/ production goods	production goods/ durable-consumer goods	Consumer goods/ Production goods/ Durable consumer goods/ High technology goods
	(Periphery → Core)	Primary products	Primary goods/ consumer goods	Primery goods/ consumer goods	**Consumer goods/ Production goods/ Durable-consumer goods**
	Periphery				Primery goods/ consumer goods
Kondratiev's Long waves		The first wave (1700-1844~51)	The second wave (1844~51-1890~96)	The third wave (1890~96-1948)	The fourth wave (1948- present)
In addition: Amsden's Late comers' technology features		Invention	Innovation/application of science to production		Learning/ borrowed technology and improvement in productivity

(*Source* Kim -J 1988: 18). The original figure has been modified in the "forms of international division of labor" column. Kim adds the row of "political and economic conditions" as indicators of the characteristics of industrialization by generation. The final row of late comers' technological features was the one that the author cited from Amsden 1989 and Amsden 1991).

Note * In Kim's original table, it is "large firms", but here it is displayed as "firms".

fourth generation is the industrialization of developing regions in the second half of the twentieth century, especially NIEs and others. The drivers of industrialization in each generation were Gerschenkron's theory of step-by-step institutions, with the first generation being private enterprises, the second generation being banks and large private enterprises, and the third generation being the state and private corporations. Then, in the fourth generation, foreign companies will be added. The union of the state, foreign companies, and domestic enterprises is the starting point for industrialization. In relation to the world system, Wallerstein's three-tier structure can be divided into four-tier structures. The United Kingdom, which carried out the first generation of the Industrial Revolution, is the core, and subsequent industrialization is subdivided into semi-core type, semi-periphery type, and the fourth generation is subdivided into periphery type in order of difference in time relationship with the United Kingdom. A major feature of the Fourth Generation is that industrialization is subject to even stronger constraints due to the experience of colonial rule.

In this way, the international division of labor also changes with each generation. The first generation of British industrialization led to an international division of labor between consumer goods and primary commodities. In the countries of the second and third generations, the advent of modern industry led to an international division of labor between production goods and durable goods and primary commodities and consumer goods. The industrialization of the second half of the twentieth century, the fourth generation, gave rise to the international division of labor between production goods, durable consumer goods, and advanced technology products, and consumer goods, production goods, and durable consumer goods. Of course, the surrounding developing regions still have an international division of labor that exports consumer goods and primary commodities. Incidentally, the core technology of this industrialization will be addressed by the step-by-step invention, innovation, and learning identified by Amsden.

Kim also adds his interesting explanation of the industrialization of the fourth generation, which he explains: The fourth generation of industrialization in countries such as South Korea and Taiwan is a development of the "reverse Lewis mode". Sir William Arthur Lewis, a Nobel laureate in economics and economist born in the British Windward Islands, described poverty in the developing world through the mechanism of "unlimited supply of labor". The developing economy consists of a modern sector and a traditional sector, and the unlimited supply of labor from the traditional sector keeps wages at the subsistence level. He took advantage of this mechanism and made "unlimited supply of capital" a hallmark of the fourth generation of industrialization. However, he also wrote that the fourth generation of industrialization creates a tendency for "the infinite supply of labor to be reproduced by the very mechanism of foreign preference" (Kim -J, 1988: 60). In other words, foreign companies that participate in promoting industrialization have a stake in low-wage labor, so the low-wage reproduction structure continues. Kim's statement is close to the argument of dependency theory that the country is stuck in underdevelopment, but the 1980s should be taken into account due to the constraints of the times. It is important to note that the industrialization of East Asia is based on the inflow of companies from developed countries, as well as capital and technology.

And from there, the challenge is set to what will open up the prospect of moving from periphery to core. As shown in Table 7.5, Kim also corresponded to each generation of Kondratieff's long-term business cycle.

By the way, Amsden and Kim's theory of industrialization in developing countries at the end of the twentieth century is a theoretical framework in which the developing countries follow the developed countries to form a "national economy". However, for the author, the important results of both are the following. In the fourth generation, the industrialization of East Asia, the role of the state, as well as the exogenous factors of multinational corporations/foreign capital and technology of developed countries, were of critical importance. This was achieved under a new international division of labor that transcended national borders.

In fact, if we look at the relationship between industrialization and the market, the characteristics of the fourth generation become even clearer. The first generation of industrialization, the British cotton industry, was achieved historically by wool traders who prevented the import of calico from the British East India Company. That was the British Industrial Revolution. The industrialization of the countries of the second and third generations was also premised on the domestic market through protectionist import substitution policies. In other words, the industrialization from the first generation to the third generation is an industrialization model based on the home market. The import substitution model has historically been the orthodox development model.

However, as we have seen in Table 7.3, in the fourth generation of industrialization in the second half of the twentieth century, both socialist and import substitution, which inherited the traditional industrialization model, all failed. What has succeeded is the industrialization model, which depends on exports, that is, developed markets, and enlists the help of foreign companies, mainly multinational corporations. This model has the characteristics of the first industrialization in history, which is premised on export to the world market. Against the backdrop of the development of science and technology, the fourth generation of industrialization would mean that the relationship between developing countries and the world market was reversed in the latter half of the twentieth century. In industrialization up to the third generation, protectionist import substitution policies were important in achieving industrialization. In the fourth generation of industrialization, securing export markets and access to technology, along with various government policies, have been key factors in its success. The industrialization of developing countries has been achieved in conjunction with the international expansion of multinational corporations in the world economy. In this relationship, there is a power struggle between the ruling and the ruled sides.

It should be noted here that a qualitative change in the structure of the international division of labor is taking place. First of all, the change in the international competition of multinational coporations is described by management guru M. Porter who points out that there are two types of international competition patterns: (a) multidomestic and (b) global competition. The latter pattern emerged after World War II. He writes:

> Some competitors may be multinational firms, but their competitive advantages are largely confined to each country in which they compete. The international industry is a collection of essentially domestic industries, hence the term multidomestic./ At the other end of the spectrum are global industries, in which a firm's competitive position in one nation significantly affects (and is affected by) its position in other nations. Rivals compete against each other on a truly worldwide basis, drawing on competitive advantages that grow out of their entire network of worldwide activities./ Industries have increasingly become global in the post-World War II period (Porter, 1990: 52).

> In a global strategy, however, a firm can choose any nation in which to assemble products, fabricate components, or even conduct research, where advantage lies./ Locational advantages often apply to individual activities. One of the potent benefits a global firm enjoys is the ability to spread different activities among nations to reflect different preferred locations. Thus, components can be produced in Taiwan, software written in India, and basic R&D performed in Silicon Valley (Porter, 1990: 57).

Porter described the global competition of American and Japanese multinationals in East Asia as "to locate and manage the value chain for selling worldwide" using the term "'value chain". Actually, "many American firms produce in the Far East (virtually all American disk drives are produced there, for example), while Japanese competitors in the sewing machine, sporting goods, electronic components, and other industries are active investors in Korea, Hong Kong, Taiwanese, and now Thai production" (Porter, 1990: 57). East Asian countries basically created major industries by incorporating (or participating) in the R&D, international division of labor and production and sales of multinational corporations, and production networks.

Incidentally, the result was the crisis of the dismantling of the traditional, self-sustaining "'national economy". The late Y. Miyazaki, one of Japan's leading economists since the 1970s until 1990s and a professor at Kyoto University, wrote that Japan's "conventional economic framework that has been steadily constructed since the Meiji Restoration" is showing signs of collapse. After the bursting of the bubble economy at the end of the 1980s, the Japanese economy suffered the following upheavals: (a) the manufacturing industry was transferred to East Asia, and the full set of subsistence industrial structures in Japan was collapsing. (b) Imports of cheap products from abroad have led to price destruction, and the price-forming mechanism centered on the domestic market has ceased to function. (c) The macro policies of the Japanese government have ceased to function. He called it "the twilight of the national economy" (Miyazaki -J, 1995).

Japan's share of manufactured goods in imports rose dramatically from 24% in 1981 to 59% in 1995. In 1994, the ratio of overseas production of electrical equipment in Japan (overseas production / [domestic + overseas production]) was 78% for color televisions, 69% for stereos, 68% for microwave ovens, 53% for VTRs, and the transfer of overseas production was in full swing with a focus on AV products with low transportation costs (METI -J, 1996: 188). Moreover, a significant increase in Japan's imports occurred in intermediate goods and capital goods. In the 1995 period, based on 1990, the growth rate by goods was 2.3 times for machine parts, 2.1 times for capital goods, and 1.8 times for consumer goods (MITI -J, 1996: 153). Needless to say, the NIEs, China, and ASEAN countries were the main exporters of these goods. Japanese companies began to import intermediate goods for machine parts and production goods from subsidiaries in East Asian countries incorporated into GVCs, as well as local companies.

In other words, the developing countries of East Asia, such as the NIEs and ASEAN countries and China, promoted industrialization, but this was characterized by the development of a new generation/stage in the international division of labor that transcended the framework of a single country.

7.4 East Asia's Industrialization and the World Economy

Since the latter half of the 1980s, export-led industrialization, which began with the NIEs, has spread to ASEAN countries such as Malaysia, Thailand, Indonesia, Philippines, China, Vietnam, and Cambodia. Moreover, the sophistication of the industrial structure was observed rapidly. How do we understand this phenomenon? In neoclassical economics, technology is freely transferred and acquired on the basis of comparative advantage. In addition, technological innovation occurs in developed countries, and developing countries are regarded as mere host regions. In the first place, theories are abstracted, and there is no need for such concrete recognition.

However, technology is a crucial factor of production in international industrial transfers. Its importance has been increasing. R. Vernon developed the product cycle hypothesis by relating the global production arrangement of a company to the life cycle of technology. Fröbel et al.'s theory of the new international division of labor also made the fragmentation of production processes and labor due to technological development a condition for the transfer of industry to developing countries.

In fact, from the beginning, Asian NIEs such as South Korea and Taiwan consciously aimed to acquire technology, and actively introduced advanced technology and developed a policy of proficiency in it. The results of Amsden and Kim, published in the late 1980s and 1990s, confirmed the process of acquisition of advanced technologies from developed countries. In this section, we will first examine the development of East Asian countries in the world economy, focusing on the acquisition of technology and the development of local companies.

7.4.1 Dynamic Comparative Advantage and Technology Learning

Economic development is achieved on a technological basis consisting of tangible assets, intangible assets, and human skills. In developing countries, technology transfer or technology introduction, especially from developed countries, plays an important role. Therefore, the development of developing countries has been discussed from the perspective of transfer or acquisition, such as FDI, import of capital goods, technical cooperation, acquisition of patents, original equipment manufacturing (OEM), and migration of people. However, technology transfer is achieved in a dynamic relationship between the technology provider and the adapter. In the following, we will consider the introduction, mastery, and development of technology, mainly from the perspective of the receiving side.

First, let's look at the basic capabilities of developing countries that can make the difference between success and failure in technology adoption and mastery.

Table 7.6 shows the basic economic indicators of developing countries, focusing on the NIEs that achieved significant industrialization in the 1970s and 1980s. NIEs have high literacy rates and levels of education, science and technology in tertiary education, and vocational education in secondary education. NIEs also account for a high proportion of active investment in R&D, imports of capital goods in trade, and FDI introduction. India has a low literacy rate and school enrollment rate, and social disparities are remarkable. It can be said that these indicators were a constraint on development. In short, the ability to absorb technology is a prerequisite for technology introduction. In the long run, it is difficult to develop without human capital.

However, the basic conditions are not sufficient conditions for industrialization and development. In relation to technology transfer, Kim proposed the "technology double gap", saying that there are two technological gaps between developed and developing countries, although they have been considered to be one in the past. There is a gap between advanced technology and transfer technology, in which lower-level technology is transferred in technology transfer by companies in developed countries, and the other is the gap between the borrowed technology of the host side and the ability of the engineers to absorb it (Kim -J, 1988: 140–178). Developing countries must follow a course that approaches the advanced technologies of developed countries by improving their capacity to absorb them. He modeled technology transfer to developing countries from the perspective of NIEs.

Figure 7.4 shows the basic model of technical mastery drawn by him. The life cycle of technology is taken on the vertical axis, and for convenience is broken down into the following four periods: 1. Pioneering period, 2. Growth period, 3.Maturity period, and 4. Decline period. The level of technology learning is given on the horizontal axis, as follows: 1. technology introduction period, 2. digestion and absorption period, 3. Application and improvement period, and 4. R&D period. The vertical axis is from the developed countries that provide the technology, and the horizontal axis is from the developing countries that receive the technology, showing the relationship between dynamic technology transfer and proficiency.

Further explanation may be needed here. The state of the technology which is to be transferred by countries and companies is indicated by the Y-axis, The life cycle of technologies is depicted as starting from pioneering, growth maturity, and finally decline. and At the same time, there is the possibility that this technology will relocate overseas or to other companies. Then, for a certain technology, an iso technology curve can be drawn that is steadily decreasing. In addition, the curve will move downward as new technologies are developed and mastered. However, from the perspective of the host country, as shown by the X-axis, the technology introduced will increase the level of technical proficiency through experience and will move in the direction of enhancing its own development capabilities. At the same time, it

Table 7.6 Technology and R&D investment indices in developing countries with a focus on NIEs 1970s-1980s

	Total capital stock [a] 1980 = 100			Human capital in 1987 or near Enrollment rate				R&D investment amount (latest value) % of GDP	Technology inflow of GDP (%)		
				Literacy rate (%)	Secondary enrollment rate of school age (%)	par 100,000			Import of capital goods 1975 - 1987	FDI inflow	Technical cooperation
	1972	1988	Increase rate (%)			No. of science and engineering students at higher education [b]	No. of vocational students at the secondary level				
South Korea	21	239	11.4	88	89	765	1970	2.3	25.7	0.9	0.1
Taiwan	n.a	n.a	n.a	92	91	795	2082	1.1	33.2	3.3	n.a
Hong Kong	n.a	n.a	n.a	77	72	318	800	n.a	39.0	7.0	0.1
Singapore	25	169	6.8	83	69	704	372	0.9	88.4	16.8	0.3
Brazil	35	100	2.9	78	38	160	1092	0.4	8.7	3.5	0.1
Mexico	61	111	1.8	90	53	453	1051	0.6	21.0	3.5	0.1
Thailand	49	147	3	79	30	n.a	648	0.3	23.6	3.0	1.4
Malaysia	33	167	5.1	70	59	85	122	n.a	34.9	9.0	0.8
Indonesia	26	177	6.8	67	39	16	626	0.3	17.2	1.5	1.1
Philippines	62	71	1.1	83	64	770	n.a	0.1	29.3	1.5	1.1
India	63	165	2.6	41	35	n.a	80	0.9	8.6	0.2	0.4
Egypt	26	184	7.1	44	69	167	1833	0.2	62.0	14.6	6.4

(*Source* Lin, 1992: 83).
Note (a) Estimates. (b) Number of students enrolled in natural science, mathematics, computer science, engineering, transportation/communication courses.

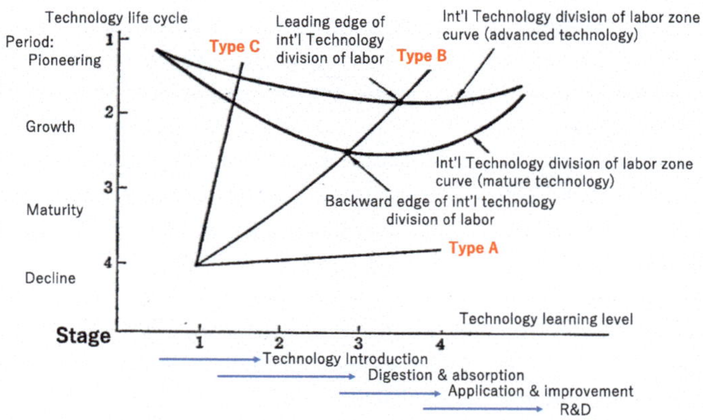

Fig. 7.4 Technology and R&D investment indices in developing countries with a focus on NIEs (*Source* Kim -J, 1988: 148, 162 Figs. 6.4 and 6.12)

will be possible to upgrade the introduction technology from standard technology to mature technology to advanced technology. It becomes a technology mastery curve that is steadily rising. Taken together, it is difficult to transfer advanced technologies at first, both on the transfer side and the introduction side. However, as mature technology becomes a standard technology, it becomes easier to transfer and learn, and development capabilities increase. Further along, relocation will be even easier. In this way, a U-shaped international transfer curve can be drawn. In other words, the barriers to transfer advanced international technology are high for both the transferee and the adopter, but on the other hand, standardized technology makes it easier for the introducer to become proficient and increases the development capability. The barriers to relocation will be lowered. Consequently, technology transfer in developed countries is divided into an iso technology curve that represents the advanced technology area (int'l advanced technology division of labor zone curve) and an iso technology curve toward maturity in the technology cycle (int'l mature technology division of labor zone curve), with the technology transfer zone in between (Kim -J, 1988: 142–162).

On the other hand, from the developing countries, there are typically three types of technical learning curves. Type A is a tracking curve that introduces the technology at the technology's decline period, and the receiving country can master the operation, production, and design techniques of the technology. This does not, however, lead to the transfer and development of the new technology. The technology learning curve is a curve that gently moves upward to the right, but never goes into the technology transfer zone.

Type B learning curve is "a case where the effect of increasing technical proficiency and promoting technology transfer is used to promote independent development and create a synergistic effect for the introduction of new technologies", and the curve is steadily upward. In other words, it is a path in which developed countries with a higher level of technology than the technical level of developing countries initially introduce and aim for mastery by introducing technologies that are in the process of maturing, repeatedly gain proficiency toward the introduction of more advanced technologies, gradually approach the acquisition of advanced technologies, and eventually lead to independence in technological development.

Type C learning curve is a case where "new technology is introduced" but the domestic mastery and indigenization are limited, and the country is almost an enclave, or it is a case of isolated production under the extreme control of a multinational corporation. The evolution to the learning process is limited, and the curve is sharply upward. As examples of each type, Kim cites India as Type A, South Korea as Type B, and Middle Eastern countries as Type C (Kim -J, 1988: 162–163). From the perspective of developing countries, the challenge is how to achieve the development of B type without falling into Types A and C.

In South Korea, the aim was to upgrade through the type-B industries as a national strategy. Of course, there were many difficulties in achieving this. A good example of Korea's heavy industrialization is the establishment of Pohang Iron and Steel Corporation (POSCO), but let's take a look at one example that is on the way to mastery. The number of internal proposals made within the company between 1974 and 1984 reached 25,534. However, it was not until the 1980s that the number of proposals increased dramatically. In 1980 there were 745 cases, in 1981 there were 1,085 cases, in 1982 there were 2,056 cases, in 1983 there were 8,756 cases, and in 1984 there were 12,635 cases. 98% of the proposals were implemented, and the breakdown of the cumulative number of proposals by breakdown was 37% related to equipment operation, 16% related to improving efficiency, 15% related to cost reduction, and 13% related to the environment and safety. The savings amounted to 44.43 billion won (fixed price in 1980) (Park -J, 1989: 180).

Incidentally, there are restrictions imposed by the provider in the introduction of technology. Kim identifies the constraints on technology adoption based on the results of a survey by the Federation of Korean Industries (FKI). Table 7.7 shows an excerpt from his table, and in the 1976–1984 survey, 39.6% of the respondents cited "market restrictions" and 23.4% "purchasing restrictions on parts and raw materials". Others were "proprietary development restriction on competitive technologies" at 13.4%, "grant back" at 13.0%, and "request for capital participation" at 8.3%. Chronological changes show that in the 1980s, regulations on the market and on suppliers of parts and raw materials increased, and the demand for capital participation also increased. Technology providers try to avoid the boomerang effect of the development of Korean companies. On the other hand, Korean companies have made various attempts to overcome these constraints at the policy level, at the corporate level, and even at the worker level.

The study is somewhat dated, but let's look at the case of Taiwan. In 1966, Taiwan was one of the first countries to establish an export processing zone in Kaohsiung to adopt a strategy of exporting labor-intensive products, but in 1980, Taiwan established a science park in Hsinchu and embarked on industrial sophistication through the formation of a high-tech industrial cluster. The Industrial Technology Research Institute (ITRI), founded in 1973, played a key role in the birth of Taiwan's high-tech enterprises. With ITRI, Taiwan has helped small and medium-sized enterprises

Table 7.7 Restrictive practices on South Korea's technology introduction

	Market restrictions	Purchasing restrictions on parts and raw materials	Request for capital participation	Proprietary development restrictions on competitive technologies	Grant back	Others	Total
1976	32.6	22.0	2.1	19.9	20.4	3.0	100.0
1980	39.6	20.9	5.5	12.1	15.4	6.6	100.0
1984	43.3	25.3	12.1	14.6	4.8	–	100.0
1976–1984 average	39.60	23.43	8.23	13.38	13.00	2.20	100.0

(*Source* Kim -J, 1988: 200).
Note Of all the data for 1976–1984, only 3 years are shown. But the average is based on all year data during 1976–1984.

(SMEs) improve their technological capabilities in semiconductor mounting, and at the same time, it has created a world-class Taiwanese company.

ITRI has acquired CMOS (complementary metal oxide semiconductor) manufacturing technology from the American firm, Radio Corporation of America (RCA, now the Technicolor SA) for a semiconductor mounting in the Science Park. In 1980, the company supported UMC's foundry business by relocating to United Microelectronics Corporation (UMC Lianhua Electronics), a firm located within the Science Park. ITRI also invited Morris Chang (Zhāng Zhōngmóu in Chinese name), who left Texas Instruments (TI) in 1984 after becoming the head of the semiconductor division of Texas Instruments (TI), to Taiwan as the head of ITRI a year later, and then established Taiwan in Hsinchu Science Park in 1987 Assisted Semiconductor Manufacturing Company (TSMC). Morris Chang has a wealth of experience in the U.S. semiconductor business, and he saw an opportunity in the high-demand foundry business of an emerging fabless venture in Silicon Valley (Soo -J, 2006: 236). ITRI, which also functions as an incubator for high-tech industries, has contributed to the formation of industrial clusters of semiconductor manufacturing in conjunction with companies.

Taiwan has nurtured a global foundry company, as well as a number of high-tech SMEs, including design houses. Thousands of scientists, mainly from the United States, gathered at the Science Park, creating a global semiconductor industrial cluster with a deep human network with Silicon Valley in the United States. Saxenian puts it this way:

> As the "brain drain" increasingly gives way to a process of "brain circulation", networks of scientists and engineers are transferring technology, skill and know-how between distant regional economies faster and more flexibly than most corporations (Saxenian, 2004: 164; Tzeng, 2006).

The acquisition of high-level human resources was also carried out as a policy in South Korea. In South Korea, the Korea Institute of Science and Technology (KIST) was established in 1966. In 1968, when a policy to support the return of scientists and engineers was adopted, a "reverse brain drain" from the United States occurred. According to an article in the Asian Wall Street Journal (April 24, 1989), 1,200 technologists have moved from the U.S. to South Korean government laboratories and universities since 1968, most of whom have returned since 1982. In the poverty of the 1950s and 1960s, talented people who went from Korea to the United States and other developed countries returned to their home countries at the stage of their own development and supported their development. The role played by the government in this process cannot be ignored (Yoon, 1992; Hirakawa -J, 1994: 48).

As mentioned above, the industrialization of Korea and Taiwan is not a simple development. The case includes various leaps and bounds that Amsden and Gereffi called dynamic comparative advantage. In any case, NIEs developed through exports. This was achieved under the international division of labor with companies in developed countries, and various attempts were made at the level of governments and corporations to support it, as well as at the level of managers and workers. However, the policies and corporate strategies differ in each country. The level of the political system will be briefly touched upon in the next section.

7.4.2 Global Value Chain and Development of Domestic Firms

The development of NIEs has been achieved through the international subcontracted production of developed companies. FDI of multinational corporations has played a major role in the development of East Asian countries, and at the same time has provided opportunities for development for local companies. The "new international division of labor" that Fröbel et al. focused on was certainly responsible for low-wage production processes, but it had a development effect on East Asian countries that went beyond that.

According to the late Liu Jinqing, a Taiwanese Professor Emeritus at Tokyo Keizai University, in the first half of the 1980s, foreign and local companies accounted for 20 percent of Taiwan's exports, and the remaining 80 percent were exports of Taiwanese companies, of which two-thirds were exports of small and medium-sized enterprises. Nearly 40 percent of electronics exports came from local OEMs, and footwear, sporting goods and handicrafts accounted for an even higher proportion(Liu, SK -J, 1989: 49, 58).

These international contracts and subcontracting relationships were the driving force behind the subsequent development of the NIEs. M. Hobday at University of Sussex, UK tracked the burgeoning export industries of South Korea, Taiwan, Singapore and Hong Kong, focusing on the enterprise level, and found that the above-mentioned international consignment and subcontracting relationships have become channels for local enterprises to become technical mastery and development.

Table 7.8 shows the development path of the local company that he advocated. Local companies in NIEs first learn the assembly process of standard goods and simple goods through original equipment manufacturers (OEM). At this stage, the TNC/buyer outsources production, provides technology and know-how, packages the produced products, and sells them under the brand. However, local companies eventually master this production technology and move to own-design manufacture or original design manufacturing (ODM). Local companies acquire product innovation skills and acquire design capabilities on their own. TNCs, on the other hand, buy products, add value to their own brands, and sell them. As technology proficiency progresses, local companies design and produce complex products on their own, conduct R&D, and even organize sales networks under their own brand names to add value and sell them. It is in the own-brand manufacture or original brand manufacturing (OBM) stage. An example of this is a bicycle manufacturing company in Taiwan. NIEs have achieved dramatic development as local companies have mastered the technology through international subcontracted production. At the time, Hobday foresaw the future relationship between local and multinational corporations:

> It would be wrong to overemphasize the difficulties facing the latecomers in the future. Some of these appear minor when compared with those already overcome since 1960. From a starting position of poverty and backwardness the four countries have become fast-growing, highly respected international competitors. Latecomer companies have built up impressive technological competencies, finally turned to the needs of the most demanding export markets./ Hundreds of latecomer firms have narrowed the gap and are poised to make further advances towards the technology frontiers (Hobday, 1995: 203-204).

Hobday uses Fig. 7.5 to compare the degree of government intervention in the four countries/economies of the NIEs with the degree of openness to FDI and imports, and confirms the diversity of the policies of each government. While Singapore aimed to attract foreign multinationals, Hong Kong aimed to attract small-scale local companies and opened its doors to multinational corporations. Despite these differences, the four NIEs were successful. He cites four common denominators as success factors.

Table 7.8 Transition of latecomers: From OEM to ODM to OBM[a]

	Technological transition	Market transition
OEM	Learns assembly process for standard, simple goods	Foreign TNC/buyer packages, brands and distributes
ODM	Local firms designs[b] Learns product innovation skills	TNC buys, brands and distributes TNC gains PPVA[c]
OBM	Local firms designs & conducts R&D for complex products	Local firm organizes distribution, own-brand name and captures PPVA[d]

(*Source* Hobday, 1995: 114).

Notes **a** OEM stands for original equipment manufacture (or original equipment manufacturing), ODM stands for own-design manufacture (or original-design manufacturing), and OBM stands for own-brand manufacture (or original-brand manufacturing). Applies to electronics and other fast growing export markets, such as footwear and bicycles. **b** PPVA stands for post-production value-added. **c** Or contributes to the design, alone or in partnership with the foreign company. **d** In bicycles, Taiwanese firms made the full transition to OBM, unlike electronics.

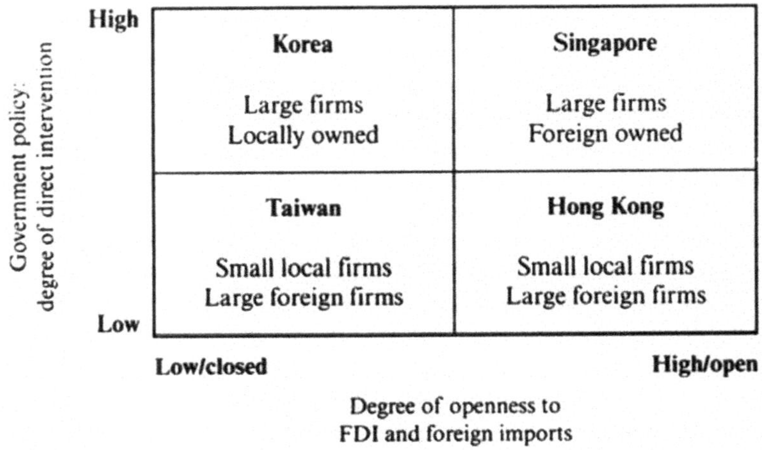

Fig. 7.5 NIEs' diversity of policy models (*Source* Hobday, 1995: 196)

(a) Governments' achieving macroeconomic stability by getting the basics right was a key factor. (b) The latecomers responded to the outward-looking, export-led industrial policies of each country. (c) Each NIE developed an appropriate educational and technological infrastructure. (d) Where and when necessary, governments intervened to ensure that the entrepreneurial base was strong enough to lead industrialization (Hobday, 1995: 198).

Each country and economy is constrained by historical conditions. Apart from that, it is difficult to enter the global international division of labor. It cannot be overlooked that there have been various attempts in this regard.

In fact, in the 1990s, a strategy to break away from the international subcontracting structure of low-value-added sectors became visible at the corporate level. In 1992, Stan Shih, founder of Acer, a Taiwanese EMS company, and his colleagues analyzed the value-added structure of traditional and computer industries to visualize the structure of the "smile curve". As shown in Fig. 7.6, the value chain structure of the Personal Computer (PC) industry has high added value in the R&D, parts, marketing, and sales departments of both left and right poles, and the assembly department in the center has the lowest structure. When he presented it in a keynote speech at the Acer Global Press Conference in 1993 (Acer News Release, Nov. 24, 2003), the smile curve began to attract worldwide attention. This is because it is a cognitive framework that is adaptable not only to the PC industry, but also to various industries, products, and the international division of labor.

The management strategy of Taiwan's PC industry is aimed at breaking away from this low-value-added sector. Acer as well as TSMC founder Morris Chang developed a corporate development strategy in line with Shih's smile curve philosophy (Huang, 2011). Both companies have created a new business model that links the manufacturing process, which is the bottom of value-added production, with R&D

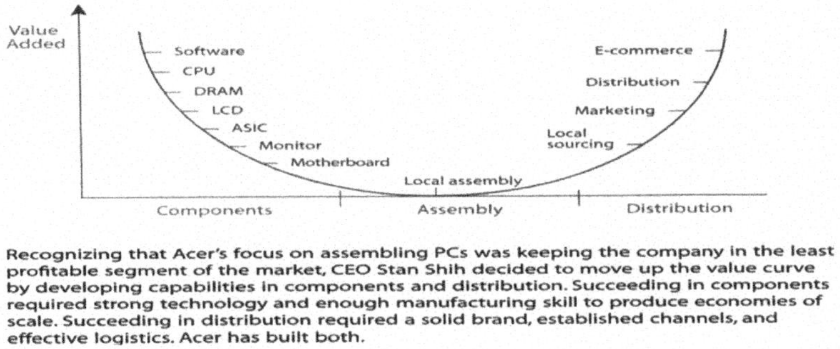

Fig. 7.6 Stan Shih' smiling curve. (*Source* Bartlett & Ghoshal, 2000: 136)

and after-sales service on the left and right. The two companies adopted a corporate strategy of not going to OBM but staying at the ODM stage and transforming into high-value-added companies. At the same time as mastering EMS, management resources were intensively invested in innovation of hardware, software, and services to add value.

Figure 7.7 shows the share of the global foundry market by company and country in 2020. In the high-tech industry, the outsourcing industry has already achieved corporate competitiveness. Taiwan's TSMC accounts for 54% of the global share of the semiconductor foundry market, followed by South Korea's Samsung with 17%. By country, Taiwan accounted for 63%, South Korea accounted for 18%, and the above two countries exceeded 80%. Obviously, the main players in the foundry market are not developed country companies. There are Taiwanese companies that go beyond mere contracting of the manufacturing process and have an advantage in the technological level and in the innovation of their business models. Incidentally, as of 2019, Taiwan holds 92% of the market share in the production of ultrafine logic ICs of 10 nm or less, and South Korea holds the remaining 8% (BCG/SIA, 2021: 35).

The structural changes that enabled the transformation of East Asian firms into high-value-added firms were theoretically developed by Gereffi and Fernandez-Stark. They say:

> In today's globalized economy with very complex industry interaction, the GVC methodology is a useful tool to trace the shifting patterns of global production, link geographically dispersed activities and actors within a single industry, and determine the roles they play in developed and developing countries alike./ providing a holistic view of global industries both from the top down and the bottle up (Gereffi & Fernandez-Stark, 2016: 6).

They organized the global and local research areas into six dimensions, as shown in Fig. 7.8 under the GVC theory.

At the level of research on the global economy/global economy, the following areas have been recognized: (1) the input–output structure of GVCs, (2) geographic scope, (3) governance structure: lead firms and industry organization, and at the level of local/national economy, (4) upgrading, (5) local institutional context, (6) The area

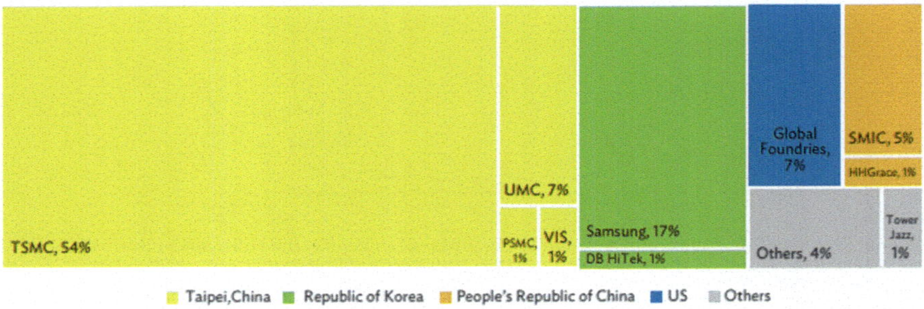

Fig. 7.7 Foundry market share tree map 2020. (*Source* ADB, 2022: 25). *Note* DB = Dongbu, HHGrace = Shanghai Huahong Grace Semiconductor Manufacturing Corp, PSMC = Powerchip Semiconductor Manufacturing Corporation, SMIC = Semiconductor Manufacturing International Corporation, UMC = United Microelectronics Corporation, US = United States, VIS = Vanguard International Semiconductor Corporation. TSMC is a semiconductor manufacturing company based in Taipei, China

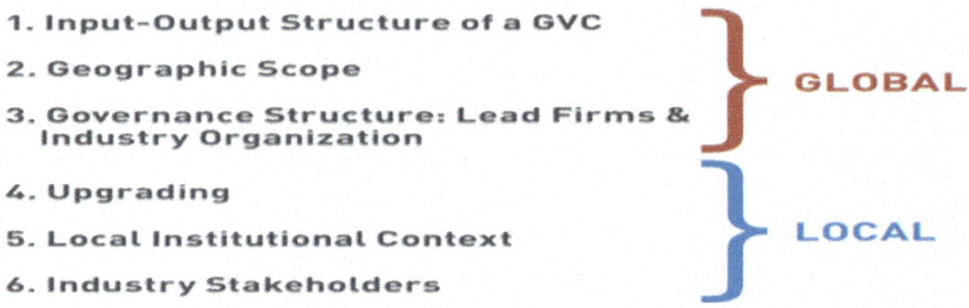

Fig. 7.8 Six dimensions of the GVC analysis (*Source* Gereffi & Fernandez-Stark, 2016: 7)

of industry stakeholders. As dimensions of (3) and (4), international relations between companies are typed from the perspective of governance.

Figure 7.9 shows the relationship between buyers and suppliers organized by Gereffi et al. into 5 types from the perspective of "governance": Market, modular, and relational. Captive, and hierarchy. These types are "determined by three variables: the complexity of the information shared between actors in the chain; how the information for production can be codified; and the level of supplier competence" (Gereffi, Humphrey & Sturgeon, 2005: 87; Gereffi and Fernandez-Stark, 2016: 10; Inomata, 2017). In the figure, as we move more to the right, the stronger the dominance of the lead company, and the more to the left, the stronger the bargaining power of the supplier. The power relationship between the lead company and the supplier company determines the type of governance. There are five types.

Market: "information on product specifications is easily transmitted, and suppliers can make products with minimal input from buyers. These arms-length exchanges require little or no formal cooperation between actors and the cost of switching to new partners is low for both producers and buyers".

Module: "governance occurs when complex transactions are relatively easy to codify". "This keeps switching costs low and limits transaction-specific investments,

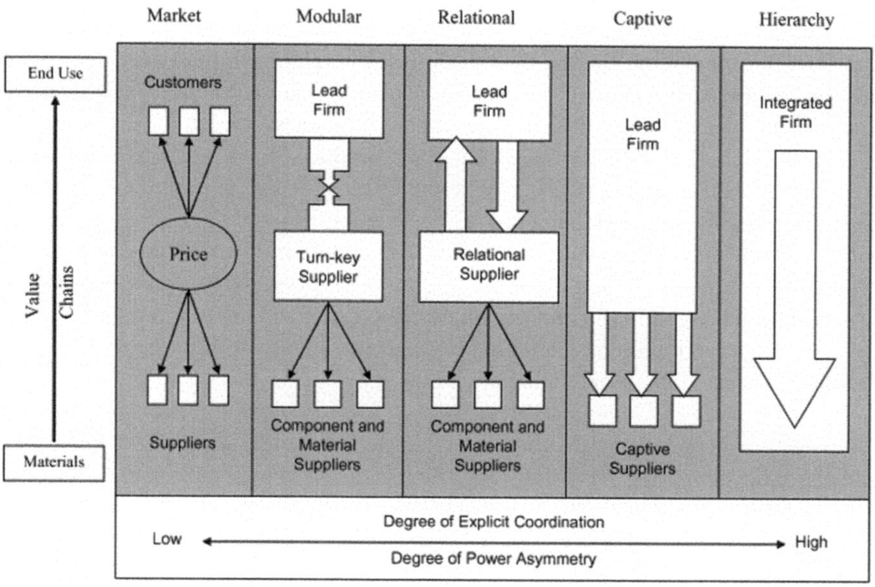

Fig. 7.9 Five global value chain governance types (*Source* Gereffi, Humphrey & Sturgeon, 2005: 89)

even though buyer–supplier interactions can be very complex. Information technology and standards for exchanging information are both key to the functioning of modular governance".

Relational: "governance occurs when buyers and sellers rely on complex information that is not easily transmitted or learned". "relational linkages take time to build, so the costs and difficulties required to switch to a new partner lend to be high".

Captive: "The power asymmetry in captive networks forces suppliers to link to their buyer under conditions set by, and often specific to, that particular buyer, leading to thick tiers and high switching costs for both parties".

Hierarchy: "This usually occurs product specifications cannot be codified, products are complex, or highly competent suppliers cannot be found. While less common than in the past, this sort of vertical integration remains an important feature of the global economy" (Gereffi & Fernandez-Stark, 2016: 10–11).

The increase in the competitiveness and bargaining power of developing countries is regarded as "upgrading", which determines the allocation of value added. In line with this framework, they conduct empirical analyses of bicycles, apparel, fresh vegetables, and the U.S. electronics industry, and seek policy upgrading in developing countries (Gereffi, 2015; Stancy & Gereffi, 2016; Bamber, Lucas et al., 2017).

The development of ICT, governed by Moor's Law,[8] dramatically changed the economies and societies of not only developed countries but also emerging and

[8] Moor predicted that the density of semiconductors would double every year, which became known as Moor's law, but it was not until 1965 that he published the rule of thumb (Moor 1965).

developing countries at the end of the twentieth century, and has further accelerated technological innovation into this century. The power relationship between the parties involved in a business changes drastically depending on the nature of the industry and product, as well as the choice of a company's business model.

The mobile phone industry is a case in point. In the early 1990s, Japanese brands dominated the PC market. The CPU was supplied by Intel, but the company turned the CPU into a module and made it a black box, standardized the interface between the parts, and sold it to a Taiwanese company. The adoption of Intel's business model of making it a platform has expanded the mobile phone market, and the market structure has changed in the blink of an eye. Intel's choice made it possible. These changes are occurring or are beginning to occur in a variety of industries, including the automotive and the semiconductors industries.

Now, Taiwanese PC manufacturers have evolved into a comprehensive supplier company by specializing in EMS and enhancing technological innovation capabilities in design, development, marketing, logistics, etc. through subcontracting of brand manufacturers (Inomata -J, 2019: 162–163). At the same time, these innovations in business models have led to the transfer of low-value-added production processes to China, making China the world's "factory".

From 1999 to 2002, foreign production accounted for 27% of Taiwanese exports of information and communication equipment. From 2011 to 2014, it accounted for 86.6%, and domestic production fell slightly to 13.4%. Most of the overseas production is done in China. Taiwan's exports of all industries fell sharply from 84.6% to 48.6% during the same period. In the 2010s, more than half of Taiwanese companies' exports were produced in China (Liu CJ, 2017: 200).

In addition, the monopoly structure of Taiwan and South Korea in the production of state-of-the-art microfabricated CPUs in the foundry market is creating a new competition for added value in GVC. Since the 1990s, new Asian companies have emerged one after another as global companies, and the nature of market competition has begun to change dramatically. There has also been a dramatic change in the international arrangement of production. But this time it brings about a new change. We'll look at this in the next section, but before we get to that, let's look at another theoretical innovation.

R. Baldwin explained the development and structural changes in East Asian countries since the 1990s with an original interpretation of changes in globalization. As discussed in Chap. 11 of this book, he argued in the early 1800s that the Steam Revolution and the subsequent Industrial Revolution divided the world into industrial and agricultural countries by allowing for a sharp reduction in the cost of trade, which he called the First Unbundling. Then, in the 1990s, the Second Unbundling occurred. Revolution in information and communication technology (ICT) has enabled fractionalization of the production process and/or slicing up the value chain. The drastic decline in communication costs removed the spatial constraints of the production process, leading to industrial relocation to developing countries. It is said that the "convergence" of the world economy has begun again.

Baldwin explains this change in the economic structure of world history from the change in the share of the seven industrialized countries and China + India.

Figure 7.10 shows this. According to this, the G7 and China + India had a share of 7 and 51% respectively in the Year 1000. However, after 1820, the share of the G7 soared and the share of China + India plummeted. In 1990, however, the trend was reversed again. The share of the G7 begins to plummet, and conversely, China + India soars. He describes this change as follows:

> For developing nations that could attract G7 production networks, the second unbundling was a true revolution. The technology transfer that everyone had hoped for in the 1970s, 1980s, and 1990s was finally happening – but not the way twentieth-century development theory said it would. Instead of building the whole supply chain domestically to become competitive internationally (the twentieth-century way), developing nations were joining global value chains to become competitive and then industrializing by densifying their participation (Baldwin, 2016: 217).

Baldwin's explanation of the development of developing East Asian countries as gaining international competitiveness through participation in global value chains, rather than the development theory of orthodox economics, which considers the development of developing East Asian countries to be the same as the construction of domestic supply chains, is convincing as a theoretical and empirical conclusion. However, the transition could be a little earlier. If you look at Fig. 7.10, you can see that the decline in the G7 market share began before 1990. His explanation for this remains ambiguous.

From Tables 7.9 and 7.10, it can be seen that the international division of labor by FDI in the electric/electronic industry in Japan in the 1960s–1970s was close to the division of labor structure described by Baldwin. During this period, Japan's major textile, clothing, and miscellaneous goods industries, as well as electrical and electronic product manufacturers, began to invest overseas. In addition, FDI for offshore purposes was rapidly increasing in FDI for electrical component manufacturing companies. In particular, more than 80% of FDI for local markets was aimed at direct or indirect exports, especially for electrical and electronic component manufacturers.

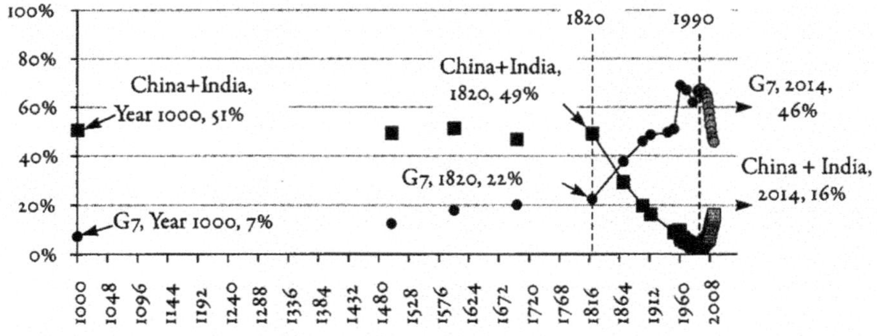

Fig. 7.10 Spot the phase transition: World GDP shares, year 1000 to 2014 (*Source* Baldwin, 2016: 81). *Notes* Data source is from World Bank database (GDP in U.S. dollars) and Maddison database (2009 version), pre-1960 with Baldwin's calculation). G7 stands for the United States, Germany, Japan, France, England, Canada, and Italy

Table 7.9 Japan's overseas investments of major electric/electronic product assembly firms by investment pattern 1960s–1974

		1960s		1970–1974						1960s–1974
		First half	Second half	1970	1971	1972	1973	1974	Total	Total
Purpose of FDI	a) Domestic market	8	13	5	7	3	0	3	18	39
	b) Domestic market & export	4	3	0	0	0	3	0	3	10
	c) Export	0	9	2	4	3	9	2	20	29
	Total	12	25	7	11	6	12	5	41	78
	b+c)/Total (%)	33.3	48.0	28.6	36.4	50.0	100.0	40.0	56.1	50.0

(*Source* Sekiguchi -J, 1976: 45).
Note *Major product assembry firms include Matsushita (present Panasonic), Hitachi, Sanyo, Mitsubishi electric and others.

In the latter half of the 1960s, mainly American multinational corporations such as Philco Ford, Admiral, RCA, Motorola, and Zenith, produced electrical and electronic equipment in the NIEs in East Asia and Mexico, and began to export them back to the United States (Helleiner, 1973: 28–31). FDI from the industry in Japan was a response to the international expansion of such American multinational companies (Sekiguchi -J, 1976: 11; Hirakawa -J, 1992: 73–85).

Baldwin's division of stage level and/or job level in production process was already confirmed in the international expansion of Japan's electric/electronic industry in the 1960s, when Fröbel et al. called it NIDL (Sekiguchi -J, 1976; Hirakawa -J, 1979: 232–237). It can be said that the fragmentation of production, which appears to be the accelerated development of ICT in the 1990s, proceeded smoothly because of this historical background. It also gave local industries opportunities to develop through a variety of channels.

In this regard, it can be seen that the question that arises in Fig. 7.9 used by Baldwin was born from the representation of the share of the developing region by China + India. The share of China + India alone will overshadow the development of the NIEs and other emerging East Asian economies. This would be indirectly reflected in the decline in the G7's share from the 1960s to the 1990s. Incidentally, there is a similar problem with the rise in the share of the G7 from the fifteenth century to 1820. The figure does not explain the upward trend of share in Europe. This is because the process of European domination of the world has begun with the expropriation of other developing regions.

In any case, the above points do not have a significant impact on the development of ICT and the theory of the second unbundling. Fröbel et al. also cited the development of IT and transportation technologies as the basis for the emergence of the NIDL. The

Table 7.10 Overseas investment patterns of Japan's electric/electronic component manufacturers 1962–1974 (Component number)

	Electric condenser			Electrical resister			Transformer coil			Audio components (Speaker · earphone etc.)			Mechanical device			Electron tube			Semi-conductor			Total		
	A1	A2	B	A1	A2	B	A1	A2	B	A1	A2	B	A1	A2	B	A1	A2	B	A1	A2	B	A1	A2	B
1962–65	2	2	2	0	0	0	0	4	3	0	2	3	0	0	2	0	0	0	2	0	0	4	7	11
1966–70	9	7	0	4	1	2	3	3	3	9	1	1	5	0	2	1	4	0	7	1	0	38	23	8
1971–1974	18	12	0	9	2	2	21	7	0	10	4	1	11	2	1	5	2	2	6	2	1	80	31	8
A. Offshore type																								
A1	29			13			24			19			16			6			15			122		
A2		20			3			14			7			8			6			3			61	
Total A	49			16			38			26			24			12			18			183		
A/(A+B) %	91%			80%			86%			84%			83%			92%			95%			87%		
Total	54			20			44			31			29			13			19			210		

(*Source* Sekiguchi, -J. 1976: 58–59. The table shows the data by year. Organized by the author).

Note 1. A: offshore type, **A1:** export to Japan and third countries. **A2:** entry into the market for finished products for export. B: local market type.

2. The total number of items is for the amount of entry that is known to the contents, and not for locally produced items by all the companies in the market.

acceleration of ICT began in the 1990s, but structural changes in the global economy began to occur in the 1960s. It seems safe to assume that Baldwin's turning point began in the 1960s and 1970s.

7.4.3 The Technological Development of NIEs and Economic "Upgrading"

As we see in Chap. 2 of this book, in the 1990s, there was a lot of interest in the economic integration of East Asian countries and the emergence of a middle class. Table 2.3 also points out that the spatial relationship between global production and consumption has led to a new stage of development in emerging economies, particularly in East Asia. In other words, developing countries in East Asia have moved from the export-led investment (NIEs) type of development stage to the potentially bigger market economy investment (PoBMEs) type of development stage.

In fact, since the 1990s, and especially since the beginning of this century, middle-class people in emerging economies have begun to assert themselves by rapidly increasing their incomes, even though their consumption levels are quantitatively and qualitatively lower than those of developed countries. Multinational corporations in developed countries began to view the markets of the BRICs, ASEAN and emerging economies as promising markets for the future, and began to develop new entry strategies for emerging economies. It is symbolic that all of the world's automobile companies have begun to expand into China. And in this market, a cluster of local companies had begun to grow.

In the fields of economics and business administration, we became interested in the sources of competitiveness in emerging countries, especially East Asia. In the early 2010s, Tomoo Marukawa, a professor at the University of Tokyo, called it "catch-down" technological progress (innovation) to refer to the special technological developments in developing countries that have occurred since the turn of the century. He proposed the term as a neologism to refer to technological progress in which "companies from less developed countries have become the implementers", "a type of technological progress that is different from the technological catch-up of conventional developing countries (which has been happening in China and India in recent years)" (Marukawa -J, 2014: 49).

He focused on the launch of the Nano passenger car developed by India's Tata conglomerate in 2009, video CDs in China, which were largely forgotten by technological progress in developed countries, guerrilla mobile phones ("Shānzhài shǒujī"), which attracted dramatic attention for a period of time at the turn of the century, and the dramatic spread of products such as electric bicycles and anime products. These manufacturing technologies did not catch up with the technologies of developed countries, but on the contrary, they were products based on older technologies in terms of generations, but it was a fact that they could be established as a business in the local market. For a period of time around the 2010s, Yamazaite machines were exported from the Middle East to India, Southeast Asia, Latin America and Africa. Its sales volume exceeded 200 million units, and at its peak, the number of smartphone mobile phone manufacturers was said to be 2,000 or 3,000, and its global market share was 15% (Tei -J, 2013; Takase & Takaguchi -J, 2020: 136).

The center of this production was Shenzhen, China. In 1978, when China began its reform and opening up, Shenzhen was designated as a special economic zone, and the population increased dramatically from 314,000 in 1979 to 13,438,800 at the end of 2019. Initially, production in this special economic zone was on the condition called PMACT (i.e. processing with supplied materials, manufacturing with supplied drawings and samples, assembling with supplied parts and compensation trade). In 1983, Sanyo Electric, a Japan company, entered the market, and in 1984, the company established a joint venture, Huaqiang Sanyo, to produce radios, radio cassettes, tape recorders, and other products. In 1985, Epson built a printer factory. In 1989, Hitachi established Seg Hitachi and began producing radios and radio cassettes. In the 1990s, South Korea's Samsun built a large-scale factory in Huizhou City, next to Shenzhen, and Foxconn Technology, a subsidiary of Taiwan's Hon Hai, built a large-scale factory in Shenzhen, and Shenzhen grew into a world industrial cluster for electronic products.

In 2003, Taiwanese company MediaTek sold a set of system-on-chip (SoC) and firmware for future phones, and countless companies in Shenzhen began to use the chips to make large quantities of low-quality but low-cost mobile phones. They were called "Shanzhai" mobile phones because they were mostly counterfeit goods, unlicensed and unbranded goods. Shanzhai is a word that means "mountain fortress" or "mountain camp" (Takase and Takaguchi eds. -J, 2020: 134–135).

Shanzhai Mobile phones began to boom in the 2010s. However, in the second half of the 2010s, Shenzhen's assessment changed 180 degrees. It will become regarded as the most innovative industrial cluster in the world. "With the rise of smartphones, most of the Shanzhai manufacturers have fallen, but there are also cases where they have developed into large companies" (Fujioka & Takaguchi -J, 2020: 136).

Marukawa notes the exceptionally high number of patents in Shenzhen. In 2014, the number of patents in China reached 31,077, following 78,129 in Beijing and 39,133 in Shanghai. There is a strong correlation between the number of university faculty members in each province in China and the number of invention patent applications (R2 = 0.78). However, in Shenzhen, there are only two universities, and the number of invention patents is 46 times higher than the theoretical value. He concludes that the large number of invention patents in Shenzhen cannot be explained by local resources, and that it is the convenience of being able to concentrate various resources such as human resources, funds, parts, and materials from home and abroad, including smuggling (Marukawa -J, 2017).

A paper co-authored by Junichi Fujioka, a Japan contract company manager in Shenzhen, states that as Shenzhen developed as an industrial city, "as a result of the relocation of low-value-added factories to the suburbs, a dual ecosystem of the core responsible for innovation and the outer periphery responsible for manufacturing was completed. By flexibly using methods that are different from Western-style IP management, an ideal environment for the manufacturing industry has been created" (Fujioka & Takaguchi -J, 2020: 147–148).

Drawing on the work of Kai Kajitani, a Chinese economic researcher in Japan, he points out the coexistence of three different layers of intellectual property rights. The first is the "modern layer" that utilizes intellectual property rights represented by patents. This includes global telecommunications equipment manufacturers Huawei, ZTE, Xiaomi, and OPPO. Then there is the "pre-modern layer" that ignores intellectual property rights. Emerging manufacturers that appear one after another in Shenzhen, such as Shanzhai makers. Lastly, there is the "postmodern layer" that seeks to promote innovation through the involvement of various people, rather than surrounding technology with patents. The mixture of these various companies has created a tremendous and innovative industrial cluster (Fujioka & Takaguchi -J, 2020: 140).

Needless to say, there are government incentives giving birth to new companies. In 2014, Shuāng chuàng (Establishment of the Masses) policy[9] was introduced, and subsidies for venture companies were introduced. Through local government funds, venture companies obtained investments (Fujioka & Takaguchi -J, 2020: 140, 156).

What we would like to draw attention to here is that China's growing domestic market has become a foundation for innovation and has given rise to companies that are globally competitive. In addition, these companies are gaining competitiveness by flexibly utilizing the system of technological hegemony in developed countries. This dramatic shift from the so-called "Shanzhai" mobile phone to the "Shenzhen phenomenon" does not occur anywhere in East Asia. However, it can be said that this is a contemporary characteristic of the development of R&D and innovation at the PoBMEs stage.

Incidentally, while Taiwan, South Korea, and China have joined the group in the development of advanced technologies, the development of ASEAN countries is heavily dependent on the FDI of multinational corporations, and the formation of domestic innovation ability has been delayed. However, a strong correlation between economic growth and domestic innovation capability has been observed in developing countries, and the importance of the role of governments in the accumulation of innovation ability has been recognized. UNCTAD also emphasizes the importance of technology in development (Singh, 2007: 429). In the development of developing countries, including ASEAN countries, the experience of East Asia, starting with the Asian NIEs, must be learned.

[9] "Shuāng chuàng" is an abbreviation for "Mass Entrepreneurship and Mass Innovation", and is said to be an initiative proposed by Premier Li Keqiang of the State Council at the Davos Conference in September 2014.

7.5 Concluding Remarks

In this chapter, Various approaches to industrialization and economic development in East Asia, starting with the East Asian NIEs, were introduced and examined in three main categories. From there, it was confirmed that industrialization and development were not limited to the dimension of export-led policies, but that the role of the government was significant, and at the same time, it was related to the global production activities of companies in developed countries. Through comparisons with various development attempts in the world in the latter half of the twentieth century, we highlighted the characteristics of industrialization and development within a global network, which are different from existing experiences. Since the turn of the century, this feature has been confirmed by the emergence of new theories.

The development of this developing region, as the term BRICs emerged in this century, is understood in terms of China and India, among others, and can be traced back to the industrialization and development of the Asian NIEs since the 1960s. This led to the industrialization of the PoBMEs stage to this day, as described in Chap. 3. In this development, the importance of technical mastery and accumulation has been pointed out, and at the same time, the importance of innovation, including business models, has been noted.

How do we understand the relationship between development and governments in the world economy and the global economy, and the relationship between the world economy and the economies of each country? As was shown in the previous section, Greffi et al. indicated research areas at both the global and local levels. In other words, the industrialization and development of emerging economies can only be achieved by connecting the two levels of the world economy and the national economy.

In this respect, governments in developing countries can basically only develop their policies within the framework of their borders. Hegemons and their allies have an advantage over their own companies in the establishment of international rules, but developing countries do not have such power. They have no choice but to adopt a support policy that opens up the upgrading channel in accordance with the rules, given the global networks of GVCs. This must be achieved even in the face of fierce international competition.

To reiterate, it is important to recognize that the development of East Asian countries today has reached the stage of export-led development in the second half of the twentieth century, as well as the historical generational recognition that Kim called the fourth generation. The same is true for emerging economies and the developing countries that are following suit. On the premise of entering a new global division of labor, an export-led industrialization policy that properly recognizes the role of the government must be sought. The industrialization and development of emerging Asian economies is entering a new stage, including regionalist international cooperation, as discussed in Chap. 9.

References

*Documents with a symbol (-J) after the author's name are Japanese documents

ADB. (2022). Asian economic integration report 2022: Advancing digital services trade in Asia and the Pacific. Metro Manila: Asian Development Bank.

Acer News Release. (2003). Acer's Stan Shih: Empowering technology—Making your life easier, November 24.

Abegglen, James, C. (1994). *Sea change: Pacific Asia as the new world industrial center*. The Free Press.

Akamatsu Kaname -J. (1944). Keizai shin chitsujo no keisei genri (Principles of formation of a new economic order). Tokyo: Rison Sha, July.

Akamatsu, K. -J. (1965). *Sekai keizai ron (The world economy)*. Kunimoto Shobo.

Amin, S. (1976). *Unequal Development*. Monthly Review Press.

Amsden, Alice, H. (1989). *Asia's next giant: South Korea and late industrialization*. Oxford University Press.

Amsden, A.H. (1991). Diffusion of development: The late-industrializing model and greater East Asia. *The American Economic Review*, *81*(2) (May).

Gerschenkron, Alexander. (1962). *Economic backwardness in historical perspective: A book of essays*. Belknap Press of Harvard University Press.

Baba, Hiroji -J. (1991). Gendai sekai no nihon kaisya-shugi (The contemporary world and Japan's company-ism). *Institute of Social Science*, University of Tokyo (ed) Gendai nihon shakai (Contemporary Japanese society). Tokyo: University of Tokyo Press.

Baba, Hiroji -J. (1995). Sekai taisei ron to dankai ron (World System Theory and Stage Theory). In Kudo, A. ed. *Nijisseiki shihonshugi (Capitalism in the 20th century)*. The University of Tokyo Press.

Baba, H.-J. (1997). *Shin shihonshugi ron: Shikaku tenkan no keizaigaku (New capitalism: The economics of altered perspectives)*. Nagoya University Press.

Balassa, B. (1981). *The newly industrializing countries in the world economy*. Pergamon Press.

Balassa, B. (1985). The role of foreign trade in the economic development of Korea. In: Galenson, Walter (ed) Foreign trade and investment: Economic development in the newly industrializing Asian countries. Wisconsin: the University of Wisconsin Press.

Baldwin, Richard. (2016). The great convergence: Information technology and the new globalization. *Cambridge, Massachusetts, and London: Belknap Press of Harvard University Press*.

Bamber Penny, Jack Daly, Gary Gereffi. (2017). The Philippines in the coffee global value chain. *Center on Globalization, Governance & Competitiveness, Duke University*.

Bamber Penny, Lukas Brun, Stacey Frederick, Gary Gereffi. (2017). Global value chains and economic development. *Joint Project between Global Value Chain Center (GVCC), Duke University and Korea Institute for Industrial Economics & Trade (KIEP)*.

Bartlett Christpher A, Ghoshal Sumantra. (2000). Lessons from late movers, Harvard Business Review, March-April.

BCG/SIA. (2021). Strengthening the global semiconductor supply chain in an uncertain era. Boston Consulting Group/ Semiconductor Industry Association, April. https://web-assets.bcg.com/9d/64/367c630944l1b6e9e1407bec0dcc/bcgxsia-strengthening-the-global-semiconductor-value-chain-april-2021.pdf.

Bernard Mitchell, John Ravenhill. (1995). Beyond product cycles and flying geese: Regionalization, hierarchy, and the industrialization of East Asia. *World Politics*, *47*(2).

Blomqvist, Hans, C. (1997). *Economic interdependence and development in East Asia*. Praeger.

Bradford Jr, Colin, I. (1982). The rise of the NICs as exporters on a world scale. In: Turner, Louise, Neil McMullen et al. eds., The newly industrializing countries: Trade and adjustment, London, Boston: Allen & Unwin for the Royal Institute of International Affairs.

Bradford Jr, Colin, I., & Branson, William, H. (eds). (1987). Overview. In: Bradford Jr, C.I, & Branson WH (eds). Trade and structural change in Pacific Asia. The University of Chicago Press.
Breen, Michael. (2011). Men of Steel: The founding history of POSCO, The Korean Times, February 6.
Cumings, Bruce. (1984). The origins and development of the Northeast Asian political economy: Industrial sectors, product cycles, and political consequences. *International Organization, 38*(1), Winter.
De Backer, Koen. (2011). Global value chains: Preliminary evidence and policy issues. OECD DSTI/IND (2011)3 For Official Use.
Economic Planning Board, Japan -J. (1994). Sekai keizai hakusho (White paper on the world economy). Tokyo: Okura Sho Insatsukyoku (Printing Office of Ministry of Finance).
Ernst, Dieter. (2006). Searching for a new role in East Asian regionalization: Japanese production networks in the electronics industry. In: Katzenstein, Peter J, and Takashi Shiraishi (eds) Beyond Japan: The dynamics of East Asian Regionalism. Ithaca and London: Cornell University Press.
Frank, Andre, G. (1966). *The Development of Underdevelopment*. New England Free Press.
Frank, A. G. (1967). *Capitalism and Underdevelopment in Latin America*. Monthly Review Press.
Fröbel Folker. (1982). The current development of the world-economy: Reproduction of labor and accumulation of capital on a world scale. *Review, 5*(4) (Spring).
Folker, F., Jürgen, H., & Otto, K. (1977). *Die neue international Arbeitsteilung: Strukturelle Arbeitslosigkeit in den Industrieländern und die Industrialisierung der Entwicklungsländer*. Rowohlt Taschenbuch Verlag GmbH.
Fröbel, F., Heinrichs, J., & Kreye, O. (1980). *The new international division of labour*. Cambridge University Press.
Fujioka, J., & Takaguchi, K. -J. (2020). "*Haado-uea no seichi*" "*Shinsen no himitsu*" *(Holy land of Hardware, the secret of Shenzhen)*. In: Takasu, M., & Takaguchi, K. -J (Eds.). Puroto taipu shiti: Gurobaru inobesyon to Shinsen (Prototype City: Global innovation taking place in Shenzhen), Kadokawa.
Gereffi, Gary. (1989). Rethinking development theory: Insights from East Asia and Latin America. *Sociological Forum, 4*(4).
Gereffi, G. (2015). Global value chains, development and emerging economies. Research, statistics and industrial policy branch Working Paper 18/2015, Vienna: UNIDO.
Gereffi, G., Humphrey John, Sturgeon Timothy. (2005). The governance of global value chains. *Review of International Political Economy, 12*(1).
Helleiner, G.K. (1973). Manufactured exports from less-developed countries and multinational firms. *The Economic Journal, 83*(329).
Henderson, J. (1989). *The globalization of high technology production*. Routledge.
Hirakawa, H. -J. (1979). 'Chushinkoku' no yushutsu shiko gata kogyoka to nihon shihon (Export-oriented industrialization in 'middle-advanced countries' and Japanese capital. *Meiji Business Review, 25*(2).
Hirakawa, H. -J. (1992). NIES: Sekai shisutemu to kaihatu (NIEs: World system and development), Tokyo: Dobunkan.
Hirakawa, H.-J. (1994). Higashi ajia NIEs ni okeru kogyoka: Gijutu hatten to kokusai gijutsu iten (Industrialization in Asian NIEs: Technology development and international technology transfer). In: Hirakawa H and Park Ilu (eds) Ajia NIEs: Tenkanki no Kankoku, Taiwan, HonKon, Shingaporu (Asian NIEs: South Korea, Taiwan, Hong Kong, and Singapore in transition). Kyoto: Sekai Shiso Sha.
Hirakawa, H.-J. (1997). Higashi ajia kogyoka dainamizumu no ronri (The logic of industrialization in East Asia. In: Kasuya, S (ed) Higashi ajia kogyoka dainamizumu (Industrialization dynamism in East Asia). Tokyo: Hosei Daigaku Shuppan Kyoku.
Hirakawa, H. (1999). East Asia's industrialization and the currency and financial crises within the world economy. *Journal of International Economic Studies*, 13.
Hobday, Michael. (1995). *Innovation in East Asia: The challenge to Japan*. Edward Elgar.

Hori, Kazuo -J. (1994a). Shokuminchi no dokuritsu to kougyo no sai hensei-Taiwan to kankoku no jirei (Colonial independence and industrial reorganization: The cases of Taiwan and South Korea) In: Nakamura, S. (ed.) Higashi ajia shihon shugi no keisei: Hikakushi no shiten kara (The formation of East Asian capitalism: From the perspective of comparative History. Tokyo: Aoki Shoten.

Hori, K.-J. (1994b). Higashi ajia NICs seiritsu no jouken (Conditions for establishing East Asian NICs (Newly industrializing countries), Kyoto University/Kyungpook National University, Korea, Joint Academic Symposium "Structure of East Asian capitalism", Kyoto University, Kyodai Kaikan, December 13–14.

Huang, Tien-Lin. (2011). Editorial: The 'smile curve' and the import of quality. Taipei Times, April 1, 2011.

Imaoka, H. Ohno, K., & Yokoyama, H. -J. (eds.) (1985). Chushinkoku no kogyo hatten: Fukusengata seicho no ronri to jissyo (Industrial development in middle-advanced countries: Theory and proof of dual-track growth). *Tokyo: Institute of Development Economies (IDE).*

Inomata, Satoshi. (2017). Analytical frameworks for global value chains: An overview. In: GVC development report 2017, *World Bank.*

Inomata, S.-J. (2019). Gurobaru baryu cheene (Global value chains). Tokyo: Nihon Keizai Shimbun Sha.

Itagaki, H. -J. (1997). Nihonteki Keiei/ Seisan shisutemu to higashi ajia (The Japanese management/ production system and East Asia). Kyoto: Mineruve Shobo.

Johnson, Chalmers. (1985). Political institutions and economic performance: The government-business relationship in Japan, South Korea, and Taiwan. In: Scalapino, Robert A, Sato S, and Watanabe J (eds) Asian economic development: Present and future, Institute of East Asian Studies, California: University of California.

Kasahara, Shigehisa. (2004). The flying geese paradigm: A critical study of its application to East Asian regional development, UNCTAD Discussion Papers (Munich Personal RePEc Archive *MPRA Paper* No. 21881), April.

Kim, Young-Ho -J. (1988). Higashi ajia kogyoka to sekai shihon shugi (East Asia's industrialization and world capitalism: The fourth generation of industrialization). Tokyo: Toyo Keizai Shimpo Sha.

Kojima, Kiyoshi. (1973). A macroeconomic approach to foreign direct investment. *Hitotsubashi Journal of Economics, 14*(1).

Lin, Wuu Long. (1992). Some aspects of cooperation in the effective transfer and development of technology, Industry of Free China.

Liu, Shin-Kei. (1989). Taiwan no chushokigyo mondai to kokusai bungyo (Small-, medium- enterprises issues in Taiwan and international division of labor). *Ajia Keizai (Asian Economies) (IDE-JETRO), 30*(12).

Liu, Chin-Jui. (2017). The development of the Taiwanese ICT hardware industry: With focus on "Cross Strait" division of labor. In: Hirakawa, H. et al., (eds) Innovative ICT industrial architecture in East Asia, Tokyo: Springer.

Marukawa, T. -J. (2014). Hatten tojokoku no kyacchi-daun gata gijutsu shimpo ('Catch-down' innovations in developing countries). *Ajia Keizai, 55*(4).

Marukawa, T. -J. (2017). Chugoku Shinsen ni okeru jigyo soushutsu to inobeshon (Business creation and innovation in Shenzhen, China).f Japan Scholarly Association for Asian Management 24th National Conference Common Topic Report PPT, Sendai: Tohoku University.

Milton, F., & Freedman, R. (1980). *Free to Choose*. Harcourt Brace Jovanovich Inc.

METI -J. (1996). Tsusho hakusho (White paper on international trade). *Ministry of Trade and Industry*, Japan.

METI -J. (1999). Tsusho hakusho (White paper on international trade). *Ministry of Trade and Industry.*

METI -J. (2004). Tsusho hakusho (White paper on international trade). *Ministry of Economy, Trade, and Industry, Japan.*

Ministry of Foreign Affairs, Japan -J. (1986). Keizai kyoryoku no genjou to mondaiten (Present situation and problems of economic cooperation). Gaimusho (Ministry of Foreign Affairs).

Yoshikazu -J. (1995). *Kokumin keizai no tasogare: "fukugyo fukyou" sonogo (Twilight of the national economy : After the "compound recession*"). Asahi Shimbun Sha.
Moor, Gordon, E. (1965). Cramming more components onto integrated circuits. *Electronics, 38*(8), April 19.
Nakamura, S. -J. (1991). Kindai sekaishi zo no sai kousei: Higashi ajia no shiten kara (Reexamining the image of modern world history: From an East Asian perspective). Tokyo: Aoki Shoten.
Oman, C. (1984). *New forms of international investment in developing countries.* OECD.
Park, Woo-Hee -J. (1989). Kankoku no gijutsu hatten (Technological Development in South Korea). Tokyo: Bunshin Do.
Porter, Michael E. (1990). *The competitive advantage of nations*, The Free Press.
Saxenian, Annalee. (2004). *The Silicon Valley Connection: Transnational Networks and Regional Development in Taiwan*, China and India. In: D'Costa, Anthony P., Sridharan, E. (eds.) India in the Global Software Industry (pp.164–192).
Samir, A. (1974). *Accumulation on a World Scale.* Monthly Review Press.
Sekiguchi, H. -J. (1976). Wagakuni minseiyo denshi kiki sangyo no takokusekika senryaku (Multinational strategy of Japan's consumer electronics industry). *Tokyo: Institute of Developing Economies (IDE).*
Singh, Lakhwinder. (2007). Innovations, high-tech trade and industrial development: Theory, evidence and policy. In: Mavrotas, George and Anthony Shorrocks eds., Advancing development: Core themes in global economics, New York: Palgrave Machillan.
Soo, Hsien-Yang -J. (2006). Taiwan haiteku chushokigyo no seicho (Growth of Taiwan's high-tech SMEs) In: Hirakawa, H. Liu Shinkei, & Choi Yong-Ho eds., Higashi ajia no hatten to chusho kigyo (East Asia's development and small and medium-sized enterprises), Tokyo: Gakujutsu Shuppankai.
Stacey, F., & Gereffi, G. (2016). *The Philippines in the electronics & electrical global value chain, Center on Globalization.* Duke University, May.
Suehiro, Akira, -J. (1995). Ajia kogyoka no dainamizumu (the dynamism of Asia's industrialization), Kudo, A ed., Nijusseiki shihon-shugi (Capitalism in the 20th century), Tokyo: University of Tokyo Press.
Takase, Masakazu, Takaguchi Kota eds. (2020) Puroto taipu shitii: Shinsen to sekaiteki inobasyon (Prototype city: Shenzhen and global innovation), Tokyo: Kadokawa.
Tei, Ka -J. (2013). Sumatophon jidai no 'Shānzhài' keitai denwa ("Shanzhai" mobile phone in the smartphone era). Kaigai kenkyuin repouto (Foreign researcher report), Tokyo: IDE-JETRO.
Tzeng, Rueyling. (2006). Reverse brain drain. *Asian Population Studies, 2*(3), November, https://doi.org/10.1080/17441730601073821O
Wallerstein, I. (1979). *The Capitalist World-economy.* Cambridge University Press.
Watanabe, T. -J. (1985). Seicho no ajia Teitai no ajia (Growing Asia and Stagnated Asia). Tokyo: Toyo Keizai Shimpo Sha.
Watanabe, T. -J. (1991). Aija no dainamizumu wo dou toraeruka (How to grasp Asian dynamism). In: Watanabe T, Kajihara H, Takanaka, K., Ajia sogoizon no jidai (Asia's age of interdependence). Tokyo: Yuhikaku.
Watanabe, T.-J. (2004). Shohyo: Kojima Kiyoshi cho "Gankogata keizai hatten ron (Dai 1 kan, Dai 2 kan". *Ajia Keizai, 45*(9).
Westphal, Larry, E. (1978). The Republic of Korea's experience with export-led industrial development. *World Development, 6*(3), 347–382.
World Bank. (1981). *World Development Report 1981.* International Bank for Reconstruction and Development.
World Bank. (1993). *The East Asian Miracle: Economic Growth and Public Policy.* World Bank policy research report, Oxford University Press.
World Bank. (1997). *World Development Report 1997*, IBRD.
Yokota, Kazuhiko -J. (1992). ASEAN shokoku no boueki kouzo. In: Ota, Y., & Urata, S. (Eds.). *ASEAN no Keizai, Nihon no yakuwari (ASEAN's economy and Japan's role)*, Yuhikaku
Yoon, Banf-Soon, L. (1992). Reverse brain drain in South Korea: State-led model. *Studies in Comparative International Development, 27*(1), Spring.

Chapter 8
The Road to and from the East Asia's Currency and Economic Crisis

Abstract The Asian financial crisis, which began in Thailand in July 1997, quickly spread to neighboring countries in East Asia, Hong Kong, South Korea, and the following year, Russia and Latin America. Countries in crisis were forced to accept IMF conditionality in order to receive emergency loans, and structural reforms were pursued. But that prescription didn't stop the crisis, it only made it worse. Because the crisis was different in nature from previous experiences of economic crises in developing regions of Latin America, the IMF's prescription for countries in crisis was strongly criticized. As for the causes of the crisis, there was a sharp conflict between the two perceptions: one was that of the IMF and mainstream economics, looking for the causes in institutions and policies of Asian countries; and the other, that of anti-mainstream economists, with an interpretation that focused on the international liquidity of capital and looked for the cause to be excess liquidity in short-term capital. East Asian countries have accepted the structural reforms of the IMF on the one hand, and on the other hand, they have recognized the risks posed by unilateral dependence on international organizations such as the IMF, and have come to seek institutionalization of regional cooperation to avoid them.

Keywords Asian monetary fund · Asian currency and economic crisis · Capital mobility · Crony capitalism · New Miyazawa Initiative · Financial instability

8.1 Introduction

East Asia's economies were thrown into a harsh crisis beginning with the Thai baht's depreciation in July 1997. The enthusiasm that had been felt for East Asia's economic growth before the currency and economic crisis almost seemed to disappear.[1] However, in 1999, optimistic views that the currency and economic crisis in

[1] The president of the Institute of International Economics, C. Fred Bergsten, wrote in an article in 1999: "Not too long ago, there was much debate over whether the next hundred years would be the 'Japanese' or 'Asian' century. Now, that looks less likely. The 'European century' seems a more likely prospect, or even a 'second American century'" (Bergsten, 1999: 33).

H. Hirakawa and F. C. Maquito, *The Dynamics of Asian Economic Development*,
https://doi.org/10.1007/978-981-97-3106-0_8

East Asia was over, or out of the worst stage, had begun to appear.[2] Actually, the recovery from the crisis took place much faster than expected, though there was still a huge amount of unemployment and degradation of employment conditions in the crisis-hit countries, such as Indonesia and South Korea, where political and social instability continued.[3] The outbreak of the currency and financial crisis in East Asia and its course since then was far from the expectations of almost all economists, policy makers and ordinary people.

What made the Asian countries fall into the currency and economic crisis? How did the countries affected by the crisis recover from it? Though there was still a crucial difference in understanding the currency and economic crisis among economists and policy makers, the policies for overcoming it were converging. The programs imposed on the affected countries by the International Monetary Fund (IMF), which had been strongly supported by the United States, had been loosened to some extent, on the one hand, while there had been discussions regarding regulation and monitoring of short-term capital movement, which has been free internationally. And among East Asian countries and people, the necessity of a regional financial system and cooperation had begun to be considered.

In this paper, we will begin by briefly looking at the impact of the currency and economic crisis on East Asian economies and societies, next, describe the transition of main or popular understandings of the crisis, and consider an international and regional currency system to prevent another crisis from taking place, from the viewpoint of East Asia.

8.2 The Impact of Currency and Economic Crisis on Asian Countries

On July 2, 1997, the day after the people of Hong Kong celebrated the return to China under "one country, two systems" with joy, the baht began to crash in Thailand. The currency crash quickly spread to neighboring Malaysia, the Philippines, and Indonesia, and then northward to Hong Kong and South Korea, leading to the Asian currency crisis. Thailand, Indonesia and South Korea were forced to accept

[2] The managing director of the IMF, Michel Camdessus, said, on April 25, 1999 that the financial crisis that had hit most of world's emerging market economies "seems to be over", and the Financial Times, which published the article, explained, saying that "his [Camdessus] remarks before this week's IMF spring meetings reflected a growing optimism among international economic policymakers that the worst of the turmoil is now behind them" (Financial Times, April 26, 1999).

[3] The International Labour Organization (ILO) issued a Press Release on March 4, 1999, describing the social consequences of East Asia's financial crisis. It said, its social consequence "has exceeded all forecasts and shows few signs of revering, in spite of the stabilization of financial indicators, such as currency and equity prices". "The social implications of the crisis have become enormous, with unemployment, underemployment and poverty rising steeply" (ILO's Millennium Priorities to be aired at Budget Hearings, ILO/99.4).

International Monetary Fund (IMF) conditionality in order to obtain emergency loans.

But the IMF's traditional prescription of high interest rates and austerity measures in crisis countries failed to end the crisis. In 1998, the currency crisis, which was thought to be confined to Asia, spread to Russia and Latin America. In Indonesia, the crisis has deepened into an economic crisis, a social crisis, and even a crisis of regime change. Financial institutions in crisis countries were burdened with large amounts of non-performing loans, and crisis countries were forced to restructure their financial sectors under the IMF's conditionality.

According to the World Bank report, liquidity support in the wake of the crisis reached 18 percent of GDP in Indonesia, 13 percent in Malaysia, 20 percent in Thailand, and 5 percent in South Korea, and the ratio of non-performing loans to total loans in 2000 was 58.7 percent in Indonesia (May), 23.2 percent in Malaysia (June), 30.6 percent in Thailand (September), and 16.4 percent in South Korea (June). The closure of financial institutions was 69 out of 237 banks in Indonesia, 1 in 15 banks and 59 out of 91 financial corporations (FC) in Thailand. The temporary nationalization of banks amounted to 12 banks in Indonesia, 1 in Malaysia, 4 in Thailand and 4 in South Korea. Across the region, some 70 banks and more than 250 financial institutions have been closed" (World Bank, 2000: 71–72).

Table 8.1 shows that in the first half of the 1990s, lending to emerging economies in the global financial markets was directed exclusively toward Asia. It came to a sudden halt in the third quarter of 1997, and then it began to rise, peaking in East Asia in the first half of 1998.

In contrast, lending to Latin America, which was plunged into a debt crisis in the 1980s, was almost non-existent throughout the first half of the 1990s, and even increased when the Asian currency crisis began in 1997. The impact of the Asian currency crisis was not felt until the second half of 1998 、 and the impact was small. Bank for International Settlement 69th Annual Report (1999) wrote as follows: "the data present a qualified and in many respects surprising picture for Latin America. Flows of bank credit to Latin America remained strong even as the crisis spread rapidly throughout Asia in the second half of 1997″ (BIS, 1999: 34). This raises questions about what this means, and what is the crisis that has arisen in Asia.

Looking back, Thailand has long adopted a dollar-peg system and at the same time pursued a policy of financial liberalization, which was generally lauded. That changed dramatically. At the end of June 1997, just before the onset of the crisis, the exchange rate was 1 dollar to about 25 baht. However, when the Thai government abandoned the dollar peg system on July 2 due to a short-selling offensive by hedge funds, it fell to the level of 1 dollar to 29 baht on the same day, and to the level of 1 dollar to 32 baht at the end of the same month. In response to the Thai government's request for assistance, the IMF agreed to provide a total of $17.2 billion[4] in aid at a support meeting held in August, but the baht sell-off did not subside. In January

---

[4] The IMF's support for the Thailand conference is described in Sect. 8.4 of this chapter.

Table 8.1 International bank lending* of emerging market economies

	Average 1990–95	1996	1997				1998				1999	June 1997	December 1999
				First half	Q3	Q4		First half	Q3	Q4		Outstanding liabilities	
	In billion of US dollars, at an annual rate												
Asia**	37	80	5	74	−8	−109	−96	−103	−94	−32	−53	480	315
of which: China	7	13	10	13	21	−1	−11	−6	−25	4	−15	85	68
Crisis countries***	28	58	**−10**	**49**	**−39**	**−96**	**−83**	**−96**	**−59**	**−43**	**−35**	**329**	**190**
Latin America	1	29	31	27	43	40	−8	30	−32	−24	−16	284	280
Russia	1	6	10	8	17	6	−6	12	−43	−6	−8	54	44

(*Source* BIS, 1999, 2000).
Notes: * Exchange rate adjusted change in claims of BIS reporting banks. ** Excluding Hong Kong and Singapore. *** Indonesia, Korea, Malaysia, the Philippines, and Thailand.

of the following year, the exchange rate depreciated by more than 50%, reaching 1 dollar = 56 baht. The currency crisis is contagious to Indonesia. In June 1997, \$1 = 2,446 rupiah collapsed to 14,000 rupiah six months later in January 1998, and Indonesia's exchange rate fell to less than one-fifth. The average exchange rate of the Korean currency in the past year until June 1997 was 1 dollar to about 850 won, but by the end of December it had fallen to 1 dollar to 1,700 won.

The currency crisis immediately spilled over into the stock market. From Fig. 8.1, it can be confirmed that the currency crisis spread to the stock market and spread to neighboring countries one after another. The decline in stock prices was greater than that of currencies. Thus, the Asian currency crisis plunged into an economic crisis.

Table 8.2 shows the GDP growth rates of major East Asian countries in the second half of the 1990s. From this, we can see that the major countries in the region have suffered a significant economic setback due to the crisis. The year-on-year GDP growth rates in 1998 were −10.4 percent in Thailand, −13.2 percent in Indonesia, −7.5 percent in Malaysia, −6.7% in the Republic of Korea, and followed by Hong Kong −5.1 and −0.5 in the Philippines (ADB, 2000). The unemployment rate also rose. In 1998, Thailand's unemployment rate increased 3.5 times, from 0.9 to 3.4% in the previous year, and the rest of the world jumped as well. South Korea went from 2.6 to 6.8%, Indonesia from 4.7 to 5.5%, and Malaysia from 2.4 to 3.2%.

According to ESCAP, "the most acute and widespread impact of the Asian financial crisis on the labour market was the fall in real wages as inflation quickly eroded their nominal value". Nominal wages in Indonesia continued to rise between 1997 and 1998, but real wages fell by 30%. The rate of decline in real wages in Thailand was about −1% in 1997 and −7% in 1998. South Korea fell by −10% in 1998 (ESCAP, 2003: 40).

The incidence of poverty increased in all the countries. In Indonesia being the hardest hit, 18.2% of population were classified as being poor in 1999 as compared with 11.3% in 1996. In Thailand, the shares increased from 11.4% in 1996 to 13.0% in 1998, and 15.9% in 1999. "The Republic of Korea's incidence of poverty among urban worker's households increased from 3% in the fourth quarter of 1997 to 7.5% in the third quarter of 1998 (ESCAP, 2003: 41).

According to ILO's World Employment Report 2001, "as of 2001, as much as one-third of the world's workforce of three billion people are unemployed or underemployed. Of these, about 160 million people are openly unemployed, 20 million more than before the onset of the Asian financial crisis in 1997, and despite strong signs of economic recovery in most of Asia" (ILO News, 2001).

Incidentally, a currency and economic crisis broke out in the very country that was hailed as the "East Asian miracle" a few years ago. Again raising the question of why the currency crisis occurred.

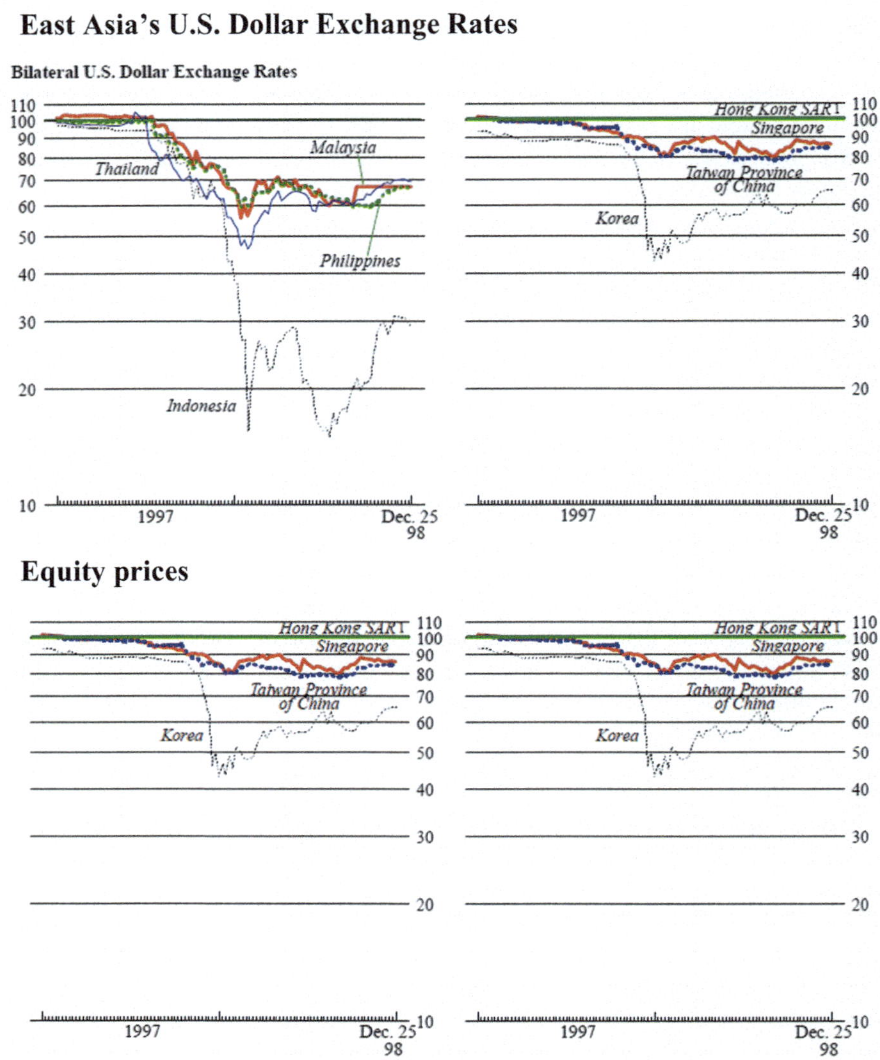

Fig. 8.1 Bilateral U.S. dollar exchange rate and equity prices in selected Asian Economies (*Source* IMF, 1999). *Note*: In U.S. dollars per currency unit: logarithmic scale. January 1, 1996 = 100

8.3 Understanding East Asia's Currency and Economic Crisis and Its Transition

In this section, we will trace the controversy between neoclassical economics and non-neoclassicals on Asian currency and the economic crisis.

Table 8.2 Rates of GDP growth and unemployment in main countries affected by the Asian currency and economic crisis 1995–2000 (%)

	GDP growth rates						Unemployment rates					
	1995	1996	1997	1998	1999	2000	1995	1996	1997	1998	1999	2000
Thailand	8.9	5.9	−1.8	−10.4	4.1	4.5	1.1	1.1	0.9	3.4	3.0	2.4
Indonesia	8.2	7.8	4.7	−13.2	0.2	4.0	7.2	4.9	4.7	5.5	6.4	6.1
Malaysia	9.8	10.0	7.5	−7.5	5.4	6.0	3.1	2.5	2.4	3.2	3.4	3.1
Philippines	4.7	5.8	5.2	−0.5	3.2	3.8	8.4	7.4	7.9	9.6	9.4	10.1
ROK	8.9	6.8	5.0	−6.7	10.7	7.5	2.0	2.0	2.6	6.8	6.3	4.1
Hong Kong	3.9	4.5	5.0	−5.1	2.9	5.0	3.2	2.8	2.2	4.7	6.3	5.0
Ref. China	10.5	9.6	8.8	7.8	7.1	6.5	2.9	3.0	3.1	3.1	3.1	3.1

(*Source* ADB, 2000: 242 Table A1; ADB, 2001: 16).

8.3.1 Popular Understanding of the Crisis and Controversies

What made the Asian crisis take place? Many interpretations have been offered. Among them was a loss of competitiveness and overproduction. For example, the Chinese renminbi's depreciation in January 1994, and the yen's depreciation beginning in the second half of 1995 made the currencies of Thailand, South Korea and other countries, stronger compared to China's and/or Japan's, which meant a loss of relative competitiveness of the Association of Southeast Asian Nations (ASEAN) and NIEs.

The idea of overproduction is that the East Asian countries increased investment too rapidly into productive capacity after the second half of the 1980s, especially in the first half of the 1990s, and "the drive to expand capacity and market shares may be seen in the increase in the ratio of investment to output from already high levels, which was facilitated by the availability of relatively low-cost foreign funding" (UNCTAD, 1998b: 61). But these views fail to explain why the crisis spread throughout East Asia, and thereafter to Russia and Latin American countries, as a currency and financial crisis. Actually, it does not seem to be true that China's currency depreciation stopped Thailand's exports from increasing. As for the idea of over-investment, though its manufactured exports were largely microelectronics, Singapore was not affected by the currency crisis, as South Korea was. These observations can explain partly the cause of the crisis in particular countries.

Incidentally, the popular understanding of and interest in the East Asian crisis have changed during the two years following the crisis. By briefly describing the transition of the main understanding, we can inquire into the main causes of the crisis and policy changes.

First, as the currency and economic crisis, which broke out in Thailand on July 2, 1997, spread to Malaysia, the Philippines, Indonesia and so on, MIT professor Paul Krugman's paper 'The Myth of Asia's Miracle' which was published at the end of

1994, immediately drew public attention because it appeared to have foreseen the crisis in Asia.

In the previous year, 1993, the World Bank's famous report, The East Asian Miracle had been published, the growth rates of East Asian economies were very high, and confidence in East Asia's growth was at its peak, Krugman, conscious of the work of the World Bank, used the term "myth" in his paper's title instead of "miracle" used by the financial institution. He pointed out that "East Asian growth seems to be driven by extraordinary growth in inputs like labor and capital rather than by gains in efficiency", and that it was "like that of the Soviet Union in its high-growth era" (Krugman, 1994: 70). In actuality, the Soviet Union had collapsed in the last month of 1991; this fact continues to shock the world, and Krugman's paper was treated sensationally by economists and policy makers who believed in the growth potential of East Asia. The crisis brought back memories of his assertion when it struck.

But Krugman denied that his paper explained the current crisis, and remarked that the scenario he had thought up was different from that of the East Asian crisis[5] (Krugman, 1998a; Nihon Keizai Shimbun -in Japanese, October 20, 1997. Hereafter referred to as Nikkei -J).

The widely-accepted understanding of the East Asian crisis was that the East Asian capitalist model was the cause of the crisis. International financial institutions, United States officials, the IMF staff, and neoclassical economists, those who belonged to the orthodoxy in economics, seemed to support this kind of understanding. It appeared immediately after the currency and economic crisis broke out in Thailand, and became widely accepted as the crisis spread to Indonesia, Malaysia, and even to South Korea through the summer and fall. As a result, quite a few Asian areas researchers and journalists in East Asia seemed to support this view.

According to this view, the Asian crisis stemmed from a state-led or bureaucracy-led mode of development, crony capitalism or nepotism, which could not cope with the changing current markets. Their way of economic management led by Asia's governments, supplied a great sum of money to a small number of political or military leader's families' businesses and big businesses (like the Chaebols in South Korea), which, in turn, could make investments or overinvestments without regard for efficiency. Naturally the corruption among political leaders and businesses spread widely and made the economy inefficient.

For example, early in December 1997, the vice chairman of Goldman Sachs International, Robert Hormats, in an interview about "Japan and Korea in the midst of the financial crisis", commented that "Asian neo-mercantilism - the strategy of

[5] Krugman said: "It seems safe to say that nobody anticipated anything like the current crisis in Asia. True, there were some Asia skeptics—including myself—who regarded the claims of an Asian economic miracle as overstated, and argued that Asia was bound to run into diminishing returns eventually. … But even pessimists expected something along the lines of a conventional currency crisis followed by at most a modest downturn, and we expected the long-term slowdown in growth to emerge only gradually. What we have actually seen is something both more complex and more drastic" (Krugman, 1998a: first paragraph).

closed financial sectors, high tariffs and aggressive export promotion – had hit a wall" (Newsweek, December 1, 1997).

U.S. Treasury Secretary, Robert Rubin defended IMF policy against criticism, stating that:

> The Asian crisis is essentially one of confidence. The best way to restore investor's confidence is to reform financial institutions, restructure corporations overburdened by debt, and prohibit governments' telling banks to lend to favored companies. Healthier banks could begin lending again to power an economic revival (Wall Street Journal, June 30. 1998).

The U.S. Treasury Under Secretary, Larry Summers stated that:

> (This crisis) is profoundly different because it has its roots not in improvidence but in economic structures. The problems that must be fixed are much more microeconomic than macroeconomic, and improve the private sector more and the public sector less (Financial Times, February 20, 1998; cited from Singh, 1998: 1).

And the Managing Director of the IMF, Michal Camdessus and the Chairman of the U.S. Federal Reserve, Greenspan have expressed similar views (Singh 1998: 1; Nikkei evening ed. -J, May 28, 1998).

Of course, the IMF initially pursued the structural reform of the Asian capitalist model with such an understanding. It required the countries not only to accept the traditional prescriptions of tightening financial expenditures, maintaining high interest rate policies, and so forth, but also to accept new prescriptions including greater market opening to foreign capital, removals of subsidies, and amendments of employment related laws.

Incidentally, another criticism of the East Asian state-led mode of development seems to have come out mainly from Japan. East Asian states, as late comers, were able to develop their economies under high growth rates, making effective use of limited resources through industrial and other policies. However, in spite of having reached the stage where the removal of regulations was inevitable, they continued intervening in the market. This error brought about the crisis.

However, it can be said that this understanding is one that applies to Japan's case of state-led development as much as it does to other East Asian developing countries. It clearly differs from the criticism of the East Asian development model made by neoclassical economists who consider the market to be synonymous with the discipline of economists. In the view of the neoclassicists, there is no room for a staged approach.

At any rate, the criticism of the East Asian development model was strongly critiqued by many prominent economists, among them Harvard University Professor Jeffery Sachs, a professor at the same university and President of the National Bureau of Economic Research (NBER) Martin Feldstein, Columbia University Professor Jagdish Bhagwati, and Cambridge University Professor Ajit Singh etc.

Sachs wrote, in a paper in collaboration with Steven Radelet, that "the Southeast Asian currency crises of 1997 are not a sign of the end of Asian growth but rather a recurring—if difficult to predict—pattern of financial instability that often accompanies rapid economic growth" (Radelet & Sachs, 1997: 45).

Ferdstein criticized the IMF:

> The IMF is now acting in Southeast Asia and Korea in much the same way that it did in East Europe and the former Soviet Union: insisting on fundamental changes in economic and institutional structures as a condition for receiving IMF funds. It is doing so even though the situations of the Asian countries are very different from those of the former Soviet Union and Eastern Europe. Since Korea's total foreign debt was only about 30 percent of GDP (among the lowest of all developing nations), this was clearly a case of temporary illiquidity rather than fundamental insolvency. Moreover, since the current account deficit was very small and rapidly shrinking, there was no need for the traditional IMF policy of reduced government spending, higher taxes, and tight credit (Feldstein, 1998: 22, 24).

Actually, there are other difficult points to settle in understanding the East Asian development model as the cause of the crisis. The first question is: if the East Asian development model brought about the crisis, why did it have a contagion effect on Russia, Latin America, and even to the U.S.? The second question is: why has East Asia remained as a world growth center for the last several decades? As Stiglitz pointed out, "this is a single crisis against a record of thirty years of remarkable growth".[6]

Perhaps, as the development model of East Asia is considered to be different from the Anglo-American model of capitalism among IMF economists and American government staff, they were confused into thinking that the East Asian model was the cause of the crisis. Why do many area researchers and journalists, even in East Asia, support this view? Their tendency to focus mainly on internal factors seems to lead to a conclusion which disregards international factors. But as the crisis broke out, the East Asian model became an issue, though the model itself had not brought about the crisis. This understanding leads to a reversal of the causal sequence. Actually, this understanding seemed to lose its influence gradually after the Russian crisis in the summer of 1998 and Brazil's policy change into a floating exchange rate system in January 1999.

A third understanding drawing attention recently is one that stresses policy errors and/or sequence errors in the liberalization of the Asian countries affected by the crisis. World Bank staff, policymakers, and IMF staff seem to support this kind of understanding, which can be outlined as follows. Asian countries continued to increase short-term debt in an irrational way under dollar peg exchange rate systems, creating a bubble economy there. Explicit guarantees by East Asian governments created a "moral hazard" for both foreign and Asian domestic banks, and allowed them to lend and borrow great sums of money without regard for risk. But when the increase of exports nearly dried up in those countries in 1996, and foreign banks and investors saw the increase in those countries' current balance deficit, they lost confidence in the growth in East Asian countries, and consequently withdrew large sums of money abruptly. This precipitated the currency and financial crisis.

---

[6] Joseph Stiglitz wrote, "We seem to be ignoring the fact that this is a single crisis against a record of thirty years of remarkable growth. Although a significant setback, the current turmoil does not seem likely to permanently reverse the gains of the past quarter century. We are unjustifiably treating the occurrence of a crisis as compelling evidence of a fundamentally malfunctioning economy. No economy since the beginning of capitalism has escaped fluctuations. The historical record, in fact, shows that East Asia has had less such fluctuations than other parts of the world – hardly evidence of a striking vulnerability in the economies" (Stiglitz, 1998a).

The World Bank had already assumed a rather critical attitude, from the 1980s toward IMF support programs which mainly consisted of tax increases and higher interest rates, claiming that such prescriptions would make it difficult for the private sectors to invest in the long term, and would prevent developing countries from achieving economic growth.[7] On September 11, 1997, the institution approved a loan of U.S.$15 million to Thailand, which had been affected by a currency and financial crisis, for improving the structure, resiliency, soundness of the financial sector and so forth (World Bank, 1997).

In a speech at the annual meeting of the World Bank and the IMF held in Hong Kong on September 23, President James D. Wolfensohn said that the Bank was scaling up its work to restructure banking and financial systems in developing countries. He also outlined a plan to meet what he called "the challenge to inclusion", focusing on strengthening the social safety net to narrow the gap between rich and poor (Wolfensohn, 1997). The Annual Report of the World Bank (1998) explained the East Asian crisis as follows:

> While the chief factors contributing to the crisis differed from country to country, there were common characteristics: failure to contain demand and a boom in lending resulted in large current account deficits and property and stock market bubbles; the rigid nature of currency regimens encouraged foreign borrowing leading to imprudent exposure to foreign exchange risk by banks and corporations; and lax prudential rules and supervision of financial sectors led to sharp depreciation in the quality of bank's loan portfolios. These sectors were compounded by shortcomings in the way countries allocated their resources, including state-directed lending, nepotism, skewed industrial structures, and limits on foreign participation and competition (World Bank, 1998: 22).

The World Bank considered that the cause of the crisis was the adoption of liberalization on capital before building healthy domestic financial systems. The World Bank's chief economist on the East Asia region, Masahiko Kawai, expressed a similar view:

> It is 'order' that is important. Former and traditional orders have overlooked the point that the building of strong and healthy domestic financial systems was made prior to the liberalization of capital movements. (Then) if abrupt and large inflows and outflows occurred, the financial system could avoid hypertrophy of financing, sudden credit contraction, and partial paralysis of financing (Kawai -J 1998).

The Asian Development Bank has taken the same view (ADB, 1999c). It expressed the same interpretation in its annual report, *Development Outlook 1999*.

> The Asian crisis showed that when countries open up their capital accounts without effective supervision and regulation of financial intermediaries, they become more vulnerable to crisis, because the access to foreign capital magnified the weakness and distortions of the domestic financial system. This suggests that financial liberalization must be carefully sequenced (ADB, 1999a: 39; ADB, 1999c).

---

[7] According to S. Shirai, the World Bank criticized the IMF's prescriptions in World Development Report 1984 (Shirai -J, 1999: 166).

Since 1998, the IMF has changed its understanding from defects in the East Asian development model to sequencing misses in liberalization and relaxed its conditionalities.[8] As for the origin of the East Asian crisis, IMF First Deputy Managing Director Stanley Fischer stated the following:

> The key domestic factors that led to the present difficulties appear to have been: first, the failure to dampen overheating pressures that had become increasingly evident in Thailand and many other countries in the region and were manifested in large external deficits and property and stock market bubbles: second, the maintenance of pegged exchange rate regimes for too long, which encouraged external borrowing and led to excessive exposure to foreign exchange risk in both the financial and corporate sectors; and third, lax prudential rules and financial oversight, which led to a sharp deterioration in the quality of banks' loan portfolio. As the crisis unfolded, political uncertainties and doubts about the authorities' commitment and ability to implement the necessary adjustments and reforms exacerbated pressures on currencies and stock markets (IMF, 1998a).

Though Fischer pointed to global factors as reasons behind the crisis in East Asia, he claimed they were only secondary. He said that "although the problems in these countries were mostly homegrown, developments in the advanced economies and global financial markets contributed significantly to the buildup of the imbalances that eventually led to the crisis". This meant that huge sums of private capital accumulated in advanced countries had flowed to emerging markets in search of high interest (IMF 1998a). Therefore, the following measures are needed to overcome the crisis: "liberalization of the capital account must be carried out in an orderly, properly sequenced manner, carefully married to a strengthening of the domestic financial system" (IMF, 1998b).

Berry Eichengreen, a professor at the University of California, Berkely and also Senior Policy Advisor in the IMF's Research Development, and Michael Mussa, Director of the IMF's Research Development, also point out in a collaboration in a joint magazine published by the IMF and the World Bank that:

> The most important point to recognize in the sequencing of capital market liberalization is the danger of precipitously removing restrictions on capital account transactions before major problems in the domestic financial system have been addressed./ As problems in the domestic financial system, they point to; (a) inadequate accounting, auditing, and disclosure practices in the financial and corporate sectors that weaken market discipline, (b) implicit government

[8] In October 1997, the IMF imposed on the Indonesian government an economic restructuring program as a conditionality, which the goal of government financial balance to 1% of GDP, and on the 1st of the next November, it forced the closure of 16 financial institutions. However, it amended the goal of government financial balance to minus 1% of GDP in January1998, because of the worsening economy. In Thailand, the IMF eased the government financial expenditure from plus 1% of GDP in 1997 to minus 2%in February 1998 in order to strengthen its social safety net, as Thailand's economy continued to worsen in spite of the implementation of conditionalities. In South Korea, though the initial condition on government financial balance was plus 0.2% of GDP, it was relaxed to minus 1.7% in May 1998 (Shirai -J, 1999:150-160). According to the South China Morning Post on May 5, 1998, IMF Managing Director M. Camdessus in Singapore backed Singapore Finance Minister Richard Ho who "had blamed the East Asian crisis on countries that rushed to liberalize their financial systems and capital accounts without first putting adequate safeguards in place". Therefore, the South China Morning Post used as its headline, "IMF joins critics of rapid reform".

guarantees that encourage excessive, unsustainable capital flows, and (c) inadequate prudential supervision and regulation of domestic financial institutions and markets, which open the way for corruption, connected lending, and gambling for redemption (Eichengreen & Mussa, 1998: 19)

This interpretation criticizes the free movement of capital. It has after then been widely accepted and was advocated by Malaysian Prime Minister Mahathir Mohamad who criticized the billionaire financial investor, Gorge Soros first on July 26, 1997 (Nikkei -J, July 27, 1997). Mahathir "blamed Soros and other foreign fund managers for causing this summer's currency crisis" and even called Soros a "moron". The dispute between Mahathir and Soros reached its peak at the World Bank and IMF meeting in Hong Kong in September 1997. According to the Wall Street Journal, "with finance officials around the world looking on anxiously, Mahathir blamed Soros for Malaysia's current economic crisis". While Mahathir said "I am saying that currency trading is unnecessary, unproductive and immoral. It should be stopped. It should be made illegal", Soros disclaimed responsibility for Malaysia's foreign exchange woes, and called Mahathir's suggestion "so inappropriate that it doesn't deserve serious consideration" (Wall Street Journal, September 2, 1997). On the day of the dispute of the two, according to the Financial Times, confidence in Southeast Asian markets was undermined, especially Malaysia, and Malaysia's currency recorded 'another historic low (Financial Times, September 2, 1997).

The problem of speculation using short-term capital was submitted as an economic argument by Columbia University Professor Jagdish Bhagwati, when he published his article, 'The Capital Myth' in *Foreign Affairs* in the May/June issue of 1998. Bhagwati pointed out the essential difference between free trade and free capital movement.

Many assumed that free capital mobility among all nations was exactly like free trade in their goods and services, a mutual-gain phenomenon. Freeing up trade is good, why not also let capital move freely across borders? However, the claims of enormous benefits from free capital mobility are not persuasive. Capital flows are characterized, as the economic historian Charles Kindleberger of the Massachusetts Institute of Technology has famously noted, by panics and manias (Bhagwati, 1988:7, 8, 1999: 33).

World Bank Senior Vice President, Joseph Stiglitz declared the following:

More generally, there is little evidence that full capital-account liberalization contributed to investment or growth. What is clear is that short-term capital flows increase volatility, which is bad for growth. Our research shows that countries that have gone further in financial liberalization, including capital-account realization, are more likely to experience a financial crisis (Stiglitz, 1998).

Paul Krugman, MIT Professor describes that:

It is possible in principle that a loss of confidence in a country can produce an economic crisis that justified that loss of confidence --- that counties may be vulnerable to what economics call 'self-fulfilling speculative attacks'. And, while many economists, me included, used to be skeptical about the importance of such a self-fulfilling crisis, the experience of the '90s in Latin America and Asia has settled those doubts, at least as a practical matter (Krugman, 1998d).

Finally, in September, he came to recognize the significance of regulations on the free movement of capital.

> If Asian nations did adopt currency controls, they'd have to brace themselves for an even rougher ride. Any chance of attracting new foreign investment would disappear. The financial markets would probably go into another swoon. But the damage, though painful, would be only temporary (Krugman, 1998c: 38).

Incidentally, in August 1998, prior to Krugman's acceptance of currency controls, the United Nations Conference on Trade and Development (UNCTAD) criticized the IMF, saying that "tightening monetary policy may simply intensify the stampede, further understanding creditworthiness and increasing the risk of default", and proposed debt moratoria, and capital controls as essential tools to provide "the breathing space needed to design a debt reorganization plan". UNCTAD also insisted that flexibility on the introduction of capital controls should be permitted as "an indispensable part of developing countries' armory of measures for the purpose of protection against international financial instability" (UNCTAD 1998d, 1998b).

In this context, on September 1, 1998, Malaysia decided to implement capital controls despite of criticism from the IMF, neoclassicalists, U.S. officials, and many newspapers. Krugman essentially accepted Malaysia's decision in an "open letter to Prime Minister Mahathir" on the same day.

Bhagwati put forward Krugman's argument further and analyzed the structure driving the liberalization of capital movements worldwide. He concluded that "Wall Street has exceptional clout with Washington for the simple reason that there is a definite networking of like-minded luminaries among the powerful institutions – Wall Street, the Treasury Department, the State Department, the IMF, and the World Bank most prominent among them". He called it the Wall Street-Treasury complex (Bhagwati 1998: 11).

Of course, the IMF attempted to refute Bhagwati's argument, but its counterarguments appeared to remain on the level of a general explanation that the liberalization of capital movements can supply money to a country where capital is in short supply (Anjaria, 1998:142–143). U.S. Federal Reserve Chairman Alan Greenspan offered, in a speech in Washington, his view of the East Asian Crisis, that it was like a milestone which was unavoidable in the market economy (Nikkei, evening edition -J, May 28, 1998).

In summary, there are several major interpretations of the Asian financial and economic crisis. Influential views have changed sharply, though at present the last two perspectives are involved in a hot dispute. In the initial stage, domestic factors in the affected countries in East Asia were strongly pointed out as the main causes of the crisis. And later, international factors have been given more attention.

In actuality, capital liberalization in East Asia has been carried out mainly forcibly under the IMF's and United States' leadership (Kawai and others, 1996: 2–3, 9). Capital liberalization in the region has been a natural part of globalization, which contains policies that transition economies have adopted. The currency and economic crisis in East Asia was not limited to the region, but spread out to Russia and Latin American countries, etc. As UNCTAD insisted, the East Asian crisis is part of an increased frequency of financial crises in both the developed and developing countries, which have taken various forms (UNCTAD, 1998b: Chap. 3). Therefore, the cause of the Asian crisis should not be sought inside East Asia. Instead, it is natural to think that its cause is the financial globalization that has been led by the United States and the IMF. Market volatility and vulnerability have stemmed from the capital account liberalization itself. From a moral standpoint, the IMF and the United States, who forced globalization, should take much more responsibility for the crisis than the affected countries in East Asia.

Incidentally, financial globalization has been pushed forward since around the second half of the 1980s, following the internationalization of production led by transnational firms in the 1960s, the great advances in information technologies since the 1970s have made it easy to integrate operations all over the world, and the accumulation of a huge amount of capital in the advanced industrial economies, especially the United States, in the 1980s. Needless to say, the globalization of the real economy has already come into existence. It would be impossible to return to the age of the national economy. We can no longer think about economic development based on a national economy isolated from the world economy. Accordingly, the problem is not globalization per se, but global standardization.

If we consider the issue in this way, it is easy to understand that some countries in East Asia seem to have begun the process of recovery faster than expected. Part of the huge amounts of capital which is created in stock and financial markets in the United States and other advanced economies has moved back to some East Asian countries again. We should realize that crises and booms no longer depend on a single country's economic indicators.

8.3.2 Subsequent Arguments Regarding Liberalization and Regulations on Short-Term Capital Movement

Asia's currency and economic crisis was followed, through a contagion effect by the Russian financial crisis and the Latin American crisis, showing that the current liberalization of capital flows is very volatile. Then, after the near-collapse of a famous American hedge fund, Long Term Capital Management (LTCM), in September 1998, the regulation of short-term capital movements became an important point of discussion (Motoyama -J, 1999). Strengthening the monitoring of financial institutions, especially hedge funds, information disclosure on the activities of highly-leveraged financial institutions, monitoring of international capital movements, and some form of regulation of capital movement are just some of the issues now under examination among the IMF, World Bank, and other international financial institutions, as well as various governments.

In October 1998, British Prime Minister Tony Blair in a speech in Hong Kong, said that funds which secretly manipulate unprecedented volumes of capital cannot be seen by national governments or international financial organizations, and therefore that we need new rules. Even the famous American speculator George Soros, in a speech in Washington, took a position in the controversy against free capital movements, saying that it would not be wise to approve the complete liberalization of capital movements (Nikkei Evening ed. -J October 6, 1998; ditto, October 25, 1998). In the United States Congress as well, arguments against short-term capital movements were raised. In Europe, it is said that the Chief of the European Central Bank's supervisory committee proposed a limit on the amount borrowed on hedge funds, a fundamental prohibition of European banks from holding a stake in hedge funds, and so forth (Nikkei -J, October 13, 1998).

The Japanese government has insisted that excess liquidity and overdependence on the U.S. dollar were the main causes of the East Asian currency crisis, and therefore that some regulations of large-scale and speculative short-term capital outflows and disclosure of hedge funds were needed.

The Japanese government developed an idea of building an international financial supervisory organization and floated this proposal at a meeting of proxies of the G7 finance ministers and central bank governors. The organization was expected to be an independent one, integrating supervisory divisions separated from the IMF, the World Bank and the Bank of International Settlements (BIS), and its role would be: (a) to monitor financial surveillance systems in each country, (b) to offer technical advice to the financial divisions of each country and exchange financial information between them, (c) to supervise international investors including hedge funds, (d) to gather information and conduct surveys on international capital movements, and so forth (Nikkei -J, November 1, 1998). At a summit meeting of Asia Pacific Economic Cooperation (APEC) held in Kuala Lumpur, Malaysia in November 1998, there was a controversy on whether speculation by investors should be regulated or not, mainly between the United States and East Asian countries. Though no concrete results came from discussions, Malaysia, China, and Japan insisted on regulations against free capital movements, while the United States opposed them (Nikkei -J, November 11, 1999).

The Asian Development Bank also changed its view of what kind of financial liberalization should be adopted by the affected countries, from a reckless to a prudential one. The Asian Development Bank describes in its latest annual reports.

> The Asian crisis showed that when countries open up their capital accounts without effective supervision and regulation of financial intermediaries, they become more vulnerable to crisis, because the access to foreign capital magnifies the weakness and distortions of the domestic financial system. This suggests that financial liberalization must be carefully sequenced (ADB, 1999a: 39).

Moreover, even the government of the United States, which has long opposed any restrictions on capital movements, is changing its attitude towards accepting some restrictions on short-term capital movements, according to a correspondent of the Nihon Keizai Shimbun in Washington who sent to Japan an account of U.S. Treasury Secretary Robert Rubin's address on April 21, 1999. It was written that to regulate excess capital movements and speculative trading, Rubin had expressed the idea of asking the financial institutions to disclose information on their investments in hedge funds and other financial institutions. He also said that in some circumstances regulations on private banks' dealings in foreign exchange and making short-term foreign currency borrowings, as well as government control of foreign debts in emerging markets, would be needed (Nikkei -J, April 22, 1999).

Thereafter, on April 29, the President's Working Group on Financial Market, chaired by Rubin submitted a report, which "argued that Congresses give two financial regulators, the Securities and Exchange Commission (SEC) and the Commodity Future Trading Commission (CFTC), more authority to collect and verify the accuracy of information about unregulated affiliates of securities and future firms, including those that enter into financial contracts with hedge funds". The report also recommended that the SEC issue new rules requiring public companies to disclose any material exposure to hedge funds and other financial institutions that rely heavily on borrowed money (Washington Post, April 29, 1999). In the United States, the government was trying to strengthen the government's monitoring of financial institutions to ensure sound markets.

As for the IMF, UC Berkeley Professor Barry Eichengreen, who was Senior Policy Adviser in the IMF's Research Department, expressed his views in his work:

> I am explicit about the need for Chilean-style capital-inflows taxes as the only effective solution to this problem for the vast majority of developing countries (Eichengreen, 1999: 6).

But, according to him, "there is a crucial distinction between controls that seek to prevent international financial transactions from taking place at any price and taxes that merely seek to correct the price for discrepancies between private and social cost. Taxes are not prohibitions" (Eichengreen, 1999: 51).

In addition, at a meeting of G7 Financial Ministers for the Köln Economic Summit, held in Frankfurt in June 1999, controls of capital outflows were agreed upon reluctantly. The report said,

> (Emerging countries) need to pursue sound macroeconomic policies, including sustainable exchange rate regimes and prudent fiscal policies. A high priority should also be given to strengthening emerging economies' financial sectors and supervisory regimes. [And also] capital account liberalization should be carried out in a careful and well-sequenced manner, accompanied by a sound and well-regulated financial sector and by a consistent macroeconomic policy framework.
>
> The use of controls on capital inflows may be justified for a traditional period as countries strengthen the institutional and regulatory environment in their domestic financial systems. [As for] controls on capital outflows, they may be necessary in certain exceptional circumstances (G7 Finance Ministers to the Köln Economic Summit, 1999; Nikkei -J, June 13, 1999).

Even though Eichengreen asserts that Chilean-style capital-flow taxes do not contradict the discipline of neoclassical economics, and the Köln Economic Summit approved controls on capital flows (though only in certain exceptional circumstances), it was clear that such views had retreated compared to the view of the Washington consensus and neoclassical economics, which assert almost complete freedom of the market.

8.4 The East Asian Currency and Economic Crisis and Japan

In this section, we will discuss the Thai financial support meeting, and the New-Miyazawa Initiative as Japan's financial support framework for the crisis-hit countries.

8.4.1 The Emergency Thailand Financial Support Meeting in Tokyo in August 1997 and the Asian Monetary Fund

In the 1990s, Japan needed to carry out Asian policies from a new point of view. The boom of investment by Japanese companies in the East Asian region since the second half of the 1980s has played a part in integrating the economies of the Asian newly industrializing economies (NIEs), the ASEAN countries, and China through the growth of intra-Asian trade. Though Japan's rate of manufactured imports as a percentage of total imports was 31% in 1985, this rate increased to more than 50% in 1989, then attained around 60% in 1995. Moreover, Japanese banks, who had close linkages with Japanese companies in East Asia, advanced into the region, to expand their own financial businesses and supply huge sums of money. However, the currency and economic crisis then broke out. Japan was simultaneously facing the bursting of the bubble economy in the 1990s, and almost all Japanese banks had huge amounts of bad loans, and in addition, following Japan's financial "big bang", it found itself mired in a depression in the wake of the bursting of the bubble economy. Japanese banks faced difficulties not only in their domestic businesses but also in East Asia businesses. It seems that the Japanese government had no choice but to deal seriously with the currency crisis in East Asia, mainly in order to support its own banks. This led the Japanese government to adopt prompt countermeasures.

After the baht began to depreciate on July 2, 1997, an emergency meeting of countries planning to give financial support to Thailand was held in Tokyo on August 11. At this meeting, which the United States declined to attend (Ito -J 1998: 53), the participating nations, at the request of the Thai government, agreed to a U.S. $12.7 billion package of financial support for Thailand. Out of this U.S. $12.7 billion, Japan agreed to contribute U.S. $4 billion, Australia, Hong Kong, Singapore, and Malaysia U.S.$1 billion each, and Indonesia and Korea U.S. $0.5 billion each. Subsequently, China pledged to contribute U.S. $1 billion, and the World Bank and Asian Development Bank U.S. $1.5 billion and 1.2 billion respectively (IMF, 1997a).

Inside Japan, there had been some opinion that Japan should provide financial support to Thailand, even if it had to do it alone. Therefore, the international agreement was much appreciated in Japan. Japan had several reasons to support Thailand. First, Japan is proud of its position as an advanced country in Asia, and recognized this as a good chance for it to assume leadership in Asian politics. Secondly, the Bank for International Settlement (BIS) had granted private loans in Thailand amounting to US$70.3 billion by the end of 1997, and Japanese private banks had loaned more than half this, or US$37.5 billion. Because of this, the Japanese government needed to help the Japanese banks to finance this huge amount of money. Thirdly, this support was considered useful for the internationalization of the yen.[9]

However, for other Asian countries/regions, this agreement to support Thailand had another significance. Many East Asian countries participated in making the financial support package together, in the form of international or Asian regional cooperation. This means that each country was becoming convinced of the existence of common interests and that there was the common realization that they were in a dangerous situation.

In this meeting, there was another important proposal. A proposal to establish an Asian Monetary Fund (AMF) was made mainly under Japan's leadership, in response to the Thai government's request. The first idea was that the IMF would be an international institution giving emergency financial support to the countries affected by the currency crisis, and would be independent from the IMF. On September 21, Japanese Finance Minister Hiroshi Mitsuzuka explained the Japanese idea about the fund at an informal meeting of Japan-ASEAN finance ministers held in Hong Kong.

By this time, Japan had changed the plan, increasing the number of participating countries by adding China and South Korea to ASEAN as member countries. The fund would be managed in cooperation with the IMF (Nikkei -J, September 22, 1997). This plan was further adjusted according to differences of opinion expressed by concerned countries during a series of international meetings on financial issues held in Hong Kong in September, consisting of the IMF-World Bank Annual Meeting, G-7 Meeting, and so forth (Nikkei -J, September 24, 1999). In the beginning, the plan was to establish the Asian Monetary Fund (AMF) with US$50–60 billion in funding, and to establish it within 1997, so it could act as a regional complement to the IMF. The funding was later increased to $100 billion, "half of which was to come from Japan and the remainder from PRC; Hong Kong, China; Singapore; and Taipei, China" (ADB, 1999a: 44).

However, the AMF was mainly proposed by the Japanese government and supported by the ASEAN countries, but faced strong opposition from the United States and the IMF. The opponents' argument was that AMF financing of the countries affected by the crisis could encourage moral hazards, on the one hand, and the leadership or political power Japan would get through the IMF would threaten the United States' political supremacy, on the other hand. The Wall Street Journal said as follows:

> Mr. Rubin (U.S.) Treasury Secretary and Mr. Summers (Deputy Treasury Secretary) feared the fund would offer big loans with less-stringent conditions than the IMF's and would threaten U.S. economic supremacy. Treasury officials worked the corridors of Hong Kong's convention center and the city's private dining room to slow the Japanese plan's momentum.

---

[9] The chief managing director of The Japan Research Institute, Mikio Wakatsuki, said regarding the meeting of countries planning to make financial support to Thailand, that it was necessary for Japan to make it easy to use the yen internationally in response to Asian countries' needs (Wakatsuki -J, 1997: 18).

China, South Korea, and other nations suspicious of Tokyo's ambitions leaned toward the U.S.' (Wall Street Journal, September 24, 1998).

In the end, in a Manila meeting of proxies of finance ministers and central bank governors from fourteen countries held on November 18–19, 1997, Japan abandoned its proposal. The Asian Development Bank explained as follows:

> Despite strong support from Malaysia, the proposal did not get far. Only two months after it had first been suggested, it was turned down. One objection was the fear that finance support without any conditions attached would raise the risk of moral hazard. Another risk was a lack of coordination and potential conflict with the IMF (ADB, 1999a: 44).

Though the Asian Development Bank's report did not specifically name the United States, Japan mainly met with the opposition of the United States, and was obliged to give up the plan, notwithstanding the fact that some ASEAN member countries supported it.

8.4.2 The New Miyazawa Initiative in 1998

8.4.2.1 The New Miyazawa Initiative as a Bilateral Assistance

On October 3, 1998, Japan's government announced "a New Initiative to Overcome the Asian Currency Crisis", which carried the name of the Finance Minister, Kiichi Miyazawa. The initiative was "a package of support measures totaling US$30 billion, of which US$15 billion will be made available for the medium- to long-term financial needs for economic recovery in Asian countries, and another US$15 billion will be set aside for their possible short-term capital needs during the process of implementing economic reform".

The Japanese government itemized four targets that crisis-hit Asian countries would implement using medium- to long-term financial support.

(a) Supporting corporate debt restructuring in the private sector and efforts to make financial systems sound and stable.
(b) Strengthening the social safety net.
(c) Stimulating the economy (implementation of public undertaking to increase employment)
(d) Addressing the credit crunch (facilitation of trade finance and assistance to small- and medium-sized enterprises)

When the New Miyazawa Initiative was announced, governments such as Thailand and Indonesia in East Asia quickly expressed their approval. Furthermore, prominent persons such as World Bank Vice President J. Stiglitz and Harvard University Professor J. Sachs supported Japan's New Miyazawa Initiative. Naturally, the Japanese government publicized the initiative aggressively but carefully. Three days after the first statement, on October 6, State Secretary of Finance Sadakatsu Tanigaki delivered a statement by Finance Minister K. Miyazawa at the fifty-third Joint

Annual Meeting of the IMF and the World Bank. In his statement, while criticizing the IMF's prescriptions,[10] Miyazawa proposed the New Miyazawa Initiative as "a new scheme of financial assistance totaling some U.S.$30 billion to be provided as Japan's bilateral support". His statement was an expression that the Japanese government was determined to provide bilateral support in opposition to the United States and the IMF.

On December 15, 1998, in his speech "Towards a New International Financial Architecture" at the Foreign Correspondents Club of Japan, Tokyo, Miyazawa proposed. Some concrete ideas about mechanisms for providing quicker and greater liquidity, out of which there were reinforcing functions of the IMF, and establishing regional currency support mechanisms. That is to say, (a) the IMF could create a new facility that would be precautionary as well as quick in disbursement when needed, (b) the IMF could borrow in the market as the institution is granted the capacity to do so by its articles, (c) it is appropriate to consider establishing regional currency support mechanisms, and so forth.

In the last idea (c), he referred to the New Miyazawa Initiative for the Asian countries affected by the crisis, then, he said, "I am hoping that this initiative could lead to further discussions toward a regional currency support mechanism of the type that I just mentioned" (Ministry of Finance, Japan, 1998).

Needless to say, the United States' and the IMF's attitude toward the New Miyazawa Initiative would be decisive in whether it succeeded or not. For that reason, the Japanese government changed the AMF to the New Miyazawa Initiative, and seemed to have found the right timing to start it in order to have it accepted by the U.S. and the IMF.

In contrast with the AMF, which was planned as an international institution, the New Miyazawa Initiative would be bilateral support, even though Finance Minister Miyazawa admitted that the New Miyazawa Initiative could in time develop into some kind of regional currency fund and a wider internationalization of the yen (Business Times, Singapore, October 5, 1998). This means that while bilateral assistance lessens the room the United States and the IMF to express opposition, and gives Japan's government a freer rein, it is only Japanese assistance, rather than a regional agreement or institution of collaboration.[11]

There were actually quite a few cases of the Japanese government giving financial support in the form of assistance, co-financing, parallel loans, and so forth with

---

[10] Miyazawa criticized the IMF, saying that "on a macroeconomic policy level, there are cases where the Fund's traditional prescription that combines fiscal balance improvements with tightening the monetary policy is not appropriate. I say this because in many cases nowadays a currency crisis or international payments difficulties do not stem from current account deficits".

[11] Q&A about the New Miyazawa Initiative to overcome the Asian Currency Crisis: A5. "The AMF, discussed last year, was a multilateral scheme focused on the stabilization of currency. The New Miyazawa Initiative, announced this October, mainly consists of bilateral support focused on assisting Asian countries affected by the currency crisis in overcoming their economic difficulties and contributing to the stability of international financial markets" (MOF, Japan, 1999).

the World Bank, the IMF and the Asian Development Bank. For example, it is co-financing with the World Bank a yen loan for banking system reform project equivalent to approximately US$300 million, which the Japanese government announced to the Philippine government in 1999, as well as yen loan of the same amount for a Metro Manila air quality improvement sector development program, also co-financed with the Asian Development Bank. A yen loan equivalent to approximately US$1500 million was extended to Indonesia in February 1999, as a parallel loan with the IMF/Extended Fund Facility and co-financed with Asian Development Bank and the World Bank.

In fact, on the day, December 16, 1998, that the New Miyazawa Initiative started, involving financial support initially to Thailand and Malaysia, Japan's Prime Minister Keizo Obuchi, in Hanoi, called for greater cooperation without involving Western powers. However, because of its involvement in Iraq and the impeachment proceedings, the Clinton administration could not offer any comments (Far Eastern Economic Review, December 31, 1998).

In this connection, by early May 1999, a total of U.S.$17 billion in financial support to East Asian countries had been announced under the New Miyazawa Initiative. The support was made first to Malaysia and Thailand, in December 1998, thereafter to Indonesia in January 1999, to Indonesia and the Philippines in February, to Malaysia and South Korea in March. The Japanese government was planning to add Vietnam to the qualifying countries for the Miyazawa loans. In September of the same year, an exchange of notes was signed with the Vietnam government to provide JP¥ 20 billion (about U.S.$ 170 million) as part of the New Miyazawa Initiative (MOF Press Release, 1999; GRIPS -J, 2002: 12). In addition to this, on March 25, 1999, the Asian Development Bank approved the establishment of an Asian Currency Crisis Support Facility, established by Japanese contributions of JP ¥7.5 billion (US$625 million equivalent at an exchange rate of US$1 to JP¥ 120) in cash for interest payments and technical assistance grants, and JP¥ 360 billion (U$3 billion equivalent) in government notes for guarantees in fiscal year 1998, under the New Miyazawa Initiative (MOF Press Release, March 23, 1999; ADB, 1999b). This facility's purpose was to assist the crisis-hit countries in overcoming their immediate economic difficulties.

In the preceding part of this section, we confirmed the relation between the AMF and the New Miyazawa Initiative. The New Miyazawa Initiative appeared as a substitute for the AMF, which Japan was forced to adopt due to opposition from the IMF and the United States. The Japanese government does not seem to realize the difference between the two initiatives, especially because the latter was accepted rather successfully. But we have reservations about its form, as we will see in the following section.

8.4.2.2 Significance and Problems of the New Miyazawa Initiative

It is now clear that financial liberalization, as led mainly by the IMF and the United States, has caused market volatility and weakened stability. Bhagwati's assertion that there is a difference in quality between the liberalization of goods and services and that of capital mobility, and UNCTAD's approval of debt moratoriums and capital controls as essential tools for countries affected by crisis, were prompt reflections of this reality. Therefore, the management of free short-term capital movement must be pursued at the international level. While information disclosure by financial institutions, and especially hedge funds, is needed, capital controls by host developing countries should naturally be approved. Malaysian type of capital controls should be approved as an experiment, just as in the Chilean case. Capital controls should not be condemned.

The East Asian crisis is now a new type of financial crisis, as Camdessues said "the crisis of the 21 century". East Asian countries have high saving rates, stable financial conditions, and low inflation rates. But despite of this, a financial crisis broke out.

In general, medium- to long-term capital is crucial in the process of economic growth of developing countries. Criticism of the Asian development model notwithstanding, these countries did manage to induce multinational corporations' foreign direct investment and offered manufacturing bases to their affiliates, and in addition, built a framework for supplying domestic savings to manufacturing industries. These systems allowed East Asian countries to grow for more than three decades.

Globalization, as driven by the IMF and the United States, or the Washington Consensus, takes lightly the role of medium- and long-term capital in latecomers. On the one hand, the IMF neglects responsibility or LTCM moral hazard on the lending side, international financial institutions, and, on the other hand, stresses the responsibility or moral hazard of the borrowing side, developing countries. Moreover, the IMF had been possessed by the illusion that structural reform of the crisis-hit countries could be easily attained by imposing its programs.[12] Although the IMF now recognizes that restrictions on the free flow of capital have some effect, it can be said that the perception of liberalization and structural reform has not fundamentally changed.[13]

---

[12] Vice Minister of Finance for International Affairs Eisuke Sakakibara, at the Manila Framework Meeting in Melbourne, Australia in March 1999, spoke as follows. His comment was much to the point: "For example, there were more than fifty items of structural reform required in the program for Indonesia, including reforms of the food distribution system. I doubt whether all these reforms were absolutely necessary to resolve the crisis. The reform measures were also too ambitious, as evidenced by the closure of 16 banks in Indonesia in a matter of a few days without adequate protection for depositors. Structural reform is not something that can be implemented by a single decision by the decision-maker, like a change in interest rate" (Reform of the International Financial System, http://www.mof.go.jp).

[13] J. Stigliz criticized that even though the 2020 COVID-19 crisis destabilized the currencies of emerging market and developing countries (EMDCs) through capital outflows, the IMF simply "recommended CFMs (capital flow management measures). only as a last resort, after a government had exhausted all other possibilities."Despite the fact that the IMF acknowledged that "capital controls can indeed be effective under certain circumstances" after the Asian financial crisis, in the end, this policy has not been achieved to this day, "owing to resistance from IMF shareholders, financial lobbies, and intransigent economists inside and outside the institution" (Stiglitz & Gallagher, 2022).

The New Miyazawa Initiative seems to have been accepted by the crisis-hit countries. This is because the IMF's unreasonable programs worsened the economies of East Asian countries, and the New Miyazawa Initiative was considered to be a set of support measures for governments and private sectors in difficulties caused by the IMF's programs. In a situation of credit crunch prompted by the IMF's belt-tightening policy of high interest rates and fiscal balance improvements, even many healthy companies became doomed to bankruptcy. Goals such as supporting corporate debt restructuring in the private sector, implementing public works to increase employment, strengthening the social safety net and addressing the credit crunch were easily accepted.

Certainly, there is a dilemma. Such loans may partly help crony capitalism, and allow ineffective economic systems to survive. However, this does not mean that everything should depend on the market. As much as possible, the Japanese government must listen seriously to the voices of people and governments in East Asia (Hirakawa, 1999a).

The New Miyazawa Initiative is "a more modest revised proposal" compared to the AMF proposal in 1997 (ADB, 1999a: 44). The transformation of the AMF, which would have been multinational cooperation, to the New Miyazawa Initiative, which was bilateral cooperation between Japan and other East Asian countries, means that Japan gained increased discretion. As Miyazawa himself pointed out, in his statement of December 15, 1998, when he said that it was a step to future development, the New Miyazawa Initiative needs to be developed into a regional public organization with East Asian perspectives. The AMF initiative was hardly discussed until the 2010s, when Kawai (2015) and Hyun and Paradise (2019), both in ADB publications, suggested the formation of an AMF to foster a regional cooperation system that is more sensitive to the East Asian region's situation. This has prompted the emergence of various kinds of regional cooperation.

8.5 Groping for a New Regional Financial Cooperation Order in East Asia

In this section, in the wake of the Asian financial crisis, we will review the development of regional cooperation by the governments of East Asian countries.

8.5.1 Necessary of a Regional Financial System

We must understand that essentially East Asia's financial and economic crisis does not stem from internal factors, rather from financial globalization. As the currency and economic crisis spread beyond East Asia to Russia, Latin America, and even to the U.S., the essence of the crisis has become ever clearer.

Incidentally, it was unreal for East Asian countries to adopt traditional and domestic-centered development strategies. Industrialization and economic growth in East Asia since the 1960s have been realized only by the region's open development policy to the world economy. While transnational enterprises, which have become major main actors in the world economy, spread their production sites worldwide thanks to progress in transportation and telecommunication as well as production technologies, East Asian countries lured them to invest, and in doing so became integrated in their worldwide production networks. By doing so, East Asia gained the chance to industrialize and to develop their economies through exports.

However, after the second half of the 1980s, financial liberalization was carried out, driven mainly by the United States, and the age of globalization of finance came into existence. Institutional investors and hedge funds that manipulated huge amounts of capital accumulated in the advanced industrial countries and/or augmented the capital through leverage increases actively enlarged their financial business. Astonishing progress in information technology helped this financial globalization. In the same period, East Asian countries adopted financial liberalization policies mainly under IMF guidance. The free movement of capital or globalization of finance, was underpinned by the Washington consensus, or the "Wall Street-Treasury complex" (in the words of Bhagwati, 1998), or the "Wall Street-Treasury-IMF complex" (in the words of Wade and Veneroso 1998). Washington consensus' belief that the market is best[14] seemed to be strengthened by the collapse of the socialist countries, and the industrialization and economic success of the export-led newly industrializing economies in East Asia. However, as a result of the financial liberalization, the crisis then broke out in East Asia.

Therefore, the development of the real economy in East Asia should be considered to be a fruit of the globalization of production since the 1960s. In this sense, single nation-based economic development is impossible (Hirakawa, 1999b). The problem is not globalization but global standardization.

At any rate, the currency and economic crisis should be managed by international cooperation systems beyond national boundaries, in accordance with the nature of the crisis. However, the currency and financial crisis have characteristics which strongly impact on the real economy. Therefore, the social safety net has gained more attention, and economic reforms have had to be implemented prudentially, in balance with the social burden on people. In spite of this, the IMF has clearly neglected regional realities and imposed its own programs which worsened the state of the economies. Of course, East Asian societies have their own histories and conditions, as every society has. Prescriptions for economic reforms cannot be implemented successfully if they neglect the peculiarities of societies. In the East Asian region, it is ideal that an organization which is familiar with the societies implement reforms prudently.

At the Köln Economic Summit, although the strengthening of financial regulation in industrial countries was discussed and attention was focused on supervisors

[14] Bhagwati wrote, regarding the belief in free capital movements, "free capital mobility among all nations was exactly like free trade in their goods and services, a mutual gain phenomenon" (Bhagwati, 1998: 7-8).

and regulators of highly leveraged institutions, there are still no concrete regulations. There are no mechanisms to cope with crises occurring because of free capital movements. Regional financial cooperation or organizations are needed in order to prevent a region from falling into crisis because they understand the real society. Needless to say, an effective mechanism to bring about currency stability had to be worked out, and done in cooperation with the IMF, the World Bank, and other international institutions.

8.5.2 Groping for the Stability of East Asian Currencies

The stability of East Asian currencies is crucial for their development, because the region's economic development has been attained within the world economy. However, it is quite difficult to stabilize currencies. For example, the fluctuations in 1998 of the yen against the dollar ranged 36 yen between the lowest 147.64 yen, recorded on August 11, and the highest, 111.45 yen, on October 8, a particularly great fluctuation occurred from August to October, indicating that international factors were moving the yen's exchange rate. Even in Japan, which produced 14% of the world's gross domestic product (GDP) in 1997, there were huge fluctuations. It should therefore be considered impossible for developing countries to absorb such large fluctuations of exchange rates, because they have adopted export-led policies that lowered their resistance against fluctuations.

Many kinds of systems for keeping currencies stable have been proposed. Eichengreen, who examined the history of currency systems, concluded that only two exchange systems would be able to survive in the twenty-first century: flexible exchange rate systems or a currency union. Pegged rate systems, adjustable hedging systems "target zone systems, and managed floating rate systems as well as, of course, fixed rate systems would continue to face difficulties as capital movement increased and globalization developed" (Eichengreen -Japanese translation, 1997: 68).

In actuality, Europe launched the euro in January 1999, opening a new step for the currency unions, on one hand, while on the other, many developing countries have moved from dollar pegged systems to floating rate systems. In particular, Latin American countries depend enormously on the dollar. "Dollarization" was taking place there both in policy and de facto.

Since Brazil changed to a floating rate system in January 1999, its currency had depreciated, putting more pressure on the Argentine peso to depreciate. Under these situations, Argentina's central bank governor announced a plan to adopt the dollar as its currency. A newspaper in Japan, Nihon Keizai Shimbun said:

> Argentina will make progress on dollarization, replacing the local currency with the U.S. dollar in the future. Argentina will ratify a treaty on dollarization with the United States several years hence, and a currency union of the dollar will be built throughout the Americas. Argentina will be the core of dollarization (Nikkei -J, January 23, 1999).

The Washington Post said that some Latin American countries were engaged "in quiet conversations about adopting the dollar as their currency, as a way of achieving financial stability and faster growth". Argentina, El Salvador, Panama, and Mexico too are actively considering dollarization and,

> The finance ministers of eight Central American countries are scheduled to meet in July 1999 to discuss the pros and cons of dollarization. Officials in Washington, and Latin America must reckon with the *de facto* dollarization of Latin America. Latin Americans already hold a majority of their savings in dollars, and in countries such as Argentina, Bolivia, Peru and Uruguay, at least 70 percent of all banking assets and liabilities are now dollar-dominated (Washington Post, April 28, 1999).

It is said that an interim committee of the IMF stressed the merits of a dollar-centered currency exchange system in its conclusion (Nikkei -J, May 1, 1999). According to the Financial Times, U.S. Treasury Secretary Rubin, in a policy speech before a recent meeting of leading finance officials of the G7, stated that he opposed pegged exchange rate systems. The Times wrote:

> Big international financial packages led by the International Monetary Fund should, as a general rule, no longer be used to support pegged exchange rates. Crises in Asia, Russia, and Brazil have all stemmed from pegged exchange rates that proved unsustainable. Mr. Rubin said emerging economies should adopt either a flexible exchange rate or a strong institutional mechanism such as a currency board that would fix a credible rate (Financial Times, April 22, 1999).

In contrast with Europe and Latin America, the future of international exchange rate systems in East Asia remains unclear. The annual report 1999 of the Asia Development Bank refers to the Asian exchange rate systems, the future of which is still uncertain.

The countries of East Asia certainly had an interest in the single European currency. In September 1997, during the crisis, the issue of a single currency came up for discussion at the meeting of finance ministers of East Asian countries (Nikkei -J, May 2, 1999), and the birth of a single European currency increased interest in such a currency in East Asia.

In an interview by Mainichi Shimbun Editor in Chief Minato Kido of Malaysian Prime Minister Mahathir Mohammad on January 11, 1999, Mahathir claimed that an international currency was now needed in Asia as the euro was born, he said the yen should shoulder the role (Mainichi Shimbun -J, January 12, 1999). On January 11, some bankers from Asian nations that had been severely affected by the region's financial crisis suggested that Asia might someday end up with a single currency similar to the euro, though they acknowledged this would not happen anytime soon, if at all. Some of the central bankers also expressed the opinion that "a single currency for Asia might someday be in the cards", though, according to the Japan Times, they were "far from ready to seriously consider such a step" (Japan Times, January 12, 1999).

Thereafter, at an international conference entitled the Future of Asia held in June 1999, and organized by Nihon Keizai Shimbun Sha, Philippine President Joseph E. Estrada insisted that "an East Asian common currency" be seriously considered in order to reduce over-dependence on the U.S. dollar (Nikkei -J, June 25, 1999).

However, interest in a single currency for East Asia seems to have cooled. A certain high-ranked official of the Monetary Authority of Singapore remarked that concrete discussion of a single currency for East Asia had not progressed thereafter. "As economic differentials between East Asian countries cannot be compared with those between European countries, there is no reality of any single currency for East Asia" (Nikkei -J, May 2, 1999).

Discussions at the start, however, were actively undertaken. As Mahathir pointed out, the yen's role was expected to increase gradually. The Japanese government had also seriously, and with a sense of crisis, begun to embark on the internationalization of the yen since the birth of the euro. Japanese Finance Minister Hikaru Matsunaga, at a meeting of Finance Ministers of APEC member countries held in Canada, in May 1998, announced the internationalization of the yen, and in July, two months later, at the Council on Foreign Exchange and Other Transactions of the Ministry of Finance launched a Sub-council on the Internationalization of the yen, which submitted an interim report in November. On December 22, the Ministry of Finance stated it would step up the internationalization of the yen mainly through two measures: (i) the inducement of competitive price auctions for financing bills (FBs), and (ii) the enforcement of tax reforms related to the internationalization of the yen.

Thereafter, Minister of Finance K. Miyazawa made a statement celebrating the birth of the euro on the first day of its launch, January 1, 1999, in which he pointed to the importance of the internationalization of the yen to pull the East Asian countries out of the crisis.[15]

Furthermore, on April 21, 1999, the Council on Foreign Exchange and Other Transactions submitted a report, stating that a currency basket exchange rate system for East Asian countries was desirable both for the internationalization of the yen, and for East Asian countries to stabilize their currency exchange rates. "The Asian currency crises beginning in 1997 exposed at a stroke the critical risk of linking a currency to the dollar without considering the level of that economy's trade and investment ties with other economies". Therefore, East Asian countries should adopt a currency basket system to lessen the exchange risks, the report said (Council on Foreign Exchange and Other Transactions, Japan, 1999).

Although the United States opposes currency basket systems,[16] it seemed that East Asian countries were generally showing a tendency to adopt such systems. On May

[15] Miyazasa's statement of January 1, 1999 was as follows: "Today marks the birth of a new currency, the euro, which I very much welcome. This is a great step forward towards a closer Economic and Monetary Union which has been made possible by the European countries' efforts in the past 30 or so years. We acknowledge the importance of the internationalization of the yen in light of global economic and financial developments such as the Asian financial crisis" (https://www.mof.go.jp).

[16] The Asian Development Bank observed as below. "In Europe, for instance, it is likely that more countries will ultimately adopt the euro. In Latin America, Argentine policymakers are taking dollarization seriously. In Asia, the future is much more uncertain, and political and practical hurdles to any regional currency union are high. Yet the costs of excessive volatility and competitive devaluation are an important concern in Asia's highly open economies. ... Although the post-crisis period has seen a general movement toward greater exchange flexibility, the diversity in exchange rate regimes continues. This suggests that Asian economies are unlikely to see complete uniformity in exchange rate management soon" (ADB, 1999a: 42).

1, 1999, at a meeting of finance ministers of Japan, China, South Korea and ASEAN countries held in Manila, there was agreement that they would argue the usage of the yen, for market stability and for strengthening the economic relation between Japan and the other countries. They also expressed approval, one after the other, for currency basket systems using the yen, euro, and others. In regard to this, the Nihon Keizai Shimbun commented that this drew a clear line of demarcation against the conclusion of the IMF's interim committee which stressed the merits of a dollar-centered currency exchange system (Nikkei -J, May 1, 1999). Of course, basket currency systems may be less stable than currency unions and face Eichengreen's grim forecast, but still they must be considered a step forward. Nevertheless, one thing is clear: Japan should consider its role in East Asia and try to increase this role, not only for Japan, but also for East Asia in general.

8.5.3 Grouping Toward Regional Cooperation in East Asia

Could it be possible to achieve the internationalization of the yen? It was true that Japan produced 14% of the world's GDP and was the biggest economy in Asia at that time. But Japan's share in the total trade of 9 East Asian countries, consisting of major 4 ASEAN member countries (Thailand, Indonesia, Malaysia, and the Philippines), 4 Asian NIEs, and China was only 16% in 1997. The figures for the United States and the 15 European Union member countries were 17%, and 14%, respectively. Japan's share in total exports and imports of the 9 ASEAN member countries (the ASEAN 4 plus Singapore, Brunei, Vietnam, Laos and Burma) were 13.4% and 19.0% (Council on Foreign Exchange and Other Transactions, Japan, 1999). Japan's share is rather small, considering the geographical proximity between Japan and other East Asian countries.

However, quite a few Japanese firms' affiliates and multinational affiliates from other advanced industrial economies and NIEs had developed businesses in East Asian countries, and they had been rapidly increasing intra-East Asia regional trade. If Japan could stabilize the yen's rate against the U.S. dollar, it could open its domestic market to East Asian countries much more than now, and the internationalization of the yen would progress. For this, Japan would have to become convinced of the significance of East Asian economies and try to build close organic economic relations with them. But even though Japan would decide to pursue the internationalization of the yen, it would be difficult to achieve it. It still at that time maintained the negative legacy of the Great East Asia Co-Prosperity Sphere from the period of World War II. In due consideration of this history, Japan needed to win the trust of East Asian countries and for that reason, Japan would have to make a decisive decision like abolishing the yen, just as, with the birth of the euro, Germany decided to abolish the Deutsch mark.

Anyway, it was significant that Japan, along with other East Asian countries, was working to build a regional cooperation system like an Asian Monetary Fund (AMF).

A policy change from an AMF to the New Miyazawa Initiative was a big step for the Japanese government to gain the trust of other Asian countries.

Since 1998, the idea of a Japan-South Korea Free Trade Zone has been emerging and has drawn much attention. It was also a big step for the future of East Asia, even though it was not realized. We are aware that we, until recently, did not have any concrete economic cooperation systems in the Northeast region, like the ASEAN Free Trade Area in Southeast Asia. The Japan-South Korea Free Trade Zone was first proposed by the South Korean government at a Japan-Korea ministerial conference in November 1998, and joint research between research institutes in both countries regarding the feasibility of a Free Trade Zone has been going on since then. The Korea-Japan and Japan-Korea Business Conference held in Seoul in April 1999, took up this proposal for serious discussion.

Korean government and business interests have expressed strong expectations for the Free Trade Zone (Nikkei -J, May 7, 1999). However, one Japanese newspaper said that Japanese business interests are taking a cautious attitude toward the idea of a free trade zone, because Japanese businesses have faced a long domestic recession, and suffer from excessive capacity and debt (Nikkei -J, May 7, 1999). South Korean businesses were also afraid of excessive imports from Japan. Though the negotiations were subsequently suspended, it became a catalyst for various regional FTAs that followed.

Incidentally, any strengthening of East Asia's regional cooperation raised tensions with the United States. In actuality, the United States' attitude toward the birth of the euro was irrational. Institute for International Economics Director C. Fred Bergsten pointed out that even if Europe's proposal was constructive, United States officials opposed it simply because it has not been made by the United States, and he diagnosed this behavior of his own country "schizophrenia".[17] In our experience, the opposition would be stronger toward East Asia than toward Europe.

The United States refused to attend the meeting of countries planning to give financial support to Thailand, and opposed the AMF. Though it did not reject the New Miyazawa Initiative, it was very sensitive to things through which Japan or other East Asian countries try to take the initiative. At its annual meeting in May 1999, the ADB approved the establishment of a facility, called the Asian Currency Crisis Support Facility (ACCSF), for which funding would be raised through contributions to the ADB by the Japanese government under the New Miyazawa Initiative. The ADB was supplying emergency relief to South Korea and other countries in the midst of the crisis by reassigning financial funds for long-term loans; this was an attempt to institutionalize it.

[17] Bergsten writes: On the one hand, the United States claims that Europe (and, during better times, Japan) should assert greater international responsibility and "share the burdens of leadership". On the other hand, its revealed preference is to try to maintain American dominance even while asking others to pay the bill and to exploit national differences within Europe whenever possible. One senses that some American officials resist European or other international ideas simply because they originated elsewhere. Whatever the cause, the administration has responded with studies in difference or outright hostility to constructive European trade and monetary proposals (Bergsten, 1999: 301).

However, as Japanese newspapers commented and showed obvious anxiety, the field of emergency relief had become "one where the IMF has taken leadership". In fact, the United States and European countries resisted this institutionalization. The reason for their opposition was the argument that the ADB should be an institution supplying long-term loans (Asahi Shimbun -J, May 4, 1999). Behind the United States' opposition was it feared that Japan would augment its political influence in the region through the ADB (Nikkei -J, May 3, 1999).

Both Japan and other East Asian countries had grown within the Asia–Pacific economy after World War II. This structure had not changed fundamentally. Even though Japan was at that time opening its market much more to East Asian countries, still the United States was trying to retain its position as a major political power and major market supplier. Cooperation and conciliation between East Asia and the United States were needed.

Globalization itself was not the problem; rather the problem was the way of globalization. It is safe to say that the IMF's imposition of structural reforms on crisis-hit East Asian countries was a rough-and ready method. Clearly, the way globalization was done must be considered. In developing areas, social costs should be minimized. In East Asia, "after those tumultuous years, many middle-income countries pushed back against the IMF's drive for capital-market liberalization and 'self-insured' against capital-flow volatility by accumulating foreign exchange reserves and implementing capital-account measures" (Stiglitz 2022). They also started thinking seriously about protecting the region from a recurrence of the currency and economic crisis through regional cooperation (Hirakawa, 1999c).

8.6 Concluding Remarks

A number of East Asian countries liberalized their capital markets in the 1990s after "incessant prodding by U.S. advocates of globalization" and fell in the Asian financial crisis (Gyohten 2006: 72; Crowley 2017: 225). Growing countries in East Asia "became magnets for footloose private capital" due to the liberalization of the capital market which they asked, and hedge funds and international monetary institutions did also business using short-term capital.

Many Asian banks and investors borrowed low-interest short-term funds abroad in foreign currencies and invested the funds in illiquid, high-interest long-term domestic projects. It was fund-raising with the risk of so-called "double mismatching". As a result, when real estate prices soared, the bubble economy began to fade, and exports stopped growing, international banks and hedge funds refused to roll over the short-term loans of their lenders, and instead began to recover funds. This led to a devaluation of the local currency and a crisis in the local banking sector. This negative chain of events led to the Asian currency crisis. ADB 50 Annual Journal sums up countries in East Asia as having "miscalculated the monstrous force of globalization" (McCawley, 2017: 225).

The IMF, the U.S., and mainstream economists initially blamed domestic factors in crisis countries for the causes of the crisis, even stating that "currency crises as an opportunity to force fundamental structural and institutional reforms on countries" (Feldstein, 1998: 32). The regulation of highly liquid short-term capital would have been the direction that should have been aimed at in the reform of the international financial system. It didn't go in that direction. The IMF, the U.S., and mainstream neoliberal economics were at the time in a delusion of market mechanisms. As Harvard University Professor, Dani Rodrik wrote, in his book titled The Globalization Paradox in 2011, Anne O. Krueger delivered a Presidential address at the 109th meeting of the American Economic Association in 1997, in which she questioned herself the "issue of how the principle of comparative advantage could have been so blithely abandoned. With hindsight, it is almost incredible that such a high fraction of economists could have deviated so far from the basic principles of international trade" (Krueger, 1997: 11).

Actually, "Economists have long agreed that capital flows, from countries where capital per worker is abundant and has a relatively low real rate of return to countries where capital per worker is scarcer and has a higher real rate of return, could benefit both capital-sending and capital-receiving countries". "In either case, the country would obtain a bundle of goods and services with larger capital inputs than would be achievable in the absence of trade in goods and capital flows. But if "trade in capital" is all that is involved in capital flows, the form of the capital flow should be immaterial- whether long-term bonds issued in the receiving country, long-term commercial bank lending, foreign purchase of equities in the local share market, or FDI" (Ito, & Krueger, 2000: 3).

The communiqué issued by the Interim Committee of the Board of Governors of the International Monetary Fund of the IMF/World Bank Joint Meeting, held in Hong Kong in September 1997, which was in the midst of the Asian currency crisis, called for further liberalization. It pointed out that the "recent turmoil in financial markets has demonstrated again the importance of underpinning liberalization with a broad range of structural measures, especially in the monetary and financial sector, and within the framework of a solid mix of macroeconomic and exchange rate policies, the Committee reiterated its view that an open and liberal system of capital movements, and adopted the Statement on "the Liberalization of Capital Movements Under an Amendment of the Fund's Articles" (IMF, 1997b).

Under these circumstances, East Asian countries in the midst of the currency crisis chose to address the risk of financial liberalization through regional cooperation. In November, two months after the above meeting, a meeting of deputy finance ministers and central bank governors from 14 countries held in Manila abandoned the AMF concept and instead agreed on the Manila Framework, which would strengthen the IMF's response capabilities and establish regional surveillance. Its objectives were to prevent a recurrence of the crisis and to stabilize currencies.

Incidentally, 1997 happened to be the 30th anniversary of the formation of ASEAN, and China, Japan, and South Korea, after "incessant prodding by U.S. advocates of globalization" were invited to the ASEAN Summit Meeting in December of the same year, where they exchanged views on currency issues. A year later, the

ASEAN + 3 leaders decided to hold another summit meeting on a regular basis, and in May 2000, the ASEAN + 3 Finance Ministers agreed to establish the Chiang Mai Initiative. It was a response to the occurrence of liquidity difficulties that could hinder the ability of a country in the region to make external payments. One of the objectives was to provide a short-term accommodation of foreign currency funds by other countries in the form of currency swaps in the face of a liquidity crisis. The other was to create a collective financial support system aimed at stabilizing foreign exchange and financial markets by restraining sharp fluctuations in exchange rates. East Asia recognized the need to strengthen regionalism in order to maintain an international voice in the East Asian region in response to the trend toward regionalism advancing in the West during this period.

Thus, the 3rd ASEAN + 3 Summit in November 1999 issued the first ever "Joint Statement on East Asia Cooperation", confirming cooperation in economic, social, cultural, and political areas, and in financial areas, the promotion of "self-reliance and support mechanisms" in finance (ASEAN, 1999). The Asian currency crisis provided a major impetus for regionalism in East Asia at the beginning of the twenty-first century.

This was, however, not to be the last financial crisis. In 2008, the Lehman Shock triggered the global financial crisis that began in the United States. In 2009, the Economist published a special feature entitled "an astonishing rebound" (The Economist, August 13, 2009) on the economic recovery of emerging Asian countries after the Asian currency crisis of 1997–98 and the dotcom bust of 2001. Both the IMF and the World Bank are now more cautious than in the past with regard to capital liberalization and structural reforms. However, in the 1990s, liberalization was nakedly recommended, and this basic recognition still holds true today. It can be confirmed once again that the Asian currency crisis was a crisis brought about by such liberalization policies and thus became an opportunity for regionalism.

References

**Documents with a symbol (-J) after the author's name are Japanese documents*

ADB. (1999a). *Asian development outlook 1999*. Asian Development Bank.

ADB. (1999b). ADB approves new US $3.06 billion facility to aid Asia's currency crisis-hit countries. *News Release* no.14/99, March 23.

ADB. (1999c). ADB report says economic outline outweighs capital control and protectionism. *News Release* no.22/99, April 19.

ADB. (2000). *Asian development outlook 2000*. Asian Development Bank.

ADB. (2001). *Key indicators of developing Asia and Pacific countries*. Oxford University Press.

Anjaria, Shailendra J. (1998). The capital truth: What works for commodities should work for cash. Foreign Affairs, *77*(6), November/December.

ASEAN. (1999). Joint statement on East Asia cooperation. 28 November 1999 https://asean.org/joint-statement-on-east-asia-cooperation-28-november-1999/.

BIS. (1999). *69th Annual Report 1998–1999*, April 1, 1998- March 31, 2000. Basel: Bank for International Settlement, June 7.

BIS. (2000). *70th* April 1, 1999- March 31, 2000. Basel: Bank for International Settlement, June 5.

Bergsten, C Fred. (1999). America and Europe: Clash of the titans? *Foreign Affairs, 78*(2), March/April.

Bhagwati, Jagdish. (1998). The capital myth: The difference between trade in widgets and dollars. *Foreign Affairs, 77*(3), May/June.

Council on Foreign Exchange and Other Transactions, Ministry of Finance, Japan. (1999). Internationalization of the Yen for the 21st century. April 20 https://www.mof.go.jp/english/about_mof/councils/customs_foreign_exchange/e1b064a.htm (Accessed: Oct. 19, 2022).

Dunsmuir, Lindsay. (2017). IMF calls for fiscal policies that tackle rising inequality. Reuters, October 11 https://www.reuters.com/article/imf-g20-inequality-idUSL2N1ML16B.

Eichengreen, Barry -J. (1997) *Niju-ichi seiki no kokusai tsuka seido (Japanese translation of "International monetary arrangements for the 21st century"*, 1994). Tokyo: Iwanami Shoten.

Eichengreen, Barry. (1999). *Toward a new international financial architecture.* Washington D.C.: Institute for International Economics.

Eichengreen, Barry, & Mussa, Michael. (1998). Capital account liberalization and the IMF. *Finance and Development, 35*(4), December.

ESCAP. (2003). *Bulletin on Asia pacific perspectives 2002/2003.* Economic and Social Commission for Asia and the Pacific, New York: United Nations.

Feldstein, Martin. (1998). Refocusing the IMF. *Foreign Affairs, 77*(2), March/April.

GRIPS -J (2002) Nihon no tai betonamu kaihatsu kyoryoku: Hinkon sakugen wo tomonau ko-han na seicho heno shien (Japan's development cooperation to Vietnam: supporting for broad growth with poverty reduction). *GRIPS Development Forum,* Tokyo: National Graduate Institute for Policy Studies.

G7 Finance Ministers to the Köln Economic Summit. (1999). Report of G7 finance ministers to the Köln economic summit 1999. Cologne, Germany, 18–20 June http://www.g8.utoronto.ca/finance/fm061999.htm.

Gyohten, Toyoo. (2006). The future of Asia. In: Indermit, G., Yukon H., & Kharas, H. (Eds). *East Asian visions: Perspectives on economic development*, Washington DC and Singapore: World Bank and Institute of Policy Studies.

Hirakawa, H. (1999a). The Asian Monetary Fund and the New Miyazawa Initiative, Paper presented at economic sovereignty in a globalizing world: Creating a people centered economics for the 21st century. March 23–26, Chulalongkorn University, Bangkok, Thailand (Reprint: in Singer, Sir Hans, Hatti, Neelamber, & Tandon, Rameshwar (eds.) (2006). *Newly industrializing countries after Asian Crisis*, Delhi: B.R. Publishing Corporation).

Hirakawa, H. (1999b) East Asia's industrialization and the currency and financial crises within the world economy. *journal of International Economic Studies*, Institute of Comparative Economic Studies (Hosei University, Tokyo), no.13

Hirakawa, H. (1999c). East Asia's currency and economic crisis and a new financial and cooperation Order: A view from Japan, Paper presented at Conference on "Toward a New International Financial Order", October 6–8, Taegu, Korea. In: (Reprint) Singer, Sir H., Hatti, N. & Tandon, R. (Eds.), (2006). *Newly industrializing countries after Asian Crisis.* B.R. Publishing, Delhi, India,

ILO News. (2001). ILO's world employment report 2001: Despite improved employment outlook, digital divide looms large. *Press Release*, January 21.

IMF. (1997a). IMF approves stand-by credit for Thailand. *Press Release* no.97/37, August 20.

IMF. (1997b). Communique of the interim committee of the board of governors of the international monetary fund. *Press Release* 97/44, September 21.

IMF. (1998a). *The Asian crisis: A view from the IMF: addressed by Stanley Fischer, First Deputy Managing Director of the IMF*. January 22 https://www.imf.org/en/News/Articles/2015/09/28/04/53/sp012298.

IMF. (1998b). The IMF and developing countries: from myths to realities—Address by Alassane D. Ouattara. November 10.
IMF. (1999). *The IMF responses to the Asian crisis: A fact sheet.* January 17 (This factsheet is no longer being updated. The information it contains may, therefore, no longer be current).
Inman, Phillip. (2020). IMF boss says global economy risks return of Great Depression. The Guardian, January 17 https://www.theguardian.com/business/2020/jan/17/head-of-imf-says-global-economy-risks-return-of-great-depression.
Ito, Takatoshi –J. (1998). Ajia no tsuka kiki to IMF (The Asian currency crisis and the IMF). In: Research Institute for Finance and Monetary Policy (ed.) *ASEAN no kinyu to zaisei no ayumi*, Tokyo: Policy Research Institute, Ministry of Finance, Japan.
Ito, T., & Krueger, Anne O. (2000), Introduction. In: Ito, & Krueger, (Eds.) *The role of foreign direct investment in East Asian economic development.* Chicago and London: the University of Chicago Press.
Kawai, Masahiro -J (1998) *Keizai kyoshitsu: Chiikiteki na kyocho no wakugumi wo (Toward a framework of regional cooperation).* The Nihon Keizai Shimbun, November 4.
Kawa, M., & Quick General Institute eds –J. (1996). *Ajia no kinyu/shihon shijo: Jiyuhka to sougo izon (Financial and capital markets in Asia: Liberalization and interdependence).* Tokyo: Nihon Keizai Shimbun Sha.
Krueger, Anne O. (1997). Trade policy and economic development: How we learn. *American Economic Review, 87*(1).
Krugman, P. (1994). The myth of Asia's miracle. *Foreign Affairs, 73*(6).
Krugman, P. (1998a). What happened to Asia? For a conference in Japan. January http://web.mit.edu/Krugman/
Krugman, P. (1998b). An open letter to Prime Minister Mahathir. September 1 http://web.mit.edu/Krugman/.
Krugman, P. (1998c). Saving Asia: It's time to get radical, Fortune, September 7.
McCawley, Peter. (2017). *Banking on the future of Asia and the Pacific: 50 years of the Asian Development Bank*, The Philippines: Metro Manila.
MOF, Japan. (1998). *Towards a new international financial architecture: Speech by Mr. Kiichi Miyazawa*, the Ministry of Finance at the Foreign Correspondents Club of Japan. https://www.mof.go.jp/english/policy/international_policy/new_international_financial_architecture/e1e057.htm.
MOF, Japan. (1999). Q&A about the New Miyazawa Initiative to overcome the Asian Currency Crisis (New Miyazawa Initiative). Ministry of Finance, Japan https://www.mof.go.jp/english/policy/international_policy/financial_cooperation_in_asia/new_miyazawa_initiative/my001.htm.
MOF Press Release. (1999). ODA loan to Viet Nam—to support economic reform of Viet Nam. September 29 https://www.mofa.go.jp/announce/announce/1999/9/929.html.
Motoyama, Yoshihiko -J (1999). Fudo teki tanki gaishi kisei no mosaku (Groping for regulation of floating short-term foreign capital). *Sekai Keizai Hyoron (World Economic Review), 43*(1).
Radelet, Streeten, & Sachs, Jeffery. (1997). Asia's reemergence. *Foreign Affairs, 76*(6).
Singh, Ajit. (1998). Asian capitalism and the financial crisis. *MPRA Paper* no. 54932, August 19 https://mpra.ub.uni-muenchen.de/54932/.
Shirai, Sayuri –J. (1999). *Kensho IMF keizai seisaku (Checkback of IMF economic policies).* Tokyo: Toyo Keizai Shimpo Sha.
Stiglitz, Joseph. (1998). Road to recovery: Restoring growth in the region could be a long and difficult process. Asia Week, July 17.
Stiglitz, J., & Gallagher, K. P. (2022). The IMF's unfinished business. *Policy Syndicate*, March 7 https://www.project-syndicate.org/commentary/imf-review-must-embrace-capital-controls-by-joseph-e-stiglitz-and-kevin-p-gallagher-2022-03.
UNCTAD. (1998a). *World investment report 1998: Trends and determinants. United Nations Conference on Trade and Development*, New York: United Nations.
UNCTAD. (1998b). *Trade and development report 1998.* United Nations.

UNCTAD. (1998c). Changes emerge in foreign investment into Asia. November 2, *UNCTAD Press Release* TAD/INF/2779.
Wade, Robert, & Venerosos, Frank. (1998). The Asian crisis: The high debt model versus the Wall Street-Treasury-IMF complex. *New Left Review*, no.228, March/April.
Wakatsuki, Mikio –J. (1997). Ajia tsuuka kiki to kinyu kyocho (The Asian financial crisis and financial cooperation). *Kokusai Kinyu (International Finance Journal)*, Tokyo: Institute of Foreign Exchange and Trade Research, no.992, September 15 issue.
Wolfensohn, James D. (1997). The challenge of inclusion: World Bank President James D. Wolfensohn addresses the Annual Meetings, Hong Kong. September 23 (no file number) http://hdl.handle.net/10986/26154.
World Bank. (1993). *The East Asian miracle: Economic growth and public policy*. World Bank. Oxford University Press.
World Bank. (1997). World Bank supports implementation of financial reform in Thailand. *Press Release* no.98/1480/EA.
World Bank. (1998). *Annual report 1998*. World Bank Group.
World Bank. (2000). *East Asia: Recovery and beyond*. World Bank Group.

Chapter 9
Advancing Regionalism and Economic Cooperation in Asia

Abstract This chapter provides a historical overview of regional cooperation and regionalism pursued in Asia, particularly in East Asia, with a focus on the contemporary period. Specifically, it traces the development of regional cooperation and regionalism from Japan's conception of the Greater East Asia Co-prosperity Sphere in the first half of the twentieth century to the postwar period. The study will examine how regional cooperation has dramatically developed through institutionalization, which was triggered by the Asian currency crisis, and how it has been influenced by and linked to regional integration in the West. Furthermore, we will confirm that the emergence of new structures in this century has brought about a further phase of change, and we will examine its current characteristics and challenges.

Keywords AFTA · ASEAN+3 · East Asia Summit · Economic integration · Greater East Asia Co-Prosperity Sphere · RCEP · Regionalism · TPP (CPTPP)

9.1 Introduction

The late 2010s and 2020s can be described as a period of dramatic qualitative change in the world and East Asian economies. Regional cooperation or regionalism has shifted from intra-regional cooperation to a policy of regional integration within the global economy, and a breakaway from the U.S.-centered world order created throughout the second half of the twentieth century appears to be underway. Moreover, with the U.S. abandoning its Asia policy under the Trump administration and the subsequent COVID-19 pandemic further accelerating this structural change, we can say that we are moving into a new phase of Asian economic regionalism.

This chapter first briefly traces the development of East Asian regionalism from the 1940s to the 1950s. Next, the formation of the basic conditions for East Asian regionalism in the 1960s is reviewed, and the development of regionalism or regional cooperation from the 1970s to the Asian currency crisis of the 1990s is examined, divided into two parts by the Plaza Accord of 1985. Furthermore, the institutionalization of East Asian regional cooperation after the Asian currency crisis, especially in

H. Hirakawa and F. C. Maquito, *The Dynamics of Asian Economic Development*,
https://doi.org/10.1007/978-981-97-3106-0_9

the beginning of this century, will be examined, as well as the structure of promotion of the mega FTA/EPAs in the broader region that became prominent in the 2010s. Finally, we will take a bird's eye view of Asian regional cooperation and regionalism over the past century or so, and mention the achievements and challenges of economic integration and regionalism in contemporary East Asia.

9.2 Regionalism in the 20th Century and Its Development

This section will review the development of regional cooperation and regionalism in three phases in order to put today's regionalism and its institutionalization in a broader perspective, briefly mentioning the Japanese concept of the Greater East Asia Co-prosperity Sphere in the first half of the twentieth century and the Colombo Plan, the first cooperation mechanism after World War II. The institutionalization of regional cooperation and its development in the 1960s will also be reviewed.

9.2.1 Regional Integration Concepts and Decolonization Under 20th Century Imperialism

Japan's attempts at economic integration in Asia during the period from the early twentieth century to World War II included Japan's conception of the Greater East Asia Co-prosperity Sphere, which, after winning the Sino-Japanese War in 1894 and the Russo-Japanese War in 1904, enhanced Japan's tendency toward aggression in Asia,

The Japanese Foreign Minister Yōsuke Matsuoka formally announced the idea of the Co-Prosperity Sphere on 1 August 1940, in a press interview.[1] In 1941, Japan entered the Greater East Asia War (World War II), advocating the construction of a vast "Greater East Asia Co-Prosperity Sphere" (GEACPS) that would stretch from Northeast Asia up to the "South" (Southeast Asia). It was a war in which Japan, as a "have not country" without resources, sought to create a self-sufficient economic zone. Ideologically, the war was justified by the liberation of Asia, which had been colonized or anti-colonized by the Western powers.

In November 1943, Japan held the "Greater East Asia Conference" in Tokyo and issued the "Greater East Asia Joint Declaration". The participants included representatives from the "Manchukuo (a puppet state created in 1932 by Japan)", the Republic of China (WāngJīngwèiZhèngquán), the Philippines and Burma, whose independence Japan had recognized, as well as India, whose provisional government had been recognized as an observer. The Declaration defined the Greater East Asia War as a war to "free Greater East Asia from the fetters of the United States and Great Britain" and called for respect for independence and mutual assistance. The

[1] James L. McClain, Japan: A Modern History p 470 ISBN 0-393-04156-5.

second Greater East Asia Conference could not be held due to the worsening war situation.

In fact, Japan's war confused the liberation of Asia with Japanese domination of Asia, and increasingly tended toward the latter. The anti-Japanese independence movements that emerged throughout Asia, when viewed from the Japanese perspective, lead to the conclusion that the war was self-righteous and a justification for aggression[2] (Yasuda -J, 1990; Hirakawa -J, 2015). This is evidenced by the fact that the distrust created among Asian nations by the invasion imposed restrictions on Japan's Asian policies for a long time afterward.

However, from the perspective of the Asian peoples colonized by the West, the Japanese invasion brought about disappointment and distrust of Japan, but at the same time, by causing them to question the absolute superiority of the West, it provided an opportunity for the Asian peoples to rise up toward independence after Japan's defeat in the war. This fact cannot be denied. Lest we inadvertently throw the baby out with the bathwater, it should be noted that there was a thinking in Japan that was aligned with a more genuine GEACPS. Japan's fear of colonization from Western powers drove it to its over 200 years of isolationism or virtual autarky from 1603 to 1868. As Western powers came to pry open her ports, Japan was forced to accept various unequal arrangements, which, as was the practice then toward latecomers, did not afford her the luxury of protecting domestic industries, and provided special privileges to the Western businesses operating within Japan. It was not only after Japan's annexation of Formosa (now Taiwan) and South Korea, and her victory against the Russian Baltic fleet during the Meiji Restoration that Japan was able to regain a more equal footing with the Western powers.

Since the Meiji Restoration of 1868, Japan has been torn between "*Datsua*" (getting out of Asia) and "*Koa*" (prospering with Asia). The path chosen, however, by Japan in the early part of the twentieth century was *datsua* and an integration with the world economy (Serizawa, 2015).

Japan's involvement in global trade already had the strategic features of the Flying Geese type of development to be observed by Akamatsu in the early 1930s. Japan was import-substituting for labor-intensive and capital-intensive goods, wherein industries established in South Korea and Taiwan, then colonies of Japan, were uncompetitive but were supported by protectionist walls. Japan was promoting the export of labor-intensive consumer goods, causing a surge of cheap imports from Japan by the Southeast Asian countries. This was initially welcomed by the powerful lobbies in the colonized countries, as it allowed them to sustain the low wages. With the World Depression of the 1930s, however, the colonial powers turned towards protectionist measures to shield ailing businesses in the mainland and the colonies. This rise in protectionism put at risk the ability of Japan to continue waging its war in China, and inadvertently supported the strategic proposal of the hawkish elements in Japanese

[2] Japanese researcher Toshie Yasuda examines the Greater East Asia Conference and its declaration in detail based on historical documents and concludes that the "liberation of Asia" in the declaration was a deception. In addition, she confirms the fact that the anti-Japanese national independence movement in the Japanese occupied territories was one of the reasons for Japan's defeat in the war (Yasuda -J, 1990: 416-417).

politics to secure the sources of raw materials and markets in Southeast Asia through the use of military means.

The Manchurian incident of 1931 and the consequent disengagement of Japan from the League of Nations in 1933 saw the rise of popularity of Pan Asianism, practically ignored during the datsua decades, within the Japanese government (Aydin, 2008). Pan Asianism provided the underlying idea of the GEACPS, and is an ideology that propagated the liberation and unity of all Asian peoples (Matthiessen, 2011).

Perhaps emboldened also by the "benign neglect"[3] of the U.S. with regards to Japan's incursions in China, the Japanese imperial army pushed south from Manchuria to northern and further to southern Indo-China. This finally prompted the U.S, as well as the British and the Dutch, to freeze Japanese assets in the U.S., enforcing a de-facto oil embargo on Japan on August 1, 1941 (U.S. time). Almost a day before that on August 1, 1941 (Japan time), Japanese Foreign Minister Matsuoka Yosuke formally introduced the GEACPS to the general public.

It was unfortunate that the Japanese military under war conditions was entrusted with implementing the GEACPS. The consensus within the Japanese government over its details was not reached until 1943, which by then was too late, as Japan was starting to lose the war (Yellen, 2019). Even with such a consensus, it is doubtful that the vision could be effectively implemented given the lack of well-functioning administrative machinery in the colonies.

According to Matthiessen (2011), there were two thoughts of Pan Asianism in Japan that were both influential on Japanese government policy making. One is the exoteric Pan Asianism, which was represented by the Dai Ajia Kyōkai (1933-End of WWII), and the other is the esoteric Pan Asianism, which was represented by the Shōwa Kenkyūkai (1933–1940). Both were advisory bodies to the Konoe Fumimaro administration. While both streams recognized the need for solidarity with Asian peoples, the esoteric stream viewed this to be a more challenging program, and was more open to the use of punishment when confronted with resistance. The mixed reception of Southeast Asian nations to GEACPS and invading Japanese imperial forces effectively validated both streams. Even in the Philippines, there were those who ascribed to Japan's Pan-Asianism, but they were not really able to rally support for this cause given that American ideals have already been deeply entrenched within Philippine society.

Despite it being branded as propaganda, GEACPS is said to have contributed to the ending of an imperial world order, and instilling in the erstwhile colonies the confidence of extricating themselves from their colonial masters.[4] It took decades for ASEAN members to overcome the trauma of Japanese occupation. It is now quite clear, however, that Japan and the sovereign members of ASEAN could work together as equals towards a genuine GEACPS[5] that would sustain peace and prosperity for the Greater East Asia region.

[3] U.S.-Japan trade continued to be strong even in the politically tense years of the 1930s. See Nakagawa (2010).

[4] For a fuller discussion, see Aydin (2008).

[5] See Singh (2002) for the discussion of the evolution of ASEAN's views towards Japan after WWII.

After the end of World War II, Asian colonies became independent one after another. The first regional cooperation initiative involving the newly independent countries was the "the Colombo Plan for Cooperative Economic Development in South and Southeast Asia".[6] In the Plan's establishment, the Indian Ambassador to China (the National Government at Nanking and later to the People's Republic of China in Peking between 1948 and 1952), Kavalam Madhava Panikkar sent "a memorandum to the English and Australian ambassadors, the main argument of which was that without immediate and adequate help in the economic field, the political structure of South-East Asia would provide no more than a frail barrier to the expansion of communism". Their joint proposal for a Commonwealth Ambassadors Meeting was the beginning (Panikkar, 1955: 55–56; Fisher, 1971: 301). In fact, India's initiative in the formulation of the Colombo Plan was significant (Nowik, 2013: 123; Watanabe, -J, 2014: 29). After India became politically independent in 1947, Prime Minister Jawaharlal Nehru, at the request of the Fourth Commonwealth Prime Ministers Conference in 1949, changed the name of the "British Commonwealth of Nations" to "the Commonwealth of Nations". The Colombo Plan was adopted by the Commonwealth Finance Ministers' Conference in London in that year, followed by the Commonwealth Conference on Foreign Affairs in 1950 (London). The Colombo Plan was officially launched at the Commonwealth Conference on Foreign Affairs in 1950 (Colombo) after the Commonwealth Finance Ministers' Conference in London that year, and began its activities the following year in 1951. The founding members were the seven Commonwealth nations: Australia, Britain, Canada, Ceylon (now Sri Lanka), India, New Zealand, and Pakistan (Colomb Plan Home page. Accessed Jan.16, 2022).

By the way, the name change to Commonwealth demanded by India was an event related to the basic philosophy of the organization. Watanabe writes about it that the character of the Commonwealth of Nations became "not a centralized system of domination by suzerain Britain as it had been before the war, but an equal and complementary relationship among the Commonwealth countries, which also sought a cooperative relationship with UN agencies" (Watanabe -J, 2014: 25, 29). The nature of the cooperation reflected the perceptions of development economics at the time. The Colombo Plan, therefore, was followed by the participation of South and Southeast Asian countries: the United States and Laos in 1951, Burma (now Myanmar) and Nepal in 1952, Indonesia in 1953, Japan, the Philippines, and Thailand in 1954, and Malaysia in 1957 (Nowik, 2013: 124). Incidentally, as of 2023, the number of participating countries is 28. The nature of the Colombo Plan is described today as follows.

> The Colombo Plan is a partnership concept of self-help and mutual-help in development aimed at socio-economic progress of its member countries (https://colombo-plan.org/overview/ Accessed Jan.18, 2022).

---

[6] The name was changed, due to adopting a new constitution in 1977 when its members grew to 27 nations, beyond the group of the commonwealth nations and expand the scope of its activities, to "The Colombo Plan for Cooperative Economic and Social Development in Asia and the Pacific" (The Colombo Plan Secretariat, History https://colombo-plan.org/history/).

It goes without saying that the establishment of the Colombo Plan was born with the intention of preventing the shift to communism. Asia at that time was the poorest in the world and the domino of communism was a real threat; the participation of the U.S. in the Colombo Plan in 1951 was a reflection of that, and the accession of Japan with the support of the U.S. was also aimed at the same thing. In any case, the participation of the U.S. enabled it to secure the largest budget on behalf of its former colonial power, the United Kingdom, which was in the midst of a pound crisis. Thus the transfer of physical capital and technology took place. Airports, roads, railroads, dams, hospitals, and fertilizer plants were built, while mutual technology transfer and skilled development among member countries were emphasized (Nowik, 2013: 124; Watanabe -J, 2014: 39; Hatano & He -J, 2014: 301). Indeed, technical assistance was a modest but near-ideal form of mutual support and self-help and mutual assistance for the newly independent member states. Kazuo Kaneko, an official in the Asian Bureau of the Japanese Ministry of Foreign Affairs, described the plan in 1957 as follows.

> In general, the member countries of the Colombo Plan are capitalist countries, so there is no reason for them to provide capital assistance that is not profitable at all. There is only a difference in whether the aid is intended to sow seeds for the distant future or for immediate transactions. In this respect, technical assistance is extremely simple and straightforward. Supplying technology to a country that lacks it and raising the level of that technology is advantageous in the long run from the viewpoint of the donor country, and from the viewpoint of the recipient country, it is meaningful to save the country from an immediate crisis. Although technical assistance is modest, there is less fear of so-called strings attached than with capital assistance, and this was most consistent with the ostensible objectives of the Colombo Plan (Kaneko -J, 1957: 66).

Kaneko's eyes on countries that have just gained independence from colonies seem to somewhat look down on the member countries, but in any case, they are on the side of Japan to help. However, the Colombo Plan's emphasis on technical assistance has shifted its attention to the independence of emerging and independent developing countries in Asia. This perspective eventually leads to social development down to the community level. Incidentally, in the twenty-first century, the current areas of cooperation in this plan are the following four permanent programmes. Drug Advisory Programme (DAP), Capacity Building Programme, Gender Affairs Programme (GAP), Environment Programme (Colombo Plan Home Page. Accessed Jan.20, 2022). The characteristics of self-help from the beginning of the project seem to have been inherited by the Colombo Plan, which emphasizes social development.

What was the significance of the Colombo Plan? Kaneko points out the following three points. (1) Formulation of policies in South and Southeast Asia, (2) Provision of a forum for economic discussions, and (3) Establishment of a centralized provision system through technical assistance mechanisms. In other words, the greatest significance is that it functioned as an international organization for cooperation among the developing countries of southern Asia and the developed countries of Northern and southern Asia, involved in development cooperation, mainly in line with the position of emerging developing countries.

Kaneko explains why the Colombo Plan has become a regional cooperation organization in the Asia–Pacific region as follows.

> If Japan came out, it would inevitably be held responsible for the war in some way, if the United States came out, it would be stigmatized as economic domination, and if the Soviet Union or the Chinese Communist Party came out, it would have become a major conflict. It was only because of the tilt of the eaves that Britain was able to provide a forum for discussions on economic development in South and Southeast Asia without causing much discontent (Kaneko -J, 1957: 66).

Incidentally, in the Colombo Plan, which was organized amid the decline of British national power, the treatment of Japan was on the agenda from the beginning. In the end, with the expectation of becoming a donor, he accepted the idea that "Commonwealth countries should open not only China but also the entire Asian market to Japan in order to prevent Japan from demilitarizing and rearmament, and to encourage economic reconstruction". The threat of communism and the expectation of economic aid paved the way for Japan's accession.

The Colombo Plan's response worked in Japan's favor in two ways. One reason is that, despite losing the war, "Japan also sought to open the Asian market through economic cooperation as a new 'factory of Asia' while dispelling the image of economic aggression before the war" (Watanabe -J, 2014: 39). The other is to return to the international community through participation in the Colombo Plan. This was Japan's greatest wish at the time (Murakami -J, 1960: 11). Japan joined the Colombo Plan in 1954 with the "backing of the United States"[7] and from 1955 was able to begin accepting trainees and sending experts as a government-based technical cooperation (MOFA, 2001: 11; JICA HP: about ODA. Accessed Jan.16, 2022). While the participating countries looked to Japan for its technological capabilities and assistance in lifting itself out of poverty, Japan gained a foothold in returning to the international community in Asia, where distrust of Japan is deep-rooted. The fact that Japan had no war reparations issue between India, Pakistan, and Ceylon further raised expectations for accession (Hatano & He -J, 2014: 302, 315). Incidentally, in 1954, Japan became an official member of ECAFE.

1956 was the year that Japan's "White Paper on the Economy" wrote that "[Japan] is no longer post-war." Under the scrutiny of Japan by Asian countries, steady technical assistance was an ideal form of assistance for Japan at that time, as it was a return to the international community and economic development.[8]

[7] During the Cold War in the 1950s, the United States supported development through trade for the reconstruction of Japan in opposition to the opposition of Asian countries, such as the United Kingdom, France, and the Netherlands, which had a strong distrust of Japan. Whiteman states that the U.S. supported Japan's trade with the ECAFE region for obvious reasons and that "The SCAP representatives to ECAFE meetings virtually became a salesman for Japanese goods" (Whiteman, 1963: 236).

[8] To commemorate the 50th anniversary of the establishment of the Colombo Plan, the White Paper on Japan's ODA 2021 summarizes the major contributions made to the development of Asia by Japan's ODA, which began with the technical cooperation of the Colombo Plan. "Overall, Japanese assistance has made a major contribution—through human resources development and the improvement of economic and social infrastructure—to the rapid economic development process that became known as the 'Asian Miracle'" (MOFA, 2001: 11).

Looking back, the Colombo Plan was launched with the aim of economic and social development in the impoverished Asian region, and based on the idea that the emerging participating countries of Asia would cooperate for development on an equal footing. The Colombo Plan's work was a humble but pivotal form of self-reliance in poverty-stricken Asia. It can be said that this was the vitality that continued to this day. At the same time, it was an important first step in the reconstruction of Japan and its return to the international community.

9.2.2 The 1960s: The Development of Two Asian Regionalisms

Failure of the OAEC Establishment Initiative and the Establishment of ASEAN

The 18th session of the United Nations Economic Commission for Asia and the Far East (ECAFE) in March 1962 was expected to realize the concept of the Organization for Asian Economic Cooperation (OAEC). In January of the same year, ECAFE Secretary General U Nyun, who was born in Myanmar, presented a proposal for the establishment of the OAEC to the member countries, and in March 1960, the 16th General Assembly of ECAFE asked U Nyun to formulate a concept for promoting regional economic cooperation (Whiteman, 1963: 299), and in response to his request, he established the "Three-member Committee of Experts on Asian Economic Cooperation". This is because it was based on the final report of one of the members of the committee, Saburo Ōkita of Japan.

The final report recommended cooperative measures such as preferential tariffs, the establishment of multilateral payment mechanisms to address trade imbalances among countries, and long-term contracts for agricultural and mineral resources, and the OAEC was the organization to achieve these objectives. However, the newly independent countries of Asia at that time did not materialize despite their expectations due to the emphasis on economic policies by each country, distrust of the major powers in the region, and Japan's consideration for the United States and its wariness of the fiscal burden. In the end, the 1962 ECAFE General Assembly in Tokyo failed to even put OAEC on the official agenda (Whiteman, 1963: 291–294: 330–335; Hoshiro -J, 2007: 3).

According to Hoshiro Hiroshi, a Japan researcher at the University of Tokyo who examined in depth Japan's response to the OAEC policy-making process, Japan's decision on the OAEC was "Japan's financial concerns and the protection of agriculture" and "the Minister of Agriculture (Minister of Agriculture and Forestry) in particular expressed a stance of opposition to trade between Japan and Asia itself." Japan's diplomacy is largely influenced by the intentions of the United States. However, at that time, the Japanese government had decided on a policy of opposition before the United States conveyed its intention to oppose it (Hoshiro -J, 2007: 16).

Incidentally, the same report also proposed the establishment of an Asian Development Bank for the provision of development financing. In addition, ECAFE Executive Director U Nyun played an important role in the founding of the ADB. He "led the talks" at preparatory meetings held in Bangkok, Manila, and Wellington (New Zealand) from 1963. Thus, in 1966, the ADB was established. Japan had high hopes that the ADB's headquarters would be in Tokyo, but in the end it was Manila, Philippines. However, Takeshi Watanabe, a former Japanese finance bureaucrat who played a major role in the preparation process, was appointed as governor (Nakao -J, 2017: xii).

In the 1960s, other countries in the Cold War structure that belonged to the liberal camp moved to establish various international organizations. The Asian Foreign Ministers' Meeting (ASPAC) proposed by then-South Korean President Park Chung-Hee is one of them. ASPAC began in Seoul in 1966 and lasted until 1972.

ASEAN was also formed in 1967. In addition to the Cold War structure, Southeast Asia had complex ethnic and racial problems, and had been a region of constant conflict until then. In 1961, the Commonwealth of Malaya Prime Minister Tunku Abdul Rahman announced a plan to establish a "Malaysia" that included Singapore in the British Channel Colony, as well as Sabah and Sarawak on the island of Borneo. Independence was achieved in 1963, but Indonesia criticized the plan as a British "neo-colonialist project" and adopted a policy of "confrontation" with military action. The policy of "confrontation" lasted until 1966. The Philippines also claimed Sabah, and conflicts continued with Britain and Malaysia. During this period, Singapore became independent from Malaysia in 1965. In the 1960s, the Vietnam War began in 1965 with the bombing of North Vietnam, and the fighting intensified.

Amid the threat of communism and unstable regional international relations, the five countries of Indonesia, Malaysia, the Philippines, Singapore and Thailand agreed to establish ASEAN, "strengthening the economic and social stability of the region and ensuring their peaceful and progressive national development', and 'to ensure their stability and security from external interference in any form" (ASEAN Declaration, Aug. 8, 1967). However, although the summit had to wait until 1976 and economic cooperation was not embarked on until later, the birth of ASEAN was a decisive event in the formation of the international order in Southeast Asia. Susumu Yamakage, an ASEAN scholar in Japan, sees ASEAN during this period as a system for political security cooperation (Yamakage -J, 1991: 114–115).

Japan's Proposal for an Asia–Pacific Economic Community

The 1960s also saw the emergence of regionalism in Japan that extended to the Pacific Ocean. Japan was increasing its national power through rapid economic growth, and interest in the Asia–Pacific region was increasing. Morinosuke Kajima, who advocated "Pan-Asia" as a peaceful regionalism before World War II, began advocating an "Asia–Pacific Community" in 1964 in response to the development of the EEC (Kajima -J, 1964a, b: 34–35).

The United Kingdom applied to join the EEC, which was established in 1957, and Greece became an associate member in 1961.[9] The annual World Economic Report 1961 of Japan's Economic Planning Agency (now the Cabinet Office) reported:

> If the United Kingdom is admitted membership, not only Denmark and Norway, which have already announced their accession, but also Austria, Switzerland, and Sweden, which are politically neutral countries, will become associate members, and Portugal will also join (Economic Planning Agency -J, 1961: Part 1, Chap. 3).

The following year, in 1962, the EEC made steady progress in institutional integration, including the reduction of tariffs within the region, the elimination of quantitative restrictions on industrial products, and the Common Agricultural Policy (Economic Planning Agency -J, 1961, 1962). In 1967, the executive bodies of the three communities, the EEC, the European Coal and Steel Community (ECSC), and the European Atomic Energy Community (Euratom), were merged to form the European Community (EC). Against the backdrop of these developments in Europe, Japan developed a concept of Asian economic integration with the United States and Canada. Kajima wrote about the importance of the Asia–Pacific Community as follows:

> If the Asia-Pacific Economic Community is formed, so to speak, as an Asian version of the EEC, U.S. President Johnson's development plan for Southeast Asia, ECAFE's various development plans, the Colombo Plan, and the plans of local countries will be promoted more effectively (Kajima -J, 1966a: 7).
>
> Over the past year or two, a sense of regional solidarity has rapidly strengthened among the liberal countries of Asia, and it is attracting attention as a new trend in Asia. The Ministerial Conference for Economic Development in Southeast Asia and the Asia-Pacific Ministerial Conference (ASPAC) are held regularly every year, and the Asian Development Bank was also launched. More recently, the Association of Southeast Asian Nations (ASEAN) was formed consisting of five countries: Thailand, the Philippines, Malaysia, Singapore, and Indonesia, and although Japan, Australia, New Zealand, and the United States and Canada are expected to participate in the near future. The Pacific Basin Economic Cooperation Council (PBEC)[10] is also attracting attention. Recently, the diplomatic line of Eisaku Sato and Takeo Miki has greatly expanded the concept of the Asia-Pacific region and is trying to greatly promote the role of the only developed country in Asia in the formation of such a regional community. This concept is exactly what I envisioned for the Asia-Pacific Community (Kajima -J, 1968: 9).

In fact, Morinosuke Kajima, Eisaku Sato, Takeo Miki, and Kiichi Miyazawa proposed the concept of an "Asia–Pacific Organization" in 1969 (Oba -J, 2004: 212). Miki, who was foreign minister under the Sato cabinet at the time, paid attention

---

[9] Great Britain applied for full membership in 1961. However, at this time, it did not materialize due to the opposition of the then French President de Gaulle. Denmark, Ireland and the United Kingdom joined the EU in 1973 (the first expansion). Greece in 1981 (second expansion), Spain and Portugal in 1986 (third expansion), and Australia, Finland and Sweden in 1995 (fourth expansion).

[10] PBEC was established by the President of the Japan Chamber of Commerce and Industry T. Tadashi Adachi Japan President of the Japan Chamber of Commerce and Industry, was proposed by the President of Bradford Cotton Company and others, and was inaugurated in Tokyo in April 1967 with the participation of private economic representatives from Japan, Australia, New Zealand, Canada, and the United States. It is an APEC affiliated organization (PBEC Fast Facts).

to the "Free Trade Area of the Pacific (PAFTA)" concept advocated by Kiyoshi Kojima, a professor at Hitotsubashi University at the time, and set out to realize the Asia–Pacific concept. Kojima describes the background of the PAFTA concept and its subsequent development as follows:

> For about one and a half years from 1964, he participated in the joint research of Professor Balassa. The results were later published. During this joint research, I felt a sense of crisis about what would happen to the economic development of the Pacific Rim region, even though the development of the European Community was wonderful, would the region be left behind? This was the beginning of the Pacific Economic Bloc concept. In November 1965, Mr. Saburo Okita held a conference entitled "Trade and Development in Underdeveloped Countries" at the Japan Economic Research Center. It was here that my vision of the "Common Pacific Market" was first introduced. In March-April 1967, Mr. Takeo Miki, then Minister of Foreign Affairs, was attracted to my proposal for the Pacific Community, and asked me to come out to see if an international conference of scholars could be held in order to promote the idea. He visited the United States, Canada, the United Kingdom, Australia, and New Zealand, and had a brief meeting with key people. In January 1968, I became the chairman of the organizing committee and started the Pacific Trade and Development Conference (PAFTAD) at the Japan Center for Economic Studies. Although I expected it to be a one-time conference, the interest and enthusiasm of the participants was strong, and it became a unique kind of conference that has survived and developed to this day (Kojima -J, 1984: 513–514).

Kojima also wrote:

> My 1965 paper entitled "The Pacific Common Market and Southeast Asia" became the founding of the Pacific Economic Community = Pacific Economic Zone Formation Movement. This paper led to the establishment of our PAFTAD = Pacific Conference on Trade and Development in Tokyo in 1968 under the direction of Mr. Takeo Miki, then Minister of Foreign Affairs, and has continued to conduct basic research on the Pacific Rim economy to this day (Kojima -J, 1990: i).

Although the Asia–Pacific Community of Kajima and the Pacific Economic Community of Kojima had the same target area, there was a significant difference in the perception of what the community should be. Kajima, a diplomat, politician, and business manager, literally conceived of a community of interstate cooperation. On the other hand, economist Kojima proposed that the "five advanced countries of the Pacific" (the United States, Canada, Japan, Australia, and New Zealand) form an economic integration like a free trade area and jointly explore a policy of economic cooperation with Southeast Asia (Kojima -J, 1990: 1).

There was a difference in the basic perception of Asian regionalism. It is a question of who will take the initiative, but the concept of regional cooperation for development has emerged from both Japan and ASEAN.

9.2.3 *The 1970s to the 1990s: Two Coexisting Regionalisms*

The Nixon Shock and East Asia

From the 1970s until the Asian financial crisis of 1997, there were two major changes in the international and regional political and economic environment in the world and in Asia. Regional cooperation or regionalism in Asia emerged in line with the changes of the 1970s, and took a major turn with the Plaza Accord in 1985.

First, let's take a look at the major changes that took place in the world and Asia in the 1970s. In August 1971, the U.S. stopped converting gold and dollars, the so-called Nixon shock. Then, in October 1973, the first oil shock broke out, and the world economy entered a phase of serious stagnation. The exchange rate regimes of major advanced economies shifted from fixed exchange rates to floating exchange rates, and the International Monetary Fund/General Agreement on Tariffs and Trade (IMF/GATT) regime collapsed. In East Asia, China's accession to the United Nations was realized in 1971, followed by a visit by U.S. President Richard Nixon and the normalization of diplomatic relations with Japan with China the following year. In 1973, the Vietnam War came to an end with the conclusion of the Paris Agreement, but in 1976, North and South Vietnam were unified to form the Socialist Republic of Vietnam.

However, at a time when the world economy was stagnating, the Newly Industrializing Economies (NIEs) were growing their industrial exports and achieving economic growth.[11] It was in 1979 that the Overseas for Economic Cooperation and Development (OECD) focused on emerging economies that were increasing exports of manufactured goods, calling them Newly Industrializing Countries (NICs).

Japan, a developed country in the region, has continued to grow since the 1960s, rapidly increasing its economic power to become a major country in the world. Japan completed its last post war reparations to the Philippines in 1976, and in 1977 announced a five-year doubling plan to double its official development assistance (ODA) in five years. However, due to the appreciation of the yen immediately afterward, in 1978 the government formulated the first medium-term target of doubling the 1.42 billion U.S. dollars in ODA in 1977 by 1980.

The Plaza Agreement and East Asia

The year 1985 was a watershed. In Europe and North America, there was another big change. In Europe, in June 1985, the European Council of the European Community (EC) published a white paper on the internal market ("Competing the Internal Market: White Paper from the Commission to the European Council"), and in February of the following year, the Single European Act in Luxembourg. The signing of the SEA paved the way for the formation of the European Union (EU) six years later. The 1992 EC summit signed the Maastricht Treaty, and the EU was formally established in 1993. In 1999, a common currency, the euro, was born.

---

[11] The development of NIEs was mentioned in Chap. 2 and discussed in detail in Chap. 6.

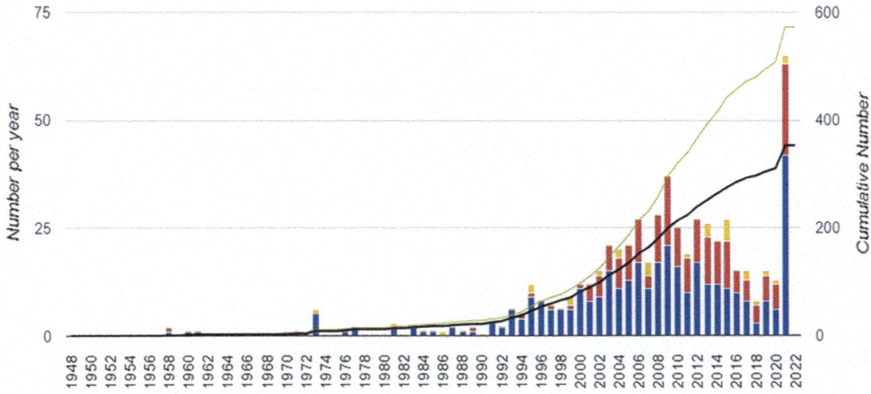

Fig. 9.1 EPAs/FTAs currently in force by year of entry into force, 1948–2022. (*Source* WTO Secretariat).
Note Notifications of EPAs/FTAs: goods, services & accessions to an FTA/EPA are conducted separately. The cumulative number lines show the number of EPAs/FTAs/notifications currently in force

In the United States, the U.S.-Canada Free Trade Agreement was signed in 1989, and in 1992, Mexico joined the North American Free Trade Agreement (NAFTA). In addition, the Free Trade Area of the Americas (FTAA) initiative was launched by U.S. President George H.W. Bush. The FTAA did not materialize in the end, but President Clinton took over the concept following Bush, and in 1994, the 1st Summit of Americas was held by 34 countries in the Americas, excluding Cuba, and it was agreed to conclude an FTAA by 2005. The third summit meeting in 2001 also confirmed the conclusion of the FTAA by January 2005.[12] In other words, in the late 1980s and 1990s, the movement toward economic integration was gaining momentum in the developed economic regions.

Figure 9.1 shows the annual evolution of FTAs/EPAs notified to the WTO. In the 1990s, it could be seen that the number of cases began to increase steadily.[13]

Major changes have also occurred in East Asia. When the Plaza Accord was concluded at the Finance Ministers and Central Bank Governors Meeting of the Five Industrialized Countries in 1985, Japan's yen exchange rate soared, and a foreign

[12] However, an agreement on the FTAA was not reached until 2005. The Online dictionary Britanicca explains why:'A major stumbling block in the negotiations was the Latin American countries' disapproval of domestic subsidies by the U.S. government, particularly in the agricultural sector. Also, the Latin American countries were less willing than the United States to extend the agreement beyond issues of market access to include rules regarding trade in services and intellectual property' (Britannica: Free Trade of the Americas).

[13] The WTO refers to the commonly used free trade agreements (FTAs) as regional trade agreements (EPAs). However, this expression has a strong image of geographical integration, and FTAs are generally used to indicate the details of tariff elimination or reduction. On the other hand, EPAs (Economic Partnership Agreements) are often used because they often include not only tariffs but also intellectual property protection, investment rules, e-commerce, and so forth. Japan has come to generally use EPAs.

direct investment (FDI) boom in East Asia occurred. In 1989, the Tiananmen Square Massacre occurred in China, which embarked on reform and opening up in 1978, but China decided to open up with Deng Xiaoping's Southern Tour in 1992. In East Asia in the late 1980s, the international environment related to Japan and China was undergoing drastic changes, which led to de facto economic integration.

In East Asia, regional cooperation with ASEAN on the one hand and Japan and Australia on the other hand led regional economic cooperation initiatives. In what follows, I will review the development of regional cooperation and regionalism in East Asia roughly in two periods, one from the 1970s to the mid-1980s and the other one later than this period.

ASEAN Regional Cooperation and Its Development

Following the reunification of North and South Vietnam in 1976, ASEAN embarked on economic cooperation. Until then, each ASEAN country had been aiming for import-substitution industrialization. Regional economic cooperation was added to this. From 1985 onwards, a new industrialization policy was promoted to accept more foreign companies (Shimizu -J, 1998; Hirakawa, 2018: 79–81).

The first summit meeting held in 1976, 10 years after the formation of ASEAN, was mainly aimed at addressing the international environment after the end of the Vietnam War. The summit adopted the Treaty of Amity and Cooperation in Southeast Asia (TAC), reaffirmed territorial integrity, non-interference in internal affairs, and settlement of disputes by peaceful means, and added principles to ASEAN, which does not have a basic treaty (Yamakage -J, 2001: 117–118). At the same time, the summit put economic cooperation on the agenda. The leaders signed the Declaration of ASEAN Concord and set out to implement the ASEAN Industrialization Project (AIP), which had been discussed at the ASEAN Economic Ministers' Meeting the previous year. The project promises that countries will work together to investigate the construction and study of factories such as urea, superphosphates, potassium potash, diesel engines, soda ash, and newsprints. At the Second Economic Ministerial Meeting held in March 1976, the AIP and the ASEAN Preferential Trade Scheme (APT) were adopted (Joint Press Statement, ASEAN, 1976).

The Second ASEAN Heads of Government Meeting in 1977 confirmed starting the construction of an ammonia-urea project in Indonesia in 1978 as soon as the feasibility studies were completed. It also greenlighted the finishing, as soon as possible, other projects, such as an ammonia-urea project in Malaysia, a diesel engine project in Singapore, a rock salt-soda ash project in Thailand, and a phosphatic fertilizer in the Philippines." They also noted that pre-feasibility studies would be undertaken on other possible ASEAN industrial projects namely, heavy duty rubber tyres, metalworking machine tools, newsprint, electrolytic tin plating, TV picture tubes, fisheries and potash" (Joint Communique, ASEAN, 1977).

However, most of the projects ended in failure. Countries pursuing import-substitution industrialization policies have failed to reconcile their interests with their own industrialization (Shimizu -J, 1998: 51–54). In 1977, the APT system was established to impose a 50% most-favored-nation tariff on imports within the ASEAN region. However, the system did not function effectively because the regional division of labor structure had not been created. This state of affairs lasted until the early 1980s (See Fig. 2.3).

ASEAN's economic cooperation did not begin to move in substance until the Third ASEAN Summit in December 1987. At the Third Summit, it was reaffirmed that ASEAN countries should attract FDI in order to introduce capital and technology.[14] The following year, the Economic Ministerial Meeting in 1988 decided to establish the ASEAN BBC (Brand-to-Brand Complementation) scheme. The BBC would grant a 50% tariff concession to the domestic procurement of foreign car companies for their own brands. In 1996, the BBC became an ASEAN Industrial Cooperation (AICO), which allowed preferential tariffs of 0–5% for domestic procurement by companies other than automobile companies.

In the 1990s, in addition to economic integration in Europe and the Americas, China's rapid growth attracted FDI from all over the world. This prompted a sense of urgency to accelerate integration in ASEAN (Hirakawa -J, 2014: 42). The Fourth ASEAN Summit in December 1992 decided to establish an ASEAN Free Trade Area (AFTA) and adopted a scheme to establish the Common Effective System of Preferences (CEPT) and reduce tariffs to 0–5% over the next 15 years. AFTA was launched in January 1993, and in 1994 it was rescheduled to be completed by 2003, five years ahead of the original schedule. The Sixth Summit Meeting in December 1998 was a "bold step" in the midst of the Asian financial crisis, and the completion date was moved up by another year to 2002. By 2002, the government decided to reduce the tariff on all CEPT scheme items to 0–5% (ASEAN Secretariat, 1998). Intra-regional trade within ASEAN will become more active.

ASEAN also moved to expand its membership during this period. There were five original members, with Brunei Darussalam joining in 1984, but in the 1990s all the so-called latecomer ASEAN countries in the Indochina Peninsula were approved for membership. Vietnam was added in 1995, Laos and Myanmar in 1997, and Cambodia in 1999, bringing the total number of member countries to 10. While being conscious of the rapid growth of China, it can be said that ASEAN has pursued the formation of an economic zone that maintains and expands its global influence as a regional international organization representing the Southeast Asian region.

Japan and Australia in Asia–Pacific Economic Cooperation

Within East Asia, Japan and Australia, as advanced economies, moved to institutionalize regional economic cooperation. In 2011, the late Professor Emeritus Ippei Yamazawa, who was the Japan representative of the Asia Pacific Economic Cooperation (APEC) Group of Eminent Persons, recalled the Asia–Pacific cooperation as follows.

---

[14] The Joint Communiqué states:'Recognizing the role of foreign investments as an effective source of capital inflow and modern technology, the Heads of Government reaffirmed their commitment to promote investment opportunities in the ASEAN countries, to adopt measures that would attract direct foreign investments into the region, and to encourage intra-ASEAN investments'.

APEC's 21 member economies	Date of joining
Australia	6-7 Nov 1989
Brunei Darussalam	6-7 Nov 1989
Canada	6-7 Nov 1989
Chili	11-12 Nov 1994
People's Republic of China	12-14 Nov 1991
Hong Kong, China	12-14 Nov 1991
Indonesia	6-7 Nov 1989
Japan	6-7 Nov 1989
Republic of Korea (South Korea)	6-7 Nov 1989
Malaysia	6-7 Nov 1989
Mexico	17-19 Nov 1993
New Zealand	6-7 Nov 1989
Papua New Guinea	17-19 Nov 1993
Peru	14-15 Nov 1999
Philippines	6-7 Nov 1999
Russia	14-15 Nov 1999
Singapore	6-7 Nov 1999
Chinese Taipei (Taiwan)	12-14 Nov 1991
Thailand	6-7 Nov 1989
United States of America (USA)	6-7 Nov 1989
Vietnam	14-15 Nov 1998

Fig. 9.2 APEC members map and list (*Source* https://www.mapsofworld.com/apec-member-economies.htm and https://apec-flows.ntu.edu.tw/)

In 1978, Prime Minister Masayoshi Ohira called for the "Trans-Pacific Solidarity Initiative" in his inaugural address, and Pacific cooperation expanded from discussions among businessmen and economists to politicians, diplomats, scholars of international relations, area researchers, and journalists. A research group of young scholars, bureaucrats, and businessmen was organized to identify the report, and the "Trans-Pacific Solidarity Initiative" report (1979) was prepared. Mr. Okita was appointed as the chairperson. In January 1980, Prime Minister Ohira and Foreign Minister Saburo Okita visited Australia and New Zealand, and with the support of Australian Prime Minister Fraser and New Zealand Prime Minister Muldoon, the first Pacific Economic Cooperation Conference (PECC) was held in September, hosted by President Crawford of the Australian National University. Five developed countries (Japan, the United States, Canada, Australia, and New Zealand), five ASEAN countries, and South Korea participated. Each country sent a tripartite representative of businessmen, academics and former bureaucrats. Prof. Kojima was invited to the first and second PECC meetings on behalf of the PAFTAD conference. The PBEC (Economic Commission for the Pacific) became the mother body for sending businessmen and PAFTAD for academics. In this way, "APEC was formally established as an intergovernmental consultative body in November 1989 as a result of the efforts of Australia and Japan" (Yamazawa -J, 2011: 68–72).

Initially established with 12 countries, APEC has 21 members, including China, Hong Kong, and Taiwan in 1991, Mexico and Papua New Guinea in 1993, Chile in 1994, and Peru, Russia, and Vietnam in 1998 (Fig. 9.2).

The first APEC Ministerial Meeting was held in Canberra, Australia. Its characteristics are, as J. Ravenhill points out, that it is quite unique and "open regionalism" (Ravenhill, 2001, 2007: 94). There is no discrimination between countries within and outside the region. With the addition of the United States, the country's strong initiative gave rise to "open liberalism." However, APEC has become a forum where trade and investment liberalization is promoted rather than economic cooperation.[15]

[15] The initial initiative of then Australian Prime Minister Fawke, who proposed APEC, excluded the United States. There was a backlash from the United States, which led to it becoming a member. As a result, APEC initially became more of a gathering that promoted trade and investment liberalization rather than economic cooperation. In fact, the U.S. was indifferent to economic cooperation and

APEC Ministerial Meetings have been held annually since then, and the Bogor Declaration was adopted at the 1994 APEC Ministerial and Economic Leaders Meeting in Indonesia, which called for trade and investment liberalization for advanced economies by 2010 and for developing economies by 2020. This event can be said to have been the culmination of trade liberalization in East Asia in the 1990s, as economic globalization was being promoted.

Incidentally, as for the establishing of APEC, Australian Prime Minister Fawke took the initiative. Japanese journalist, Y. Funabashi laments that while Australia "has been happy to take full credit, giving its political leaders a boost domestically and giving the nation a higher profile internationally", "Tokyo's activism has been obscured for two reasons":

> Internally, Japan's Foreign Ministry remains skeptical of MITI's motivation in creating the body and continues to struggle with MITI over its shape and future. Externally, Japan has been concerned about the perceptions Japan's neighbors, particularly ASEAN nations, would have over its activism, given the legacy of its past region-building exercises (Funabashi, 1995: 66).

On the other hand, by excluding the United States at the conceptual stage, Australia not only enhanced its posture toward Asia, but also made the United States recognize the importance of Australia. Funabashi writes:

> There were strong reasons for Australia to exclude the United States, at least initially. By courting Asian nations first, Australia could claim another victory in its "Asianization" drive... Canberra calculated that the exclusion would force North America to take notice of Australia and the Asia Pacific region at large (Funabashi, 1995: 63).[16]

Japan's Pacific Economic Cooperation initiative was born out of the enjoyment of growth with the United States as its main market. Politically and economically, Japan pursued its own initiatives under "open liberalism" with the addition of the United States. For Australia, it was also of great significance to strengthen its relationship with a growing Asia. The theory that supported this concept was the so-called Akamatsu Flying Geese Theory advocated by economist Kiyoshi Kojima in Japan. However, the perception of this theory changed from the initial theory of the Pacific to the theory of Asian development led by Japan.

Looking back, Japan's government economist Saburo Okita explained the development of Asia at an international conference on Pacific Economic Cooperation held in Seoul in 1985 using the flying geese theory, which triggered international interest in it.[17] Okita focused on international transfer, which is considered to be a sub-form of Akamatsu's flying geese theory, and explained the development of East

---

tried to push for the liberalization of trade and services through APEC even more than GATT. For this reason, ASEAN insisted on a consensus system and opposed the United States (Kinoshita -J, 2002: 179).

[16] Funabashi quoted Prime Minister Hawke as saying that the real reason for Australia's initial exclusion of the United States was unclear. 'There were some in [ASEAN], particularly Malaysia, who had a well-developed antipathy towards the United States, and Malaysia certainly would have preferred to exclude the Americans' (Funabashi, 1995: 63).

[17] The flying geese theory of Akamatsu is discussed in more detail in Chap. 11.

Asia. However, the logic was that U.S. industry was transferred to Japan, which in turn gradually spread industrialization to East Asia (Okita, 1985). In other words, he proposed the flying geese theory as a theory of Asia–Pacific development.

Following in the footsteps of Okita, there are no studies that attempt to add the role of the United States to the flying geese theory (Ozawa, 2009). However, the theory of the flying geese soon came to be regarded as a theory of Asian development that placed Japan at the head of the flying geese pattern. Japan was concerned that the appreciation of the yen after the Plaza Accord would hollow out the Japan economy, but it soon led to a boom in direct investment by Japanese companies in Asia. This will lead to the development of the NIEs, ASEAN and even China. In the 1990s, the flying geese theory, along with Akamatsu's name, was published in the White Paper on Japan's Economy (Economic Planning Agency -J, 1994a, b) and the UNCTAD report (UNCTAD, 1994, 1995, 1996), the flying geese pattern of development came to be recognized as the flying geese development of East Asia, where Japan flies as the lead goose rather than the United States.

Funabashi, who viewed the establishment of APEC with high expectations as "Asia–Pacific fusion," uses the flying geese theory to note that the development of East Asia has provoked various reactions not only in Japan's perception of Asia, but also in the United States and other Asian countries.

> Japan's official emphasis on the "Flying Geese" model is often pointed to as proof that Tokyo is attempting to create an army of little mercantilist Japanese in the region. The fact that many Asian nations have endorsed the Japanese model has given American trade policy makers the jitters./ In modern history, Japan's pursuit to dominate a Greater East Asia Co-Prosperity Sphere revealed this hierarchical mindset, which has been well-suited to bilateral relationships and alliances and has allowed Japan a high comfort level in its Anglo-Japanese and U.S.-Japan alliances. Japan's view of Asia, and its own role in it, is challenged by new economic realities. The old flying-geese analogy has been updated by a Chinese scholar, who compared the Asian economy to a train with Japan leading the front car and China pushing as a caboose. Yet another conception portrays the Asian economies as elevators at different levels, where Japan has ascended to the top, the "four tigers" are at the next highest level, and the industrializing economies such as Malaysia are rapidly following. At any rate, the traditional leader-follower dynamic between Japan and Asia is becoming more complex. Over the past two decades, Asia has undergone tremendous transformation, as the development of the NIEs progressed through the 1970s, democratization took root in the 1980s, and APEC, with the ground-breaking Bogor Declaration, paved the way for liberalization in the 1990s. During this progression, the tensions and ideological passions that used to inflame North-South relations have become subdued. The LDCs are now more self-confident. The infrastructure that Japan's ODA helped install has propelled further growth. As a result, Japan is increasingly more comfortable with its own role in the region (Funabashi, 1995: 37–38, 234).

A detailed discussion of the Flying Geese Model will be left to Chap. 12, but there was no doubt about the importance of Pacific trade for the countries of East Asia, including Japan. However, this development, while including mixed reactions to Japan and other East Asian countries, has brought confidence in development and forced the United States to reconsider its perception of Asia.

Seeking Economic Cooperation in Asia

In fact, the concept of regional cooperation in Asia, which overtook the United States, was put forward in the early 1970s. The Nixon shock made the decline of U.S. national power clear to everyone. This led to the aforementioned Morinosuke Kajima's early return to Asianism. In the wake of the Nixon shock in the United States on the one hand and China's return to the international community on the other, he saw that in 1972 Asia was "gradually moving toward 'Pan Asia'". He advocated the "Union of Asian States" (Kajima -J, 1972). However, the idea of a federation of Asian nations was too early ahead of its time (Hirakawa -J, 2011: 32).

In fact, the collapse of the IMF-GATT regime gave birth to the United States, which created markets using dollars under a floating exchange rate system, and brought about development in East Asia. Although trade friction arose between Japan and the United States, both Japan and the NIEs enjoyed development with the United States as a huge market. The Pacific Economic Bloc was being born. This is how APEC was born. Australia's move was to take advantage of its growth structure.

In the 1990s, regionalism emerged from the developing ASEAN region. As mentioned above, since the late 1980s, economic integration has accelerated in both Europe and the Americas. Is it okay for Asia to continue as it is? The question was promptly answered by Malaysia's Prime Minister at the time, Mahathir bin Mohamad. According to Funabashi, Mahathir was suspicious that Japan and the United States were behind the proposal for Australia to establish the APCE, and was reluctant to include the United States. In late 1990, when Chinese Premier Li Peng visited Kuala Lumpur, Mahathir proposed to him the East Asian Economic Group (EAEG), which was limited to East Asian countries. Moreover, the proposal was "not a bottom-up by the bureaucracy of the Malaysian government, but an idea that came out of Mahathir's own head" (Funabashi, 1995: 57, 68; Sudo, 2002: 100). In fact, Mahathir says:

> We had in mind only a forum at the level of heads of governments, where common economic and trading problems could be discussed and resolved or a common stand decided for the Group when discussing international trade regimes with other regions. Of course, we knew this proposal could be modified when ASEAN meetings considered it./ We felt such an East Asian group was necessary because the smaller countries of Southeast Asia, even when we acted as the ASEAN Group, were no match for the European Union and the countries of the North American Free Trade Agreement (NAFTA) when negotiating trade and other economic matters. Together with the three Northeast Asian countries, however, the small economies of Southeast Asia would have sufficient clout to get a fair deal from Europe and North America (Mahathir, 2006: 13).

However, the United States and Australia, which were excluded from the group, strongly objected to the EAEG, saying it was protectionist and would divide APEC. The EAEG changed its name to the Economic Consultative Council for East Asia (EAEC), but Japan did not participate and it was unsuccessful. At this time, the attempt at East Asian regionalism was partially stalled (Hirakawa, 2004: 21–22).

However, the ASEAN countries continued to carefully pursue the summit of East Asian countries without the United States. The first meeting of the Asia-Europe Meeting (ASEM), proposed by then-Prime Minister Goh Chok Tong of Singapore, was held in Bangkok in March 1996, and Japan, China, and South Korea were added to ASEAN as Asian participants in consideration of the diplomatic balance with Europe. Its members were the same as those of the EAEG.

In January 1997, the 30th anniversary of the founding of ASEAN, Japan's Prime Minister Ryutaro Hashimoto, who visited ASEAN, proposed a regular meeting between the leaders of Japan and ASEAN, and ASEAN agreed to invite the leaders of Japan, China, and South Korea to a summit to be held in Kuala Lumpur in December of the same year. Prime Minister Hashimoto's proposal sought ASEAN's understanding of the review of the Japan-U.S. defense guidelines that were underway in Japan at the time, and intended to take advantage of diplomacy with China, which strongly opposed the review. However, ASEAN added China and South Korea in consideration of the political balance between Japan and China, and established a meeting between ASEAN and Japan, China, and South Korea (Hirakawa, 2004: 22).

In 1994, the ASEAN Regional Forum (ARF) was established as a dialogue forum for political and security issues in the Asia–Pacific region. The ARF is the only intergovernmental forum in the Asia–Pacific region. As of 2022, there are 26 participating countries + the EU. ASEAN has always pursued international diplomacy in order to avoid being left on the periphery of ASEAN in a developing Asia. Eventually, this would become a basic policy of "ASEAN centrality". The ARF is one of the outcomes.

Looking back at the 1990s, in 1993, the World Bank published a report, "The East Asian Miracle," with the support of Japan. The report is the pinnacle of de facto integration in Asia. When the Asian financial crisis hit Asia in 1997, East Asian countries were held responsible and subjected to strong criticism. This will revitalize the regionalism and economic integration efforts in the region, and pave the way for institutionalization that supports de facto economic integration.

In the next section, we will look at the institutionalization of regional economic cooperation in the wake of the Asian financial crisis.

9.3 The Asian Currency Crisis and the Institutionalization of Regionalism

In this section, we will review the efforts for regional cooperation and economic integration that have progressed rapidly in the wake of the Asian financial crisis.

9.3.1 The Outbreak of the Asian Currency Crisis and the Institutionalization of Regional Cooperation in East Asia

The ASEAN+3 summit in December 1997 was coincidentally held in the midst of the Asian financial crisis. In July of the same year, the Asian currency crisis[18] began with the collapse of the baht in Thailand, and quickly "infected" East Asian countries and economies such as Malaysia, Indonesia, the Philippines, Hong Kong, and South Korea.

The U.S., the International Monetary Fund, and mainstream economists initially blamed the currency crisis on the failure of the policies of the countries in crisis, as well as the flaws in their institutions and organizations, and condemned Asian capitalism by calling it "crony capitalism". Thailand, Indonesia, and South Korea, which were in crisis, accepted conditionality in order to obtain emergency IMF loans, but both the IMF and the United States forced the crisis countries to liberalize trade and investment, not to mention financial liberalization (Feldstain, 1998: 24). The crisis was seen as an opportunity to impose structural reforms. APEC, which promotes liberalization, has been indifferent to countries in crisis, and even the Asian Development Bank (ADB) was initially slow to act.

For this reason, the Japanese government allocated the largest amount of emergency relief at the Tokyo Conference on Assistance to Thailand at the IMF's call in the month after the outbreak of the Thai baht crisis in July 1997, and in September launched the Asian Monetary Fund (AMF) initiative. When this initiative was frustrated by opposition from the United States and the IMF, Japan tried to respond to the demands of the crisis countries by announcing the so-called "New Miyazawa Initiative", in October 1998, this time to overcome the Asian currency crisis (Hirakawa, 1999).[19]

The Japanese business community also took the opportunity of the Asian currency crisis to confirm the integration of the Japanese economy and the East Asian economy. In August–September 1999, after the crisis, the Ministry of Foreign Affairs (MOFA) established "Mission for Revitalization of Asian Economy" under the leadership of the Chairman of the Japan Federation of Employers' Associations (Nikkeiren)

---

[18] The Asian currency crisis was discussed in more detail in Chapter. 7.

[19] The amount of assistance agreed at the Tokyo Conference on IMF assistance to Thailand totaled $17.2 billion, and Japan and the IMF shared the same amount of $4 billion, for a total of $8 billion. Japan's Ministry of Finance explained the Shin-Miyazawa Initiative as follows: "New Miyazawa Initiative, in order to assist Asian countries in overcoming their economic difficulties and to contribute to the stability of international financial markets, Japan stands ready to provide a package of support measures totaling U.S.$30 billion (equivalent yen), of which U.S.$15 billion (equivalent yen) will be made available for the medium- to long-term financial needs for economic recovery in Asian countries, and another U.S.$15 billion (equivalent yen) will be set aside for their possible short-term capital needs during the process of implementing economic reform". It was implemented from December 1998, and by February 2000, a total of 21 billion dollars worth of yen had been provided, mainly to countries in crisis (Ministry of Finance, Japan Home Page. Accessed Jan.18, 2022).

and Chairman of the Board, Hiroshi Okuda of Toyota Motor Corporation to Asian countries, including South Korea. The report defined East Asian countries, including Japan, as "a community with a common fate" and reported on the reconstruction assistance and cooperation (Mission for Revitalization of Asian Economy, 1999).[20]

Incidentally, the failure of the AMF initiative could be attributed in part to the U.S. being wary of Japan's growing influence in Asia, the IMF's wariness of losing its own policy influence in Asia, and China's and South Korea's distrust of Japan. Thus, the response to the Asian currency crisis eventually resulted in an agreement on the Manila Framework, which included strengthening the IMF's response capacity and establishing regional surveillance. The expansion of Japan's influence was suppressed. However, the countries of East Asia took this opportunity to raise their interest in regional cooperation, that is, regionalism.

In December 1998, a year after the crisis, the leaders of ASEAN, Japan, China, and South Korea agreed to hold the ASEAN+3 summit on a regular basis, at which South Korean President Kim Dae-Jung proposed the establishment of the East Asia Vision Group (EAVG) to deepen regional cooperation. In conjunction with the meeting, the ASEAN+1 summit was also regularized.

The momentum for regional cooperation in East Asia is evident in the first-ever "Joint Statement on East Asian Cooperation" at the Third ASEAN+3 Summit held in Manila in November 1999. The statement called for cooperation in a wide range of fields, including economic, social, cultural and political fields. In monetary and financial cooperation, the promotion of a "self-reliance and support mechanism" was confirmed through the ASEAN+3 framework, and in line with this agreement, the ASEAN+3 Finance Ministers' Meeting in May 2000 agreed to establish the Chiang Mai Initiative (CMI) to provide currency to countries in times of emergency. The AMF concept, which collapsed due to opposition from the United States and the IMF, and a common currency for East Asia, following the example of the euro, were also discussed.

In terms of financial cooperation, following the Chiang Mai Initiative, efforts were made to foster the region's bond market. In August 2003, the Asian Bond Markets Initiative (ABMI) was launched under the ASEAN+3 framework. In addition, the Board of Directors of the Central Bank of East Asia and Oceania established the dollar-denominated Asian Bond Fund (ABFI) in June 2003, and the Asian Bond Fund (ABF2) denominated in local currencies was established in December of the following year (EMEAP Press Release June 2, 2003, Dec.16, 2004, May 12, 2005).

At the 4th ASEAN+3 Summit held in Singapore in November 2000, the host country, Goh Chok Tong, proposed the establishment of an East Asia Summit to which ASEAN would invite the establishment of an East Asia Summit and the formation of an East Asia Free Trade and Investment Area at the same time. South Korean President Kim Dae-jung proposed the establishment of an East Asia Study

[20] ASEAN has had an ASEAN swap agreement as a financial support scheme since 1977 and stand-by credit in the 1980s, but it was only in the tens of millions of dollars and did not work in practice. In addition, not only South Korea, which has fallen into a crisis, but also China, which avoided the crisis by regulating foreign exchange transactions, recognized the need for regional cooperation in order to deal with the instability caused by globalization.

Group (EASG) to study these proposals. The EAVG's report "Towards an East Asian Community" was submitted to the 5th ASEAN+3 Summit in Brunei Darussalam in November 2001, and the "Final Report of the EASG" was submitted to the 6th ASEAN+3 Summit in Phnom Penh in November 2002. Asian Free Trade Aria (EAFTA), promotion of investment on SMEs, and establishment of an East Asia Investment Area (EAIA) were proposed. The summit also recommended the establishment of EAFTA and EAIA in the future, as well as the establishment of an East Asia Summit (EAS) (EAVG, 2001; EASG, 2002).

In November 2004, the 8th ASEAN+3 Summit held in Vientiane decided to host the EAS in 2005. As for the members of the EAS, Australia, New Zealand, and India, which met the conditions presented by ASEAN,[21] joined to form the ASEAN+6. Thus, in December 2005, the first East Asia Summit was held in conjunction with the Ninth ASEAN+3 Summit. The 11th ASEAN+3 Summit held in November 2007 issued the Second Joint Statement on East Asian Cooperation.

From the 3rd ASEAN+3 Summit in 1999, the China-Japan-South Korea Trilateral Summit was held in the form of a luncheon, and from that year the Finance Ministers' Meeting, the Economic Ministers' Meeting in 2000, the Labour Ministers' Meeting and the Agriculture and Forestry Ministers' Meeting in 2001, and the Tourism Ministers' Meeting and the Energy Ministers' Meeting in 2002 have been held regularly every year.

What is the relationship between the newly created conference and the existing conference, and how will it be managed? The ASEAN+3 Summit in 2005 affirmed that it is the "main instrument" for the formation of an East Asian Community, and at the same time ASEAN is the "driving force". The first East Asia Summit (EAS) also stipulates that the summit can play an "important role" in building an East Asian community, that the meeting will be held annually, and that the ASEAN chair will be the chair. In the framework of East Asian cooperation between ASEAN, ASEAN+3 and the EAS, "ASEAN centrality" has been incorporated into the system.

Figure 9.3 illustrates the relationship between the ASEAN-centered regional cooperation system and the economic integration concept. In this way, in addition to APEC, which was born in 1989, the newly institutionalized ASEAN+3 and the EAS collaborated to create a framework for promoting their respective economic integration initiatives. These were the fruits of the currency crisis.

Incidentally, ASEAN has played a major role in the development of Asian regionalism. Because ASEAN is a collection of small countries, there is always a risk of being buried among the major powers. In order to overcome this, ASEAN created the principle of "ASEAN centrality" and paved the way for the development of balanced regionalism in East Asia through "conference diplomacy" that transcends regional limits.

---

[21] Three criteria for participation in the East Asia Summit which was established by ASEAN were: 'First, participant countries must sign the ASEAN Treaty of Amity and Cooperation (TAC). Second, they must be a formal dialogue partner of ASEAN. Third, they must have substantive cooperative relations with ASEAN' (Tanaka, 2006).

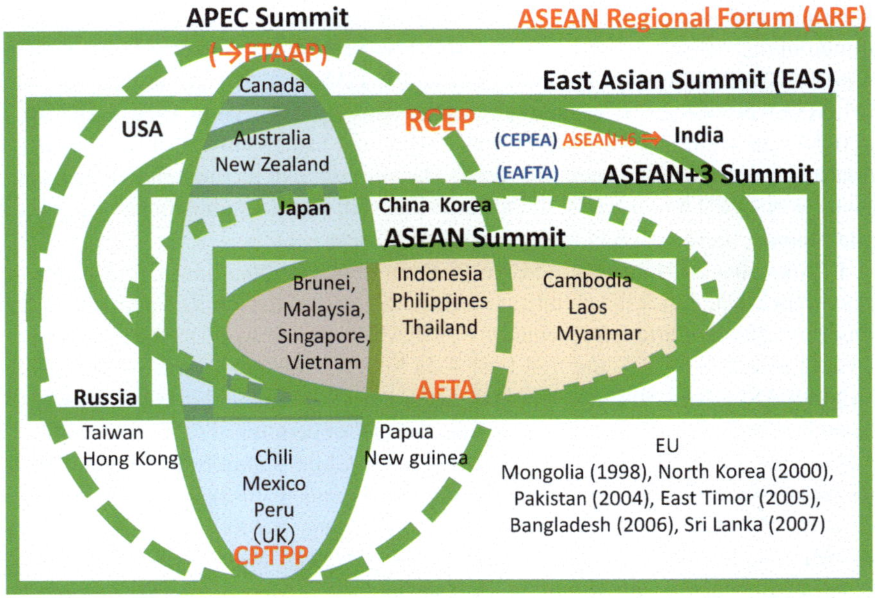

Fig. 9.3 Regional institutionalization and integration centering East Asia as of 2023 (*Source* made by Hirakawa). *Note* AFTA stands for ASEAN Free Trade Area, APEC: Asia Pacific Economic Cooperation, CEPEA: Comprehensive Economic Partnership in (for) East Asia (ASEAN+6), CPTPP (11): Comprehensive and Progressive Agreement for Trans-Pacific Partnership, FTAAP: Free Trade Area of the Asia Pacific, RCEP: Regional Comprehensive Economic Partnership

In the next section, we will look at the multi-layered regional cooperation initiative.

9.3.2 ASEAN Community and Economic Integration

With regard to ASEAN's regional integration, we have already seen the reduction of AFTA's tariffs in the previous section. The AFTA tariff reduction, which began in 1992, was flexible in that the six ASEAN countries and the four latecomers would achieve liberalization in stages according to their respective reduction schedules, rather than a uniform rule, but the target year was moved forward twice, and it was almost achieved in 2002.

The following year, in 2003, the Ninth ASEAN Summit adopted the Declaration of ASEAN Concord II (Bali Concord II), setting the building of the ASEAN Community as a new goal. The ASEAN Community was built through three pillars: the ASEAN Security Community (ASC), the ASEAN Economic Community (AEC), and the ASEAN Socio-Cultural Community (ASCC). The AEC is at the heart of the community and aims for the "realisation of the end-goal of economic integration as outlined in the ASEAN Vision 2020" (Bali Concode II).

In the 12th ASEAN Summit Meeting held in the Cebu, Philippines in January 2007, ASEAN agreed "to accelerate the establishment of an ASEAN Community by 2015 as envisioned in the ASEAN Vision 2020 and the ASEAN Concord II" and "to hasten the establishment of the ASEAN Economic Community by 2015 and to transform ASEAN into a region with free movement of goods, services, investment, skilled labour, and freer flow of capital" (ASEAN Summit, 2007; Ishikawa, 2021a: 28). In November of the same year, the 13th ASEAN Summit formulated Blueprint 2015, in line with which the AEC almost achieved its goals in 2015.

As at 31 October 2015, 469 of the 506 AEC scorecard measures, which includes the 54 highly priority measures (HPMs), were implemented, leading to a 92.7% overall implementation rate by all 10 ASEAN Member States. As the full set of measures that have been previously committed, including those that are not identified as HPMs totals 611 measures, the implementation rate of the full AEC Scorecard stood at 79.5%, or 486 out of 611 measures (ASEAN Secretariat, 2015a: 9–10).

The most advanced part of the AEC was the reduction of tariffs on goods. "The trade liberalization rate (percentage of tariff lines subject to elimination) of ASEAN trade in goods agreement (ATIGA) stands at 98.6%, a rate that is as high as that of the TPP ATIGA's weighted average. ATIGA's weighted average effective applied tariff rate dropped to 1.4% in 2018" (Ishikawa, 2021a: 29).

The ASEAN Secretariat acknowledged that the AEC Blueprint 2015 was a substantial success, citing tariff reductions and trade promotions, the trade in services liberalization agenda, investment liberalization and promotion, and the removal and adjustment of capital market regulations. And as a milestone towards further economic integration, AEC Blueblind 2025 will be announced (ASEAN Secretariat, 2015b: 1). The Blueprint 2025 sets the following goals:

> The AEC Blueprint 2025 will build on the AEC Blueprint 2015 consisting of five interrelated and mutually reinforcing characteristics, namely: (i) A Highly Integrated and Cohesive Economy; (ii) A Competitive, Innovative, and Dynamic ASEAN; (iii) Enhanced Connectivity and Sectoral Cooperation; (iv) A Resilient, Inclusive, People-Oriented, and People-Centered ASEAN; and (v) A Global ASEAN (ASEAN Secretariat, 2015b: Para 1).

Figure 9.4 is a summary of the economic integration that ASEAN has promoted over the past half century. As Japan's ASEAN researcher Ishikawa points out, ASEAN's regional and economic cooperation has long been negatively evaluated, and the AEC's goals have sometimes been viewed as "optimistic and fanciful". However, the AEC believes that gradualism has been the key to ASEAN's success, He also describes this as "gradual and flexible liberalization over time while setting high goals" (Ishikawa, 2021a: 38). Especially since the 1990s, it has mainly aimed to attract Japanese companies and even regional companies. This ensured the development of ASEAN. The AEC's policy was not only ASEAN's internal policy, but also its external policy beyond ASEAN.

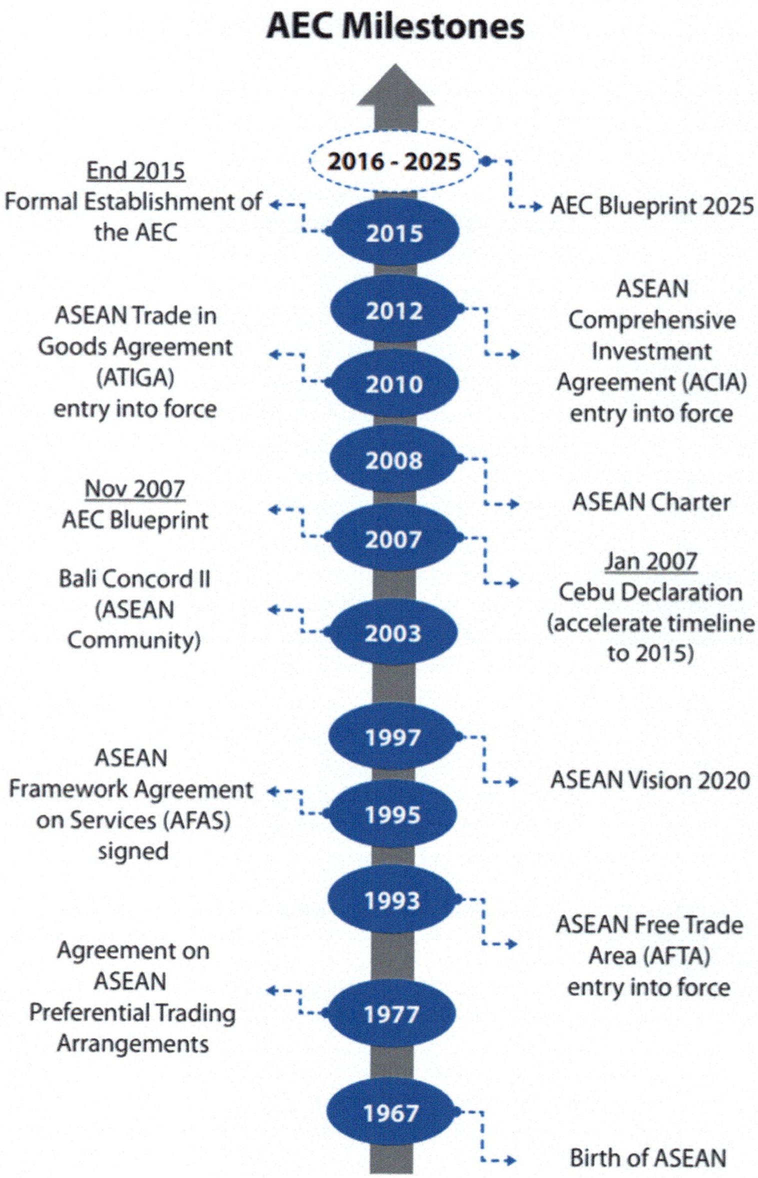

Fig. 9.4 ASEAN Economic Community milestone (*Source* ASEAN Secretariat, 2015a: 4)

9.3.3 Two "East Asian Community" Initiatives

The ASEAN+3 Summit in 1999 issued the first-ever "Joint Statement on East Asian Cooperation", and the 2002 ASEAN+3 Summit was established in accordance with the EAVG's "Towards an East Asian Community" and the EASG's final report as a proposal to build an East Asian Community and support the East Asian Free Trade Area (EAFTA) and the East Asian Investment Area, which was set as a regional goal.

However, the East Asian Community was involved in the constituent countries, and there was a struggle for leadership among Japan, China, and South Korea. In January 2002, then-Prime Minister Junichiro Koizumi of Japan delivered a policy speech in Singapore, where the Japan-Singapore Economic Partnership Agreement (JSEPA) was signed, proposing "a community that acts together and advances together." His proposal was subsequently regarded as a proposal for an East Asian Community, but it was different from ASEAN's and China's vision of an East Asian Community.

Koizumi envisioned that the ASEAN+3 plus Australia, New Zealand, and India as the constituent countries of the EAS, which the Japanese Ministry of Foreign Affairs called the "extended East Asian community". However, in his and MOFA's proposal for an Asian Community, they used "Asian community", with a lower case "c", instead of "Asian Community", with an upper case "C". According to a Japanese former UN diplomat, M. Taniguchi, the term "community" means "abstract and vaguely refers to regional cooperation" (Taniguchi -J, 2004: 34–35). The MOFA had also used the Japanese Katakana word "komyunitii" for "community", not the Kanji word "kyodotai" (Community). The Katakana word "community" is abstract in the Japanese sense of the word and refers to a mere gathering, while the Kanji word "kyoudotai" is associated with the meaning of a society with tools and rules. Ultimately, it was not until 2004 that Japan began to consider the 'Community' discussed in ASEAN and ASEAN+3. The policy report of the Council on East Asian Community (CEAC) describes the change in the Japanese Government's perception of 'community' as follows.

> The Japan Government has adopted the slogans "a community that acts together and advances together" (Koizumi's speech in Singapore in January, 2002), "Building an East Asia community" (the Japan-ASEAN Commemorative Summit in December 2003), and "an East Asia Community" (Koizumi's speech at the United Nations in September 2004, and Koizumi's policy in January 2005), and the concept of an "East Asian community" is gradually coming to the fore while changing the wording (CEAC, 2005: 10).

In East Asia, there was a reality that changed Koizumi's proposal from a mere gathering to an "East Asian community." CEAC Chair Kenichi Ito explains the background to the establishment of the Council in Japan in 2005 as follows:

> Looking at East Asia as a whole, I think the term "East Asian Community" has been talked about since about 10 years ago. Therefore, Japan has recently realized this and is surprised and is trying to respond in a hurry, but I think the reality is that Japan people are approaching this word with the feeling that they will not miss the bus (Ito, -J, 2005: 3).

In fact, Koizumi's proposal to ASEAN was made as a response to China's announcement at the ASEAN+3 summit held two months earlier in November 2001 that it would conclude an FTA with ASEAN within 10 years. At the ASEAN-Japan Commemorative Summit held in Tokyo in December 2003, the Tokyo Declaration was issued, proclaiming "deepening East Asia cooperation for an East Asian community (which is outward looking)" (MOFA, 2003). Strangely, however, the decision was made in the absence of the leaders of China and South Korea. Japan was shocked that China's outreach to ASEAN was going beyond Japan's expectations. In his speech to the United Nations General Assembly in 2004, Koizumi also referred to the proposal for an "East Asian Community".[22]

Incidentally, at the ASEAN+3 summit in November 2004, Japan and China were engaged in a leadership struggle over the EAS member countries. At that time, Japan recommended Australia and New Zealand as participating countries, and finally India, which was recommended by Singapore, joined to form the ASEAN+6 summit.

When the first EAS was held in December 2005, the Japanese media reported on the struggle for leadership between Japan and China.[23] In relation to the EAS member countries, Japan's intention to check China gave rise to the ASEAN+6 framework (Hirakawa -J, 2015: 39). The U.S. Secretary of State and the Russian Foreign Minister were invited to represent the leaders of the United States and Russia at the 5th EAS in Hanoi, and the leaders of the United States and Russia became official members from the 6th EAS in 2011. It can be confirmed that ASEAN exercised a flexible and skillful "conference diplomacy".

In the next section, we will look at the struggle for leadership over the economic integration plan.

9.4 East Asian FTAs/EPAs Moving from Bilateral to Mega

In the 1990s, East Asia began to move rapidly from de facto economic integration to institutionalized economic integration. The Asian currency crisis was the catalyst. Economic integration as regional cooperation went not only bilaterally, but also to mega economic integration. In this section, we will trace the history of economic integration that has spread to bilateral, multilateral, and mega EPAs/FTAs since the beginning of this century, and consider the background, prospects, and challenges.

[22] On September 21, 2004, Prime Minister Koizumi said in his speech at the General Debate of the United Nations General Assembly, "Building upon ASEAN+ 3, I have advocated the idea of an "East Asia Community" (Koizumi, 2004).

[23] Related headlines of the major newspapers in Japan were: "Japan-China Leadership Battle" (Asahi -J December 4, 2005), "Tug of War of East Asian Community: China/Japan and the U.S. Trying to Hold Back" (Nikkei evening edition -J December 8, 2005), and "Japan and China Struggle for (East Asian Community) Leadership" (Mainichi -J December 14, 2005).

9.4.1 Progress in Bilateral Regional Economic Integration

Throughout the 1990s, ASEAN promoted economic integration through the institutionalization of AFTA. However, it did not extend to the institutionalization of economic integration in East Asia. The Asian currency crisis will change the situation. After the crisis, countries that would become nodes of Asia–Pacific trade began to lobby Japan for an FTA. In addition, China, which has succeeded in joining the WTO, will begin to make its moves. As the momentum for negotiations increases, ASEAN will play a pivotal role in regional integration. ASEAN, which is a collection of small countries, consciously pursues this role.

First, let's review the background to the substantial shift in Japan's FTA policy. In August 1998, then vice minister for international affairs of MITI, N. Hatakeyama, received the first FTA proposal from Mexican Commerce and Industry Minister, Herminio Blanco. In response to this, an FTA research team was organized within the Ministry of Economy, Trade and Industry. However, the report was not completed by the time of the visit of Mexican President Ernesto Zedillo in November of the same year, and discussions were not ready (Hatakeyama, 2002: 24–25). However, at the end of the same month, at the Japan-ROK Ministerial Meeting, South Korea proposed an FTA to Japan. In response to the proposal, Japan began joint research by research institutes in both countries.

Japan's Ministry of Economy, Trade and Industry (METI) is thus reconsidering its WTO-focused trade policy. In the 1999 edition of the White Paper on International Trade, the FTAs were held to be consistent with the GATT/WTO free trade system, and the previous view that FTAs were protectionist was revised. The following year, the 2000 edition of the White Paper on International Trade, emphasized the advantages of FTAs. At an international symposium hosted by JETRO in March 2001, while emphasizing the basic policy of Japan's multilateral free trade policy, the senior reprasentative of METI emphasized the peculiarities of East Asia, stating that "Japan, China, South Korea, Taiwan, and Hong Kong in China are the only countries in the world's top 30 GDP countries and regions that have not joined any FTAs" (JETRO, 2001). In effect, it was a change in the course of trade policy. The joint research on the Japan-South Korea FTA became a joint communiqué in May 2000, industry-government-academia joint research began in July 2002, and intergovernmental negotiations began in 2003. However, negotiations have been suspended since the end of 2004.

South Korea, which proposed an FTA to Japan, actively moved to conclude the FTA. Negotiations with Chile were concluded in October 2002 and entered into force in April 2004. In October of the same year, negotiations with Singapore were concluded, and the law entered into force in 2006. Negotiations on the South Korea-ASEAN FTA began in October 2004 and entered into force in 2007. Since 2005, it has begun preliminary negotiations with the United States (signed in 2007) and Canada beyond the East Asian region. The trade liberalization measures between Japan and South Korea have been substantially realized with the entry into force of the Regional Comprehensive Economic Partnership Agreement (RCEP) in February 2022.

Following South Korea, Singapore proposed an FTA to Japan in December 1999, and the Japan-Singapore New Era Economic Partnership Agreement (JSEPA) was signed in January 2002, which entered into force in November of the same year. There is no issue of open markets for agricultural products between Singapore and Japan. This led to an early conclusion. Singapore began negotiations with Chile in 1999 and Canada, Mexico, the United States, Australia in 2000, and reached an agreement with New Zealand in August 2000. The FTA with the United States was signed in May 2003.

China followed. Chinese Premier Zhu Rongji proposed an FTA to ASEAN at the China-ASEAN Summit in November 2000, when China-ASEAN was expected to join the WTO, and at the China-ASEAN Summit in December 2001, the month before the official accession to the WTO, an agreement was reached to conclude an FTA within 10 years, and the following November 2002 summit meeting signed the Framework Agreement for Economic Cooperation. Meanwhile, at the ASEAN+ 3 Summit, Japan and South Korea proposed FTA negotiations.

Japan was inspired by China's moves. Then-Prime Minister Junichiro Koizumi visited Singapore in January 2002 and signed the JSEPA, proposed an Economic Partnership Agreement with ASEAN countries, and issued a joint statement on the Comprehensive Economic Partnership (CEP) at the ASEAN+3 summit in November 2002 to establish an economic partnership within 10 years as soon as possible. The following year, on the occasion of the ASEAN+ 3 summit in November 2003, the "CEP Framework" was signed. Negotiations on a bilateral FTA with the Philippines began in December 2003, an agreement in principle was reached in November of the following year, and signed in May 2006. An agreement in principle was reached with Malaysia in May 2005 and entered into force in July 2006.

Thus, since the beginning of this century, there has been a rush of FTAs/EPAs in East Asia. According to the database of ADB's Asian Regional Integration Center, the number of FTAs concluded, negotiated, and proposed by East Asian countries and economies increased tenfold from 10 in 2001 to 103 in 2007 (Kawai & Wignaraja, 2008: 118). In 2022, there are 187 in force, 25 in agreement but not yet in force, and 58 in negotiation. In descending order of the number of countries in force, Singapore 26, China 19, South Korea 17, Malaysia 16, Thailand 14, Vietnam 14, and Indonesia 12 (ADB Asian regional integration center Database).

The focus here is on ASEAN. Figure 9.5 compares the efforts of East Asian FTAs/EPAs between 1997 and 2007. Until the Asian financial crisis, FTAs/EPAs were limited to ASEAN. It can be seen that after the currency crisis, it spread throughout East Asia, with ASEAN as the core. In other words, South Korea and Singapore, which proposed FTAs to Japan, and China, which was assured of membership in the WTO, moved to conclude FTAs in the East Asian region, which in turn led to Japan's aggressive FTA policy. At the core of the agreement was ASEAN, which supported the international production networks of multinational corporations. Singapore, Malaysia, Vietnam, and other countries have also participated in

MEGA FTAs/EPAs in the Asia–Pacific region, further promoting economic integration. East Asia will become one of the world's poles for the institutionalization of economic integration (Fig. 9.6).

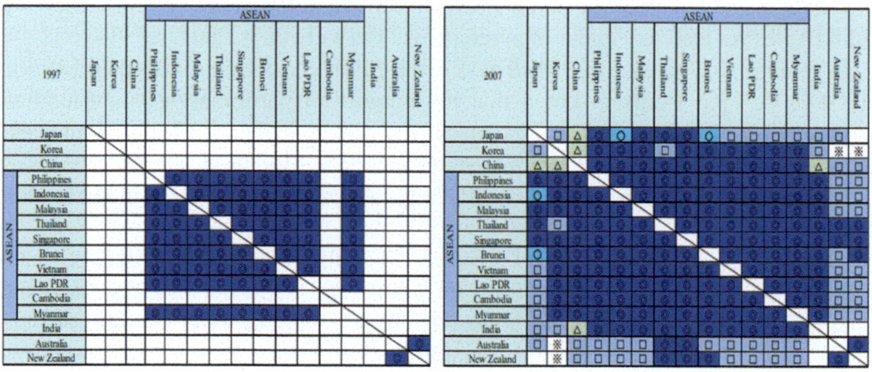

Fig. 9.5 Status of efforts towards FTA/EPA in East Asian region in 1997 and 2007 (*Source* METI, Japan, 2007: 172). *Notes* ◎ Signed or (partially) implemented: ○ Broad agreement/conclusion, □ (In negotiation (or agreement to launch negotiations), △ Government-participated joint research or conclusions ongoing (including FTA/EPA among multiple countries). ⋇ After agreement at the leader level, South Korea will implement joint research with Australia and New Zealand through private-sector research initiatives. 2007 Data is as of April 2007

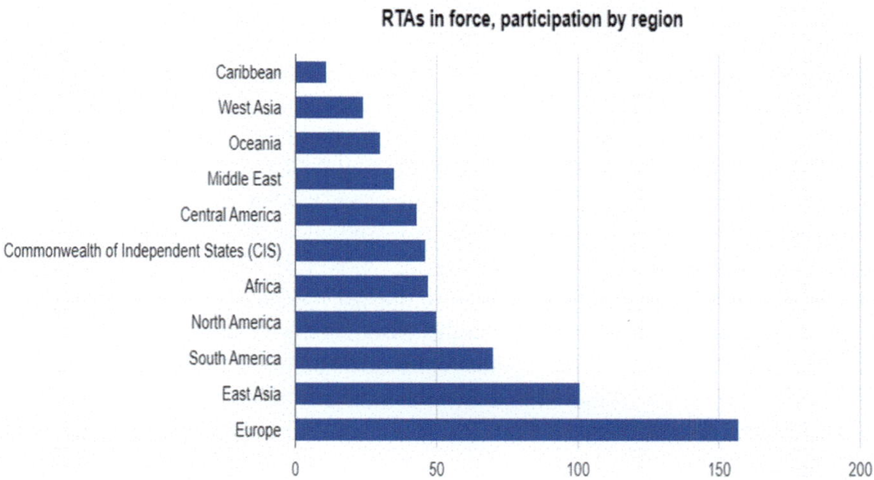

Fig. 9.6 FTAs/EPAs in force by region as of February 10, 2022 (*Source* WTO. https://rtais.wto.org/UI/charts.aspx). *Note* The composition of regions may be found in the RTA database User Guide. FTA/EPAs (RTAs) involving countries/territories in two (or more) regions more than one are counted. "Korea" refers to South Korea

Figure 9.4 shows the regional breakdown of global FTAs/EPAs notified to the WTO as of February 2022.[24] East Asia now has the second largest number of agreements in the world, with 100 agreements, after Europe.

By the way, why did the countries of East Asia move toward concluding FTAs and EPAs instead of stopping at the WTO's multilateral free trade system? And why did FTAs/EPAs lead to a chain of agreements? Let's check it again.

In general, the increase in FTAs/EPAs in the 1990s can be summarized as follows. In 1996, C. Fred Bergsten noted that the number of participating countries had increased to well over 100 (124 at the time). The principle of GATT is unanimity, and an increase in the number of member states makes it difficult to reach a consensus (Bergsten, 1996: 106). In fact, the GATT Uruguay round, which began in 1986, took until 1994.

There is also the issue of WTO consistency. In the first place, FTAs/EPAs have protectionist aspects that are contrary to multilateral trade liberalization, and the conditions for their conclusion are attached to Article 24 of the GATT (GATT Article XXIV-5). In other words, existing signatories should not aggravate existing terms of trade with non-signatories. However, it still gives rise to the advantage of trade between signatories, and the possibility of replacing trade with non-signatories with trade with signatories. This is the so-called "trade diversion effect". Non-signatory countries will be handicapped in exports. In contrast, trade volumes among the signatory countries are expected to increase through liberalization. This is the so-called "trade promotion effect." Together, FTAs/EPAs are expected to expand trade, while non-FTAs and EPAs are likely to contract. This is the mechanism by which the conclusion of FTAs/EPAs creates a ripple effect on non-signatories.

But there are more specific reasons for East Asian economic integration. East Asia fell into the Asian currency crisis in 1997. Yet in the midst of the crisis, the APEC Economic Leaders' Meeting in Vancouver, Canada, in November agreed on "early voluntary sectoral liberalization in 15 sectors" (EVSL) on trade liberalization. This is because neoliberal economic ideas dominated in foreign policies of the United States. However, EVSL eventually failed to make progress (Scollay & Gilbert, 2001: 7–8; Munakata -J, 2001: 98–99). APEC's inability to effectively deal with currency crises has weakened its influence (Kawai & Wignaraja, 2008: 120), while the momentum for regional cooperation within the East Asian region has increased. This gave impetus to the promotion of FTAs/EPAs. The instability associated with globalization has made East Asia aware of the need for regional cooperation, and FTAs/EPAs as economic cooperation have been promoted based on this recognition.

In addition, the conclusion of FTAs/EPAs reflected the characteristics of regional economic integration. Looking back, the economic integration of East Asia in the 1990s was achieved by the establishment of cross-border production networks by Japan and NIEs companies. FTAs/EPAs can reflect the needs of such companies. In addition, diplomatic and strategic factors related to the interests of major countries in the region will also be considered. It is mainly a struggle for leadership between

[24] The WTO refers to FTAs/EPAs as Regional Trade Agreements (RTAs), but FTAs/EPAs are used in this document.

Japan and China. In the next section, we will look at the moves that East Asian countries are moving toward wide-ranging mega-FTAs/EPAs.

9.4.2 ASEAN+3 and APEC Wide-Area FTAs/EPAs Initiatives

The move toward FTAs/EPAs, which accelerated early in the century, eventually resulted in the conclusion of two wide-area Mega FTAs/EPAs. These are the Regional Comprehensive Economic Partnership Agreement (RCEP) and the Comprehensive and Progressive Agreement for Trans-Pacific Partnership (CPTPP).

RCEP as a MEGA FTA In November 2002, the 6th ASEAN+3 Summit met with the final report of the East Asia Study Group (EASG) and adopted the East Asia Free Trade Area (EAFTA) and East Asia Investment Area (EAIA) initiatives as medium- and long-term cooperation goals of the report. It approved the promotion of investment by small and medium-sized enterprises. However, two ideas for free trade in East Asia have been proposed.

The two ideas are the "ASEAN+ 3 Free Trade Agreement" (EAFTA) and the "Comprehensive Economic Partnership in East Asia" (CEPEA). EAFTA was proposed at the ASEAN+ 3 Economic Ministerial Meeting (EMM) in November 2004, and the Phase 1 study started in April 2005. The results of Phase 1 research were reported at the ASEAN+ 3 Economic Ministerial Meeting in August 2006, and the research was completed in June 2009 after Phase 2.

CEPEA officially began in January 2007 when the second EAS meeting held in Cebu, Philippines, agreed to start the Phase 2 study (EAS, 2007: 12). The results of CEPEA's Phase 2 study were completed in July 2009. The results of the two studies were submitted to the ASEAN+ 3 EMM and the EAS EMM respectively for approval in August. However, "ASEAN was unable to decide which proposal to support so it attempted to bridge the two" (Hamanaka, 2014: 10).

One of the differences between the two initiatives is the composition of the participating countries. EAFTA is an FTA of ASEAN+3 member countries and was promoted by China, and CEPEA is promoted by Japan with ASEAN+6 member countries including Australia, New Zealand and India in China's proposal. There is the issue of the initiative ownership between China and Japan.

Another point appears in relation to the name. In conclusion, China focused on trade liberalization of goods, while Japan emphasized liberalization of investment and intellectual property rights (Hamanaka, 2014:10). That's why it is called the EPA. Its main objective is to support the activities of multinational corporations that have promoted de facto economic integration in East Asia through the international division of labor. We can get a glimpse of the differences in positions between the United States and China.

Incidentally, the ASEAN+ 3 Summit in Hanoi in October 2010 agreed to have the "four ASEAN Plus Working Group that were tasked to look into the recommendations of the studies on the East Asia Free Trade Area (EAFTA) and the Comprehensive Economic Partnership in East Asia (CEPEA) in Parallel" (APT Summit, 2010). Four

ASEAN Plus Working Groups (APWGs) were particularly in the areas of rules of origin, tariff nomenclature, and customs procedures, and economic cooperation.

Furthermore, ASEAN leaders, "taking into account the joint proposal of Japan and China, decided to establish ASEAN Plus Working Groups in the areas of Trade in Goods, Trade in Services, and Investment" noting in particular that the Working Group on Trade in Goods, that would be set up in early 2012, would also be tasked to follow-up on the outcome of the APWGs on Rules of Origin, Tariff Nomenclature, and Customs Procedures" (ASEAN Plus Three Summit, 2011). However, the 19th ASEAN Summit resolved "to establish an ASEAN-led process by setting out principles under which ASEAN will engage interested ASEAN FTA partners in establishing a regional comprehensive economic partnership agreement (RCEP)" (ASEAN Secretariat, 2012). RCEP was, based on the initiative of ASEAN, a group of small countries, counter-proposal to the joint proposal by Japan and China.

Thus, the 20th ASEAN Summit in April 2012 and the 5th China-Japan-Korea Trilateral Summit in May 2012 agreed to launch the RCEP by the end of the same year. The launch ceremony for the RCEP negotiations was held in Phnom Penh, Cambodia in November 2012 (MOFA, 2012). Subsequently, the acceleration of negotiations was confirmed at the APEC Economic Leaders' Meeting in Lima Peru in November 2016, and four years later, in November 2020, it was signed. However, since India declined to participate, the number of signatories was reduced to 15. Subsequently, the RCEP completed domestic procedures in ten countries in November 2021 and entered into force in January 2022.

The signing of the RCEP in November 2020 had a major impact on the world. Once the signing took place, the world's media reported it as the birth of the world's largest mega FTA. ADB explains the significance of RCEP as accounting for 29% ($25.8 trillion), 30% (2.3 billion) of the world's population, and 25% ($12.7 trillion) of global trade in goods and services,[25] states its significance as follows.

> RCEP will be the world's biggest free trade agreement (FTA) measured in GDP—larger than the Comprehensive and Progressive Agreement for Trans-Pacific Partnership (CPTPP), the European Union, the MERCOSUR trade bloc in South America, and the recent United States–Mexico–Canada Free Trade Agreement. RCEP is the first multilateral agreement to include the PRC and it establishes the first free trade agreement between the PRC and Japan, and Japan and the Republic of Korea (ADB, 2020: 1).

Figure 9.7 shows a map of RCEP participating countries. Negotiations have been held at ASEAN+6. This was the first EPA in history to cover almost all of East Asia. For India, which did not sign, special measures were taken to exempt it from negotiations. This is the reason why India has a different color in the figure.

APEC and FTAAP as a Goal In East Asia The conception of the ASEAN+ 3 and ASEAN+ 6 frameworks proceeded in parallel, culminating in the RCEP integration proposal. But there is another important Pacific economic cooperation framework. APEC was established in 1989. Since the 1990s, APEC has pursued an FTA for the Pacific Rim, or Asia–Pacific. Under the strong influence of the United States, the

[25] Data is from World Bank's World Development Indicators. 2019 data for GDP and population, and 2018 for trade in goods and services.

Fig. 9.7 Countries participating in the RCEP (*Source* Hutt, & Crispin, 2020)

Bogor Declaration was issued in 1994 advocating trade and investment liberalization, and at the APEC Summit in Vancouver in November 1997, the BOGOR Declaration was issued, and an 'early voluntary sectoral liberalization (EVSL) was agreed upon. However, due to the Asian currency crisis, hopes for APEC were dashed, and as a result, it did not produce results. Work on it started again in 2006.

Hanoi's 14th APEC Economic Leaders' Meeting in November 2006 "agreed to make every effort for realizing APEC's goals of free and open trade and investment" (APEC, 2006). In addition, the 17th APEC Summit in Singapore in 2009 and the 18th Summit in Yokohama in 2010 agreed on the construction of a future trade and investment-free trade zone. Leaders' declarations defined the FTAAP as the Asia–Pacific regional integration that deals with "next-generation" trade and investment, stating:

> 2009 Declaration:We will continue to explore building blocs toward a possible Free Trade Area of the Asia Pacific (FTAAP) in the future. An analytical study by officials shows that there are significant economic benefits from an FTAAP, as well as the challenges of establishing such an agreementq. We look forward to the progress update from Ministers and officials next year on the outcomes of the exploration of a range of possible pathways to achieve FTAAP (APEC, 2009).

> 2010 Declaration: We will take concrete steps toward realization of a Free Trade Area of the Asia-Pacific (FTAAP).... An FTAAP should be passed as a comprehensive free trade agreement by developing and building on ongoing regional undertakings, such as ASEAN+3, ASEAN+6, and the Trans-Pacific Partnership, among others. To this end, APEC will make an important and meaningful contribution as an incubator of an FTAAP by providing leadership,

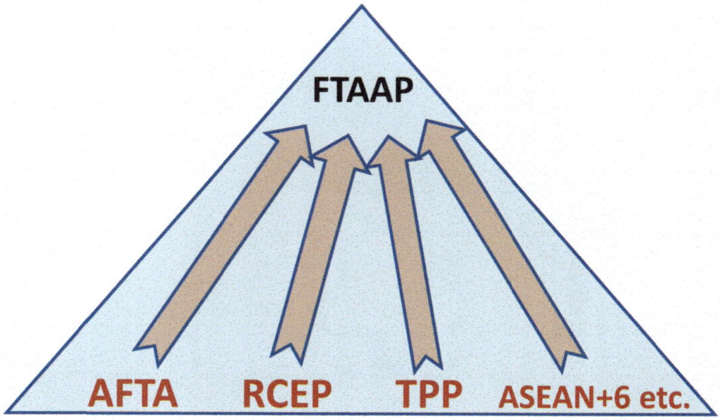

Fig. 9.8 Pathways to FTAAP (*Source* the Ministry of Finance, Japan. *Note* AFTA: ASEAN Free Trade Area, RCEP: Regional Comprehensive Economic Partnership. TPP: Trans-Pacific Partnership

> and intellectual input into the process of its development, and by playing a critical role in defining, shaping, and addressing the "next generation" trade and investment issues that FTAAP should contain. APEC should contribute to the pursuit of an FTAAP by continuing and further developing its work on sectoral initiatives in such areas as investment; services; e-commerce; rules of origin; standards and conformance; trade facilitation; and environmental goods and services (APEC, 2010a).

The APEC Economic Leaders' Meeting specifically announced the "Pathways to FTAAP" and stipulated the relationship between the FTAAP and other economic integration schemes. This is shown in Fig. 9.8. APEC's strong will to liberalize trade and investment, however, was left to ASEAN+3 and ASEAN+6, which had begun negotiations and studies, as well as to the Trans-Pacific Partnership Agreement (TPP), which will be discussed later. The FTAAP was described as "a major instrument" to achieve APEC's regional economic integration (REI) and was touted as "an important and meaningful contribution as an incubator".

However, the time lag increases the likelihood that a situation of coexistence of FTAs/EPAs with different conditions of integration will arise. This phenomenon is called by Jagdish Bhagwati as the "spaghetti bowl phenomenon" or "spider's web" (Bhagwati). The FTAAP was positioned as an EPA formed by the Asia–Pacific Economic Bloc that ultimately avoided this spaghetti phenomenon.

The FTAAP will be further expanded at the APEC Beijing meeting in November 2014. The Chinese Presidency of the FTAAP has shown a willingness to build an FTAAP, with the statement inserting the text "endorse Beijing Roadmap for APEC's Contribution to the Realization of the FTAAP" and including the 2012 agreement in Vladivostok of lowering tariffs related to environmental goods by the end of 2015. Not only that, but China has proposed a roadmap to achieve the FTAAP by 2025. However, the proposal was strongly opposed by the United States and Japan, who were concerned about the impact on the TPP during negotiations. In the end, the statement replaced the phrase "2025" with "as early as possible" and stated that it would aim to achieve the FTAAP (APEC, 2014: Para 12–15; Umada -J, 2017: 253).

The U.S. and Japan followed suit, with an emphasis on the TPP negotiations and the intention to reflect its provisions in the FTAAP (Umada -J, 2017: 254). Since then, the two negotiations, the Trans-Pacific Partnership (TPP) and the Regional Comprehensive Economic Partnership (RCEP), have progressed intertwined.

The start of negotiations on the China-Japan-Korea (Trilateral) FTA was agreed upon at the China-Japan-ROK summit meeting in Beijing in May 2012, and the commencement of negotiations was announced at the ministerial meeting in Phnom Penh in November 2012. The first round of negotiations began in March 2013 and was held 16 times by November 2019 (MOFA Press Release Nov. 29, 2019), but no agreement was reached. Incidentally, in November 2023, a spokesperson for China's Ministry of Commerce announced at a regular press conference that the company would aim to resume China-Japan-Korea FTA negotiations as soon as possible (CGTN Japanese Dec.1, 2023).

U.S. Withdrawal from TPP12 and Entry into Force of TPP11 (CPTPP)

Brunei, Chile, New Zealand, and Singapore signed the Trans-Pacific Strategic Economic Partnership Agreement (TPSEP or P4) in July 2005, which entered into force in 2006. In September 2008, then-U.S. President George W. Bush announced his participation in the agreement, and Australia, Peru, and Vietnam joined the agreement, making it a total of eight negotiating countries (USTR, 2008). However, substantial negotiations will begin in March 2010. Barack Obama, who was inaugurated as the new president of the United States in January 2009, announced his participation in the White House in November 2011, and the first meeting of the negotiations was held in March. The U.S. saw the TPP as a broad-based membership, having the high standards worthy of a twenty-first century trade agreement, and a vision to achieve increased exports of U.S. goods and employment by incorporating the world's fastest-growing regions.

Malaysia joined the TPP in October 2010. It was aimed at concluding the TPP by the 18th APEC Hanoi Economic Leaders' Meeting in November 2011, but it did not materialize. However, when then Japan-Prime Minister Noda announced at the 19th APEC Summit in Honolulu in 2011 that "negotiations to join the TPP" had begun, Canada and Mexico followed suit. Canada and Mexico joined the TPP negotiations in June 2012, and Japan joined the negotiations in July 2013 under the new Abe administration. The TPP has now reached 12 countries.

In October 2015, the TPP negotiations reached an agreement in principle, and the TPP signing ceremony of 12 member countries took place in Auckland in February 2016. However, in January 2017, Donald Trump, who campaigned on the "America First," platform won the presidential election. As soon as he took office, he signed an executive order to withdraw from the TPP.

Following the withdrawal of the United States, the remaining 11 TPP countries held the TPP Ministerial Meeting in Chile in March of the same year, with the initiative of Prime Minister Abe of Japan, and in May the Ministerial Meeting in Vietnam discussed early entry into force, and reached an agreement in principle at the Ministerial Meeting in Da Nang in November of the same year. The March 2018 Agreement was signed in Chile under the name of the Comprehensive and Progressive Agreement for Trans-Pacific Partnership (CPTPP or TPP11) and entered into force in December 2018.

According to 2000 data from the IMF and the United Nations, the CPTPP is about $10.6 trillion in total GDP, 13% of total world GDP, about 500 million people, and about $5 trillion in trade. As we will see in the next section, it is considered to be "a free and fair economic zone based on the rules of the twenty-first century" (TPP Headquarters at the Cabinet Secretariat Office 2021).

9.4.3 Economic Effects of RCEP and CPTPP

One month before the RCEP entered into force in January 2022, UNCTAD released a report estimating its impact on the global economy. According to the report, 90% of the US$2.3 trillion of goods traded in the RCEP region will be tariff-free, increasing the total GDP of member countries by 2 percent. Overall, the increase in trade value due to tariff reductions is US$41.8 billion, of which 60% is generated by trade diversion and 40% by trade creation. In this way, the RCEP economic zone becomes the center of gravity of the global economy. In addition, the increase in trade value is concentrated in the three countries of East Asia, in descending order of effectiveness as follows: Japan is $20.2 billion, China is $11.2 billion, and South Korea is $6.7 billion. The effects will be concentrated in the three Northeast Asian countries that have not been able to conclude FTAs with each other so far (UNCTAD, 2021: 5, 13).

There is a study by Petri and Plummer that uses GTAP to simulate the impact of the CPTPP and RCEP, the US-Sino trade war initiated by the Trump administration, and the coronavirus pandemic on the global economy in 2030 (Petri and Plummer 2020a). Figure 9.9 summarizes the scale of the increase in the trade value. If there is no US-Sino trade war, the CPTPP will increase trade by US$147 billion in 2030, RCEP15 by $186 billion, and India by $53 billion. However, the trade war will reduce the CPTPP's effectiveness, reducing global income by $301 billion, and the CPTPP effect by $26 billion from pre-war forecasts to $121 billion. The effect of RCEP will increase by $23 billion to $209 billion. India, which did not join the RCEP, is expected to remain unaffected.

Of course, this increase or decrease in the amount of trade is not equally distributed or shared. The biggest global benefits of the CPTPP will go to Japan with $46 billion in grains, followed by Canada with $22 billion, Malaysia with $21 billion, Mexico with $16 billion, and Vietnam with $11 billion. "China will be the most adversely affected, with estimated losses of $10 billion". RCEP-induced benefits of $186 billion will go largely to China with $85 billion, followed by Japan with $48 billion, and Korea with $23 billion respectively (Petri & Plummer, 2020a: 11).

In 2030 losses due to the ongoing trade war are as follows. China's exports to the U.S. will fall to 72% of the baseline export value ($1006 billion) and $723 billion. U.S. exports to China will also fall to $193 billion, or 46% of the baseline ($420

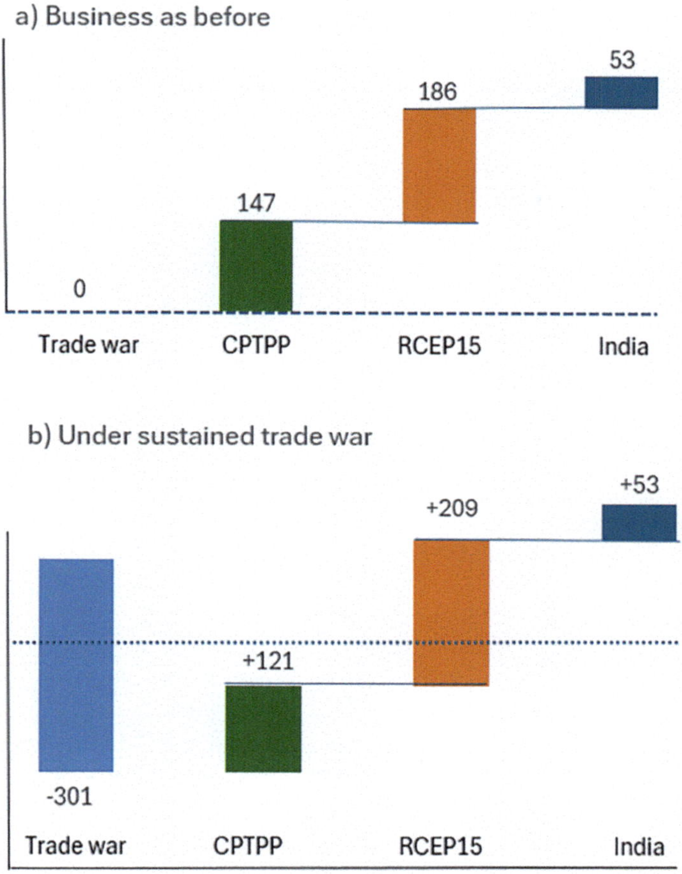

Fig. 9.9 Global income effects of Asia–Pacific trade policies in 2030 (income gains/losses in billions of US dollars (*Source* Petri and Plummer 2020a: 4). *Note* CPTPP (11): Comprehensive and Progressive Agreement for Trans-Pacific Partnership. RCEP: Regional Comprehensive Economic Partnership. Note: "Business as before" assumes a return to a pre-trade war path: "Sustained trade war" assumes a path defined by post-Phase 1 tariffs. Bars show incremental effects of adding each policy to all previous policies. The policy denoted "India" involves adding India to the RCEP15 agreement to form RCEP16

billion). The trade wars will affect global trade as a whole (Petri & Plummer, 2020a: 16–17).

The following sentences are part of their summary.

- RCEP will be economically significant with or without India, and indeed more significant than the CPTPP, with especially important benefits for China, Japan and South Korea.
- RCEP will reorient trade and economic ties away from global linkages toward regionally focused relationships in East Asia.
- RCEP will make larger contributions to global and regional welfare in the context of a trade war than under business-as-before assumptions (Petri & Plummer, 2020a: 5)

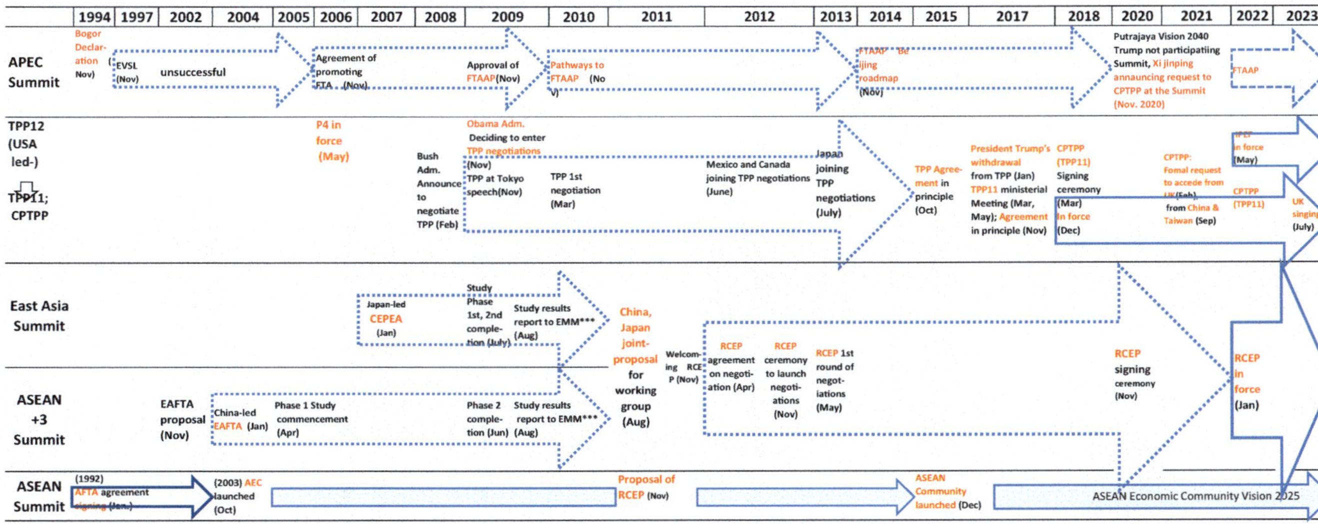

Fig. 9.10 Development of FTAAP, TPP, RCEP and others (*Source* created by Hirakawa). *Note* CEPEA: Comprehensive Economic Partnership in East Asia. EAFTA: East Asia Free Trade Area. EMM: Economic Ministerial Meeting. EVSL: Early Voluntary Sectoral Liberalization. FTAAP: Free Trade Area of the Asia–Pacific. IPEF: Indo-Pacific Economic Framework for Prosperity. P4: Trans-Pacific Strategic Economic Partnership. RCEP: Regional Comprehensive Economic Partnership. TPP: Trans-Pacific Partnership. CPTPP (=TPP11): Comprehensive and Progressive Agreement for Trans-Pacific Partnership. Month in parenthesis is the month in which negotiations began, signed, and entered into force. The P4 initially included four countries (Singapore, New Zealand, Chili, and Brunei), and then the following countries participated in the negotiations: USA, Australia, Peru, Vietnam (Mar. 2010), Malaysia (Oct. 2010), Mexico, Canada (June 2012), and Japan (July 2013)

The Asia–Pacific economic structure, they predict, in 2030 will have a significant economic impact on East Asia, regardless of whether there is a U.S.-Sino trade war or not. Moreover, the trade war and COVID-19 will further enhance the significance of the economic effects in East Asia. In any partnership agreement, Japan, China and South Korea will receive the greatest economic benefits (welfare). As the title of their paper suggests, the consequence of the trade war and COVID-19 is practically that "East Asia decouples from the United States". This conclusion is broadly consistent with the UNCTAD study.

9.5 Characteristics and Structure of East Asian Economic Integration

In this section, we will review the background to the conclusion of the RCEP and CPTPP, their promotion structure, and their characteristics.

9.5.1 Promotion Structure of RCEP and CPTPP

The impact of the CPTPP and RCEP on the global economy is enormous. However, as we have seen in the previous section, regional integration in Asia was inspired by the regional integration movements in Europe and the United States, and began rather late. It has now, however, become one of the poles of regional integration. This section examines the significance and characteristics of the CPTPP and RCEP, the mechanisms for promoting wide-ranging mega-FTAs/EPAs in East Asia, and examines the current achievements and challenges of economic integration in East Asia and the Asia–Pacific.

Looking back, the impetus for the establishment of the CPTPP was the start of the TPP negotiations in the United States. Substantive negotiations began with President Obama's decision in November 2009. The U.S. has been promoting economic integration through APEC. Despite this, why was there a move to promote the TPP at this time? What should be noted is the timing of FTAEA and CPAEA promoted by China and Japan.

Figure 9.10 shows the development of major EPAs/FTAs in the Asia–Pacific region, which summarizes the mechanisms for promoting regional economic integration to date. Regional cooperation (regionalism) after the Asian financial crisis moved towards economic integration as its main goal. The ASEAN+3 summit agreed on the formation of EAFTA. China was the first country to move to promote this initiative. At the suggestion of China, research on ASEAN+3 FTAs began in 2004. However, Japan did not agree with this proposal, and in early 2007 submitted a CEPEA proposal for ASEAN+6 countries to the EAS, initiating research in this area. The results of the two proposals were submitted to the ASEAN+3 Summit and the EAS in August 2009, respectively. However, neither proposal includes the United States.

In the previous section, the FTAAP was confirmed in two APEC Leaders' declarations in 2009 and 2010, with the United States exclusively promoting trade liberalization through APEC. However, this does not avoid the risk that East Asian integration, excluding the United States, will take precedence. This is the background that prompted the Obama administration to embark on the realization of the TPP concept. The start of TPP negotiations in November 2009 coincided with this timing. However, the position of the TPP in relation to China has changed since then. Let's take a look at the changes below.

President Obama visited Japan immediately after announcing his participation in the TPP negotiations, and in his speech in Tokyo, he described the TPP as "a regional agreement that will have broad-based membership and the high standards worthy of a 21 century trade agreement. "At the same time, he stated that the "United States does not seek to contain China, nor does a deeper relationship with China mean a weakening of our bilateral alliances" (Obama, 2009). Thus, in 2011, the TPP became the Obama administration's Asia–Pacific strategy. A press release from the White House on November 12, 2011 announced that 'The TPP is a key element of the Obama Administration strategy to make U.S. engagement in the Asia–Pacific region a top priority' (White House Office of the Press Secretary 2009). "Secretary of State Hillary Clinton framed the TPP as the centerpiece of the United States' strategic pivot to the Asia–Pacific region" (McBride et al., 2021).

In fact, the Obama administration's initial TPP policy focused on U.S. exports of goods and job growth, with the focus on increasing U.S. exports and employment, bearing in mind the move toward FTAs in East Asian markets and assuming that China would be a country to be included in the future. This is probably the intention behind the "broad-based membership" pointed out in Obama's participation in the TPP negotiations. A March 2012 study report by the U.S. Congressional Research Service (CRS) (Obama Administration's "Rebalancing" towards Asia) also described the importance of the TPP and China:

> U.S. efforts to proactively influence the region's path toward economic integration are focused on the ongoing TPP negotiations. As envisioned by the Office of the U.S. Representative, a free trade agreement between the nine negotiating parties will form the basis for a broader agreement that eventually could include all the economies of the Asia-Pacific region, including China.… /The participation of Japan, the world's third-largest economy and a regional power, would significantly raise the economic and strategic impact of the TPP. Canada and Mexico also have begun consultations to join the negotiations (CRS, 2012: 22).

Japan, Canada, and Mexico joined the negotiations after the release of the report, but the intention of the U.S. TPP was to liberalize trade throughout the Asia–Pacific, including China. This is expected to lead to APEC's FTAAP.

However, during this period, China was rapidly building up its military capabilities, and in 2013, it launched the Belt and Road Initiative, which led to a change in its attitude toward the outside world. Hitoshi Tanaka, a former diplomat in Japan, wrote in a September 2012 newspaper article about the change in China's attitude toward the outside world:

> China's attitude toward the outside world has been changing over the past 40 years. In 2010, it took tough measures in a territorial dispute in the South China Sea and unilaterally took measures against a Chinese fishing vessel off the Senkaku Islands (with a Japan Coast Guard patrol boat) that gave the impression of an extremely aggressive external stance (Tanaka, -J, 2012).

The U.S. perception of China has begun to change, and the position of the TPP has also changed. The U.S. will not only secure the Asian market through the formulation of its own rules, but at the same time, it will strengthen its tendency to keep China in check. President Obama's emergency statement on the agreement in principle on the TPP showed this recognition. He explained the significance of the TPP as follows.

> When more than 95 percent of our potential customers live outside our borders, we can't let countries like China write the rules of the global economy. We should write those rules, opening new markets to American products while setting high standards for protecting workers and preserving our environment (Obama, 2015).

Following the agreement in principle on the TPP, Japan has shown a similar recognition. An article signed by Japan Keizai Shimbun editorial board member Yasuhiko Ota titled "Determination for Pacific Rim Growth" explains its significance as follows:

> The focus of heated negotiations (in Japan) is not necessarily the essence of the trade agreement. While it is essential to open up markets to increase imports and exports of goods, the real heart of the Trans-Pacific Partnership (TPP) lies in the establishment of novel international rules that have never existed before. In the background is the rise of China. A superpower with a military presence in the South China Sea and a wide range of state-owned Gulliver companies. There is a glimpse of an unstable future in which China's romantic overture and brawn are crucial. Japan's defeat in the bidding of the Shinkansen bullet train in Indonesia is symbolic of this (Nikkei- Ota signed article -J, Oct. 6, 2015).

The first half of the 2010s was a turning point in this perception of China. Obama's start of TPP negotiations put a lot of pressure on Japan. Japan's participation in the TPP negotiations was met with strong opposition from within Japan. The ruling party in Japan at this time was the Democratic Party of Japan, and both administrations, Naoto Kan and his successor Noda Yoshihiko, announced that they would consider joining the TPP before participating in the APEC summit. As the Prime Minister of the host country of APEC in 2010, Kan announced in October 2010 that he would consider joining the TPP. The day before Noda participated in the APEC (Hawaii) meeting in November of the following year, he announced that he would "enter into consultations with the countries concerned to participate in the TPP negotiations" (Asahi Shimbun -J, Nov.11.2011) and informed President Obama of the start of the talks.

However, after the Liberal Democratic Party (LDP) won an overwhelming victory in the December 2012 general election by criticizing the TPP. Prime Minister Shinzo Abe, who became prime minister, announced his participation in the TPP in March of the following year, easily reneging on his promises, and officially participated in the negotiations in July. Prime Minister Abe's process of joining the TPP shows typical disregard for election promises and a willingness to follow the U.S. by LDP politicians in Japan, but in any case, there is no doubt that there was a strong intervention (foreign pressure) from the U.S. in Japanese politics.

However, the crux of the matter lies elsewhere. Japan was forced to participate late in the TPP negotiations, and there was a sense of crisis that the United States would force it to make significant concessions in trade liberalization. To that end, the negotiating card with the United States was the promotion of regional integration in Asia, including China. Abe tried to gain an advantage in joining the TPP negotiations by proposing economic integration without the United States. This led to a proposal to set up a working team for a joint FTA with China in August 2011. The result was a counter-proposal of the RCEP by ASEAN.

In April 2012, Indonesia proposed the Regional Comprehensive Economic Partnership (RCEP) as an ASEAN proposal, which led to the launch ceremony of negotiations in November 2012, and negotiations began the following year. It is ASEAN centrality that plays an important role in RCEP (see Box).

Box: Notes on RCEP and ASEAN Centrality An important feature of RCEP is ASEAN's centrality. This is very much in line with the ASEAN Community Vision whereby ASEAN deepens its integration among member nations, through the principle of non-interventionism and respect for diversity, and prevents the marginalization of ASEAN in regional and world affairs. This centrality should not be construed as hegemonic ambition[26] on the part of ASEAN

This centrality has geopolitical and economic significance. Geopolitically, ASEAN centrality, as a neutral broker, has brought the East Asian countries to agree on a multilateral trade agreement. With regards to this, Petri and Plummer write:

> RCEP, often labeled inaccurately as "China-led," is a triumph of ASEAN's middle-power diplomacy. The value of a large, East Asian trade agreement has long been recognized, but neither China nor Japan, the region's largest economies, were politically acceptable as architects for the project. The stalemate was resolved in 2012 by an ASEAN-brokered deal that included India, Australia, and New Zealand as members, and put ASEAN in charge of negotiating the agreement. Without such "ASEAN centrality". RCEP might never have been launched (Petri & Plemmer, 2020b).

Moreover, M. Cook affirms the ASEAN centrality in providing a venue for the three East Asian countries to discuss regional issues:

> RCEP is the latest example of ASEAN facilitating greater contact and cooperation between China, Japan and Southeast Asia for the benefit of East Asia. In 1997, in the midst of the Asian Financial Crisis, ASEAN established the ASEAN+ 3 process bringing together the ten ASEAN member states and China, Japan and South Korea. The ASEAN+ 3 process provided a conducive environment for the three ASEAN dialogue partners to start trilateral meetings between themselves. However,

[26] Such a perspective appears in Mueller (2019), which finds a threatened ASEAN centrality in the sense that ASEAN is concretely able to exercise leadership in the trade negotiations.

the leaders of China, Japan, and South Korea have met more frequently and regularly at the 22 ASEAN+3 Summits held since 1997 than they have at the irregularly scheduled and frequently postponed China-Japan-[South] Korea trilateral summits. ASEAN+3 has become the most active ASEAN-led broader grouping as has been shown during the ongoing Covid-19 pandemic (Cook, 2020).

From an economic standpoint, RCEP represents the largest FTA thus far in terms of the income and trade of participating countries. More relevant to ASEAN centrality, however, is in imbuing to the agreement a flavor that is distinctly ASEAN. Shiro Armstrong and Peter Drysdale, in a study on RCEP and ASEAN published by the Economic Research Institute for ASEAN and East Asia (ERIA) in March 2022, describe this as follows:

> While the RCEP agreement does not have some of the disciplines of other agreements such as the CPTPP, it does represent a large commitment to economic liberalisation by East Asia. It allows developing countries in the arrangement to phase in their liberalisation over considerable periods of time, in contrast to many other FTAs, while still ensuring an endpoint of substantial liberalisation across a comprehensive range of goods and services. That approach recognises the wide range of economic development and market conditions found in member countries and helps countries meet commitments through cooperation rather than with the threat of punishments or sanctions (Armstrong & Drysdale, 2022: 8).

Similarly, F. Kimura writes:

The commitments under RCEP are made in the 'ASEAN Way', with slow movers allowed a grace period to achieve the same goals. This is sometimes called the '10 minus x' approach in the context of ASEAN economic integration, meaning that the 10 nations that make up ASEAN are not necessarily required to progress at the same pace. This is criticised as being too lenient, but in this way ASEAN has successfully achieved deeper economic integration where others have failed (Kimura, 2022).

Composed of countries that are different in terms of development, culture, and politics, ASEAN has developed a respect for such diversity. Such an ASEAN flavor of the RCEP implies an acceptance towards the adoption of an effective industrial policy by member countries, where temporary but strategic protection of local industry

For example, in the case of the Philippines, a call to tread carefully in the legislative deliberation of RCEP was still being raised at the beginning of 2022, despite ratification by President Duterte last September 2, 2021. The Department of Trade and Industry, however, has assured that the Philippines could always invoke the Safeguard Measures Law or Republic Act 8800 containing the necessary remedies for laws that may be affected by the treaty (Tan, 2022).

ASEAN centrality would, therefore, introduce a tolerance for the adoption of industrial policies of the RCEP members. This could be viewed as a source of strategic complementarity of ASEAN to the Flying Geese dynamics that has contributed very well to the region's integration.

However, in Japan, distrust of China increased at about the same time as the RCEP negotiations, and at the stage of agreement in principle on the TPP, converging to the U.S. perception of China. Once Japan became a negotiating country in the TPP, Japan preferred to effectively proceed with the TPP negotiations over the RCEP.

From China's point of view, RCEP is close to accepting Japan's proposal. This is because it will effectively become a framework for ASEAN + 6. However, even though China's economy surpassed Japan to become the world's second largest economy in 2010, there was a general perception that China's economy could not withstand the conditions for joining the TPP. If this is the case, it seems that China has decided that it would be better to join the RCEP on a joint proposal with Japan and consolidate its foothold in East Asian FTAs in terms of its policy toward the United States. Around 2010, Japan and China agreed on the RCEP policy toward the United States.

ASEAN, of course, must avoid getting bogged down in the competition between Japan and China for economic integration initiatives. That was the RCEP's proposal to guarantee ASEAN centrality.

However, in January 2017, President Trump withdrew from the TPP. It was a 180-degree rejection of the Obama administration's Asia policy. The result was the conclusion of the Comprehensive and Progressive Agreement for Trans-Pacific Partnership (CPTPP) by the remaining 11 countries. The member countries that have already agreed to the TPP, like Japan, recognized that they could not afford to exploit the TPP as a card against China. In order to avoid dependence on China and China's excessive influence, the CPTPP framework is absolutely necessary. The 11 countries rushed to conclude the CPTPP, hoping for the return of the United States in the near future.

On the other hand, the U.S. withdrawal from the TPP was seen as an opportunity for China to move toward regional integration in East Asia. The RCEP negotiations were agreed in principle in March 2018, one year after Trump's withdrawal from the TPP. Shintaro Hamanaka, a researcher at the Institute of Developing Economies in Japan, sees the situation as follows. Taking advantage of the U.S. withdrawal from the TPP, China rushed to conclude the RCEP and persuaded ASEAN to create a situation in which the RCEP could be signed without Japan. Japan faced a situation where it could not say no to the conclusion of the RCEP (Hamanaka -J, 2020). Hamanaka's understanding is disputed in Japan. In fact, the CPTPP reached an agreement in principle in November 2017. Japan had no reason to delay RCEP either.

Incidentally, at the 2014 APEC Beijing Meeting, China was positive about promoting the FTAAP. The announcement of the Beijing Roadmap shows this. The Trump administration's withdrawal from the TPP has created the conditions for China to step up its offensive toward regional integration. Since this period, the U.S. and China have changed their offensive and defensive positions due to trade liberalization.

Figure 9.11 shows a comparative diagram of the economic scale of the world's major FTAs/EPAs, taken from a paper by the Atlantic Council. This diagram reveals the importance of China. In order of economic size, it will be followed by RCEP, USMCA, EU, and CPTPP, but if China is added to the CPTPP, the world's first and second largest economic integration, surpassing the United States, will emerge in Asia, and China will sit at the center of it. The United Kingdom applied to join the CPTPP seven months before China's formal application for membership

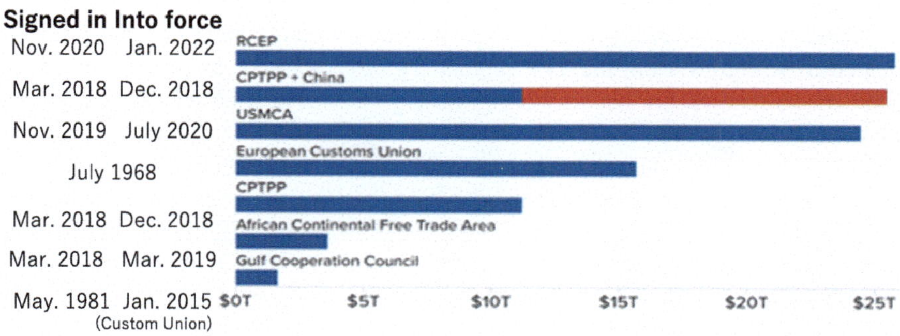

Fig. 9.11 Global trade blocs: Total GDP of member economies (*Source* Graham 2021. "Date signed" and "in force" mainly from the official site of each institution). *Note* RCEP: Regional Comprehensive Economic Partnership, CPTPP (11): Comprehensive and Progressive Agreement for Trans-Pacific Partnership, USMCA: US-Mexico-Canada Agreement. The red bar shows China's GDP Share

in September 2021, the accession process began in June, and its official membership was confirmed in March 2023.

Following China's application for membership, Taiwan immediately moved to apply. At the end of 2021, South Korea and Ecuador also announced their participation. The CPTPP and RCEP will have a significant impact on the global economic structure. Moreover, China's application to join the CPTPP will have an enormous impact not only on the economy but also on international politics. The impact on regional cooperation in Asia will be even greater. Let us now reconsider these points.

President Joe Biden's administration, which was inaugurated in January 2021, launched the Indo-Pacific Economic Framework (IPEF) in May 2022 with 13 countries as an alternative to Trump's withdrawal from the TPP, which removed the ladder to Asia through economic integration. The IPEF is a cooperation framework that is intended to compete with China, but it aims to cooperate on four pillars: trade, supply chains, clean economy and fair economy. Since its inauguration, ministerial meetings have been held vigorously, and a summit meeting was held in November 2023, and negotiations have been concluded in three areas except trade.

9.5.2 Asian Economic Integration and China

In November 2020, when Chinese President Xi Jinping announced his intention to join the CPTPP at the online APEC Economic Leaders' Meeting, interest in China was renewed. Various opinions are heard regarding how this application for membership is viewed.

On the other hand, there are those who argue that the degree of liberalization required by the CPTPP is at a level that China cannot meet, and that the membership application is simply for pretenses. On the other hand, there are those who say that China's application for membership is serious. In fact, when President Trump decided to withdraw from the TPP in January 2017, China's Ministry of Foreign Affairs had already expressed its willingness to join the TPP. In May 2020, at a press conference after the end of the National People's Congress, Premier Li Keqiang made a "positive" statement about joining the CPTPP. While it is unlikely that negotiations on joining the CPTPP will be short-lived, what is certain is that, on the one hand, the CPTPP will have a negative effect on China, as confirmed in the previous section, and on the other hand, the withdrawal of the United States will provide an opportunity to expand China's influence. It would not be wrong to assume that the Xi Jinping leadership will make a strategic decision to apply for membership.

With China's application in mind, let us review some basic differences between the CPTPP and RCEP. The first is the quality of the CPTPP, which is generally considered to be highly liberalized. With the withdrawal of the United States, the TPP was renamed CPTPP, but it is not just a name change. The remaining 11 countries that were left moved to conclude the CPTPP in a timely manner in order to contain the unrest. The conclusion of the agreement was limited to the minimum necessary amendments, and measures were sought in the hope of a return of the United States. The method was to resort to the "suspension" of the commitments that countries had made to the United States. When the U.S. returns, it will basically reinstate its commitments to the U.S. A report by the Congressional Research Service (CRS) reported that the Suspension of TPP provisions under the CPTPP is as follows:

> In order to preserve U.S. interest in the TPP, Japan, which led the CPTPP negotiating process, pushed for the CPTPP to suspend 20 provisions where consensus could not be reached, rather than amend them. The parties agreed to suspend 20 provisions, which primarily were sought by the United States and agreed to by other countries in return for access to U.S. markets. This was especially true in the area of intellectual property rights (IPR) …./ In the investment chapter, investor-state-dispute-settlement (ISDS) is suspended with respect to investment screening (e.g., the criteria by which a party approves an investment), and also with respect to investment agreement between a host state government and an investor. These changes potentially could lead to a requirement to use domestic courts and apply domestic laws to resolve some investment disputes, counter to long-standing U.S. objectives in bilateral investment treaties and FTAs. In e-commerce, the parties suspended the obligation to review *de minimis* tariff levels on express shipments. The party also removed a provision to "promote compliance" with local labor laws in the procurement of goods or services, and one section of a provision related to the prohibition against illegal trade in wildlife. In the event of the return of the United States to the agreement, reinstatement of the suspended provisions would require consensus among the existing parties (CRS Insight, 2018: 2).

In the above report, there are 20 items that are frozen, but 22 items are counted in the Japan study (for example, Ishikawa -J, 2021a, b). In any case, this freeze was applied only to cases in which the other country allowed the U.S. to open its market in exchange for accepting the strong demand of the United States, and the difference in the number of frozen items does not change the evaluation or perception of the situation.

Half of the frozen items (11 items) are related to intellectual property rights and are incorporated into the U.S.-ROK FTA. Other frozen items included two items related to government procurement, three items related to dispute settlement including two items related to investor-state disputes (ISDS), two items related to trade in services and investment such as e-commerce, three items related to government procurement, one item related to state-owned enterprises, one item related to the environment, and one item related to transparency of pharmaceuticals and their equipment. Examining its characteristics, Ishikawa summarizes it as follows. "The CPTPP freeze items are rules-related," and in terms of market access, "the TPP's provisions and commitments were kept intact." "Key rules such as e-commerce, intellectual property, state-owned enterprises, and labor are maintained", and the TPP's high rate of liberalization (Table 9.1) remains unchanged in the CPTPP. The degree of liberalization of trade in goods reaches 98% (Ishikawa -J, 2021a, b: 5, 17).

Next, let's compare the RCEP, which China has already acceded to, and CPTPP. The RCEP has 20 chapters and CPTPP has 30 chapters, which is 1.5 times the number of chapters in the RCEP. It can be seen that the CPTPP is a more detailed provision. Table 9.2 shows chapters that differ in the relevant provisions of the two agreements and those that are not covered. The CPTPP does not recognize the RCEP-approved positive lists in the chapter on investment and cross-border trade in services. In other words, the provisions of the CPTPP are more stringent. In e-commerce, the bill includes a ban on tariffs on electronic transactions, which are not included in the RCEP. State-owned enterprises, labor protection and environmental regulations are not covered by RCEP. Intellectual property rights are subject to ratification of international agreements. In other words, the CPTPP provides for a higher level of liberalization than RCEP. The CPTPP has frozen items, but there has been no definitive degradation, so the above assessment is generally correct.

So, is it possible for China to join the CPTPP? The barriers to clearing many items, such as the chapters on state-owned enterprise, e-service, and labor, are not low. However, it cannot be said that it cannot be cleared. In fact, China has already made some commitments in RCEP that go beyond the CPTPP hurdle. Ishikawa (2021a, b) pointed out that China has already granted national treatment in the investment chapter of the RCEP. China has not recognized national treatment in any previous FTAs and investment agreements at all, and also recognizes the prohibition of demand for the implementation of specific measures (performance demand), the prohibition of royalty regulation, and the prohibition of technology transfer requests. In e-commerce, China accepted (1) not to require data localization, and (2) not to

Table 9.1 TPP (CPTPP) tariff elimination rate (%) of negotiating member as for signing time of agreement

Country	Japan	USA	Canada	Australia	NZ	Singapore
Item rumber base	95	100	99	100	100	100
Trade value base	95	100	100	100	100	100
Country	Mexico	Chili	Peru	Malaysia	Vietnam	Brunei
Item rumber base	99	100	99	100	100	100
Trade value base	99	100	99	100	100	100

Source TPP Headquarters at the Cabinet Secretariat Office, Japan -J (2015).

Table 9.2 The main differences between the CPTPP and RCEP

Major issues	CPTPP chapter(s)	RCEP chapter(s)	CPTPP content	Expected RCEP differences
Investment	9	10	National treatment. MFN treatment, compensation for expropriation. rules for financikal transfers, bar performance requirements, investor—state dispute settlement (ISDS) with improved safeguards for public welfare regulations: phaseout of equity limits in some countries	Instead of negative lists also permits positive lists for exceptions: ISDS provisions will not be activated unless members decide to do so three years after the agreement is signed.
Cross-border trade in	10, 11, 13	8	Disciplines on market restrictions, local presence requirements, regulations, criteria for service providers: special provisions for financial services in enhancing offerings, and for telecommunications services on interconnection, roaming	Instead of negative lists also permits positive lists for exceptions
Electronic	14	12	Prohibition of customer duties on electronic transmissions, discriminatory treatment of digital products: legal framework for e-commerce; limited restrictions on cross-border transmission of data and location of computing facilities	No coverage of cross—border data flows and data localization requirements; no moratorium on customs duties on electronic
State—owned enterprises (SOEs) and designated monopolies	17	–	Definition of state-owned enterprises and designated monopolies; limits on noncommercial assistance to SOEs	State-owned enterprises not covered
Intellectual property (IP)	18	11	Commitments to ratify international agreements on intellectual agreements on intellectual property; suspension of US-promoted provisions for expand provisions for expanded IP protections under TPP	

(continued)

Table 9.2 (continued)

Major issues	CPTPP chapter(s)	RCEP chapter(s)	CPTPP content	Expected RCEP differences
Labor	19	–	Commitments to implement laws and regulations supporting ILO Declaration on Labor Rights; institutions for review and a Labor Council for monitoring	Not covered
Environment	20	–	Recognition of multilateral environmental agreements; provisions on ship pollution, biodiversity, invasive species, marine fisheries, conservation	Not covered

Source Petri and Plummer 2020a: 7–8, partly cited). Petri and Plummer 2020a: 20–9).

interfere with the free flow of data (Ishikawa -J, 2021b: 40). Considering that RCEP was signed about two and a half years after the CPTPP, it is China's response that may have been based on joining the CPTPP.

A joint study by a team in Japan that comprehensively examined China's CPTPP application in relation to its domestic policy concluded that its purpose was to build a Chinese "institutional spoken right" (Zhìdù xìng huàyǔ quán), or "discourse power embedded in the system.“ The ultimate goal of China's accession to the CPTPP is for China to establish international rules (Watanabe, Kamo et al. -J, 2021). According to their research, China is hampered in the modern world under U.S. hegemony because of its non-capitalist political system, and the transformation of that system is the goal. That is what led China to decide to apply for membership in the CPTPP. If this is the case, China must be exploring all possibilities for accession.

New accession to the CPTPP requires consensus among all parties. At this stage, members Singapore, Malaysia, Vietnam, and Chile have welcomed or supported China's accession, while Japan and Australia have strong negative views. Canada and Mexico have a problem with Article 32.10 of the USMCA, which they signed with the United States in 2018. The USMCA signed with the United States under the Trump administration had a so-called "toxin clause" that stipulates that if a contracting country enters into FTAs with a non-market country, other parties can terminate the FTA (Lan, 2020). It means that neither Mexico nor Canada can basically admit China's accession to the CPTPP without the consent of the United States. The toxin clause is considered a violation of WTO rules, but Canada and Mexico need to clear it as the struggle for supremacy between the United States and China intensifies. The Accession of the United Kingdom to the CPTPP in July 2023 will also raise the hurdles for China to join.

There is also the Taiwan issue. Taiwan is in a better position than China in terms of economic openness when it joins. In the case of joining the CPTPP, Taiwan is eligible to apply, although the provisions themselves were created in consideration of the complex relationships in international politics. Nevertheless, China, an applicant country, strongly opposes Taiwan's accession.

As mentioned above, there are many issues to be addressed on the issue of China's accession to the CPTPP, and there is a strong possibility that China's accession to the CPTPP will be negotiated in the medium to long term. In any case, not only the success or failure of China's accession to the CPTPP, but also the negotiation process itself will be affected by the global economy and the international order. At this stage, it is difficult to predict whether China's accession will succeed or fail.

9.6 Concluding Remarks

Focusing on East Asia, this chapter provides a bird's eye view of the development of regional cooperation and economic integration, from Japan's Greater East Asia Co-Prosperity Sphere concept, which challenged the Western powers, to the development of regional cooperation and economic integration by newly independent countries after World War II, to the conclusion and entry into force of mega-ETAs/FTAs like the current CPTPP and RCEP.

Regionalism in East Asia has developed regional cooperation in tandem with the trend of regionalism in Europe and the United States, while at the same time responding to structural changes associated with economic development in the region. There were two currents in its promotion. One is the trend of regional cooperation that emerged from the developing regions of Southeast Asia, which was seen in ASEAN until the 1990s, and the other is the trend of regional cooperation from the developed economic regions of Japan and Australia. These were the concepts of regional cooperation centered on Southeast Asia and regional cooperation spreading to the Asia–Pacific region.

However, from the late 1980s to the beginning of this century, a new structure emerged. In the wake of the appreciation of the yen in Japan, intra-regional direct investment by Japan companies, followed by NIEs, ASEAN companies, and Chinese companies, led to the development of the regional international division of labor and the development structure of East Asia centered on China.

However, in 1997, the Asian currency crisis broke out. The countries of East Asia have taken this opportunity to take regionalism to a new level. They urged the institutionalization of regional cooperation with ASEAN as the center. The ASEAN+ 3 Regional Cooperation Framework and the East Asia Summit were born. Under this framework, ASEAN, Japan, and China mainly competed to promote regional integration.

Incidentally, in East Asia, regional cooperation has always been developed within the framework of U.S. policy in Asia throughout the twentieth century and until the first half of the 2010s. With the birth of APEC in 1989 and the beginning of this century, the U.S. has played a strong role in promoting the TPP. The Obama administration at the time conceived the TPP with a rising China in mind. However, President Trump, who was inaugurated in 2017, has effectively abandoned his Asia policy.[27] It is tantamount to removing the constraints imposed by the United States on Asian regionalism.

President Trump's Asia–Pacific structure has changed the structure of the U.S.-Sino trade war and the U.S.-Sino struggle for hegemony. At the APEC Economic Leaders' Meeting in November 2018, Vice President Mike Pence criticized China in place of President Trump, who was absent, and a joint communiqué was not released due to the US-Sino confrontation. The APEC Economic Leaders' Meeting in Chile, scheduled for November 2019, was canceled, and the 27th APEC Economic Leaders' Meeting hosted by Malaysia in November 2020 was held online due to the coronavirus pandemic. However, President Trump did not participate in the summit, and in contrast, President Xi Jinping announced that he would "actively consider joining the CPTPP". In fact, China applied for membership in September 2021. The U.S. and China took contrasting stances.

The same summit announced the APEC Putrajaya Vision 2040, which aims to create "an open, dynamic, resilient and peaceful Asia-Pacific community by 2040" and sets new goals to replace the Bogor Declaration of 1994. Regarding trade and investment there, it said:

> We will further advance the Bogor Goals and economic integration in the region in a manner that is market-driven, including through the work on the Free Trade Area of the Asia-Pacific (FTAAP) agenda which contributes to high standard and comprehensive regional undertakings. We will promote seamless connectivity, resilient supply chains and responsible business conduct (APEC, 2020).

In January 2021, the Biden administration was inaugurated in the United States, and Trump's era of "America First" has passed for the time being. Biden is returning to multilateralism and returning to the Asia–Pacific. However, a U.S. return to the CPTPP is almost impossible amid deep rifts in U.S. society. The goal of achieving an FTAAP in APEC is also aimed at China's influential position in place of the United States.

How does this composition relate to regionalism in Asia? China, which is becoming more powerful, is aiming to actively participate in the Asia–Pacific economy and shape its rules, as seen in its application to join the CPTPP. Furthermore, as we saw in Chap. 3, China is actively working to form its own economic zone through the Belt and Road Initiative. In his keynote speech at the 3rd BRI International Cooperation Forum held in October 2023, Xi boasted of the achievements of the BRI over the past 10 years, saying that the BRI extends from Eurasia to Africa and Latin America, and that more than 150 countries and more than 30 international organizations have signed the BRI's joint construction documents. Foreign Minister Wang Yi, who presided over the forum, expressed China's determination to "open a

---

[27] In the first three months of his presidency, President Trump held a total of 50 telephone conversations with foreign leaders and 15 face-to-face meetings with foreign leaders, but none with ASEAN leaders (Cook & Storey, 2017). He also had 32 meetings with leaders in the 11 months from January to November 2019, but, with the exception of a meeting with Singaporean Prime Minister Lee Hsien Loong in New York in March, he had no meetings with ASEAN leaders. There were no talks. He hardly participated in the ASEAN+ 3 Summit and the EAS, and did not seem to place any importance on the ASEAN (Storey & Cook, 2020; Ide -J, 2022: 200–201).

new stage in high-quality joint construction" of the BRI and its future deployment (People's Daily Online Oct.19, 2023). Amid the worsening US-Sino conflict and the worsening economic downturn at home, China will not give up its external offensive in the name of the BRI.

On the other hand, Japan and Australia are strengthening their Quad cooperation with the addition of India and the United States. The United States, Japan and Australia in particular are moving toward strengthening cooperation in the future to counter China. As China's influence has increased in ASEAN, there has been a difference in the positions of member countries. There are those becoming increasingly dependent on China, such as Laos and Cambodia, and countries that are at odds with each other over the South China Sea issue, such as Vietnam and the Philippines. While the emergence of a military regime in Myanmar has created a challenge of decentralization in ASEAN regional cooperation. However, ASEAN continues to try to strengthen its own raison d'être by launching its own Indo-Pacific vision (ASEAN, 2019). The attempt is to avoid excessive dependence on either the U.S. or China, and to pursue the possibility of an Indo-Pacific economic bloc in which both sides aim to develop within the framework of ASEAN centrality.

Will Russia's war in Ukraine, which began in February 2022, and the Israeli-Hamas war in October 2023, swallow up Asian regionalism at the inter-state level, or will it lead to divisions in conflict with China, or will it give birth to a new regionalism? Conflicts between the U.S. and China are crucial, but at the same time, in addition to the two countries, a new entity "Global South" may be involved in the emergence of a framework for regionalism and development. The birth of Asia for peace and prosperity is absolutely necessary.

References

Documents with a symbol (-J) after the author's name are Japanese documents.

ADB. (2020). Regional comprehensive economic partnership: Overview and economic impact. *ADB Briefs*, no.164, Asian Development Bank, December

APEE. (2006). *2006 leaders' declaration, Chairman's statement of the 13th ASEAN Plus Three Summit*. November 18.

APEC. (2009). *2009 leaders' declaration*. Singapore, November 14.

APEC. (2010a). *2010 leaders' declaration*. Yokohama, November 13.

APEC. (2010b). Pathways to FTAPA. November 14.

APEC. (2014). *2014 leaders' declaration*. Beijing, November 11.

APEC. (2020). APEC Putrajaya vision 2040. https://www.mofa.go.jp/mofaj/files/100117818.pdf.

APT Summit. (2010). Chairman's statement of the 13th ASEAN Plus Three Summit, Hanoi. October 29.

Armstrong, S., & Drysdale, P. (2022). The economic cooperation potential of East Asia's RCEP Agreement. *Journal East Asian Economic Review*, 26(1), March.

ASEAN. (2012). *Joint communique, The Second ASEAN Head of Government Meeting*. Kuala Lumpur, August 5, 1977.

ASEAN. (2023). *ASEAN Outlook on the Indo-Pacific*. https://asean.org/asean2020/wp-content/uploads/2021/01/ASEAN-Outlook-on-the-Indo-Pacific_FINAL_22062019.pdf.

ASEAN Plus Three Summit. (2002). *Final report of the East Asia study group*. Phnom Penh, Cambodia, November 4.

ASEAN Plus Three Summit. (2011). *Chairman's Statement of the 14th ASEAN Plus Three Summit*. Bali, November 18.

ASEAN Secretariat. (1998). *Statement on Bold Measures* 6th ASEAN Summit. Hanoi, December 16.

ASEAN Secretariat. (2012). *19th ASEAN Summit: ASEAN Framework for regional comprehensive economic partnership*. June 12.

ASEAN Secretariat. (2015a). *A blueprint for growth: ASEAN economic community 2015: Progress and key achievements*. Jakarta.

ASEAN Secretariat. (2015b). *ASEAN economic community: Blueprint 2025*. Jakarta.

ASEAN Summit. (2007). *Chairperson's statement of the 12th ASEAN Summit H.E. the President Gloria Macapagal-Arroyo "One caring and sharing community"*.

ASEAN Summit. (2011). *Chair's Statement of the 19th ASEAN Summit Bali*. November 17.

ASEAN. (2019). ASEAN Outlook on the Indo-Pacific. https://asean.org/wp-content/uploads/2021/01/ASEAN-Outlook-on-the-Indo-Pacific_FINAL_22062019.pdf

Aydin, C. (2008). Japan's Pan-Asianism and the Legitimacy of Imperial World Order 1931–1945. *The Asia-Pacific Journal: Japan Focus, 6*(3).

Bagwatti Jagdish, N. (1986). *Export promoting trade strategy: Issues and evidence*. World Bank Development Policy Issues Series ERS7, October.

Bergsten, C. F. (1996). Globalizing free trade. *Foreign Affairs, 75*(3), May/June.

CEAC, -J. (2005). *Seisaku houkoku Higashi Ajia kyodotai koso no genjo, haikei to nihon no kokka senryaku* (*Policy Report: Status quo and background of East Asia Community Initiative and Japan's state strategy*). Higashi ajia kyodotai hyougikai (The Council on East Asian Community), August.

Cook, M., & Ian, S. (2017). The trump administration and Southeast Asia: Limited engagement thus far. Institute of Southeast Asian Studies, *Perspective*, no. 27, April 27.

Cook, M. (2020). *Affirming ASEAN's East Asian centrality*. ISEAS Commentary—2020/183, November 16, https://www.iseas.edu.sg/media/commentaries/affirming-aseans-east-asian-centrality/ (Accessed April 16, 2022).

CRS: Manyin, M. E., Daggett, S., Dolven, B., Lawrence, S. V., Martin, M. F., O'Rourke, R., & Vaughn, B. (2012). *Pivot to the pacific? The Obama Administration's "Rebalancing" toward Asia*, CRS Report for Congress, Congressional Research Service, 7–5700, March 28.

CRS Insight. (2018). TPP countries sign new CP TPP agreement without U.S. Participation. Congressional Research Services Insight, IN10822

EAS. (2007). Chairman's statement of the second East Asia Summit Cebu, Philippines. East Asia Summit, 15 January https://asean.org/%EF%BB%BFchairmans-statement-of-the-second-east-asia-summit-cebu-philippines-15-january-2007/.

EAS. (2011). ASEAN Community in a global community of nations. In *Chairman's statement of the 6th East Asia Summit, Bali, Indonesia*, November 19, 2011.

EASG. (2002). *Final report of the East Asia Study Group*. ASEAN+4 Summit, November 4, 2002, Phnom Penh, Cambodia

EAVG. (2001). *Toward an East Asian Community: Region of peace, prosperity, and progress*. East Asia Vision Group Report.

Economic Planning Agency -J. (1994a). *Sekai keizai hakusho (White paper on world economy)*. Keizaikikakucho (current Cabinet Office, Japan).

Economic Planning Agency -J. (1994b). *Keizai hakusho (White paper of economy, Japan)*. Keizaikikakucho (current Cabinet Office, Japan).

Economic Planning Agency, Japan –J. (1961). *Showa 36 nen, Nenji sekai keizai houkoku* (*Annual Report on the world economy* FY 1961). Economic Planning Agency, Japan.

Economic Planning Agency, Japan –J. (1962). *Showa 37 nen, Nenji sekai keizai houkoku* (*Annual Report on the world economy* FY 1962). Economic Planning Agency, Japan.
Feldstein, M. (1998). Refocusing the IMF. *Foreign Affairs, 77*(2), March/April.
Fisher, C. A. (1971). Containing China? II. Concepts and Applications of containment. *The Geographical Journal, 137(*Part 3), September.
Funabashi, Y. (1995). *Asia pacific fusion: Japan's role in APEC*. Institute for International Economics.
Graham, N. (2021). *The RCEP ratification and its implications*. Econographics. Atlantic Council, December 3 https://www.atlanticcouncil.org/blogs/econographics/the-rcep-ratification-and-its-implications/ (Accessed February 20, 2022).
Hamanaka. S. (2014). Trans-Pacific Partnership versus Regional Comprehensive Economic Partnership: control of membership and agenda setting. *ADB Working Paper Series on regional economic integration*, no.146. December.
Hamanaka, S. (2020). *IDE sukuea Sekai wo miru me: RCEP syomei ha naniwo imisuruka-Chikeigaku teki mikata* (*IDE square Views to the world: What does RCEP signing mean? geomorphologic views*). Institute of Developing Economies (IDE-JETRO), November.
Hatakeyama, N. (2002). Viewpoint: Short history of Japan's movement to FTAs. *Journal of Japanese Trade and Industry, 21*(6), November/December.
Hatano, S., & He, H.U., -J. (2014). Koronbo puran wo meguru shiensenryaku to sono henyo (Supporting strategy around the Colombo Plan and its transformation). In S. Watanabe (Ed.), *Koronbo puran* (*The Colombo plan*). Hosei Daigaku Shuppan Kyoku.
Hirakawa, H. (1999). The Asian Monetary Fund and the Miyazawa Initiative. Paper presented at the Conference on "Economic Sovereignty in a Globalizing World: Creating people-centered alternatives for the 21st century", 23–25 March, Chulalongkorn University, Bangkok, Thailand.
Hirakawa, H. (2004). Globalization and regional cooperation in East Asia. In: Hirakawa, H. & Kim, Y.H. (Eds.). *Co-design for a new East Asia after the crisis*, Springer Verlag.
Hirakawa, H. -J. (2008). Higashi ajia chiiki togo niokeru ASEAN no yakuwari (The role of ASEAN on regional integration in East Asia). *Kokusai Ajia Kyodotai Jaanaru* (*Journal of International Asian Community*) *1*(1), November.
Hirakawa, H. -J. (2011). Higashi ajia no hatten to yureru nihon no taigai hatten seisaku (East Asian development and Japan's vacillating foreign development policies between East Asia and Pacific Asia). *Azia Kenkyu* (Asian Studies), (*Japan Association for Asian Studies*), *57*(3), July.
Hirakawa, H. –J. (2014). Kozo tenkan no sekaikeizai to higashi ajia chiiki no seidoka (Structural change of the world economy and institutionalization of the East Asian region). In H. Uemura, H. Uni, A. Isogai, T. Yamada (Eds.), *Tenkanki no ajia shihonsyugi* (*Asian capitalism at a turning point*). Fujiwara Shoten.
Hirakawa, H., -J. (2015). Nihon no higashi ajia seisaku to ajiakan no hensen - Kindai kara gendai made - (Japan's East Asian policy and Transforming Asian view). In *Herausgegeben von Urs Matthias Zachmann und Christian Uhl, Japan und das Problem der Moderne, Wolfgang Seifert zu Ehren, München*. IUDICIUM Verlag GmbH.
Hirakawa, H. (2018). Transformation of the world economy and institutionalization of the East Asian region. In: R. Boyer, H. Uemura, T. Yamada, & L. Song (Eds.), *Evolving diversity and interdependence of capitalism*. Springer Japan.
Hoshiro, H., -J. (2007). 1962 nen no ajia kyodotai: OAEC koso to nihon ("An Asian Community" in 1962: The Proposal for the OAEC and Japan). *Ajia Kenkyu, 53*(1), January.
Hutt, D., & Crispin, S.W. (2020). RCEP trade pact heralds dawn of the Asian Century. *Asia Times*, November 15 https://asiatimes.com/2020/11/rcep-trade-pact-heralds-dawn-of-asian-century/.
Ide, F., -J. (2022). Beicyu no taikoku kan tairitsu to kokusai chitsujo (Conflict between superpowers, US and China, and international order). In S. Nakamoto, & H. Muramatsu (Eds.), *Beicyu masatsu no seiji keizaigaku* (*Political economy of USA-Sino Friction*). Koyo Shobo.
Ishikawa, K., -J. (2018). Beikoku no TPP ridatsu to CPTPP goui no igi (US's TPP withdrawal and meanings of CPTPP agreement). In Institute for International Trade and Investment (ITI) (Ed.),

TPP11 to ASEAN no boueki, toshi, sangyo heno eikyo (*The Impact of TPP 11 and ASEAN on trade, investment, and industry*). ITI, March.

Ishikawa, K. (2021a). The ASEAN community and ASEAN economic integration. *Journal of Contemporary East Asia Studies, 10*(1).

Ishikawa, K., -J. (2021b). *Chugoku to Taiwan ga CPTPP kanyu wo shinsei* (*China and Taiwan applied for CP TPP*). Kaikakusha, December issue.

Ito, K. -J (2005). *Higashi ajia kyodotai no yume to genjitsu: Dreams and Realities of an East Asian Community* (*A Lecture record at the Ajia shinzen koryu kyoukai*). The Council on East Asian Community.

JETRO, -J. (2001). *Ajia no chiiki keizaitogo no tenbo: 2000 nendo ajia keizai togoka forum kaisai houkokusho* (*Report of Prospects for Asia's regional economic integration: In Asian economic integration Forum*). Economic Information Division, Japan External Trade Organization (JETRO), March.

Joint Communique, ASEAN. (1977). 1977 *Joint Communique of the second ASEAN Heads of Government Meeting*. https://cil.nus.edu.sg/wp-content/uploads/2019/02/1977-Joint-Communique-of-the-Second-ASEAN-Heads-of-Government-Meeting-1.pdf.

Joint Press Statement, ASEAN. (1976). *1976 Joint press statement of the 2nd ASEAN Economic ministers' meeting*. https://cil.nus.edu.sg/wp-content/uploads/2019/02/1976-2nd-AEM.pdf.

Kimura, F. (2022). A framework for ongoing commitments to RCEP success. *East Asia Forum Quarterly, 'East Asia's Economic Agreement', 14*(1). January-March.

Kajima, M. -J. (1964a). Ajia taiheiyo kyodotai wo teisyo suru (Advocate Asia-Pacific Community). *Keidanren Geppo* (Japan Business Federation Monthly Report), January.

Kajima, M. -J. (1964b). *Genzai no gaiko mondai* (*Current diplomacy issues*). Kajima Kenkyujo Shuppankai.

Kajima, M. -J. (1966a). Nihon no hatasubeki kokusaiteki yakuwari (International role of Japan to take). *Kokusai Jihyo* (*International Times Review*) (9), January.

Kajima, M. -J. (1966b). Jo (Preface). In: Kajima Peace Institute (Ed.), *Dai ikkai Kajima Heiwa Sho jusho no kiroku - Jushosha Kudenhofu Karerugi Haku* (*the Record of the First Kajima Peace Award: Awardy Coudenhove-Kalergi*). Kajima Institute of International Peace Press.

Kajima, M. -J. (1972). *Gaiko ron senshu 5: Pan Ajia heno michi* (*Selected works on diplomacy 5, Pathway to Pan Asiaism*). Kajima Institute Press.

Kaneko, K. -J. (1957). Koronbo keikaku no seika (Results of the Colombo Plan). *Ajia mondai* (*Asia Issues*), *6*(5), April.

Kawai, M. & Wignaraja, G. (2008). EAFTA or CEPEA: Which way forward? *ASEAN Economic Bulletin, 25*(2), August.

Kinoshita, T. -J. (2002). ASEAN10 to nicchu kan FTA no tenbo (ASEAN 10 and the prospect of Japan-China-Korea FTA). In: S. Urata (Ed.), *FTA Gaidobukku* (*A Guidebook of FTA*). Japan External Trade Organization.

Koizumi, J. (2004). Address by H.E. Mr. Junichiro Koizumi, Prime Minister of Japan, at the Fifty-Ninth Session of the General Assembly of the United Nations: A new United Nations for the new era. September 21, United Nations.

Kojima, K. -J. (1984). Kojima Kiyoshi meiyo kyoju jisaku nenpu (Professor Emeritus Kiyoshi Kojima's self-made chronology). *Hitotsubashi Ronso* (*The Hitotsubashi Review*), *92*(4).

Kojima, K. -J. (1990). *Zoku taiheiyo keizaiken no seisei* (*Continuation Issue: Generation of Pacific economic zone*). Bunshindo.

Lan, G. (2020). The "Poison Pill" in the USMCA: The erosion of WTO principles and its implications under a US-China trade war. *Vanderbilt Journal of Transnational Law, 53*(4), October.

Mahathir, M. (2006). Let Asians build their own future regionalism. *Global Asia, 1*(1), September.

Matthiessen, S, (2011). The perception of the Philippines in Japanese Pan-Asianism from the Meiji-Era until the wake of the Pacific War. *GEMC Journal*, March 1

McBride, J., Andrew, C., & Anshu, S. (2021). What's next for the Trans-Pacific Partnership? Council for Foreign Relations. September 20 https://www.cfr.org/backgrounder/what-trans-pacific-partnership-tpp.

Mahathir, M. (2006). Let Asians build their own future regionalism. *Global Asia, 1*(1), September.

METI, Japan. (2007). *White paper on international trade 2007*. Ministry of Economy, Trade and Industry.

Mission for Revitalization of Asian Economy. (1999). Report of the Mission for Revitalization of Asian Economy: Living in Harmony with Asia in the Twenty-first Century. Ministry of Foreign Affairs of Japan, November.

MOFA Japan. (1998). A new initiative to overcome the Asian currency crisis - New Miyazawa Initiative. Ministry of Finance Affairs, Japan https://www.mof.go.jp/english/policy/international_policy/financial_cooperation_in_asia/new_miyazawa_initiative/e1e042.htm.

MOFA Japan. (2001). Japan's official development assistance: White paper 2001. Ministry of Foreign Affairs, Japan.

MOFA Japan. (2003). Tokyo declaration for the dynamic and enduring Japan-ASEAN partnership in the new millennium https://www.mofa.go.jp/region/asia-paci/asean/year2003/summit/tokyo_dec.pdf.

MOFA Japan. (2012). Announcement of the launch of negotiations for the regional comprehensive economic partnership (RCEP). November 20 https://www.mofa.go.jp/announce/announce/2012/11/1120_03.html (Accessed February 20, 2020).

MOFA Japan. (2019). *Press releases: Sixteenth round of negotiations on a free trade agreement among Japan, China and the Republic of Korea*. MOFA, Japan.

Mueller, L. Maximilian. (2019). ASEAN contrarily under threat – the cases of RCEP and connectivity. *Journal of contemporary East Asian studies*. 8(Issue 2).

Munakata, N. (2001). Nihon no chiiki keizaitogo seisaku no seisei (Generation of Japan's regional economic integration policies). In: Munakata, N. (Ed.), *Nicchu kankei no tenki - Higashi ajia keizai togo heno chosen* (*Turning point of Japan-China relations - Challenges to an East Asian economic integration*). Toyo Keizai Shinposha.

Murakami, K. -J. (1960). Koronbo puran (The Colombo Plan). *Gaimusho Chosa Geppou* (*Monthly research of Ministry of Foreign Affairs, Japan*), *1*(7).

Nakagawa, R. (2010). Japan-U.S. trade and rethinking the point of no return toward Pearl Harbor. *Ritsumeikan Annual Review of International Studies,* 2010. ISSN 1347-8214. vol.9, pp. 101–123.

Nakao, T. (2017). Forward. In: P. McCawley, *Banking on the future of Asia and the Pacific: 50 years of the Asian Development Bank*. Metro Manila: ADB.

Nowik, M. (2013). Colombo plan: From India's initiative on foreign assistance to regional organisation in Asia and the Pacific. *Research papers of Wroclaw University of Economics,* 294.

Oba Mie, -J. (2004). *Ajia taiheiyo chiiki keisei heno dotei* (Road of forming Asia Pacific region). Minerva Shobo.

Barack, O. (2009). *Remarks by president Obama at suntory hall* (p. 14). The White House Office of the Press Secretary.

Obama, B. (2015). Statement by the president on trans-pacific partnership (p. 5). *For Immediate Release*. The White House Office of the Press Secretary, October.

Okita, S. (1985). *Special presentation: Prospect of the Pacific economies. Paper presented at the fourth pacific economic cooperation conference: Issues and opportunities*, Korea Development Institute, April 29- May 1.

Ozawa, T. (2009). *The rise of Asia: The 'Flying-geese' theory of tandem growth and regional agglomeration*. Edward Elgar.

Panikkar, K. M. (1955). *In two Chinas: Memoirs of a diploma*. George Allen & Unwin.

Petri, Peter A., & Plummer, M. G. (2020a). East Asia decouples from the United States: Trade war, COVID-19, and East Asia's new trade blocs. PIIE Working Paper 20–9, Peterson Institute for International Economics, June.

Petri, P. A., & Plummer, M. G. (2020b). RCEP: A new trade agreement that will shape global economics and politics. Brookings, November 16, 2020. https://www.brookings.edu/blog/order-from-chaos/2020/11/16/rcep-a-new-trade-agreement-that-will-shape-global-economics-and-politics/ (accessed April 16, 2022).
Ravenhill, J. (2001). *APEC and the construction of Pacific rim regionalism.* Cambridge University Press.
Ravenhill, J. (2007). From poster child to orphan: The rise and demise of APEC. UNISCI Discussion Papers, no. 13, January ISSN 1696-2206.
Scollay, R., & Gilbert, J. P. (2001). New regional trading arrangements in the Asia Pacific? *Institute for International Economics.*
Serizawa, T. (2015). Japanese Solidarity Discourse on the Philippines during the Second World War. *Philippine Studies: Historical & Ethnographic Viewpoints, 63*(1), 71–100.
Shimizu, K., -J. (1998). *ASEAN chiiki keizai kyoryoku no seijikeizaigaku ASEAN.* (*Political economy of ASEAN economic cooperation*). Minerva Shobo.
Singh, B. (2002). ASEAN's Perceptions of Japan: *Change and continuity Asian survey. 42*(2), 276–296. ISSN: 0004-4687.
Storey, I., & Malcolm, C. (2020). The trump administration and Southeast Asia: Half-time or game over? *Institute of Southeast Asian Studies, Perspective,* (112), October 7.
Sudo, S. (2002). *The international relations of Japan and South East Asia.* Routledge.
Tan, Alyssa Nicole, O. (2022). Senator backs go-slow approach to RCEP, says Philippines not ready, *Business World,* January 27, 2022. https://www.bworldonline.com/economy/2022/01/27/426404/senator-backs-go-slow-approach-to-rcep-says-philippines-not-ready/ (accessed April 16, 2022).
Tanaka, H. (2006). ASEAN+3 and East Asia Summit: A two-tiered approach to community building. *East Asia Insights toward Community Building,* (1), January.
Tanaka, H. -J. (2012). *Chugoku to dou mukiauka: Takokukan de juhsoteki wakubumi wo, Keizai kyoshitu* (*How to face China: Toward multilateral framework, Economics Classroom*). Nihon Keizai Shimbun, September 26.
Taniguchi, M. -J. (2004) Higashi Ajia kyodotai (An East Asia Community). Tokyo: Iwanami Shoten
TPP Headquarters at the Cabinet Secretariat Office, Japan, -J. (2015). PPT material: TPP ni okeru kanzei kosho no kekka (Results of tariff negotiations on TPP). October 20 https://www.cas.go.jp/jp/tpp/tppinfo/2015/pdf/151020_tpp_kanzeikousyoukekka.pdf (Accessed February 20, 2023).
TPP Headquarters at the Cabinet Secretariat Office, Japan, -J. (2021). PPT Material: Kan taiheiyou paatonashipu ni kansuru hokatuteki oyobi senshinteki na kyotei (TPP11) (Comprehensive and progressive agreement on Pacific-Rim partnership: TPP 11). https://www.cas.go.jp/jp/tpp/tppinfo/kyotei/tpp11/pdf/2110tpp11_gaiyou_koushin.pdf (Accessed March 3, 2022).
Umada, K. -J. (2017). Ikisaki fumei to natta TPP to FTAAP (TPP and FTAAP with uncertain future). In K. Ishikawa, K. Umada, K Shimizu (Eds.), *Kensho Ajia Keizai* (*Inspection Asian economy*). Bunshindo.
UNCTAD. (1994). Trade and development report, 1994, UNCTAD
UNCTAD. (1995). Trade and development report, 1995, UNCTAD
UNCTAD. (1996). Trade and development report, 1996. UNCTAD
UNCTAD. (2021). *A new center of gravity: The regional comprehensive partnership and its trade effects.* United Nations for Trade and Development.
USTR. (2008). *Trade Facts: United States to negotiate participation in Trans-Pacific Strategic Economic Partnership.* Office of the United States Trade Representative, September 2006.
Watanabe, M., Kamo, T., Kawashima, F., & Kawase T., -J. (2021). Chugoku no CPTPP sanka ishi hyomei no haikei ni kansuru kosatsu (Considering background of China's statement of intention to participate in the CPTPP*). RIETI Policy Discussion Paper Series* 21-P-016, Research Institute of Economy, Trade and Industry, Japan, September 11.
Watanabe, S. -J. (2014). Igirisu no datsu shokuminchika to koronbo puran (De-colonization of England and the Colombo plan). In W. Shoichi (Ed.), *Koronbo puran: Sengo ajia kokusai*

chitsujo no keisei (*The Colombo Plan: Formation of post-war international order in Asia*). Hosei Daigaku Shuppan Kyoku.

White House (Office of the Press Secretary). (2011). *For immediate Release Fact sheet: The United States in the Trans-Pacific Partnership*. November 12.

Wightman, D. (1963). *Toward economic cooperation in Asia: The United Nations Economic Commission for Asia and the Far East*. Yale University Press.

Yamakage, S. -J. (1991). *ASEAN - Shinboru kara shisutemu he* (*ASEAN: From symbol to system*). University of Tokyo Press.

Yamakage, S. -J. (2001). ASEAN no kihon rinen no doyo (Upset of ASEAN basic philosophy). In S. Yamakage (Ed.), *Tenkanki no ASEAN - Aratana kadai heno chosen* (*ASEAN at a turning point: Challenging new issues*). Kokusai Mondai Kenkyusho.

Yamazawa, I. -J. (2011). Taiheiyo kyoryoku kara APEC 2010 made—Kojima Kiyoshi kyoju no sendoteki kenkyu no hattenn wo tadotte—(From Pacific cooperation to APEC 2010: following up the development of advancing research by Professor Kiyoshi Kojima). *Kokusai Keizai* (*Journal of Japan Society of International Economics*) (62).

Yasuda, R. -J. (1990). "Daitoa kaigi" to "Daitoa kyodo sengen" wo megutte (On the assembly of Greater East-Asiatic nations and the Joint Declaration in 1943). *Hogaku Kenkyu* (*Journal of Law, Politics, and Sociology*), *63*(2), February.

Yellen, J. (2019). *The greater east Asia co-prosperity sphere: When total empire met total war*. Cornell University Press.

Chapter 10
The Historical Roots of Unshared Growth: The Case of the Philippines

Abstract This chapter considers the historical roots of the Philippines' developmental malaise, despite having an excellent head start over many other countries in East Asia. Moreover, it was observed that the Philippines has gone through the traditional patterns of economic development. Her post-war development could be clearly marked with the traditional phases of importation, import-substitution industrialization, and export-oriented industrialization. In terms of sectoral contributions, the Philippine economy could also be seen as moving from agriculture, then industry (manufacturing), and then services. Despite this, development of the Philippines has lagged behind its cohorts in Southeast Asia, suggesting an underlying weakness in the seemingly good patterns it went through in the course of her post-war development. We focus in this chapter on the lack of strategic sequencing which could be ultimately traced to the very skewed distribution of income and wealth in the country.

Keywords Economic development history · Strategic sequencing · Unshared growth

10.1 Introduction

In Chap. 6, we discussed how the Philippines was actually involved in triggering the controversial East Asian Miracle (EAM) report published by the World Bank in 1993. Ironically, the Philippines was not considered as one of the eight highly performing East Asian economies covered in the EAM report, despite its being at the geographical center of the region consisting of both northeast and southeast Asia, which the World Bank refers to simply as "East Asia". This exclusion could be attributed to the Philippines inability to have achieved "shared growth" over the three-decade period of the 1960s up to the 1980s. "Shared growth" was coined in the EAM report, and is the hallmark of the eight miracle economies of the report. It refers to a high rate of development, measured by GDP per capita, that is accompanied by improvements in income distribution. It could be argued that even if the EAM report is updated, the Philippines would still find it difficult to be included as one of the

H. Hirakawa and F. C. Maquito, *The Dynamics of Asian Economic Development*,
https://doi.org/10.1007/978-981-97-3106-0_10

miracle economies. In this chapter, we examine what could be the historical roots of this unfortunate performance.

10.2 Historical Context of Philippine Economic Development

10.2.1 Development Features (Post War)

The Post-War economic development of the Philippines could be broadly divided into four phases: (1945 to 1950) agricultural, (1950 to 1970s) import-substitution industrialization, (1980 to 1990s) export-oriented industrialization, and (1990s to present) deindustrialization. As it can be seen, the Philippines seem to have followed a conventional path in development.

Figure 10.1 shows the shares of agriculture, industry, and services to GDP of the Philippines. As could be seen, agriculture per se was dominant over manufacturing for only a couple of years after the war. The trend for agriculture, however, has been generally downwards since then. Manufacturing's share, on the other hand, exhibited a rising trend even slightly dominated services in the mid-1970s. It peaked sometime in 1980, and from thereon was on a downward trend. In contrast, services share since 1980 shifted to an upward trend from a relatively stable trend.

This more or less fits with the description, which will be discussed in more detail below, of the various phases in the economic development of the Philippines. There is a period of relative stability of shares of agriculture and manufacturing during the agricultural phase of 1945–1950. Manufacturing shares started to be uptrend during the import-substitution industrialization phase of the 1950s to 1970s, which also corresponded to the downtrend in agricultural shares. During the export-oriented industrialization phase from the 1980 to the 1990s, however, manufacturing shares went down, reflecting the ineffectiveness of that phase to invigorate manufacturing. In contrast to this, services was able to recover its share at the end of the war sometime during the end of the export-oriented industrialization phase. The share of services was well on its new upward trend during the de-industrialization phase from the 1990s up to the present. Manufacturing shares, on the other hand, seems to have shifted to a more downward trend during the 1990s.

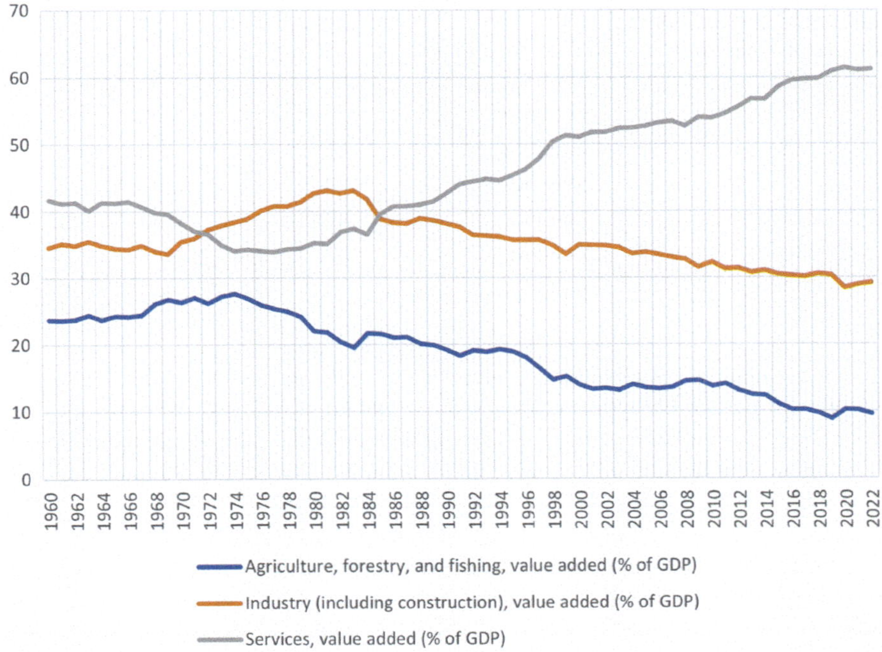

Fig. 10.1 Sectoral shares in total income (*Source of Data* World Bank)

10.2.2 Pre-modern Phase: 1500s to 1940

To understand the Agricultural Phase of Philippine economic development, one has to review the long history of the Philippines being under foreign rule. The Philippines was first discovered by Europeans on March 16, 1521 by a Spanish expedition, headed by a Portuguese named Ferdinand Magellan, whose expedition was the first to circumnavigate the globe. The Philippine Islands, as it was called by its European discoverer, became a colony of Spain. It then became a colony of the United States when it defeated Spain in 1898. During the American colonization, the Commonwealth of the Philippines was created in preparation for independence, which came on July 4, 1946, as originally scheduled despite the Japanese occupation of the islands from 1941 to 1945.

As a Spanish colony, the Philippines' economic role up to the 3rd quarter of the eighteenth century was mainly to sustain an entrepot trade through the so-called Manila Galleons transporting goods across the Pacific between Manila and Acapulco until 1815, under a tariff-free regime. The Spanish did not find spice or minerals sufficient enough to induce efforts to develop local production. The entrepot trade, however, was insufficient to sustain the colony, which had to depend on a subsidy from Spain. It was not until the 4th quarter of the eighteenth century that efforts to develop the local economy began in earnest.

Table 10.1 GDP per capita (1990 international $)

Country	1820	1870
Malaysia	603	663
Philippines	704	776
Singapore	615	682
South Korea	600	604
Taiwan	499	550
Thailand	646	n.a

(*Source* Angus, 2003: 154).

A great deal of infrastructure projects were undertaken during the nineteenth century that put the Philippine economy and standard of living ahead of most of its Asian neighbors and even many European countries at that time. Among them were a railway system for Luzon, a tramcar network for Manila, and the Puente Colgante (now known as the Quezon Bridge), Asia's first steel suspension bridge.

A Western evaluation of the Spanish colonization was mainly positive. As John Crawfurd put it in his History of the Indian Archipelago, in all of Asia the "Philippines alone did improve in civilization, wealth, and population under the colonial rule" of a foreign power. This is corroborated by Table 10.1, which shows that the Philippines had a higher GDP per capita in the early and later 1800s than all the East Asian economies given in table, which includes economies that have currently reached high-income status (i.e., Singapore, Taiwan, and South Korea).

Against the wishes of the Philippine revolutionaries, the Philippines was ceded to the U.S. from Spain in the 1898 Treaty of Paris. Conflict eventually erupted in 1899, as the 1st Philippine Republic declared war on the U.S. The Philippine-American war ended in 1902, with the capture of the President of the nascent Republic, but hostilities in far-flung regions continued until 1913.

As a U.S. colony, the Philippines trade, as can be seen Table 10.2, generally was on an upward trend, from an average yearly total trade value of about $125 million in the 1903–05 period to about $249 million in the 1936–40 period. There was a steady shift, however, from a dependence on European markets to American markets. Early in the U.S. colonial rule, the shares of export to and import from Europe were, on the average, 40.8% of total exports and 33.0% of total imports. On the other hand, the U.S. accounted for 41.6% of exports and 15.5% of imports. Near the start of hostilities with the Japanese empire, we could see from Table 10.2 that the U.S. already dominated Philippine trade, accounting, on average, for 78.4% of exports and 66.4% of imports. In contrast, Europe accounted, on average, for only 10.1% of exports and 11.3% of imports.

Spanish colonial rule led to a dualization of the economy, the main features of which largely remain to this day.

> Colonial economic development resulted in a dual economy in which a relatively modern commerce-oriented sector grew alongside a traditional, technologically backward, subsistence agricultural sector. Not only were these sectors economically isolated, but the ownership of the modern sector tended to be vested in the economically rational Chinese minority

Table 10.2 Shares in Philippine foreign trade by region, 1903–1940

Year	Export				Import			
	Yearly ave	Europe %	America %	Asia %	Yearly ave	Europe %	America %	Asia %
1903–05	63,334	40.8	41.6	15.0	62,293	33.0	15.5	43.8
1906–10	69,558	45.4	37.4	14.7	66,739	34.9	24.8	33.0
1911–15	100,014	40.2	43.2	14.8	104,362	20.3	46.9	27.2
1916–20	225,991	21.0	62.2	15.8	191,188	6.6	61.1	29.1
1921–25	235,469	18.8	69.3	11.0	204,512	10.0	59.8	27.5
1926–30	298,051	15.0	75.7	8.4	256,024	12.6	62.6	22.4
1931–35	203,892	9.5	83.6	5.7	166,026	12.2	64.3	21.1
1936–40	233,975	10.1	78.4	8.9	214,927	11.3	66.4	19.0

(*Source* Nagano, 2015: 44–45). *Note* Yearly averages are in thousands of pesos.

> as well as in the dominant Western minority. Business acumen and a high marginal propensity to save and invest productively were richly rewarded by the laissez-faire economy exported to the Philippines in the latter part of the colonial period. Such qualities were slow to appear in the tradition-dominated Philippine society, and Filipinos tended to stand by and watch the alienation of their economy (Golay, 1961: 0, 9).

Since the early part of the U.S. colonization, "Filipinos have tried to use the economic powers of the state to initiate industrial development." Such efforts became more aggressive as the country gained independence. This is most likely in reaction to the marginalization of Philippine entrepreneurs during the colonial period. The Philippines was a Commonwealth from 1935 to 1946, when the "principle of government participation in directly productive economic activity became firmly established".

Table 10.3 shows the primary commodities that mainly comprised the exports of the Philippines for most of the U.S. colonization period. As did the Spanish, the Philippines was not really known as a major source of spice or minerals. The top crop export was Manila hemp in the early years but was deposed by sugar in the later years. As could be gleaned from Table 10.2, most of these exports went to U.S. markets.

10.2.3 Agricultural Phase: 1945 to 1950

The Bell Trade Act of 1946 provided the funds and market for the agricultural commodities needed by the Philippines to recover from the ravages of war. By 1949, it became evident that war rehabilitation funds were not able to compensate for the growing imports, prompting the government to embark on an import-substitution industrialization. For this purpose, import quotas and foreign exchange controls were in place until the 1960s.

Table 10.3 Composition of total export of the Philippines (%)

Year	Manila hemp	Sugar	Copra	Coconut oil	Tobacco	Total
1901–05	67.5	11.6	8.9	0.0	7.5	95.5
1906–10	51.8	15.6	18.9	0.3	9.2	95.8
1911–15	39.2	20.2	22.4	2.6	8.8	93.2
1916–20	35.5	19.5	5.8	17.8	10.6	89.2
1921–25	20.4	29.2	13.5	14.7	8.2	86.0
1926–30	18.2	31.6	12.0	15.9	5.8	83.5
1931–35	8.1	53.2	8.4	10.1	6.0	85.8
1936–40	10.9	42.4	10.6	9.9	4.4	78.2

(*Source* Nagano, 2015: 46).

Table 10.4 Percentage shares of export products to total exports

Product	1937–40	1947–49	1950–52
Coconut	25.3	68.2	46.2
Sugar	40.3	9.0	20.9
Abaca & cordage	12.2	12.3	15.4
Tobacco & Mfrs	4.3	0.7	0.8
Embroideries	3.6	1.8	1.8
Metals, ores, & concentrates	4.4	1.7	6.3
Logs, timber, & lumber	3.4	0.8	4.3
Canned pineapple	1.4	0.7	2.6
Others	5.1	4.8	1.7

(*Source* Golay, 1961: 45).

Table 10.4 shows the composition of Philippine exports for this phase. It could be readily seen that primary commodities continue to dominate.

10.2.4 Import-Substitution Industrialization (ISI) Phase: 1950s to 1970s

The ISI phase started out as a measure for addressing a balance of payments crisis that materialized in 1949. These measures quickly evolved into a plan for industrialization through import-substitution. Considering that the Philippines was coming out from a relatively free trade regime under U.S. colonial rule, the protectionist policy environment of an ISI strategy would seem like a complete reversal of policies. One way for the balance of the crisis to have been solved would have been to promote the earning of foreign exchange through exports.

Maxfield and Nolt (1990) argue coherently that ironically it was the U.S. that aggressively pushed for the ISI strategy. This was actually the agenda of the Bell Mission that was sent by the U.S. government to the Philippines in 1950. This was the origin of an intensive U.S. effort to promote ISI, which contradicts the conventional wisdom that ISI was the policy of the Third World economic nationalists in opposition to U.S. liberalism. In fact the ISI initiative came from the two sectors of U.S. society generally most associated with liberal trade, the executive branch of government and internationalist business.

This irony makes sense when one understands the business strategy associated with ISI. The largest U.S. manufacturers expected to benefit from ISI in two ways, first because it stimulated export demand for the intermediate products of U.S. heavy industry such as steel, petroleum, and sophisticated machinery, and second because it enabled many firms to reap monopoly profits by investing in assembly and finishing plants in protected ISI markets.

The lobbying of internationalist business in the U.S., on top of the growing protectionism in the U.S., which finds its roots in the Great Depression, eventually directed the U.S. government to support an ISI strategy for the Philippines. Against such overwhelming forces, proponents for exports and free trade, the incumbent policy, in the Philippines were not able to stem the tide of a protectionist strategy.

Against this backdrop, it is quite easy to understand the basic features of the ISI strategy of the Philippines:

a. There was no priority for manufacturing for export, and, hence, posing no threat to foreign markets. The export structure of the Philippines did not change significantly during the ISI phase. The top ten exports in 1969 were basically the same major export products in 1949. Six of these "accounted for 36% of total exports in 1949 and 32% in 1970", namely, sugar, coconut oil, desiccated coconut, canned pineapples, veneer, and plywood. "The other four major export products accounting for 50% of the value of exports in both 1949 and 1950 are copra, abaca, logs and lumber, and copper concentrates".
b. Industrialization was capital-intensive. Baldwin (1975) reports that between 1950 and 1968, the capital-labor ratio in Philippine manufacturing was estimated to have more than doubled from 61 to 142. This was prompted by the policy of facilitating the importation of capital goods, and, hence, helped exporters of such goods
c. Industrialization did not promote backward integration, which did not help the proponents of exports in the Philippines.

Table 10.5 shows that the top four export product categories (i.e., coconut products, sugar products, logs, lumber & plywood, and copper & gold) held a majority position in exports until the 1970s.

Table 10.5 Percentage shares in total exports 1965–1980

Product	1965	1970	1975	1980
Coconut	34.0	18.6	20.3	14.0
Sugar	18.5	17.2	26.9	11.4
Logs, lumber & plywood	22.7	24.2	9.4	6.6
Copper & gold	5.9	16.9	12.6	13.5
Pineapple & bananas	1.8	2.5	5.0	3.6
Electrical equipment & components	0.0	0.0	2.0	11.6
Garments	0.0	0.0	4.4	8.6
Other non-traditional manufactures	5.8	10.9	11.5	16.2
Others	11.3	10.4	7.9	14.5

(*Source* NEDA, Philippine statistical yearbook 1987).

10.2.5 Export-Oriented Industrialization Phase: 1980s to 1990s

The shift from the inward-looking ISI strategy to an outward-looking export-oriented industrialization (EOI) is said to have occurred in 1970, with the enactment of the Export Incentives Act of 1970 and the floating of the Philippine peso in 1969. Nevertheless, "the general pattern of protection remained the same during the 1970s." Despite the political turmoil of the 1980s, there was a steady dismantling of protectionist policies. It started with a series of tariff reductions and other protectionist policies, wherein the effective protection rate for the manufacturing sector fell from an average of 108% in 1983 to 75% in 1988.

As could be seen from Table 10.6, the traditional exports continued to dominate the export structure of the country in the 1970s. In that decade, we can see the start of the exportation of electrical equipment & components, and garments, as well as the steady rise in non-traditional exports. By 1980, the share of the top four traditional exports was down to 45.5%.

This trend continued into the 1980s. Table 10.6 shows that manufactured exports were on the uptrend and dominant since the middle of the 1980s.

10.2.6 De-Industrialization Phase: 1990s to Present

From Fig. 10.1, we can see that divergence in the shares of the agriculture and manufacturing sectors started in the 1980s. There was a relative stabilization in the share of manufacturing until the mid-1990s, after which it continued to decline, accelerating the divergence with the services sector. One very possible cause of this divergence is the growth of the Business Processing Outsourcing (BPO) business prompted by developments in Information and Communications Technology (ICT).

Table 10.6 Percentage share of export products in total exports

Product	1985	1986	1987	1988	1989	1990
Coconut products	10.1	9.8	9.9	8.2	6.9	6.1
Sugar and products	4.0	2.1	1.2	1.0	1.4	1.6
Fruits and vegetables	5.5	5.7	4.9	4.3	4.1	4.0
Other agro-based products	5.9	7.5	6.6	6.8	5.8	5.3
Forest products	4.3	4.2	4.2	3.7	2.5	1.2
Mineral products	12.3	11.1	8.1	10.8	10.6	8.8
Petroleum products	2.0	1.9	2.3	2.3	1.2	1.9
Manufactures	54.8	55.2	60.0	61.3	66.4	69.7

(*Source* Maquito's calculations. Basic data: BSP).

A report of the Central Bank of the Philippines in 2012 begins with an appreciation for the importance of BPO in the growth of services.

> The expansion in the services sector during the past decade has been largely influenced by the rapid development in information and communication technology (ICT) services, notably in contact centers and other business process outsourcing (BPO). Recognizing the industry's contribution to employment generation, investments and foreign exchange earnings, and given the comparative advantage of the country's workforce in these type of services, the government's thrust to promote the development of was articulated in the Philippine Development Plan (PDP) 2005–2011 and its successor PDP 2011–2016.

The spurt of the ICT-BPO sector could actually be traced back to the jump in activity following the subprime crisis in the late 1990s. The BPO industry has been in the Philippines since the late 80's but on a limited scale. It was only in 1992 that business process outsourcing started in the country in a major way with the entry of Accenture. Other big names followed. Sykes, which is the first multinational BPO firm in the Philippines, started operations in 1997. Then came PeopleSupport in 1998, eTelecare in 2000, and ePLDT and Ventus in 2006. Today, the key players in the industry also include Convergys, JP Morgan Chase, 24/7 Customer Philippines, Telephilippines, and Teletech, among others.

Magtibay-Ramos, et al. (2008) points to the early half of the new millennium as the period when the industry practically took off, to wit:

> While BPO began in the 1990s, it was only in the early part of the new millennium that outsourcing opportunities gained ground in the Philippines. During the period 2000 to the first half of 2006, the cumulative amount of investment projects registered under the Philippine Board of Investment and the Philippine Economic Zone Authority reached U.S.$830 million, corresponding to a total of 420 investment projects. Of these, 3 per cent were investments in contact centers while 35% were investments in software development projects.

The industry experienced a period of uncertainty during the global crisis of 2008–2009. Concerns were raised on the Philippine BPO industry's capacity to survive the slowdown in America and Europe. During that time, there were two possible market reactions. First, companies in the West could reduce exposure to outsourcing because of the general decline of economic activity. Second, companies in the West could recognize the cost-saving potential of transferring business activities to low-cost areas, i.e. BPO destinations. These reactions operated in opposite directions, causing some doubt on the future of BPO as a corporate model and of the BPO industry in the Philippines.

A major impetus for the acceleration of the BPO sector in the Philippines is the BPO deployment of U.S. financial institutions in the Philippines. This was particularly the case of the subprime crisis that hit the U.S. in the late 2000s. U.S. financial companies reeling from the crisis were forced to outsource their business processes abroad in order to cut costs and somehow survive the crunch. Amidst worries that the subprime crisis (ground zero: U.S.) will be triggering a reduction of investments to emerging economies, U.S. financial institutions are coming in strong into the Philippine ICT-BPO sector riding on the wave of cost-cuttings following the crisis. Two such cases were JP Morgan Chase and the American International Group.

10.2.7 No EAM Report Part II

Figure 10.2 shows that the Philippines had a GDP per capita of $1,070 in 1950, second only to Malaysia's $1,559. In the same year, the Philippines had a higher GDP per capita than Indonesia ($840) and Thailand ($817), and even South Korea ($854) and Taiwan ($924). By 2010, the gaps had widened, with the Philippines having the lowest GDP per capita among the three other ASEAN countries shown in Fig. 10.2: the Philippines with $3,204 against Indonesia's $4,722, Malaysia's $10,094, and Thailand's $9,372. The Philippine GDP per capita was certainly much lower than that of South Korea ($21,701) and Taiwan ($23,292). Over the 60-year period, the Philippines had the lowest Compound Annual Growth Rate (CAGR) of 1.7%, compared to the 2.9% of Indonesia, the 3.2% of Malaysia, and the 4.2% of Thailand.

The GDP per capita of the ASEAN member states for 2021 and 2022 are shown in Tables 10.7 and 10.8, respectively. Not only is the gap between the Philippines and its cohorts (Indonesia, Malaysia, Thailand) maintained, but it could be seen that a latecomer ASEAN member state, Vietnam, has now overtaken the Philippines in terms of GDP per capita.

Moreover, the Philippines continues to exhibit one of the worst distributions of income as shown in Table 10.9. Compared to the latecomer ASEAN member states, it has the worst distribution of income.

It has been over twenty years since the publication of the East Asian Miracle Report of the World Bank, wherein shared growth was used to describe the performance of the Highly-Performing East Asian Economies. After all these years, the numbers in Fig. 10.2 and Tables 10.7, 10.8, and 10.9 indicate that shared growth continues to elude the Philippines.

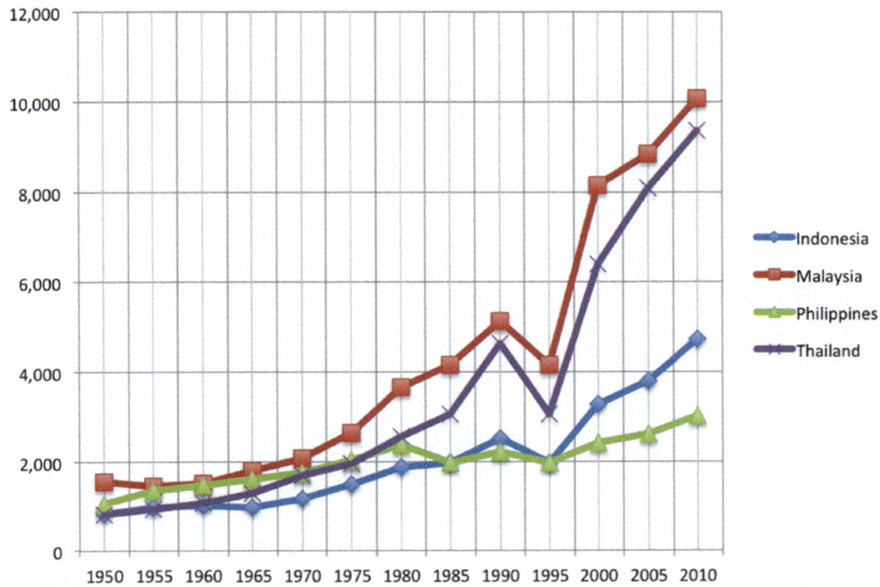

Fig. 10.2 Five-year GDP per capita of four early ASEAN countries (1990 international Geary-Khamis Dollars) (*Source* Maddison 2013)

Table 10.7 ASEAN GDP per capita for 2021

Rank	Country	Population in million	GDP nominal millions of USD	GDP nominal per capita USD	GDP (PPP) millions of USD	GDP (PPP) per capita USD
7	Myanmar	53,550	65,160	1,216	239,354	4,469
8	Cambodia	16,589	27,421	1,653	78,658	4,967
9	Laos	7.371	18,552	2,514	62,642	8,488
4	Philippines	109.991	393,612	3,571	1,011,099	9,175
6	Vietnam	98.328	366,201	3,724	1,134,024	11,533
1	Indonesia	272.270	1,186,067	4,356	3,566,283	13,099
—	ASEAN	667.393	3,358,605	5,045	9,070,441	13,626
2	Thailand	69.947	513,165	7,336	1,343,727	19,209
5	Malaysia	33.358	372,754	11,399	970,748	29,686
10	Brunei	0.461	19,915	44,808	29,687	66,795
3	Singapore	5.840	396,992	72,794	635,270	116,487

(*Source* IMF 2021 data).

Table 10.8 ASEAN GDP per capita for 2022

Rank	Country	Population in million	GDP nominal millions of USD	GDP nominalper capita USD	GDP (PPP) millions of USD	GDP (PPP) per capita USD
7	Myanmar	53.886	56,757	1,053	261,170	4,846
8	Cambodia	16.767	29,912	1,784	89,570	5,600
10	Laos	7.477	15,304	2,046	69,843	9,207
6	Philippines	111.570	404,261	3,623	1,171,162	10,497
5	Vietnam	99.462	406,452	4,086	1,321,249	13,284
1	Indonesia	274.859	1,318,807	4,798	4,036,878	14,687
—	ASEAN	672.397	3,657,636	5,439	10,316,112	15,342
2	Thailand	70.078	536,160	7,650	1,482,347	21,152
4	Malaysia	32.993	407,923	12,364	1,134,671	34,391
9	Brunei	0.442	16,639	37,667	31,142	70,500
3	Singapore	5.637	466,789	82,807	719,080	127,563

(*Source* IMF 2022 data).

Table 10.9 Gini coefficient of some ASEAN countries

Country	Year	Gini
Indonesia	2022	37.9
Lao PDR	2018	38.8
Malaysia	2018	41.2
Myanmar	2017	30.7
Philippines	2021	40.7
Thailand	2021	35.1
Vietnam	2020	36.8

(*Source* World Bank Database).

10.3 Lack of Strategic Sequencing

Despite a generally good start in the late 19th and the first half of the twentieth centuries, the Philippines has lagged behind its ASEAN cohorts entering the twenty-first century. There have been proposed of course a host of reasons for such lack-luster performance, but in this chapter, we focus on a strategic logic that is well known in development economics but apparently not applied by policy makers in the Philippines. This is essentially the logic of strategic sequencing.

In Chap. 6, we looked at the ODA-FDI-EXIM trinity of Japanese international engagements, with their underlying economic philosophies. We saw the varying degrees by which the Philippines responded to such engagements: relatively high with Japanese ODA, mixed with Japanese FDI, and relatively low with Japanese

EXIM dynamics. The generally mixed response of the Philippines to this ODA-FDI-EXIM trinity suggests that there is a failure of strategic sequencing in the development policies of the Philippines.

The strategic sequencing suggested in Chap. 6 is that of the Flying Geese model, which consists of the following phases of industrial development: importation → import-substitution industrialization → export-oriented industrialization → reversed importation. The Flying Geese model also includes a shift from more labor- to more capital-intensive industries.

Another strategic sequencing well-known in development economics is the Petty-Clarke Law, wherein a country's development focus shifts from agriculture, and then to industry (manufacturing), and finally to services. We first look at this type of strategic sequencing, before the one suggested by the Flying Geese model.

10.3.1 Dichotomy of Import-Substitution and Export-Oriented Industrialization

Philippine industrial policy exhibits a marked tendency to view import-substitution and export-oriented industrialization as two inherently separate policies. The export-oriented industrialization phase is generally seen as a measure to correct an evidently failed import-substitution phase.

> One of the most significant changes in development policy thinking among developing countries in the past decades was the shift from a purely import-substituting industrialization policy to a more outward-looking export-oriented strategy. Owing primarily to the dissatisfaction with the former policy in achieving multiple goals of development, a number of developing countries have opted for a change in terms of increased dependence on the export market to relieve the constraints to growth. In this respect, the Philippines was no exception (Tecson 1983: 386).

The flagship program of the Export-Oriented Industrialization (EOI) in the Philippines, and in many developing countries, was the Export Processing Zones (EPZs), which became the epitome of how EOI was separated from all other economic policies of the past. In fact, these were often referred to as export "enclaves" (Warr, 1987, 1989). The EPZs in the Philippines have gone through two generations of evolution.

> These first generation economic zones (or ecozones) followed the traditional model where they are essentially enclaves outside of the country's "normal customs territory" with production of locator firms being meant almost entirely for the export market and with their intermediate and capital inputs being allowed to come in free of duty and exchange controls.
>
> Republic Act (RA) 7916 enacted in 1995 replaced the traditional model with the second-generation model, the special economic zone. RA 7916 expanded the objectives for the establishment of ecozones by including the establishment of forward and backward linkages among industries in and around the ecozone, promoting greater financial/industrial linkage between the Philippines and the rest of the world through technology transfer, and broadening the geographic dispersion of industries. The SEZ model is more liberal than the EPZ model in the sense that SEZ locators need not produce exclusively for the export market. Registered enterprises in SEZs are also allowed to engage in a wider range of activities in addition to

manufacturing, such as commercial/trade services, utilities and infrastructure development, and tourism (Manasan 2013: 2).

Despite the attempt to escape from its enclave character, "backward linkages of SEZ enterprises have remained at a low level" (Manasan, 2013: 5), and remains poorly integrated to the local economy (Foreign Investment Advisory Service, 2008). Noting that SEZs are also devices for attracting FDI, the separation of import-substitution and export-oriented industrialization could also be seen in references to two distinct types of FDI. Needless to say, these would be import-substitution and export-oriented FDI (Mercado-Aldaba, 1994).

From a sectoral perspective this dichotomy of import-substitution and export-oriented industrialization would not be problematic. Traditional trade theory would tell us that at any time, a country would have an exporting and importing sector based on its comparative advantage profile. A crucial problem, however, arises when this dichotomy persists from a temporal perspective, which as could be noted from our review of Philippine industrial policy above, is precisely the perspective that we are conducting our review. As per that review, Import-substitution indeed preceded export-oriented industrialization in the Philippines.

The industrial upgrading component of the Flying Geese model tells us that an industry's strategic development should proceed from importation, to import-substitution, export-orientation, and then reverse importation. The driving force underlying this development is the international competitiveness of the industry, which starts from practically nil at the importation stage, rises as the industry goes through the import-substitution stage, peaks at the height of export-orientation, then finally declines paving the way for reverse importation. The transition from import-substitution to export-orientation follows a similar logic to the infant industry argument, wherein infant industries are protected from foreign competition to prepare them ultimately for such competition. From a temporal perspective, therefore, there should be no dichotomy between import-substitution and export-promotion. The temporal dichotomy of these two stages in the Philippine experience produced an import-substituting sector that continues to be infantile despite decades of protection, and an export-oriented sector that has basically weak linkages to other sectors of the economy.

To further illustrate this point, let us use the International Competitiveness Coefficient (ICC) found in the Flying Geese literature.[1] The ICC for an industry j is computed as follows.

$$ICC_i = \frac{X_i - M_i}{X_i + M_i}$$

where

X_i = value of exports of industry i.
M_i = value of imports of industry i.

[1] For example, see (Daisuke, 2005).

The ICC takes a value between −1 and 1, and could be used to indicate at which stage of the Flying Geese model a certain industry is at any moment. Table 10.10 below summarizes the correspondence between the ICC and the Flying Geese model stages.

It is to be noted that the ICC, if it is to match the evolution of the various phases of the Flying Geese model, should progress from a value of negative one, move towards one, and eventually decline. There is a transition from the import-substitution to the export-oriented phase. This could be anywhere between the ICC values of negative one and positive one, wherein the industry starts exporting and/or substituting imports with local production. For our purposes, however, we define the transition point between import-substitution and export-oriented phases to correspond to the ICC zero value. An ICC value above zero corresponds to a stage where the industry has become a net exporter, and therefore considered as being in the export-oriented stage. On the other hand, an ICC value less than zero corresponds to a net importing stage, where local production has already begun to displace some of the imports, and therefore is considered as import-substitution.

Table 10.11 below tabulates the ICC for the Philippine manufacturing industries using input–output tables for various years from 1961 to 2018. It could be readily seen that there is a preponderance of negative values, supporting the commonly held belief of perpetually uncompetitive industries that seem to be mired in the import-substitution stage. Looking more closely, however, a few bright spots emerge. Some industries appear to cleanly go through the FGM sequence of moving from importation, import-substitution, export-orientation, and finally reverse-importation, namely: Wearing apparel & made-up textile goods; Furniture and fixtures; and Electrical machinery. There are other industries that displayed periods of positive ICC, but these were considered to be too erratic and, therefore not too suited to be cited as examples of good strategic sequencing.

Table 10.10 ICC phase definitions

ICC	Occurs when	Flying geese model stage
Negative one	Zero exports; imports only	Full importation
Negative but not equal to negative one, and less than zero	Exports are less than imports	Import-substitution
Zero	Exports are equal to imports	Transition point
Positive but not equal to positive one, and greater than zero	Exports are greater than imports	Export-oriented
Positive one	Exports only; zero imports	Full exportation
Declining towards negative values	Exports declining and/or imports increasing	Reverse importation

(*Source* Authors).

Table 10.11 International competitiveness coefficients for industrial sectors, 1961–2018

Industry	1961	1965	1969	1974	1979	1985	1988	1994	2000	2006	2012	2018
Food manufacturing industries	0.03	−0.01	0.24	0.55	0.35	0.18	0.34	0.06	−0.32	0.19	−0.31	−0.38
Beverage industries	−0.79	−0.78	−0.36	0.00	−0.70	−0.31	−0.32	−0.42	−0.76	−0.54	−0.61	−0.89
Tobacco manufactures	−1.00	0.59	−0.23	0.53	−0.51	−0.40	−0.64	−0.68	−0.34	0.79	0.39	0.61
Manufacture of textiles	−0.96	−0.52	−0.99	−0.75	−0.39	−0.66	−0.51	−0.66	−0.78	−0.29	−0.44	−0.48
Wearing apparel & made−up textile goods	**−0.99**	**−0.48**	**0.58**	**0.49**	**0.85**	**0.41**	**0.29**	**0.77**	**0.78**	**0.47**	**−0.17**	**−0.38**
Products of wood, cane & cork, except furniture	0.87	0.89	0.93	0.96	0.99	0.96	0.95	0.67	0.20	0.26	0.74	0.14
Furniture and fixtures	**−0.36**	**0.31**	**0.35**	**0.82**	**0.99**	**0.99**	**0.99**	**0.96**	**0.73**	**0.54**	**0.22**	**−0.09**
Paper and paper products	−1.00	−1.00	−0.94	−0.85	−0.89	−0.56	−0.74	−0.75	−0.58	−0.44	−0.46	−0.57
Printing, publishing and allied industries	−0.99	−0.98	−0.79	−0.90	−0.97	−0.72	−0.45	−0.71	−0.58	−0.56	−0.19	−0.19
Leather and leather products	−1.00	−0.98	−1.00	0.06	−0.23	−0.27	0.17	0.20	−0.09	−0.17	−0.46	−0.37
Rubber products	−1.00	−0.98	−0.83	−0.90	−0.93	−0.80	−0.14	−0.57	0.18	0.01	−0.21	−0.32
Chemicals and chemical products	−0.75	−0.26	−0.46	−0.21	−0.01	−0.23	−0.27	−0.43	−0.55	−0.56	−0.42	−0.33
Products of petroleum and coal	−1.00	−0.67	0.02	−0.72	−0.77	−0.49	0.13	−0.57	−0.20	−0.29	−0.78	−0.32
Non−metallic mineral products	−1.00	−1.00	−0.83	0.01	−0.34	0.00	−0.66	−0.24	−0.21	0.30	−0.54	−0.89
Basic metal industries	−1.00	−0.97	−0.86	−0.88	−0.67	0.49	−0.39	−0.07	−0.35	0.12	−0.15	−0.64
Metal products	−0.99	−0.99	−0.97	−0.97	−0.85	−0.90	−0.79	−0.40	−0.39	−0.29	−0.49	−0.53
Machinery, except electrical machinery	−1.00	−1.00	−0.99	−0.98	−0.98	−0.89	−0.87	−0.85	−0.33	−0.36	−0.41	−0.43
Electrical machinery	**−1.00**	**−1.00**	**−0.95**	**−0.96**	**−0.41**	**−0.04**	**−0.13**	**0.00**	**0.26**	**0.20**	**0.23**	**−0.33**
Transport equipment	−1.00	−1.00	−0.97	−1.00	−0.92	−0.76	−0.89	−0.52	−0.31	−0.39	−0.24	−0.62
Miscellaneous manufacturing industries	−0.95	−0.93	−0.58	−0.75	−0.38	0.10	−0.19	−0.32	0.04	−0.07	0.11	−0.33

(*Source* Philippine statistics authority). *Note* Bold highlighted industries refer to industries that appear to follow the FGM strategic sequencing.

10.3.2 Premature Industrialization and Deindustrialization

A second form by which there is a lack of strategic sequencing in Philippine development policy is the premature manner by which industrialization and deindustrialization were conducted. It is a well known observation in development economics that countries generally go through a process that starts with agriculturalization, followed by industrialization, and finally by servitization, also known as the Petty-Clark Law.[2]

There appears to be "premature industrialization", which we define as a situation where industrialization is strongly pursued before conditions that lead to the structural transformation of the agricultural sector have been created. We shall return to this later below.

Felipe et al. (2012) also points to the related problem of early de-industrialization. De-industrialization refers to the long-term decline of the share of manufacturing to total income. It being early implies its initiation at a development stage earlier than that at which it occurred in the advanced industrial nations.

One of the earliest observations of early deindustrialization was in the UN Trade and Development Report of 2003 [UNCTAD 2003] regarding the decrease in the share of employment in the manufacturing sector of developing countries in Latin America in the 1990s. [UNCTAD 2003] cites [Rowthorn, Rawasmamy 1999] which defined the critical per capita income at which deindustrialization typically becomes a clear trend to be between $8000 and $9000 (measured in 1986 prices). It observes that the decline in relative importance of manufacturing activities in most developing countries in Latin America occurred at much lower levels than the critical range.

[UNCTAD 2003] tends to view this deindustrialization as undesirable. It argues against the interpretation that this deindustrialization is a desirable shift away from the past import-substitution industrialization (ISI) undertaken by Latin American countries, to a development that leverages their comparative advantage in natural resources and pursues an outward orientation. The argument is that most Latin American countries that have deindustrialized have not really experienced an acceleration of growth that would accompany a successful shift from the inward-looking orientation of the ISI. Moreover, the report compared the deindustrialization of resource-rich Scandinavian countries in the 1960s and found that the Latin American countries were at a much higher level of deindustrialization.

Figure 10.3 shows the share of employment to total employment in the Philippine manufacturing sector based on available data. Although, there was a dip in employment share in the first half of the 1980s, this could not be really considered as deindustrialization given that the share of manufacturing value-added to GDP was relatively stagnant during this period (see Fig. 10.1), and given that there was a later rise in manufacturing employment share. We mark the deindustrialization phase to have started around 1997, when the manufacturing employment share seems to have peaked. Since the GDP per capita of the Philippines at this time was much lower than the critical $8000, this further confirms that the Philippines entered an early deindustrialization phase around the 1990s.

---

[2] See Clark (1940) and Kuznets (1971).

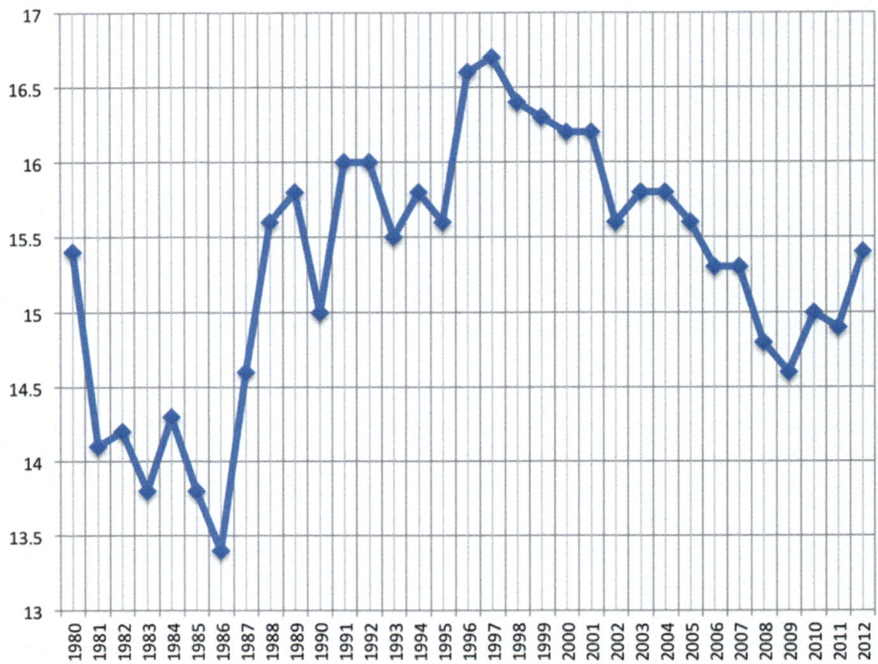

Fig. 10.3 Manufacturing employment share to total employment (*Source* International Labour Organization, Key Indicators of the Labour Market database)

[Tregenna September 2011] provides a distinction between a less problematic deindustrialization (LPD) and a more problematic deindustrialization (MPD). In the LPD, the drop in manufacturing employment in levels or share to total employment is largely due to decreasing labor-intensity in manufacturing, while in MPD, it is largely due to the drop in manufacturing value added level and share to total GDP. Tregenna (2011) argues that LPD is less problematic by appealing to the theory of Kaldor and the structuralist economists, which stresses that manufacturing is a solid engine of growth given its dynamic economies of scale, forward and backward linkages, strong properties of learning-by-doing, innovation and technological progress, and importance in the balance of payments. A drop in manufacturing employment due to a decrease in the sectoral share of manufacturing is considered more problematic because of the possibility that the economy is being deprived of the Kaldorian properties that make manufacturing an engine of growth.

The three Kaldorian laws suggest three general patterns of an "engine of growth". We investigate to what extent these properties could be found in the agriculture, industry, and services sectors of the Philippines.

1st Kaldor Law: the faster the growth of the sector, the faster is the growth of the total income. A linear specification of this law is as follows

$$\text{Ggdp} = \text{a1} + \text{a2 Gi}$$

where Ggdp is the annual growth rate of real GDP, Gi is the annual growth rate of the real value added of sector i (i.e., agriculture, industry, and services)

An alternate specification of the 1st Law is as follows

$$\text{Ggdp} = \text{a1} + \text{a2}(\text{Gi} - \text{Gj})$$

where Gj is the annual growth rate of the real value added of the sectors other than sector i. Note that a2 is anticipated to be a number between zero and one.

2nd Kaldor Law (a.k.a. Kaldor-Verdoorn Law): the faster the growth of the sector, the faster is the growth of that sector's productivity. A linear specification of this law is as follows

$$\text{Gprodi} = \text{b1} + \text{b2 Gi}$$

where Gprodi is the annual growth rate of the average labor productivity of sector i

3rd Kaldor Law: the faster the growth of the sector, and lesser the growth of employment in the other sectors, the faster is the growth of the total income. A linear specification of this law is as follows

$$\text{Gprodgdp} = \text{c1} + \text{c2 Gi} + \text{c3 GLj}$$

where Gprodgdp is the annual growth rate of the overall average labor productivity, and GLj is the annual growth rate of employment in sector j not equal to i.

This 3rd Law is related to the Less Problematic Deindustrialization mentioned by Tregenna and the positive deindustrialization mentioned by Rowthorn and Wells, wherein the decline in employment share or level of manufacturing is due to productivity increases in that sector. This is essentially what is happening, for example, in the case of a growing services sector accompanied by reductions in employment in the manufacturing sector.

The three Kaldor Laws specify three possibly interrelated features of an engine of growth. Firstly, the engine's (excess) growth should be positively related to the growth of the overall economy (1st Law). This relationship does not simply stem from an accounting relationship wherein the value added of a sector is part of total income. It touches on the crucial structural features of the engine of growth wherein there are improvements in the engine's labor productivity due to static and dynamic effects (2nd Law) and/or overall improvements in productivity due to transfer of resources to the engine of growth from other sectors of the economy (3rd Law). The detailed study of these effects, however, are beyond the scope of this study.

The above laws were tested using Philippine data. Gi is the growth rate of the value added, at constant prices, of one of the three sectors, i.e., agriculture, industry, and services. The value added data were collected from the National Statistical Coordination Board of the Philippine government. The data was originally available quarterly, and was aggregated into annual data. Gprodi is the growth rate of the average labor productivity of one of the three sectors. This was calculated as the ratio of real value added of one sector to the amount of employment in that sector. Employment rate (as a percentage of total employment) by sector was obtained from the World Development Indicators. The total labor force data were obtained from two sources. Annual data for 1990 to 2010 was taken from the World Development Indicator, while that for 1980 to 1990 was taken from the Philippine Department of Labor and Employment (DOLE). The two series of labor force data were spliced at the overlapping year of 1990, from which the ratio of the World Development Indicator value to the DOLE value was used as a factor to adjust the DOLE values from 1980 to 1989. The employment per sector was computed by multiplying the employment rate by the labor force. Gprodgdp is the growth rate of the overall average labor productivity, which was computed as the ratio of the real GDP to the labor force Growth rates were calculated using the midpoint average formula Estimates guided by the Kaldor Laws were basically done using OLS estimation. All the three sectors were estimated for all the patterns suggested by the three Kaldor Laws. This would ensure that there is no bias in identifying any sector as an engine of growth.

The summary results of the application of these laws to the case of the Philippines are as follows.

The results of the estimation based on the 1st Kaldor Law in Table 10.12 show that the (excess) growth of the value-added of industry is the only sector that is positively and significantly related to the growth of total income. This implies that the industrial sector remains an engine of growth for the Philippine economy.

The estimates based on the 2nd Kaldor Law in Table 10.12 indicate that the growth of the average labor productivity of all three sectors are positively and significantly correlated to their respective sectoral growth rates. It could be observed that the industrial sector's b2 estimate is furthest from the value of one, suggesting that the growth of labor productivity in this sector is associated with increases in this sector's employment, which in turn could come with the absorption of labor from the other sectors (Basu & Budhiraja 2021). Given that the estimated b2 for agricultural and, more visibly, services is close to one implies that such labor absorption in these two sectors is not as prominent as that in the industrial sector.

Table 10.12 Results of Kaldor Law-guided estimations

Kaldor law	Estimated coefficient	Agriculture	Industry	Services
1st law (alternate specification)	a2	−0.576***	0.761***	−0.878***
	Goodness of fit	0.400	0.647	0.384
2nd law	b2	0.952***	0.818***	0.999***
	Goodness of fit	0.538	0.512	0.574
3rd law	c2	0.607***	0.597***	1.118***
	c3	−0.302	−1.120***	−0.628***
	Goodness of fit	0.254	0.899	0.842

(*Source* Authors). *Notes* *** significant to the 1% level. Estimates for the 1st Law used annual data from 1982 to 2010.

The estimates based on the 3rd Kaldor Law in Table 10.12 show that, for all three sectors, the overall average labor productivity is positively and significantly related to sectoral growth rate and negatively and significantly related to growth of employment in the other sectors. The service sector's growth in output appears to have the highest correlation with overall labor productivity, followed by industry, and then agriculture. In terms of implied labor absorption, the industry sector appears to have the highest correlation with overall labor productivity, followed by the service sector. The agricultural sector appears to have no significant labor absorption effect, likely due to it being essentially a supplier of surplus labor.

The Kaldor-guided estimations, therefore, suggest that:

1. Growth in the industry sector is associated with higher growth rates in the overall output, while growth in the agriculture and service sectors could not be associated with higher growth rates in the overall output (1st Law);
2. Growth in the industry sector's output is associated with higher employment in this sector, and higher growth rates in this sector's labor productivity. Although having a positive and significant correlation with their respective sector's labor productivity, growth of output in the agricultural and service sectors appear to be less associated with growth in their sector's employment (2nd Law);
3. Growth in the industry sector's output and implied labor absorption (due to decrease in employment in the other two sectors) are associated with higher overall labor productivity (3rd Law).

In short, the Kaldor Law estimates suggest that the industrial sector continues to be an engine of growth, despite the fact that the Philippine economy has already moved ahead to the service phase, as indicated by the dominant share of service sector output in total income. This would suggest a premature type or early deindustrialization that could have detrimental effects on the whole economy's long-term growth.[3]

One major detrimental effect would be to retard the structural transformation of the agricultural sector. In this study, we focus on the structural transformation as defined by the Lewis Turning Point (LTP). While the LTP appears not to garner much attention in the Philippines, it is relatively more popular in the rest of Asia.[4] The structural transformation that is associated with the LTP is the transformation of a traditional agricultural sector into a modern one, thereby eradicating the dual nature of the economy. Such a transformation is promoted in part by an industrialization that absorbs the surplus labor from the traditional agricultural sector.

In this study, we consider an industrial sector that is unable to foster such transformation within a sufficient amount of time as indicative of premature industrialization. To put this into more concrete terms, let us look at the East Asian countries that have

[3] A similar observation is made by (Olamade & Oni, 2016), based on a panel data analysis of 28 African countries over the period 1981–2015 wherein the manufacturing sector had a declining share in GDP. Applying various estimation techniques, they concluded that 1st Kaldor Law applied in the case of the African countries, and warned that a continued contraction of manufacturing share would be detrimental to long-term growth of African countries.

[4] See for example, (Minami et al., 2014; Zhang et al., 2011; Cai & Du, 2011 and Bairagi & Kamal, 2019).

Table 10.13 Comparative LTP features

Country	LTP year	Agricultural share in GDP, %	Per capita GDP (US$ at 2015 prices)
China	2002–2010	13.3−9.3	2,557.9−5,647.1
Japan	1960	9	6,260.7
South Korea	1975	24.5	2,905.6
Philippines	Not yet as of 2022	9	3,528.0

(*Sources* LTP Year of NIEs: Minami et al., 2014; Zhang et al., 2011 among others; Bai, 1982.[5] Agricultural share in GDP, per capita GDP: World Bank Database). *Note* The agricultural share and per capita GDP are taken for the LTP year. In the case of the Philippines, these values are for 2022.

Table 10.14 LTP year estimates for China

TLP year	References
2003	(Zhang et al., 2011; Cai and Du, 2011)
2002–2004	(Liu, 2015)
2004	(Fang et al., 2016)
2010[a]	(Wei & Kwan, 2018)
2020–2025	(Das & N'Diaye, 2013)
Not yet passed	(Minami et al., 2014)

Note [a]China's eastern and north-eastern regions passed the turning point by 2010, while the central region is approaching this point and the western region remains far from it.

reached their LTP. (Minami et al., 2014) report that the NIEs (China, Japan, and South Korea) have already reached their LTP. We use this as the basis for defining an appropriate level of LTP. Table 10.13 summarizes the critical features of the LTP of the NIEs, including the Philippines for reference.

LTP Year is the year the TLP was reached.

The LTP year of China is much debated. Table 10.14 summarizes the estimates that we were able to find.

For this study, we chose to lean towards the estimates of the Chinese scholars (topmost four rows) on the premise that they are "insiders" who would have more access to better data. Hence, the LTP years range from 2002.

Table 10.13 shows that the agricultural shares at LTP Year ranges from 9 to 24.5. Given that agriculture shares decline as an economy transforms, the Philippines is just about at the brink of its TLP, benchmarking it with the NIEs. However, at its current situation, the Philippines is still considered to be a dual economy. As per recent estimates, the real wage differential between the agricultural and non-agricultural sectors remains large (Cerutti, 2021). In other words, even with industrialization at full swing right after the war, the agricultural sector remains unintegrated to the rest of the economy, implying premature industrialization.

[5] In Korean, but referred to in English by (*First Turning Point*, n.d.).

10.4 Conclusion: Unshared Growth as a Critical Factor

Why then did the Philippines experience lack of strategic sequencing as implied by the dichotomy of import-substitution and export-oriented industrialization, as well as premature industrialization and premature deindustrialization?

There would most likely be a host of answers to this important question, but we focus on one that is not really paid the attention that we think it deserves. Recall from Table 10.1 that the Philippines was a relatively prosperous nation even in the late nineteenth century, and that from Tables 10.7 and 10.8, we see that it has now fallen behind its ASEAN cohorts, and in fact overtaken by one of the late member countries of ASEAN. This long-term phenomenon is reminiscent of the reversal of fortune thesis of (Acemoglu et al., 2002).

> In prosperous and densely settled areas, Europeans introduced or maintained already-existing extractive institutions to force the local population to work in mines and plantations, and took over existing tax and tribute systems. In contrast, in previously sparsely settled areas, Europeans settled in large numbers and created institutions of private property, providing secure property rights to a broad cross section of the society and encouraging commerce and industry. This institutional reversal laid the seeds of the reversal in relative incomes. But most likely, the scale of the reversal and the subsequent divergence in incomes are due to the emergence of the opportunity to industrialize during the nineteenth century. While societies with extractive institutions or those with highly hierarchical structures could exploit available agricultural technologies relatively effectively, the spread of industrial technology required the participation of a broad cross section of the society-the smallholders, the middle class, and the entrepreneurs. The age of industry, therefore, created a considerable advantage for societies with institutions of private property. Consistent with this view, we documented that these societies took much better advantage of the opportunity to industrialize.

In the Philippines, the existence of extractive institutions rather than institutions of private property, which promoted the participation of a broad cross-section of society, is quite pervasive. (Lanzona, Jr., 2019), for example, attributes the slow implementation of the agrarian reform program in the Philippines to institutions that endow de facto political power to the powerful elites resulting in the elite capture of institutions. Through a systematic comparison of the agrarian reform in the Philippines with the more successful ones in South Korea and Taiwan, (You, 2014) essentially corroborates elite capture in the implementation of said program in the Philippines. He tracks the root to inequality that leads to corruption through policy capture and political clientelism (patron-client relations). The existence of detrimental lobbying in the industrial sector is confirmed by Aldaba (2005) in the form of policy reversals in the government's liberalization thrust since the 1980s, resulting in some industries still receiving a high rate of protection. Such policy reversals are pushed only by selected industries that have strong lobbying groups. Moreover, the performance of these protected industries remain dubious. Here we clearly see the roots of the Philippines' unshared growth. There could be no doubt that it has undermined her democracy, as well as industrial and development policies.

References

Acemoglu, D., Johnson, S., & Robinson, J. A. (2002). Reversal of fortune: Geography and institutions in the making of the modern world income distribution. *The Quarterly Journal of Economics, 117*(4), 1231–1294.

Aldaba, R. M. (2005). Policy reversals, lobby groups and economic distortions. *PIDS Discussion Paper, 2005*(4).

Angus, M. (2003). *Development centre studies the world economy historical statistics: Historical statistics*. OECD Publishing.

Bai, M.-K. (1982). Structural changes of the Korean labor market. *Journal of Economics, 21*(1), 571–621.

Bairagi, S., & Kamal, M. (2019). Is Bangladesh's economy approaching the Lewis turning point? *South Asia Economic Journal, 20*(1), 19–45. https://doi.org/10.1177/1391561418822208

Baldwin, R. E. (1975). *Foreign trade regimes and economic development: Philippines*.

Basu, D., & Budhiraja, M. (2021). What to make of the Kaldor-Verdoorn law? *Cambridge Journal of Economics, 45*(6), 1243–1268. https://doi.org/10.1093/cje/beab027

Cai, F., & Du, Y. (2011). Wage increases, wage convergence, and the Lewis turning point in China. *China Economic Review, 22*(4), 601–610. https://doi.org/10.1016/j.chieco.2011.07.004

Cerutti, E. M. (2021). *The agricultural exodus in the Philippines: Are wage differentials driving the process?* IMF eLibrary. Retrieved November 27, 2023, from https://www.elibrary.imf.org/view/journals/001/2021/220/article-A001-en.xml

Clark, C. (1940). *The conditions of economic progress*. MacMillan.

Daisuke, H. (2005). The "Catching up" process of manufacturing in East Asia. *IDE Discussion Paper, 22*.

Das, M., & N'Diaye, P. (2013). Chronicle of a decline foretold: Has China reached the Lewis turning point? [WP/13/26]. In *IMF Working Paper*. Retrieved November 27, 2023, from https://www.imf.org/external/pubs/ft/wp/2013/wp1326.pdf

Fang, Y., Fan, Q., & Zeng, L. (2016). Transformation strategy of the three industries in China at the Lewis turning point. In *2016 International Conference on Industrial Economics System and Industrial Security Engineering (IEIS)*. IEEE Xplore. Retrieved November 27, 2023, from https://ieeexplore.ieee.org/document/7551855

Felipe, J., Abnon, A., & Kumar, U. (2012). Tracking the middle-income trap: What is it, who is in it, and why? *Levy Economics Institute, Working Paper*, (715).

First turning point. (n.d.). K-Developedia. Retrieved November 27, 2023, from https://www.kdevelopedia.org/Development-Overview/all/first-turning-point--109.do

Foreign Investment Advisory Service. (2008). *Special economic zones: Performance, lessons learned, and implications for zone development*. World Bank.

Golay, F. (1961). *The Philippines. Public policy and national economic development*. Cornell University Press.

Kuznets, S. (1971). *Economic growth of N*. Harvard University Press.

Lanzona, L. A., Jr. (2019). Agrarian reform and democracy: Lessons from the Philippine experience. *Millennial Asia, 10*(3), 272–298. https://doi.org/10.1177/0976399619879866

Liu, D. (2015). Has the Chinese economy passed the Lewis turning point? *Journal of the Asia Pacific Economy, 20*(3), 404–422. https://doi.org/10.1080/13547860.2015.10541672003-2204

Manasan, R. G. (2013). Export processing zones, special economic zones: Do we really need to have more of them? *PIDS Policy Notes*, (2013–15), pp. 1–8. https://pidswebs.pids.gov.ph/CDN/PUBLICATIONS/pidspn1315.pdf

Maxfield, S., & James, H. N. (1990). Protectionism and the internationalization of capital: US sponsorship of import substitution industrialization in the Philippines, Turkey and Argentina. *International Studies Quarterly*, 49–81.

Mercado-Aldaba, R. A. (1994). *Foreign direct investment in the Philippines: A Reassessment*. PIDS.

Minami, R., Makino, F., & Kim, K. S. (Eds.). (2014). *Lewisian turning point in the Chinese economy: Comparison with East Asian countries*. Palgrave MacMillan.

Nagano, Y. (2015). *State and finance in the Philippines, 1898–1941: The mismanagement of an American colony*. NUS Press.
Olamade, O., & Oni, O. (2016). Manufacturing and economic growth in Africa: A panel test of Kaldor's first growth law. *Journal of Economics and Sustainable Development, 7*(22), 126–140.
Ramos, N. M., Estrada, G., & Felipe, J. (2008). An Input-output analysis of the Philippine BPO industry. *Asian-Pacific Economic Literature, 22*(1), 41–56. https://doi.org/10.1111/j.1467-8411.2008.00211.x
Rowthorn, R., & Rawasmamy, R. (1999). Growth, trade, and industrialization. *IMF Staff Papers.*
Tecson, G. R. (1983). Trade and promotion policy in Philippine industrial development. *The Developing Economies, 21*(4), 386–414. https://doi.org/10.1111/j.1746-1049.1983.tb01160.x
Tregenna, F. (2011) Manufacturing productivity, deindustrialization, and reindustrialization. *UNU-WIDER Working Paper, 2011*(57).
Warr, P. G. (1987). Export promotion via industrial enclaves: The Philippines' Bataan export processing zone. *The Journal of DEvelopment Studies, 23*(2), 220–241. https://doi.org/10.1080/00220388708422028
Warr, P. G. (1989). Export processing zones: The economics of enclave manufacturing. *The World Bank Research Observer, 4*(1), 65–88. https://doi.org/10.1093/wbro/4.1.65
Wei, Z., & Kwan, F. (2018). Revisit China's Lewis turning point: An analysis from a regional perspective. *Asian Economic Journal, 32*(4), 333–357. https://doi.org/10.1111/asej.12162
You, J. (2014) Land reform, inequality, and corruption: A comparative historical study of Korea, Taiwan, and the Philippines. *The Korean Journal of International Studies, 12*(1), 191–224. https://doi.org/10.14731/kjis.2014.06.12.1.191
Zhang, X., Yang, J., & Wang, S. (2011). China has reached the Lewis turning point. *China Economic Review, 22*(4), 542–554. https://doi.org/10.1016/j.chieco.2011.07.002

Chapter 11
Decentralization in the Philippines: From Inclusive to Shared Growth

Abstract Chapter 11 (co-written with Damcelle Torres-Cortes) elaborates on a mechanism by which the problem of skewed distribution of income and wealth in the Philippines could be solved: decentralization. The chapter is essentially a meta survey of related literature on decentralization and its relation to shared growth, as manifested in the two socio-economic goals of efficiency and equity. We find that more rigorously done studies tend to reveal the positive contribution of decentralization on efficiency. On the other hand, decentralization was observed to have an aggravating effect on equity, suggesting the need for the implementation of countermeasures. It was noted, however, that inter-regional competition may help mitigate the widening of the income/wealth gap.

11.1 Introduction

In Chap. 9 (Historical Roots), egalitarian, as against extractive, institutions are important for broad based growth, or what we refer to as shared growth in this book. We consider mechanisms for shared growth as potent means to counteract such extractive institutions. One principle that we deem could contribute to shared growth is decentralization, which, broadly defined, fosters growth outside of the traditional growth centers of a national economy.

According to a World Bank study (East Asia Decentralizes),[1] the Philippines and fellow Archipelago, Indonesia, were the early adopters of decentralization in East Asia. In the Philippines, the Local Government Code (Republic Act No. 7610) was enacted in 1991. This law legislates the "transferring control and responsibility of delivering basic services to the hands of local government units (LGU). It aimed to enhance provision of services in the grass roots level as well as improve the efficiency

[1] "World Bank (2005). East Asia Decentralizes: Making Local Government Work. Washington, DC. © World Bank. https://openknowledge.worldbank.org/handle/10986/7492 License: CC BY 3.0 IGO."

H. Hirakawa and F. C. Maquito, *The Dynamics of Asian Economic Development*,
https://doi.org/10.1007/978-981-97-3106-0_11

in resource allocation. Further, it sought to widen the decision-making space by encouraging the participation of stakeholders, especially in the local level".[2]

How has fiscal decentralization fared since then? One way to answer this question is to take a look at a major pillar of Philippine decentralization, namely, the Internal Revenue Allotment (IRA), which is now referred to as the National Tax Allocation, since the redefinition of the tax base in 2022 following a Supreme Court ruling. For the purpose of this chapter, however, we will focus our attention to the IRA. Two standard measures of performance are employed: the vertical and horizontal imbalances. The vertical imbalance (efficiency) refers to the gap between national and sub-national funds and the cost of the functions devolved from the national government to the LGU. The horizontal imbalance (equity), on the other hand, refers to disparity in development among different LGUs.

We can associate shared growth to the two socio-economic goals of efficiency and equity. "Growth", as we idealize it, stems from the efficient allocation of resources, while "shared" refers to the equitable distribution of income and wealth. In the case of the Philippines, the absence of shared growth has reached disturbing proportions.

As could be seen from Table 11.1, the Philippines trails behind its original ASEAN cohorts. Its income leans closer to the GDP of younger ASEAN member states, and has even put us in the same category as the later batch of ASEAN countries. In fact, Vietnam already surpassed the Philippines in terms of GDP per capita in 2020. From Table 11.2, we can see that the Philippine Gini Coefficient is worse than that of the lower income ASEAN countries.

We can reframe the vertical and horizontal imbalances in terms of efficiency and equity, or shared growth. Efficiency refers to the ability of LGUs to utilize available funds to pay for the devolved public services. The higher the efficiency, the smaller the vertical imbalance, for the same amount of resources. Equity, on the other hand, is very much related to horizontal imbalance. Greater equity implies that disparities among LGUs in terms of economic development tend to be lower.

Let's consider two prominent criticisms of the IRA. The first one asserts that the IRA tends to widen the horizontal imbalance: "lack of an equalizing feature in the IRA distribution formula so that disparities in the fiscal capacities of LGUs are not adequately addressed, thereby widening the geographic disparities in human development outcomes and level of economic development" (Manasan 2007: 2). A second one essentially asserts that the IRA tends to widen the vertical imbalance: "vertical imbalances leading to the inadequacy of the IRA to fund the expenditure functions assigned to them" (ibid.: 2). It is related to the other criticism pertaining to the "disincentive effects on local revenue generation" (ibid.: 2). The LGU's high dependence on IRA is taken to be symptomatic of the lack of incentive to be self-reliant through the generation of local revenue.

[2] Explanatory Note. Bill No. 2575. (2008, August 28). An Act Reverting to the National Government the Discharge of Functions and Responsibilities Devolved to Certain Local Government Units, Amending for the Purpose of Republic Act No. 7160, Otherwise Known as the Local Government Code of 1991. http://legacy.senate.gov.ph/lisdata/82027399!.pdf.

Table 11.1 GDP of ASEAN countries estimates as of 2018

Country	Population in million	GDP nominal millions of US$	GDP nominal per capita US$	GDP (PPP) millions of US$	GDP (PPP) per capita US$
ASEAN	6,50,494	28,91,020	4,444	85,55,573	13,155
Indonesia	2,65,316	10,05,268	3,788	34,95,920	13,176
Thailand	69,182	4,90,120	7,084	13,23,209	19,126
Malaysia	32,446	3,47,290	10,703	9,99,835	30,815
Singapore	5,661	3,46,621	61,230	5,56,219	98,255
Philippines	1,07,018	3,31,678	3,099	9,56,030	8,933
Vietnam	94,575	2,41,434	2,552	7,07,620	7,482
Myanmar	52,832	71,543	1,354	3,59,107	6,797
Cambodia	16,253	24,141	1,485	70,265	4,323
Laos	6,777	18,230	2,690	53,912	7,955
Brunei	0	14,695	33,824	35,456	81,612

(*Source* IMF 2018).

Table 11.2 Gini coefficients for various East Asia countries

Country	Rank	Distribution of family income-Gini index	Date of information
Philippines	44	44.4	2015 est.
Cambodia	77	37.9	2008 est.
Laos	86	36.7	2008
Vietnam	98	34.8	2014

(*Source* Central Intelligence Agency 2018).

Both criticisms, if valid, effectively question the ability of IRA, as embodied in its formula for determining the allocations, to contribute to efficiency and equity, and, therefore, to shared growth. Maquito (2017), however, questions the bases of these criticisms, and therefore leaves open the possibility that the IRA, as it stands, could indeed contribute to shared growth. The first criticism, related to the horizontal balance, assumes that a rise in IRA causes a rise in income, even though there is the possibility that a rise in income causes a rise in IRA. It is this second possibility where the higher IRA could be seen as a reward for higher income that should be welcomed. The second criticism, related to vertical imbalance, also appears to fly in the face of positive correlations between IRA and (current) internal revenue collections (Maquito 2017) and local sources of income (Luna and Maquito 2020).[3]

In order to further investigate the effect of fiscal decentralization on horizontal and vertical imbalances, we undertook a systematic review of literature, the methodology

[3] "Decentralization, Land Value Taxes, and Shared Growth in the Philippines" paper presented at the 5th Asia Future Conference held on January 10–12, 2020 in Alabang and UPLB.

for which is discussed in the next section. This is followed by sections presenting the results of the horizontal imbalance-related survey and then the vertical imbalance-related survey. In the final section, we present our synthesis of the results.

11.2 Systematic Review of Literature Methodology

The Philippines' primary vehicle for intergovernmental transfers, the IRA,[4] has been subject of various research probing its use, sufficiency, and impact. But like many fiscal governance interventions, the IRA's effects on sub-national spending and contributions to local development are contingent on several internal and external determinants (Sepulveda, 2011). Moreover, the IRA's multiple policy objectives elicit divergent views about its role in development. Local government leaders value the allotment as a major source of income, funding delivery of the bulk of basic services to communities. Data shows that on average the IRA comprises 60 to 75% of the annual operating budgets of LGUs (Guevara, 2000; Manasan, 2007). More recent experience of LGUs reveal growing dependence.[5] This casts doubt on the expected stimulative or incentivizing effects of the IRA. It also bolsters the claim that such transfers promote fiscal dependency, which can compromise the local autonomy that the IRA supposedly promotes.

Decentralization's mixed results (Abimbola, 2019; Sepulveda, 2011) and noted uncertainties in the impact of IRA on local development (Panao, 2020) prompted us to scrutinize previous studies to synthesize and analyze premises, methods, and findings about the consequences of IRA through a systematic literature review. This "research of research" (Whittemore & Knafl, 2005) methodology originates from and has been widely used in the medical field to sift through inferences from clinical trials. Its application has nonetheless expanded to the social sciences to analyze both quantitative and qualitative research. Systematic reviews have evolved to distinct approaches to social science research: traditional, extended and/or adapted, and integrative (Victor, 2008).

Integrative review served as our literature review process for this study. Unlike the traditional approach to systematic reviews, the integrative method suits the nature of published works on the IRA, which rarely relies on randomized control trials. The extended/adapted review still had strong links to the traditional approach, giving less flexibility in the appraisal of resources. The integrative approach allowed for a "more iterative process" as well as "purposive sampling and appraisal of evidence"

[4] IRA is the term used in the Local Government Code of 1991 for the share of local governments in national taxes. The 2018 Supreme Court ruling in the Mandanas mandated that the IRA shall include a proportionate share from customs duties as well. In light of this decision, the IRA is now properly referred to as "National Tax Allotment" (NTA). In this chapter, IRA and NTA are used interchangeably.

[5] In a September 2021 forum where authors shared initial results of the study, a provincial administrator presented figures confirming that close to 90% provincial revenue in the past 3 years are sourced from the IRA.

(Victor, 2008). It also enabled cross-review of studies with diverse methodologies-i.e., qualitative and quantitative; experimental and non-experimental–"to capture the context, processes and subjective elements of the topic" (Whittemore & Knafl, 2005: 548, 553).

Such adaptability of integrative reviews is also the source of critiques concerning possible bias and weak methodological rigor in drawing conclusions from surveyed literature. To address these concerns, we followed Whittemore and Knafl's (2005) five-stage framework: (a) problem identification; (b) literature search; (c) data evaluation; (d) data analysis; and (e) presentation. These stages build on Cooper's (1998) guide for systematic reviews and incorporate strategies for strengthening the integrative review process. Though Whittemore and Knafl's framework has been developed for studies in the field of healthcare, particularly nursing, the methodology has been adopted and applied to the social sciences.

In this section, we describe how we applied each of the five steps in the integrative analysis framework to understand the relationship between fiscal decentralization and shared growth. We also take the opportunity to explain in this section the justification for and the operationalization of variables considered in the study.

11.2.1 Problem Identification

The first step of integrative review involves the standard procedure in any research exercise. Careful framing of the variables in consideration and the relationships subject of inquiry is crucial to delineate the scope and aims of the study. Though Whittemore and Knafl (2005) did not recommend a specific tool for refining variables, we used the PICO framework to streamline the research problem and facilitate literature review. PICO stands for the four search parameters: population, intervention, comparison, and outcome. There are other approaches such as PICOS, which adds the study design as the fifth sifting criterion; and SPIDER, which considers the sample, phenomenon of interest, design, evaluation, and research type. These enhance sensitivity and specificity in database search (Methley et al., 2014). Our interest in fiscal decentralization, and shared growth in the Philippines narrowed down our scope, making PICOS and SPIDER appealing. However, to ensure that we generate ample country-specific references, we relied on the PICO to cast a wider net, and filtered the results in subsequent iterations to identify the most relevant papers.

Drawing from general interest on fiscal decentralization's possible contribution to shared growth, we limited our inquiry to the Philippines not only because it is a context we are most familiar with, but for two other important reasons. First, the Philippines is touted as a "fast starter" (World Bank, 1993) of decentralization in East Asia as it institutionalized and went full steam with decentralization in 1991 through a national policy, the Local Government Code (LGC). The progress and consequences of two decades of distribution of powers and resources particularly through intergovernmental transfers deserves an intimate analysis. Second, the fiscal transfer scheme is undergoing an "expansion" or more accurately, fuller implementation as a result of a 2019 Philippine Supreme Court ruling in the Mandanas-Garcia case. The pronouncement increases the constitutionally mandated share of all LGUs, thereby infusing more funds for public services at the grassroots by 2022. A practical appreciation of the relationship of fiscal transfers with local economic development is thus all the more imperative to guide how a bigger share of the pie can be used to promote shared growth. More on this Mandanas-Garcia case and its implications in the concluding portion of this chapter.

Population

Applying the first element of PICO, the study's population covers the basic subnational or local government units (LGUs) in the Philippines across all levels of governance as identified by the LGC. As of this writing, these include 81 provinces, 1466 cities, 1488 municipalities, and 42,046 barangays (Philippine Statistics Office, 2020), with provinces as the biggest and barangays as the smallest political-geographical units. The country is also subdivided into 17 regions. These are not autonomous local entities acknowledged by the LGC, and do not have their own elected officials and revenue-raising powers. Composed of contiguous provinces, regions serve as administrative units mostly for development planning and coordination. In this study, while regions do not have corresponding IRA allocations, they nonetheless have become units of interest because many socio-economic indicators of shared growth are often aggregated per region.

Intervention

The intervention in question is the IRA, the Philippine's primary inter-governmental transfer scheme under the LGC. Fiscal decentralization takes several forms apart from national transfers, and even national transfer arrangements vary per country (Bahl & Linn, 1994). The LGC promotes fiscal autonomy by imbuing LGUs with corporate powers to levy taxes and fees, contract loans and engage in economic development activities. But the IRA has been the primary source of local income based on a system of fund allocation that has remained the same since 1991. This is despite several recommendations to revisit its formula (Manasan, 2007) to make the fund distribution more equitable and sensitive to contextual variations across. LGUs.

Figure 11.1 is the standard illustration of the IRA mechanism. Under the LGC, 40% of national taxes collected by the central government are automatically released to LGUs based on the mandated percentage share of each category of LGU (vertical formula). Municipalities get the largest share (34%) from this 40% presumably because the bulk of devolved services are at their level. Provinces and cities each have 23% even though provinces cover a bigger geographical jurisdiction, and cities, which are 18 times more than provinces in number, have more revenue raising powers.

Within each category of LGUs, the distribution further follows a horizontal formula which takes into account population in the case of barangays, and population plus land area for provinces, cities and municipalities. Though the formula remains unchanged, the absolute equivalent of the 40% share increased by around 70% in fiscal year 2022. This is because the total national internal revenue income

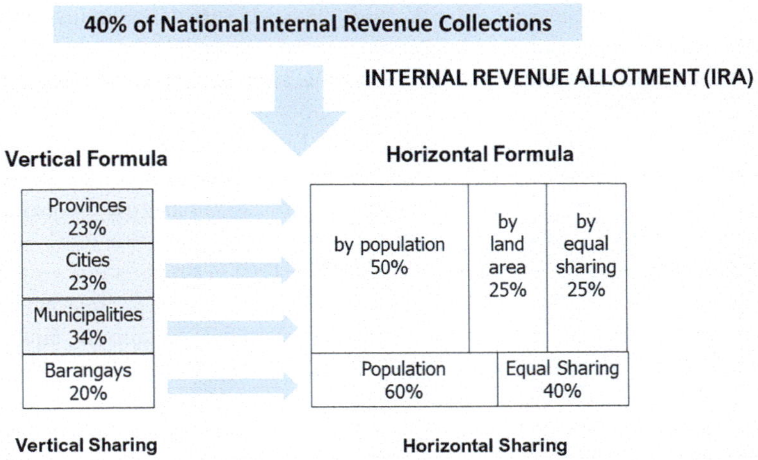

Fig. 11.1 Internal revenue allotment formula. (*Source* JICA, 2009)

that serves as the base or denominator for computing the total IRA increased as a result of the previously mentioned Mandanas-Garcia case. Through petitions filed by local officials and LGU associations, the Philippine Supreme Court in that case clarified that the IRA base should include customs duties, which had been omitted in the sum of national taxes since the implementation of the LGC.

Comparison

As for the third element in the PICO framework, the comparison relevant to the study involves shared growth in LGUs with and without fiscal decentralization, specifically the IRA. Since the IRA is anchored on the decentralization system under the LGC, comparing pre- and post-1991 local development scenarios proved sensible. This was not the only approach available though. Econometrics and other empirical methods have been likewise applied in previous studies to evaluate associations. Accordingly, the integrative review searched for scholarly research published after the LGC's enactment and those which pertained to investigating the relationship between fiscal decentralization and equitable development in the Philippines. The comparison thus centered on varying findings regarding the IRA's contribution to shared growth, and the bases therefore.

Outcomes

Treating IRA as the intervention, we looked into one of its specific outcomes. The IRA is linked to a range of economic, social and political consequences, intended and unintended. We focused our interrogation on shared growth. Shared growth is sometimes used interchangeably with inclusive growth as both call for a holistic understanding of development by integrating pro-poor and pro-marginalized orientations. Both concepts challenge traditional economic development indicators which fail to measure quality of life and how certain individuals and groups are left behind despite a rise in national income. The World Bank has clarified that inclusive growth "refers to both the pace and distribution of economic growth" (Anand et al., 2013: 1), the latter reflecting equity considerations. Inclusiveness is considered a broad concept that "encompasses equity, equality of opportunity, and protection in market and employment transitions" (Lanchovichina & Lundstrom, 2009: 2). Despite this conceptual breadth, shared growth is the term most associated with "income distribution schemes" (Lanchovichina & Lundstrom, 2009: 2). Analyzing the East Asian Miracle in eight high-performing economies, the World Bank previously defined shared growth as rapid growth with equity. Maquito (2017) supports this view based on clarifications during the 14th Annual Global Development Conference of the Asian Development Bank in Manila in 2013: shared growth pertains to "equality of outcomes" while inclusive growth refers to "equality of opportunities". This is not to say that shared growth dispenses with increases in real income because distribution presumes the existence of resources to be allocated. Shared growth thus involves reducing the gap between the rich and the poor alongside poverty alleviation. Accordingly, for purposes of the study, we chose the term shared growth as it accurately captures our inquiry on fiscal decentralization as a strategy for (re)distributing both power and resources. Our overarching research question is thus: does IRA contribute to shared growth?

To operationalize the inquiry, we translated shared growth into two of its most essential aspects: efficiency, which reflects growth, and equity which highlights the shared aspect of growth. This presents a deconstructed interpretation of shared growth as an increase in income that adequately addresses human development needs, and at the same time benefits the entire population and not just a select few. In other words, shared growth entails two things: (1) the ability to provide relevant, quality, and timely goods and services at the least cost and with the least waste using minimum resources, and (2) ensuring that everyone, especially the marginalized, has access to and benefits from such goods and services, at par with the rest of the population. These twin goals align with widely held motivations behind fiscal decentralization and are typically translated as *vertical* and *horizontal fiscal im/balance* (Manasan, 2020). We use the latter terms in the study.

Vertical fiscal imbalance Efficiency denotes optimal use of resources, with numerous measures and indicators in the field of development economics. In the context of decentralization, efficiency presupposes the availability of resources for financing goods and services at the local level. Of particular interest to our inquiry is what fiscal federalism refers to as "vertical fiscal balance". Such balance exists "when transfers to subnational authorities combined with their own revenues (and borrowing) are sufficient to finance their expenditure responsibilities" (Boadway & Eyraud, 2018: 6). Implied in this notion of balance is the concept of vertical fiscal gap or the difference in locally-generated revenues and the total spending of local governments. National transfers like the IRA are common sources for filling the gap though it is not the only means. Local governments can also meet the deficit through subnational borrowing. The idea is that not all development spending should be exclusive to local or national entities. Subsidiarity, responsiveness, and accountability call for fiscal decisions at the local level. But goods and services that are best provided through economies of scale and risk-distribution may be better left to the central government (Boadway & Eyraud, 2018). In the Philippines, the LGC delineates expenditure responsibilities. Though the same code empowers local governments to raise their own revenues, most are not able to do so and rely on the IRA (Manasan, 2007; Panao, 2020). In this context, understanding the relationship between the IRA and the efficiency aspect of shared growth seeks to examine studies that touch on the vertical fiscal balance and answer the first research question: does the IRA contribute to vertical fiscal balance in the Philippines?

Horizontal fiscal imbalance As for the equity aspect of shared growth, we considered the concept of "horizontal fiscal balance" which is achieved when vertical fiscal balance exists not only in the aggregate, but also across subnational jurisdictions (Boadway & Eyraud, 2018). Horizontal fiscal balance is premised on the public finance principle of horizontal equity or equal treatment of equals. The reality of fiscal transfers is that some local governments may receive more or less funding than what is needed to cover devolved expenditures or provide comparable quality of services. While the situation can be traced to pre-existing disparities in local resources and fiscal capacities (Courchene et al., 2000), fiscal transfers–when blind to such uneven landscape–can exacerbate divergences in regional and per capita income. This is of particular interest in the Philippines given the country's archipelagic configuration, the resulting heterogeneity in natural resources and vulnerabilities among localities, and the growing overall income inequality. Interrogating horizontal fiscal imbalance in the context of the IRA prompts a closer look at the core purpose of intergovernmental transfers, i.e. to reduce inequalities across local governments, and the redistribution dimension of shared growth. In our study, exploring the relationship between the IRA and the shared aspect of growth seeks to analyze studies on the redistributive and equalizing effects of national transfers. Hence, we expressed our second research question as: does the IRA contribute to horizontal fiscal balance in the Philippines?

11.2.2 Literature Search

Guided by the articulated questions on the IRA and fiscal and horizontal and fiscal imbalance in the Philippines, we conducted an online database search of relevant academic studies. Given the geographic specificity of the study, we tried to expand the source of scholarly articles by searching twelve (12) local and international database sites which offered institutional access based on our university affiliations. The selection was limited to original peer-reviewed journal articles to ensure disciplinal validation. Only those published in English from 1991 onwards were considered, to cover the period after the enactment of the Local Government Code of 1991 which mandated the IRA.

One challenge encountered in dealing with multiple databases was the variations in the search functions of each source. For instance, the Philippine eJournals did not have the usual advanced search option that could refine coverage to a target period

Table 11.3 Search results from online databases

Online database	Search results	
	Round 1	Round 2
EBSCO research databases	206	76
Emerald insight	14	10
JSTOR	57	25
Philippine eJournals	1434	18
Project MUSE	21	12
Proquest	39	30
SAGE journals	76	29
ScienceDirect	80	51
SpringerLink	35	25
Taylor & Francis journals	233	99
WILEY online library	227	67
Oxford academic journals	227	32
Total	2,649	474

(*Source* Authors).

or a specified word string. To maintain consistency across different databases, we purposely broadened the initial search terms to *Philippine fiscal decentralization* (without quotation) in titles, abstracts, key words, and contents of relevant articles. This wide net also enabled us to capture more articles from the initial search despite the specificity of our research query.

Table 11.3 presents the number of articles yielded from this first round of search (Round 1). For databases which yielded more than 300 articles, an advanced search was undertaken using the search terms "*internal revenue allotment*" (with quotation) to narrow down the initial search results. We set such a threshold for another layer of search for practical reasons, i.e. to save us from a manual, article by article check to confirm the relevance of several hundred articles. This additional protocol applied to Proquest but not to Philippine eJournal which had limited search functionalities. Since our interest is in the Philippines, the second round of the search (Round 2) aimed to sift the results for studies relating to the country of focus. This involved title and abstract review by each of the researchers to select articles that focused on the Philippine case, or analyzed cross-country data that included the Philippines.[6] As shown in Tables 11.1 and 11.3, this second filtering process led to a more manageable set of 474 articles. Using Mendeley as a library management platform, a total of 51 duplicates were removed.

[6] One article by Sepulveda and Martinez-Vazquez (2011), which analyzed cross-country panel data, did not indicate the countries included. Researchers corresponded with one of the authors who confirmed that the Philippines was included in the study.

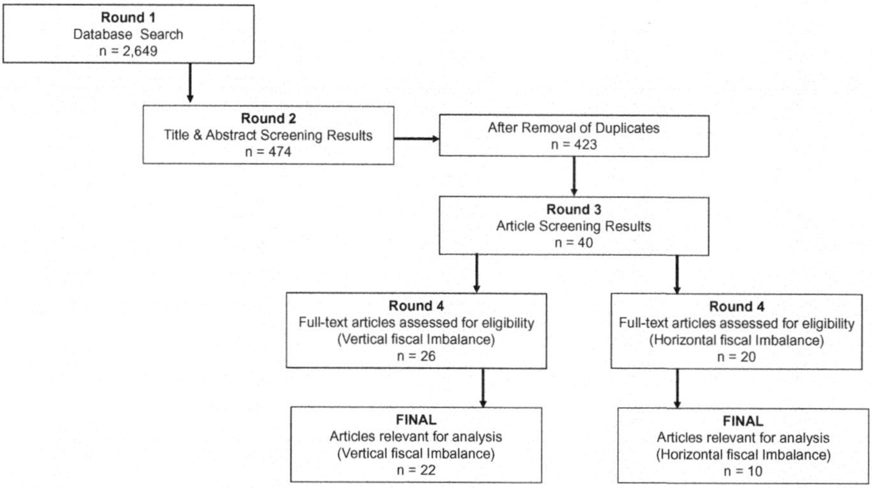

Fig. 11.2 Overview of the integrative review data collection process. (*Source* Authors)

11.2.3 Data Evaluation

Researchers then cursory read the 423 articles to identify 40 papers that directly and indirectly pertained to fiscal decentralization and shared growth (Round 3). Past this stage, each researcher independently screened the articles to shortlist the final studies eligible for assessment (Round 4). One researcher (Maquito) identified 22 articles on the relationship between the IRA and vertical fiscal imbalance, while the other (Cortes) selected a final set of 10 papers discussing the relationship between IRA and horizontal fiscal imbalance. Excluded in the process were studies that merely mentioned the variables without linking them, directly or indirectly. We considered studies of various methodologies (quantitative, qualitative, and mixed) and reserved a discussion of their distinctions in the analysis. A total of 32 articles were identified as relevant to the research questions on vertical and horizontal fiscal imbalance. An overview of this data collection procedure is presented in Fig. 11.2.

11.2.4 Data Analysis and Presentation

Each author analyzed the selected articles for vertical and horizontal imbalance separately. To lend consistency in the treatment of the studies, we adopted a common data extraction template detailing characteristics and observations–including the methodology, variables, and their relationship-on each article in an Excel spreadsheet.

Mindful of varying approaches for establishing the relationship of variables, we adapted the classification used in a 2016 study of Channa and Faguet. Their research also employed a systematic review of decentralization literature, but focused mainly on quantitative evidence and health and education mechanisms and efficiency outcomes in developing countries. They qualified their approach as a "quality adjusted review" to discriminate among scholarship based on the credibility of evidence presented. This led them to catalog their selected literature into four tiers distinguished based on the rigor of the empirical method applied to "evaluate the causal effects of decentralization in service delivery" (Channa & Faguet, 2016: 201). The spectrum ranged from Rank 1 studies characterized as having a Strongly Credible Identification Strategy to Rank 4 as Less Credible, expressing preference for robust econometrics in evaluating the quality of evidence (see further discussion on the ranking in Sect. 11.4). For our purposes however, we applied Channa and Faguet's categories to organize and qualify findings–and not to exclude studies from the analysis–since we have at the outset broadened our scope to include articles of diverse research approaches. Accordingly, we refer to each class as "level", instead of "rank" to emphasize classification over order. Table 11.4 presents the categories of literature we followed for analysis.

We provide separate discussions about horizontal and vertical fiscal imbalance, using both tabular and narrative presentations of the studies selected and their findings. As the nature of the research on these topics vary, we examine in the next section the themes and pathways through which decentralization contributes to efficiency and equity aspects of shared growth.

Table 11.4 Categories of literature selected decentralization vis-à-vis horizontal and vertical fiscal imbalance

Category	Description
Level 1	Quantitative studies that employ a "valid comparison group", which have limited endogeneity concerns. These include application of the gold standard for establishing causality, i.e. randomized control trials
Level 2	Quantitative studies that apply quasi-experimental designs and compare groups with efforts to address some endogeneity concerns. These include research using "panel estimates in a fixed effects model"
Level 3	Quantitative studies based on comparison groups that are not robust, and contain endogeneity bias. These include research using cross-sectional or panel data with fixed or random effects
Level 4	Quantitative studies based on "self-selected populations" using "less sophisticated" empirical methodologies. These include research with serious endogeneity challenges, as well as qualitative studies

(Adapted from Channa and Faguet, 2016).

11.3 A Systematic Review of Literature on Horizontal Imbalance (Equity)

The survey of literature relating to the relationship between IRA and horizontal imbalance yielded a pre-final set of 20 journal articles.[7] These included publications that one way or the other had conclusions or commentaries, whether as main arguments or as *obiters*, regarding the relationship of the two variables of interest, i.e. fiscal decentralization (FD as the broad concept for IRA) and horizontal fiscal imbalance (HI). As discussed in the section on the integrative review methodology, given specific interest in the Philippines, the survey was limited to studies that focused on the Philippine case or considered cross-country data which included the Philippines.[8]

A careful reading led to the exclusion of 10 articles based on the strict application of the relevance criteria. Relevance was determined not just based on what a study had to say about the association of variables but also on how such was established. Our research considered both qualitative and quantitative approaches. Regardless of the method, only the articles which considered both FD and HI as variables and which sought to establish, no matter how loosely or tangentially, their relations appeared. In other words, excluded in the final analysis were articles that: merely associated FD with HI as a general observation without relating the variables; measured either FD or HI only; or did not refer to HI as a disparity but instead considered other socio-economic factors that could directly or indirectly influence horizontal inequality.

The final 10 articles subject of the analysis are listed in Table 11.4 according to their publication years. All except for one (the most recent) were quantitative studies which employed different statistical methods ranging from descriptive comparisons[9] to sophisticated techniques using data on the Philippines alone,[10] or cross-country.[11] While all the selected literature measured FD and HI, their indicators varied. Some considered FD as part of a larger decentralization process, which includes political devolution. Others measured FD based on local income or revenue. Two studies used proxy indicators for overall inequality such as land value divergence[12] and health outcomes.[13] The period covered likewise varied across years before and after the time the IRA was instituted through the adoption of the LGC.

---

[7] This includes one study (Diana 2008) selected based on the supplementary chain literature review.

[8] Rodriguez-Pose authored and co-authored numerous publications on fiscal transfers and equity, but the studies yielded from the database searches did not include them as these were not about the Philippines. Cross-country data were often about Latin American states and other contexts that did not include the Philippines.

[9] Akita & Pagulayan (2013); Capuno (2012); Balisacan et al., (2006).

[10] Silva (2005); Balisacan & Hill (2006); Diana (2008); Capuno (2012); Akita & Pagulayan (2013); Yeeles (2015).

[11] Shankar and Shah (2003); Sepulveda & Martinez-Vazquez (2011); Lessman (2012); Abimbola et al., (2019).

[12] Capuno (2012).

[13] Abimbola et al., (2019).

11.3.1 Pathways

Before categorizing the 10 articles into Channa and Faguet's four levels of literature, it is useful to present briefly the pathways through which we can examine the possible effect or contribution of fiscal decentralization and horizontal equity. Appreciating these pathways guided further analysis of the literature to surface patterns and nuances in the findings.

Theoretically, it could be that FD and HI are mutually exclusive and have no association. Development literature however does not support this and assumes the contrary. This is evident in the motivations behind the subnational distribution of budgets which has been a feature, although to varying extent and mechanisms, in almost all governance systems. Economics and political science peddle decentralization, both administrative and fiscal, as strategies of national development (Andriesse, 2017; Bahl & Linn, 1994; Sepulveda & Martinez-Vazquez, 2011). Moreover, a common justification for FD is its ability to promote equity in incomes and services among subsidiary entities.

This assumption provides the basis for the first pathway which captures FD's **equalizing effect**. An idealized view of FD has underpinned the Philippines' IRA policy as a mechanism for reducing regional disparities. The rationale is that with funds regularly earmarked for and infused into local government alongside the authority to independently raise local income through taxes and fees, each LGU will have sufficient means to provide goods and services necessary to achieve development goals. The IRA's supposed stimulative effects are also designed to contribute to its redistributive role (Shah 2006). Studies have shown that fiscal transfers are associated with increased subnational spending, which is expected to translate to more and better goods and services.

The equalization promise however encounters the reality of pre-existing disparities, which offers the counter argument of the second pathway or the FD's **negative distributional effect**. Not all LGUs start equal. They differ in initial income, leadership, talent pool, infrastructure, taxing capabilities, natural resources and disaster vulnerability, among many others. An across the board fiscal transfer like the IRA, enable these asymmetries to favor richer localities over poorer ones, making less developed LGUs lag even more than their already well-off counterparts (Capuno, 2002; Panao, 2020). For instance, the National Capital Region and neighboring provinces enjoy a broad tax base of the urban population, business and industry, as well as the highways, ports and bridges that enable production of goods and services, and generation of income. One of the poorest provinces, Agusan del Sur.[14] does not have access to these inputs and will not have the same efficiency to produce comparable goods and services despite having the similar proportional share from the national income. Inequitable results are further traced to the formula for the IRA itself (Guevara, 2000; Manasan, 2007). The computation for each LGU's share factors in

[14] Based on the Official Poverty Statistics of the Philippines, Philippine Statistics Authority (First Semester 2021). https://psa.gov.ph/sites/default/files/2021%201st%20Poverty%20Stats_Full%20Publication_17Dec2021_rev5.pdf.

Table 11.5 Categories of articles based on Channa & Faguet's level of literature (*Source* Authors)

Level	No. of articles	Articles
Level 1	0	–
Level 2	4	(Shankar & Shah, 2003; Sepulveda & Martinez-Vazquez, 2011; Lessman, 2012; Yeeles, 2015)
Level 3	2	(Silva, 2005; Diana, 2008)
Level 4	4	(Balisacan et al., 2006; Capuno, 2012; Akita & Pagulayan, 2013; Ambimbola et al. 2019)
Total	10	

population and land area, but remains blind to the uneven realities on the ground. In addition, central governments are seen to have greater capacity and efficiency to undertake large scale redistribution efforts (Sepulveda and Martinez-Vazquez, 2011). Hence, central to local fiscal transfers divert the needed national resources to do so, exacerbating local disparities.

Different studies demonstrate how each pathway operates but the third pathway captures what scholars refer to as inconclusive or **mixed effects**. Decentralization is a complex intervention (Abimbola 2019; Hill, 2008) involving nonlinear processes. Its impacts are often mediated by other factors that can facilitate or hinder achievement of development outcomes. Accordingly, whether FD will address or exacerbate income disparities will depend on existing structural inequities across LGUs, the design of the fiscal transfer, the strength of institutions, and socio-political dynamics.

We apply the three pathways to illuminate how the selected literature of diverse methodological rigor explain the contribution of FD to HI. We acknowledge that such may only be one side of interrogating FD-HI relations, which may also involve ways through which HI could impact fiscal decentralization. The negative distributional effect depicts this dimension with pre-existing asymmetries mediating FD's consequences. We, however, do not go beyond this in our examination which is premised on fiscal decentralization, specifically the IRA, as the *a priori* intervention. We accept this starting point and one-way attention to FD and its impact on HI to be a important research limitation.

We now turn to applying the categories of Channa and Faguet (2016) in analyzing the 10 selected articles, as shown in Table 11.5. Although nine out of ten articles employed quantitative methods, not one study met the Level 1 criteria of having authentic comparison groups or robust research design for establishing causality. This was not surprising given the intricacies of fiscal transfers and the variations in their intent and design.[15] The articles fall under Levels 2 to 4 as follows, and are examined in the succeeding section.

[15] See Bahl and Linn (1994) for a comprehensive discussion of different typologies of intergovernmental transfers.

11.3.2 Level 2 Literature

Figure 11.3 compares the four articles that fall under Level 2. All of them employed statistical tests to establish association, including standard regression analysis. However, unlike Level 3 studies, their methodologies took into account a number of factors to manage endogeneity. Shankar & Shah controlled for population and level of development; Sepulveda & Martinez-Vazquez controlled for GDP, education, political system, age, urban population and ethnic fractionalization. Lessman controlled for GDP, number of regions, country size, unemployment, trade openness, ethnic fractionalization and urban population. Yeeles employed subgroup decomposition to compare inter- and intra- regional inequalities. All studies used the Gini coefficient as a measure of inequality likely because of the availability of data alongside other indicators on horizontal inequality. An exception is the study of Sepulveda and Martinez-Vazquez whose analysis relied on the Gini coefficient only. Except for Yeeles whose object of study was solely the Philippines, the rest involved cross country panel data across several years, with Lessman and Yeeles using a shorter timeframe but more recent data from a decade since IRA implementation.

Interestingly, three out of the four Level 2 studies had general findings supporting the first pathway. All these three used other HI indicators apart from the Gini Index. Sepulveda and Martinez-Vazquez's statistical analyses, though based on the Gini coefficient as the sole measure of HI, may still be considered most robust and unbiased for covering data of 56 states over 22 years and controlling for endogeneity. Lessman considered almost similar controls and the same sample size but explored different indicators for both FD and HR, although his indicators covered the broader notion of

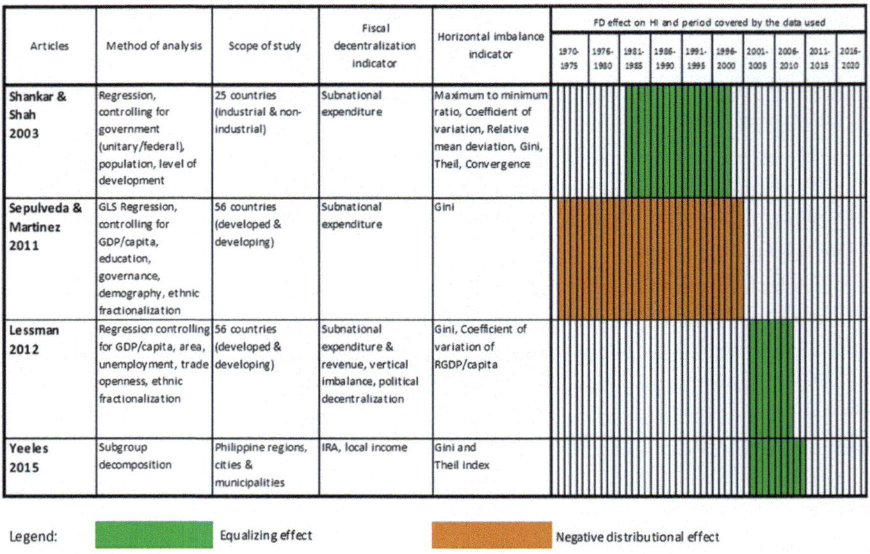

Fig. 11.3 Comparison of Level 2 papers. (*Source* Authors)

decentralization to include political devolution. Though Lessman used cross country figures from 1980 to 2009, Philippine data was limited to 6 years from 2002 to 2008, 10 years after the LGC adoption.

It is worthy to note that the main findings were qualified. Shankar & Shah tested if decentralized fiscal arrangements widen regional inequality by comparing regional income disparities in federal and unitary states. In their study, the Philippines was considered a unitary state absent a federal structure of governance in its devolution system. They found that "federal countries do better in restraining regional inequalities, because of the political risk those disparities pose for such countries" (2013: 1). The implication is that fiscal decentralization is more a political than an economic tool, which can nonetheless create a more equitable society. Lessman likewise found that decentralization decreases regional inequalities in general. However, panel data estimation using interaction variables of decentralization and GDP per capita revealed that the effect of fiscal transfers depends on a country's level of economic development. Developed economies benefit from the equalizing effect while less developed ones may suffer from a negative distributional effect. Lessman interpreted this finding to be based on higher efficiencies and greater mobility in developing countries.

Focusing on the Philippines as a case study, Yeeles also inferred that overall intergovernmental transfers have an equalizing effect among LGUs: "IRA does reduce LGU per capita income across national space" (2015: 399). He arrived at this conclusion by looking into spatial income inequalities among regions. He saw such inequalities to be relatively stable at least from 2001 to 2010, inclusive and exclusive of IRA transfers. He however observed that while inter-regional disparities remain the same, inequalities within regions, i.e. rural vs. urban centers and across districts, and inequalities are more pronounced. This is consistent with the observations of Balisacan et al., (2006) (to be discussed in Level 4 literature discussion) that inequalities in the Philippines are accounted for by intra- rather than inter-regional differences. Yeeles nonetheless absolves the IRA from the blame for much granular inequities, saying that "there is no immediate evidence that transfers are the cause of horizontal inequalities or contributing to a worsening of the inter-LGU fiscal situation" (2015: 400).

The lone finding of negative distributional effect was from Sepulveda and Martinez-Vazquez who have both done numerous rigorous research on decentralization and poverty. Like Lessman, they used panel and cross-country data of 56 countries[16] over a long period, the bulk of which predates IRA implementation. They correlated fiscal decentralization (expenditure decentralization measured as share of local government expenditures over total national government expenditures) with income inequality (Gini coefficient), while controlling for specific-country effects. Their analysis derived a positive and statistically significant relationship which indicated that "by itself, fiscal decentralization worsens inequality in the distribution of income" (2011: 333). But using an interaction term representing government size (defined as government share in the GDP), they qualify their observation in that the

[16] The article did not enumerate the included countries but email correspondence with one of the authors (Martinez-Vazquez) confirmed that data on the Philippines was part of the analysis.

effect of FD depends on the size of the government sector. In large governments (at least 20% government share in GDP), FD has an equalizing effect. Smaller governments suffer the negative distributional effect. The explanation lies in the capacity of central governments to engage in expansive redistribution roles when they are of a sufficient size.

11.3.3 Level 3 Literature

Two publications fall under the Level 3 category, namely the studies of Silva (2005) and Diana (2008). (See Fig. 11.4 below for a summary comparison of the articles). Both involved Philippines case studies and used standard correlation to examine how the IRA explains inequalities across regions and provinces, without the sophistication of controlling for endogenous variables. Although the studies used different indicators and covered different periods of data, both supported the negative distributional effect of the IRA.

Silva looked into disparities in socioeconomic indicators among political regions in the country before and after LGC implementation. He observed a "temporal coincidence in between devolution and increased regional disparities" and that "Philippine devolution in its present form contributes to (or even exacerbates) regional disparities" (2005: 414). This happens both directly and indirectly by interacting with other related factors. His findings echo the negative distributional narrative where marginalized LGUs who lack capacity and resources to begin with, fail to keep up with progressive LGUs who receive the same share of fiscal transfers.

Diana (2008) studied a shorter time frame, a decade after IRA institutionalization. Her approach to determine the impact of IRA on horizontal imbalances was straightforward: simple correlation between per capita IRA and average daily income. This inquiry was part of her general examination of the impact of the IRA on Philippine provinces. She found IRA to be counter-equalizing based on the consistently positive correlation coefficients.

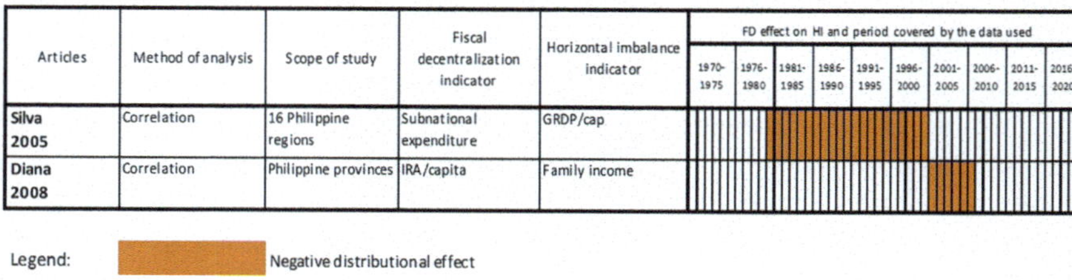

Fig. 11.4 Comparison of Level 3 papers. (*Source* Authors)

11.3.4 Level 4 Literature

This last category includes four articles, one of which is qualitative and is the most recent among the ten articles in our integrative review.

From Figure 11.5, it could be seen that the 2019 study of Abimbola and colleagues involved a systematic review of 51 publications concerning 51 countries and the impacts of decentralization on health system outcomes, including equity. Their synthesis of evidence centered on unpacking contextual factors and mechanisms that enable or hinder decentralization's contribution to health system equity. Accordingly, their paper did not make a definite position as to the equalizing or counter-equalizing effects of FD. Their premise and conclusion was that FD indeed has mixed effects depending on how a host of contextual realities (e.g. design of fiscal transfer, ease of migration, inter-LGU competition, civil society participation, elite pressure, accountability mechanisms) impinge on the three mechanisms of voting with the feet, close to the ground, and watching the watchers to shape equity in health services.

Two other studies (out of the four under Level 4) support the mixed effects finding. Balisacan et al., (2006), and Akita and Pagulayan (2013) both employed quantitative approaches in their analyses of Philippine regional data. They are however categorized under the lowest tier or methodological rigor because for purposes of determining the effects of IRA on HI, they merely looked at trends of inequalities before and after the adoption of the LGC. Baliscan and Hill were interested in broad regional disparities in the Philippines and ascertaining if the country is becoming more spatially related over time. They conducted an inter-regional comparison of socio economic indicators (GRDP, poverty, Gini ratio, life expectancy, literacy, education, HDI, population and migration, infrastructure, among others) from 1986 (pre-LGC) to 2005 (post-LGC). They found large regional disparities across all indicators. They found some presence of convergence (areas with close if not equal incomes) but noted that the trends were sensitive to the selection of administrative

Articles	Method of analysis	Scope of study	Fiscal decentralization indicator	Horizontal imbalance indicator	FD effect on HI and period covered by the data used									
					1970-1975	1976-1980	1981-1985	1986-1990	1991-1995	1996-2000	2001-2005	2006-2010	2011-2015	2016-2020
Balisacan & Hill 2006	Trend analysis	Philippine regions & provinces	Subnational expenditure, Decentralization policies	GRDP, Gini ratio, Regional price variations, Convergence				Mixed effects	Mixed effects	Mixed effects	Mixed effects			
Capuno 2012	Correlation	Philippine provinces & cities	Decentralization policies	Clustering of land values, Moran test statistics				Negative distributional effect	Negative distributional effect	Negative distributional effect				
Akita & Pagulayan 2013	Trend analysis	Philippines regions	Decentralization policies	Bi-dimensional decomposition of GRDP/capita, Theil index		Mixed effects	Mixed effects	Mixed effects	Mixed effects	Mixed effects	Mixed effects	Mixed effects		
Abimbola, et al. 2019	Qualitative, meta-analysis of studies	51 publications	Health system decentralization	Health system equity	Equalizing effect	Equalizing effect	Equalizing effect	Equalizing effect	Equalizing effect	Equalizing effect	Equalizing effect	Equalizing effect	Equalizing effect	

Legend: Equalizing effect; Negative distributional effect; Mixed effects

Fig. 11.5 Comparison of level 4 papers. (*Source* Authors)

boundaries. This means that the extent of income inequality largely varies depending on the politico-geographic unit used in the analysis. They acknowledged the mixed effects of FD based on literature explaining how center-region relations and quality of local governance affect equitable growth, and also from their own finding that income disparities across regions have remained largely unchanged before and after the institution of the IRA. After all, the Philippines is not yet fully decentralized given LGUs' dependence on the central state for decisions and resources.

Out of the four articles in Level 4, only Capuno (2012) observed a negative distributional effect. Like Abimbola et al., he did not measure the usual income inequality but examined regional disparities based on land prices over a fourteen year period before and after IRA implementation (1986–2000). His premise was that spatial clustering of land values may be indicative of development patterns across provinces and cities. He utilized the Moran statistic to test for convergence. While such an approach is quantitative, there was no statistical test or systematic comparison utilized to test the relationship of land price distribution (as a proxy for equality) and FD; hence, the Level 4 classification. Nonetheless, by comparing spatial distribution of land values pre- and post-LGC implementation, Capuno found a consistent pattern of divergence and pockets of clustering in Metro Manila and nearby areas. This trend has been indicative of further agglomeration economies under decentralization, where progressive cities like Makati receive a standard IRA share like the rest while earning billions for serving as the country's central business district. Like Guevara (2000), Capuno traces this phenomenon to the IRA formula which apportions a greater share for bigger land areas and more populous LGUs, regardless of their capacity to raise local income or govern.

11.3.5 Some Observations

Overall, the ten studies examined in this review demonstrate the three different pathways by which FD impacts HI. While four out of ten studies point to a negative distributional effect, such a simple majority must not be easily accepted as the prevailing view. Organizing the studies based on Channa and Faguet's categories reveals that Level 2 or the more rigorous research support the equalizing effect of fiscal transfers. In contrast, standard correlations without controls for endogeneity under Level 3 literature support the negative distributional effect. As expected and consistent with Channa and Faguet's observations, general trend and qualitative analyses produce more uncertain results. The mixed effects capture this by accounting for a range of contingencies that can mediate the impact of the IRA. This confirms the intricate operation of fiscal transfers in bringing desired developmental outcomes.

Likewise worth noting is how the type of data used in the studies relate to findings. Among Level 4 literature, the studies that supported an equalizing effect used other income inequality indicators other than the Gini coefficient. There is however no similar observation on the kind of indicator used to quantify fiscal decentralization, whether based on local expenditure or revenue, or IRA share. This demonstrates the complexity of the variables under study, especially horizontal fiscal imbalance. Martinez (1999) notes that unreliability of measuring such imbalance in terms of revenues or expenditures alone. High revenues may be driven by tax collection efforts more than real income. Similarly, expenditures can be misleading as they can be impelled by the existence of vulnerable groups, or in the Philippines special circumstances such as disaster or election spending. According to Martinez, horizontal imbalance on the revenue side can be more accurately represented by fiscal capacity or the size of potential tax base. Expenditures can also be adjusted for expenditure needs to present a more realistic and comparable picture. But there is usually a lack of data so researchers rely on less accurate proxies.

There is no discernible pattern in the IRA's impact based on the unit of analysis, i.e. whether the study used cross-country or Philippines specific figures, or whether the comparison was inter- or intra-regions. Nevertheless, the observations of Balisacan and Hill (2006) and Capuno (2012) regarding granular disparities at lower subnational levels deserve attention in future studies. This is especially because most of the studies relied on regional comparisons, perhaps due to availability of data. While regions are administrative and economic subdivisions, they are not the jurisdictional units endowed with devolved political and fiscal powers under the LGC.

Another remarkable observation is that studies that utilized data from 2001 onwards, or a decade since the implementation of the IRA, tend to favor IRA's redistribution feature. This is particularly true for Level 2 research, which as earlier discussed involve more robust research methodologies. While the LGC which institutionalized the IRA was enacted in 1991, its implementation happened incrementally. In fact, full devolution is still being pursued in light of the Mandanas-Garcia ruling of the Supreme Court. Decentralization is indeed a process that no matter how fast-tracked requires consistent and patient implementation. As Shankar & Shah (2003) revealed, federalized structures produce less inequalities than centralized ones. It is likewise possible that the IRA's effects can only be felt after years or in this case a decade. Interaction variables such as the size of government (Shankar & Shah 2003) and level of development (Lessman 2012) relate to how fiscal transfers affect income disparities. The Philippines' increased government spending and improved economy especially after 2003 may explain the IRA's egalitarian contributions.

11.4 A Systematic Review of Literature on Vertical Imbalance (Efficiency)

The survey protocol yielded 22 papers related to vertical imbalance, with two studies for Level 1, six studies for Level 2, three studies for Level 3, and 11 studies for Level 4. This section presents the results of these papers and its discussion, in four subsections.

11.4.1 Level 1 Literature

Unlike the horizontal imbalance (equity) review, there are two papers in the Level 1 category, which involve the use of Randomized Controlled Trial (RCT): Channa and Faguet (2016) and Capuno and Schustereder (2015).[17]

Channa and Faguet (2016) was not an RCT but was a multi-country, including the Philippines, review of related literature that covers papers using RCT. We, however, do not replicate this review, but simply distill the relevant results, of which there are two. (Our review, therefore, could be considered as an independent one that is more focused on the experience of the Philippines.) One is the confirmation that influential studies on the effects of decentralization produce mixed results. Another is that a survey of related literature that considers the quality of the methodology reveals the pattern that "higher-quality evidence indicates that decentralization increases technical efficiency across a variety of public services, from student test scores to infant mortality rates" (Channa & Faguet, 2016: 199). Technical efficiency here refers to "the production of more or better public goods by a decentralized government for a given set of inputs" (Channa & Faguet, 2016: 201–202). "Higher-quality evidence" refers to studies categorized as utilizing strongly credible identification strategies.

Channa and Faguet (2016) ranked the reviewed literature into the following four categories, according to the rigor of the methodology used.

Rank 1: Strongly Credible Identification Strategy.

- Research that contains a valid comparison group
- Work that is likely to have extremely limited endogeneity concerns
- Studies such as randomized control trials fall in this category

Rank 2: Strongly Credible Identification Strategy.

- Research that is able to construct a reasonable comparison group
- Work that specifically attempts to address sources of endogeneity and is mostly successful in its attempt
- Studies using quasi-experimental designs such as difference in differences and instrumental variables fall in this category
- Studies using panel estimates in a fixed effects model while controlling for more than one socio-economic covariate and more than one covariate from the health/education production function may also fall here

Rank 3: Somewhat Credible Identification Strategy.

- Research that attempts to construct a comparison group but with limited success
- Work that is likely to continue to suffer from some endogeneity biases in spite of efforts at mitigation

[17] Given the higher quality of the literature related to vertical imbalance, we dispense, in this section, with a deeper analysis of the papers, such as those given for Figs. 11.3, 11.4, and 11.5 for the horizontal imbalance literature.

- Studies based on cross-sectional data but using specific techniques to create a comparison groups fall in this category
- Studies using panel data with random effects or between effects models may fall in this category
- Papers using difference in differences but without providing support of parallel trends, papers using IV not considered particularly strong and papers using fixed effects but with very limited covariates may fall in this category

Rank 4: Less Credible Identification Strategy.

- Research that bases findings on self-selected populations
- Work that is likely to suffer from serious endogeneity challenges
- Studies based on cross-sectional data that do not use any other sophisticated methodology to address endogeneity fall in this category

It should be noted that Channa and Faguet (2016) did not cover qualitative research since they considered a cross comparison of such studies to be intractable. Our systematic review generally follows the stress on methodological rigor orientation of the Channa and Faguet survey. Our Levels 1 and 2 generally correspond with the Ranks 1 and 2 of Channa and Faguet. Our Level 3 is a combination of Ranks 3 and 4 of Channa and Faguet, while our Level 4 contains the qualitative studies. We included qualitative studies for the insights that they provide on the factors related to decentralization and vertical imbalance.

Capuno and Schustereder (2015) utilized RCT to answer a research question that is less directly related to our research question than Channa and Faguet (2016) is. It, however, is more direct in that it focuses on the case of the Philippines, covering 12 municipalities and cities, with eight acting as treated and four as control subjects. The period covered is 2001–2003; hence, the subjects are already under the decentralized regime. Treated subjects are LGUs that conveyed an index of governance to its citizens and local officials. This index is a "composite of ten subjective and objective indicators that assess the performance of the local government in terms of expenditure priorities, how well it meets its constituency's demand for public services, and the extent of public consultations" (Capuno and Schustereder 2015: 523). In essence, their study examined the responsiveness of citizens and local officials to being exposed to information about local governance.

The findings of Capuno and Schustereder (2015) show mixed results: only four out of the nine responsiveness indicators (namely, desired changes in local public services, mayor responds to barangay needs, mayor responds to complaints, and mayor can be approached for personal needs) showed significant correlation with the treatment, but were surprisingly negative. This, however, does not to detract from the results of Channa and Faguet (2016), which addresses a different but more direct question related to decentralization and vertical imbalance. Citizen and local official responsiveness to governance performance indicators, the concern of Capuno and Schustereder (2015), is conceptually one more step away from vertical balance than technical efficiency, the concern of Channa and Faguet (2016).

11.4.2 Level 2 Literature

There were six studies considered as Level 2 literature, which are quantitative studies that considered causality although not quite at the level of rigor of Level 1 literature. With the exception of one, the other five studies found generally positive effects of decentralization on the vertical imbalance.

Utilizing panel data estimation methods for 63 countries from 1960–2007, Im (2010) found a negative relationship between the GDP growth rate and political/ fiscal decentralization. Even when dividing into income groups, the negative relationship was found to be significant except in the case of developed nations. Applying pooled estimation of cities and municipalities for average values over 2011–2015 while addressing the issue of endogeneity, Canare and Francisco (2019) found that decentralization, as measured by the share of local revenues to total LGU revenues, is negatively related to poverty, and much more so in the case of the poorer LGUs. Using panel data estimation methods for 80 Philippine provinces for 2006, 2009, and 2012, Canare (2021) found that fiscal decentralization, as measured by the share of local revenue share to total local expenditures, has a stable and significantly positive effect on welfare, as measured by income per capita and the Human Development Index, but not on poverty. Moreover, the better the governance, as measured by the Good Governance Index published by the Philippine Statistics Authority, the higher the impact of fiscal decentralization on welfare. Using regression analysis, which dealt with the endogeneity problem, for various models covering 587 to 1,363 municipalities, Kelekar (2012) found that "on average, an increase of one percent of neighboring local government expenditure is associated with an increase of 0.1073% in the level of health spending of a given region" (p. 25). Using panel data estimation methods for 65 low-and middle-income countries including the Philippines for the period 1980 to 1997, Khaleghian (2004) found that decentralization is associated with higher immunization coverage rates in low-income countries, but lower coverage rates in middle-income countries. The turning point for the GDP per capita was estimated to be around 1,400 US$ (in 1995 prices). Since the Philippine GDP per capita from the World Bank even in 2015 prices was 778.1 for 1980 and 1288.6 in 1997, the Philippines could then be considered a low-income country for which the positive relationship between decentralization and immunization applied.

The evidence from this category, therefore, leans in favor of a positive relationship between decentralization and vertical imbalance in the Philippines. The lone dissenting study, Im (2010), may be too aggregated or too indirect in its dependent variable to be of significance. While Khaleghian (2004) was also cross-country, it provided a way of discerning the case of the Philippines. Dependent variables for the four favorable studies were also more directly related to public services (health services spending and immunization) and to welfare (poverty, income per capita, and HDI).

Using an endogeneity-adjusted regression analysis of 209 innovations by 48 Philippine cities and municipalities over the period of 2004 and 2008, Capuno (2011) found that fiscal capacity, as measured by LGU budget per capita, has a positive but diminishing relationship with innovations. There is no explicit relation between innovations and vertical imbalance. But one possibility is suggested by looking at the definition of innovations. In Capuno (2011) "each respondent was asked to identify her LGU's six top or best innovative programs, with three of them in expenditures services and the other three in revenue or public administration services. The innovations could be an output (e.g., health insurance service), process (e.g., simplified business licensing procedure) or organizational (e.g., wider people's consultation). The key distinction is that the service was supposed to be new and significantly improved compared to previous or current ones (p.54)". There is, therefore, a possible positive effect on vertical imbalance since innovation leads to an efficiency improvement (decreasing cost for the same amount of service or more service for the same amount). Inter-LGU networks also appear to be good for innovations, while exposure trips do not.

Inter-LGU competition was raised in two of the above-mentioned studies. The spatial effects found by Kelekar (2012) was considered to be a manifestation of competition among LGUs for health resources. On the other hand, Canare (2021) mentions the "unintended consequence" of a possible increase in inequality among LGUs, since lower income LGUs tend to have lower benefits from decentralization.

The possibility of an optimal level of decentralization was raised by Khaleghian (2004), Capuno (2011) and Canare and Francisco (2019), beyond which the positive gains from decentralization start to wane. Capuno (2011) found that innovations no longer increase beyond a certain point of fiscal capacity. Canare and Francisco (2019) cited economies of scale and the rise of corruption as possible factors that may hinder further decentralization.

11.4.3 Level 3 Literature

There are three studies considered as level 3 literature, which is mainly quantitative but of lesser rigor than the other two levels in establishing causality. All three studies found some positive aspects associated with decentralization.

Using regression analysis across Philippine cities in 2013, Canare (2016) found a stable positive relationship between IRA and health and social security/services expenditures. Moreover, it was found that one peso increase in IRA and locally sourced revenues would be accompanied by a one peso increase in city government expenditures. Although these were larger than usually expected, the effect of inter-local funds or funds from other LGUs was estimated to be about 2.5 times larger. Canare (2016) posits this to be due to the conditionalities attached to inter-local funding, such as earmarking for specific uses and counterpart funding. Nevertheless, inter-local funding remains to be a very small part of city revenues.

Estimating probability models for Philippine cities and municipalities over the period of 2001–2010, Capuno (2013) found that the increase in IRA is one of the factors driving the conversion of a municipality into a city. Population density was not. Moreover, conversion contributed to the political longevity of the initiating local government executives or their affiliates. Capuno (2013), however, notes that the additional benefits of gerrymandering will in time vanish. As more municipalities convert to cities, the IRA share of each becomes smaller, thus making the quest for cityhood less attractive.

Using regression, which captured spatial effects on 96 Philippine cities in 2008, Estrada (2012) found that fiscal policies on education and basic services displayed spatial effects; that is, these affected similar policies of neighboring LGUs. No spatial effects, however, were found for taxation and health/nutrition policies. Such spatial effects contribute to reducing both vertical and horizontal imbalances. This evidence tends to support the "political yardstick competition" theory of Besley and Case (1995), wherein local public policy may react to the policy of neighboring jurisdictions, in effect "benchmarking against others to identify superior and more effective approaches tested in other LGUs in the delivery of public services, taxation policies, and of areas in which they can improve" (Estrada, 2012: 134). The evidence, however, does not seem to support tax mimicking among local governments under the "Tiebout model" of tax competition.

11.4.4 Level 4 Literature

Our survey yielded eleven papers that could be considered generally qualitative in approach and in coverage. As expected, the findings are mixed. Notably, compared to the literature categories above, more Level 4 studies provide poor assessments of decentralization and its impacts on vertical imbalance.

Abimbola et al., (2019) conducted a survey of 51 decentralization-related studies covering 25 countries, including the Philippines, and three decentralization mechanisms (voting with feet, close to the ground, and watching the watchers) that could affect LGU efficiency. Voting with feet involves inter-LGU competition, which was found to produce efficiency losses on the part of poorer LGUs. For instance, patients gravitate to the health services provided by richer neighbors, who in turn enjoy efficiency gains brought about by economies of scale. Moreover, when poorer LGUs are not able to generate local revenue, they are often forced to charge user fees. The "close to the ground" mechanism refers to the devolution of authority to the LGU. When this is adequately done, the LGU could be more efficient in terms of adoption of proper services and provision of incentives. "Watching the watchers" refers to the accountability of lower level to higher level of government units. This has been found to contribute to enhancing efficiency of LGUs where such mechanisms are properly functioning.

Balisacan et al. (2006) also provided a survey of findings on three local governance mechanisms. With regards to "voice", they observed that local government elections in the Philippines have generally not been an effective instrument for exacting accountability, but activist or high-quality LGUs can make a difference. As for the mechanism of "exit", they found that the impact of this mechanism remains unclear, and that interregional migration in the Philippines is extensive, although the principal explanatory factor appears to be relative income levels, that is migrants selecting richer regions rather than necessarily better-governed ones. With regards to the mechanism of "neighborhood effect", they assert that the evidence of positive neighborhood effects is not compelling: well and poorly governed LGUs are frequently contiguous, even allowing for the possibility of lagged demonstration effects.

On the subject of funding, Bautista (2012) gave a generally poor assessment of the ability of LGUs to attract Public Private Partnerships (PPPs) as an additional source of funding. He attributes this to: the reality on the ground of LGUs not being able to finance PPPs without external financing such as loans from Government Financial Institutions or ODA grants; the lack of clarity on the oversight responsibilities and devolved functions of LGUs; and the lack of capacity to demonstrate project feasibility and high rates of returns to private investors.

Du (2017) gave a poor assessment of the viability of good governance in the Autonomous Region of Muslim Mindanao (ARMM) under federalism, considering that decentralization appears to stop at the regional level, with poor accountability (public funds easily become private funds) and financial management skills of the leaders. Despite the huge influx of funds from various sources, ARMM is one of the poorest regions in the country.

Lakshminarayanan (2003) concluded that after five years of implementation of devolution, gains in health outcomes at the national level remained unexceptional in many LGUs. This is attributed to: a hurried devolution process; the national health agency's resistance to devolution; improper definition of services; mismatch of cost and revenues of devolved functions; and lack of capacity building.

Shair-Rosenfield (2016) identified the factors causing the low quality of governance and public services as follows: lack of financial resources; weak accountability of local executives to their electorates; and persistence of patronage politics. Based on expert opinions, Liwanag and Wyss (2018) identified a set of hindering/facilitating factors on the effect, albeit mixed, of decentralization in the health sector.

The remaining qualitative studies tend to provide a positive note. Sumbalan (2007) asserted that fiscal decentralization improved the provision of medical services in Bukidnon, a province in Southern Philippines. This was mainly attributed to the political will to carry out reforms to improve administration of public health services. Hospitals are treated as income centers to ensure that services are improved and reimbursements from public health insurance are maximized. Based on case studies of two small Philippine municipalities, Atienza (2004) found that people's participation proved to be the most crucial variable in actual improvements in local cases of health service delivery. Porley and Gabito (2018) validated this more specifically in the case of Civil Society Organizations.

Bahl and Linn (1994) provided a taxonomy of the eight most popular forms of intergovernmental transfer in various LDCs. Type B, the type of transfer, which is most preferred in terms of national, local, and joint considerations, uses a fixed share of the national or state tax to determine the total divisible pool, and divides this amount using a formula. It is the type being used in the Philippines through the IRA, and is preferred in terms of minimizing the vertical imbalance since it enables the LGU to have control over local finances (non-earmarked funds), efficiently plan budgets (anticipate receipts), and increase the adequacy of fund flows (versus funds determined *ad hoc*). Type B is also preferred for equalizing services and fiscal capabilities among LGUs since it allows the national government to set the parameters of the formula, and applying it uniformly across a certain LGU category.

11.5 Synthesis

Our survey yields two key considerations in designing and implementing decentralization policies: the tradeoff between efficiency and equity; and decentralization's mixed results. Studies have voiced concerns that pushing efficiency, and hence, shrinking the vertical imbalance could inadvertently widen the horizontal imbalance as more capable LGUs pull away from the less capable. The observed mixed results tend to cast doubt on the effectiveness of decentralization efforts to address both vertical and horizontal imbalances. Either of these observations would be enough to throw decentralization policy makers into a state of paralysis. From a macroscopic perspective, this may well be occurring in the case of the Philippines. Despite being branded by the World Bank as a "fast starter" in decentralization and nearly 30 years of decentralization under its belt, the Philippines continues to suffer from efficiency and equity issues, or the absence of shared growth.

To address the trade-off issue, it is recommended that two independent but related policy instruments be employed to separately target efficiency and equity. There should be no hesitation to promote efficiency where LGUs could push ahead. At the same time, a separate policy instrument should be employed to address the equity issue.

An example of the latter instrument is the development equalization fund. Manasan (2020) found that "the incremental IRA due to the April 2019 SC IRA ruling 66 out of 81 provinces (or 81.5%), 43 out of 145 cities (or 29.7%) and 161 out of 1,489 municipalities (or 10.8%) will not be enough to allow them to provide comparable levels of re-devolved PAP [Programs, Activities, Projects] services" (p.12). Her recommendation is to adopt "equalization grants to address the horizontal imbalance problem" (p.13).

Another strategy to address the trade-off issue is the adoption of "two-birds-with-one-stone" (2B1S) policies. In fact, the equalization fund, as proposed by Manasan (2020), could be such a policy given that it has the following design considerations that ultimately contribute to enhancing LGU fiscal efficiency:

1. The grants should be unconditional and given in lump-sum so they can be used "without limitation and constraints" as if they are local revenues. This allows better matching of services to local needs, for as long as service packages do not become too small.

2. Grants should "not create negative incentives for revenue mobilization... neither should they induce inefficient expenditure choices." The idea is not to simply help increase income but to expand fiscal capacity.
3. Allocation "should be simple and transparent" and "not be subject to political manipulation or negotiation in any of its aspects." This ensures that LGUs will not shirk in their efforts to provide public services, and can be held accountable by citizens.
4. Grants should not result in the diminution of existing unconditional transfers. This reduces disincentives to access the fund, and mitigates efficiency losses due to poor governance (Manasan, 2020: 13).

These design parameters are remarkably similar to the features of a Type B intergovernmental transfer discussed by Bahl and Linn (1994) as contributing to local government fiscal efficiency.

Our integrative review points to at least two other 2B1S strategies. One would be the active utilization and promotion of innovation networks. Based on Capuno (2011), such networks enhance the efficiency of LGUs by driving LGU innovation, and promoting the sharing of innovations among LGUs. This presents the possibility of catching up (advantage of latecomers). The neighborhood or spatial effects found by Estrada (2012) suggests another 2B1S strategy. The "political yardstick competition" model of Besley and Case (1995) further confirms that local public policy may react to the policy of neighboring jurisdictions. Modeling and benchmarking can spur diffusion of good local governance practices.

True to form, the Philippines appears to be living up to its reputation as a "fast starter" in the sense that compared to Indonesia and Thailand (Cortes & Maquito 2022), the Philippines is pushing ahead in its budgetary reform with the Supreme Court Ruling of 2018 in Mandanas-Garcia. The additional IRA mandated by the SC ruling will be funded by unfunding the PAPs that were supposed to be done by the LGUs but were being implemented by and financed through national government agencies. The unfunded PAPs will then be re-devolved to the LGUs concerned.

With respect to the mixed results found by our review, trends in the conclusions of studies examining vertical and horizontal imbalances suggest the importance of methodology in evaluating decentralization. Evaluation results tend to be more "unmixed" or conclusive as more rigorous methodology is employed in clarifying the causality among the research variables. In fact, the pattern that emerges is that decentralization has positive effects on efficiency and equity, particularly over time or years after the LGC's full implementation.

One crucial upshot of this observation is for evaluations to be done using methodologies that are more rigorous in establishing causality. As our survey shows, such methodologies appear to be not popularly employed. Any evaluations using such methodologies can equip policy makers to see beyond the fog of mixed results and craft policies based on clear evidence.

The mixed results issue also suggests that decentralization efforts should be taken on a case-by-case basis. This essentially goes beyond the differing capabilities of LGUs, and requires looking at the willingness of LGU leadership and constituents to embrace and promote decentralization. Studies have shown that even the poorest or fiscally-strapped LGUs could find ways to improve their situation, such as by involving the private sector including civil society organizations, networking with other LGUs for best practices or even financial assistance, and enabling entrepreneuring local chief executives. Scarce resources could be better channeled to such LGUs. Cortes and Maquito (2022) observed in the cases of the Philippines, Indonesia, and Thailand that LGUs, when adequately empowered, could contribute to reducing the vulnerability and raising societal resilience against crises such as pandemics.

Cities are important engines of economic development due to their ability to exploit economies of scale and connectivity to the rest of the world. These qualities, however, are the very same reasons that make cities super spreaders in the event of an outbreak. Excessive population density leads to congestion, marked by overcrowding especially in the low-income sectors of the city. Major cities would most likely become hubs that attract high flows of people and goods from abroad. To counteract this, it is imperative to intensify decentralization so as to have a wider distribution of connections. This will serve as well to strengthen localized means of production for essential provisions such as food and medical supply chains, and build regional resilience to sudden shocks in global supply chains (UN-Habitat, 2021).

References

Abimbola, S., Baatiema, L., & Bigdeli, M. (2019). The impacts of decentralization on health system equity, efficiency and resilience: A realist synthesis of the evidence. *Health Policy and Planning, 34*(8). https://doi.org/10.1093/heapol/czz055

Akita, T., & Pagulayan, M. S. (2013). Structural changes and interregional income inequality in the Philippines, 1975–2009. *Economics & Management Series*. https://cir.nii.ac.jp/crid/1570572702937374464?lang=en

Anand, R., Mishra, S., & Peiris, S. J. (2013). Inclusive growth revisited: Measurement and determinants. *Economic premise*, no.122. https://openknowledge.worldbank.org/handle/10986/22618

Andriesse, E. (2017). Regional disparities in the Philippines: Structural drivers and policy considerations. *Erdkunde, 71*(2), 97–110. https://doi.org/10.3112/erdkunde.2017.02.01

Atienza, M. E. L. (2004). The politics of health devolution in the Philippines: Experiences of municipalities in a devolved set-up. *Philippine Political Science Journal, 25*(48), 25–54. https://doi.org/10.1080/01154451.2004.9754256

Bahl, R., & Linn, J. (1994). Fiscal decentralization and intergovernmental transfers in less developed countries. *Publius, 24*(1), 1–19. https://doi.org/10.2307/3330701

Balisacan, A. M., Hill, H., Piza, S. F. A. (2006). Regional development dynamics and decentralization in the Philippines: Ten lessons from a 'fast starter'. *Journal of Southeast Asian Economies*. https://crawford.anu.edu.au/acde/publications/publish/papers/wp2006/wp-econ-2006-14.pdf

Bautista, L. (2012). Alternative approach to local economic development: A case for fiscal decentralization through a localized public-private partnership. *BEL Journal*. https://ejournals.ph/function/author.php?id=3832

Besley, T., & Case, A. (1995). Incumbent behavior: Vote-seeking, tax-setting, and yardstick competition. *American Economic Review, 85*(1): 24–25.

Boadway, R., & Eyraud, L. (2018). *Designing sound fiscal relations across government levels in decentralized countries* (IMF Working Paper No. 18/271). https://www.imf.org/en/Publications/WP/Issues/2018/12/10/Designing-Sound-Fiscal-Relations-Across-Government-Levels-in-Decentralized-Countries-46425

Canare, T. (2016). The relationship between IRA and local government expenditures: Evidence from a cross-section of Philippine cities. *Philippine Political Science Journal, 37*(3), 167–189. https://doi.org/10.1080/01154451.2016.1236476

Canare, T. (2021). Decentralization and welfare: Theory and an empirical analysis using Philippine data. *Public Sector Economics, 45*(1), 93–123. https://doi.org/10.3326/pse.45.1.3

Canare, T., & Francisco, J. P. (2019). Decentralization, fiscal independence, and poverty in the Philippines. *Public Budgeting & Finance, 39*(4), 94–117. https://doi.org/10.1111/pbaf.12241

Capuno, J. J. (2002). Philippines, in P. Smoke and Y.-H. Kim (Eds.), *Intergovernmental Fiscal Transfers in Asia: Current Practice and Challenges for the Future*. Manila: Asian Development Bank.

Capuno, J. J. (2011). Incumbents and innovations under decentralization: An empirical exploration of selected local governments in the Philippines. *Asian Journal of Political Science, 19*(1), 48–73. https://doi.org/10.1080/02185377.2011.568243

Capuno, J. J. (2012) Agglomeration and sub-regional disparities under decentralization: Evidence of spatial clustering of land values in the Philippines. *Review of Urban & Regional Development Studies, 24*(3): 106–120.

Capuno, J. J. (2013). Fiscal transfers and gerrymandering under decentralization in the Philippines. *Lex Localis-Journal of Local Self-Government, 11*(3), 409–429. https://doi.org/10.4335/11.3.409-429(2013)

Capuno, J. J., & Schustereder, M. M. G. (2015). The correlates of local government responsiveness under decentralization: Do performance ratings matter in the Philippines? *International Journal of Public Administration, 38*(7), 521–532. https://doi.org/10.1080/01900692.2014.949747

Channa, A., & Faguet, J. (2016). Decentralization of health and education in developing countries: A quality-adjusted review of the empirical literature. *World Bank Research Observer, 31*(2), 199–241. https://doi.org/10.1093/wbro/lkw001

Cooper, H. (1998). *Synthesizing research: A guide for literature reviews* (3rd ed.). Sage Publications.

Cortes, D. T., & Maquito, F. C. (2022). Implications of full devolution on vertical and horizontal gaps in fiscal decentralization: The case of a fast starter. *Proceedings: Compilation of Full Papers and Short Papers, The 6th Asia Future Conference*. Atsumi International Foundation.

Courchene, T., Martinez-Vazquez, J., McLure Jr, C. E., & Webb, S. B. (2000). Principles of decentralization. In M. M. Guigale & S. B. Webb (Eds.), *Achievements and challenges of fiscal decentralization: Lessons from Mexico* (pp. 85–122). The World Bank. http://www1.worldbank.org/publicsector/learningprogram/Decentralization/achievementsandchallengesCH1.pdf

Diana, M. E. (2008). The impact of internal revenue allotment on Philippine Provinces. *National Tax Research Center Tax Research Journal, 20*(6): 1–32.

Du, E. C. (2017). Federalizing the autonomous region in Muslim Mindanao. *Progressio Journal on Human Development, 11*(1), 80–96. https://ejournals.ph/article.php?id=13487

Estrada, R. D. (2012). Estimation of interdependent behavior of city government units of the Philippines using the Les Model. *International Journal of Business and Management, 2*(1), 132–153.

Guevara, M. M. (2000). Decentralization and economic development: The Philippine experience. *Hitotsubashi Journal of Economics, 41*(2), 97–109. https://doi.org/10.15057/7712

Hill, H. (2008). Globalization, inequality, and local-level dynamics: Indonesia and the Philippines. *Asian Economic Policy Review, 3*(1): 42–61.

Im, T. (2010). Does decentralization reform always increase economic growth?: A cross country comparison of the performance. *International Journal of Public Administration, 33*(10), 508–520. https://doi.org/10.1080/01900692.2010.509712

Japan International Cooperation Agency (JICA). (2009). *The study on the improvement of internal revenue allotment (IRA) system in the republic of the Philippines*.

Jimenez, E., & Paqueo, V. (1996). Do local contributions affect the efficacy of public primary schools? *Economics of Education Review, 15*(4), 377–386. https://doi.org/10.1016/S0272-7757(96)00029-5

Kelekar, U. (2012). Do local governments interact fiscally while providing public health services in the Philippines? *World Medical & Health Policy, 4*(2), 1–33. https://doi.org/10.1515/1948-4682.1233

Kelekar, U., & Llanto, G. (2015). Evidence of horizontal and vertical interactions in health care spending in the Philippines. *Health Policy and Planning, 30*(7), 853–862. https://doi.org/10.1093/heapol/czu086

Kelekar, U. (2012). Fiscal competition in health spending among local governments in the Philippines. *WHO South-East Asia Journal of Public Health, 2*(3), 198. https://apps.who.int/iris/handle/10665/329799

Khaleghian, P. (2004). Decentralization and public services: The case of immunization. *Social Science & Medicine, 59*(1), 163–183. https://doi.org/10.1016/j.socscimed.2003.10.013

Lakshminarayanan, R. (2003). Decentralisation and its implications for reproductive health: The Philippines experience. *Reproductive Health Matters, 11*(21), 96–107. https://doi.org/10.1016/S0968-8080(03)02168-2

Lanchovichina, E., & Lundstrom, S. (2009). *Inclusive growth analytics: Framework and application,* Policy Research Working Paper 4851. https://documents1.worldbank.org/curated/en/771771468180864543/pdf/WPS4851.pdf

Lessmann, C. (2012). Regional inequality and decentralization: An empirical analysis. *Environment and Planning A: Economy and Space*, *44*(6), 1363–1388. https://doi.org/10.1068/a44267

Liwanag, H. J., & Wyss, K. (2018). What conditions enable decentralization to improve the health system? Qualitative analysis of perspectives on decision space after 25 years of devolution in the Philippines. *PLoS ONE, 13*(11), 1–20. https://doi.org/10.1371/journal.pone.0206809

Luna, C. Z., & Maquito, C. F. (2020). Decentralization, Land Value Taxes, and Shared Growth in the Philippines. *Paper Presented in the 5th Asia Future Conference*

Manasan Rosario, G. (2007). *IRA design issues and challenges* (No. 2007–09). Philippine Institute for Development Studies Policy Notes. ISSN 1656−5266

Manasan, R. G. (2020). *Fiscal sustainability, equity, and allocative efficiency in the light of the 2019 Supreme Court ruling on the LGUs' share in national taxes,* Discussion Paper Series No. 2020–18. https://pidswebs.pids.gov.ph/CDN/PUBLICATIONS/pidsdps2018.pdf

Martinez-Vazquez, J., & Timofeev, A. (2010). Decentralization Measures Revisited. International Studies Program Working Paper 09–13. Andrew Young School of Policy Studies, Georgia State University, USA.

Maquito, F. C. (2017). Decentralization, the internal revenue allotment, and shared growth: An examination of correlations. *Journal of Public Affairs and Development, 4*: 109–142.

Methley, A. M., Campbell, S., Chew-Graham, C., McNally, R., & Cheraghi-Sohi, S. (2014). PICO, PICOS and SPIDER: A comparison study of specificity and sensitivity in three search tools for qualitative systematic reviews. *BMC Health Services Research, 14*, 579. https://doi.org/10.1186/s12913-014-0579-0

Panao, R. A. L. (2020). Beyond flypaper: Unconditional transfers and local revenue generation in the Philippines, 1992–2016. *International Journal of Public Administration, 44*(15), 1341–1354. https://doi.org/10.1080/01900692.2020.1759628

Philippine Statistics Office. (2020). Philippine standard geographic code. https://psa.gov.ph/classification/psgc/downloads/SUMWEBPROV-SEPT2020-CODED-HUC-FINAL.pdf

Porley, J., & Gabito, S. L. (2018). Making decentralization work for the poor: Synergistic coproduction of housing services for informal settlers in Manila and Quezon City. *Luz Y Saber, 12*, 47–60. https://research-manila.letran.edu.ph/article/134.

Sepulveda, C. F., & Martinez-Vazquez, J. (2011). The consequences of fiscal decentralization on poverty and income equality. *Environment and Planning C: Government and Policy, 29*(2), 321–343. https://doi.org/10.1068/c1033r

Shair-Rosenfield, S. (2016). The causes and effects of the local government code: Locked in the status quo of weakly decentralized authority. *Journal of Southeast Asian Economies, 33*(2), 157–171. https://www.jstor.org/stable/44132299

Shah, A. (2006). Local Governance in Industrial Countries. Public Sector Governance and Accountability. Washington, DC: World Bank.

Shankar, R, & Shah, A. (2003). Bridging the economic divide within countries: A scorecard on the performance of regional policies in reducing regional income disparities. *World Development, 31*(8): 1421–1441.

Silva, J. A. (2005). Devolution and regional disparities in the Philippines: Is there a connection? *Environment and Planning C: Government and Policy*, *23*(3), 399–417. https://doi.org/10.1068/c051

Sumbalan, A. T. (2007). Local governance of devolved hospital services: The Bukidnon model. *Liceo Journal of Higher Education Research, 5*(1). https://link.gale.com/apps/doc/A284553850/AONE?u=googlescholar&sid=googleScholar&xid=e9d718bc

UN-HABITAT. (2021). *Cities and pandemics: Towards a more just, green and healthy future.* United Nations Human Settlements Programme. https://unhabitat.org/cities-and-pandemics-towards-a-more-just-green-and-healthy-future-0

Victor, L. (2008). Systematic reviewing. *Social Research Update, 54*, 1–4. https://sru.soc.surrey.ac.uk/SRU54.pdf

Whittemore, R., & Knafl, K. (2005). The integrative review: Updated methodology. *Journal of Advanced Nursing, 52*(5), 546–553. https://doi.org/10.1111/j.1365-2648.2005.03621.x

World Bank. (1993). *The East Asian miracle, economic growth and public policy.* Oxford University Press.

World Bank. (2005). *East Asia decentralizes: Making local government work.* https://openknowledge.worldbank.org/handle/10986/7492

Yeeles, A. (2015). Intergovernmental fiscal transfers and geographical disparities in local government income in the Philippines. *Southeast Asian Economies*, *32*(3), 390–401. https://www.jstor.org/stable/44132216

Part III
Toward a Better-Balanced Economic Development

Chapter 12
Akamatsu's Flying Geese Model of Development in East Asia and Beyond

Abstract In this chapter, we shall discuss the development as well as changes accompanying the birth and succession of the Flying Geese Model, which has garnered attention with regards to thinking on East Asia's economic development since the second half of the 1980s. This model was given birth by Kaname Akamatsu in the 1930s. Due to the series of developments of East Asian countries in the 1960s, it evolved from research that was mainly advanced by Akamatsu and his successors to a globally-acclaimed veritable East Asian Development Theory by the second half of the 1980s. Interest and thinking on the model, however, greatly changed from Akamatsu's original German historical approach to modern economics approaches, as well as into an East Asian development model that is led by Japan. In this chapter, we return to the original problem statement of the Flying Geese Model, and consider the significance and issues of Akamatsu's Flying Geese Model in today's context.

Keywords K. Akamatsu · Flying Geese model · China · Japan · K. Kojima

12.1 Introduction

Amidst the development achievements of East Asian countries, from the second half of the 1980s to the 1990s, the Flying Geese Model (FGM) has gained worldwide recognition as a theory to explain the development of the East Asian region. Up to then, an economic development model, which had influence only within Japan, piqued global interest. This was because, from the point of view of an economics that analyzes individual national economies, an analytical approach of the development of the East Asian region was also a big issue. The FGM was seen as a response to this issue.

Derived from Kaname Akamatsu empirical research of latecomer Japan's industrialization in the 1930s, the FGM, since the second half of the 1980s, became the theory of the continuous regional development of various East Asian countries. However, the approach for explaining or the manner of perceiving Akamatsu's FGM

H. Hirakawa and F. C. Maquito, *The Dynamics of Asian Economic Development*,
https://doi.org/10.1007/978-981-97-3106-0_12

significantly differed between the 1930s and the 1960s. The FGM was refined to match the dramatic changes in the academic world after the Second World War.

The reality of the East Asian economy, however, is once again dramatically changing. How should the FGM adjust to this reality? The effectiveness of thinking about the economy based on original empirical work is once again sought after.

In this chapter, we will track the birth and development of Akamatsu's FGM, as well as the changes therein in its exposition and issues of concern, so as to shed light on the features within the original FGM and its successors. In the second section, we shall establish the background and developments that led to the global interest on Akamatsu's FGM. In the third section, we shall consider the basic problems and conceptualization of Akamatsu which led to the birth of the FGM in the 1930s. Furthermore, we shall track the exposition of the FGM that emerged under new appearances in the 1950s and the 1960s, and compare the newly developed theory with Akamatsu's original FGM. In so doing, we shall observe the model's transformation into a theory of East Asian development that is led by Japan. In the fourth section, we shall consider some points that should be discussed in relation to the FGM, and finally summarize the present day issues and significance of the FGM.

12.2 The International Acceptance of the Flying Geese Model

Since the economic development of East Asian countries accompanying the second half of the 1980s, the FGM of the late Japanese economist Kaname Akamatsu (1896–1974) became an instant international sensation. The late Kiyoshi Kojima (1920–2010), Professor Emeritus of Hitotsubashi University, perceived the FGM as "one of the general theories of economic development", and explained the international acceptance of Akamatsu's FGM in the post-war era in terms of the first period covering the 1960s and the 1970s, and the second period from the second half of the 1980s.

In the first period, Akamatsu's own English paper on the FGM was published in 1961 and 1962, and was named as the "catching-up product cycle" (CPC) following the product life cycle (PLC) hypothesis of R. Vernon in 1973. It was a period that discussed the development of East Asian countries.

In actuality, the 1960s was a period giving rise to the issue of creating a new world economic order with the increasing danger of global protectionism as the American dollar crisis deepened while Europe and Japan were achieving economic growth. In Japan, the Association for World Economic Studies (AWES)[1] in November 1969 inaugurated the "Long-Term Prospects of World Trade" project, which aimed to explore the expansion of world trade in the next 15 years, and published the six volumes of "1985 World Trade". In 1972, its first volume "Japan's Trade Structure

[1] The AWES is an organization established in 1954, supported by the government and powerful businesses, and has at its core Japan's international economics researchers.

and Development" was issued under the supervision of a Professor at Hitotsubashi University, Kojima. This was the fruit of tens of research meetings over two years, and was an exploration into the ideal method of Japan's future export industry amidst the global economy (Kojima -J, 1972a: 3).

In the first volume, Akamatsu gives a synthesis of Japan's Flying Geese development in the first chapter, while Kojima, in the second chapter, compares the FGM with the main theories of Europe and America on the international division of labor. In that chapter, Kojima considered Vernon's Product Life Cycle model and Hecksher-Ohlin's Factor Endowment model as being limited to a "one-industry, one-product" partial analysis, and sought to overcome such limitations through a dynamic model of industrial development using the FGM (Kojima -J, 1972b). He also studied the difference in the character of the FDI of American and Japanese firms, and reached the conclusion that Japan's FDI "harmoniously promotes the restructuring of North–South trade" (Kojima -J, 1972c: 147).

This project's achievement would be the crowning point of the FGM's first period. Kojima named the FGM as the CPC model, and, as the development of the East Asian economy was starting, analyzed the theory and policy of the upgrading of the Japanese economy's industrial structure, using the FGM. This was reported in a book he edited, which was also published abroad in English (Kojima, 1973a, 1973b). Kojima's first-generation and Akamatsu's 2nd-generation pupil, the late Yamazawa Ippei (1973–2018), Professor Emeritus of Hitotsubashi University and who is also member of the APCE Conference of Eminent Persons, was in charge of the that report's third chapter on "Industrial Development and Foreign Trade".

In a 1990 paper, Yamazawa explains the naming of the FGM as follows. In an English paper published in February 1973, Kojima "renamed the pattern as catching-up product cycle after its association with the product cycle model of Vernon (1966). The new name conveys more precisely the underlying mechanism of industry development ... , but the original name has gained greater popularity because of its poetic image" (Yamazawa, 1990: 4).

In the second period, the Fourth Pacific Economic Cooperation Conference held in Seoul in 1985 started with a special presentation by the late Saburo Okita (1914–1993). Formerly with the Ministry of Foreign Affairs, he was known as a celebrity among bureaucrat-economists since the post-war recovery period of Japan. In his speech, he used the FGM to explain the development of various East Asian countries. Kojima observed that "since then, the FGM became extremely famous, highly-esteemed, and popularly used not only in Japan but also various Asia–Pacific countries, international institutions, conferences, governments, businesses, and media" (Kojima -J, 2000a, 2003b: 5). In short, interest on the FGM was different from that it received in the first period, as it became accepted as development theory of East Asia.

Entering the 1990s, Japan's Economic Planning Agency (now, the Cabinet Office) and the Ministry of International Trade and Industry (MITI: now, the Ministry of Economy, Trade and Industry: METI) have been using the FGM to explain the East Asia regional development in government reports such as white papers on the economy, global economy, and trade (Economic Planning Agency -J, 1994a, 1994b; METI -J, 2001).

Even international institutions began introducing the FGM in relation to the development of South Korea and Taiwan. The 1993 issue of UNCTAD's Trade and Development Report for the first time touched on the 'flying geese pattern", while the 1995 issue of the World Investment Report widely covered the "flying geese" paradigm. In Part II of Chap. 2 of the Trade and Development Report 1994, the first section of "Integration and industrialization in East Asia" explained in detail "the flying geese paradigm". Within the academe, the FGM became widely known, as interest on it grew since the 1980s. Sweden's Hans C. Blomqvist explains as follows.

> The concept of the 'Flying Geese' goes back to the time before World War II, but has been little known by Western economists until recently. ... The reason for the recent interest in the model by Western economists is no doubt the rapid ascendance of several East Asian countries to a status of important industrial producers and actors in international trade. As this development is frequently seen as a 'miracle', scholars have been keen to look for explanations, even unconventional ones, for what is going on in this region (Blomqvist, 1997: 13).

Incidentally, it is interesting to note that the World Bank's report "The East Asian Miracle" was published in 1993, which was about the same time as the reassessment of the FGM, but was not mentioned in the report. The FGM was considered as a separate theory to explain regional integration in East Asia. Moreover, from the new perspective of the development of today's East Asian newly industrializing economies, research has emerged viewing the FGM to be an old model (Baldwin, 2016).

How should we actually assess the FGM? Should we dispose of it as old-fashion in this greatly changing global and Asian economies? As both the world and Asia changes, it is but natural that the interest of researchers changed. The changes in the East Asian economy have been particularly large. Looking back, however, the FGM was born amidst greatly changing times nearly a century ago, regained interest half a century later, and has survived even to this day. As an economic development theory of Asia, it has provided good insights to future developments. Below, we would like to once again consider the significance of the FGM, as we take a comprehensive review of the model, going all the way back to its birth.

12.3 The Birth and Succession of Akamatsu's FGM

In this section, we will discuss the birth and succession of Akamatsu FGM. Born in the 1930s, Akamatsu's FGM at one time considered a large-area economic zone as being the same as the Greater East Asia Co-Prosperity Sphere. The defeat of Japan of course derailed the construction of the Greater East Asia Co-Prosperity Sphere. Since the 1950s, however, amidst the development of East Asia following Japan, the FGM was revived through the efforts of Akamatsu and his pupil Kojima. Through the addition of Kojima's new approach, new theories were vigorously advanced by the 1970s. At the same time, the interest in the FGM shifted from research on Japan's industrialization to research on the regional development of various East Asian countries. What manner of development theory is the FGM that includes both? We shall observe the features of this development and the problem awareness at the birth of the FGM.

12.3.1 Akamatsu's FGM: Prototype and Its Problem Awareness

Akamatsu FGM starts with his discovery of regularities in import, production, and export that arose from the industrialization of latecomer Japan. It is 1935. The regularity, which was discovered from research on the development of Japan's wool industry, was completed in a paper, published two years later, on the cotton industry. This could be said at the completion of the primary model.

However, in the discovery of the FGM, two problems, which he confronted from the 1920s and after the 1930s, were involved. One was the basic recognition of the regularities in latecomer Japan's industrialization and another was the empirical approach of economics.

With regards to the former, Akamatsu had an unwavering perspective throughout his life. In his speech at the 38th founding anniversary of Hitotsubashi University in 1960 and in his paper published in 1974, a year before his death, he consistently explained the FGM as related to the "heterogenization and homogenization of the world economy." Let us confirm this from his words.

> The first naming of the FGM of industrial development came from concluding in my 1935 manuscript "Trade Trends of Our Wool Industry" that "We could formulate, in one industry, an FGM of import, production, and export". As it is said, the theoretical analysis of the FGM is insufficient. This model, however, is a partial theory of the historical approach to what I call the world economy's heterogenization (division of labor) and homogenization (competition)…. Moreover, such heterogeneous relation and homogeneous relations, as in a seesaw game, gradually becomes more sophisticated such that the center of the theory is in high level heterogenization and high level homogenization (Akamatsu -J, 1974: 155, 156–157).

Such awareness could be confirmed from Koide Yasuji's recollections. Koide was Akamatsu's assistant, during his Nagoya Higher Commercial School days, and was charged with collecting and organizing the economic statistics, such as Japan's foreign trade and production.

> It was one morning in Showa 10 (1935), as our survey of our country's wool industry was proceeding to its research on trade. When I requested the good professor to take a look at the graphs I drew of the statistics that I could collect, the idea of a flying geese pattern came to him. Needless to say, this was an idea that was based on "the heterogenization and homogenization of the global economy" which he has nurtured for many years (Koide -J, 1975: 302).

Fig. 12.1 The Picture of a Flying Geese flock that Akamatsu put in his book (*Source* Akamatsu -J, 1974). *Note* The picture is labeled as "Dawn's Geese"

For the reader's reference, we present the photo in Fig. 12.1. Akamatsu inserted this photo in a book during his last years as the scenery that came to his mind as he looked at the patterns of import-production-export. In the caption to this photo, he writes "I hope that this photo at the beginning of the book would be a reminder of the origins of the 'Flying Geese' naming" (Akamatsu -J, 1974: v).

The Heterogenization and Homogenization of the Global Economy

What is the "heterogenization and homogenization of the global economy"? A 1932 paper is all about this. It gave a historical overview of the development of capitalism that started in England. "Observing the pre-war trade shares of England, Germany, France, and the US as well as Japan, it saw how today's major capitalist countries industrialized vis-a-vis other agricultural countries, somehow forming a heterogeneous relationship of the global economy. ... We can observe that in the industrialization of these countries the reflection of a particular pattern in the changes of the trade shares". Moreover, it states that "the tendencies, which appeared in the industrialization of China, India, and the like, was once experienced by Japan, and in the industrialization of latecomer countries, beginning with primary industries, is today moving the global economy towards homogenization" (Akamatsu -J, 1932: 259, 270).

Akamatsu recognizes the patterns in the changes of the trade structure, looking at the history of capitalism mainly from the perspective of latecomer countries. He writes that such patterns could be seen not only in Japan, but also in other countries such as China and India. Heterogenization of the global economy here refers to the change in trade relations with other countries from primary to manufactured goods, and also to the change in the international division of labor. due to the Industrial Revolution in England. Homogenization refers to the entry into a competition relation of the latecomer countries that have successfully industrialized and have become more similar in trade structure. At the same time, the heterogenization and homogenization that arise from such competition change the trade relationship to higher levels of heterogenization and homogenization. In short, Akamatsu, throughout his life, always held the viewpoint that considered the industrialization of latecomer countries within the history of the global economy, as well as the changing relationships and advancements therein.

Another issue that Akamatsu confronted was related to the methodology or epistemology of economics. We can see this in his 1937 paper, which is considered as the one that finally gave birth to the FGM. The title of that paper, which deals with the development of Japan's cotton industry, is unexpectedly "The Synthetic Dialectics of Japan's Economic Development", and allocates about two-thirds of its depiction to the "synthetic dialectics" (Akamatsu -J, 1937).

There is a reason for his stress on "synthetic dialectics" over simple dialectics. If we were to simplify, it is a recognition method that perceives the development process as the integration at a higher dimension of matters that are understood to be in conflict with each other. Under such a recognition method, he tried to reach an integrated understanding, on the one hand, of the materialistic dialectics of Marxism, which was then dominant and considers human ideas as reflected in things, and on the other hand, of the confirmation of the activeness of human ideas from the position of Hegel. Such awareness was gained from his experience in the 1920s.

He graduated in April 1919 from the Kobe Higher Commercial School (now Kobe University), entered the Tokyo Higher Commercial School (now Hitotsubashi University), and critically learned Marxism under Fukuda Tokuzō. At that time, Akamatsu had a strong interest in the labor movement, which is probably why he studied under Fukuda Tokuzō. This is because Fukuda was a researcher who studied under the German historian Lujo Brentano, and obtained his doctorate from Munich University.

Akamatsu became an instructor at the Nagoya Higher Commercial School in April 1921, and from March 1924 up to July 1926, was mainly studying in Germany. On his way home, however, he passed by America, which shifted his interest to research the industrialization of then latecomer Japan within the global economy. Before he went on foreign study, he was to handle "commercial policy" at Nagoya. This is why his goal in studying abroad was about "building the academic foundations of economic policy" (Akamatsu -J, 1975: 24).

As such, he would eavesdrop at Berlin University on the lectures of German Historian Economist Werner Sombart, and read Rudolf Stammler's *Wirtschaft und Recht* (Economy and Law), 1896 (Akamatsu -J, 1975: 26). At Heidelberg University, he participated in the seminar of Neo-Kantian Philosopher Heinrich John Rickert, and "he wrote a critical paper on Hegel's position up to Rickert's Neo-Kantism, published it in a German philosophy journal, from which he arrived on the idea of synthetic dialectics (Akamatsu -J, 1958: 501). In short, he came to consider that a concept, which is born from reality (intuitive reality) and is then put to work on reality, gives birth to a new reality (ideal reality). This came to be expressed as "synthetic dialectics".

As returning home to Japan drew closer, Akamatsu was ordered by the school head of the Nagoya Higher Commercial School, Dr. Ryusei Watanabe, to pass by America from April to June of 1926, where he visited Harvard's faculty of commerce and learned about its case method, among other things, and also went on site visits to the Industry Research Center and the Economic Research Center, which studied such things as management surveys and business cycles. It was there that Akamatsu came upon a big inspiration, which became a souvenir from his study abroad (Akamatsu, 1958: 501). The inspiration was about the fusion of synthetic dialectics, which he arrived at Heidelberg University as a research method, and Harvard University's empirical economics method. In short, it is conducting empirical research of economic theory building based on empirical data. Upon returning home, he right away recommended to School Head Watanabe the establishment of a survey research center, which materialized as Nagoya Higher Commercial School's "Industry Survey Section". He reflects on this as follows.

> The economics, which we are about to enter as empirical science, should not start from a priori concepts, but from intuitive phenomena gained from experience. Is it not this very survey research center that would be the road leading to the composition of scientific concepts from grasping the intuitive phenomenon in this experience. ... This idea came to me when I tied together Hegel and Harvard's empirical research (Akamatsu -J, 1975: 34).

With this thinking, he very quickly launched on the research published by N.D. Kondratieff on the theory of business fluctuations and long-term fluctuations, and in 1939 linked the long-term economic fluctuations with the "heterogenization and homogenization of the global economy". He published a theory on the correspondence of heterogenization and homogenization with their respective long-term fluctuations. This was included in his 1944 doctoral dissertation in the first chapter (second part) "Theory of the Formation of a New Economic Order" and in the second chapter "The Heterogenization and Homogenization of the Global Economy" (Akamatsu -J, 1944).

12.4 The Birth of FGM

In this way, the establishment of the Industrial Survey Section and its research brought about the FGM of the industrialization of latecomer Japan. For Akamatsu, the essential development process, as well as recognition process and research, which are inherent in the awareness of objective reality, the development of history, economics methodology, and every matter, are understood to be synthetic dialectics. As such, the regularity, where import, production, and export are consecutive, was extracted and discovered through the empirical research on latecomer Japan's industrialization.

> Except for Japan's unique silk making and tea industries, we can see the growth of import industries. ... We can summarize the various development phases as follows: phase 1 as the era of importation of finished goods; Phase 2 as the era of the rise of local production and decline of finished goods importation; and Phase 3 as the era of export industrialization of local goods. This is what I call the flying geese industrial development of Japan, since importation, production, and exportation come after another, separated in time, flourishing one after the other.
>
> Such an FGM of industrial development is a synthetic dialectic process. The expansion of imported finished goods faces the contradiction brought about by the weakening or decline of local industry due to the concentration of citizen's buying power on imported finished goods. The power to stop this contradiction, for one, lies in the natural flow of capital to the highly profitable manufacturing industries of imported goods, as well as the promotion of this movement by the state's economic policy. Hence, the expansion of imported finished goods cannot avoid changing to the rise of self production, in rejection of the above contradiction. ...In order to prevent the importation of finished goods, it becomes necessary to import the means of production, by which self production is established. As a primary motive, self-production, for as long as it is earnestly pursued, will stir up state protectionist policies, by which it is promoted. The fusion of the primary motive and the promotional motive will reject imports and establish self production. What comes next is the self-production of the means of production. During this stage, machinery and tools are adopted to the foundations of Japan through discovery and improvements that remove the contradictions and inappropriateness of foreign means of production. It is during this stage that establishment of the export industry is completed (Akamatsu -J, 1937: 197–198).

As such, Akamatsu concludes that Japan "clearly showed a flying geese-like development of imports-production-exports with regards to cotton thread, cotton cloth, spinning machinery, as well as all machineries and tools...[he] also saw a flying geese pattern in the self production being established from cotton thread and then to cotton cloth, and then to spinning machinery, and then to other machineries and tools." However, "self production must overcome this contradiction through low prices and labor costs. Here lies the death struggle in the era of establishing self production" (Akamatsu -J, 1937: 207, 209).

Bloc Economics and the Greater East Asia Co-Prosperity Sphere

His problem of interest, however, at this time was taken hostage by the environment of the era. Japan's industrialization gave rise to homogenization in global trade, intensifying market competition. Moreover, there are two coping policies taken. One is the creation of new industries, and another one is the widening (creation of blocs) of the economy. Amidst the intensification of the competition among imperialist countries, Japan also heads into the construction of economic blocs. Continuing on from the conclusions of the FGM, the 1937 paper adds the following supplementary statement, "the acquisition of raw materials as production factors is finally taking on an importance" (Akamatsu -J, 1937: 207).

As Japan's interest expanded to the Chinese continent in the 1930s, Akamatsu, at the core of his awareness of the "Japanese people", steadily became a subject. Although not central to our evaluation of the FGM, Box 12.1 briefly clarifies Akamatsu's posture on the Greater East Asia Co-Prosperity Sphere. The FGM then becomes an FGM led by the Japanese people. The problem of raw materials becomes a bridge to the Greater East Asia Co-Prosperity Sphere as an economic bloc. In his

1938 paper "Industrial Control Theory" and 1942 co-authored paper "General Theory of National Defense Economy", Akamatsu grasped the historical importance of the Greater East Asia Co-Prosperity, as he developed a stronger totalitarian thinking. He co-authors a paper published in June 1943 with Kojima entitled "Global Economy and Technology", in the introduction of which, he writes as follows.

> This paper was mainly the result of Kojima Kiyoshi's efforts in preparation of the essence of our co-authorship of the issues that we regularly discuss in our research office. ...Now, I have come to the South under the Greater East Asian War, and have partially taken the side of the military government.
>
> At the end of this book, I feel deeply moved to experience the Greater East Asia wide-area economy up close, as I look at its prospects. I would like to immerse myself for a while into the reality of the south, and reflect whether reality will move or should be moved as we anticipate January 1943 (Akamatsu, & Kojima -J, 1943: 2–3).

Box 12.1: Akamatsu and the Greater East Asian Co-Prosperity Sphere

As for Akamatsu's posture toward the Greater East Asian Co-Prosperity Sphere and the Greater East Asian War, Ihza thinks Akamatsu was a fervent supporter (Ihza Mahendra -J, 1998), A. Ikeo and T. Otsuki, on the other hand, think he was reluctant to cooperate to the point of being in opposition (Ikeo -J, 2008; Otsuki -J 2010), since a war between the US and Japan will be lost. Relying on Ikeo and Ōtsuki, Kasahara states that it is unclear as to how Akamatsu viewed the advance of Japanese imperialism (Kasahara, 2019: 186). Akamatsu leaned towards absolutist thinking in the 1930s (Akamatsu -J, 1937), and it cannot be denied that he cooperated with the Greater East Asian War in line with state policy. Owing to his synthetic dialectics thinking, he understood that a bloc economy was a natural conclusion to the industrialization of latecomer Japan. Moreover, Akamatsu was influenced by Hegelian philosophy, which regarded world history as the self-development of a unified "absolute spirit" of subjective spirit (mind, soul, consciousness) and objective spirit (law, morality, human morality). Moreover, Hegel's advocacy of the "absolute spirit" was regarded as "embodied as an emperor" and "Japan people" in Japan, and regarded its absolute superiority in Asia. In other words, a "conversion of faith" of other Asian peoples is considered to be quite natural. The contradiction, which Akamatsu is unable to recognize here, is that the "conversion of faith" is not natural and actually entails free choice (Hirakawa -J, 2013, 2021).

He wrote this introduction as the Director of Research of Japan of the Japanese Inspectorate General of Military Government, Southern Army. Moreover, this awareness of the problem was vividly shared in the July 1944 issue of "The Forming Principles of an Economic New Order", which became his doctoral dissertation. The whole paper became the theoretical system of synthetic dialectics, with the early part on "synthetic dialectics of a new economic order", and the latter part on the "synthetic dialectics of world economic development and formation". The first part discussion includes "the deployment principle of economic control' (Chap. 6), "the economic system of a military state" (Chap. 10), while the latter part includes "the heterogenization and homogenization of the world economy" (Chap. 3), and "the historical necessity of the formation of a bloc economy" (Part 2, Chap. 8).

The criticism of Akamatsu's FGM as propaganda for the Greater East Asia Co-Prosperity Sphere could be due to Akamatsu's leanings towards a controlled economy, and the unification of his bloc economics and the Greater East Asia Co-Prosperity Sphere. Akamatsu sought convergence of the formation of a Japan-led economic bloc, in other words the Greater East Asia Co-Prosperity Sphere, with the FG development of industrialized Japan. This, we dare say, is his leap from the theory of latecomer industrialization to Japanese imperialism, an academic unification to Japan's affairs at that time.

The Birth of the Kojima Theory

Kiyoshi Kojima, a disciple and co-author of Akamatsu during the war, evaluates the theory of the FGM after the war, stating only briefly that it was "buried during the Great War (= Greater East Asia War)" (Kojima -J, 2000a: 8). The fact of the co-authorship of Akamatsu and Kojima (Akamatsu, & Kojima -J, 1943) is also not mentioned. The reason for this is that, as we will see later, his awareness of the problem of the flying geese model was theorized in modern economics after the war, and there was also a sense of guilt in linking it to the Greater East Asia Co-Prosperity Sphere.

At the same time, however, Kojima had already come to think of Akamatsu's flying geese model in a larger framework by the 1970s. This is because Japan achieved high economic growth in the 1960s, and the international environment was changing dramatically as NIEs countries such as South Korea and Taiwan began to develop. Moreover, Japan is directly involved in its development. The perspective of international transfer of the FGM has emerged as an even more realistic issue. In the report of the 1972 Long-Term Outlook for World Trade project, Kojima wrote:

> Dr. Akamatsu's... development consists of the following three interrelated empirical studies, which form one unified theory. The first is the geese of industrial development, the second is the heterogeneity and homogenization of the world economy, and the third is the proximity and remoteness of trade areas. As will gradually become clear, since the first proposition is fundamental, and the second and third are external forms of phenomena, the unified theory of the three parties is also named here the "flying geese theory of industrial development" (Kojima -J, 1972b: 28).

Kojima's description of "Three Empirical Studies" here shows his basic understanding of the flying geese theory. The first empirical study is the study of the basic theory of Akamatsu, but the second "heterogeneity and homogenization" has two concepts, says Kojima. One is the relationship between "whether the industrial structure of a country and a particular foreign country becomes heterogeneous or homogeneous", and "this is probably the basic type of heterogeneity and homogenization" or "typical type". The other is that the historical heterogeneous relationship between the industrial nation of the nineteenth century between Britain and the agricultural countries changed to a relationship of "greater or lesser homogeneity", as industrialization spreads worldwide in the twentieth century. He says, "This can be seen as a variant of heterogeneity and homogenization" (Kojima -J, 1972b). Kojima tried to interpret Akamatsu's "heterogenization and homogenization of the world economy" as a reflection of the industrialization of one country in relation to other countries, rather than changes in the framework of the world economy accompanying the development of capitalism.

An explicit explanation for the third area of empirical research cannot be found, but there are references to the European Economic Community (EEC), European Free Trade Association (EFTA), and Latin American Free Trade Association (LAFTA), which were born in the 1960s. In these regional integrations, "trade between industrialized countries, which should have been homogeneous and conflicting, is increasing rapidly. A theory of competitive horizontal trade between industrial goods, which is different from complementary vertical trade, such as industrial goods versus primary goods, must be developed" (Kojima -J, 1972b: 32), indicating that intra-industrial trade is being kept in mind. In addition, Kojima once co-authored with Akamatsu to envision the economic sphere with trade in neighboring areas as Asian trade and trade in remote areas as trade with developed countries (Akamatsu & Kojima -J, 1943: 487–503). If we refer this to the third empirical study, it is likely that he had in mind whether the center of gravity should be East Asia or the United States in the future outlook of the Japan economy. This consideration was included in the flying geese theory.

In this century, Kojima writes that there are three phases of geese-type economic development. The first phase is the "catch-up process of one country's development", the second phase is the "international propagation of geese-type industrial development", and the third phase is the "geese-type development of the world economy".

The difference between the arrangements of Kojima in 1972 and in his later years seems to reflect the difference in the international economic environment surrounding Japan. The second phase of 1972 was focused on FDI into East Asia, which began with the industrialization of Japan. In its final years, the focus became the regional integration and development mechanism of East Asia in the 1990s. The third phase involves the structure of the global economy in addition to regional integration. Kojima examines this issue by using examples from Pax Britannica to Pax Americana, and the world order of today and the role of Asia within it (Kojima -J, 2004: i). The development of the less developed Asian countries will lead to the homogenization of the world economy. Nevertheless, heterogeneity for development is required. As can be seen in the formation and development of the EEC, economic integration and development are also issues in East Asia. Kojima inherited Akamatsu's awareness of the issue of the times.

At the end of 1974, Akamatsu passed away. And Kojima took over this task.

In the next section, I will confirm the multilayered cognitive structure of Akamatsu's flying geese theory as a theory of industrialization of latecomer countries, which are connected to the world economy.

12.4.1 The Basic Model of Akamatsu's Flying Geese Theory

Detailed tabulation and charting of Japan's imports, production, and exports since the Meiji period and the 1870s have been used consistently since Akamatsu's "Heterogenization and Homogenization of the World Economy" in 1932. However, it was not until the 1950s after the war that the regularization is considered to have reached the level of completion.

In his 1956 paper "The Flying Geese Development of Japan's Industry", he added another flying geese-type of development to the previous flying geese theory, saying, "Finally, one of the most important geese forms is that the geese-type development of one industry in each country appears one after another with a time lag due to the different stages of development of the latecomer countries". At the same time, the existence of the decline period was confirmed as imports would begin again at the stage of industrial development, and the example of England was cited (Akamatsu -J, 1956: 71). In 1937, the pattern of the flying geese development of latecomer and Japan industries was defined by the development of imports, production, and export by cotton yarn, cotton cloth, spinning and weaving machinery, and machines and tools, and "from semi-finished products to finished products, and then to finished means of production" (Akamatsu -J, 1937: 207).

In other words, through an empirical examination of the sophistication of the industrial structure of Japan in the 1950s, we confirmed a total of three types of flying geese theories: the succession of the development of "import, production, and export" of industry, the "upgrading from consumer goods to industrial goods, from crude products to refined products", and "international transfer of industry".[2] Three types of flying geese were mentioned as a description in a 1932 paper. In 1935, the patterns of the flying geese theory were recognized. The first two types were recognized in 1937, and the third type was recognized in a paper in 1956, and the original flying geese theory was completed. These were published in English in 1961 and 1962 to the world (Akamatsu, 1961, 1962).

The above conceptual diagrams of the flying geese model are shown in Figs. 12.2, 12.3 and 12.4. Figure 12.2 shows the industrial development of consumer and capital goods published in a 1961 paper. Figure 12.3 is the basic model of industrial development published in a paper in 1962. For the cotton yarn, cotton cloth, spinning and weaving machinery, and machines and tools industries, the curves for imports, production, and exports are drawn with a time lag. In short、 the first basic pattern is 'the sequence of import-domestic production-export', the second pattern is 'the sequence from consumer goods to capital goods and from crude and simple articles to complex and refined articles', and, the third pattern is "the alignment from advanced nations to backward nations" shown in Fig. 12.4 (Akamatsu, 1961: 208, 1962: 15). Of interest, however, is Fig. 12.4 listed in the literature of the 1970s (Akamatsu -J, 1974: 175). In this figure are shown only the countries where the industrialization of the latecomers has progressed from importing countries to production and export

[2] In Akamatsu's (1956) paper, he used the expression "variation" rather than "secondary form".

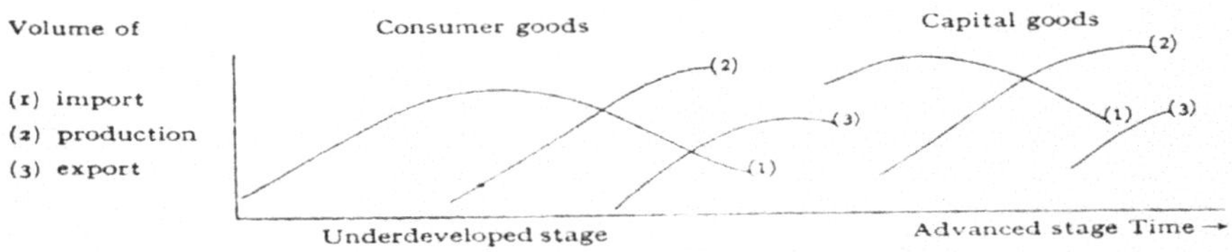

Fig. 12.2 The Flying Geese development from consumer goods to capital goods in a nation (*Source* Akamatsu, 1961: 206; Akamatsu -J, 1974: 175)

processes. This may mean that his awareness of the problems in his later years was still on the industrialization of latecomers.

Thus, the names of the three patterns were also named as follows in 1965.

> The successive importation, production, and exportation of an industrial product is called the basic form of the flying geese model, and the secondary forms are the succession from consumer goods to capital goods and from crude products to refined products. Furthermore,

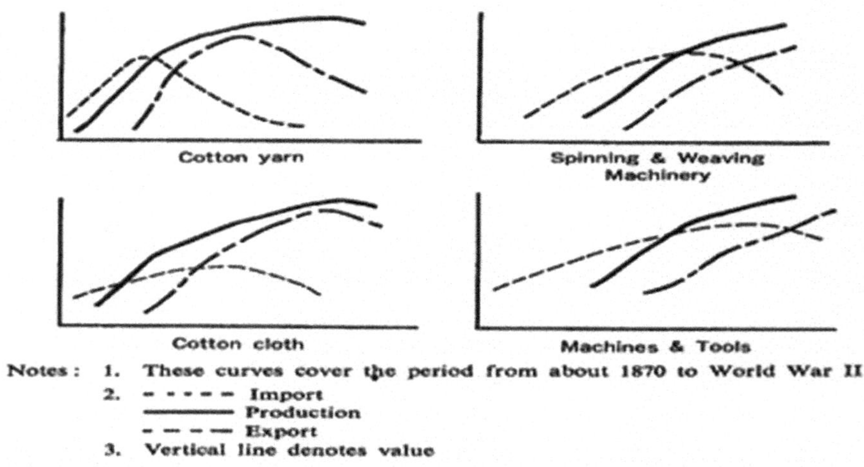

Fig. 12.3 Fundamental Flying-Geese pattern (*Source* Akamatsu, 1962: 12)

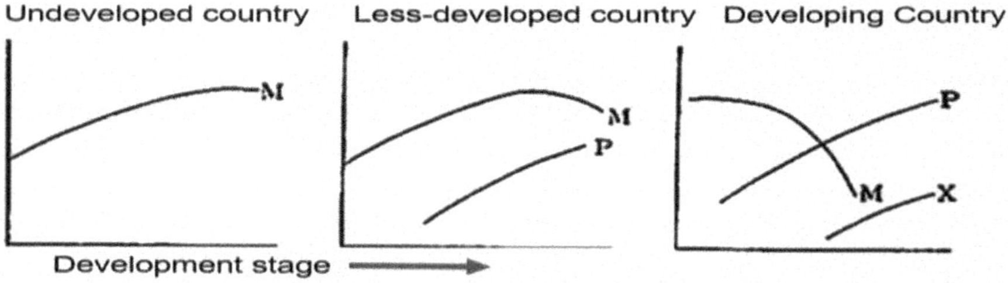

Fig. 12.4 Flying-Geese pattern by development stage (*Source* Akamatsu -J, 1974: 175). *Note* M = import, P = production, X = export

the series of countries at each stage of development, with the most developed countries as the leading group, can also be called a secondary form of the flying geese pattern (Akamatsu -J, 1965: 173).

The basic form is the succession of imports, production, and exports in industrial development, while the secondary forms are the industrial upgrading from consumer goods to production goods (for now, the secondary form 1) and the industrial transfer from the most advanced countries to the follower countries (the secondary form 2). The basic form and the secondary form 1 are, in this order, domestic development phenomena, while the secondary form 2 is the phenomenon of internationalization.

In addition, the following statement, given in the 1956 paper as the "observed goal of industrial development" in the flying geese model, has implications for how it should be read.

From the perspective of the exporting country, we must pay attention to the future demand for exports and the conversion of exported goods. Of course, not all countries will have the same flying geese pattern of development, not all latecomer countries will complete the flying geese pattern of development of all industrial products, and not all later geese will always be able to overtake the earlier geese. In particular, when national industrial protection policies are enforced, it is possible to rapidly increase domestic production, to significantly reduce imports, and to encourage exports, and thus the flying geese pattern can be promoted by national policy (Akamatsu -J, 1956: 72).

The above statement is reproduced in the 1972 paper, but we note that such a statement points out an important observation. In particular, what kind of development is meant by the first sentence following "of course" if it is not "the same flying geese pattern of development in all countries"? In any case, it is worth noting that Akamatsu points out an intriguing observation.

12.4.2 Succession and Development of Akamatsu's Flying Geese Model

After World War II, the economics community in Europe and the United States changed dramatically. Akamatsu later recounted these changes as follows.

Although I was able to return to the faculty at the end of 1948, after I had been approved for teaching and public service, the trends in the economics community had changed dramatically. The German historical school, which we had followed, had completely fallen to the ground, and Keynesian or Marxian thought was taking over the academy like a wildfire, so to speak (Akamatsu -J, 1975: 51).

Upon his return to research, Akamatsu enthusiastically absorbed the latest research results of modern economics and development economics in Europe and the U.S., and began to participate in international academic circles. The "Synthetic Dialectics" was re-launched as a research methodology, with all references to the Japanese people disappearing. Together with his disciple, Kojima, Akamatsu embarked on a renewed theorization of the flying geese model. Akamatsu himself completed his original theory through his research on Japan's industrial upgrading. Schröppel and Nakajima (2003) call Kojima's attempt "Westernization of the Flying Geese Model". Kojima recounted the following in 1972, 1975, and 2000.

> Both the flying geese theory and the product cycle theory are extremely excellent ideas based on empirical research, but theoretically they are incomplete, and there are still many aspects that need to be supplemented and improved. Dr. Akamatsu's vision is truly outstanding and is highly regarded worldwide. However, the empirical analysis of some industries has been conducted, and the basic form of the goose pattern has been nicely drawn, but not enough theoretical modeling and analysis of the driving factors have been done yet (Kojima -J, 1972b: 27, 31).
>
> Dr. Akamatsu was very concerned about this comment (see above). ... Kojima proposed a model in which both the basic form (efficiency of production) and the secondary form (diversification of production) of the flying geese theory are based on the progress of capital accumulation in a country, or in other words, the increase in the capital-labor ratio (Kojima -J, 1975: 233).
>
> From the perspective of Dr. Akamatsu's synthetic dialectics, it is an adequate theorization. However, it is far from the theorizing of modern economics, wherein formalization or modeling is done by means of a system of mathematical equations. In a paper by Kojima (1958), he attempted to clarify the basic type (efficiency of production) and its variant or subtype (diversification of production) of the flying geese pattern of industrial development by combining the neoclassical growth theory and Heckscher-Ohlin's theory of factor proportion (Kojima -J, 2003b: 19–20).

With expectations on Kojima's research, Akamatsu admitted that "the theory of the flying geese pattern is not well analyzed theoretically, as pointed out by Kojima" (Akamatsu -J, 1974: 156). In his 1960 Hitotsubashi University 83rd anniversary lecture, Akamatsu related the theory to "the heterogenization and homogenization of the world economy" and stated,

> The "heterogeneity and homogeneity of the world economy", which was inspired by my empirical research in Nagoya (Higher School of Commerce), and the "flying geese pattern" of economic development in the less developed countries, form the core of my understanding of the world economy to this day. It is remarkable that Professor Kiyoshi Kojima has brought to bear the scalpel of modern theory on the "flying geese pattern" and is attempting to theorize the most difficult historical events. It is extremely interesting to see his attempt to start from history, advance to theory, and then to synthesize theory again on a historical grounding (Akamatsu -J, 1960: 101).

The flying geese pattern modeled by Akamatsu was reinterpreted by Kojima using modern economic methods. Kojima considers that the "flying geese pattern" of development "emerges successively" at three levels or phases, and proceeds to theorize the theory of the flying geese pattern.

The first phase is the basic form. However, Kojima's basic model is an integration of Akamatsu's basic form and the first secondary form, and is "the catch-up process of a country's economic development, namely, the streamlining of production (starting with imports and increasing production and then exports) and the diversification and upgrading of the industrial structure". He called this the "First Kojima Model". According to him, it is "based on the factor proportions theory (or Heckscher-Ohlin theorem), which is in the tradition of international trade theory", but it is "static economics that assumes that the production function and demand function are given and unchanging". They cannot be used as they are. Owing to this, he aimed to construct an "inter-temporal dynamic economics (Dynamics)" that deals with the continuous fluctuation of production factors (labor and capital) over time, allocating them to multiple industrial sectors as capital accumulation progresses. He called this the "dynamic proposition" of the flying geese model (Kojima -J, 2004: 23).

The second phase corresponds to the second of Akamatsu's sub-phase. In East Asia, industries are propagating internationally one after another in the order starting from the labor-intensive light industry, to the capital-intensive heavy chemical industry, and then to capital- and knowledge-intensive machinery industry (high-tech), separated by time from the leading country to the following country. Kojima calls this phase "the international propagation of the flying geese industrial development or the globalization proposition", and sees it as being achieved through FDI by Japanese firms. He calls it the "Second Kojima Model".

Incidentally, Kojima assumed that there is a third phase in the flying geese pattern, namely, the "flying geese development of the world economy", which is classified as a historical order and structure as follows. "(1) Pax Britannica (1820–1914), (2) Interwar period (1920–1940), (3) Pax Americana I (1945–1971), (4) Transitional period (1972–present): collapse of Bretton Woods regime (1971), the fall of the Berlin Wall, the end of the Cold War, and the formation of a new world economic order in the twenty-first century (would it be Pax Americana II?)" (Kojima -J, 2004: i).

The economic development of the less developed countries is achieved within the global economy. The less developed countries must obtain development within the international order and institutions of that era. The construction of such a development model is an important area of research. The study of this phase is not generally treated as a theory of the flying geese pattern. However, Kojima includes the third phase in the research area of the flying geese model, which he calls "agreed specialization". This is because it is a realistic issue for the development of East Asia. In the following sections, We will look at the development of Kojima's theory.

Catching-Up Product Life Cycle Hypothesis and Fundamental Flying-Geese Paradigm

When R. Vernon published his Product Life Cycle (PLC) theory in (1966), Kojima developed a theory that the flying geese theory was a catch-up theory from the side of latecomers, relying on Vernon's research. Of course, this was what Akamatsu expected. Akamatsu wrote, "Both of these theories (the flying geese theory and the PLC hypothesis) are two sides of the same coin as seen from the perspective of the less developed countries and the developed countries" (Akamatsu -J, 1975: 3).

In 1972, Kojima made a comparison between the flying geese theory and the PLC theory, and in 1973, he named the flying geese theory the catch-up product cycle (CPC) and published an English paper to gain recognition within mainstream economics, especially in Europe and the United States. He wrote,

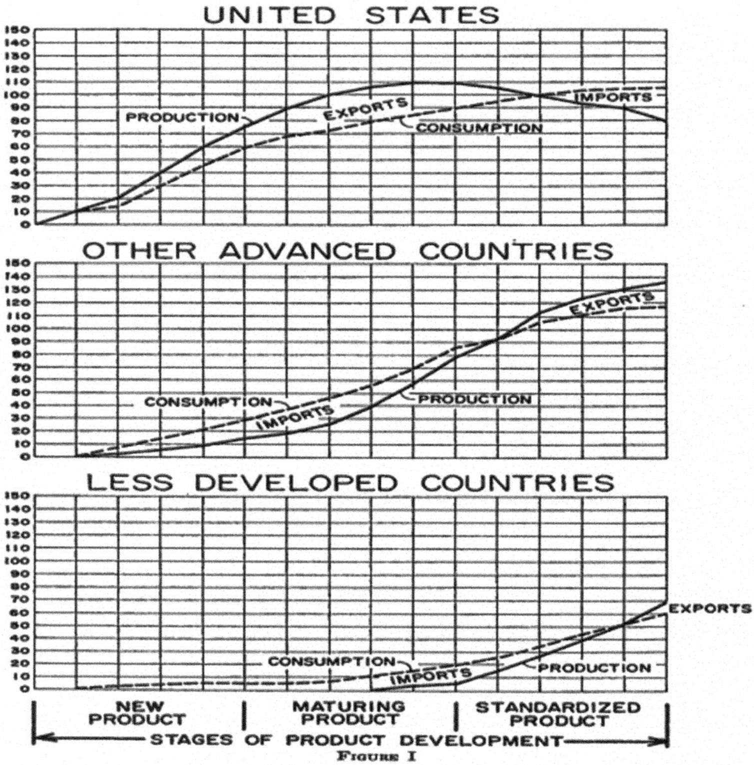

Fig. 12.5 Vernon's product life cycle model (*Source* Vernon, 1966: 199)

> Recently Professor Vernon's "product cycle" theory has become well-known, but in Japan Dr. Akamatsu, Professor Emeritus of Hitotsubashi University, propounded a "catching-up product cycle" theory as early as the mid-1930s. He originally called it the "wild geese-flying pattern" (Ganko keitai) of industrial development in developing countries (Kojima, 1973a: 9).

Let us first confirm these models by presenting two conceptual diagrams, first the product-life-cycle hypothesis and then Kojima's flying geese model.[3]

Figure 12.5 is Vernon's PLC model. The figure illustrates the pattern of the overseas expansion of the U.S. MNCs in relation to the life cycle of their products. In the U.S. economy, where technology is superior to other developed countries and wages are high, MNCs first develop and produce new products in the U.S., which are soon exported. As products reach maturity, they begin production in other advanced countries to which they originally exported, and eventually export from there. At this stage, the U.S. begins importing maturing products. When products reach the standardization stage, they begin production in less developed countries, which have always been their export destinations, and eventually begin exporting from there.

[3] Note that Schröppel and Nakajima (2003: 214 and 218) also have two figures, Figs. 12.5 and 12.6.

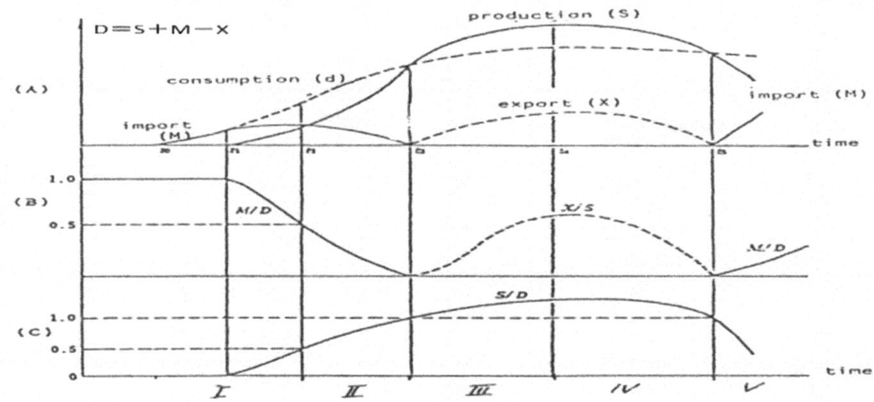

Five development Stages
I Introductory II import substitution III export IV mature V reverse import

Fig. 12.6 Yamazawa's catching-up product cycle development of an industry: A schematic diagram (*Source* Yamazawa -J, 1984: 74)

In 1972, Kojima compared and examined the flying geese theory and the PLC hypothesis, focusing on the differences in the nature of investment between Japanese and American firms (Kojima -J, 1972b, 1972c). The following year, he published it as an English paper (Kojima, 1973a, 1973b). Thus, Kojima began to argue that the development of East Asia was being realized by FDI by Japanese firms.

FDI by Japanese firms begins with small, comparatively inferior industries. FDI in the U.S., on the other hand, is investment by oligopolistic firms in advanced industries. Therefore, Japanese FDI is trade-oriented because Japanese FDI promotes comparative advantage, while U.S. FDI is anti-trade oriented because U.S. FDI replaces its exports with production in its destination market (Kojima -J, 1972b; Kojima, 1973a). It was the trade-oriented FDI of Japanese firms that enabled the export-led development of East Asian countries. Subsequently, Kojima named the former PROT-FDI and the latter ANT-FDI[4] (Kojima -J, 2003a).

I. Yamazawa was highly praised by Kojima: "My protege Ippei Yamazawa's doctoral dissertation, 'Japan's Economic Development and the International Division of Labor' (1984), is a further refined version of the theory of the Flying Geese Pattern" (Kojima -J, 2003b: 17). That dissertation further elaborated on Japan's economic development using long-term statistics. Figure 12.7 shows the catch-up PC theory, or in other words, the basic form of the flying geese model.

As seen in panel (A) of Fig. 12.6, the figure consists of two curves for consumption and production, following Vernon's PC diagram, showing changes in imports,

[4] PRO-Trade FDI does not just mean it promotes exports but rather it promotes trade in such a way that countries specialize in producing and exporting goods in which they have comparative advantage. This type of trading, according to the theory of comparative advantage of Ricardo, leads to a global trading system that is efficient in the sense that a larger amount of goods are produced for the same amount of resources.

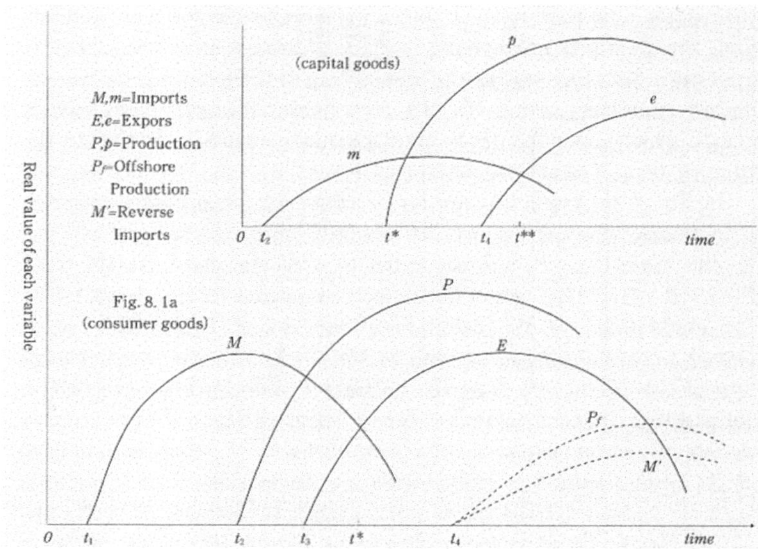

Fig. 12.7 **1a** and **1b** Kojima's Flying Geese pattern of industrial development (*Source* Kojima, 2000b: 378)

production, and exports at five stages of development. Panel (B) shows the indicators that define each of these stages. Stage II, import substitution, is 0.5–0, Stage III, the export stage begins, the value of export (X)/production (S) is characterized by M/D having values between 0 and 1.0, and Stage IV, maturity, begins at the peak of the production curve (S). Finally, Stage V, reverse import, occurs, this time with M/D rising from 0 to 1.0. In panel (C), the S/D curve shows the gradual development from domestic demand substitution to export surplus and its decline.

As Yamazawa points out, this diagram is only an idealized diagram, but it illustrates the reverse importation stage, which Akamatsu and Kojima only described, and shows Akamatsu's basic form of a certain good or a certain industry as a whole.

Thus, Yamazawa attempts to elucidate the internal mechanism of this development in line with Kojima's problem conception. He pointed that at introductory phase, learning effects in both consumption and production is important, and at import substitution and export phases, the growth of demand (both domestic and export) and decreasing unit cost of production, in which decreasing cost is realized through (a) operation on a large scale, (b) adoption of better technology, and (c) accumulated experience in both labor and management skills is important (Yamazawa -J, 1984: 75; Yamazawa 1990: 7).

Kojima also later drew the conceptual diagram in Fig. 12.7-1a and 1b. In this diagram, reverse importation is also taken into account. Kojima then explains. "In Fig. 12.7-1a, the import of consumer goods (X) increases from t_1 to t_2. At t_2, domestic demand becomes large enough to set up optimal scale plants, making it possible for profitable domestic production to begin. Thus, at t_2, the P-curve starts to increase in

Fig. 12.1b, and the imports (m) of capital goods (Y) also rise as shown in Fig. 12.1b". In addition, offshore production of consumer goods (X) begins. The curve of offshore production (Pf) followed by reverse imports (M′) is drawn from T4[5] (Kojima -J, 2000b: 379).

Incidentally, Kojima's conception of the flying geese pattern was also Akamatsu's conception in his final years. Akamatsu's last essay before his death, published in Sekai Keizai Hyoron (World Economic Review) six months after Akamatsu's death, was titled "The Flying Geese Theory of Foreign Investment."

> About 30 years later (after the publication of the "Flying Geese Pattern" in 1935), scholars at Harvard University in the U.S. published their Product Cycle Theory. The Theory posited that exports (X) by developed countries would trigger foreign production (Pf), which would eventually lead to reverse imports (M'). This is what is meant by the transnational corporation's re-exportation to its home country. Both of these theories (the flying geese theory and the product cycle theory) are the flip side of the same trade pattern as seen from the perspective of the less developed and developed countries. The U.S. invests in innovative capital-intensive industries abroad, while Japan initially invested in labor-intensive industries in less-developed countries, which are gradually becoming more sophisticated capital-intensive industries (Akamatsu -J, 1975: 3).

Akamatsu shares Kojima's argument linking PROT-FDI by Japanese firms with his interpretation of the development of less developed countries. At the end of the above essay, Akamatsu writes that both the U.S. and Japan are now suffering from the same problem of reverse importation, pointing out that the development of East Asian countries is causing the hollowing out of American and Japanese industries, and that the need for further production of "refined products" and development of advanced industries is a countermeasure to this problem. The report also pointed out the need for further production of "refined products" and development of advanced industries as countermeasures. This was a proposal for "heterogenization". Thus, Akamatsu entrusted Kojima with the legacy and development of his theory.

Akamatsu's legacy was also carried on independently by T. Ozawa, a professor at the University of Colorado. He supported the Akamatsu-Kojima school with his own development of the flying geese theory, and Fig. 12.8 shows a conceptual diagram of the flying geese pattern of development, which Ozawa analyzed differently from Kojima. As the diagram shows, the characteristics of the transformation of key industries and their FDI investment patterns due to Japan's industrial upgrading are explained by stage, respectively.

2nd Sub-Form of the Flying Geese Model: International Transfer of Industry

In 1985, S. Okita gave a speech at the Pacific Cooperation Forum on the flying geese theory (Okita 1985). In line with the development of East Asia, a number of regional researchers were already analyzing the development of East Asian countries, and catch-up industrialization was being actively discussed. The flying geese theory was garnering a lot of attention while influencing such studies. Thus, the central argument

[5] In the paper published in 2009, the last year of Kojima's life, a slight modification was made: t4 in Fig. 12.1a was rewritten as t** and the start of offshore production was shifted backward from t4 (Kojima -J, 2009: 6).

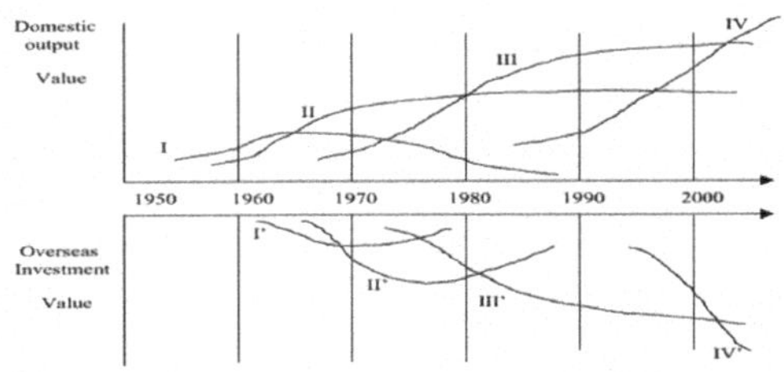

Stages of industrial upgrading (a leading-growth-sector model)

- I Labor-driven "Heckscher-Ohlin" industries (e.g., textiles)
- II Scale-driven "nondifferentiated Smithian" industries (e.g., steel)
- III Component-intensive, assembly-based industries (e.g., autos and early-generation electronics)
- IV Innovation-focused R&D-intensive "Schumpeterian" industries (e.g., new materials, biotechnology and latest-generation electronics)

Phases of overseas investment

- I' Low-wage-labor-seeking "elementary" FDI
- II' Resource-seeking and house-cleaning FDI
- III' Assembly-transplanting/market-seeking FDI (inclusive of low-wage-seeking FDI in parts/components/accessories and low-end products)
- IV' Alliance-seeking (strategically networking)) FDI in production, marketing and R&D

Fig. 12.8 Japan's industrial upgrading and overseas investment: comparative advantage recycling (CAR) as adaptive efficiency enhancement (*Source* Ozawa 2001: 475, This figure was first presented in 1993). *Note* The above trend curves are not drawn to exact scale—for illustrative purposes only. Output and FDI may be alternatively expressed in percentage terms when the trends are empirically verified

of the flying geese theory moved toward theorizing the industrialization of the less developed countries.

Figure 12.9 illustrates the development of East Asian countries, which Kojima has depicted as the frontier of FDI. The industries of a country (Japan) diversify sequentially, become more efficient, and develop in a geese pattern. Industry X is textiles and other labor-intensive goods, Industry Y is capital-intensive goods such as steel and chemicals, and Industry Z is capital- and knowledge-intensive goods such as machinery. Each industry represents a key industry, and many subdivisions and items are assumed within this category. The developed country (Japan) will increase the sophistication of its comparative advantage industries from X to Y to Z to a more advanced industry Z′ along the passage of time (I → II → III → IV), and at the same time transfer its comparatively inferior industries to the NIEs → ASEAN → China… through PROT-FDI. East Asia will continue to develop through this mechanism in which Japanese firms will play a role (Kojima, 2000b: 385–6; Kojima -J, 2003: 213).

Thus, the flying geese model comes to be depicted in a more purified form.

Figure 12.10a and b are concept figures of the flying geese model, posted by Ippei Yamazawa in the final report of the project "The Interdependence of Economic Development Between Asian Economies" which was instituted within the Economic Planning Agency (now the Cabinet Office) Economic Research Institute since 1990, and under the supervision of Yamazawa (1993: 21). Like Fig. 12.6, the vertical axis is S/D and the horizontal axis is time. Then, Fig. 12.10a shows the diversification and sophistication of industries in late-starting countries over time, and b) similarly shows the international movement of an industry from one country to another.

After explaining this figure (Fig. 12.10), Yamazawa presents S/D curves based on empirical evidence for Japanese cotton textiles, steel products, automobiles, and industrial machines for 110 years since 1870 (Economic Planning Agency, 1993:

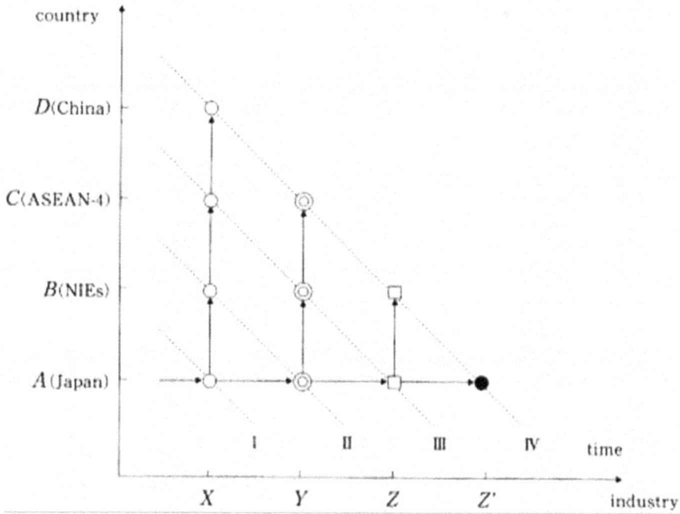

Fig. 12.9 Investment frontier in Kojima's Flying Geese pattern of industrial development (*Source* Kojima, 2000b: 386)

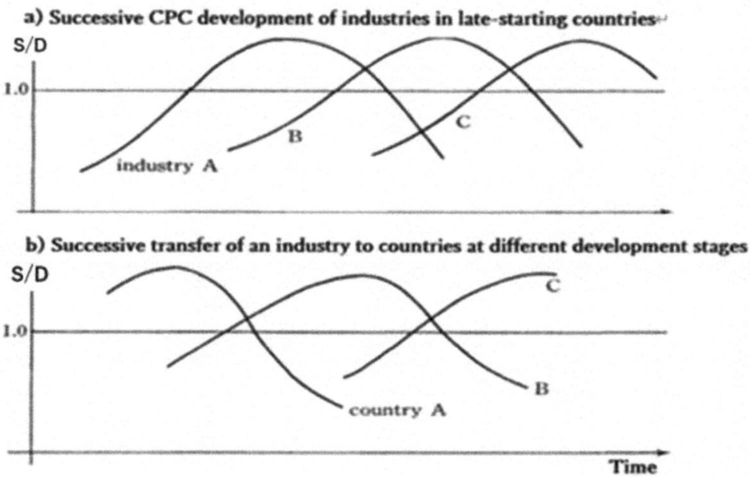

Fig. 12.10 **a** and **b** Variations of Catching-up Product Cycle development (*Source* Yamazawa, 1990: 11, 1993: 21). *Note* D=S+M-X, S means production

21). The S/D curves show that these industries developed in the order of imports, domestic production, and exports.

Thus, the characteristics of East Asian economic integration through trade can be concretely illustrated with actual statistical support. Japan's Economic White Paper (Economic Planning Agency -J, 1994a, b) used the RCA index to calculate the degree of export coupling between the U.S., Japan, and the rest of Asia, confirming the deepening interdependence. It also used the trade specialization coefficient, expressed as (exports − imports)/(exports + imports) × 100, to show the stepwise changes in the trade structure of East Asia. It is shown in Fig. 12.11. The Economic White Paper explains as follows.

> The trade specialization coefficient is the ratio of the trade balance of a good to its trade value ((exports − imports)/(exports + imports)), with a positive value indicating an excess in exports and a negative value indicating an excess in imports. First, we can see that the order of countries (or regions) is Japan, NIEs, ASEAN, and China, and the order of industries is non-durable consumer goods, durable consumer goods, and capital goods, and that the coefficient of specialization has been increasing, decreasing, and then turning negative. Thus, we can clearly observe a flying geese type of development, with the leading country (Japan) followed by shifting the weight of its industry to higher value-added fields one after another. In particular, the process of following the latecomers, ASEAN and China, has been significantly shortened (Economic Planning Agency, Japan -J, 1994a).

Thus, the flying geese theory literally became widely known and accepted as a theory to explain the development of East Asia.

Figure 12.12a and b is a figure widely circulated today as the Akamatsu's flying geese model. In addition, comparative advantage is basically reflected in cost.

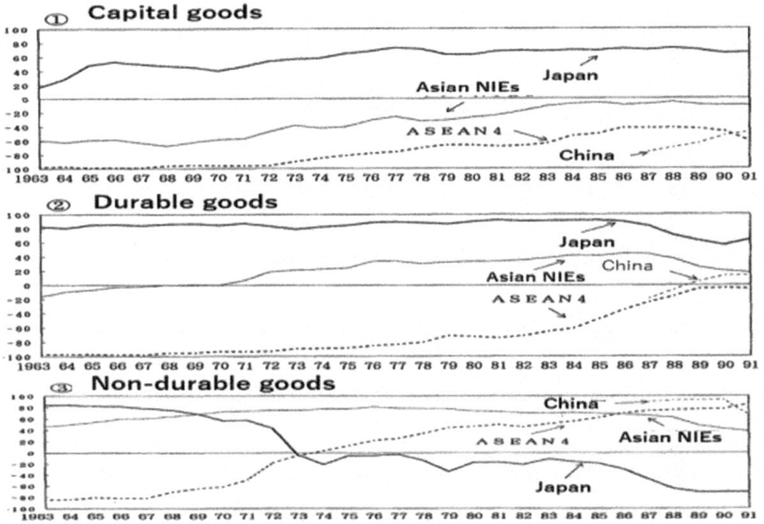

Fig. 12.11 Trade coefficients for Japan, NIEs, ASEAN4, and China by commodity (1963–1991) (*Source* Economic Planning Agency -J, 1994a: Fig. 3-1-13). *Note* 1. Compiled by the AIDXT of the Institute of Developing Economies. 2. Trade Specialization Coefficient = (Exports − Imports)/(Exports + Imports) × 100. NIEs: Hong Kong, South Korea, Singapore, Taiwan and ASEAN4: Indonesia, Malaysia, Philippines, and Thailand

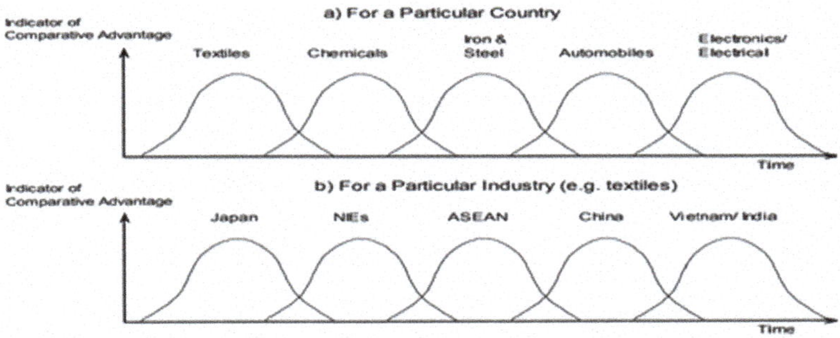

Fig. 12.12 Asia's Flying-Geese pattern of economic development a) For a particular county, b) For a particular industry (*Source* Kwan, 2002: 4)

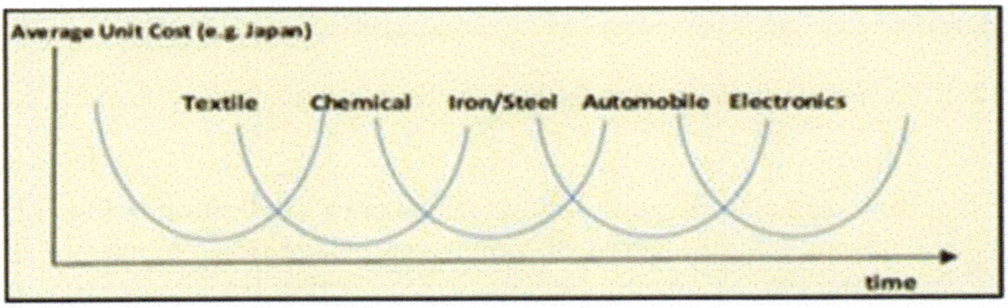

Fig. 12.13 Average unit cost of Asia's Flying-Geese pattern of economic development Single-Country-Multiple-Product/Sector framework (*Source* Kasahara, 2019: 58)

Recently, Kasahara (2019) has created a cost diagram that reverses the above diagram to better understand this[6] (Fig. 12.13).

At the beginning of this century, the picture was further simplified: D. Hiratsuka of the Institute of Developing Economies, JETRO, drew a convincing picture of the stage of development of each country's industry, using the value of (exports − imports)/(exports + imports) as the international competitive coefficient (ICC). This is shown in Fig. 12.14a–d.[7] He implicitly assumes that "by observing the simple ICC index over time, assessed by product or by industry, the domestic demand and supply gap can be discussed". The ICCs for each country's industry in this table are calculated based on three-year moving averages from 1990 to 2001. Data are taken from the UN SITC, third revised edition (SITC-R3), for 43 product groups. In Fig. 12.14b apparel, c synthetic fiber, and d electronics parts are three industries selected for convenience by the authors of this chapter. From this figure, it is easy to see the stage of development of each country's industry (Hiratsuka -J, 2003; Hiratsuka, 2005: 4).

[6] Kasahara (2019) is a doctoral dissertation, and the list of references gives a vast literature on the flying geese model.

[7] Hiratsuka presented his first study using the ICC index at the ASEAN-Japan Research Institute Meeting in October 2002 in Bangkok.

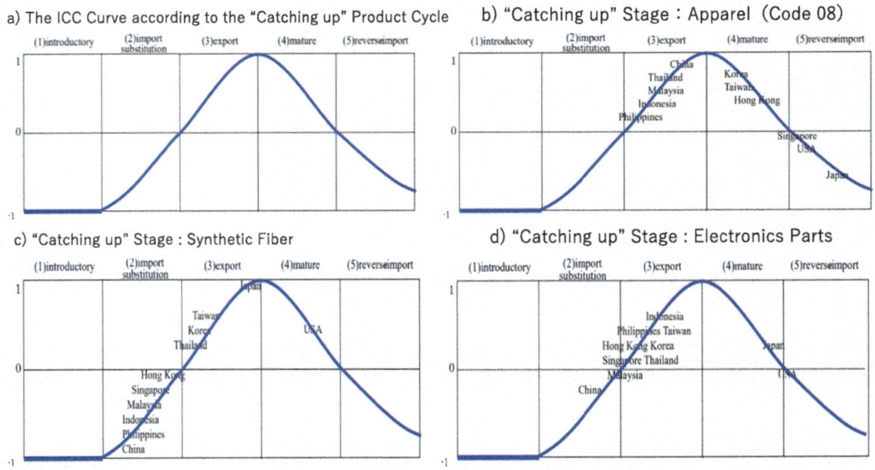

Fig. 12.14 ICC curves according to the 'Catching-up' product cycle (*Source* Hiratsuka, 2005)

Note that this stage classification follows Yamazawa's definition in Fig. 12.6, but a closer look reveals a modification of Yamazawa's definition. Yamazawa defined the beginning of the import substitution phase in stage II as 0.5 on the M/D and S/D scales. In contrast, Fig. 12.13 begins at −1. Similarly, Kwan's Fig. 12.12 shows the vertical axis as the indicator of comparative advantage, but it seems more appropriate to use the index of international competitiveness (ICC index). The reason why the peaks are capped is because they are ICC coefficients.

As we have seen above, the initial interest in the flying geese theory was a basic type consisting of less developed countries and Japan, but interest eventually shifted to a secondary type involving the development of the region through the international transfer of industry. What is interesting is the way the conceptual diagram of the basic type was drawn. Initially, three curves were shown for imports, production, and exports, followed by two curves for consumption and production, and eventually a single ICC curve was used. To be sure, such reduction of curves could be considered as innovative. There is the risk, however, of oversimplification such that some dynamics of the model are ignored. Nevertheless, the ICC is used throughout this book, signifying its usefulness in illustrating the flying geese model based on trade data. We feel that there should be no problem in using such simplifications for as long one bears in mind the dynamics underlying the model. Ignoring these underlying dynamics has apparently led to a loss of interest in actual development policies, which are important for latecomers to adopt.

Kojima's Principle of Agreed Specialization/Coordinated Production and Neoliberal Economics Criticism

In his later years, Kojima devoted his energies to researching the third phase of the flying geese theory in order to develop a general theory of the industrialization of

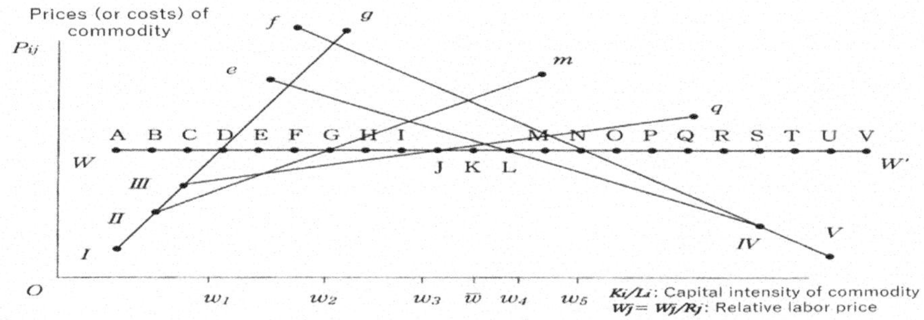

Fig. 12.15 Kojima's Asia Pacific trade map (*Source* Kojima -J, 2004: 84; Kojima 2005). *Note* The title of this figure was World Trade Map in the 2005 English paper. Kojima has changed the title to "Asia Pacific trade map" in his subsequent Japanese paper (Kojima -J, 2009: 29). We use the title from the Japanese article as the title for this figure

East Asian countries as it has materialized. The problems resulting from the industrialization of East Asian countries were considered from a different perspective, involving the harmonious international division of labor in the face of intensifying competition. Kojima calls it the Third Kojima Model (Kojima -J, 2004: 108).

If the less developed countries succeed in industrializing one after another, their industrial structures will eventually become homogeneous, producing similar products, and intensifying market competition. The heterogeneity that was the basis of a more peaceful international division of labor virtually disappears. A theoretical construction and policies are required to meet these challenges. Kojima argued that a framework that avoids such excessive competition and allows development to continue is ultimately based on the principles of agreed specialization and coordinated production.

In the 2000s, Kojima constructed a model of the international division of labor that enables the optimal allocation of resources (factors of production) in a country's economy with the trade structure of Asia–Pacific countries in mind, and published it in the Journal of Asian Economics, vol. 16 in 2005. Figure 12.15 is a model that explains agreed specialization.[8]

However, before going into the explanation of Fig. 12.15, there is something that must be confirmed up front. Kojima uses the Heckscher-Ohlin theorem to explain the establishment of the agreed international division of labor based on the country-two goods model. He explains it as follows.

> In a national economy (value system), prices of goods and factors are homogenized according to the cost of production or productivity of the factors. There, the "cost-of-production law" prevails. This was the "law of domestic value" of the classical school. In trade between countries, however, the price of a commodity is determined by the equilibrium of reciprocal demand between the two countries, where the value of exports = the value of imports. In this case, the price of an element (typically labor) is not homogenized internationally.

[8] Kojima devoted a considerable amount of time to the construction of this model, including the use of Lerner's diagram (Lerner 1952).

> Ohlin introduced differences in comparative production cost patterns based on the factor endowment ratios as an important factor causing differences in value systems. This is the so-called H=O proposition. However, Ohlin argued that this is not the case for the domestic value system. However, Ohlin did not consider it to cause differences between the domestic and international value laws. He considered that international trade could also be treated as a problem of the general equilibrium price system. In this respect, I (Kojima), who supports the classical school, have a very different view (Kojima -J, 2006c: 46).
>
> Although he introduced the H–O proposition, or factor proportions theory, as a representative of the strict existence of differences in value systems, Ohlin failed to appreciate its important implications and concluded that the principle of a general equilibrium price system holds true both domestically (same value system) and internationally, and that there is no need to distinguish between national value laws and international value laws. (This) is the critical point on which we disagree with Ohlin. In Ohlin's view, the "international division of labor/profits of trade" based on the principle of relative competition would dissipate into thin air. ... In order for a global general equilibrium price system to be established, the remuneration of resources, especially labor (wage rates), must also be globally uniform. ... However, wage rates (or, more generally, factor prices) do not equalize among different value systems. This is why the "international law of value," the principle of relative competition, is essential. In emphasizing the principle of relative competition, we part company with Ohlin and go back to the classical school of thought (Kojima -J, 2006c: 49).

Kojima explains the comparative advantage of each country in international trade based on the Ohlin proposition, but it is based on his own interpretation.

Now let us look at Fig. 12.15. On the vertical axis is P_{ij}, i.e., the cost of good i in country j, and on the horizontal axis are two measures: the capital intensity by good (production per unit) K_i/L_i and the country-specific factor price ratio $w = W_j/R_j$. Then, under the principle of "one price for one commodity", a line is drawn where all goods are quantities that can be produced for one dollar in the common currency (US dollar). Thus, the competitive goods are positioned at one of the points on the W-W′ line according to the factor intensity of each country.

Furthermore, when the marginal competitive advantage (MCA) line is drawn for each country (Roman numerals I–V), two types of advantage lines are drawn. In low-income developing countries (I–III), labor-intensive goods (e.g., good B) become cheaper and thus become competitive advantage goods (i.e., exportable goods), and the MCA line rises steadily. In contrast, in developed countries (IV and V), capital-intensive goods (e.g., S and U goods) become competitively superior (= exportable goods) because they are cheaper relative to labor-intensive goods, and the MCA line falls steadily. Kojima divides the MCA lines with different slopes into two types: a low-wage developing country type competitive advantage line (D-type CA) and a high-income advanced economy-type competitive advantage line (A-type CA). Here, the A-type CA line is called "competitive advantage pattern reversal", emphasizing its significance as a new discovery by Kojima[9] (Kojima, 2005; Kojima -J, 2006c: 188–202). The conversion of the MCA pattern from D-type to A-type is indicated in the figure as a conversion in the range of J → K → L goods. It is noted that South

[9] Kojima explains this finding as follows. In the Heckscher-Ohlin model, a 'comparative costs' reversal occurs when "the W/R (factor price ratio) is <1 (labor is undervalued) and when it is >1 (capital is undervalued).This is something I had not noticed before, and if it can be mathematically proven, it is a remarkable finding" (Kojima -J, 2004: 87–88).

Korea and Taiwan converted from D-type to A-type in the 1990s (Kojima -J, 2006c: 201–203).

The industrialization of the less developed countries, enabling them to catch up, thus actually intensifies competition as similar industrial products are produced in each country. The proposed method of adjustment is the agreed specialization of Kojima. Competing countries can profit together through a coordination of countries of what to produce.

Kojima's achievement in the tension between theory and reality is described as follows.

> The new world economic order must be based on the principle of relative competition, which realizes the benefits of coexistence and co-prosperity in the international division of labor in accordance with the theory of comparative advantage. Ricardo-Mill's two-country, two-goods barter model is based on the "principle of relative competition", which realizes the coexistence and co-prosperity benefits of the international division of labor according to the theory of comparative advantage. That is, if the international division of labor is such that a country specializes in the production of comparatively superior goods and exports them, and instead reduces the production of comparatively inferior goods and imports them, it will be able to obtain more of the importable good at a lower cost than it would have been in the pre-trade situation where the two goods are produced together. The two countries can reciprocally obtain these "import benefits" (benefits of coexistence and co-prosperity). However, to make this happen, international coordination is necessary to establish terms of trade (international exchange ratio of the two goods) and trade balance. ... If the catching-up of the less developed country is rapid, the two national economies will become homogeneous and can produce similar goods with equal comparative advantage. At such time, if firm A in country I specializes in good Y, and firm B in country II specialize in good X, respectively, the scale of production will expand in both countries, production costs will decline, a new comparative production cost differential will be generated, and the division of labor within the industry will be created. This is agreed specialization. This is the "coordination" that is necessary when the demand for imports, which had been produced in each country, is now left to the production of the other country (Kojima -J, 2004: ii, iii).

Kojima, by the way, identified PROT-FDI in comparatively inferior industries or firms in Japan as the "bearer of the international propagation of flying geese development. He then explains agreed specialization as follows.

> The term "agreement" or "discussion" may sound like hyperbole and an anti-market mechanism. Actually, it is not. Rather, it is an aspect or an extension of the intra-corporate work that firms do on a daily basis. It [agreed specialization] ultimately depends on the strategy of market driven multinationals according to the dynamic comparative advantage principle (Kojima -J, 2003a: 28, 6).

The above description gives us the impression that agreed specialization can be realized through free competition. However, his conclusion is not so. The keyword is "dynamic comparative advantage", which implies that a country currently does not have a comparative advantage in a certain industry but could have a comparative advantage in that industry with time. The policy recommendation here is for countries to aim for industries which have the potential of having a comparative advantage.

This is a question of international order. We have already discussed regionalism and regional cooperation in Asia in Chap. 9 of this book, where we saw how Kojima's vision of a Pacific economic zone eventually, after some twists and turns, came to fruition in Asia Pacific Economic Cooperation (APEC). The initiative in the formation of APEC in 1989 eventually passed from Japan to Australia, but Kojima was skeptical of that country's Prime Minister Hawke's (1929–2019) call for the formation of APEC. He believed that the interests of the developed countries were strongly emphasized and the perspective of cooperation for the development of developing countries was neglected (Nakauchi -J, 2010: 54–55).

Kojima writes that APEC "has become an odd mixture for the Pacific Rim countries", and that they "want to form their own economic development community in East Asia while maintaining a close cooperative relationship with the United States, which is expanding and deepening its own huge economic zone in the Americas" (Kojima-J 2004: 164). This idea then moves toward the recognition of a tripolar world structure through the development of Asia. In other words, the world economy in the twenty-first century will consist of three poles: the EU, the FTAA (Free Trade Area of the Americas), and the Asian Economic Community (AEC).

The theoretical underpinnings of this concept are vividly illustrated in the following narrative.

> Note that not only international trade, but also foreign direct investment (FDI) and the cooperative division of labor are all mechanisms of "relative competition" based on the comparative cost of production theory (Ricardo). One of Kojima's contributions was to point that out. If the terms of trade between two countries are determined in the middle of the comparative cost of production theory, two-way trade will be created, in which both countries can always import and export, and both sides can gain the benefits of coexistence and co-prosperity. In other words, imports and exports are always reciprocal activities. In this respect, it differs greatly from the principle of absolute competition, in which a price war is fought for each good and the other party is defeated (Kojima -J, 2004: iii).

Kojima also writes as follows.

> In the barter model, the production cost ratio of Goods Y and X in Country I must always be considered in pairs, as in the comparison of the production cost ratio of Goods Y and X in Country II. Therefore, looking at each good separately (in terms of partial equilibrium analysis), country I has the production of good Y and country II has the production of good X, and absolute competition is fought to overcome the production of the other country. This has recently come to be called competitive advantage. With the shift from the barter model to the monetary economy model, the former concept of comparative advantage and relative competition has been forgotten, and the latter concept of competitive advantage and absolute competition has come to dominate. Herein lies a serious problem that needs to be reflected upon and re-examined (Kojima -J, 2004: 69).
>
> International economic transactions are based on the "principle of relative competition" to bring about profits and prosperity. In the real monetary economy, however, which consists of many countries and many goods, "absolute price competition" dominates, where prices are converted at the exchange rate and expressed in a common currency (e.g., US dollar), and the goal is to maximize profits (profit) by buying from cheap places and selling to expensive places. The "principle of relative competition" is then forgotten. This is where the problem arises (Kojima -J, 2004: v).

Thus, Kojima summarizes his theory of international order.

(i) In an absolute price-competitive market, the logic of the strong dominates. Relative competition that reciprocally gives other countries opportunities to operate is not taken into consideration. This is American unilateralism.

(ii) Multiple individual transactions by goods do not guarantee a contractual agreement to reach an equilibrium between supply and demand. In order to balance the national trade, an integrated entity, the state (fiscal and monetary authorities), apart from the myriad of individual traders, must initiate balance of payments adjustment measures.

(iii) The state must be responsible for macroeconomic adjustment by bringing the exchange rate to an appropriate level, adjusting domestic fundamentals, and restoring the balance of payments to equilibrium (Kojima -J, 2004: v).

When the Soviet Union collapsed in 1991, capitalism took the world by storm. In economics, neoclassical economics espoused market fundamentalism, and the "Washington Consensus" came to dominate. In the midst of this historical situation, Kojima rejected the neoclassical theory of absolute competition and returned to the trade theory of classical economics, emphasizing the importance of the mechanism of relative competition. He even advocated reform of the GATT/WTO, including the dollar-centered "reconstruction of the international currency and exchange rate system", and even wrote that this was "one of Kojima's contributions" (Kojima -J, 2004: 80).

At the end of this section, we must point out another decisive observation that Kojima reached.

> East Asian countries are beginning to reflect on the extent to which they can continue their export-led growth methods that rely on foreign capital and technology. Instead of such "sham development", they must turn to "self-sustained economic development" through investment based on their own savings, self-sustained technological innovation, and self-sustained enterprise. This is especially true for China's inland development. Here, too, we find the limitations of the international transmission method of flying geese development. However, the acceptance of foreign direct investment is only a driving force for the economic development of subsequent countries and is only a small part of the total investment. We must be careful not to go too far, but it is still essential to make effective use of foreign investment while taking optimal openness into consideration (Kojima -J, 2003a, 2003b: 293).

In retrospect, Akamatsu pointed out the necessity of a regional economic zone theory at the end of the 1930s and directly linked it to the Greater East Asia Co-prosperity Sphere. In contrast, Kojima, against the backdrop of regional integration in East Asia from the end of the twentieth century to the early twenty-first century, can be said to have aimed to construct a peaceful regional integration model for East Asia, while being aware of the risk of homogenization. As such, he must have been reminded of Akamatsu's experience with the Greater East Asia Economic Bloc. He had essentially written the book "World Economy and Technology" as the joint one with Akamatsu during the war in 1943, and had discussed an East Asian economic sphere (Akamatsu & Kojima -J, 1943). "World Economy and Technology", is a book published jointly with Akamatsu during the war, and was essentially written by Kojima on Akamatsu's behalf (Akamatsu & Kojima -J, 1943). Here, he is seen to once again develop his own theory of the East Asian economic sphere.

However, Kojima's arrival at the point of his theory of the "flying geese pattern" has posed a direct challenge to the world of academia, where neoliberal economics has been gaining strength since the 1990s. At the same time, Kojima acknowledges the "limits of the international transmission method of flying geese development" and reaffirms that the less developed countries themselves must win their own development, even if their development is achieved within the given international environment. As an economist who respects empirical facts and follows Akamatsu's vision, Kojima seems to have dared to write a narrative, which is even confrontational to his own assertions.

12.5 Akamatsu-Kojima Flying Geese Model: Some Discussion Points

In this section, we will attempt to organize the various evaluations, criticisms and discussions of the flying geese model inherited from Akamatsu to Kojima, and through them, consider the vitality of this model.

12.5.1 The Flying Geese Model and Dialectical Epistemology

First of all, let us examine the birth of Akamatsu's theory of the flying geese pattern by going back to the methodology of economics. One of the issues I would like to touch upon is the influence of the German School of History. In his doctoral dissertation submitted to the University of Tsukuba in 1998, Indonesian Yusron Ihza pointed out the similarity between Akamatsu's theory of the four stages of national economic development and Friedrich List's "System of National Economy", which was published in 1841. In the National Economic System, List identified a first stage in which domestic agricultural products are exported and foreign industrial products are imported, a second stage in which industrial products are imported and domestic industry develops, a third stage in which domestic industry increases its supply to the domestic market, and a fourth stage in which industrial products are exported and raw materials are imported. Akamatsu first mentioned List's narrative after the war in a 1961 English paper (Akamatsu, 1961: 207; Akamatsu -J, 1972: 17), but Dr. Ihza noted that Akamatsu may have "adapted [List's] ideas to Japan" (Ihza Mahendra -J, 1998: 13–14).

In 2000, Kojima examined the relationship between List and Akamatsu. He concluded that "we have no doubt of Dr. Akamatsu's originality" based on how Akamatsu became aware of List's narrative as mentioned just above. According to Kojima's verification, Akamatsu first received information about List from his junior economist, Yoichi Itagaki, in 1956, and mentioned it in a 1961 paper. Kojima not only confirms this in Itagaki's literature (Itagaki -J, 1963: 433), but also writes that he himself confirmed this point directly from Itagaki (Kojima, 2003a, 2003b: 13). However, Otsuki's detailed study on Akamatsu found that Akamatsu had already referred to List's work in his wartime since 1940, and pointed out that Ihza misunderstood Akamatsu, noting the difference in their interests (Otsuki, 2010: 97–98, 104–106).

Equally noteworthy is a 1931 paper by German economist Walther Hoffmann, which Akamatsu pointed out with comments in the same 1961 paper. In his 1961 English paper, Akamatsu pointed out that Hoffmann had studied the process of economic development in capitalist countries by country, and had investigated two subforms of the flying geese theory: the development of the consumer goods industry into the capital goods industry, and the transfer of industry overseas. He adds that in his 1972 Japanese paper, Hoffmann "does not, however, describe any one form of import, production, or export on a country-by-country basis (Akamatsu, 1961: 208; Akamatsu -J, 1972: 17, 1974: 169). Incidentally, the "form" mentioned here could be said to be the basic form of the flying geese theory.

Schröppel and Nakajima (2003) point out that Hoffmann, in his 1931 article, had described many of the basic features of Akamatsu's flying geese theory, confirming the influence of the German historical school in this regard (Schröppel & Nakajima, 2003: 206). One of the authors of this book, Hirakawa, shares a view close to that of Schröppel and Nakajima. At the same time, it is important to note that, historically speaking, capitalism, beginning in the United Kingdom, has shown certain commonalities in the development paths of industrialization in Germany, Japan, and even the United Kingdom. Akamatsu had captured the whole picture in his 1932 paper. Akamatsu's and Hoffmann's findings overlap in time. A reasonable interpretation is that Akamatsu arrived at his hypothesis of the flying geese pattern at the same time as Hoffmann, when Akamatsu put into practice in the industrial research office of the Nagoya Higher School of Commerce the empirical research methods that he had developed at Heidelberg and Harvard universities in the 1920s. Incidentally, the Nagoya area was one of Japan's leading textile industry clusters at the time.

Akamatsu also notes that Albert O. Hirschman, in his "Strategy of Economic Development" (1958), describing the development of the less developed countries, likens the import substitution process to "the fairy tale of the cannibal demon" and that "the 'creative role' of imports is played in a manner similar to that seen in ancient tragedies." Akamatsu's own description of the process of import substitution in his 1937 article is "astonishingly similar to Hirschman's conception", he writes. Akamatsu continues as follows.

> He [Hirschman] thinks very dialectically here, likening the role of imports to an ancient Greek tragedy. From the beginning, I have considered the development of imports, domestic production, and exports dialectically (Akamatsu, 1974: 163).

Akamatsu's discovery of the flying geese pattern was the result of his dialectical awareness gained in Germany.

Table 12.1 is a comparative table of the differences between Akamatsu's approach of the flying geese model, and Kojima, Vernon, and neoclassical theory, as organized by Schröppel and Nakajima (2003). As can be seen, Akamatsu's main concept is linkage, whereas the "Western theory" approach, typical of neoclassical theory, is factors of production and resources. While Akamatsu acknowledges the role of the state, the other three approaches are generally negative. The dialectic's cognitive framework is unique to Akamatsu. It confirms the uniqueness of the Flying Geese Theory.

However, work has been done to fill in the theoretical gaps in the flying geese model from the perspective of neoclassical economics through an analysis based on Kojima's theory of factor endowments. The two approaches have developed in a mutually complementary manner. This is where we can see one aspect of the vitality of the Flying Geese Model.

Here, we would like to point out another characteristic of the flying geese model in relation to the dialectical epistemology. This is the tension between the theory of the flying geese model and empirical research. Before World War II, Akamatsu linked his theory of a broad economic zone directly to the theory of the Greater East Asia Co-prosperity Sphere by linking it to the Japanese people crowned by the emperor through the speculative logical development of the dialectic of synthesis. However, his methodology of economics is based on reality, or intuitive reality.

Akamatsu synthesized the inspiration he had gained at Heidelberg and Harvard, and his belief was that "economics as an empirical science should not be launched from a priori concepts…but from intuitive events given by experience" (Akamatsu -J, 1975: 34). Kojima sought an ideal international division of labor based on the factor endowment theory of H–O theory, but he was also always conscious of verification by data based on reality. His PROT-FDI in his CPC theory was not accepted

Table 12.1 Major differences between theories of economic development (Adapted from Schröppel and Nakajima, 2003: 222)

	Flying geese approach		Product cycle theory	Neoclassical theory
	Akamatsu	Kojima/ Yamazawa[b]	Vernon	
Main concept	Linkages	Factors (economy specific)	Resources (firm-specific)	Factors (capital and labor)
Driving force of development	Demand	Supply	Supply	Supply
Country development	Dynamic	Dynamic	Static	Static
Product/industry development[a]	Dynamic[c]	Dynamic[c]	Dynamic	Static
International trade	Moderate protectionism	Free trade	Moderate protectionism	Free trade
Industrial policy	Comprehensive	Limited	Limited	None
Dialectical view	Yes	No	No	No

(Adapted from Schröppel and Nakajima, 2003: 222).

Note [a] Added "industry", [b] added "Yamazawa", [c] changed "Static" to "Dynamic". However, the three places marked with Asterisk were re-edited at the authors' own discretion.

by the mainstream of economics (Blomqvist, 1997: 9, 23), but it was a modeling that showed one aspect of reality in the development of East Asia. It was only because of his judgment backed by reality that Kojima even wrote in his last days that the development of East Asia through PROT-FDI by Japanese firms was a "sham development," and pointed out the limitations of his interpretation of the flying geese theory that they must turn from their export-led growth methods that rely on foreign capital and technology to "self-sustained economic development" (Kojima, 2003a, 2003b: 293).

Akamatsu's empirical analytical method, which emphasizes the relationship between historical long-term perspectives and economic phenomena and economic realities through a synthetic dialectic, sheds light on issues that cannot be found in mainstream Western theories. And it is this awareness of the issues that has given rise to the uniqueness of East Asian economic development.

12.5.2 The Characteristics of the Flying Geese Theory as a Theory of Industrialization of the Less Developed Countries

In the 1930s, Akamatsu developed the theory of the flying geese pattern as a theory of industrialization for Japan, which was then a latecomer. In the 1980s, Saburo Okita introduced it as a theory of East Asian development (Okita, 1985), and it became a theory of East Asian development alongside the neoclassical theory of free trade, and the "mainstream perspective on East Asian growth experience". Moreover, the flying geese theory, like neoclassical theory, "shares their positive view of capitalism's power to promote industrialization in smooth, non-contradictory, and egalitarian fashion" (Hart-Landsberg & Burkett, 1998: 87–88). T. Ozawa likened the FGM to a Pacific economic zone led by the United States and followed harmoniously by East Asian countries.

> The U.S. itself was once a second goose, along with Continental European nations, emulating Great Britain, where the Industrial Revolution originated. Hence, learning-based catch-up is nothing new. What makes Japan's and the rest of East Asia's experience rather distinct from any previous ones, however, is that both the leader and follower nations have more deliberately and more cooperatively engaged in regional growth—the U.S. in particular has helped Asia develop by providing technology, capital, and markets, while the Asian governments have actively orchestrated export-led outer-focused industrialization (Ozawa, 2001: 474).

The trade structure of East Asian countries is called the growth triangle structure, which increased the possibility of forming an Asia–Pacific economic zone in the 1980s (Aoki -J, 1987; Hirakawa -J, 1992). As discussed in Chap. 9, Kojima himself had put forth the concept of a Pacific economic zone, and Ippei Yamazawa was deeply involved in the development of APEC. Okita's recognition of the flying geese model mentioned above was an Asia–Pacific economic zone similar to that of Ozawa.

However, it came to be seen as a theory that explained the integration of a region multilayered with NIEs, ASEAN, China, and late-ASEAN countries at different stages of development, with Japan in the lead (Kasahara, 2004: 10). At the same time, various criticisms and questions from early political science, history, and other disciplines were directed at the East Asian development theory, with Japan leading the way. B. Cumings, a prominent East Asian political scientist who was one of the earliest to focus on the flying geese theory, saw the development of South Korea and Taiwan not as the development of national economies, but as a development within a political-economic historical relationship that deeply involved Japan and the U.S. (Cumings, 1984). Barnard and Ravenhill pointed out that the development of the East Asian region is not import-substituting development, nor are the major export markets formed from the reverse imports of developed countries in the region, and that the hierarchy of the international division of labor through FDI is missing (Barnard & Ravenhill, 1995). Some studies have emerged that examine the flying geese theory, going back to Akamatsu's theory of the Greater East Asia Co-prosperity Sphere (Ihza Mahendra, 1998). One of the authors (Hirakawa) also pointed out the fact that East Asian NIEs developed without following the basic form of Akamatsu's flying geese theory, although at the same time they are heavily dependent on FDI by Japanese firms (Hirakawa -J, 1997: 9; Hirakawa, 1999: 7).

In the 1990s, the World Bank reported on the "East Asian Miracle", which was experiencing remarkable development. It even exhibited the characteristics of "shared growth" (World Bank, 1993). One of the main driving forces was undoubtedly Japan's FDI, which led to the acceptance of the flying geese theory of East Asian development.

Looking again at the theoretical developments, we can see that the area of interest in the flying geese theory has changed during the succession from Akamatsu to Kojima. Its characteristics may be summarized as follows.

(i) The interest of Akamatsu's theory of the flying geese pattern was the industrialization of Japan (as a latecomer), and the subject of industrialization was the Japanese economy and Japanese industry. However, Kojima's interest was to Japan and extended to the international transfer of industrialization to subsequent developing countries.

(ii) The flying geese theory after Kojima clarified the mechanism by which Japan, now an advanced country, advanced its industrial structure, and transferred industries, which had lost their comparative advantage, to less developed countries. While PROT-FDI by Japanese multinationals accelerated the transfer of industries, on the other hand, the less developed countries accepted industries that had a comparative advantage due to low wages. This was explained as if industrialization was automatically achieved.

(iii) Akamatsu's interest in the specific industrial development of the less developed countries, which had been the focus of Akamatsu's early research, became purely an analysis of a theoretical model based on Kojima's numerical data.

(iv) Since it was assumed that Japan would transfer international production of comparatively inferior industries and eventually move into a phase of reverse importation, it was implicitly accepted that Japan would be the major market. This was seen as a theory of regional economic integration in East Asia.

(v) Akamatsu focused on the industrialization of Japan, a latecomer, and emphasized import-substitution policies. Kojima similarly emphasized "catching-up" as a theory of "industrialization of the less developed countries," but because he extended his flying geese theory to the less developed countries following Japan, he introduced the possibility of pro-trade FDI, which comes from the more advanced countries to the latecomer countries, as a way of hastening the latecomer industry's upgrading and moving out of the import-substitution phase into the export phase.[10]

(vi) As Figs. 12.9, 12.10, 12.11, 12.12, 12.3 and 12.14 show, interest in the less developed countries was concentrated in import/export data. Akamatsu's flying geese theory refers to a basic type of import, production (import substitution), and export. However, Kojima changes his interpretation of the flying geese pattern to refer to the shape of its flock, wherein each one of the geese becomes a latecomer country with a "national economy,"

(vii) Akamatsu considered it as a theory of industrialization for Japan, a latecomer country, but Kojima came to see the flying geese theory as a "general theory of economic development" (Kojima, 2003b: i).

Japan's Economic White Paper (1994) uses Kojima's CPC theory of economic development in East Asia and writes as follows.

> Changes in the comparative advantage dynamics can be explained by the product cycle theory. In other words, considering a country that starts producing a certain good (first mover country), (1) initially, the domestic industry grows through import substitution, (2) as domestic production capacity increases, the country expands overseas through exports, (3) as the technology for the good matures, exports of the first mover country decrease and imports increase as the second mover country follows the same path of import substitution and export (4) The first mover country invests directly in the second mover country, where wages are relatively low, while promoting import substitution for goods that require even higher technology. This process is called "flying geese development" because it resembles a flock of geese flying in the sky (Economic Planning Agency -J, 1994a: 302–305).

The above quotation explains that both the first- and second-mover countries adopt import-substitution policies and follow the basic form of the flying geese pattern of development consisting of import, production (import substitution), and export, with development through FDI from the first-mover countries.

However, the major development policies of East Asian countries are diametrically opposed to those of Akamatsu and Kojima. In addition, in the actual development of East Asia, there were widespread cases in which the import and import substitution phases, the basic form of the flying geese theory, were either very short-lived or production and exports suddenly started without going through these processes. The electronics and electrical industries were a good example (Yokota -J, 1992:

[10] See Ozawa (2007) for a discussion of this matter, even as he points out that Akamatsu's points in his FGM has been proposed by Western economists such as Krugman, ignorant of Akamatsu's prior work.

81–84). This fact was recognized by Kojima and Ozawa (UNCTAD, 1995: 260). However, it was simply perceived as an acceleration of industrial relocation by Japanese multinationals.

Furthermore, there was strong criticism that the flying geese theory, like the neoclassical theory of comparative advantage, has become a theory of harmonious East Asian development, but ignored the problem of industrial hollowing out in developed countries due to industrialization in less developed countries. That criticism was also largely ignored. In fact, Toshio Watanabe, involved in this issue, criticizes Kojima's position in his 1995 paper.. Kojima writes that the Japanese economy is less import-dependent and closed, and that this feature is common to "catching up economies" including South Korea and Taiwan. If so, Watanabe points out the contradiction, asking, "How does this assertion by Professor (Kojima) square with the forward trade-oriented East Asian development model?" (Watanabe -J, 2004: 57).

Eventually, despite various criticisms, the flying geese theory came to be regarded as a theory of East Asian development that emerged with Japan in the lead. At the same time, it became widely accepted in Japan among economists and policy elites involved in aid administration (Schröppel & Nakajima, 2003: 223–226).

The Flying Geese Theory as an East Asian Development Theory of Japan

After a period of high growth in the 1960s, Japan maintained steady growth even in the 1970s, when the world economy fell into a period of low growth, and FDI by Japanese firms increased steadily. Against this backdrop of Japan's economic development, Akamatsu and Kojima continued to disseminate their theory of the flying geese pattern to the rest of the world, while their disciples, mainly in Japan, accumulated studies one after another toward country- and industry-specific verification of the flying geese theory.

Blomqvist, relying on Korhonen's (1994) study of Akamatsu, states: "In Japan, he was remarkably influential during the whole postwar period, and his ideas were guidelines for those responsible for the Japanese industrial reconstruction after the war" (Blomqvist, 1997: 14; Kohonen, 1992: 68). Schröppel and Nakajima confirm the influence of the flying geese model in Japan with a quote from Jomo's article, "Akamatsu's 'flying geese' model was the development orthodoxy among Japanese economists and intellectuals in the early and mid-1990s" (Jomo, 2001: 476; Schröppel & Nakajima, 2003). K. Akamatsu has been a leader in various controversies and has occupied a solid position in the Japanese economic community since the end of World War II. However, it was not until the late 1980s that the theory of the "flying geese pattern" gained wide acceptance among Japanese scholars of Asia.

Toshio Watanabe, then professor at Tsukuba University, led the debate on Japan's economic development in Asia throughout the 1970s and 1980s.[11] Watanabe applied

---

[11] In the Japanese theory of East Asian economic development or industrialization, there was an interpretation of neo-dependency development influenced by Marxist economics and the Latin American subordination school, such as Andre Gander Frank and Samir Amin. The idea was that

the concept of "advantage of latecomers" from A. Gerschenkron's study of latecomers to the rapid development of South Korea and other Asian NIEs, and at the same time, he called the "great spurt" "compressed growth" and attributed its development to the fact that the NIEs had "social capabilities" that made it possible. Here, social capabilities included skilled labor and technological level, entrepreneurial capacity, and administrative capacity (policy change capacity) (Watanabe -J, 1979: 22). In the late 1980s, when economic development continued from the NIEs to ASEAN, China, and so on, he named the regional growth as a "chain succession of structural transformation", and expressed that this was possible because the region had "transformational capacity"—competent bureaucracy, entrepreneurial management capacity, and excellent labor force. The terminology was changed to "transformative capacity" - a competent bureaucracy, entrepreneurial management capacity, and excellent labor force. Furthermore, in the 1990s, he renamed East Asia "Western Pacific," and in its regional development, gave it the clever phrase "Asianizing Asia" (Watanabe -J, 1999), providing one controversial axis after another for Japanese East Asian economic theory.

However, as the flying geese theory gained international recognition, Watanabe's research came to be interpreted as basically the same as Kojima and Yamazawa's. The main reason for this, paradoxically, seems to be the mastery of the narrative that Watanabe arrives at in his theory of East Asian economic integration. He explains it as follows.

> The Western Pacific is the region depicted by a structure in which the less developed countries respond quickly to the trade and investment opportunities created by structural changes in the developed countries, transforming their own structures while "tracking" the developed countries with higher growth rates (Watanabe -J, 1991: 193).

Moreover, to explain the above, Watanabe points out that Japan has shifted to domestic demand-led growth due to the strong yen and that East Asia is moving toward regional integration (Watanabe -J, 1979; Watanabe -J, 1985). In this way, Watanabe's theory of East Asia's "chain succession of structural transformation" is a brilliant case of development in line with the fundamentals of modern economics, and even loses the distinction between the flying geese theory and neoclassical economics. The UNCTAD's Report 1996 wrote: "The increasing economic integration of East Asia through intra-regional trade and investment" has, in fact, erased the uniqueness of Watanabe's theory and made the originality of the flying geese theory stand out.

> A main lesson that emerges from the assessment (of this pattern) is that there is considerable scope for developing countries at different levels of industrialization to benefit mutually from the flying geese pattern of trade and FDI. As long as they pursue appropriate industrial and technology policies, these countries can move up the industrial hierarchy through accelerated capital accumulation and the adaptation of advanced technology in such a way that shifts

---

developing countries would only be responsible for low-wage production processes, and that the gap between them and developed countries would not be narrowed, but rather widened. However, it lost its influence after the late 1980s as the development of East Asian countries was realized. For more on regional integration of East Asian economies, see Chapter 6 of this book.

> competitiveness to the mutual advantage of all countries and does not lead to unmanageable domestic dislocations and adjustment problems, or to trade frictions. Consequently, there is considerably more scope for South-South cooperation in industrial development than is generally believed (UNCTAD, 1996: 78).

We can think of another reason why the flying geese theory was accepted. It was the fact that Akamatsu and Kojima were in an overwhelmingly advantageous position in Japan in terms of training their successors, including foreign students. Hitotsubashi University has an Institute of Economic Research, which Akamatsu was involved in establishing, which fostered successors in the tradition of empirical research. These successors accumulated country-specific, industry-specific, and theoretical research on the flying geese theory through studies at institutions of higher education as well as at the Institute of Developing Economies, a leading empirical research institute in Japan.

Japan's ODA and Overseas Assistance Institutions

By the way, after Japan's rapid growth in the 1960s, the country quickly advanced to become one of the world's major industrialized countries from the 1970s onward. Japan rapidly increased its presence in the international community.

From the late 1970s, Japan dramatically increased its ODA, and for the eight years between 1993 and 2000, Japan surpassed the U.S. to become the world's largest ODA donor. By the end of the 1970s, Japan was becoming known for its trinity of ODA, FDI and trade. Japan's White Paper on Economic Cooperation states that Japan was extending "comprehensive economic cooperation in Asia that integrates aid, direct investment, and imports (trade)" (MITI, 1979: 2, 89).

And this is precisely the reason why the flying geese theory had a significant impact on ODA policy makers. In the early 1970s, Kojima had already argued, with Vernon's CPC theory in mind, that direct investment by Japanese firms would help Asia achieve industrialization. Aid could help Japanese investment and promote trade. Indeed, the flying geese theory would serve as the basic theory for Japan's comprehensive Asian policy.

However, Japan's aid delivery method was loan-oriented, and there was a strong relationship with the private business sector in providing aid. As a result, Western countries and civic activists have strongly criticized Japan's aid as "aid with strings attached" and driven by commercialism. Japan came to be criticized for its purpose of helping Japanese firms internationalize and taking away markets from Western firms, while imposing repayment obligations on the borrowing country through the provision of yen loans. Support for large-scale infrastructure construction also became an issue as global environmental problems also came to the forefront of attention. With untied ODA loans, the Japanese government argued that the "request principle" of economic cooperation in granting ODA loans would raise developing countries' awareness of their own interests and encourage "self-help efforts." The development of East Asian countries, which were recipients of aid, made this argument quite persuasive.

In short, the Flying Geese Theory has given legitimacy to Japan's Asia policy and its own aid activities among those involved in aid.

However, this means that Japan has developed its own unique economic cooperation approach among the Development Assistance Committee (DAC) members of the OECD, which is different from that of Europe and the United States. Japan-World Bank controversy occurred in the 1980s with the World Bank's structural adjustment lending (SAL) to developing countries. In September 1990, the World Bank criticized Japan's two-step loan (TSL) program, in which Japan provided loans to financial institutions in the Philippines, which in turn provided loans to small and medium-sized enterprises and the agricultural sector in the Philippines. In October of the following year, the Overseas Economic Cooperation Fund (OECF) of Japan published "Issues Related to the World Bank's Structural Adjustment Approach: Proposals from Key Partners" (OECF occasional paper, no. 1). The differences in the perception of development between the two organizations became apparent.[12]

The Japanese position was vigorously buttressed by Toru Yanagihara. A physics major at the University of Tokyo, he worked at the Institute of Developing Economies and studied economics at Yale University's Graduate School of Economics. Yanagihara was a member of a study group organized by Prof. Ishikawa Shigeru at Hitotsubashi University and another link to the Akamatsu lineage. He was also a member of a study group organized by Ishikawa at the MOF and served as a direct conduit for Ishikawa's ideas to the OECF research team headed by Shimomura. He also "played a key role in monitoring its progress" in the preparation of the World Bank report "The East Asian Miracle", funded by the Japanese government (Terry, 2002: 82, 86).

Yanagihara calls the Japanese development approach the "ingredients approach" (Yanagihara -J, 1992: 25) and later the economic system approach (ESA) to describe the differences between it and neoclassical economics. Yanagihara explains the difference between the ESA and neoclassical economics.

> We take a historical, evolutionary perspective of the economic system approach (ESA). The neoclassical paradigm, modeled after classical physics, is essentially ahistorical and non-evolutionary. Its analytical approach is too mechanistic and deterministic to be able to capture essential elements of interactions among actors and thus misses important strategic issues in the course of economic development/ Why is ESA needed? ... Development is all about change and changes need to be understood in terms of adaptation of a system to its internal as well as external conditions. More substantively, ESA is needed because reduced-form, response function presentation of neoclassical economics is totally inadequate as a basis of policy design (Yanagihara, 1997: 1, 2).

Yanagihara and Susumu Sanbonmatsu held an international symposium at the Institute of Developing Economies (IDE) in January 1997, where Yanagihara further elaborated the Economic System Approach (ESA) as a Japanese development theory. He divided the economic development paradigm/approach into four categories: (a) Historical School (Stage of Development Approach), (b) Neoclassical School (Market-friendly Approach), and (c) New Institutional Economics (Market-enhancing approach), and (d) ESA. And Yanagihara distinguished four approaches to development. At one extreme is "Framework" Thinking/Functionalism, which includes the Market-friendly Approach (Neoclassical economics, World Bank's East

[12] This controversy is discussed in detail in Chap. 6.

Asian Miracle approach) and the subsequent Market enhancing Approach, and at the opposite extreme is "Ingredients" Thinking/Realism, which includes the Historical Approach (Industrial Composition, stages of development) and the ESA. He emphasized the effectiveness of the ESA (Yanagihara, 1997: 14–15).

He describes the historical approach of Japanese development theory and its significance as follows.

> The historical approach, the 'ingredients' thinking shaped under the influence of the German Historical School. It conceptualizes an economy as the sum total of its constituent parts ('ingredients') typically identified with productive sectors or industries. It envisages the process of economic development in terms of changing proportions of productive activities within a national economy. This approach, descriptive and crude as it may be, attempts to capture the dynamic process of economic development in its totality and to identify historical sequences observed in the course of development/The 'historical approach', represents a quintessentially non-theoretical perspective in that propositions it generates, often in regard to stages of development defined in terms of changes in industrial composition over time, are typically in the nature of summarization of empirically observed regularities with virtually no mention of underlying functional relationships. This approach may nonetheless be important, or even indispensable, in capturing the course of development of productive capacities as a historical process and in broadly identifying possible interactions between changes in productive capacities and in institutional factors (Yanagihara -J, 1997: 4, 9, 14).

As such, he finally divided the East Asian economy into "three tiers according to income level as well as the sophistication of the economic system". The first tier consists of Japan, the second tier consists of Taiwan and South Korea, and the third tier, ASEAN3, Malaysia, Thailand, and Indonesia. He then explained the development of the region in relation to the flying geese theory as follows.

> Regional economic configuration in East Asia is often captured by the "flying geese" metaphor. In fact there are two versions to the flying geese metaphor. One is macroscopic relating to the relative positions of national economies in the level of development (often measured by GNP per capita). The other is microscopic in the sense that attention is focused on a particular industry or even a product. In this microscopic approach the sequence of exports of a certain product or a product group is traced over time for each economy and then superimposed to see a sequence and interrelation of events on a regional scope/These two versions of the flying geese metaphor are logically interrelated (Yanagihara, 1997: 32–33).

Ishikawa who played a major role in Japanese development theory and with whom Yanagihara attended his seminar, also summarizes the conflict between the World Bank and Japan as follows.

> The World Bank believed that as long as control and planning were suspended the market economy would be revived, and once the market economy was revived, it would surely achieve industrialization on its own. We believe that the market economy not only stops the controlled economy, but will not appear unless the government lends its support to foster and strengthen it. Industrialization must be planned and protected in its initial stages (Ishikawa -J, 2002).

Like Ishikawa, Kenichi Ohno, a professor at the National Graduate Institute for Policy Studies (GRIPS) involved in aid to Vietnam and other developing countries, has also expressed strong criticism of the World Bank's neoclassical economics aid formula, based on his practical experience.

> The World Bank, which is supposed to lead development policy, appears to be intellectually divided, with both old neoclassical adherents who thoroughly reject the term "industrial policy" and economists who are comfortable promoting industrial policy with certain conditions attached. For us, while there may be some academic significance in continuing to fight the remnants of the Washington Consensus, it is not essential to the task of setting out practical development actions in developing countries. Theory must be supported by practice, and practice must guide theory/...countries that have succeeded in catch-up industrialization in the past have generally done so through self-learning, imitation, experimentation, trial and error, and so on. This is because there was no orderly guidance or textbooks for policy formation (Ohno -J, 2013: 36–37).

Japanese aid has long had a field-oriented tradition, with a dimension separate from government aid policy. Akamatsu also developed his theory of the flying geese theory on the basis of economic thinking that was clearly different from neoclassical Western economics, but Japanese economists and policy makers directly involved in aid were conducting policy from a practical, field-oriented standpoint. Akamatsu and Kojima's theory of the flying geese theory linked theory and policy, both micro and macro, to support their actions. They were supported both theoretically and practically by the flying geese theory.[13]

But this position was ultimately not understood by World Bank economists. According to R. Terry, during the IDE international symposium in 1997, the World Bank's Policy Research Department head, Lyn Squire provided formal comments, and "he criticized the paper's lack of an analytical framework or any empirical tests in support of the concept". After that, Lyn, in a personal capacity, cited this problem. "It was extremely difficult to understand what he [Yanagihara] was saying—to the point where it was difficult to frame my comments. I think the difficulty is when you have research that is not confronted by the data—research which may have some political motivation" (Terry, 2002: 95). In the end, the ESA, which shared Akamatsu's flying geese theory and its approach, was seen only as a Japanese policy theory. Thus, when the Asian currency crisis broke out in Thailand six months after the international symposium, Japan's assertion of its development theory rapidly lost momentum.

In the last part of this section, I would like to introduce an interesting interpretation of the flying geese theory: according to T. Kenderdine of the Australian National University, the flying geese theory is a dominant trade and industry theory of East Asian economic development in the late twentieth century. It is a Keynesian economic theory and was the political tool for the industrialization of East Asia by Japan, an "historical and geopolitical theory, not economic theory, geopolitical theory, not an economic one" (Kenderdine, 2018: 437). His interpretation will be discussed again in the next section, but Kojima's "general theory of economic development", or

---

[13] S. Ishikawa describes the characteristics of Japanese economic cooperation (assistance) as follows. The merit of Japan's yen loans is that, in the formation and implementation of the projects covered by yen loans, the staff or consultants of the Japanese donor agency promoted serious joint research and discussion with the staff of the recipient country on an equal footing, and this contributed to improving the project results, On the other hand, there is the transfer of technology and knowledge betweenI often encountered such facts in the field of aid, and felt that this is the Japanese style of aid activities (Ishikawa, 2002).

flying geese theory, is seen by Kenderdine as a theory of Japan's Asian policy. His understanding also captures one aspect of the flying geese theory.

12.5.3 Changes in the Structure of the International Division of Labor and the Flying Geese Theory

In this century, various debates have arisen regarding the validity of the flying geese theory. Martin Ford, in his book, *Rise of the Robots* writes that "as technology advances, we can expect that more and more of the routine tasks now performed by offshore workers will eventually be handled entirely by machines" (Ford, 2015: 121) We anticipate the future disappearance of unskilled labor, including much skilled labor. That possibility is certainly possible in the long run (Hallward-Driemeier & Nayyar, 2019). But first, we need to examine the reality of the situation, including developing countries.

Of particular interest is Baldwin's theory of the international division of labor. He views economic globalization in the context of a long-term history and understands it as follows. Historically, the economy has been confined to a narrow geographic space of production and consumption by three limiting factors: high trade costs, high communication costs, and high face-to -face costs. This first limitation was exceeded at the beginning of the nineteenth century with the development of transportation technology and the Industrial Revolution. Trade costs fell and international trade flourished. This he calls "globalization's first unbundling".

In the 1990s, the development of ICT facilitated the transfer of knowledge and technology by removing the constraints of high communication costs. The way of industrial production, which had been limited to developed countries, changed, and some stages of the production process and jobs began to be transferred to developing and emerging countries. This is "Globalization's second unbundling". Thus, the industrialization of the less developed countries has changed from "orderly flying-geese formation" to "something that looked more like a flock of starlings" (Baldwin, 2016: 269). He writes as follows.

> The development ladder or sequencing perspective is thoroughly embedded in many people's thinking about industrialization. /Before North–South production unbundling took off around 1990, the sequencing concern was aptly described with the "flying geese" model of development /The flying geese also depict an international specialization dimension. The lead country,goose, typically taken to be Japan, accumulates competencies that allow it to attain competitiveness in sectors on the lower rungs. This opens the door for the next goose in line. The first wave of followers (Hong Kong, Singapore, Taiwan, and Korea) was called the newly industrializing countries or, more colorfully, the "four dragons". Countries in the second wave (Thailand, Philippines, Indonesia, and Malaysia) were called the "four tigers".
>
> The traditional view of import substitution and orderly development-ladder thinking became increasingly irrelevant with production unbundling. All of a sudden, geese at the very back of the formation started exporting what used to be considered sophisticated parts. The evolution was not following a sector-by-sector logic but a stage-by-stage logic, so the strict sequencing of yesteryear broke down (Baldwin, 2016: 267–269).

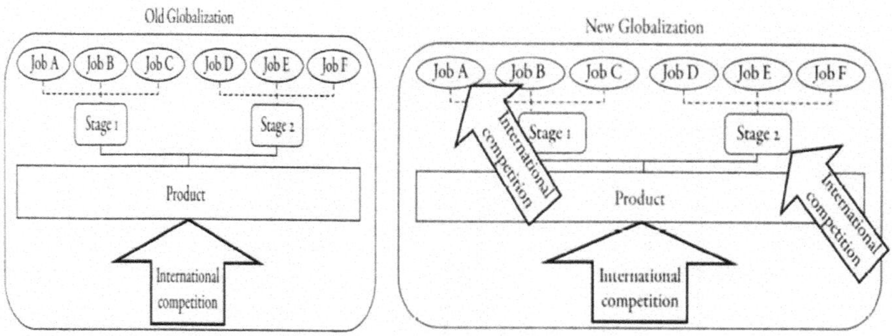

Fig. 12.16 Old globalization and new globalization (*Source* Baldwin, 2016: 166). *Note* Before the second unbundling, firms could be viewed as "black boxes" since global competition pitted one nation's products against another's, as shown schematically in the top panel. More open trade spurred the fortunes of some firms while spiking the fortunes of others, but the firm was the finest level of disaggregation worth looking at. Since most firms in a sector stood or fell together, globalization analysts tended to focus on sectoral impacts—for example, globalization hurt low-tech, labor-intensive sectors in G7 nations while helping their high-tech, high-skill sectors. The fortunes of sectors tended to be shared with the productive factors used most intensively in the sectors, so labor skill groups were also a useful aggregate for analytic purposes (not shown in diagram)

What does it mean that the second unbundling changed the sector-level logic to process-level logic?

Baldwin says that the second unbundling advanced international competition from the product level to the level of stages and jobs (occupation), as shown in Fig. 12.16. The traditional international market was a competitive relationship between products. But with the development of ICT, the production process is now more fragmented, layered, and fragmented. The international division of labor has deepened to the level of stages or jobs (occupations) that make products.[14] Multinational corporations are building international value chains (GVCs) and offshoring their production processes to ensure efficient production.

Developing countries then have no choice but to industrialize by participating in these GVCs; until the 1980s, developing countries had to gain a comparative advantage at the product level. But with the second unbundling, they can now industrialize by producing specific components. Baldwin writes: "The new ability shifted the sequencing question from "what sector" or "what product" to "what stage" or "what part". The switch meant that the big push could be done in small nudges for those developing nations that managed to join global value chains" (Baldwin, 2016: 266). However, "the ability to join an international supply created a new development trap" (Baldwin, 2016: 270).

[14] The writer is sympathetic to Baldwin's theory of the second unbundling. However, the author believes that the international division of labor structure was smoothly developed in the 1990s with the development of ICT, due to the fact that the form of entry of Japanese firms into NIEs in the 1960 and 1970s was already a transfer of stages or jobs (Hirakawa -J, 1992). This is dealt with in Chap. 7.

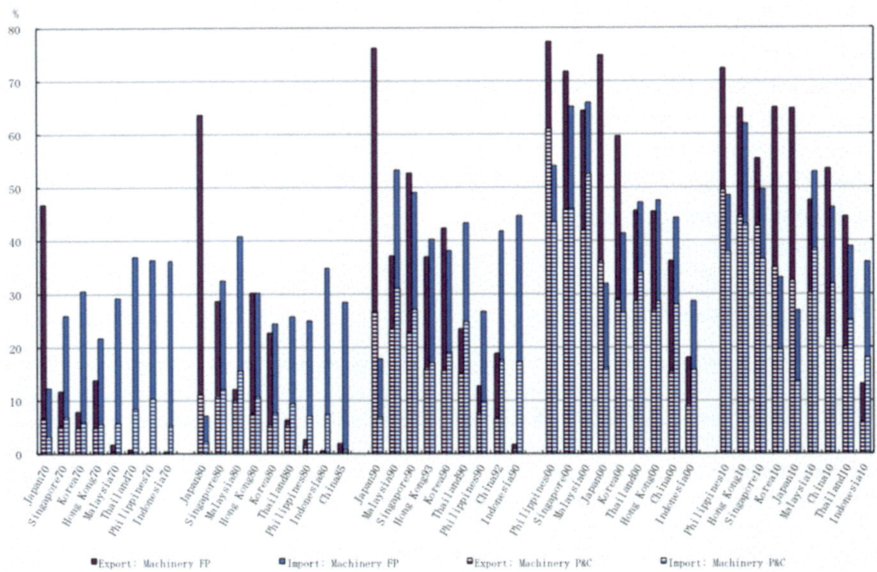

Fig. 12.17 Shares of machinery in the total exports/imports to/from the World, 1970–2010 (*Source* Kimura, 2019). *Note* The data for 1970 and 1980 and those after 1990 are based on SITC and HS commodity classification, respectively

Trade in intermediate goods can be traced back to the 1960 and 1970s, as confirmed in Chap. 7 of this report, when trade in intermediate goods began to be observed in the trade of East Asian countries. Figure 12.17 shows the composition of trade in finished goods and intermediate goods in East Asian countries by decade since the 1970s, confirming the rapid growth of trade in intermediate goods since the 1990s. Fukunari Kimura, Professor at Keio University, Japan, who created this figure, also considers the flying geese theory as a theory of "sectoral" development, based on Baldwin's theory of second unbundling.

If so, is the flying geese theory an analytical framework of a bygone era? Tran Van Tho, a Vietnamese economist from Hitotsubashi University, disagrees with Baldwin's assertion that the flying geese theory is a theory of the past because the industrial structure has become more sophisticated since the 1990s and the international division of labor is now at the process level rather than the sector level. He defines the flying geese theory as "a theory that explains the dynamic international division of labor with goods and industries as units", while fragmentation theory and Baldwin's theory that explains the division of labor between processes as "a theory of the international division of labor with production processes and operations as units". If the market for parts and intermediate goods can be identified, they can all be regarded as industries, and can be analyzed within the framework of the flying geese theory. However, since production processes and tasks are not "industries", their cross-border location and outsourcing can be explained by the fragmentation theory. In short, both flying geese theory and fragmentation theory can explain the development and division of labor in modern Asia" (Tran -J, 2019: 88).

However, regarding the vertical division of labor at the process and component level, Tran points out that Japanese synthetic fiber firms had already developed vertical division of labor in South Korea, Malaysia, Indonesia, and other countries in the 1970 and 1980s, and that fragmentation is not a new phenomenon, merely one that did not become common due to the weak trend toward free trade at the time. In other words, Tran argues that trade in components and intermediate goods already occurred before the 1990s, and he attributes this to differences in trade policy instead of ICT, which Baldwin emphasizes (Tran -J, 2019: 86).

Figure 12.18 illustrates the Asian Development Bank's calculation of the average export composition of industrial products by technology level for major East Asian economies on a value-added basis for the period 2013–2017. From this, the ADB confirms the validity of the flying geese theory by showing that, in general, high-income economies produce high-value-added products and middle-income economies export middle-value-added products. At the same time, we note that countries overlap at similar value-added levels, indicating a more complex international division of labor. We describe it in the following narrative.

> Generally, the graph shows that high-income economies have a larger share of more complex goods in their export basket, whereas middle-income economies have a larger share of mid-complexity goods. This reinforces the "flying geese" model often used to signify the pattern of industrialization in the region, which generalizes dynamic patterns of industrial catch-up. In this process, industries relocate from advanced to developing economies sequentially, starting in light industries requiring lower technology, such as footwear and garments. But, at the same time, we can observe the emergence of intra-industry trade in addition to inter-industry trade: Fig. 12.18 shows overlapping export patterns in each product sophistication level. This indicates that the inter-economy and interindustry "flying geese" development model evolved over time into a more complex and dynamic structure of intra-industry regional and global value chains (ADB, 2020: 158).

Baldwin emphasizes that the development of Stage and Jobs in developing countries is possible at a stroke by joining the global value chain (GVC) of multinational corporations, and not the development of an ordered set of industries, as in the flying geese theory. He says it has metaphorically changed from a flock of geese to a "flock of starlings". But multinationals had begun trading in intermediate goods before the 1990s, and their division of labor did not ignore wage levels or the quality of labor. They set up the international division of labor with wage levels in mind and with a focus on productivity, and from a more macroscopic perspective, there is an international pecking order of technological levels.

In the end, the evaluation of the Flying Geese Theory depends on how one perceives it: the development of ICT has gradually changed the industrial structure and the nature of the international division of labor since the period that Fröbel et al. called New International Division of Labour (NIDL) (see Chap. 6). And now, with the emergence of China as a huge economy, another change is underway. The authors also discussed the development mechanism of East Asia in Chaps. 3 and 7, pointing out the shift from NIEs to PoBMEs type of development.

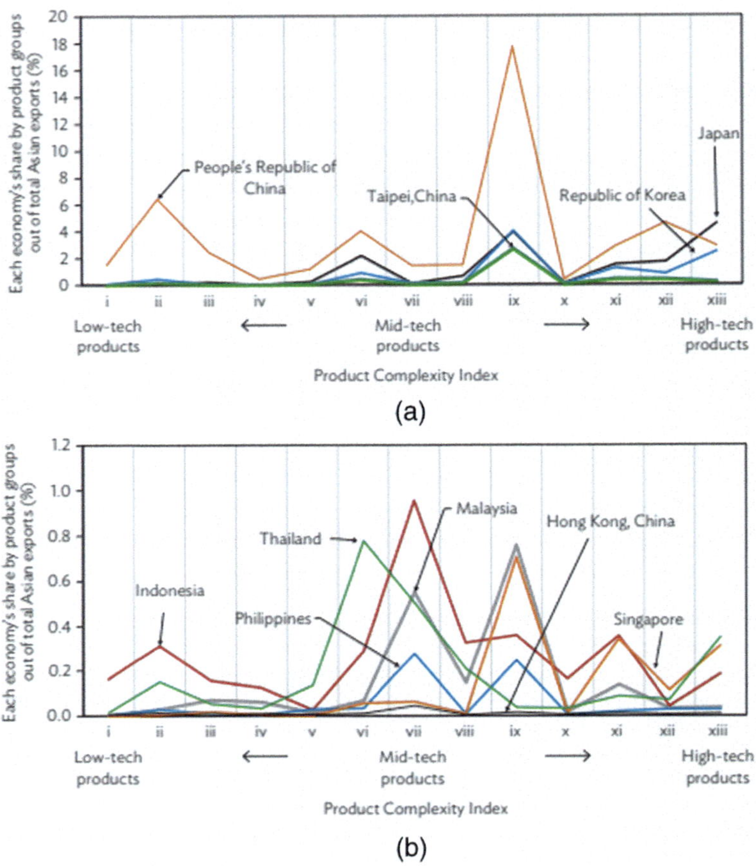

Fig. 12.18 The Flying Geese pattern of Asian exports (Average for 2013–2017) (*Source* ADB 2020: 157). *Notes* Data are for manufactured exports on a value-added basis, averaged for 2013–2017. Input–output data are used to calculate value added. The y-axis depicts each economy's exports of a product group as a share of total Asian exports of all product groups. Total Asian exports is based on 24 economies. The x-axis represents the following product groups, arranged by increasing complexity: (i) leather and footwear, (ii) textiles and textile products, (iii) manufacturing not elsewhere classified (nec) and recycling; (iv) wood and products of wood and cork; (v) other nonmetallic minerals; (vi) basic metal and fabricated metal; (vii) food, beverages and tobacco; (viii) rubber and plastics; (ix) electrical and optical equipment; (x) pulp, paper, printing, and publishing; (xi) chemicals and chemical products; (xii) machinery, nec; and (xiii) transport equipment

The significance of the Akamatsu Flying Geese Theory lies not in its validity, but rather in its recognition and perspective that attempts to grasp the totality of this major global economic change from a historical perspective. Yanagihara attempted to develop it as an ESA. In an era of drastic change, the strength of the Flying Geese Theory lies in its perspective and research methodology, which is rooted in reality, and broadened to include historical perspectives for theorizing. Let us discuss this point again in the next section.

12.6 Akamatsu's Flying Geese Theory and the Development of Less Developed Countries

The flying geese theory, on the other hand, was Akamatsu's attempt to empirically capture the industrialization and economic development of Japan as a latecomer in the first half of the twentieth century, while being aware of its historicity. That development had a basic form and two sub-forms. In East Asia, the subject of this research, on the one hand, Japan went from a latecomer to an advanced country and eventually became a capital exporter, and on the other hand, the latecomers achieved industrialization one after another and economic integration progressed. During this period, interest in the flying geese theory has shifted from the basic form to the international transfer of industries in the secondary form. And FDI by Japanese firms played a major role in that transfer. Kojima's development of the geese pattern theory certainly represents one direction of development.

However, if we go back to the starting point of the flying geese theory, there remains the perspective of reconsidering the catch-up of new latecomer countries in line with the actual situation, including the basic form. Akamatsu's research in the 1930s shows that extremely detailed individual data on trade goods were collected and painstakingly analyzed (Akamatsu -J, 1932, 1935). Akamatsu's (1956) narrative, mentioned at the end of Sect. 12.3.2 of this chapter, pointed out the need to examine the flying geese type development of the latecomer countries following Japan. Kojima emphasized the importance of PROT-FDI, and if so, it would not be surprising if the flying geese pattern development was assumed to be modeled by adding FDI as well as imports for the less developed countries following Japan. At the very least, the relationship with the basic form of the less developed countries following Japan should have been an issue for consideration.

Focused on internal innovations in the development of Asian NIEs in the 1990s. Hobday writes that the Flying Geese Model is "the first model to account systematically for inter-country trade and technology connections", and "Japan is undeniably important", but "the model fails to give due recognition to the distinctive indigenous efforts of the four dragons to accumulate technology and to export overseas" (Hobday, 1995: 11). He identifies a problem with the post-Kojima theory of the flying geese pattern, in which the position of the less developed countries has disappeared. Directly linking the sophistication of Japan's industrial structure to the theory of development of the less developed countries is a generalization of the theory, but it is out of step with Akamatsu's positivist economics. In other words, the elaboration of the final flying geese theory relies too much on the Japanese experience as a developed country. This seems to be one reason why Akamatsu's successors have been less sharp in their criticism of neoclassical economics, which takes the market as the panacea. It was probably Baldwin and Kenderdine who exploited this pitfall of the flying geese theory.

Baldwin turns to the dramatic changes in the international division of labor resulting from the "second unbundling", and the nature of industrialization in the developing countries. He also touched on the advantages and limitations of industrialization in the less developed countries. According to him, unlike the development of industry assumed by the flying geese theory, participation in GVCs is a condition for industrialization in the less developed countries today. Neoclassical economics and even the national economic framework assumed by Akamatsu's theory of the Flying Geese Model have been revised. The development of latecomer countries requires two sets of policies. First are "policies that convince the foreign firms that they can safely do business in the developing nation", and the second are policies that remove "hindrances to cross-border flows of the things that are needed to keep the international production network running as a network" (Baldwin, 2016: 272).

Incidentally, in Chap. 3 and even Chap. 7 of this book, the authors confirm that the development of East Asia in the 1960–90s was achieved by the international expansion of multinational corporations, and explain that the intra-East Asian market is now the basis of development, which we call PoBMEs type of development (Hirakawa -J, 1992; Hirakawa et al., 2017: Chap. 2; Hirakawa, 2018: Chap. 3).

The less developed East Asian countries did not create their own conditions for development as "national economies" on their own. Under the new conditions of globalization, as Baldwin points out, it is essential for the less developed countries to make efforts to industrialize their own economies. Akamatsu makes a similar point based on Japan's experience in extracting the basic form of the flying geese pattern. It is a dialectical narrative, but the "establishment of self-production" of imported industries "was the usual struggle, the overcoming of contradictions" (Akamatsu -J, 1937: 207). The same challenge remains the same in today's less developed countries.

Satoshi Inomata of IDE/JETRO, Japan, and others have been working to clarify the structure of the international division of labor by analyzing an international input–output table that combines the input–output table of each country with international trade data. They develop the ideas of G. Gereffi, a development sociologist who developed the global value chain (GVC) theory from the commodity chain, and Baldwin, who developed the unbundling theory mentioned above, argue that "the development of transportation technology and information and communication technology accelerates the international transfer of technology. As a result, many developing countries have achieved economic sophistication at a much faster pace than traditional development theory assumes". At the same time, he is concerned about the emergence of a new North–South problem, the problem of disparity between the less developed and the most developed countries. Nowadays, it is increasingly difficult for less developed countries to catch up due to (i) the importance of labor productivity, (ii) changes in the mass production product market due to diversification of consumption preferences, (iii) the need to address environmental issues, and (iv) the need to respond to the automation of production due to technological innovation (Inomata -J, 2019: 168–167, 211–212). What is clear is that, as Baldwin, Inomata, and we have pointed out, the less developed countries must now overcome their own challenges on the basis of the international ruling conditions. To this end, they must not stop at passive responses to the given conditions, but must take active measures to build up their own competitiveness. Therein lies the new role of the flying geese theory.

Kenderdine, by the way, approaches the flying geese theory from a completely different perspective.

> The theory was first used as a justification for the Greater East Asian Co prosperity Sphere, then to explain Japan's reindustrialization and springboard into Asian markets, and was finally codified into the Asia Pacific Economic Cooperation free trade area (Kenderdine, 2018: 438).

He summarizes the "One Belt, One Road" (BRI) concept adopted by President Xi Jinping as China's alternative to the flying geese pattern, which he sees as Japan's policy theory for the formation of a broad economic zone. China's outward direct investment (ODI) is different from the FDI that Kojima's flying geese theory emphasizes."China's FDI is not driven by chasing lower costs of labour in regional economies but rather by global geoeconomics strategies" (Kenderdine, 2018: 442). China, through its "One Belt, One Road" policy, will become a "global geoeconomic, geo-industrial and geopolitical power" in the future. He also foresees a "realignment of twenty-first century economic history from the Pacific to the Indian Ocean" (Kenderdine, 2018: 450, 451). He uses the expression "Death of the East Asian goose" to describe the flying geese theory. But it evokes the image of a new goose taking flight.

If the theory of the flying geese pattern had been free to consider the industrialization and economic development of the less developed countries following Japan in line with their realities, as Akamatsu emphasized, a new theory of the flying geese pattern development of the less developed countries could have been developed. Given the current state of the academic world of economics, it is understandable that this would be extremely difficult. However, if the original Akamatsu's theory of the flying geese pattern of development had been applied to the industrialization of the less developed countries, and the theory had been extracted from the industrialization of East Asian countries using data, it is possible that the theory of the flying geese pattern of development in Asia would have been born. The GVC theory and China's BRI could have been examined in the context of the development of the flying geese theory. It would have provided a guideline for development policy. In this sense, Akamatsu's flying geese theory left behind "economics as an empirical science" and its economic methodology as a legacy. The economics methodology, which aims to theorize in line with reality, has not faded away.

In today's dramatically changing global economy, it is a fiction to assume that interpretations based on abstract theories are the only truth. Rather, theories and policies based on reality are required. Standing at the present moment, we must expand our analytical framework to the basic and secondary forms formulated by Akamatsu's theory of the flying geese pattern, as well as to the realm of historical world economic structure, which Akamatsu called the "heterogenization and homogenization of capitalism" and Kojima called the third phase of the flying geese pattern, and pursue the development of less developed countries from this perspective.

To repeat the last point, as both Baldwin and Inomata and we have pointed out, the given conditions for industrialization and development of the less developed countries have changed today. The industrialization of the less developed countries is catch-up industrialization, which can only be specifically accomplished within the framework of the capitalist world economy. This was true in Akamatsu's time and remains true today. And today, participation in GVCs is probably a necessary condition for the development of the less developed countries. But it is not a sufficient condition. The development of policy and technological human competitiveness must be explored in relation to the industrialization of the less developed countries. Active responses from the perspective of the less developed countries are indispensable.

The succession of the flying geese theory from Akamatsu to Kojima has given life to Akamatsu economics for nearly a century. Now it will be necessary to reverse the process, returning to Akamatsu's starting point. From the approach of the German historical school, Akamatsu extracted empirical laws in late industrialization. Now it is time to go back to the starting point once again, reexamine various theoretical and empirical achievements of the current world economy from a historical perspective, and envision a theory and policy for the development of latecomer countries. This would be the rebirth of a new theory of the flying geese pattern, which should be a joint work with the people of the less developed countries.

References

A symbol (-J) after the author's name are Japanese documents

ADB. (2020). *Asia's journey to prosperity: Policy, market, and technology over 50 years*. Asian Development Bank.

Akamatsu, K. (1961). A theory of unbalanced growth in the world economy. *Weltwirtschaftliches Archiv, Band 86, Heft, 2*, 196–217.

Akamatsu, K. -J. (1932). Sekai Keizai no ishitsuka to doshituka (Heternization and homogenization in the World Economy). *Shogyo Keizai Ronso (Journal of Commerce and Economy, Nagoya Higher Commercial School), 10*, Part 1.

Akamatsu, K. -J. (1935). Wagakuni yomo kogyohin no boeki susei (Trade trend of our country's wool industry products). *Shogyo Keizai Ronso (Journal of Commerce and Economy, Nagoya Higher Commercial School), 13*, Part 1.

Akamatsu, K. -J. (1937). Wagakuni keizai hatten no sogo benshoho (Synthetic dialectics of our country's economic development). *Shogyo Keizai Ronso (Journal of Commerce and Economy, Nagoya Higher Commercial School), 15*, Part 1.

Akamatsu, K. -J. (1944). *Keizai shin chitsujo no keisei genri (The forming principles of an economic new order)*. Riron Sha, July.

Akamatsu, K. -J. (1956). Wagakuni sangyo hatten no ganko keitai—Kikai kigu kogyo ni tsuite (Types in the development of our imported industries—With special reference to the machine tool industry). *Hitotsubashi Ronso (Hitotsubashi Review), 36*(5).

Akamatsu, K. -J. (1958). Jisaku nenpu (Self-made chronology). In Collection Publishing Committee of commemorative papers for Dr. K Akamatsu's 60th birthday (Ed.), *Keizai seisaku to kokusai boeki (Economic policy and international trade)*. Shunju Sha.

Akamatsu, K. -J. (1960). Hitotsubashi no dento ni okeru keizaiseisaku: Hitotsubashi daigaku souritsu 83 shunen kinen koen (Economic policy in Hitotsubashi tradition: A lecture commemorating the 83rd anniversary of the founding of Hitotsubashi University). *Hitotsubashi Ronso (Hitotsubashi Review), 44*(1).

Akamatsu, K. (1962). A historical pattern of economic growth in developing countries. In *The Developing Economies Preliminary Issue, no. 1* (pp. 3–25). Institute of Developing Economies, March–August.

Akamatsu, K. -J. (1965). *Sekai keizai ron (The World Economy).* Kunimoto Shobo.

Akamatsu, K. -J. (1972). Nihon sangyo hatten no ganko keitai. In Sekaikeizai Kenkyu Kyokai/ Kojima K (supervised) *The world economy in 1985*, Volume 1: Japan's trade structure and development. Shiseido.

Akamatsu, K. -J. (1974). *Kin haika to kokusai Keizai (Abolition of gold standard system and international economy).* Toyo Keizai Shimposha.

Akamatsu, K. -J. (1975). Gakumon henro (Academic pilgrimage). In Akamatsu's student Koijma Kiyoshi (Ed.), *Akamatsu Kaname sensei tsuito ronshu: Gakumon henro* (Prof. Akamatsu memorial paper Collection: Academic pilgrimage). Sekai Keizai Kenkyukai.

Akamatsu, K., & Kojima, K. -J. (1943). *Sekai keizai to gijutsu (World economy and technology).* Shoko Gyosei Sha, June.

Aoki, T. -J. (1987). *Taiheiyo seicho no toraiangul: Nihon, Beikoku, Ajia NICs kan no kozo chosei (Triangle of Pacific growth: Structural adjustment of Japan, USA, and Asian NIEs).* Nihon Hyoronsha.

Baldwin, R. (2016). *The great convergence: Information technology and the new globalization.* Belknap Press of Harvard University Press.

Barnard, M., & Ravenhill, J. (1995). Beyond product cycles and flying geese: Regionalization, hierarchy, and the industrialization of East Asia. *World Politics, 47*(2), January.

Blomqvist, Hans, C. (1997). *Economic interdependence and development in East Asia.* Praeger.

Cumings, B. (1984). *The origins and development of the Northeast Asian political economy: Industrial sectors, product cycles, and political consequences* (Vol.38, No. 1). International Organization, Winter.

Economic Planning Agency, Japan. (1993, March). Transmission of industrial development and international industrial adjustment. *Keizai bunseki (Economic Analysis), (Keizai Kikakucho), 129.*

Economic Planning Agency, Japan. -J. (1994a). *Heisei roku nen ban Keizai hakusho (White paper on economy 1994).* Keizai Kikakucho.

Economic Planning Agency. Japan. -J. (1994b). *Heisei roku nen ban sekai keizai hakusho (White paper on world economy 1994).* Keizai Kikakucho.

Ford, M. (2015). *The rise of the robots: Technology and the threat of mass unemployment.* One World.

Hallward-Driemeier, M., & Nayyar, G. (2019, December). *Have robots grounded the flying geese? Evidence from greenfield FDI in manufacturing.* Policy Research Working Paper 9097, World Bank Group.

Hart-Landsberg, M., & Burkett, P. (1998) Contradictions of capitalist industrialization in East Asia: A critique of "Flying Geese" theories of development. *Economic Geography, 74*(2)

Hirakawa, H. -J. (1997, March). Higashi ajia kogyoka dainamizumu no ronri (Logic of East Asia's industrialization dynamism). In Institute of Comparative Economic Studies, Hosei University Kasuya S (Ed.), *Higashi ajia kogyouka dainamizum (The East Asian industrialization dynamism).* Hose University Press.

Hirakawa, H. (1999, March). East Asia's industrialization and the currency and financial crises within the world economy. *Journal of International Economic Studies*, (13).

Hirakawa, H. -J. (2013, March). *Akamatsu Kaname to Nagoya Koto Shogyo Gakko: Ganko keitairon no tanjo to sono tenkai nikansuru ichi shiron (Kaname Akamatsu and Nagoya Higher Commercial School: An essay on the birth and development of flying geese model)* (Vol. 60, No. 4). School of Economics, Nagoya University, Keizai Kagaku (Economic Science).

Hirakawa, H. (2018). Transformation of the world economy and institutionalization of the East Asian region. In R. H. Boyer, T. Uemura, T. Yamada, & L. Song (Eds.), *Evolving diversity and interdependence of capitalism.* Springer.

Hirakawa, H. -J. (2021, November). *Nagoya Koto Shogyo Gakko to Akamatsu Kaname (Nagoya Higher Commercial School and Akamatsu Kaname).* Nagoya University Graduate School of Economics, The book commemorating the 100th anniversary of the Graduate School of Economics.

Hirakawa, H. -J. (1992). *NIES: Sekai shisutemu to kaihatu (NIEs: World system and development).* Dobun Kan.

Hirakawa, H., Takahashi, N., Maquito Ferdinand, C., & Tokumaru, N. (Eds.). (2017). *Innovative ICT industrial architecture in East Asia.* Springer.

Hiratsuka, D. -J. (2003). Nichi/ASEAN no kyousouryoku to keizai renkei (Japan and ASEANs' competitiveness and economic partnership). In I. Yamazawa, D. Hiratsuka (Eds.), *Nichi/ASEAN's economic partnership and competitiveness.* Institute of Developing Economies.

Hiratsuka, D. (2005, February). *The "Catching up" process of manufacturing in East Asia.* IDE Discussion Paper, no. 22.

Hobday, M. (1995). *Innovation in East Asia: The challenge to Japan.* Edward Elgar.

Ihza, Mahendra Y. -J. (1998). *Ganko keitai model no shinwasei (The myth of flying geese model).* Doctoral thesis. Tsukuba University.

Ikeo, A. -J. (2008). *Hyoden Akamatsu Kaname: Waga taikei wo norikoete yuke (Critical biography Akamatsu Kaname: Go beyond my theoretical system).* Nihon Keizai Hyoronsha.

Inomata, S. -J. (2019). *Gurobaru Baryu chehn (Global value chain).* Nihon Keizai Shimbun Shuppansha.

Ishikawa, S. -J. (2002, March). *Sekai ginko no kokusai kaihatu seisaku minaoshi to nihon no ODA (World Bank's international development policy review and Japan's ODA)* (Vol. 53, No. 6). Shakai Kagaku Kenkyu (Journal of Social Science, Institute of Social Science, University of Tokyo).

Itagaki, Y. (1963). *Shinpan: Seiji keizaigaku no houhou (New edition: Method of political economy).* Keisoshobo.

Jomo, S.K. (2001). Rethinking the role of government policy in Southeast Asia. In E. Stiglitz, Joseph, & Y. Shahid (Eds.), *Rethinking the East Asia miracle.* Oxford University Press.

Kasahara, S. (2004). *The flying geese paradigm: A critical study of its application to East Asian regional development.* UNCTAD Discussion Paper, no.169.

Kasahara, S. (2019). *A critical evaluation of flying geese paradigm: the evolving framework of the model application to East Asian regional development and beyond.* Ph.D. thesis at Erasmus University Rotterdam, Netherlands.

Kenderdine, T. (2018). Death of the East Asian goose and the rise of China's Geoindustrial policy. *Journal of Political Science, 23*, 437–453

Kimura, F. (2019). *(PPT material) Onshore or Offshore: Value chains in the digital age.* https://cpb-apse2.wpmucdn.com/blogs.auckland.ac.nz/dist/f/255/files/2019/09/OnOffkimuralight.pdf

Koide, Y. -J. (1975). Akamatsu sensei no gakumon to Nagoya jidai (Teacher Akamatsu's studies and Nagoya days. In Akamatsu's student Koijma Kiyoshi (Ed.), *Akamatsu Kaname sensei tsuito ronshu: Gakumon henro (Prof. Akamatsu memorial paper Collection Academic pilgrimage).* Sekai Keizai Kenkyukai.

Kojima, K. -J. (1958). Shihon chikuseki to Kokusai bungyo: Akamatsu hakase "Sangyo hatten no ganko keitai" no ichi tenkai (Capital accumulation and international division of labor: A development of Dr. Akamatsu's "Flying geese pattern of industrial development"). In: Kojima Kiyoshi hen, Keizai seisaku to kokusai boueki, Akamatsu Kaname hakase kanreki kinen ronbun shu (K. Kojima (Ed.) *Economic policy and international trade: Collection of papers commemorating Dr. K. Akamatsu's 60th birthday).* Shunju Sha.

Kojima, K. -J. (1972a). Summary. In: Kojima, K. (supervised) *Senkyuhyaku hachiju gonen no sekai keizai Daiikkan: Nihon boeki no kozo to hattenn (The world economy in 1985).* Vol. 1: Japan's trade structure and development). Shiseido.

Kojima, K. -J. (1972b). Ganko keitairon to purodakuto saikuru ron (Flying geese theory and product cycle hypothesis). In K. Kojima (supervised. 1972a) *Senkyuhyaku hachiju gonen no sekai keizai*

Daiikkan: Nihon boeki no kozo to hattenn (The world economy in 1985). Vol. 1: Japan's trade structure and development). Shiseido.

Kojima, K. -J. (1972c). Kaigai chokusetu toshi no riron to shin keitai (Theory and new form of foreign direct investment: American type and Japanese type). In K. Kojima (supervised. 1972a) *Senkyuhyaku hachiju gonen no sekai keizai Daiikkan: Nihon boeki no kozo to hattenn (The world economy in 1985).* Vol. 1: Japan's trade structure and development). Shiseido.

Kojima, K. (1973a). Reorganization of North–South trade: A Japanese model of multinational business operation. *Hitotsubashi Journal of Economics, 13*(2), February.

Kojima, K. (1973b). A macroeconomic approach to Foreign Direct Investment. *Hitotsubashi Journal of Economics, 14*(1), June.

Kojima, K. -J. (1975). Ganko keitai ron to purodakuto saikuru ron (the Flying geese model of development and product cycle theory-. In: Akamatsu Disciple (Eds.) *Gakumon henro (Academic Pilgrimage: Professor K. Akamatsu's memorial paper collection).* Sekai Keizai Kenkyukai.

Kojima, K. -J. (1984). Kojima Kiyoshi meiyo kyoju jisaku nenpu (Professor emeritus Kiyoshi Kojima's self-made chronology). *Hitotsubashi Ronso (The Hitotsubashi Review), 92*(4).

Kojima, K. -J. (2000a). Gankogata keizaihatten ron: Akamatsu original: Shinkou koku no kyacchi-appu prosesu (Flying-geese pattern of development: Akamatsu's original: Catching-up process of Emerging Economies). *Sekai Keizai Hyoron (World Economic Review), 44*(3), 47–70, March.

Kojima, K. (2000b). The "flying geese" model of Asian economic development: Origin, theoretical extensions, and regional policy implications. *Journal of Asian Economics, 11*, 375–401, October.

Kojima, K. -J. (2003a, March). Bokei/Chokusetsu toshi no Kojima meidai: PROT-FDI tai ANT-FDI (Kojima theorem of trade and direct investment: PROT-FDI vs ANT-FDI). *Surugadai Keizai Ronshu (Surugadai Economic Review), 12*(2), 1–69.

Kojima, K. -J. (2003b). *Ganko gata Keizai hatten ron, vol.1: Nihon keizai, Ajia Keizai, sekai Keizai (Flying geese pattern of economic development vol. 1: Japanese economy, Asian economy, and the world economy).* Bunshindo, May.

Kojima, K. -J. (2004). *Ganko gata Keizai hatten ron, vol. 2: Ajia to sekai no shin chitsujo (Flying geese pattern of economic development vol. 2: New order of Asia and the world).* Bunshindo, March.

Kojima, K. (2005). A reversal of "competitive advantage" pattern: Heterogenization versus homogenization. *Journal of Asian Economics, 16.*

Kojima, K. -J. (2006a). Ganko gata keizai hatten ron: kojima bajon no seika to kadai (Flying geese pattern of economic development: Kojima version's result and its problem). *Sekai Keizai Hyoron (World Economic Review),* Part 1, May.

Kojima, K. -J. (2006b). Ganko gata keizai hatten ron: kojima bajon no seika to kadai (Flying geese pattern of economic development: Kojima version's result and its problem). *Sekai Keizai Hyoron (World Economic Review),* Parts 2, June.

Kojima, K. -J. (2006c). *Ganko gata Keizai hatten ron. vol. 3: Kokusai keizai to kinyu kiko (Flying geese pattern of economic development vol. 3: International economy and financial institutions).* Bunshin Do., September

Kojima, K. -J. (2009). (Reprint version) Ganko gata keizai hatten ron: kojima basion no seika to kadai (Flying geese pattern of economic development: Kojima version's achievements and challenges) In K. Ikema (Ed.), *Kokusai Keizai no shin kozu: Gankogata hatten no shintenkara (New structure of international economy: From a view of flying geese pattern of development).* Bunshin Do, June.

Korhonen, P. (1994). The theory of the Flying Geese Pattern of development and its interpretations. *Journal of Peace Research, 31*(1)

Kwan, C. H. (2002). *The Rise of China and Asia's flying-geese pattern of economic development: An empirical analysis based on US import statistics.* RIETI Discussion Paper Series 02-E-009, July.

Lerner, A. P. (1952). Factor prices and international trade. *Economics, 25*(1).

Ministry of Economy, Trade and Industry, Japan. (2001). *White paper on international trade 2001.* METI.

Ministry of International Trade and Industry, Japan. (1979). *Keizai kyoryoku no genjo to mondaiten (Present situation and problems of economic cooperation).* MITI.

Nakauchi, T. -J. (2010). Ganko gata keizai hatten no keisho to tenkai (Inheritage and development of flying geese pattern of economic development). In K. Ikema (Ed.), *Kokusai Keizai no sin kozu: Keizai hatten ron no shiten kara (New composition of international economy: from a viewpoint of flying geese model of international economy).* Bunshin Do, June.

Ohno, K. -J. (2013). *Sangyo seisaku no tsukurikata (The way of building industrial policies).* Yuhikaku.

Okita, S. (1985). Special presentation: Prospect of the Pacific economies. *Reports of the Fourth Pacific economic cooperation Conference: Issues and opportunities.* Korea Development Institute, Soul, Korea, April 29–May1.

Otsuki, T. -J. (2010). *Akamatsu Kaname no ganko keitairon to sono tenkai: Zai Nagoya jidai to dankairon teki shiza (Kaname Akamatsu's flying geese theory and its development: His period in Nagoya and a stage-based perspective.* Doctoral Dissertation, Tokyo University of Foreign Studies.

Ozawa, T. (2001). The "hidden" side of the "flying geese" catch-up model: Japan's dirigiste institutional setup and a deepening financial morass. *Journal of Asian Economics, 12.*

Ozawa, T. (2007) Professor Kiyoshi Kojima's contributions to FDI theory: Trade, growth, and integration in East Asia. *The International Economy, 11*, 17–23.

Schröppel, C., & Nakajima, M. (2003). The changing interpretation of the flying geese model of economic development. *Japanstudien, 14*(1), 203–236. https://doi.org/10.1080/09386491.2003.11826895

Tran, Van Tho. -J. (2019). Chu Shotoku koku no wana no kadai to riron (Challenges and theories of the middle-income country trap). In: Tran, V.T., and Karikomi, S. co-authored book, *Middle income trap and China/ASEAN*, Keiso Shobo.

Terry, E. (2002). *How Asia got rich: Japan, China, and the Asian miracle.* Routledge.

UNCTAD. (1995). *World Investment Report 1995.* United Nations Conference on Trade and Development.

UNCTAD. (1996). *Trade and Development Report 1996*. UNCTAD.

Vernon, R. (1966). International investment and international trade in the product cycle. *Quarterly Journal of Economics, 80*(2), 190–207.

Watanabe, T. -J. (1979). *Ajia chusinkoku no chosen (Challenges of Asian middle-advanced countries).* Nihon Keizai Shimbun Sha.

Watanabe, T. -J. (1985). *Seicho no ajia Teitai no ajia (Growing Asia, Stagnated Asia).* Toyo Keizai Shimpo Sha.

Watanabe, T. -J. (1991). Ajia taiheiyo wo do toraeruka (How to grapse Asia Pacific). In T. Watanabe, H. Kajiwara & K. Takanaka (Eds.), *Ajia sogo izon no jidai (The age of Asia's inter-dependence).* Yuhikaku.

Watanabe, T. -J. (1999, June). *Ajiaka suru Ajia (Asianizing Asia).* Chuo Koron (Monthly). Chuo Koron Sha.

Watanabe, T. -J. (2004). Shohyo: Kojima Kiyoshi 'Ganko gata Keizai hatten ron' Daiikkan, Dai nikan (Book review: Flying geese type of economic development, vol.1, & vol.2). *Ajia Keizai, IDE-JETRO, 45*(9).

World Bank. (1993). *The East Asian miracle: Economic growth and public policy.* Oxford University Press.

Yamazawa, I. -J. (1984). *Nihon no keizai hatten to kokusai bungyo (Japan's economic development and international specialization).* Toyo Keizai Shimpo sha.

Yamazawa, I. (1990). *Flying wild-geese in the Pacific: Patterns of industrial development among Asian Countries: to deliver at the Distinguished Speakers Program.* Asian Development Bank, Manila, November 27.

Yamazawa, I. (1993). Transmission of industrial development and international industrial adjustment. In Economic Research Institute (Ed.), *Economic Planning Agency, Dynamic interdependence among the Asia-Pacific economies* . Keizai Bunseki (The Economic Analysis), no. 129, March.

Yanagihara, T. -J. (1992). Soron: Ajia taiheiyo keizaiken no seiritsu to tenkai (General: Establishment and development of the Asia-Pacific economic zone). In T. Yanagihara (Ed.), *Ajia taiheiyo no Keizai hatten to chiiki kyoryoku (Asia-Pacific economic development and regional cooperation).* IDE.

Yanagihara, T. (1997). Economic system approach and its applicability. In Yanagihara, T., & Sanbonmatsu, S., (Eds.), *East Asian development experience: Economic system approach and its applicability*. IDE.

Yokota, K. -J. (1992). ASEAN shokoku no boeki kozo (Trade structures of ASEAN member countries). In Y. Ohata & S. Urata (Eds.), *ASEAN no Keizai/Nihon no yakuwari (ASEAN economies and Japan's role).* Yuhikaku.

Chapter 13
New Structure of the Asian Economy for Trade and Resiliency

Abstract Emerging and developing economies cannot achieve development separate from the international order and the international environment created by the development stages of the capitalist market economy. Emerging and developing economies in Asia have built their own industries and societies in line with the development mechanisms of the global economy that have been given to them. This chapter summarizes the chapters discussed so far, and summarizes the development process and current status of Asian economies and their challenges. Next, we present a multi-layered cognitive framework for the world economy that takes a comprehensive bird's-eye view of its development, confirms the contemporary characteristics of development, and explores the challenges at the current stage.

Keywords Decentralization · Democracy · Localization · Local network · Regionalism · Regionalization · Globalization · Trinity of ODA-FDI-EX/IM

13.1 Introduction

This chapter reaffirms the main issues of each chapter and confirms the characteristics, destinations, and challenges of Asian economic development in the global economy.

Needless to say, the development of Asian economies has been achieved by Asian countries adapting their economies and societies to the trends of the world economy, while at the same time actively pursuing development. This process of development is not a phenomenon that can be faithfully reproduced in a test tube, under laboratory conditions. All countries and economies created by human beings do not always follow the same development path across time and space. Each has its own spatial and historical characteristics. While paying attention to these points, this book avoids excessive reliance on theory and discusses the development process of Asia in accordance with empirical facts.

Until the beginning of this century, most studies on economic development in East Asia tended to emphasize the success cases and dismiss countries and economies that

H. Hirakawa and F. C. Maquito, *The Dynamics of Asian Economic Development*,
https://doi.org/10.1007/978-981-97-3106-0_13

are not able to ride the trend. In other words, the economies that were not convenient for the mainstream theory of development were excluded from study, if not treated as separate subjects of study. Its cognitive characteristics are basically the same in the approach of the "middle-income trap" theory that emerged in the second half of the decade of the century (replaced "at the turn" with "in the second half of the decade"). This is because it discusses further development issues of "middle-income countries" based on various indicators of advanced economies. However, we have examined the development of the Asian region with a view to the fact that emerging and developing economies have been proactively pursuing the development of advanced economies in line with developments in the world economy.

This chapter begins with a summary of each chapter to describe the process of Asian economic development, its characteristics, and its challenges. Next, we conceptually grasp the relationship between the world economy and the economy and society of each country in four layers (levels) of local, national, regional, and global, and confirm the relationship in relation to development. In what follows, we will begin with a summary of each chapter of the book, and then clarify the position of developing countries among the four layers. In closing, we will briefly discuss the achievements of the Asian economy and its challenges.

13.2 Current Stage of Asia's Economic Development and Its Challenges Toward Shared Growth

Throughout this book, we have discussed the diverse development of Asian economies and the new challenges that have arisen as a result, based on empirical facts. The analytical framework has not been placed within the framework of a single country's economy, but has been examined along a time axis from the perspective of the global economy and emerging and developing economies seeking development. From there, we were able to confirm the dynamics and challenges of Asian economic development.

Let's take a look back at each chapter of the book. The five chapters of Part 1, Asian Economy and Transformation of the World Economy identify the achievements and challenges of contemporary East Asian economies. In Chap. 2, we discussed how the U.S.-Sino trade war launched by the Trump administration in the late 2010s has become more serious due to the COVID-19 pandemic that followed, and has now turned into a competition for supremacy in advanced technology between the two countries and a confrontation over national and economic security. The conflict has extended initially from trade to the realm of investment and technological development, bringing about "decoupling" in the global production network, with the emergence of China as the world's factory. It was also confirmed that COVID-19 is spreading along the global economic network, questioning the nature of the global economy itself.

Chapter 3 confirms the fact that the development of East Asia under the global economy has brought about a change in the world economic structure led by the United States. At the same time, the transformation of the leading countries from Japan to China has occurred in the structure of the East Asian region. Furthermore, it was argued that the mechanism of East Asia's development was mainly due to the international expansion of enterprises from Japan and Newly Industrializing Economies (NIEs), which gave rise to an intra-regional trade bloc characterized by intermediate goods transactions. From a spatial perspective, this development began with the NIEs and then spread to the rest of East Asia, especially among Association of Southeast Asian Nations (ASEAN) member states and China. This created internal markets in these economies, which gave rise to expectations for the future huge market among global companies, and further raised expectations for developing countries with large populations. It was in this context that the concept of the BRICs was born. Unlike the BRICs model, however, which was largely motivated by financial investment objectives, we saw a development, based largely on feedback from Japanese and other global companies operating in East Asia, that is motivated by direct foreign investment in search of abundant labor and potential bigger markets. We called this stage of development the PoBMEs stage. The world's largest economic bloc is now in Asia. And it is this development mechanism that has made China leap to become a world power.

Chapter 4 deals with the Belt and Road Initiative (BRI) launched by President Xi Jinping, who was born in China in the spring of 2013. Today, about 150 countries participate in the BRI, which can be said to be China's basic foreign diplomatic and economic strategy. Criticism of the BRI as a "debt trap" began before COVID-19, but has been intensified by the widespread debt service problems caused by the sharp decline in foreign currency earnings in developing countries due to the COVID-19 pandemic. Similarly, the confrontation between the United States and China, which was initiated by former U.S. President Donald Trump, has been further exacerbated by the outbreak of COVID-19. As a result, the diplomatic significance of the BRI for China has increased even more. Looking at the prospects for the BRI initiative, we observed three pillars of the Health Silk Road, the Digital Silk Road, and the Green BRI (Environmental Silk Road). The prospects of the health Silk Road are unclear today due to the sharp decline in vaccine exports, so it looks like the remaining two pillars will be the main areas of promotion for the BRI moving forward.

From the perspective of the global economy, the significance of China's BRI is related to the fact that the neoliberal structural reforms and privatizations adopted by the United States and international financial and aid agencies since the 1980s have effectively excluded middle- and low-income countries from development. Developed countries such as the United States and its allied international financial institutions have forced middle- and low-income countries to liberalize and privatize. The BRI initiative has opened up the possibility of infrastructure construction in those countries, which has been largely ignored by neoliberal policies. The intensification of the U.S.-Sino confrontation has recently led to a competition between the U.S., the West, and China for infrastructure aid to BRI countries, creating new development possibilities in the region.

Chapter 5 examines the development of emerging economies and developing countries that have developed the Business Processing Outsourcing (BPO) industry made possible by the development of Information and Computer Technology (ICT) and its challenges. This development is quite different from the export-driven development of industrial goods in East Asia. At the same time, it is a modern development phenomenon that is completely different from the traditional experience of industrialization in the world. On the one hand, the development of ICT has brought offshoring services to companies in the United States, the United Kingdom, and Europe, and on the other hand, it has created a BPO industry in India in South Asia and the Philippines in Southeast Asia, and has also encouraged women to participate in the labor market. At the same time, however, this development has brought the possibility of the disappearance of routine labor-intensive occupations and industries due to the rapid development of automation. The spread of remote work due to COVID-19 gave rise to expectations that it would further promote the disappearance of unskilled labor, but in fact it had the opposite effect. The BPO industry grew unexpectedly. However, the labor content of the BPO industry has changed significantly during this period. The importance of employment policies for the advancement of industrial structures has not diminished. Chapter 5 also examines whether the export-led development of ICT services in developing countries can simply replace the development of traditional manufacturing. It also touches on the challenges of "premature deindustrialization", a development issue brought about by the rise of the BPO industry.

In contrast to the above discussion of aspects of the development and growth of Asian economies, Chap. 6 focuses on the context of "shared growth" to highlight the case of the Philippines in an East Asian context. The term was coined in the controversial East Asian Miracle Report of the World Bank to describe the peculiarities of the development of eight High-Performing Asian Economies (HPAEs), in which the Philippines was not included. HPAEs were able to achieve remarkable growth alongside improvements in income distribution. The case of the Philippines in this context was elaborated through three international engagements of Japan, the premier model and advocate of shared growth. These engagements are also known as the trinity of ODA-FDI-EX/IM. Although the Philippines appeared to do relatively well in leveraging ODA and FDI, to the extent that it was able, the inability to ride on Akamatsu's flying geese dynamics which underlie Japan's trade (EX/IM) remains a challenge.

Part 2, the Results of Asia's development experiments after World War II, contains five chapters, mainly to summarize the basic structure of Asian economic development in the second half of the twentieth century. Chapter 7 summarizes the various approaches to the development of East Asia and confirms the effectiveness of the approach of latecomer industrialization in the world economy. As for the development mechanism, the mechanism of the development of the Asian NIEs was clarified. The Asian NIEs were achieved through a growth triangle structure in which products were exported mainly to the American market, while capital goods and intermediate goods for industrialization were imported mainly from Japan and exported to the United States. This growth triangle emerged when developed companies, especially Japan companies, used NIEs as production bases for labor-intensive products. They have moved capital and technology to NIEs through FDI, but on the other hand, the NIEs government has achieved export-led development through various foreign capital introduction policies, creating opportunities for the development of local enterprises. In this way, the foundation for the development of East Asia, which began with the industrialization of the NIEs, was formed. This chapter examines the development of NIEs from the perspective of placing greater emphasis on their relationship with the global economy than on the flying geese model.

In the latter half of the 1980s, the above developments expanded regionally in the wake of the Plaza Accord, an agreement to correct the appreciation of the dollar by the Finance Ministers and Central Bank Governors of the five industrialized countries (Japan, the United States, the United Kingdom, Germany, and France). The rapid appreciation of the yen due to the Plaza Accord created a wave of FDI for Japan companies in NIEs, ASEAN, China, and later ASEAN countries, and as a result, NIEs that achieved growth followed Japan companies, leading to the formation of an East Asian economic zone. Although the perception differs widely, the World Bank will call this development the "East Asian miracle". The development of East Asia, starting with the NIEs, will undergo a structural evolution to the BRICs and PoBMEs-type developments discussed in Part 1.

Chapter 8 discusses the Asian financial crisis that erupted in 1997. The Asian currency crisis, as with the coining of the term "crony capitalism", was attributed by mainstream economics and international financial institutions to the internal conditions of countries that had fallen into crisis due to the fragility of the Asian-style financial system and the wrong industrial policies. In this way, they used the crisis as an opportunity to force the emerging and developing economies of East Asia to further liberalize their economies. However, this chapter argues that the excessive liberalization of capital flows has led to excess liquidity in finance, which was the crucial cause of the crisis. Summarizing the interpretation of the Asian currency crisis, it is argued that neoliberal financial liberalization policies were the more important cause of the crisis, and clarifies that the momentum for regional cooperation in East Asia has increased as a result.

Chapter 9 examines the two origins of Asian regionalism from a historical perspective: Southeast Asia and Northeast Asia. By tracing the process of their integration since the late 1980s, we have clarified their achievements and challenges. The Asian financial crisis in 1997 struck, which accelerated the movement toward regionalism in East Asian countries. In the 2000s, on the one hand, regional cooperation conferences such as the ASEAN+3 Summit and the East Asia Summit became more institutionalized, and on the other hand, economic integration in the trade area was realized. In the 2010s, a boom in the conclusion of FTAs and EPAs led to the birth of two regional economic integrations: the RCEP, which covers almost the entire East Asian region, and the CPTPP, which covers the Asia–Pacific region. However, it was also confirmed that new challenges have arisen related to the rivalry between the United States and China.

ASEAN has played an extremely important role in regional cooperation and regional integration in East Asia. This book considers the ASEAN Way and ASEAN centrality policies developed by ASEAN to be valuable "assets" for Asia, especially

East Asia. The structural transformation brought about by the emergence of a massive China in the Asian and global economies has led to the sharpening of the U.S.-Sino confrontation and is now facing major challenges, but the significance of ASEAN's unity in overcoming these challenges is even greater. For the prosperity and peace of the Asian region, the significance of cooperation among the member countries of the East Asian region is increasing.

Chapter 10 considers the historical roots of the Philippines' developmental malaise, despite having an excellent head start over many other countries in East Asia. Moreover, it was observed that the Philippines has gone through the traditional patterns of economic development. Her post-war development could be clearly marked with the traditional phases of importation, import-substitution industrialization, and export-oriented industrialization. In terms of sectoral contributions, the Philippine economy could also be seen as moving from agriculture, then industry (manufacturing), and then services. Despite this, development of the Philippines has lagged behind its cohorts in Southeast Asia, suggesting an underlying weakness in the seemingly good patterns it went through in the course of her post-war development. We focus in this chapter on the lack of strategic sequencing which could be ultimately traced to the very skewed distribution of income and wealth in the country.

Chapter 11 (co-written with Damcelle Torres-Cortes) elaborates on a mechanism by which the problem of skewed distribution of income and wealth in the Philippines could be solved: decentralization. The chapter is essentially a meta survey of related literature on decentralization and its relation to shared growth, as manifested in the two socio-economic goals of efficiency and equity. We find that more rigorously done studies tend to reveal the positive contribution of decentralization on efficiency. On the other hand, decentralization was observed to have an aggravating effect on equity, suggesting the need for the implementation of counter measures. It was noted, however, that inter-regional competition may help in mitigating the widening of the income/wealth gap.

Chapter 12 of Part III comprehensively examines the development of the Japanese economist Kaname Akamatsu's flying geese theory, which has attracted worldwide attention since the 1980s as an explanatory theory of the development of East Asia, by going back to the theory's origins. The flying geese theory was largely established in the late 1930s. Industrialization in countries goes through the process of import-production-export development. Specifically, it clarifies the mechanism by which multi-layered industrial sophistication occurred in Japan: in the upgrading from crude products to refined products, and from low-value-added industries to high-value-added industries; and at the same time, the transfer of low-value-added industries abroad spreads along with the development.

The flying geese theory during World War II played a propaganda role in the theory of the Greater East Asia Co-Prosperity Sphere, but was revived again against the backdrop of the revival of the Japanese economy after World War II and the subsequent development of East Asian countries in the second half of the twentieth century. The empirical study of the flying geese theory by Kiyoshi Kojima, a senior disciple of Akamatsu, using modern economic models, also helped to popularize it. This theory also maintained its own theoretical position in that it allowed the import substitution stage in the early stages of industrialization in the developing countries, and also served as the theoretical policy backbone of Japan's foreign aid. Akamatsu's empirical economic methodology, which is based on the German philosophy of history, is still valid from the standpoint of the development of the developing countries. This chapter reaffirms the importance of empirical positivist research methods, which are often regarded as theories of the past due to the increasing refinement of economic analysis in this century and the emergence of new ideas. As with all theories, there is no universal theory, but from the perspective of the least developed countries, we think that the empirical positivist research method has many implications even today.

13.3 Multi-layered Understanding and Empowerment of Asian Economic Development

In the previous section, we reviewed the development of East Asia, its mechanisms, and its challenges. In this section, we will attempt to organize a cognitive framework that attempts to comprehensively understand this development.

The development of East Asian countries began with the formation of a growth triangle structure of Japan, the NIEs, and the United States. By the end of the twentieth century, this development mechanism had spread to early ASEAN countries, China, and the latecomer ASEAN countries. However, this development mechanism is also the result of East Asian countries making full use of various policies, such as the establishment of export processing zones and special economic zones, tariff and exchange rate policies, and export subsidy policies. Such policies cannot simply be classified as free trade policy as perceived by neoclassical economics. East Asian countries have created a growth triangle structure by experimenting with various policies that neoliberal economics considers protectionist, in line with the global strategy of multinational corporations. The main policy goal for these countries was to introduce capital and technology through the attraction of multinational corporations as host countries, and to secure foreign markets of the necessary size. Naturally, the policy pursued the development of local enterprises at the same time. The analysis of the flying geese theory in Chap. 12 indicates that it can be evaluated as a theory with policy implications when focusing on the relationship with Japan.

In South Asia, especially in India, a different path of development emerged than that taken in East Asia. The accelerated digitalization of the economy in developed countries due to the development of ICT has given birth to BPO industries in India, the Philippines, and other countries. Development economics examines whether a course of development that depends solely on the BPO industry is a sufficient course of development for a country's economy. In this book, we touch on premature deindustrialization and consider Potentially Big Market Economies (PoBMEs) from the perspective of world capitalism, with China and India as typical countries.

In Asia, regional cooperation has also been pursued from an early stage. Focusing on East Asia, the countries of Southeast Asia and Northeast Asia made various attempts to form regional cooperation organizations and free trade zones in the mid-twentieth century. ASEAN is a regional cooperation organization that was born in the process, and the same is true of Asia Pacific Economic Cooperation (APEC). Such a framework for regional cooperation has paved the way for the integration of East Asian economies. Cooperation and integration is likely to continue to grow.

If we position and illustrate these various attempts in the global political and economic environment, we can obtain four multilayered configurations using pyramid and network diagrams as shown in Fig. 13.1a, b. Let us first discuss the pyramid version, and return to the discussion on the network version later.

The four levels are included in the triangle diagram to see the hierarchy and direction of forces at each local and global position. Global institutions and actors have a top-down orientation, while systems and relationships at the local level are

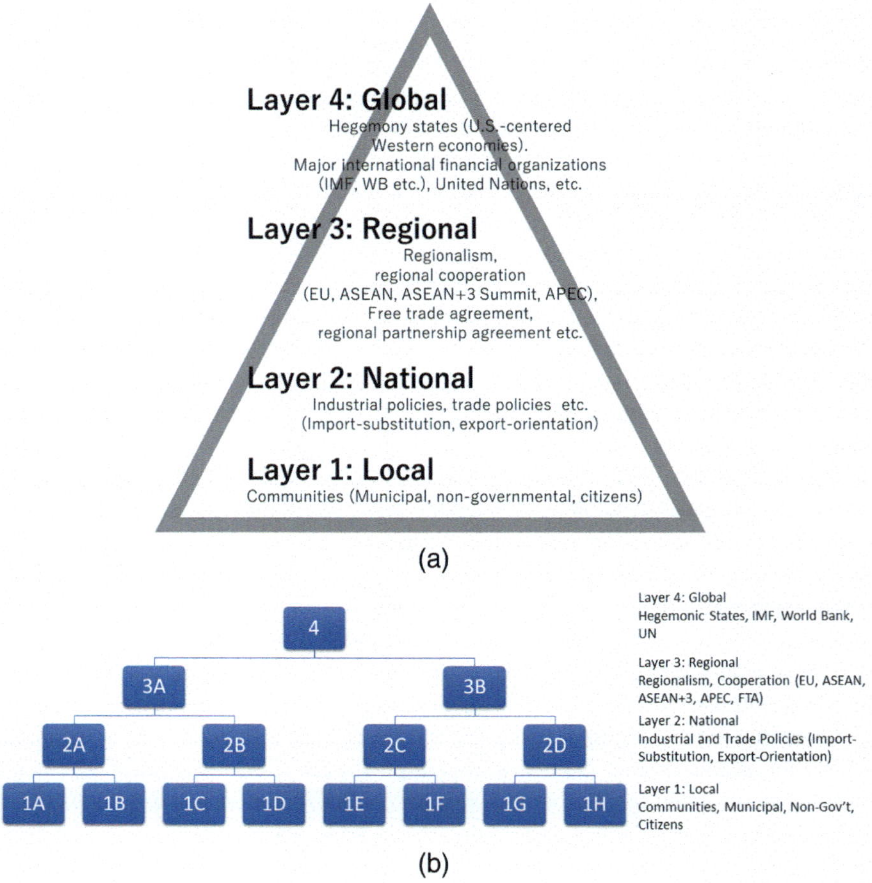

Fig. 13.1 **a** Perceptions of the four-layer structure of the world economy from the perspective of developing countries—Pyramid version **b** Perceptions of the four-layer structure of the world economy from the perspective of developing countries—Network version (*Source* Made by authors)

bottom-up. Although not rigorously defined, the BoP, which C. D. Prahalad and Stuart L. Hart, called the "Bottom of the Pyramid" and later changed to the "Base of the Pyramid," is reminiscent of the above pyramid diagram. The BoP captured the fact that 4 billion people around the world live on less than $1,500 and proposed a perspective that links this to business as a market (Prahalad & Hart, 2002). As in the BoP conceptualization, the pyramid diagram of Fig. 13.1a features a higher concentration of wealth or power as we go up the pyramid. Layer 2 nations tend to be more wealthy and powerful than local units, and Layer 3 regional institutions than Level 2 nations, and global institutions than Level 3 regions.

Now, the Layer 1 constitutes the substratum of the world, and it contains the institutions and networks of people that belong to the sphere of people's lives. This group will include community policies and activities led by local governments and non-governmental organizations, as well as their networks. Layer 2 is the national level, which includes the activities of states, domestic policies related to economic development, and external trade and monetary policies. It can be said that a country's industrial and trade policies are closely intertwined with domestic and foreign policies. Layer 3 is the regional level, which envisions various regional cooperation and regional integration attempts and networks that transcend national boundaries. This level will include cooperation frameworks such as ASEAN, ASEAN+3, the East Asia Summit, various FTAs/EPAs, and even the European Union, which is not directly discussed in this book, and the Group of 77, which attracted attention in the international community in the 1960s, mainly at the United Nations. The final layer 4 is the global layer, which includes the United States as a hegemonic power, international financial institutions such as the IMF and the World Bank, and multinational corporations with global influence and their production and procurement networks. The hegemonic state creates the international order and rules under the global strategy, and in its implementation, maintains the order and rules directly or indirectly through the use of international organizations. Global corporations are developing their global business activities in this order.

Historically, most of Asia's developing countries, like those in other regions, experienced colonization and achieved independence in the twentieth century, with few exceptions. It is the institutionalization of Layer 2 in the global economy or the international community. These newly independent countries aimed to form nation-states and national economies under the international order and rules created by the hegemonic states after World War II. Although the history of independence of the countries that were colonized during the imperialist era varies, they have acquired an independent framework for their own development through independence. The formation of a unified state of developing countries in the face of the international community was a crucial condition for development (Acemoglu & Robinson, 2012). Import substitution was seen as a common development policy in the early years of developing countries, but attempts were generally unsuccessful in the second half of the twentieth century. As discussed in this book, the developing countries of East Asia have overcome this obstacle. Developing countries were required to incorporate the technological aspects of the world economy into their development policies.

In the fourth layer, the overseas expansion of U.S. multinational corporations, and later the flow of Japanese companies to Asia, creating a physical and information network of global business activities. These activities and networks will also be included in Layer 4. And East Asia has achieved industrialization and development in cooperation with this stratum. The development of South Asia and India is related to the digitalization of the economy due to the development of ICT, but a similar structure emerges when viewed in four layers. Development has been achieved by connecting global business networks in the digitalization of the fourth-layer economy. Its development was brought about by the cooperation of Layer 4, Layer 2, and Layer 1.

The Layer 3 level includes regionalism and regional cooperation. In East Asia, in the 1950s and 1960s, attempts were made to promote regional cooperation from both Southeast Asia and Northeast Asia. In the wake of the Asian financial crisis in the 1990s, it made a leap to a framework for cooperation in the East Asian region, and the movement toward regional economic integration became active.

The network version of the four-layer structure of the world economy is shown in Fig. 13.1b. For illustration purposes, we limit the number of actors for each layer. There are eight actors for Layer 1, four for Layer 2, two, for Layer 3, and one for Layer 4. Each pair of Layer 1 actors are linked together through the Layer 2 actor, which in turn is paired and linked with another Layer 2 actor through the Layer 3 actor, which in turn is also paired and linked with another Layer 3 actor through the Layer 4 actor.

There has been a growing interest in community cooperation and cross-border networking at the local level. It is the acquisition and expansion of the power of Layer 1 and the strengthening of cooperation with Layer 3. This is shown more clearly in Fig. 13.2, using the network diagram of Fig. 13.1b. We show an example of community cooperation and cross-border networking at the local level through the link between actor 1B, belonging to country 2A, and actor, belonging to country 2B. This link helps to strengthen the link of local actor 1B to the regional actor 3A through the national actor 2A. A similar strengthening could be found in local actor 1D's link to regional actor 3A through national actor 2B.

Looking at the world structure with a focus on the development of Asia as described above, it is characteristic that the focus of development has expanded from Layer 2 in the twentieth century to Layers 3 and 1 in the twenty-first century. In other words, it shows the potential for development in the twenty-first century, and we view this as an indication of the direction of development in the twenty-first century.

Again, fourth-layer governments and international organizations maintain order, and multinational corporations use the four-layer structure to do business. On the other hand, emerging and developing countries have achieved development by developing policies and activities in line with and partly in opposition to this structure. It was, so to speak, a development of a fusion character in which the forces of top down and bottom up interact with each other. Of course, if this policy is not adequate, it will also create the possibility of the emergence and failure of a unilateral structure of control.

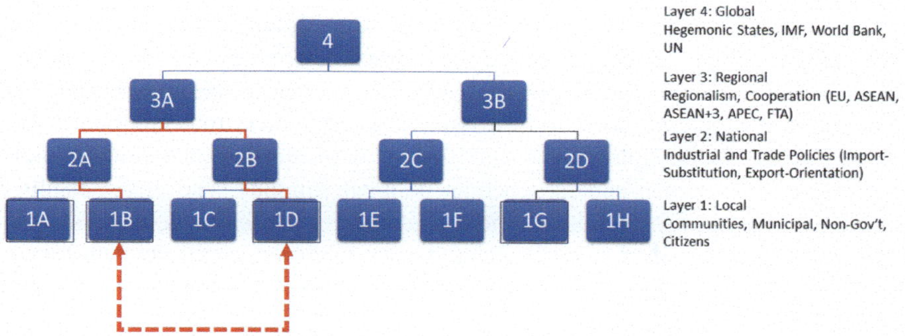

Fig. 13.2 Four-layer structure with local to local link (*Source* Authors). *Note* Red dash line indicates local-to-local linking, while other red lines indicate a strengthening of ties

Anyway, if we focus on today, Asia has achieved development and, as a result, brought about a structural transformation in the global economy in the twenty-first century. And now we are in a new phase. The hegemonic confrontation between the United States and China is intensifying, and global networks are in danger of being fragmented. On the other hand, the problem of global warming has emerged as an urgent issue, and many difficulties lie in solving it. At the same time, however, new possibilities are being introduced. The expansion of networks at the regional level and the local level, which cannot be aggregated at the national level, presents new possibilities. We must not lose sight of this direction of development.

13.4 Regionalization and Decentralization

In the course of our investigation, two forces stand out in the dynamics of East Asian development. One is regionalization, which is the process of integration in the context of globalization, and another is decentralization, whereby subnational units gain greater autonomy from the national government.

The East Asian Miracle (EAM) Report of the World Bank in 1993 coined the term "shared growth" to describe the performance of a group of East Asian economies during the period 1960 to 1990. Shared growth refers to rapid growth accompanied by improvements in distribution of income. In other words, it is a type of development that achieves efficiency (maximization of output for a given input) and equity (good distribution of income).

The EAM Report is noteworthy for the following reasons. One is that it precedes by a few decades the interest in equitable development that has recently emerged in this (21st) century, and another is that it captures an essential principle of East Asian dynamics (shared growth). It misses, however, two forces of regionalization and decentralization in East Asian dynamics that have only come to the fore even as the report was being published. Regionalization was already explained above, so in this section we will focus on decentralization.

In its 2005 report "East Asia Decentralizes: Making Local Government Work" (World Bank, 2005), the World Bank observed a widespread trend towards decentralization in East Asia since the 1990s. According to this report, there are three types of decentralization in East Asia. The fast starters (the Philippines and Indonesia) have rapidly introduced major structural, institutional, and fiscal reforms in response to a sudden and far-reaching political stimulus. The incrementalists (China and Vietnam) have taken a more piecemeal approach to decentralization. Cautious movers (Cambodia and Thailand) have established significant elements of decentralization at the formal policy and legislative levels, but there has been limited progress with implementation.

Regionalization and Decentralization have a naturally high tendency to be substitutive. Regionalization is moving towards integration, where countries form a community of nations, and homogenization, where member countries come to follow a common standard. On the other hand, decentralization is moving towards disintegration, wherein a nation is formed of many subnational communities, and heterogenization, wherein subnational communities have greater autonomy to decide and implement policies. The two forces, therefore, are in opposition or cannot co-exist. We can, however, theorize at some conditions, where these forces could be complementary, such as those given below.

The first Complementary Condition would be the proper empowerment of the state, where regional integration does not overly strengthen member states. Overly empowered states would tend to obstruct decentralization within nations. On the other hand, overly weakened states would be less able to seal international agreements and, thus, hinder regionalization. For regionalization and decentralization to be complementary, therefore, a balanced state empowerment is necessary.

The second Complementary Condition would be the existence of common principles. The sharing of common principles that are critical to the functioning of the two forces. When a nation's working principle is different from that of the international environment, international conflict tends to arise. A recent example would be the (first) Cold War, which was essentially an international conflict between Communism and Democracy, or between Centrally planned economies and Market economies. Another example is the foreign bashing of Japan after the (first) Cold War, which was essentially a conflict between different types of capitalism. Such international conflicts could be mitigated if there is a common principle driving a nation's internal workings and that of its international environment. Shared growth mechanisms promoted by Japan's international engagements complement decentralization within East Asian nations, hence, mitigating international conflicts (see Box 13.1).

Box 13.1 Shared growth mechanisms in Japan's international engagements

A common principle may be found in the principle of shared growth. This is especially evident in the case of Japanese international economic relations, consisting of the ODA, FDI, and EX/IM (trade).

Japan's ODA has adopted the self-help effort philosophy, wherein stringency, as materialized through the relatively heavier use of loans, promotes shared growth. The aspect of "shared" could be seen in the recovery of funds through loan repayments from more advanced recipient countries. On the other hand, the aspect of "growth" is promoted through incentivizing recipient countries to exert effort in order to repay the loans.

Japanese FDI contains the shared growth DNA that has contributed to Japan's achievement of shared growth. This DNA is found in its unique corporate structure called the "keiretsu", characterized by reciprocal arrangements between the firm and its various stakeholders, such as workers, stockholders, banks, and suppliers.

Japanese Foreign Trade or Export–Import (EX/IM) also contains elements of shared growth. The Flying Geese Model of Japan has been cited to have contributed to the cooperative and competitive division of labor in East Asia. Competitiveness of industries is achieved through intertemporal equity. Upstream phases in the Flying Geese dynamics lay the foundation for downstream phases, such that there is strategic continuity of industrial policies.

Based on the above discussion, it is conceivable, however, that regionalization would fail such as in the following two cases:

1. States are not adequately empowered, so that they have difficulty in reaching agreements with other states in the region
2. States may be adequately empowered but are at an impasse with other countries in the region

One possible solution is to promote the participation of subnational units in the international (regional) arena.[1] LGA (2023) finds that the more decentralized countries (ASEAN+3) tend to have a more active LGU (city) participation in regional networks. It looks at six regional networks in which ASEAN+3 countries are relatively active: ASEAN Smart City Network (ASCN); CityNet; United Cities and Local Governments (UCLG); Brunei Darussalam, Indonesia, Malaysia, Philippines East ASEAN Growth Area (BIMP-EAGA); Indonesia, Malaysia, Thailand Growth Triangle (IMT-GT); and Greater Mekong Subregional (GMS).

Table 13.1 shows the number of cities per each regional network for the ASEAN members. The ranking of each member is based on the total number of cities involved

---

[1] This is actually based on a recommendation by a study conducted by the College of Public Affairs and Development of the University of the Philippines Los Baños for the Local Government Academy (LGA) of the Department of Interior and Local Government. The study is "Baseline Study on Local Governance Systems Among ASEAN+3 Countries" and was submitted in 2023.

in the regional networks, with a rank of 1 being the highest total. It seems that the more decentralized a nation is, the higher its ranking. Among the "plus 3 countries", China appears to be the most aggressive with Japan having the lowest rank.

LGA (2023) proposes two approaches to promote the participation of Local Government Units (LGUs) in ASEAN+3 networks. One approach is Core-Driven, whereby LGUs are pulled by the ASCN pilot cities, spearheaded by Singapore. Another approach is Periphery-Driven, whereby LGUs are pulled by the cities of the sub-regional networks (such as BIMP-EAGA, IMT-GT, and GMS).

Lastly, as the pandemic has shown us, a regionalization or globalization that tends to be centralized and relies on hubs is not robust to simultaneous attacks on the hubs. As discussed in the AFC6 Roundtable (Contemplating the World from East Asian Lens), the air traffic routes tend to depend a lot on hubs for international flights. The hubs came under simultaneous COVID attack as these are points where people converge, and then spread to local points. Decentralizing such critical international networks would most likely improve its resilience against such simultaneous shocks. Here too, we can appreciate the efficacy of shared growth, which is based on the principle of decentralization.

Table 13.1 Number of cities per regional network

Countries	ASCN	CityNet	UCLG	BIMP-EAGA	GMS	IMT-GT	Total	Ranking
Brunei Darussalam	1		1	7			9	6
Cambodia	3	1			2		6	8
Indonesia	3	17	25	27		2	74	1
Laos	2				2		4	9
Malaysia	4	5	1	26		1	37	3
Myanmar	3				5		8	7
Philippines	3	21	5	35			64	2
Singapore	1						1	10
Thailand	3	1	1		10	11	26	4
Vietnam	3	5	1		15		24	5
China		8	8		12		28	1 (@P3)
Japan		2	2				4	3 (@P3)
Republic of Korea		12	2				14	2 (@P3)

(*Source* LGA, 2023: 259).

13.5 Global Society at a Turning Point and Challenges for the Development of Asia

Today, Asia and the world are at a new stage. As the first quarter of a century draws to a close, the structure of global economic development that Asia has been under pressure to change, amidst severe events occurring more frequently. A bird's-eye view of the global economy shows some of such events: the global financial crisis that began with the Lehman shock in 2008, China's rise to become the world's second-largest power in 2010, the U.S.-Sino trade war under U.S. President Donald Trump since 2018, the subsequent struggle for supremacy and the decoupling of global value chains related to U.S.-Sino advanced technology and national security, the outbreak of the COVID-19 pandemic in 2020, global border closures, and city lockdowns, the war in Ukraine due to Russia's military invasion in 2022, and the outbreak of the Israeli-Hamas war in 2023.

On the other hand, if we look at poverty and global environmental issues, since 2015, the United Nations has been pushing the sustainable development goals (SDGs) under the slogan of "leaving no one behind" toward 2030. In addition, the Principles for Responsible Investment (PRI) and Environment, Social, and Governance (ESG) have been established in the industrial world. ESG investments are actively promoted to create sustainable value.

However, the most urgent issue is global warming. Global warming was discussed in 1992 at the United Nations Conference on Sustainable Development (Rio+20) in Rio de Janeiro (Brazil), where global warming was discussed and the recognition of sustainable development was shared. At the Conference of the Parties to the Convention (COP) 3, the Kyoto Protocol was adopted. The Paris Agreement was signed in 2015 and entered into force in 2020. However, the agreement to curb greenhouse gas emissions in order to limit the temperature rise to 1.5 °C above pre-industrial levels is far from effectively being practiced. In the meantime, disasters such as extreme weather, flooding, and erosion of the land of island nations due to rising sea levels have become more frequent around the world.

At COP28 in Dubai in December 2023, nations agreed to "transition away" from coal, oil and gas. However, it will not be easy to achieve this. Asia is rapidly increasing its CO_2 emissions as it develops, and China's emissions are particularly prominent. China's emissions reached 10,081 million tonnes in 2020, or 33% of global emissions, well above the U.S. emissions' 4,258 million tons, or 13.6%. However, China's per capita emissions are 7.2 million tons, which is about 60% of the 12.8 million tons in the United States. India accounts for 6.6% of global emissions, but only 1.5 million tonnes per capita. Incidentally, Chinese President Xi Jinping announced in a video address to the United Nations General Assembly in 2020 that he would achieve carbon neutrality by 2060 with virtually zero CO_2 emissions. That promise must not be broken.

In fact, civil society movements around the world are calling for strong regulation of greenhouse gas emissions, and for "climate justice" because the biggest victims of climate change are disproportionately the most vulnerable and developing countries.

The countries of the "South" also share the severity of the problem. Carbon neutrality is an urgent issue. Science and technology are a decisive requirement for solving this problem, and the results must be shared not only by developed countries but also by Asian and developing countries. The quality of Asia's development, among other things, is being questioned.

The ideals of democracy, human rights, and inviolability of national borders epitomized by the United States in the twentieth century have been severely tarnished since the turn of the century. It is becoming increasingly clear that democracy, which many people saw as an ideal in the twentieth century, does not work well on formality alone. The emergence of President Trump in the United States and the events that followed teach us that. economic growth and the political system could not be viewed as one. China's experience teaches us that. However, China has dramatically reduced global poverty, followed by India. Both countries are typical of PoBMEs and have currently high development potential.

China seems to be trying to make its own grouping against the U.S. around the BRI and BRICS Summit, but the U.S. and Western countries are now giving diplomatic priority to these regions. India has already surpassed China in population and is clearly showing a trend to surpass China in terms of economic growth. Moreover, India has taken advantage of the U.S.-Sino confrontation and is becoming more vocal as a spokesperson for the "Global South". Incidentally, the structure of the international community is similar to that of the 1960s, when developing countries had a voice on the international arena centered on the United Nations. This time, the hegemon must take this voice seriously.

The economic development achieved by Asia has brought about a new structure of the international community. It shifts the center of gravity of the world's diplomacy and economy to the "South" side and opens up possibilities for Asia with its development prospects. But it has to be "sustainable" development. Asian countries must work together at all levels, global, regional, national, and local, towards a genuine, and therefore sustainable reduction of poverty mainly through significant reductions in the disparities in income and wealth distribution. In other words, we believe that more thrust should be given on achieving "shared growth" rather than "inclusive growth", which virtually ignores equity. A rising tide indeed lifts all boats, but a luxury liner would be more able to safely undertake longer voyages across turbulent seas compared to a raft.

We also believe that democracy and human rights are historically important human institutions. The world has no shortage of examples of the suppression of human rights. However, as a region with diverse and rich cooperative experiences, Asia has opened up the prospect of balanced social and economic development in many countries. It has also created a framework for regional cooperation. Of course, it is essential to understand the significance of self-restraint by major powers. However, if the member states continue to pursue a regional international order based on reason rather than force or threat, together with the people living there, and if the people respect diversity and at the same time promote cooperation in the direction of strengthening the power of local societies, the development of Asia will be that much more certain. The challenges are huge. However, it will be a challenge in the twenty-first century to invigorate cooperation at the local and regional levels, as well as at the global and national levels. We would like to believe that it will be effective in overcoming enormous challenges.

References

Acemoglu, R., & Robinson James, A. (2012). *Why nations fail: The origins of power, prosperity, and poverty*. Profile Books.

LGA. (2023). *Baseline study on local governance systems among ASEAN+3 countries*. Local Government Academy.

Prahalad, C. K., & Hart Stuart, L. (2002). The future at the bottom of the pyramid. Strategy+business, Issue 26, Spring.

World Bank. (2005). *East Asia decentralizes: Making local government work*. World Bank.

SPRINGER NATURE

GPSR Compliance

The European Union's (EU) General Product Safety Regulation (GPSR) is a set of rules that requires consumer products to be safe and our obligations to ensure this.

If you have any concerns about our products, you can contact us on ProductSafety@springernature.com

In case Publisher is established outside the EU, the EU authorized representative is:

Springer Nature Customer Service Center GmbH
Europaplatz 3
69115 Heidelberg, Germany

The manufacturer's authorised representative in the EU is Springer Nature Customer Service Centre GmbH, Europaplatz 3, 69115 Heidelberg, Germany. If you have any concerns regarding our products, please contact ProductSafety@springernature.com

Printed and bound by CPI Group (UK) Ltd, Croydon, CR0 4YY

30/09/2026

02225298-0018